LINUX

TCP/IP
Network Administration

SCOTT MANN
WITH MITCHELL KRELL

sgi AN SGI LINUX BOOK

PH
PTR

Prentice Hall PTR
Upper Saddle River, NJ 07458
www.phptr.com

ISBN 0-13-032220-2

90000

9 780130 322203

Y0-BZY-271

Library of Congress Cataloging-in-Publication Data available

Editorial/Production Supervision: *MetroVoice Publishing Services*
Acquisition Editor: *Mary Franz*
Editorial Assistant: *Noreen Regina*
Marketing Manager: *Dan DePasquale*
Manufacturing Manager: *Maura Zaldivar*
Cover Designer: *Talar Agasyan*
Cover Design Director: *Jerry Votta*
Series Designer: *Gail Cocker-Bogusz*
Project Coordinator: *Anne R. Garcia*

 © 2002 Prentice Hall PTR
Prentice-Hall, Inc.
Upper Saddle River, NJ 07458

The publisher offers discounts on this book when ordered in bulk quantities.
For more information, contact
Corporate Sales Department,
Prentice Hall PTR
One Lake Street
Upper Saddle River, NJ 07458
Phone: 800-382-3419; Fax: 201-236-7141
Email (Internet): corpsales@prenhall.com

Printed in the United States of America

10   9   8   7   6   5   4   3   2   1

ISBN 0-13-032220-2

Pearson Education Ltd.
Pearson Education Australia PTY Ltd.
Pearson Education Singapore, Pte. Ltd.
Pearson Education North Asia Ltd.
Pearson Education Canada, Ltd.
Pearson Educación de Mexico, S.A. de C.V.
Pearson Education—Japan
Pearson Education Malaysia, Pte. Ltd.
Pearson Education, Upper Saddle River, New Jersey

To Caitlin and Susie:
Though you no longer walk among us,
we are forever touched by the warmth
of your hearts and joy of your souls.

Contents

Chapter 2

Hardware and Network Interface Layers: Network Access   *17*

Chapter 5

The Internet Layer: IPv6   *147*

Chapter 6

The Internet Layer: Routing   *173*

Chapter 7

The Transport Layer   *235*

Chapter 9

Chapter 10

Chapter   11

Introducing Dynamic Routing Table Management   465

Chapter 12

OSPF   *547*

Chapter   13

BGP   *613*

Chapter 14

`ipchains`: Address Translation, IP Accounting, and Firewalls   *659*

Chapter 15

Netfilter: Address Translation, IP Accounting, and Firewalls *727*

Chapter 16

iproute2 And Other Routing Topics   *755*

Preface

There are a lot of documents, books, whitepapers, HOWTOs, and other guides, written about network administration generally, and Linux specifically. Indeed, I reference many of these throughout this book. There are, however, two things that these resources do not do. First, the coverage of the TCP/IP stack is usually either completely theoretical or minimized. The importance of associating implementation considerations, troubleshooting methods, and performance analysis with the functionality of each layer within the TCP/IP stack cannot be overstated. I am of the firm opinion that the theory of the stack and the application of the stack should be presented simultaneously. This I have endeavored to do in the first nine chapters.

Second, few resources provide any useful implementation information about routing table management protocols like OSPF and BGP. I have a whole bunch of horror stories relating to my early efforts at implementing OSPF and the fruits of those efforts are covered in Chapters 11 and 12. Unfortunately, I only had time to cover `gated`. At some future point, I hope to have the opportunity to add details about `zebra`. Additionally, I cover the basics of BGP as implemented by the public version of `gated` in Chapter 13. These chapters should give most modestly seasoned network administrators enough to go on to get one or more of these protocols functional.

I think that these topics alone give credence to this book. However, I tried to round out the work with some topics of general interest to network administrators. In particular, I give an introductory treatment of implementing packet filtering with `ipchains` and `iptables` in Chapters 14 and 15, respectively. I also cover some of the very exciting advanced Linux capabilities including routing policies, tunneling, and traffic control in Chapter 16.

Finally, Chapter 10 touches on the basic network applications, including DHCP, DNS, NFS, Samba, NIS, and LDAP. These topics are covered lightly with extensive reference details for further study.

I must confess that I do regret not being able to include a more thorough treatment of certain topics. In particular, the coverage of TCP, IPv6, multicast routing, and SNMP should have considerably more attention. Other areas such as coverage of `iptables` and `tc` could certainly be enhanced. On the other hand, the book is already at about 800 pages and took nine months to write (I still have a day job). So, hopefully, this a good resource as it is and a good first step toward an even better resource a year or two down the road. I certainly hope that you benefit from it.

A Note about Linux Distributions

Throughout the book, I have attempted to address a number of different Linux distributions. In particular, I specifically address Red Hat 6.2/7.0, Caldera 2.4, SuSE 6.4, and Debian 2.1. The versions for each distribution reflect the latest available at the time of this writing.

Linux Documentation

Throughout the book, I generally assume that you will know where to find the basic Linux documentation. So whenever I reference a HOWTO or Linux Guide or FAQ, I mean the document that can be found at the Linux Documentation Project (LDP) home page, namely

```
http://www.linuxdoc.org/
```

I also reference man pages by *title(section number)*. For instance, passwd(5) refers to the passwd man page found in section 5 of the manual page catalogue. More often than not, the section number is irrelevant as there is only one man page of the given name. However, sometimes, and in this particular case, there are multiple man pages related to the given name. In the case of passwd there are two pages, one in section 1 and the other in section 5. The command man passwd will bring up the man page for passwd(1). You can scroll down and eventually get to passwd(5), but

you can execute the command `man 5 passwd` to obtain the `passwd(5)` page immediately. See `man(1)` for further details.

Prerequisites

I do make certain assumptions about your knowledge. In general, I expect that
you have some knowledge of system administration and, in particular, are familiar with the following or their equivalents.

- an editor such as vi, emacs, or your favorite GUI text editor
- kernel rebuilding and the use of commands like `insmod`, `modprobe`, and
  `lsmod`
- system start/stop or start-up scripts, that is, `/etc/rc*` and `/etc/`
  `init.d/*`
- `syslog` and the `/etc/syslog.conf` file
- logical operators like `&`, `|`, and `!`

I also assume general familiarity with the Linux environment including the X
Window system and the use of the X Window manager of your choice.

Typographical Conventions

We use `courier` for Linux commands, daemons, flags, options, Web sites, etc.

We use *`courier emphasis`* for variables that are replaced with values, for
example, *`hostname`* means to replace the hostname variable with the actual host
name.

We use ***`courier bold italic`*** for hidden text such as passwords. For example,

```
foghorn login: bjt
Password: foobiebletch
```

Here, ***`foobiebletch`*** is the password and will not actually appear on the screen.

Italic is used in the text for emphasis.

I use subscripts to indicate the base of a number. For example,

10101101_2
255_8
173_{10}
ad_{16}

all represent the same value in base 2, 8, 10, and 16. I also freely interchange the terms base 2 and binary, base 8 and octal, base 10 and decimal, base 16 and hexadecimal (hex). Sometimes hex values will be represented with a preceding 0x as in 0xad or 0xAD.

I use the # prompt to indicate the root user and the $ prompt to indicate a non-root user.

When describing command syntax, anything enclosed in [ ] is optional. The | means "or" and the & means "and."

Errata and Contacts

If you discover anything that is incorrect or that is confusing or has some problem, please let me know! Send email to me at

```
linux_upat@thekeyboard.com
```

I won't always answer, but I will review any corrections, comments, and recommendations. I will post updates and corrections to

```
http://www.phptr.com/ptrbooks/ptr_0130322202.html
```

Please check the Web site once in a while for new information.

Acknowledgments

This book could not have been written without the sincere support of B.J. Wishinsky and Roger Connolly. Their willingness to grant me a leave of absence and, indeed, their enthusiastic support for this project made it possible. My sincerest thanks to you both.

I also owe a special debt of gratitude to Mitchell Krell who stepped in and provided a lot of valuable assistance when it was most needed. Mitch your contributions to this book are significant and undoubtedly have made it much better.

Mary Franz was once again a real joy to work with—her support and attention to me and this project made a huge difference. Thanks again Mary, this book wouldn't be what it is without your help.

My thanks to Noreen Regina for taking care of all the reviews and always being so pleasant. Also, to all the folks at Prentice Hall who supported this project, "thank you." I'm sure that there are many of you who I'll never know except through Mary's assurances of your efforts.

I extend a very special acknowledgment and thanks to Todd O'Boyle who, once again, provided very insightful suggestions and comments. Todd, I only wish that I had time to implement all of your suggestions! Also, my thanks to Etan Scherzer and Greg Herlein for their reviews of this material.

I'd also like to thank my family for all their support. Once again you have put up with a lot of my not being around. This will be worth it! Thanks.

1

An Introduction to TCP/IP

Perhaps the greatest advantage of Linux (and UNIX, in general) is its flexibility, especially with respect to networking. It was designed to make access easy; its use of Transmission Control Protocol/Internet Protocol (TCP/IP) networking is in harmony with that design perspective. In this chapter, we will take a look at networking from an overview perspective and introduce the TCP/IP model. We will also make a number of definitions and introduce a number of concepts that we will use throughout this book.

Computer Networking

Networks connect things together. The collection of roads throughout the United States comprises a network of paths by which vehicles can reach various points. The purpose of a network of roads is to permit people to efficiently move from one place to another. Computer networks consist of interconnected computer systems. The purpose of networking these components together is to share information and computing resources. An obvious example of a computer network is the Internet, in which millions of people access information and computer resources throughout the world. Most of the folks utilizing these resources have little notion of how those resources are made available to them or what tasks are required to provide such resources. That, after all, is the job of some computer jockey–or more formally, a system and/or network administrator.

System and network administrators own the task of ensuring that computer resources remain available. While the tasks of these two distinct roles often overlap, it is the job of the network administrator to ensure that computers and other dedicated network devices, such as repeaters, bridges, routers, and application servers, remain interconnected. In order to accomplish this task, the network administrator needs to be familiar with the software and hardware employed to effectively connect the various components. This familiarity must begin with the concept of network types and models.

Network Types

There are a number of terms used to describe different types of networks. Such terms include local area network (LAN), wide area network (WAN), campus area network (CAN), and metropolitan area network (MAN).

LAN LANs, generally speaking, are collections of interconnected *nodes*, all of which are geographically nearby, such as in the same room or in the same building. A node is any device which can be networked, like a computer (often referred to as a *system*), a printer, an appliance (web server, NFS server, etc.), or a black-box device (usually a router or switch—we define these later in this chapter). It should be noted that with the advent of layer 2 routing (see Chapter 16 for a discussion of layer 2 routing or *switching*; layers are discussed in the next section), the notion that the nodes within a LAN must be geographically close becomes untrue.

WAN A WAN is a collection of interconnected and geographically disparate nodes. Often, the major distinction between a LAN and a WAN is the use of some form of high-speed media to interconnect the nodes. Such media includes microwave, satellite, and telecommunications connections. WAN is a very general term that is often applied to collections of LANs and other WANs as well as collections of nodes. One example is the Internet, which is frequently described as a WAN—in fact, the Internet interconnects both LANs and WANs.

CAN The term CAN is usually applied to LANs or WANs that comprise the collection of interconnected nodes belonging to a single company or university/college but whose interconnection extends across many buildings.

MAN   This term is usually applied to the collection of nodes within a metropolitan area that fall under the same corporate control such as that of a telecommunications company or independent service provider (ISP).

If you think that these definitions of LAN, WAN, CAN, and MAN are a bit fuzzy, good! That's because they are! Furthermore, it's likely that they will get fuzzier as time goes on and technology presses forward.

As a consequence of the fuzziness of these terms, we define the term *local network* to mean the collection of all nodes connected via the same medium and sharing the same *network number*. We formally define network number in "IPv4 Addressing" on page 108, but for now think of sharing the same network number as meaning that no hardware or software boundaries must be crossed. In other words, nodes that share the same network number can communicate with each other without requiring the services of a *router* (router is defined in "The Internet Layer" on page 9). The definition of local network given here is synonymous with the definition of *link local scope* (defined in Chapter 5) and is quite similar to that of *broadcast domain*, which is defined in "Broadcast Addresses" on page 117.

Network Models

Let's start with a few definitions. A *network model* reflects a design or architecture to accomplish communication between different systems. Network models are also referred to as network *stacks* or *protocol suites*. Examples of network models includes TCP/IP, Sequenced Packet Exchange/Internet Packet Exchange (SPX/IPX) used by Novelle Netware, the Network Basic Input Output System (NetBIOS), which comprises the building blocks for most Microsoft networking and network applications; and AppleTalk, the network model for Apple Macintosh computers.

A network model usually consists of *layers*. Each layer of a model represents specific functionality. Within the layers of a model, there are usually *protocols* specified to implement specific tasks. You may think of a protocol as a set of rules or a language. Thus, a layer is normally a collection of protocols.

There are a number of different network models. Some of these models relate to a specific implementation, such as the TCP/IP network model. Others simply describe the process of networking, such as the International Organization for Standardization/Open System Interconnection Reference Model (ISO/OSI-RM, or more simply, OSI-RM).

OSI-RM

The International Organization for Standardization (ISO) is a worldwide body that promotes standards internationally. In the late 1970s, ISO began work on developing a standard for multivendor computer interconnectivity. The result, published in the late 1980s, was the Open System Interconnection (OSI) model. The OSI model incorporates protocols that can be used to implement a network stack. These protocols are not used extensively largely due to the popularity of the TCP/IP protocol suite. Consequently, the OSI model, with its well-defined layers, is used primarily as a reference model, hence, OSI-RM. Many network models are described by way of OSI-RM and so we provide a description of it here. The OSI-RM is depicted in Figure 1–1.

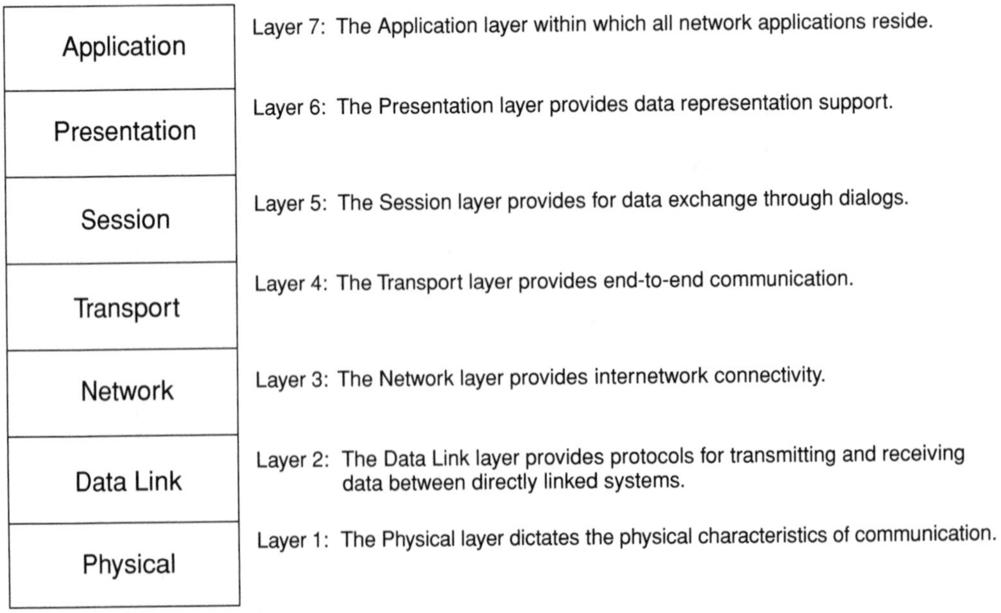

Application	Layer 7: The Application layer within which all network applications reside.
Presentation	Layer 6: The Presentation layer provides data representation support.
Session	Layer 5: The Session layer provides for data exchange through dialogs.
Transport	Layer 4: The Transport layer provides end-to-end communication.
Network	Layer 3: The Network layer provides internetwork connectivity.
Data Link	Layer 2: The Data Link layer provides protocols for transmitting and receiving data between directly linked systems.
Physical	Layer 1: The Physical layer dictates the physical characteristics of communication.

Figure 1–1   The OSI-RM

As indicated in Figure 1–1, each of the layers are numbered 1 through 7 from physical to application layer.

LAYER 7   All of the capabilities of networking begin in the Application layer. File transfer, messaging, web browsing, and other applications are in this layer. Each such application will appropriately invoke processing of data for transmission through well-defined interfaces to layer(s) below this one.

LAYER 6   The Presentation layer is responsible for data formatting. It takes care of such things as bit and byte ordering and floating point representation. Examples include External Data Representation (XDR) and Abstract Syntax Notation (ASN).

LAYER 5   The Session layer handles the exchange of data through dialog procedures or chat or conversation protocols. This layer is largely designed for mainframe and terminal communications. It has no relevance with respect to TCP/IP networking.

LAYER 4   The Transport layer is responsible for the reliable transfer of data between systems. It manages the communication session including flow control, ordering of information, error detection, and recovery of data.

LAYER 3   The Network layer owns the responsibility of delivering data between different systems in different interconnected networks (*internets*[1]).

LAYER 2   The Data Link layer provides rules for sending and receiving data between two connected nodes over a particular physical medium.

LAYER 1   The Physical layer defines the required hardware, such as cables and interfaces, for a given medium of communication, such as electrical, radio frequency, and light-based. In this way, methods for transmitting and receiving bit-streams of information are defined.

---

1. The term Internet (upper case I) is used to reference the public internetwork. The term internet (lower case i) is used to generally describe a collection of interconnected networks of which the Internet is one example.

NOTE

There is a great deal more to the OSI model than we have discussed here. For complete details on this standard, visit

```
http://www.iso.ch/cate/3510001.html
```

Also, see "For Further Reading" on page 15 for more resources on this topic.

Next, we discuss the TCP/IP model and begin our journey into the world of TCP/IP networking. We will compare it with the OSI model at the end of the next section.

The TCP/IP Network Model

The TCP/IP network model takes its name from two of its protocols, the Transmission Control Protocol (TCP) and the Internet Protocol (IP). Figure 1–2 provides a five-layer[2] representation of the TCP/IP Model. By utilizing a five-layer model, the lower four layers are numbered identically to the lower four layers of the OSI-RM model.

The lower four layers of the model represent functionality performed internally by the Linux kernel. The Application layer includes commands and daemons.

The process of initiating a network communication, like executing `telnet hostname`, causes the initiator (usually the *client*) to *encapsulate* application data, beginning at the top of the model and moving down, for the network transmission. In other words, each layer wraps the data passed to it by the previous layer with information used to determine where the packet is supposed to go and which service needs to be invoked to handle the application data itself. The information added by each layer is called a *header* when it is prefixed to the data from the previous layer, and a *trailer* when it is suffixed. On the left-hand side of Figure 1–2, you see an increasing number of rectangles as you scan down the layers. The area in gray represents the information added by each layer.

The receiving system, normally the *server*, performs the same steps except in reverse (bottom to top), *deencapsulating* the data. Each layer is responsible for

---

2. Many texts will use a four-layer representation, combining the Hardware and Network Interface layers.

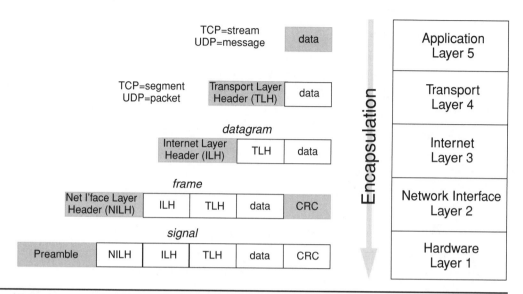

Figure 1–2   The TCP/IP Model

interpreting the header generated by the same layer on the sending system. This process is known as *peer-to-peer* communication.

The information produced during encapsulation, or read during deencapsulation by each layer is ascribed a name as shown in Figure 1–2. For Layer 5, if the underlying Transport layer protocol is the TCP, then the data produced or read by Layer 5 is called a *stream*; if the underlying Transport layer protocol is the User Datagram Protocol (UDP), then it is called a *message*. For Layer 4, if the protocol used is TCP, then the data produced or read by Layer 4 is called a *segment*. Otherwise, if it is UDP, then it is called a *packet*. The data of Layer 3 is called a *datagram*; of Layer 2, a *frame* or *cell*; and of Layer 1, a *signal*.

NOTE

The term *packet* is commonly used instead of signal and/or frame.

In the following sections, we will briefly review the information generated by each layer and its purpose.

The Hardware Layer

The Hardware layer is responsible for exactly that—hardware. This includes cables, interface cards, and repeaters. It accepts the data passed to it by the Network Interface layer and prefixes something called the *Preamble*, which is a well-known sequence of 64 bits used for synchronization purposes. When it finishes its work, it generates a *signal* to be submitted to the media (electrically-based cables in most cases). The Hardware layer also imposes the maximum transfer unit (MTU) used by the Internet layer to ensure that the Hardware layer does not get *frames*[3] that are too large or too small. For Ethernet, the MTU for the signal is 1526 octets, and the minimum signal size is 72 octets.[4]

There are two hardware devices which operate at this layer: *repeaters* and *amplifiers*. A repeater is a device with a number of ports (usually four or more) that is capable of receiving signals, filtering out noise (phenomena not related to the communication at hand), and repeating the signals to every port except the ingress (incoming) port. Amplifiers perform the same task, except that they do not filter noise. Consequently, repeaters are employed in electrical communications environments and amplifiers are employed in light-based communications environments. These devices are often called *hubs* or *concentrators*. We will discuss this layer in greater detail in Chapter 2.

The Network Interface Layer

You may think of the Network Interface layer as a collection of device drivers. Its responsibility is to prepare the data passed to it from the Internet layer for signaling. It does this by prefixing its header (indicated as NILH in Figure 1–2), computing a Cyclic Redundancy Check (CRC—a 32-bit checksum), appending the CRC to the datagram, and passing this information to the device (interface) for signaling in what is called a frame. In particular, this layer understands *physical* addresses (often referred to as Media Access Control [MAC] addresses). When using Ethernet, this is often called an Ethernet address. Physical

---

3. The data of the Network Interface layer is called a frame when it varies in size. More formally, when using Ethernet, it should be called an *Ethernet frame*. Fixed size data at this layer, such as that used by Asynchronous Transfer Mode (ATM), is called a *cell*.

4. MTU is further discussed throughout the next several chapters, but note that it is more common to quote the Ethernet frame MTU, which is 1518 octets. The minimum Ethernet frame size is 64 octets. Note that frames occur at the Network Access layer. Here we are describing the Hardware layer.

addresses are local and only need to be unique within the local network. For Ethernet interface chipsets, they are 48-bit addresses permanently written into the programmable read-only memory (PROM).

The Network Interface layer writes both the destination and source physical address into its header during encapsulation. Consequently, it is at this layer that, during deencapsulation, initial decisions are made about whether or not to continue processing an incoming frame up the stack. This is discussed in detail in Chapter 2.

There is one device associated with this layer. It is a *switch*. Switches look very much like repeaters, a piece of hardware with at least two network ports, but are more intelligent than repeaters. Since they operate at the Network Interface layer, they are able to make decisions based on physical addresses. Switches are sometimes called hubs or *bridges* or *layer 2 routers*.

NOTE

Switches are sometimes called bridges (or the other way around, if you like). Bridge is an older term that is not commonly used today. Unfortunately, the terms *switching*, *layer 2 switching*, and *layer 3 switching* all confound the issue of what is really being described. Most of the variation in the base term "switch" comes from vendors of switches and routers. An argument could be made that the proper term for the layer 2 device that is capable of making packet-forwarding decisions based on physical addresses is "bridge." A similar argument could be made for the term switch. I could coin a new term, say *swidge*, but I haven't got the courage, and, besides, it would probably make matters worse. After all, companies like Cisco aren't likely to change their terminology just because I say so.

I had to make a decision about which term to use. So I decided to use switch. Throughout this book, I will make no distinction between bridge and switch and will use the term switch to mean a layer 2 device that is capable of making packet-forwarding decisions based on physical addresses.

The Internet Layer

The Internet layer is responsible for a variety of tasks. In order to accomplish these tasks it uses three principal protocols. The Internet Protocol (IP), the Internet Control Messaging Protocol (ICMP), and the Internet Group Management Protocol (IGMP). The IP is responsible for *routing* and *fragmentation*.[5] The ICMP generates error messages, assists routing through redirection, may implement rudimentary flow control, supports the `ping` command, supports router discovery, and may generate timestamp and netmask queries and responses. The IGMP supports Internet Layer multicasting. Each of these protocols has two available versions: 4 and 6.

The device that operates at this layer is a *router*. Routers are nodes that implement the intelligence of the Internet layer protocols and forward datagrams to the appropriate *networks* or *subnetworks* (discussed in Chapter 4) based on *IP addresses* and the *routing algorithm* (described in Chapter 6). Routers are sometimes called layer 3 switches. Unfortunately, routers are also sometimes called hubs.

The Internet layer produces or reads the Internet layer header. The header contains a lot of information and, in particular, includes the source and destination IP address associated with the packet. There are two versions of the protocols in this layer: version 4 and version 6. IPv4 addresses are 4 octets while IPv6 addresses are 16 octets. These are global addresses, meaning that all nodes throughout a collection of networks that are interconnected (*internet*) must be uniquely identified by this address. Data is passed through such an internet by the process of *routing*. Routing is performed by examining a portion of an IP address in order to determine to which network the data needs to be sent (effectively the purpose of the routing algorithm). Linux systems can act as routers. This header, together with the overall functionality of the Internet layer, is largely discussed in Chapters 4, 5, and 6. Additional details of the Internet layer and Linux router functionality are given in the last six chapters of this book.

The Transport Layer

The Transport Layer is responsible for the end-to-end flow of data. There are two primary protocols used within this layer (TCP and the UDP). An application will use one or the other of these protocols for a given communication. These protocols, the headers they produce or read, and the Transport layer are described in Chapter 7.

---

5. Fragmentation applies to IP version 4 only.

The Application Layer

This is the layer where all the applications live. These applications are responsible for understanding the data format as well as interpreting the data. Example applications include the Domain Name Service (DNS), the Dynamic Host Configuration Protocol (DHCP), the Network File System (NFS), Samba, electronic mail (e-mail), the file transfer protocol (FTP), and the `telnet` utility. The Application layer is discussed in Chapter 8.

The device that operates at this layer is the *gateway*. Unfortunately, gateway is a term, somewhat like hub, that is used in many ways. We generally define it to mean a link between distinct and/or different computer networks. Often, it is used to refer to a system that is capable of converting from one network protocol stack to another, such as a system that is interconnected into both a TCP/IP network and a Netware network. Gateway is often used to refer to a system that interconnects an internal internetwork and an external network such as the Internet. Other uses of the term gateway are described as they arise.

OSI-RM and TCP/IP Model Comparison

Figure 1–3 depicts the relationship between the OSI-RM and the TCP/IP model.

The relationship between these two models at Layers 1, 2, and 3 is identical. While the diagram in Figure 1–3 shows a one-to-one correspondence at Layer 4, it should be noted that UDP does not perform all of the functions required by the OSI-RM Transport layer; we will explore this fact further in Chapter 7.

The Application layer of the TCP/IP model assumes responsibility for the Session, Presentation, and Application layer of the OSI-RM. This relationship will be detailed further in Chapter 8 and numerous subsequent chapters.

One of the advantages of depicting the TCP/IP model as a five-layer model is that we can refer to Layer 1, 2, and 3 of both models. We will do so throughout this book.

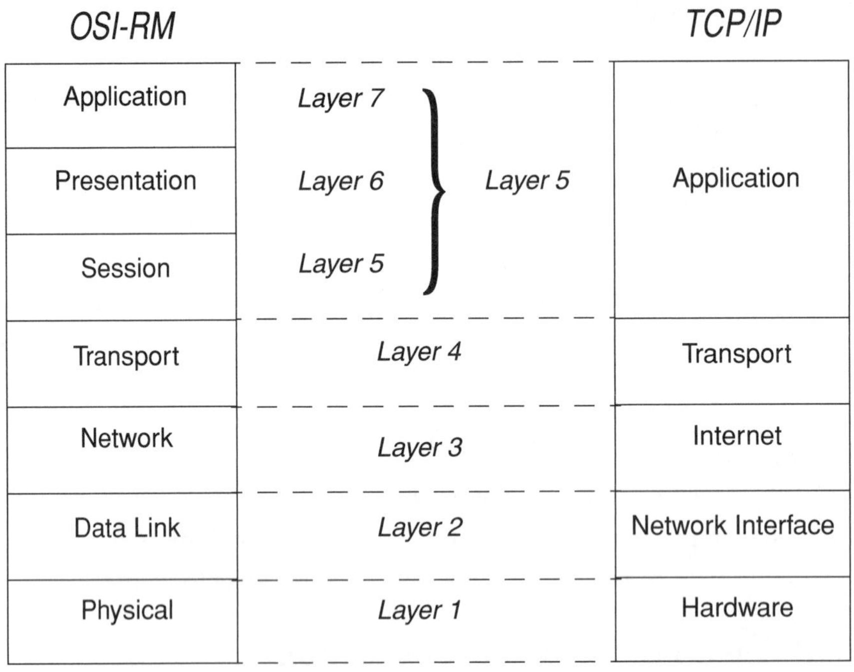

OSI-RM		TCP/IP
Application	*Layer 7*	
Presentation	*Layer 6* } *Layer 5*	Application
Session	*Layer 5*	
Transport	*Layer 4*	Transport
Network	*Layer 3*	Internet
Data Link	*Layer 2*	Network Interface
Physical	*Layer 1*	Hardware

Figure 1–3   OSI-RM and TCP/IP Comparison

The Client-Server Model

It may be rather like stating the obvious, but we define the terms *server* and *client*. A server is a network node that makes compute or data resources available. A client is a network node that utilizes server resources. Of course, for clients and servers to interact, they must be interconnected.

Nodes may act in one, both, or neither capacity of server and client. Generally speaking, from the Linux perspective, the client is the system upon which a command invoking a network-based application is executed. The server is the system on which a *daemon* is running. A daemon is a special program that responds to and handles resource requests. Throughout this book we will deal with, and further refine, these terms.

Request for Comment

The vast majority of the protocols and standards that we discuss throughout this book are embodied in a Request for Comment (RFC), more specifically, an

RFC developed and/or maintained by the Internet Engineering Task Force (IETF).

The overall controlling entity for Internet standards is the Internet Society (ISOC). The Internet Architecture Board (IAB) and the IETF both fall under the ISOC. The IETF does the actual technical work while the IAB handles a lot of the administrative details. The Internet Engineering Steering Group (IESG), also part of the ISOC, provides technical direction for the IAB and the IETF. Our interest is with the work of the IETF and, in particular, with RFCs that provide a standard that is implemented in TCP/IP networking. In addition to *standards track* RFCs (RFCs that have been approved as standards or are becoming standards), the IETF also produces informational and best current practice RFCs that provide details about the implementation and use of some technology without being a standard. You can learn more about the IETF and the associated organizations discussed in this paragraph at

```
http://www.ietf.org/
```

For complete details about IETF RFCs, please see the site

```
http://www.ietf.org/rfc.html
```

A search engine for RFCs can be found at

```
http://www.rfc-editor.org/
```

Where appropriate, we will discuss specific RFCs at various points in this book.

There is another type of RFC maintained by an organization called the Open Group. The Open Group RFCs also define standards and protocols, but are less common. For further information regarding the Open Group RFCs, please visit

```
http://www.opengroup.org/rfc/
```

Throughout this document, all RFCs are IETF RFCs unless specifically identified as an Open Group RFC.

Institute of Electrical and Electronics Engineers (IEEE)

The IEEE is a non-profit technical organization that, among other things, promotes standards for a variety of computing technologies, largely at layers 1 and 2 of the TCP/IP stack. We will be referring to their standards throughout this text. You can learn more about IEEE at their home and standards pages:

```
http://www.ieee.org/
http://standards.ieee.org/
```

Throughout this book we will reference a variety of standards from the IEEE. Table 1–1 lists the high-level IEEE standard number and its general coverage of each standard number.

Table 1–1   IEEE High-Level Standards

Standard Number	Description
802.1	High-level architectural overview
802.2	Logical link control (LLC)
802.3	Ethernet with CSMA/CD
802.4	Token bus
802.5	Token ring
802.6	MANs
802.7	Broadband LANs
802.8	Fiber optic LANs
802.9	Data and voice network integration
802.10	Security and privacy
802.11	Wireless networking

For complete coverage of these standards, see the IEEE Web sites referenced above.

There is an excellent write-up of the topics discussed in the last six chapters of this book, including the relationship between IEEE standards and the lower layer ISO standards, at

```
http://www.cs.herts.ac.uk/~simon/networks1/node1.html
```

The Internet, TCP/IP, and Other Stacks

Only a few short years ago you would have been hard-pressed to find 10 people outside of the computer industry who knew about the Internet. Today, it is nearly taken for granted.

The Internet is a global collection of WANs and LANs that are all interconnected. Participation in the Internet ultimately requires TCP/IP capability in the form of a node acting as an Internet gateway or portal. From that perspective, TCP/IP is the network stack of the Internet. There are other network stacks at play within the Internet, and indeed, in a variety of roles throughout the computer industry.

Summary

In this chapter we introduced the OSI-RM and TCP/IP model, briefly described each of their layers, and compared the two models. Additionally, we introduced the client-server model and RFCs. We also defined a number of terms that we will use throughout this text.

For Further Reading

Listed below are books and WWW resources that provide further information about the topics discussed in this chapter.

Books

Comer, Douglas E., *Internetworking with TCP/IP Vol I: Principals, Protocols, Architecture*, 3rd. ed., Englewood Cliffs, New Jersey, Prentice Hall, 1995.
Huitema, Christian, *Routing in the Internet*, Englewood Cliffs, New Jersey, Prentice Hall PTR, 1995.
Perlman, Radia, *Interconnections, Second Edition: Bridges, Routers, Switches, and Internetworking Protocols*, Reading, Massachusetts, Addison-Wesley, 2000.
Stevens, W. Richard, *TCP/IP Illustrated, Volume 1: The Protocols*, Reading, Massachusetts, Addison-Wesley, 1994.

WWW Resources

You will find OSI information at the ISO home page:

```
http://www.iso.ch/
```

IETF RFCs can be found at

```
http://www.ietf.org/rfc.html
```

and Open Group RFCs at

```
http://www.opengroup.org/rfc/
```

For IEEE standards and information, see their home page or standards page:

```
http://www.ieee.org/
http://standards.ieee.org/
```

2

Hardware and Network Interface Layers: Network Access

Network access within the TCP/IP model is controlled by the lower two layers: the Hardware and Network Interface layers. As we discussed in the previous chapter, the Hardware layer deals with physical components like network interface cards (NICs) and cables, and is responsible for the generation of signals; the Network Interface layer addresses the issue of converting the datagram (from the Internet layer) into a frame or cell and submitting it to the Hardware layer. In this chapter, we will look at these two lower layers and the functionality they provide, including NIC types and their application, device driver support, and device/device driver configuration. We will also discuss network topologies.

Generally speaking, network administrators don't expend a lot of effort dealing with the details of these lower two layers. We do need to have a basic understanding of what is happening here and a notion of how to troubleshoot problems which may arise with hardware and/or device drivers. It is from that perspective that this chapter is written.

Hardware Layer

The Hardware layer consists of the actual components which generate and carry the data communication. This fundamentally boils down to repeaters (and/or amplifiers), media (cables or air), and NICs. The role of repeaters or amplifiers is topology dependent and either extends the total distance that signals can be sent or expands the total number of nodes that are physically attached to the signaling media, or both. We will look at these devices in this and the next sections.

Cables (or air) provide the physical media by which signals are carried. There are three fundamental types of media: electrical (thinnet, thicknet, twisted-pair, serial, parallel, etc.), light-carrying (fiber-optic), and wireless (radio frequency [RF], microwave, infrared, etc.)—we will discuss various cable types later in the chapter. NICs act as the interface between the node and the communication media; they are responsible for the tasks of receiving and transmitting signals and will be discussed later in this section. First, let's take a look at the Hardware layer signal.

Figure 2–1 shows us the Hardware layer of the TCP/IP model and the breakout of the signal it generates. Note that we refer to the upper layer data submitted to this layer as the *payload*. We will use the term payload to refer to the data and headers provided by an upper layer of a model.

The Hardware layer generally prefixes the preamble before generating the signal during encapsulation. During deencapsulation, it interprets the preamble and then strips it off before passing the payload up to the Network Interface layer. The preamble is a well known sequence of bits used to synchronize communication between two nodes. This, together with the encoding scheme,[1] ensures signaling and timing synchronization.

Not all Hardware layer technologies use a preamble. For example, most implementations of asynchronous transfer mode (ATM) have no synchronization mechanism embedded in their transmissions. Instead, they rely on fixed sized *cells* and very accurate clocks at each node that are synchronized. A cell is conceptually the same as a frame except that cells are fixed in size.

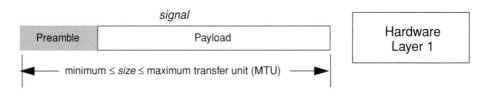

Figure 2–1   Hardware Layer of the TCP/IP Model

---

1. Encoding schemes, among other things, provide a method for synchronizing the timing in data transmissions and is dictated by the layer 2 technology implemented. See, for example, *Ethernet: The Definitive Guide* as cited in "For Further Reading" on page 52.

Notice also that Figure 2–1 specifies a *size* for the signal. This size is a range of values between the acceptable minimum and maximum for a given hardware technology. For 10 and 100 megabits per second (Mbps) Ethernet, the minimum size of the signal must be 72 octets; the maximum cannot exceed 1526 octets.[2] The latter value is called the maximum transfer (or transmission) unit (MTU). This means that Ethernet signals vary in size and so the receiving system will have to process the incoming packet to determine its payload size. The MTU is very important for routing and we will discuss it further in later chapters.

Media

There are all sorts of cables (and virtual cables) used as media for network communications. Here, we will touch on the major types and provide a bit more detail about Ethernet related media.

Electrical

Cables capable of carrying electrical signals are the most common form of network communications media. Table 2–1 lists a sample of some of the more common types of electrically based cables and the layer 2 technologies which use them.

Electrical communications fall into one of two general categories: *broadband* or *baseband*. Broadband communications provide for multiplexing of signals at different frequency ranges through the same cable. These signals may be digital, analog, or a combination thereof. Examples of technologies that utilize broadband services include cable and DSL. Baseband communications utilize the full bandwidth of the electrical media for a single digital signal. Baseband technologies are most common for local area networks like Ethernet networks.

Most network implementations today are concerned with Ethernet. With the advent of high-speed, low cost technologies (DSL and cable *modems*[3] and giga-

---

2. Once again, the MTU for an Ethernet frame is 1518 octets. The minimum Ethernet frame size is 64 octets. Note that signals are layer 1 phenomenon while frames occur at layer 2. Here, we are considering layer 1.

3. Modem is short for modulator-demodulator, a type of device that converts digital to analog signals and back again—strictly a layer 1 device. DSL and cable "modems" are really layer 2 devices and the signals are all digital for DSL and often digital for cable. Nonetheless, the use of the term modem persists in these cases.

Table 2–1   Electrical Cables Used for Networking

Type of Cable	Example Layer 2 Technology
Serial	X.25, an International Telecommunications Union-Telecommunications (ITU-T) standard and High Speed Serial Interface (HSSI)
Parallel	High Performance Parallel Interface (HIPPI), an American National Standards Institute (ANSI) standard
Coaxial	Ethernet and cable services
Twisted-Pair	Ethernet, ATM, Copper Distributed Data Interface (CDDI), digital subscriber line (DSL), and many others

bit Ethernet) utilizing Ethernet as (at least in part) their communication media, this is sure to grow even further. Consequently, we provide in Table 2–2 a list of the major Ethernet cable types.

Table 2–2   Ethernet Electrical Cable Types

Cable	Description
Thin Coaxial	A thin (0.2 inch diameter) insulated coaxial copper cable used for 10 megabits per second (Mbps) Ethernet. Also referred to as *thinnet*. This type of cable is rarely used today. Uses a Bayonet-Neill-Concelman (BNC) barrel connector still found on many NICs available today.
Thick Coaxial	A thick (0.4 inch diameter) insulated coaxial copper cable used for 10 Mbps Ethernet. Also referred to as *thicknet*. This type of cable is rarely used today. Uses a 15-pin attachment unit interface (AUI) connector or an N-series barrel connector.

Table 2–2   Ethernet Electrical Cable Types *(Continued)*

CABLE	DESCRIPTION
Category 3 Twisted-pair	A voice grade cable consisting of two or four pairs of 22–26 American wire gauge (awg) twisted wires. Supports data transmission rates of up to 10 Mbps at up to 16 megahertz (MHz). Uses a registered jack[a] (RJ) 45 connector. Also known as Cat3.
Category 4 Twisted-pair	A data grade twisted-pair cable supporting transmission rates of up to 20 Mbps at up to 20 MHz. This cable was originally designed to support 16 Mbps token ring. It is no longer widely used in favor of Cat 5. Uses RJ45 connectors. Also known as Cat4.
Category 5 Twisted-pair	A data grade twisted-pair cable designed to support transmission rates of up to 1,000 Mbps (or 1 gigabit per second [1 Gbps]) at up to 100 MHz. Also known as Cat5. This is the most widely used Ethernet cable today.
Category 5e Twisted-pair	An enhanced Cat5 cable specifically designed to support 1 Gbps Ethernet at up to 200 MHz. Also known as Cat5e.
Category 6 Twisted-pair	An emerging standard that will support significantly higher signal performance (250 MHz to 600 MHz).

a. Registered with the Federal Communication Commission (FCC).

Twisted-pair (TP) cabling is called that because each pair of wires is twisted around each other at some number of twists per foot. For data communication purposes, the most commonly used connector is the RJ45 8-pin connector. Newer twisted-pair cables can be had with the 40-pin medium independent interface (MII) connector (which then requires a NIC with that type of connector). TP cabling is normally available in unshielded (UTP) or shielded (STP) form. STP, due to its high cost, is normally only used in environments that require safeguards against electronic eavesdropping, or environments which expose the cable to a lot of electronic *noise*. Electronic noise is any electrical phenomena which generates signals that are not part of the communication.

Light-Carrying

Light-based communications operate by sending pulses (signals, if you will) of light through a light carrying medium. This mechanism requires a NIC that is capable of generating the light pulses (a laser) and receiving the light pulses together with a cable that can carry the light transmission.

Cables used for light transmissions use fiber optic plastic or glass strands that have very small diameters. These fiber optic cables are then wrapped in cladding (usually a plastic material) and an outer skin of plastic/rubber. These cables fall into one of two categories: multimode fiber optic cables (MMF) and single mode fiber optic cables (SMF). The difference between these two types of cables is the diameter of the light bearing fiber cable. The diameter of MMF cables are usually 50 micrometers (one millionth of a meter, also called a *micron*) or 62.5 microns. The diameter of SMF cables is in the range of 8 to 10 microns. SMF cables are capable of much greater transmission distances due to the fact that their diameter closely matches the wavelength of signals used for data transmission.

For a good treatment of the practical aspects of this type of media, read *Ethernet: The Definitive Guide* as referenced in "For Further Reading" on page 52.

Wireless

Wireless data communications technologies have been with us for a long time. In fact, the roots of Ethernet are found in the experimental Alohanet developed in the late 1960s, a radio frequency (RF) based data communication scheme which interconnected systems throughout the Hawaiian islands. Also, microwave and satellite communications have been bringing us data communications in various forms since the late 1950s.

The use of RF communications for local area networks has received a lot of attention in recent years and promises to provide an inexpensive alternative to traditional electrically-based local area networks in the very near future. Moreover, these technologies are being developed with interconnectivity to a variety of nodes, including TCP/IP networks, in mind. The IEEE has issued the 802.11 standard covering wireless LANs and continues to add to that standard. Other standards and specifications are still emerging with many vendors supplying RF NICs and other devices to support the demand.

For further details about this type of technology, see "For Further Reading" on page 52.

NIC Types

There are a variety of NIC types that can be used together with a layer 2 technology to implement a particular network access mechanism. For example, an ATM NIC can be used to implement ATM (no surprise there!) and an Ethernet card can be used to implement Ethernet or Novelle Netware using the Sequenced Packet Exchange/Internetwork Packet Exchange (SPX/IPX) networking model. Next we look at enabling Network Interface (layer 2) technologies and the NICs they use.

Network Interface Layer

Figure 2–2 shows the Network Interface layer and an Ethernet-like frame it either reads or generates.

Shown in gray are the headers and trailers which are prefixed and suffixed, respectively, to the payload from layer 3 by layer 2. The header consists of the destination physical address and then the source physical address. The trailer consists of the cyclic redundancy check (CRC), which is a simple 32-bit checksum of the payload and header. This frame is representative of an Ethernet or IEEE 802.3 frame. Before we get into the details of frames, let's take a look at some of the other layer 2 technologies.

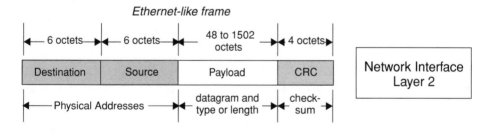

Figure 2–2   Network Interface Layer of the TCP/IP Model

Technologies

There are a great many layer 2 technologies which are implemented for a variety of purposes throughout the computing industry. We provide a list of some of the more common technologies in Table 2–3.

Table 2–3   Some Common Layer 2 Technologies

LAYER 2 TECHNOLOGY	DESCRIPTION
X.25	An ITU-T standard that has been used extensively as a wide area technology in Europe.
HIPPI	Originally designed to interconnect supercomputers through a short parallel cable, this technology evolved into a high speed backbone (800 Mbps–1,600 Mbps) over fiber. It is also used as a high speed disk interface.
Ethernet/ IEEE 802.3	Unquestionably the most common LAN technology. Supports data speeds of 10 Mbps to 1 Gbps. Efforts are underway to develop 10 Gbps Ethernet.
Token Ring	This technology supports data rates from 4 Mbps to 100 Mbps. There are two standard frame formats, IBM and IEEE 802.5. Uses a token passing scheme for media access instead of carrier sense, multiple access with collision detection (CSMA/CD). Media access is discussed in "Media Access Method" on page 28. Token ring is the nearest competitor to Ethernet.
FDDI/CDDI	A heavily adopted backbone technology operating at 100 Mbps and using IBM token ring frames. Given the advent of 100 Mbps and 1 Gbps Ethernet, Fiber Distributed Data Interface (FDDI) and CDDI are slowly being replaced, even though the emerging version 2 of the standard promises 1 Gbps performance.
Fibre Channel	Standardized by ANSI X3T11, this fiber based technology offers speeds from 100 Mbps to 1 Gbps for both networking and node to device communication.

Table 2–3   Some Common Layer 2 Technologies *(Continued)*

LAYER 2 TECHNOLOGY	DESCRIPTION
ATM	Standardized by ITU-T and other organizations, this technology represents incredible potential with data rates ranging from 25 Mbps to 10 Gbps (with lots of room for growth). This technology utilizes circuit switching, enabling it to establish virtual circuits at layer 2. Running TCP/IP over ATM is cumbersome, particularly with IPv4.
PPP	The Point-to-Point Protocol (PPP) provides for IP over serial.

Our focus will be on Ethernet since it is by far the most commonly used layer 2 technology. Throughout our TCP/IP discussions, we will provide comments about other technologies where appropriate.

The technologies of layer 2 are implemented using a particular *topology* or physical layout. In the next section, we cover the major topologies employed in networking systems together.

Topologies

There are three major LAN topologies: bus, star, and ring. Each is described in the following sections.

Bus

A *bus* topology is a collection of nodes which are interconnected by being physically attached to single cable. Thinnet and thicknet Ethernet implementations use the bus topology. The cable must be properly terminated so that the signals will behave properly on the medium. Each node interconnects to this primary cable through some mechanism. For thicknet, this is commonly accomplished through a short cable going from the node to the primary cable called a *drop* cable. For thinnet, this is commonly accomplished with a special "T" shaped BNC connector. Figure 2–3 depicts the bus topology.

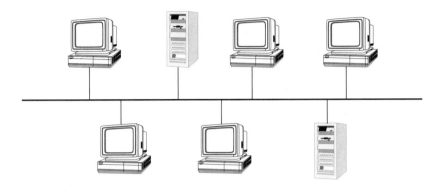

Figure 2–3   Bus Topology

Star

Star topologies are a result of the adoption of twisted-pair cabling technology. In a star topology, each node is connected to a black box, usually a repeater but sometimes a switch. In this way, the repeater or switch acts like the single cable described in the bus topology scenario. Figure 2–4 illustrates a star topology.

Most Ethernet LANs today use a star topology. Throughout the book, however, most of our diagrams will appear as if a bus topology is employed. The use of such diagrams is for clarity; for our purposes, star and bus topologies will be treated identically.

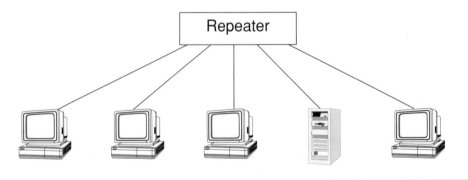

Figure 2–4   Star Topology

Ring

Ring topologies are employed to support token ring implementations such as those of FDDI/CDDI, IBM token ring, and IEEE 802.5. The distinctions between token passing methods and CSMA/CD are described in the next section. Figure 2–5 shows a ring topology.

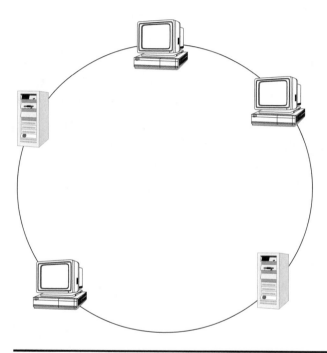

Figure 2–5   Ring Topology

Media Access Method

LAN technologies such as Ethernet and token ring utilize a shared media access method to permit the various nodes in the network access to the network media itself. Ethernet implements CSMA/CD, while token ring implements token passing. These two different methods exist to resolve network contention.

CSMA/CD

CSMA/CD permits each node connected to the physical medium to detect whether or not there is a signal on the medium (carrier sense). Each node will poll the medium for this purpose. All nodes can do this simultaneously (multiple access). Since all nodes can detect whether a signal is on the medium or not, they can determine that the medium is clear (no signal). If a node needs to transmit data, it is when the medium is clear that it will do so by sending the signal through its NIC to the communication medium. This all works fine until more than one system submits a signal at the same time. Such an event causes the signals to *collide*.

Fortunately, CSMA/CD includes collision detection (the "CD" part of the acronym). When two or more simultaneously generated signals collide, the first node to detect the collision will generate a special signal called a *jam* signal which informs all participants in the collision that their packets were destroyed and will need to be retransmitted.

The reason that the collision occurred is because the two or more nodes involved have synchronized polling periods. To avoid future collisions, whenever a node is involved in a collision it will adjust its polling period by computing a delay (using an algorithm that incorporates some randomness) that it will wait before it retransmits and starts polling again. Note that collisions and collision detection are normal operations and do not represent errors. It is only when the *collision rate* exceeds certain thresholds that there are performance problems. The collision rate is simply the number of collisions expressed as a percentage of all outbound packets.

Because of this shared approach, this type of technology implements what is called a *packet switched* network. Packet switched means that each sequential packet submitted to the communication medium may have nothing to do with each other. That is, at time t_0 a packet destined to host C is transmitted by host A, then at time t_1, the next opportunity for the medium to be used for transmission, host B sends a packet to host D. In essence, the network switches the "connection" with each packet. Contrast this with a *circuit switched* network, such as that implemented with ATM, in which a virtual circuit is established between the two communicating nodes before any data is sent. Once the circuit is complete, all data that traverses through the circuit is dedicated to the communication between the two connected nodes.

For a thorough treatment of CSMA/CD, see *Ethernet: The Definitive Guide*. For more details about ATM and circuit switching, check out some of the references in "For Further Reading" on page 52.

Token Passing

Token ring networks use a different method for sharing the medium. In a token ring implementation, in order for a node to transmit data that node must first have the token. Only one node on the given ring can have the token at any given moment in time and, therefore, only one node can communicate at a given moment in time. Therefore, collisions do not occur.

Switches

As noted in Chapter 1, switches operate at layer 2 because they are capable of reading (and sometimes writing) the contents of the frame header and trailer, and making decisions based on the information contained therein. In particular, a switch can read the destination physical address of an incoming packet and forward it to the specific port to which the device with that physical address is attached. Contrast this capability with a repeater (layer 1), which simply forwards incoming packets to all of its ports except the port on which the packet originally arrived (called the *ingress* port). In other words, repeaters have no intelligence with respect to the packets they process. Figure 2–6 illustrates this difference.

Note that Figure 2–6 shows that the repeater sends the packets to all nodes, whereas the switch only forwards packets to the specific node. If we consider a CSMA/CD implementation, such as with Ethernet, this difference alone can offer substantial performance benefits. Additional performance benefits are also realized with the use of switches because most modern switches can accommodate multiple simultaneous communications. Figure 2–6 depicts this by showing

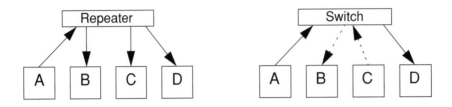

Figure 2-6   Difference between a Repeater and a Switch

A communicating with D (solid line) and C communicating with D (dashed line) simultaneously.

Switches also provide a security enhancement. Consider the case in which a *network sniffer*[4] is running on host B as depicted in Figure 2–6. In the case of a repeater, all network packets are readable by the sniffer, even those that are not destined for host B. In the case of a switch, on the other hand, the only packets that arrive at host B are those that are destined to it and so the sniffer cannot capture other packets on the LAN.

NOTE

It could be that some or all of the nodes, A, B, C, and D, shown in Figure 2–6 are LANs as opposed to individual hosts. For example, suppose that A is a host whereas B, C, and D are LANs interconnected via a bus, star, or ring topology. In such a case, the repeater behaves as previously described—forwarding all packets to all ports except the ingress port. The switch behaves in the same way as well—forwarding packets only to the port associated with the destination physical address. The difference in this case is that the switch maintains a list of the physical addresses of all the nodes within LAN B and associates them with the port to which LAN B is connected instead of associating a single physical address to that port. The switch will maintain the same sort of list for LANs C and D.

---

4. A network sniffer is a utility that is capable of capturing all the network packets on the shared medium. We discuss network sniffers in "Viewing Network Packets" on page 80.

Switches are available for a great many layer 2 technologies including Ethernet, token ring, and ATM.

Ethernet

Ethernet was originally developed in the early 1970s and eventually standardized by Digital Equipment Corporation, Intel, and Xerox (DIX). DIX Ethernet version 2 was released in 1982 and remains the standard today.

IEEE published the 802.3 standard in 1985. The significant difference (there are some minor distinctions) between Ethernet version 2 and IEEE 802.3 at that time was that where the Ethernet standard specified a 2 octet type field, the IEEE 802.3 standard defined a 2 octet length field (see Figure 2–7). In 1997, IEEE modified 802.3 to recognize both varieties of this 2 octet field, thus effectively merging Ethernet version 2 into IEEE 802.3. The purpose of the field and the differences between type and length are described in "The Type and Length Field" on page 34. Today, almost all Ethernet implementations (drivers and NICs) adhere to the IEEE 802.3 standard. Figure 2–7 depicts the Ethernet version 2 and IEEE 802.3 frames.

In Figure 2–7, we see that the two frames are nearly identical. Each frame begins with a destination Ethernet (or physical or MAC) address, followed by a source Ethernet address, followed by the 2 octet type and/or length field, followed by the datagram produced by layer 3, and ending with the CRC. We've already defined the CRC and we'll get to the datagram in Chapters 4 (IPv4) and 5 (IPv6), so for now let's describe the addresses and the 2 octet type/length field in more detail.

6 octets	6 octets	2 octets	46 to 1500 octets	4 octets
Destination Physical Address	Source Physical Address	Type	Datagram	CRC

Ethernet version 2 frame

6 octets	6 octets	2 octets	46 to 1500 octets	4 octets
Destination Physical Address	Source Physical Address	Type/ Length	Datagram	CRC

IEEE 802.3 frame

Figure 2–7   Ethernet Version 2 and IEEE 802.3 Frame Formats

NOTE

The MTU for both Ethernet and 802.3 style frames is 1518 octets. The minimum frame size is 64 octets (there is somewhat of an exception to the minimum size for 802.3ab [gigabit Ethernet over twisted-pair]—see *Ethernet: The Definitive Guide* for details). Since the header and trailer of the frames are fixed in size, the variability in the size of the frame (and, hence, the signal) is in the datagram. Thus, the imposition of the MTU most directly affects the amount of data that can be passed from layer 3 to layer 2. It is therefore the responsibility of layer 3 to ensure that the MTU is not exceeded. We discuss this further in Chapters 4 and 5.

ETHERNET ADDRESSES   An Ethernet address is 48 bits (6 octets) and is stored in silicon, usually in a read-only memory chip, on the NIC. Whenever a system initiates encapsulation and the Internet layer passes the datagram to the Network Interface layer, it will use this Ethernet address as the value to place in the source address field of the frame. When receiving a network packet, the Network Interface layer examines the destination Ethernet address and determines what to do with the packet based on that address. A destination Ethernet address may be one of three types: *unicast, multicast,* or *broadcast.* A unicast address is one that identically matches an address of a NIC. A multicast address is one which a node on the network can be configured to pay attention to. This type of address is known as a group address, since it is used to communicate to a collection of nodes simultaneously. A broadcast address is a special case of a multicast address in which all nodes are members—that is, all nodes will pay attention to a frame with the destination address set to the broadcast address.

Ethernet addresses are ordinarily referenced in colon separated hexadecimal notation. For example,

```
00:60:94:B9:83:0A
```

represents a unicast Ethernet address. Each two digits represents an octet. The leftmost three octets of an Ethernet address are assigned to specific vendors by the IEEE and are called *vendor codes* or, more formally, organizationally unique identifiers (OUI). In this example, the vendor code `00:60:94` belongs to IBM. You can get a list of these OUI assignments at

```
http://standards.ieee.org/regauth/oui/oui.txt
```

The rightmost 3 octets are, theoretically, unique to the NIC and usually reflect all or part of the serial number of the card. Occasionally, cards with duplicate addresses are found. This is unusual and, even if it does occur, is only a problem in the event that both NICs are employed in the same local network. In such a case, one of the NICs will need to have its address changed (changing the MAC address, if supported by the device driver, can be done with the `ifconfig` command, which is discussed in Chapter 4).

OH, BY THE WAY...

Not all vendors assign the Ethernet address to each NIC. Sun Microsystems, Inc. shipped systems for many years which incorporated the Ethernet address in the non-volatile random access memory (NVRAM) on each system. The proprietary Ethernet cards that Sun sold as add-on components did not even have their own Ethernet address. Only recently has Sun incorporated the capability of using Ethernet addresses on the NICs themselves. If you are using a Sun system, see the Open Boot PROM documentation for details about configuring the Sun to recognize the NIC address.

Multicast Ethernet addresses are identifiable in that they always have an odd number in the second digit of the leftmost octet when represented in hexadecimal format. For example,

```
03:00:00:20:00:00
```

is the address specified by RFC1469 as the IP multicast address. The two multicast addresses,

```
01:80:C2:00:00:00
01:80:C2:00:00:01
```

are used by switches for the implementation of the IEEE 802.1D spanning tree algorithm. You can find a fairly complete list of these types of addresses at

```
http://map-ne.com/Ethernet/multicast.html
```

An interface (a NIC or port on a switch or router) must be configured to pay attention or listen to multicast addresses.

A broadcast Ethernet address is

```
FF:FF:FF:FF:FF:FF
```

All interfaces will accept frames with this destination address unless they are specifically configured not to. The broadcast address is therefore the address to all nodes connected to the local network.

When a node receives a frame it will accept it for deencapsulation by higher layers in the stack if the destination Ethernet address identically matches the recipient's unicast Ethernet address, an Ethernet multicast address for which the node is configured, or the Ethernet broadcast address. In all other cases, the node will discontinue deencapsulation of the frame.

We have emphasized, and it is important to bear in mind, that Ethernet addresses are local addresses. Global addresses, or addresses which will get packets to other networks, are the domain of layer 3 and will be discussed beginning with Chapter 4.

THE TYPE AND LENGTH FIELD   This field contains information about the datagram carried in the frame. In the case of 802.3, when used as a length field, it contains the length in octets of the datagram (which ranges in value from 46 to 1500). Network protocol stacks such as SPX/IPX and Appletalk use the length field. When used as a type field, it contains a code which indicates the type of data being carried in the datagram. Fortunately, these fields do not overlap—the largest length value is 1500 (or 05DC in hexadecimal [hex], also represented as 0x05DC) and the smallest type code is 1536 (0x0600).

TCP/IP over Ethernet implementations expect this field to contain a type code. If a recognized type code is not found, then deencapsulation ceases. There are a great many type codes, very few of which are actually recognized by the Linux kernel. You can see a listing of the type codes at

```
http://www.isi.edu/in-notes/iana/assignments/ethernet-numbers
```

or at

```
http://map-ne.com/Ethernet/type.html
```

For the purposes of this book, we will be concerned with the type codes listed in Table 2–4.

Table 2–4   Significant Ethernet Type Codes

TYPE CODE	MEANING
0x0800	Internet protocol version 4.
0x0806	Address resolution protocol. We discuss this important protocol in the next chapter.
0x8035	Reverse address resolution protocol. This will also be discussed in the next chapter.
0x86DD	Internet protocol version 6.

Full and Half Duplex Ethernet

Half duplex Ethernet is the standard operating mode. Half duplex operation means that the same wires, or fiber, are used for both transmitting and receiving signals. *Full duplex* operation, on the other hand, means that separate wires, or fiber, are used for transmitting and receiving signals. Full duplex mode requires that both the NIC and the repeater, switch, or router be configured for that purpose. It further requires that the connection be point-to-point; that is, the cable between the node and the port on the repeater, switch, or router is not shared by any other device. Given these requirements, full duplex mode has the distinct advantage of not requiring CSMA/CD, thus providing a substantial performance improvement.[5] Full duplex Ethernet is standardized by IEEE 802.3x.

---

5. Many vendors will claim that full duplex mode leads to a doubling of throughput. Achieving such throughput requires that inbound and outbound communications are balanced.

Whether or not a particular Ethernet implementation supports full duplex mode is given in Table 2–5.

Ethernet Speeds, Distances, and Capabilities

Due to the popularity of the Ethernet networking system, a lot of flexibility and extensibility has been developed over the years. The IEEE Ethernet standard is designated 802.3. Supplements, or enhancements, modifications, improvements, etc., to the standard are designated with a single or double letter code following the 802.3 designation. For example, 802.3x is the supplement to 802.3 that specifies the full duplex standard and 802.3ab is the supplement that specifies the gigabit Ethernet over twisted pair cabling standard. There is a lot of detail in these various specifications that are not germane to our discussion. If you'd like a really thorough treatment of this topic, see *Ethernet: The Definitive Guide*.

IEEE has also specified a shorthand notation for the various types of Ethernet implementations. This shorthand notation gives us information about the performance, cabling type, and maximum cable distances. For example, 10Base5 is shorthand for 10 Mbps Ethernet, using baseband transmission, using thick coaxial cable with a maximum segment length of 500 meters. Thus, the "10" in the shorthand notation specifies the transmission speed, the "Base" indicates baseband transmission, and the "5" is for the maximum 500 meter segment over thicknet. Note that the maximum segment length indicates the maximum distance that a cable can run before a repeater is required. Table 2–5 provides an overview of the most commonly implemented Ethernet media systems, the IEEE standard or supplement in which they are defined, and their shorthand notation.

Table 2–5   Ethernet Types, Speeds, and Distances

IEEE SHORTHAND	IEEE STANDARD OR SUPPLEMENT	LOWEST GRADE CABLE REQUIRED	MAXIMUM CABLE SEGMENT LENGTH IN METERS	MAXIMUM TRANSMISSION SPEED	FULL DUPLEX MODE
10Base5	802.3	Thicknet	500	10 Mbps	No
10Base2	802.3	Thinnet	185	10 Mbps	No
10Base-T	802.3	Two pair Cat3	100	10 Mbps	Yes[a]

Table 2–5   Ethernet Types, Speeds, and Distances *(Continued)*

IEEE SHORTHAND	IEEE STANDARD OR SUPPLEMENT	LOWEST GRADE CABLE REQUIRED	MAXIMUM CABLE SEGMENT LENGTH IN METERS	MAXIMUM TRANSMISSION SPEED	FULL DUPLEX MODE
10Base-FL	802.3	Two fiber MMF	1,000[b]	10 Mbps	Yes[a]
100Base-TX	802.3u	Two pair Cat5	100	100 Mbps	Yes
100Base-FX	802.3u	Two fiber MMF	1,000[b]	100 Mbps	Yes
1000Base-CX	802.3z	Two pair STP[c]	25	1,000 Mbps	Yes
1000Base-SX	802.3z	Two fiber MMF 50 or 62.5 micron	200–275 w/ 62.5 micron cable 500–550 w/ 50 micron cable[d]	1,000 Mbps	Yes
1000Base-LX	802.3z	Two fiber MMF or Two fiber SMF	550 w/ MMF 5000 w/ SMF	1,000 Mbps	Yes
1000Base-T	802.3ab	Four pair Cat5	100	1,000 Mbps	Yes
10000Base-?[e]	802.3ae	Unknown	Unknown	10,000 Mbps	Yes

a. Special connector and configuration is required.

b. Longer distances can be achieved by using full duplex mode and/or using SMF cabling.

c. This is a specially designed high quality shielded twisted pair cable that carries no category designation.

d. Maximum distances depend on the measured bandwidth capabilities of the given cable type.

e. 802.3ae is the emerging standard for 10Gbps Ethernet. Wow!

Now that we've got a bit of information about the lower two layers, let's see how we can implement some of these technologies in Linux.

Linux Network Access Implementation

Like many operating systems, Linux utilizes special programs known as *device drivers* to enable access between the kernel and peripheral devices. Each device must have an associated device driver in order to work. NICs are no exception.

OH, BY THE WAY...

As of this writing, the version of the Linux kernel commonly found in most distributions is 2.2.1x (for instance, Red Hat 7.0 is at 2.2.17 and Debian 2.1 is at 2.2.12). This means that recompiling the kernel for NIC device driver support is generally unnecessary. This is due to the fact that loadable module support is a part of the kernel by default. Thus, as long as a device driver is written as a kernel loadable module, you will not need to rebuild the kernel, and in order to activate a module, you merely need to load the module. Of course, the modules and/or drivers need to be compiled properly. Check out

```
Kernel-HOWTO
Config-HOWTO
```

for more details about loadable modules.

If you need to relink the kernel for new device driver and/or kernel module support, or if you need to recompile the kernel, take a look at the following HOWTOs.

```
Kernel-HOWTO
Linux-From-Scratch-HOWTO
```

You may also find the *Linux Kernel Hacker's Guide* and the *Linux Kernel Module Programming Guide* useful. These guides are available at the Linux Documentation Project (LDP).

```
http://www.linuxdoc.org/guides.html.
```

The basic procedure for adding a NIC to a PC system is as follows:

1. Identify the type of network card that you need: Ethernet, ATM, FDDI, or whatever.
2. Check the Linux supported list of NICs (determining NICs that are supported by Linux is discussed on the next page) *before* you buy the hardware!
3. Gracefully shut the system down, power it off, and install the NIC in accordance with the instructions associated with the NIC and/or your computer.
4. Power the system up. If this is the first NIC in the system (if your system has an Ethernet or other network chipset built into the motherboard, that counts as the first NIC), then for many NICs, and particularly most peripheral component interface (PCI) Ethernet NICs, this is all you need to do since most drivers today autodetect the cards. This means that the Linux kernel is able to identify the card and associate the correct device driver with it and assign the proper resources for it. Proper resource includes the setting of the card's interrupt request (IRQ) and its base input/output address (I/O address). If this is the second or greater card or it is not autodetectable (such as with industry standard architecture [ISA] NICs) and/or the kernel cannot determine the correct driver, you need to go on to step 5 (manual configuration). You may also wish to manually configure all cards in a system with multiple cards to avoid potential problems with autodetect failures.
5. Configure the Linux system so that the necessary resources are allocated for and a proper device driver is associated with the NIC. An example of manually configuring a NIC appears in "Manually Configuring NICs" on page 47.

Adding a NIC to a system is normally a simple and straightforward process. Only step 5 requires a bit more work.

Linux Supported NICs

There are many different NIC types available for PC hardware. Some are supported by Linux in that a device driver is included in the kernel version or as an additional device driver with whichever distribution you are using. Others have device drivers available but not as part of the kernel or distribution, so you have to get the driver, perhaps compile it, perhaps recompile the kernel, and then you'll be able to use the driver that supports such a NIC. Still other NICs are simply not supported. The best way to find out which devices are supported before you buy one is to read the `Hardware-HOWTO`. This document will be available on your system if the documentation packages are installed. Normally, the HOWTOs are in a subdirectory of `/usr/doc`. The easiest way to find out is to execute

```
$ locate Hardware-HOWTO
```

This command will find the file or files containing the string "`Hardware-HOWTO`", if they exist. You can also get this, and all other HOWTOs, from the Linux Documentation Project (LDP) home page:

```
http://www.linuxdoc.org/
```

This document lists all the supported devices for the Linux kernel at the time it was written. It is possible that other devices have support in the kernel, but are not mentioned in the `Hardware-HOWTO` because Linux kernel and documentation updates don't always coincide. The `Hardware-HOWTO` also lists some cards which have downloadable drivers from various Web sites. Again, not all such cards will be listed.

Additional information about specific types of NICs can be found in more specialized HOWTOs. For example, you can get fairly detailed information about Ethernet NICs and drivers in the `Ethernet-HOWTO`. Further information about other types of NICs is given in Table 2–6.

Whenever a NIC is added to a Linux system, a name will be assigned to it. For example, the first Ethernet NIC is called `eth0`. Each additional Ethernet card will be given the same name but with the instance number incremented; so, the second Ethernet card is `eth1`, the third is `eth2`, and so on. These names do not have entries in any filesystem and are dynamically managed by the kernel. Table 2–6 lists some of the NIC device names, the NIC technology it represents, and the specific HOWTO associated with that type of technology.

Table 2–6   NIC Types, Names, and HOWTOs

NIC TECHNOLOGY	LINUX DEVICE NAME	HOWTO RESOURCES/NOTES
Ethernet	eth0, eth1, ...	Ethernet-HOWTO
Token Ring	tr0, tr1, ...	Token-Ring (a mini HOWTO)
Point-to-Point Protocol (PPP)	ppp0, ppp1, ...	PPP-HOWTO SLIP-PPP-Emulator (a mini HOWTO) ISP-Hookup-HOWTO ISP-Connectivity (a mini HOWTO) Note: PPP is a point-to-point connection supporting IP over serial lines and is ordinarily implemented for dial-up support.
Serial Line IP (SLIP)	sl0, sl1, ...	Ethernet-HOWTO ISP-Hookup-HOWTO NET3-4-HOWTO Net-HOWTO Note: SLIP is a point-to-point connection supporting IP over serial lines similar to PPP.
Parallel Line IP (PLIP)	plip0, plip1, ...	PLIP-Install-HOWTO PLIP (a mini HOWTO) NET3-4-HOWTO Net-HOWTO Note: PLIP is basically SLIP over parallel lines.

Table 2–6   NIC Types, Names, and HOWTOs *(Continued)*

NIC TECHNOLOGY	LINUX DEVICE NAME	HOWTO RESOURCES/NOTES
Fiber Distributed Data Interface (FDDI)	`fddi0, fddi1, ...`	Net-HOWTO NET3-4-HOWTO
loopback	`lo`	A software only interface used for testing and other support purposes. Use of this interface limits encapsulation/deencapsulation to the upper 3 layers of the TCP/IP stack.

Note the entry we've called the "loopback." This special software-only entry is always present in the Linux kernel even when no networking support is implemented. This interface is used to support networking applications when no physical networking capabilities exist (a standalone system); it is used for testing; it is also used to support other applications, such as providing a way to specify a permanent IP address when using PPP over a dial-up connection.

Linux Ethernet NIC Configuration

In order for Linux to be able to utilize a NIC, it must associate a driver with the NIC, specify a base I/O address, and specify an IRQ. First, we'll look at a NIC which is already configured and then we'll take a look at manually configuring a NIC.

Configured or Autodetected NIC

When a Linux system boots, the kernel writes boot-time messages to the *ring buffer*. The ring buffer is a small first-in, first-out (FIFO) buffer to which the kernel writes various boot-time and diagnostic messages. You can read this file with the `/bin/dmesg` command. Note, however, that since it reads a ring buffer, the boot-time messages will soon be overwritten. Consequently, you may find it useful to write this message out to a file as soon as your system has completed its boot-up cycle. You can automate such a task by placing a command like

```
/bin/dmesg > /var/log/dmesgboot
```

in a script that executes after all system start-up scripts have executed.

NOTE

As of Red Hat 6.2, support for `/bin/dmesg` is dropped from that distribution. The replacement functionality is found in the file `/var/log/dmesg` which also defeats the problem of the ring buffer traditionally used by `/bin/dmesg` being overwritten. Note, however, that if you upgrade, as opposed to reinstall, Red Hat 6.2 from Red Hat 6.0 or 6.1 `/bin/dmesg` will still be on your system.

The significance of the `dmesg` command and the associated kernel ring buffer is that if you have got a NIC already installed in your system, the kernel will report its configuration to the ring buffer at boot-time. Example 2–1 shows the pertinent output associated with the NIC on a SuSE system.

Example 2–1   NIC Related Output of `dmesg`

```
[root@topcat /root]# dmesg

<...lots of output snipped...>

eepro100.c:v1.09j-t 9/29/99 Donald Becker http://cesdis.gsfc.nasa.gov/
linux/drivers/eepro100.html
eepro100.c: $Revision: 1.18 $ 1999/12/29 Modified by Andrey V. Savochkin
<saw@msu.ru>
  The PCI BIOS has not enabled this device!  Updating PCI command 0103-
>0107.
eth0: OEM i82557/i82558 10/100 Ethernet at 0xc805b000, 00:60:94:B9:83:0A,
IRQ 14.
  Board assembly 664088-003, Physical connectors present: RJ45
  Primary interface chip i82555 PHY #1.
  General self-test: passed.
  Serial sub-system self-test: passed.
  Internal registers self-test: passed.
  ROM checksum self-test: passed (0x49caa8d6).
Receiver lock-up workaround activated.

<...lots of output snipped...>
```

In this example, what we see is that the system has a NIC installed that uses the `eepro100` driver and is assigned the interface name of `eth0`. It has been assigned a base I/O address of `0xc805b000` (the leading "0x" in this value indicates that the address is in hex), its Ethernet address is `00:60:94:B9:83:0A`, and the IRQ is `14`. You can crosscheck these values by checking the output of `ifconfig` command (described below). You can also get listings of all assigned I/O addresses by examining the file `/proc/ioports` and all assigned IRQs by looking at `/proc/interrupts`.

NOTE

The `/proc` filesystem is a pseudo filesystem maintained by the kernel. It contains a record of all configurable and many nonconfigurable kernel parameters. See "For Further Reading" on page 52 for references which detail this filesystem.

You can also verify that the device driver used for a NIC has been loaded by the kernel with the `/sbin/lsmod` command. Example 2–2 shows the output of that command.

Example 2–2   Output of the `/sbin/lsmod` Command

```
root@eeyore /root]# lsmod
Module                  Size  Used by
lockd                  30344  1  (autoclean)
sunrpc                 52132  1  (autoclean) [lockd]
eepro100               15652  1  (autoclean)
aic7xxx               136088  5
[root@eeyore /root]#
```

The output of this command lists the name of the module, followed by its size, the number of devices using it, and a reference relating to `kerneld` (in parentheses) and/or a list of referring modules (in brackets). You can learn more about `kerneld`, a utility which dynamically manages loadable kernel modules and device drivers, by reading the `kerneld(8)` man page and referencing the Kerneld mini-HOWTO. In this example, we see that the `eepro100` driver is listed, as expected. You will get entirely similar information to Example 2–2 if you examine the `/proc/modules` file.

In order to find out how the NIC card is configured for use, you can issue the `ifconfig` command. The output of `ifconfig -a` is shown in Example 2–3.

Example 2–3   Output of `ifconfig -a`

```
[root@eeyore /root]# ifconfig -a
eth0      Link encap:Ethernet  HWaddr 00:60:94:B9:83:0A
          inet addr:172.16.22.22  Bcast:172.16.255.255  Mask:255.255.0.0
          UP BROADCAST RUNNING MULTICAST  MTU:1500  Metric:1
          RX packets:64077 errors:0 dropped:0 overruns:0 frame:0
          TX packets:62328 errors:0 dropped:0 overruns:0 carrier:0
          collisions:0 txqueuelen:100
          Interrupt:14 Base address:0xb000

lo        Link encap:Local Loopback
          inet addr:127.0.0.1  Mask:255.0.0.0
          UP LOOPBACK RUNNING  MTU:3924  Metric:1
          RX packets:18 errors:0 dropped:0 overruns:0 frame:0
          TX packets:18 errors:0 dropped:0 overruns:0 carrier:0
          collisions:0 txqueuelen:0

[root@eeyore /root]#
```

NOTE

It turns out that the output of `ifconfig -a` as shown in Example 2–3 would be identical to the output of `ifconfig` (without `-a`) in this case. The difference between using and not using `-a` is that the use of `-a` will show all interfaces which are recognized by the kernel whether or not they are configured and UP. The UP flag indicates that an interface is currently configured to send and receive packets. If an interface is not up, then the UP flag will not appear and `ifconfig` will not report it, but `ifconfig -a` will. The flags, such as UP, and other arguments to `ifconfig` will be discussed in much greater detail in Chapter 4.

Notice that there are references to two interfaces: `eth0` and `lo`. The `eth0` interface is the physical Ethernet card driven by the `eepro100` driver. We know that `eepro100` is the name of the driver for `eth0` because of the output shown in Examples 2–1 and 2–2. The `lo` interface is the software only interface described in "Linux Supported NICs" on page 39. Only the first line of output for each interface deals with the lower two layers of the TCP/IP stack. There are two fields in that line, `Link encap` and `HWaddr`. In the case of `eth0`, Link encap is Ethernet, or more verbosely, the Data Link layer (of the OSI-RM model) encapsulation method is Ethernet. The `HWaddr` field is followed by the actual physical address of the device; in this case, an Ethernet address. For the `lo` interface, the `Link encap` field is set to `Local Loopback`, indicating that no encapsulation for signaling will be performed. Also, there is no `HWaddr` field for this interface since it is a software only interface.

The output fields for each of these interfaces is defined in Table 2–7.

Table 2–7   Description of Output Fields Produced by `ifconfig`

FIELD	DESCRIPTION
Link encap	The layer 2 encapsulating technology.
HWaddr	The physical address of the NIC. This address is read from the card by default (layer 1).
inet addr	The internet protocol (IP) address (layer 3).
Bcast	The IP broadcast address (layer 3).
Mask	The IP netmask, subnetmask, or supernetmask (layer 3).
flags	Flags which are turned on or off for this specific device. For example, UP BROADCAST RUNNING MULTICAST (layer 3).
MTU	The maximum transmission unit for this interface (imposed by layer 1 and applied to layer3).
Metric	A metric associated with the interface. This value is used by some routing table management protocols (like the routing information protocol [RIP]) (layer 3).
RX	Receive packet statistics (performance and troubleshooting).
TX	Transmit packet statistics (performance and troubleshooting).
Interrupt	The Interrupt Request (IRQ) signal address for the device. To see all assigned IRQs, look at the file /proc/interrupts (layer1).
Base address	The initial Input/Output (I/O) address for this device in hex. To see the full range of addresses available to this device (and all other configured devices), see the contents of /proc/ioports (layer1).
Memory	Specifies the range of shared memory addresses. This will not appear if not used, as is the case for Example 2–3 (layer1).

We will discuss the configuration of the layer 3 related fields in Chapters 4 and 5, and the meaning of the performance and troubleshooting related fields in Chapter 9. Note that the command `netstat -i` produces the same output as `ifconfig -a`, albeit in a slightly different format, as shown in Example 2–4.

Example 2–4   Output of `netstat -i`

```
# netstat -i
Kernel Interface table
Iface   MTU Met    RX-OK RX-ERR RX-DRP RX-OVR    TX-OK TX-ERR TX-DRP TX-OVR Flg
eth0   1500   0    34784      0      0      0    24014      0      0      0 BRU
```

Note that all of the statistical information displayed as output from `netstat -i` or `ifconfig -a` is found in `/proc/net/dev`. This file is managed and maintained by the kernel. It can be viewed as any ASCII file with `cat` or `more`.

Manually Configuring NICs

In order to configure a NIC, you must identify three things:

1. The correct driver for your NIC

2. An available IRQ

3. An available base I/O address

First, identify the type of card you have by searching the `Hardware-HOWTO` and `Ethernet-HOWTO` as previously mentioned. Second, determine an available IRQ. In Table 2–8, we list the IRQs and their standard hardware settings.

Table 2–8   IRQ Standard Assignments

IRQ	HARDWARE ASSIGNMENT
0	System timer
1	Keyboard
2	Cascade for second programmable interrupt controller (PIC)
3	Serial port 1
4	Serial port 0
5	Parallel port #2—often used for audio cards or NICs

Table 2–8   IRQ Standard Assignments *(Continued)*

IRQ	HARDWARE ASSIGNMENT
6	Floppy drive
7	Parallel port #1
8	Real-time clock
9	Usually redirected to IRQ 2
13	Math coprocessor
14	IDE controller #1 (ide0)
15	IDE controller #2 (ide1)
10, 11, 12	Not assigned

Looking at /proc/interrupts, which lists the IRQs and what devices are currently using them, does not list serial and parallel IRQs unless they are in active use (that is, a process has opened the port). So, if you choose IRQ 3 for a NIC, remember that you will then be unable to use serial port 1. Third, determine an available base I/O address by choosing one which is not listed as used in /proc/ioports. You can get information for the second and third item by executing the command /usr/bin/lsdev.

WARNING

Plug-and-play (PNP) ISA NIC cards can be problematic. If possible, use the DOS disk that usually comes with such cards to disable the PNP capability. Always set the IRQ and base I/O address on these cards manually.

Using /etc/modules.conf

Once you have obtained this information, simply put it in /etc/conf.modules (Red Hat 6.2, SuSE 6.4, and Debian 2.1/2.2) or /etc/modules.conf (Caldera 2.4 and TurboLinux 6.0). This file is read by /sbin/modprobe at each boot to determine which modules it should load. Example 2–5 shows an /etc/conf.modules file on a Red Hat 6.2 system.

Example 2–5   `/etc/conf.modules` File

```
[root@eeyore /root]# cat /etc/conf.modules
options eth0 irq=5 io=0x290
alias eth0 tulip
options eth1 irq=10 io=0xe800
alias eth1 3c509
[root@eeyore /root]#
```

This example file contains lines utilizing two keywords: `options` and `alias`. The `alias` keyword is used to associate a device name with a driver. The `options` keyword is used to supply optional arguments to the device driver. There are many other possible keywords in the file. See the `modules.conf(5)`[6] man page for further details.

Note that in Example 2–5, `eth0` is a card which uses the `tulip` driver and for which IRQ 5 is used and a base I/O of 0x290 is assigned. A second NIC, `eth1`, is specified. It uses the 3c509 driver, is assigned IRQ 10, and has the base I/O address of 0xe800.

OH, BY THE WAY...

You can sometimes get additional information about the options available to a driver by reading the top portion of the source code file for the driver. Often the author will put some useful comments there regarding the capabilities supported by the driver. It also usually indicates which chipsets the driver supports. Of course, while you're there, you might also want to peruse the source code itself! The source files for NIC drivers can be found in the `drivers/net` subdirectory of the source tree. For example, you would find them in `/usr/src/linux-2.2.14/drivers/net/` if you are using version 2.2.14 of the kernel.

Using LILO

You can also use the Linux loader (LILO) to manually configure NICs. For instance, to specify the IRQ and base I/O address of `eth0` as in Example 2–5, you add

```
append="ether=5,0x290,eth0"
```

---

6. Even though the file may be `conf.modules`, the man page is `modules.conf`. Actually, according to that man page, `conf.modules` has been deprecated in favor of `modules.conf`.

to each stanza in `/etc/lilo.conf` for which you want it to take effect. For further details about LILO, see the LILO mini HOWTO, and the `lilo.conf(5)` and `lilo(5)` man pages.

You can also disable autodetection in LILO. Add the line

```
append="ether=0,-1,eth0"
```

to `/etc/lilo.conf` and the kernel will no longer probe the specified device, `eth0` in this case.

Manual NIC Configuration Example

To illustrate the foregoing instructions, let's consider a specific case. Suppose that you purchase a D-Link DFE-530TX Ethernet PCI NIC that will be `eth1` on your system. It's not on the supported list, but D-Link's Web page (`http://www.dlink.com/tech/drivers`) assures you that a downloadable Linux driver can be obtained. Besides, the card has full duplex, 10/100 Mbps autosensing capabilities for a reasonable cost. So, you get the card, install it, and with some additional effort find the driver at

```
http://www.scyld.com/network/via-rhine.html
```
[7]

The instructions on that page direct you to download the files

```
kern_compat.h
pci-scan.h
pci-scan.c
via-rhine.c
```

in order to build the driver. The file `via-rhine.c` contains the driver source code, while `pci-scan.c` is a loadable kernel module that the via-rhine driver depends on. The two files ending in `.h` are header files that are included in the source code for the two modules.

After downloading these files into a working directory, you can compile them. Very frequently, compilation instructions are in the source code (ending in .c) files. These files are no exception and we can compile them with

```
# gcc -DMODULE -Wall -Wstrict-prototypes -O6 -c pci-scan.c
# gcc -DMODULE -Wall -Wstrict-prototypes -O6 -c via-rhine.c
```

This will produce the loadable modules, `pci-scan.o` and `via-rhine.o`. To test the modules, load them with `insmod`.

---

7. `http://www.scyld.com/network/` is a very good resource for many Linux NIC drivers.

```
# insmod pci-scan.o
# insmod via-rhine.o
```

In this case, `pci-scan.o` must be loaded first since `via-rhine.o` depends on it. If `insmod` reports no error messages, then you should see an association with `eth1` immediately, as shown in Example 2–6, using the `ifconfig` command.

Example 2–6   Appearance of an Interface after Loading the Driver

```
# ifconfig eth1
eth1      Link encap:Ethernet  HWaddr 00:50:BA:CA:23:25
          BROADCAST MULTICAST  MTU:1500  Metric:1
          RX packets:0 errors:0 dropped:0 overruns:0 frame:0
          TX packets:0 errors:0 dropped:0 overruns:0 carrier:0
          collisions:0 txqueuelen:100
          Interrupt:9 Base address:0xe000
#
```

Example 2–6 indicates that the loadable device driver successfully identified the new NIC card. At this point the NIC is ready to be configured—for IPv4, complete configuration of NICs is covered in Chapter 4.

In order to make these changes permanent, install the loadable modules in the appropriate source directory

```
# install -m 644 pci-scan.o /lib/modules/`uname -r`/net/
# install -m 644 via-rhine.o /lib/modules/`uname -r`/net/
```

and then place an appropriate entry in the `/etc/conf.modules` or `/etc/modules.conf` file

```
alias eth1 via-rhine
options eth1 irq=9 io=0xe000
```

or whatever is appropriate for your system.

Summary

In this chapter, we described the lower two layers of the TCP/IP stack, their functionality and responsibilities. We surveyed a number of different layer 2 technologies, especially Ethernet, defined a number of terms, and described basic network topologies. We then looked at some Linux specific implementation details, especially with respect to Ethernet, introduced the `ifconfig` and `netstat` commands, and provided information about a variety of other resources.

For Further Reading

Listed here are books and WWW resources that provide further information about the topics discussed in this chapter. They are organized topically.

Books

General and Layer 1/2 Specific

Comer, Douglas E., *Internetworking with TCP/IP Vol I: Principals, Protocols, Architecture*, 3rd. ed., Englewood Cliffs, New Jersey, Prentice Hall, 1995.

Perlman, Radia, *Interconnections Second Edition: Bridges, Routers, Switches, and Internetworking Protocols*, Reading, Massachusetts, Addison-Wesley, 2000.

Spurgeon, Charles, *Ethernet: The Definitive Guide*, Sebastopol, California, O'Reilly and Associates, 2000.

Stevens, W. Richard, *TCP/IP Illustrated, Volume 1: The Protocols*, Reading, Massachusetts, Addison-Wesley, 1994.

System Administration

Hein, Jochen, *Linux Companion for System Administrators*, Harlow, England, Addison-Wesley, 1999.

Komarinski, Mark F., and Cary Collett, *Linux System Administrator's Handbook*, Upper Saddle River, New Jersey, Prentice Hall PTR, 1998.

Nemeth, Evi, et al., *UNIX System Administration Handbook*, 2d ed., Englewood Cliffs, New Jersey, Prentice Hall PTR, 1995.

Kernel Related

Bach, Maurice J., *The Design of the Unix Operating System*, Englewood Cliffs, New Jersey, Prentice-Hall, 1986.

Beck, Michael, et al., *Linux Kernel Internals*, 2d ed., Reading, Massachusetts, Addison-Wesley, 1997.

Card, Remy, et al., *The Linux Kernel Book*, New York, New York, John Wiley and Sons, 1998.

McKusick, Marshall Kirk, et al., *The Design and Implementation of the 4.4 BSD Operating System*, Reading, Massachusetts, Addison-Wesley, 1996.

Rubini, Alessandro, *Linux Device Drivers*, Sebastopol, California, O'Reilly and Associates, 1998.

WWW and On-Line Resources

Cisco has made a plethora of technology information available to the general public. You can access this very valuable resource at their documentation home page (thanks, Cisco!).

```
http://www.cisco.com/univercd/home/home.htm
```

Charles Spurgeon wrote the outstanding book, *Ethernet: The Definitive Guide*. He also maintains a home page at

```
http://wwwhost.ots.utexas.edu/ethernet/
```

You can learn a lot about what's happening with gigabit Ethernet at

```
http://www.gigabit-ethernet.org/
```

There are a number of Web sites, both commercial and informational, that deal with the emerging wireless networking technologies. Here are a few.

```
http://www.bluetooth.com/
http://www.wi-fi.org/
http://www.homerf.org/
```

The following site provides a listing of wireless technology vendors.

```
http://www.comm-nav.com/wlan.htm
```

Information about token ring can be found at the following sites.

```
http://www.linuxtr.net/
http://www.hstra.com/
```

Information about ATM.

```
http://www.atmforum.com/
http://www.com21.com/pages/ietf.html
```

The Linux HOWTOs and Guides referenced in this chapter, and throughout this book, are available at

```
http://www.linuxdoc.org/
```

3

Between the Network Interface and Internet Layers: Address Resolution Protocol

In the previous chapter, we noted that physical or MAC addresses are local addresses and that IP addresses are global. It makes sense, then, that there needs to be a way to associate the local and global address of a given system. For IPv4, this association is handled through the address resolution protocol (ARP). For IPv6, the association is handled through ICMPv6 neighbor discovery (ND). We'll look at ND in Chapter 5. In this chapter, we will take a look at ARP functionality, managing the ARP cache, and implementing the `arpwatch` daemon. We will also describe two network sniffers, Ethereal and `tcpdump`; and briefly touch on the related reverse address resolution protocol (RARP).

ARP, RARP, and the TCP/IP Model

Figure 3–1 depicts the location within the TCP/IP in which ARP and RARP operate.

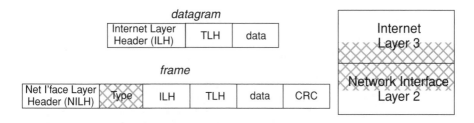

Figure 3–1   ARP and RARP in the TCP/IP Model

ARP and RARP are somewhat of an anomoly with respect to the TCP/IP model. Formally, the data used for ARP and RARP is found in the datagram which is part of the Internet layer. However, the codes which indicate that the datagram is carrying ARP or RARP data is in the type field of the Ethernet frame which is part of the Network Interface layer. The crosshatched gray areas in Figure 3–1 represent where in the frame and in the stack ARP and RARP operate.

The Purpose of ARP

As we noted in the first two chapters, whenever the process of encapsulation is initiated by an application, each layer is responsible for contributing information to the resulting packet(s). That is, the Application layer provides the data portion of the packet, the Transport layer prefixes its header, the Internet layer its header, and so forth. In order for encapsulation to proceed successfully, the information required by each layer for the purpose of constructing its header *must* be available. Most of the information required for successful encapsulation is already configured within your system, some of it as tunable kernel parameters and some of it as information determined by the algorithms which operate at each layer. But there is some information that must be provided through configuration options on the system and one piece of information (the destination physical address) that must be obtained from a remote system. The top four layers (layers 2 through 5) of the TCP/IP model are affected by this requirement.

The configurable information required for the headers of the top four layers includes the following data:

- An optional program header in the Application layer may require configurable data. For example, applications that use the remote procedure call (RPC)[1] library require the program and version number to be properly configured for generation of the RPC header.
- The source and destination port numbers for the Transport layer header.
- The source and destination IP addresses for the Internet layer header.
- The source and destination physical addresses for the Network Interface layer header.

---

1. RPC is discussed in Chapter 8.

Figure 3–2 further illustrates these required pieces of information by replacing the headers of each layer with a description of each bit of required configurable data. The configuration data is shown in gray in Figure 3–2. Note that this diagram does not fully represent the information contained in all headers—compare this illustration to that given in Figure 1–2 on page 7.

So, from where does all this administratively configurable information come? Let's examine each layer. For the Application layer, anything that must be written into the stream or message is managed by the application. In the case of RPC, both the application and the /etc/rpc file contains information necessary for successful encapsulation. Other applications will have their own configuration mechanisms.

For the Transport layer, the source and destination port numbers are either dynamically assigned by the kernel or maintained in the configuration file /etc/services. We will look at this in detail in Chapter 7.

For the Internet layer, the source and destination IP addresses are needed. During encapsulation, the source address is the IP address assigned to the host that is encapsulating the packets. A given host's IP address is stored in a distribution specific configuration file that is read at boot-time. The address is then

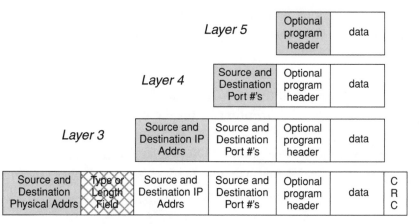

Figure 3–2   Configurable Information Required by the TCP/IP Model

stored in kernel reserved memory and can be read and/or modified with the `ifconfig` command. The destination IP address is normally obtained through a hostname resolution mechanism (i.e., `/etc/hosts` or via DNS) since the destination host is normally referred to by name and not IP address. We discuss these topics further in the next several chapters.

For the Network Interface layer, destination and source physical addresses are required. During encapsulation, the source physical address will be the one associated with the NIC that is going to transmit the signal. This address is obtained at boot-time by the device driver from the NIC and then stored in kernel managed memory. Once again, this address can be viewed and/or modified with the `ifconfig` command. The destination physical address is also required. Given the destination IP address, this address can be obtained via ARP. ARP is standardized by RFC 826.

Thus, the purpose of ARP is to provide the correct destination physical address given the destination IP address. In the case of the destination IP address being on the same local network as that of the source, the correct physical address will be the one associated with the destination IP address. In the case of the destination IP address being on another network, the correct destination physical address will be that of a router. As we will see in subsequent chapters, this means that routers are required to rewrite the destination physical address before forwarding packets to other networks. This, not surprisingly, is called *address rewriting*. The functionality provided by ARP is a *required* part of TCP/IP using IPv4.

It turns out that ARP works by maintaining a cache of associated IP and physical addresses for its local network. The cache is a storage location in memory maintained by the kernel. In order to fill the cache, ARP generates special packets using a type code of 0x0806. This type code is written into the Type or Length Field shown in the depiction of Layer 2 in Figure 3–2. In the next section, we will see how ARP fills its cache and then we'll look at viewing and manipulating the cache in "The ARP Cache" on page 65.

ARP Request/Reply

Let's suppose that a user on the host `eeyore` executes a `telnet` command in order to open a login session with the host `foghorn`. In this case, let's further suppose that all the necessary information for encapsulation is available, except for the destination physical address. After the user executes the `telnet` command, the system will check the ARP cache (described in the next section) to find an appropriate destination physical address. When this information is not found, then the host `eeyore` will issue a special ARP request packet. This is depicted in Figure 3–3. It is very important to note that encapsulation *does not proceed* until all of the previously described data is available.

The ARP request is encapsulated with all the necessary information available except the destination physical address which it doesn't have. It fills in the destination physical address with the broadcast address: `ff:ff:ff:ff:ff:ff`. Because the destination address is a broadcast, *all* of the systems on the local network will examine this request.

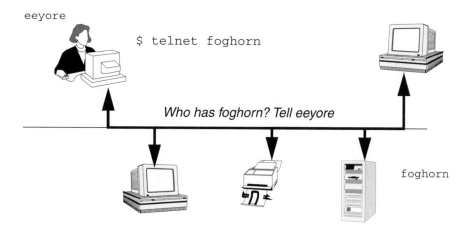

Figure 3–3 ARP Request

The ARP request and reply are encapsulated in the same way as any other network packet. The information carried within the datagram is peculiar to ARP and is generally described in Figure 3–4 for an Ethernet frame.

Figure 3–4 shows a typical Ethernet frame without its trailer and most of its header. The only portion of the Ethernet frame header shown is the 2 octet IP Type Field (see, for example, Figure 1–2 on page 7). Note that the area marked "pad" is simply extra bits to ensure that the frame meets the minimum legal size requirement (64 octets for Ethernet). In addition, we find the fields comprising the data carried in the ARP datagram. Table 3–1 describes each of the fields shown in the datagram in Figure 3–4. This table also describes the values associated with the RARP described in "A Related Protocol: RARP" on page 78. RARP uses the same format as ARP.

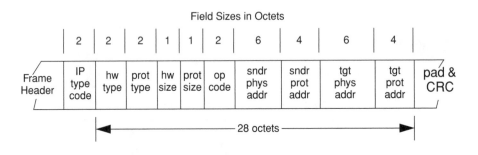

Figure 3–4   ARP Request/Reply Datagram Format

Table 3–1   The Fields in an ARP Packet

FIELD	DESCRIPTION
IP Type Code	Formally part of the frame header, this field contains the value 0x0806 for ARP and 0x8035 for RARP.
hw type	This field specifies the type of hardware address being requested. It is set to 1 for Ethernet.
prot type	This field specifies the type of protocol or software address being used. It is 0x0800 for IPv4 addresses.
hw size	This field indicates the size in octets of the hardware address. For Ethernet it is 6 octets.
prot size	This field indicates the size in octets of the protocol address. For IPv4 it is 4 octets.
op code	This field specifies the operation code. For ARP requests it is 1 and for ARP replies it is 2. For RARP requests it is set to 3 and for RARP replies, 4.
sndr phys addr	This field contains the 6-octet Ethernet address of the node initiating the request.
sndr prot addr	This field contains the 4-octet IPv4 address of the node initiating the request.
tgt phys addr	This field contains the 6-octet Ethernet address of the node replying to the request. It is always set to the broadcast address for ARP requests. This is the information sought.
tgt prot addr	This field contains the 6-octet Ethernet address of the node replying to the request.

Note that the format includes a hardware size and protocol size field. This makes the ARP data format very general and allows for application to many layer 2 technologies.

Now let's take a look at what information is carried inside the ARP packet which was generated by the example given in Figure 3–3. Figure 3–5 displays the contents of the ARP request packet in this case. Note that this information was captured by Ethereal which is discussed in "Ethereal" on page 82.

Note that the large windowpane in Figure 3–5 (the one with the "Ethernet Frame Header" and "ARP Data" references) displays the actual contents of the Ethernet frame header and the contents of the datagram, which in this case consists of the ARP data. Following the format of ARP as given in Table 3–1 on page 61, we see that the ARP request generated by eeyore causes the Ethernet frame to have a destination address of ff:ff:ff:ff:ff:ff and a source address of 00:60:94:b9:83:0a (the Ethernet address on the NIC in eeyore that is configured to use the IPv4 address, 172.16.22.22). Within the ARP data section, you can see that the filled in fields are reported by Ethereal as described in Table 3–1.

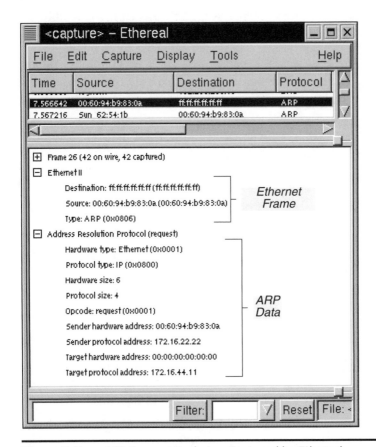

Figure 3–5   ARP Request Packet as Captured by Ethereal

The ARP request is broadcast to the local network. All systems on the network will receive and read the ARP request because it uses a broadcast for the destination physical address. However, all systems will simply destroy the packet except for `foghorn`. The packet is specifically addressed to `foghorn` at both layer 2 and 3 (it is a layer 3 unicast packet—more about that in Chapter 4). When `foghorn` receives the packet and deencapsulates it, `foghorn` recognizes that it is an ARP packet and responds with an ARP reply. This is shown in Figure 3–6.

Notice that the ARP reply is a unicast and not a broadcast packet. This is due to the fact that in the ARP request, all necessary information for unicast communication at both layer 2 and layer 3 is available to the recipient, in this case `foghorn`. Once `eeyore` receives `foghorn`'s reply, then `eeyore` will be able to go forward with the `telnet` request via unicast. Figure 3–7 shows the Ethereal captured ARP reply.

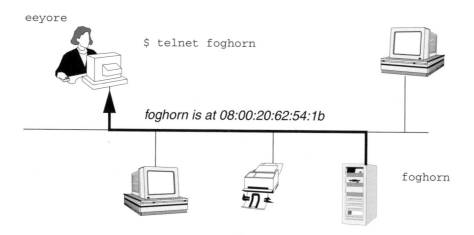

Figure 3–6   ARP Reply

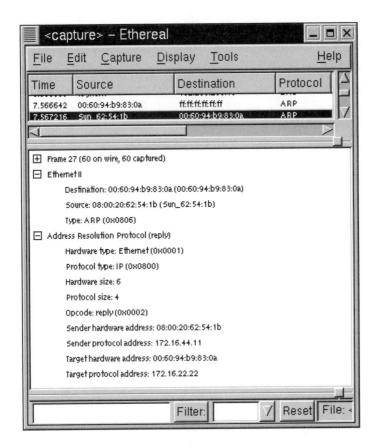

Figure 3–7   ARP Reply Packet as Captured by Ethereal

It would be terribly inefficient if this type of communication had to be executed before any other communication could commence. Fortunately, the ARP request/reply procedure is only required occasionally. Whenever an ARP request/reply sequence has been successfully completed, both of the systems involved in that communications put entries in their ARP caches. In this way, the relationship between IP address and physical address can be maintained for as long as the two systems need to communicate. ARP entries remain in the ARP cache for 3 to 4 minutes of disuse after which time they are subject to removal. If a node receives more than one ARP reply (from multiple nodes, due to multiple proxies for the same node), then the first reply received will be used and all others ignored. In the next section, we examine viewing and manipulating the ARP cache.

The ARP Cache

Viewing the ARP Cache

The ARP cache is maintained dynamically by the kernel in kernel reserved memory. You can view it with the /sbin/arp² command. When used with the -a flag, arp shows all entries in the cache. Example 3–1 displays the output of arp -a on the host eeyore.

Example 3–1   Output of arp -a

```
[root@eeyore /root]# arp -a
foghorn (172.16.77.33) at 00:A0:CC:56:0F:9D [ether] on eth0
daffy (172.16.44.11) at 08:00:20:62:54:1B [ether] on eth0
wyle (172.16.1.3) at 08:00:20:16:07:A8 [ether] on eth0
leghorn (172.16.4.18) at 00:C0:4F:2D:B4:64 [ether] on eth0
[root@eeyore /root]#
```

The output produced by arp -a is quite simple. Each line represents a record and contains the hostname (if available), followed by the IP address in parentheses, the keyword at, the Ethernet address, the layer 2 hardware type in brackets (ether for Ethernet), the keyword on and, finally, the local NIC name (eth0, in this case). Note that the ARP cache will *only* have entries of hosts on the local network.

If you have a system with multiple NICs, you will see arp -a output similar to that shown in Example 3–2.

Example 3–2   Output of arp -a on a System with Multiple NICs

```
[root@dsl-golden /root]# arp -a
atu-golden (192.111.23.153) at 00:E0:39:80:87:69 [ether] on eth0
eeyore (172.16.22.22) at 00:60:94:B9:83:0A [ether] on eth1
topcat (172.17.33.111) at 00:A0:CC:58:69:05 [ether] on eth2
wyle (172.16.1.3) at 08:00:20:16:07:A8 [ether] on eth1
roadrunner (172.17.1.3) at 08:00:20:16:07:A8 [ether] on eth2
tigger (172.17.44.11) at 08:00:20:62:54:1B [ether] on eth2
beaver (172.16.88.22) at 08:00:69:0C:C7:AD [ether] on eth1
leghorn (172.16.4.18) at 00:C0:4F:2D:B4:64 [ether] on eth1
[root@dsl-golden /root]#
```

---

2. This is the location of the arp command on SuSE, Red Hat, and Caldera. On Debian and Debian based systems, like Corel, it is found in /usr/sbin.

The difference between this example and Example 3–1 is that each entry is associated with the NIC to which the remote system is physically connected. In other words, all of the entries are local to the interface specified.

You can get very similar information by executing arp (no -a flag) as shown in Example 3–3.

Example 3–3   Output of arp

```
[root@dsl-golden /root]# arp
Address         HWtype      HWaddress          Flags  Mask   Iface
atu-golden      ether       00:E0:39:80:87:69  C             eth0
eeyore          ether       00:60:94:B9:83:0A  C             eth1
topcat          ether       00:A0:CC:58:69:05  C             eth2
daffy           ether       08:00:20:62:54:1B  C             eth1
tigger          ether       08:00:20:62:54:1B  C             eth2
beaver          ether       08:00:69:0C:C7:AD  C             eth1
leghorn         ether       00:C0:4F:2D:B4:64  C             eth1
[root@dsl-golden /root]#
```

There are two columns in the output of arp which do not appear at all in the output of arp -a. They are the Flags and Mask column. The entry in the Flags column indicates the state of the entry. There are three possible flags: C meaning the entry is complete, M meaning the entry is permanent and not subject to timeouts, and P indicating an entry is a proxy or published entry (we'll discuss the meaning of permanent and proxied entries in "Manipulating the ARP Cache" on page 67).

The Mask column is leftover from earlier kernels. It was at one time possible (in kernel versions 2.0.x and earlier) to proxy for entire networks or subnetworks. This field held the mask value for the proxied network (we discuss network masks in Chapter 4).

You can also view a single entry in the arp cache by providing a hostname as an argument. For instance, if you execute

```
# arp topcat
```

instead of simply arp, then the output will be the one entry associated with topcat. The behavior is similar if you use arp -a.

Another flag to arp that is worthy of note at this point is the -n flag. This flag suppresses IP address to hostname translation. Example 3–4 provides an illustration.

Example 3–4   Using the `-n` Flag with `arp`

```
[root@eeyore /root]# arp -an
? (172.16.44.11) at 08:00:20:62:54:1B [ether] on eth0
? (172.16.1.3) at 08:00:20:16:07:A8 [ether] on eth0
? (172.16.4.18) at 00:C0:4F:2D:B4:64 [ether] on eth0
[root@eeyore /root]#
```

There are a number of other options to the `arp` command and a complete listing is provided in Table 3–2 on page 72.

There is one other way to view the ARP cache and that is by looking at the `/proc/net/arp` file as illustrated in Example 3–5.

Example 3–5   Contents of `/proc/net/arp`

```
[root@dsl-golden /root]# cat /proc/net/arp
IP address        HW type    Flags      HW address          Mask      Device
192.111.23.153    0x1        0x2        00:E0:39:80:87:69     *          eth0
172.16.22.22      0x1        0x2        00:60:94:B9:83:0A     *          eth1
172.17.33.111     0x1        0x2        00:A0:CC:58:69:05     *          eth2
172.16.44.11      0x1        0x2        08:00:20:62:54:1B     *          eth1
172.17.1.3        0x1        0x2        08:00:20:16:07:A8     *          eth2
172.17.44.11      0x1        0x2        08:00:20:62:54:1B     *          eth2
172.16.88.22      0x1        0x2        08:00:69:0C:C7:AD     *          eth1
172.16.4.18       0x1        0x2        00:C0:4F:2D:B4:64     *          eth1
```

The only difference between this and Example 3–3 is that the hardware type (`HW type`) and `Flags` are given in hex instead of symbolically. The hex value for the hardware type `ether` is 0x01. The hex value for the `C` flag is `0x02`, for `M` it is `0x04`, and for `P` it is `0x08`.

Manipulating the ARP Cache

In addition to viewing cached entries, the `arp` command allows for the deletion of entries and the addition of temporary, permanent, and/or proxied entries.

You cannot actually directly delete an ARP entry with the `arp` command, but you can set its status to "incomplete." Doing so hastens the timeout of the entry to about one minute after which time the kernel will remove the entry from the cache. To delete an entry from the cache, use the `-d` flag to the `arp` command as shown in Example 3–6.

Example 3–6   Deleting an ARP Entry

```
[root@eeyore /root]# arp -d underdog
[root@eeyore /root]# arp -a
underdog (172.16.1.254) at <incomplete> on eth0
daffy (172.16.44.11) at 08:00:20:62:54:1B [ether] on eth0
wyle (172.16.1.3) at 08:00:20:16:07:A8 [ether] on eth0
leghorn (172.16.4.18) at 00:C0:4F:2D:B4:64 [ether] on eth0
[root@eeyore /root]#
```

Normally, you will use the delete operation for proxied or permanent entries. If you delete a dynamically generated entry that is currently in use or will be used again, then the entry will be readded the next time that host is communicated with via the ARP request/reply procedure. You can completely disable ARP on a particular interface with the `ifconfig` command. Example 3–7 shows disabling ARP for eth0 on the host `eeyore`, and then shows the output of `ifconfig eth0`.

Example 3–7   Disabling ARP on a NIC

```
[root@eeyore /root]# ifconfig eth0 down
[root@eeyore /root]# ifconfig eth0 -arp up
[root@eeyore /root]# ifconfig eth0
eth0      Link encap:Ethernet  HWaddr 00:60:94:B9:83:0A
          inet addr:172.16.22.22  Bcast:172.16.255.255  Mask:255.255.0.0
          UP BROADCAST RUNNING NOARP MULTICAST  MTU:1500  Metric:1
          RX packets:1958871 errors:0 dropped:0 overruns:0 frame:32
          TX packets:1864711 errors:0 dropped:0 overruns:0 carrier:0
          collisions:4864 txqueuelen:100
          Interrupt:14 Base address:0xb000

[root@eeyore /root]#
```

Note that before changes are made to the interface with `ifconfig`, the interface is brought down with the `down` argument. It is entirely possible to make an interface inoperable (often referred to as *hanging an interface*) if you attempt to modify it while it is still `up` (receiving and sending packets). Notice the NOARP flag indicating that ARP packets will neither be generated nor received. The `ifconfig` command is described in full detail in Chapter 4.

OH, BY THE WAY...

If ever a NIC becomes inoperable (*hung*), there are a couple things you can try to correct the problem. First, you can attempt to cycle the interface; that is, suppose eth0 is hung, then you can execute `ifconfig eth0 down` followed by `ifconfig eth0 up` and possibly correct the problem that way.

A similar approach is to cycle the network start-up script(s) (which are discussed in "Start-up Scripts and NIC Configuration Files" on page 136).

If these approaches fail, you can attempt to remove and then readd the kernel module for the device. For instance, if the driver for eth0 is the tulip driver, then execute

```
# rmmod tulip
```

The execution of the rmmod should only be done if the interface is down. However, if the NIC is hung, it may not be possible to bring the interfaces down, so try using rmmod anyway. Once you have executed rmmod, use lsmod to be sure that the tulip driver is no longer listed and therefore not recognized by the kernel. After that, you can readd the driver with

```
# insmod tulip
Using /lib/modules/2.2.14/net/tulip.o
#
```

The message will reflect the actual location of the tulip driver on your system (the only variation normally being in the kernel version, 2.2.14 in this case). Once again, use lsmod to verify the change. If this fails, you will need to reboot the system.

The most common reason for disabling ARP completely is for security. If an interface has ARP disabled, then it cannot be discovered via ARP and it is not susceptible to ARP probes (such as those generated by neped[3]). Of course, this also means that you cannot communicate with any other node unless you manually add the necessary ARP entry. You can add ARP entries with the -s flag to the arp command.

There are a number of reasons why you might need to add ARP entries. Principally, these include

- adding entries for nodes that are configured not to accept ARP packets
- adding permanent entries to avoid the timeout period
- adding proxy entries to a system

---

3. neped is a utility which attempts to detect NICs that are in promiscuous mode (defined in "The arpwatch Daemon" on page 73) and, therefore, may indicate the use of a port scanner. The use of arpwatch can cause false alarms by neped. You can obtain neped from ftp://apostols .org/AposTools/snapshots/neped/.

It's pretty clear that if a node does not or cannot reply to ARP requests, then any other node that needs to communicate with it must have a manually created ARP entry. The second item in the list points to the fact that if a node is not communicated with for the timeout period (3 to 4 minutes), then the ARP entry is removed from the cache. Suppose that you have configured a network oriented application that automatically communicates with other nodes every 10 minutes (or some number of minutes in excess of the timeout period), then, by default, each time that communication occurs an ARP request/reply sequence will need to be completed before that communication can successfully take place. Using a permanent entry for this purpose can overcome this issue and improve network performance.

The last item in the list suggests that we can add `proxy` entries to the ARP cache. As the word proxy suggests, such an entry on a system will cause that system to respond to ARP requests on behalf of the node being proxied. The primary purpose for using proxy ARP is to support nomadic connections such as PLIP, PPP, or SLIP, network address translation (discussed in Chapters 14 and 15), and network devices that do not support ARP. Let's see how we can add temporary, permanent, and proxy entries into the Linux ARP cache.

As noted previously, the `arp -s` command can be used to add entries into the ARP cache. For instance,

```
[root@eeyore /root]# arp -s leghorn 00:C0:4F:2D:B4:64
```

will add the entry for the host `leghorn` *permanently* (not subject to a timeout) into the ARP cache on the host `eeyore`. We could have used the IP address for `leghorn` instead of its hostname, and it is important to note that the IP address for leghorn must be available on your system, that is resolvable through `/etc/hosts`, DNS, NIS, or other service that can provide an IP address given a hostname (more about hostname resolution in "Hostname Resolution" on page 142). Example 3–8 shows us the output of `arp` after we have added this permanent entry.

Example 3–8   Output of `arp leghorn` Showing a Permanent Entry

```
[root@eeyore /root]# arp leghorn
Address         HWtype        HWaddress          Flags  Mask   Iface
leghorn         ether         00:C0:4F:2D:B4:64  CM            eth0
[root@eeyore /root]#
```

Now the M flag appears indicating that the entry is permanent. Notice that the output of `arp -a leghorn` is slightly different (Example 3–9), displaying the flag PERM instead of M.

Example 3–9   Output of `arp -a leghorn` Showing a Permanent Entry

```
[root@eeyore /root]# arp -a leghorn
leghorn (172.16.4.18) at 00:C0:4F:2D:B4:64 [ether] PERM on eth0
[root@eeyore /root]#
```

If you look at `/proc/net/arp` for this entry, it will show the hex value of `0x06` which has the equivalent meaning of CM.

You can add a temporary entry by using the `temp` keyword.

```
[root@eeyore /root]# arp -s leghorn 00:C0:4F:2D:B4:64 temp
```

Such an entry will be subject to the normal ARP cache timeout procedures.

If you need to set up a system to proxy ARP, one way to accomplish this is to use the `pub` argument to `arp -s`. For instance,

```
[root@eeyore /root]# arp -s leghorn 00:60:94:B9:83:0A pub
```

will add an entry to the ARP cache on `eeyore` that will cause `eeyore` to respond to ARP requests for `leghorn`. The command supplies `eeyore`'s Ethernet address as the one to associate with `leghorn`'s IP address. In that case, `eeyore` will supply its Ethernet address and effectively lie to the requesting host. `eeyore` will have to be able to properly forward the subsequent packets to `leghorn` (see Chapters 14 and 15 for examples). As of the 2.2.x kernel versions, you must also enable proxy ARP by executing

```
# echo 1 > /proc/sys/net/conf/ipv4/eth0/proxy_arp
```

This will enable ARP proxying for the NIC associated with `eth0` *only*. There will be one such file for each NIC that supports ARP on your system.

Note that in order to delete a proxy entry, you must specify the interface. For example,

```
[root@eeyore /root]# arp -d leghorn -i eth0
```

will remove the published (proxied) entry from `eeyore`'s ARP cache. Table 3–2 provides further information about the flags and arguments to `arp`.

Table 3–2   Flags and Arguments to the `arp` Command

Flag	Description
`-a`	Displays the ARP cache entries. Optionally takes a hostname or IP address as an argument in which case it displays the entry for that host.
`-d host`	Sets the entry to the specified host to incomplete causing it to be deleted within about one minute. The argument `host` may be a hostname or IP address. If multiple entries exist for the same host, specify the interface with `-i` to selectively delete.
`-s host physaddr`	Adds (sets) an entry to the ARP cache. The `host` argument may be a hostname or IP address. The `physaddr` argument must be a physical address. By default, an entry added using this flag is permanent and will not be removed until the next reboot or removal with `-d`. There are two optional arguments that can be used with this flag. They are `temp` and `pub`. The `temp` argument causes the added entry to be subject to the standard timeout. The `pub` argument serves to publish (proxy) the entry.
`-Ds host ifname`	Adds an entry to the ARP cache using the physical address associated with `ifname`. The `ifname` argument must be replaced with the name of a local NIC, like eth0, eth1, etc. This flag can use the `temp` and `pub` arguments like `-s`.
`-f`	Causes ARP to get its entries from the file `/etc/ethers`. You can override the use of `/etc/ethers` by specifying a different file after the `-f` flag. The file must have one physical address, IP address, and optionally the argument `temp` or `pub` per line, separated by spaces or tabs. The `arp` command with the `-f` flag could then be invoked by a start-up script to survive reboots.
`-v`	Adds debugging output. Useful if you are tracing the code.
`-i ifname`	Specifies the interface. Replace `ifname` with eth0, eth1, etc. Can be used with any other flag. This flag can be very useful on a system with multiple interfaces and when you want to specifically publish an entry to a particular network.

Table 3–2   Flags and Arguments to the `arp` Command *(Continued)*

FLAG	DESCRIPTION
`-n`	Suppress hostname to IP address resolution.
`-H` *type*	Specifies the hardware type. The default is Ethernet, specified by `ether` in place of *type*.

The `arpwatch` Daemon

If you manage even a modestly sized network, obtaining physical addresses for all of the nodes on your network(s) can be a tedious task. The `arpwatch` daemon can help. It collects physical address/IP address pairs and writes them to a file. It does this by putting the specified NIC into *promiscuous* mode—meaning that the NIC will read all signals, even those that are not addressed to it.

The `arpwatch` daemon is publicly available from its home page:

```
http://www-nrg.ee.lbl.gov/
```

It was written and is maintained by the folks at Lawrence Berkeley National Lab's Network Research Group and is copyrighted by the Regents of the University of California. The latest version is 2.1a4. You may also be able to find this utility precompiled and prepackaged for the distribution of your choice. For example, a Red Hat package manager (RPM) package can be found at

```
ftp://ftp.redhat.com/redhat-6.2/i386/RedHat/RPMS/arpwatch-2.1a4-
19.i386.rpm
```

or one of its mirrors.

If you cannot find a precompiled version, fear not! Compiling `arpwatch` is easy. After downloading, uncompressing, and extracting the tar file from the `arpwatch` home page, you need only execute

```
# ./configure
```

in the directory in which the source exists. The `configure` utility is from the folks at GNU's not UNIX (GNU[4]) and is designed to make compiling on different platforms very simple. For more information about `configure`, see *Programming with GNU Software* as cited in "For Further Reading" on page 89.

---

4. To learn more about GNU and the GPL go to `http://www.gnu.org/`.

Running `configure` will create a `Makefile` that is suitable for your operating system and hardware. Once `configure` is complete, you need simply run

```
# make
# make install
```

That's it! Note that, by default, `arpwatch` and its associated files will get loaded in subdirectories of `/usr/local`. You can change this by giving configure the appropriate arguments. Run

```
# ./configure --help
```

to view the available configuration options. Also, if you are unfamiliar with `make`, see *Programming with GNU Software*.

NOTE

It is sometimes the case that problems arise when attempting to compile and install publicly available software. We cannot cover every conceivable issue, but we'll provide an example here.

Suppose that you want to install `arpwatch` on SuSE 6.4. The `arpwatch` software depends on `libpcap`, which is not compiled and installed by default on SuSE 6.4 (but, if you've installed everything, it will be found in source form as the file `libpcap-0.4a6.tar.gz` in `/usr/src/packages/ SOURCES/`). So, after you have obtained, compiled, and installed `libpcap` (also available from `http://www-nrg.ee.lbl.gov/`—it uses `configure` and should be easy to compile), you then set out to configure and compile `arpwatch`. At this point, you will discover that the compilation fails with missing header errors. That's because the two header files, `pcap.h` and `net/bpf.h`, are not in locations where the `make` utility can find them. The solution in this case, is to copy those two files from the `libpcap` source directory to the `arpwatch` source directory and then the compilation and installation of `arpwatch` should go fine.

Once `arpwatch` is installed, you first need to create the database file and then run the daemon. We will assume a top-level directory of `/usr` (as opposed to the default `/usr/local`, which means that we configured it with `configure --pre-fix=/usr`). Example 3–10 illustrates initially running `arpwatch`.

Example 3–10   Starting the `arpwatch` Daemon

```
[root@eeyore /root]# touch /var/arpwatch/arp.dat
[root@eeyore /root]# /usr/sbin/arpwatch -f /var/arpwatch/arp.dat
[root@eeyore /root]#
```

Before running the `arpwatch` daemon, the file to which it writes its database must first exist, hence, the use of the `touch` command. Notice that we invoke `arpwatch` with `-f` so that we can tell it to write its database to `/var/arpwatch/arp.dat`. By default, `arpwatch` first looks in `/usr/arpwatch` (because we used `/usr` as our `prefix`) and then in the current working directory for an `arp.dat` file. If it does not find one, it will silently terminate. `arpwatch` reports this and all of its activities to `syslog` via facility `daemon`. So, check your `/etc/syslog.conf` file to see where `daemon` messages get written and look there. For purposes of our discussion, we will assume that `daemon` messages get written to `/var/log/messages`.

After the `arpwatch` daemon has been running for a while it will begin to report what it has found in the `arp.dat` file. Example 3–11 shows a sample arp.dat file.

Example 3–11   Sample `arp.dat` File

```
[root@eeyore /root]# more /var/arpwatch/arp.dat
0:a0:cc:56:f:9d     172.16.1.2      948494413   sgitux2
0:60:94:b9:83:a     172.16.22.22    960083084   eeyore
0:69:2:9:b:3        172.16.22.22    948494423   eeyore
0:20:af:dc:28:1f    172.16.1.254    960083084   underdog
8:0:20:62:54:1b     172.16.44.11    960083104   daffy
8:0:69:c:c7:ad      172.16.88.22    960083104   beaver
8:0:20:16:7:a8      172.16.1.3      960082884   wyle
0:c0:4f:2d:b4:64    172.16.4.18     960082738   leghorn
[root@eeyore /root]#
```

There are four tab separated fields in each record (line) in the file. From left to right, they are: Ethernet address, IP address, an internally used date stamp, and the hostname. As you can see, this file can be very useful for record-keeping purposes and for identifying Ethernet/IP address pairings for utilities such as DHCP. You can allow this file to automatically build slowly over time or you can remove all the entries from the system's ARP cache and then ping[5] each host on the local network.

---

5. The `ping` command is discussed in "The `ping` Utility" on page 196.

The `arpwatch` daemon also reports certain special events. These events are listed in Table 3–3.

Table 3–3   Special Events Generated by `arpwatch`

SPECIAL EVENT	DESCRIPTION
`new activity`	The reported Ethernet/IP address pair has been used for the first time in six months or more.
`new station`	The reported Ethernet/IP address pair has not been seen before.
`flip flop`	The reported Ethernet address has changed from the most recently reported Ethernet address to the second most recently reported address associated with the same IP address. This is common in DECnet environments.
`reused old ethernet address`	The reported Ethernet address has changed to the third or greater most recently reported address associated with the same IP address.
`changed ethernet address`	The Ethernet address previously reported with this IP address has changed.

The events in Table 3–3 are not reported to the `arp.dat` file. Rather, they are reported to `syslog` via the `daemon` facility and via e-mail to the root user on the system on which `arpwatch` is running. Example 3–12 illustrates some of the special events as written to `/var/log/messages`.

Example 3–12   Records written to `/var/log/messages` via `syslog` by `arpwatch`

```
Jun  3 19:25:33 eeyore arpwatch: arpwatch startup succeeded
Jun  3 19:25:33 eeyore kernel: device eth0 entered promiscuous mode
Jun  3 19:25:33 eeyore arpwatch: listening on eth0
Jun  3 19:26:07 eeyore arpwatch: changed ethernet address 172.16.22.22
0:60:94:b9:83:a (0:69:2:9:b:3)
Jun  3 19:26:24 eeyore arpwatch: new station 172.16.1.3 8:0:20:16:7:a8
```

We see two special events in Example 3–12. First, a record of a changed Ethernet address and, second, a record of a new station. As noted before, these messages will also be reported via e-mail. If you run `arpwatch` with the `-d` flag, they will be reported to the terminal, not e-mailed, but the output is identical. Note that the `-d` flag also suppresses daemonization of `arpwatch` (it will run in the foreground). Example 3–13 illustrates the use of `arpwatch -d`.

Example 3–13   Special Events Reported to the Terminal by `arpwatch -d`

```
# arpwatch -d

From: arpwatch (Arpwatch)
To: root
Subject: new station (sylvester)

          hostname: sylvester
        ip address: 172.17.1.254
  ethernet address: 0:e0:29:16:d0:68
   ethernet vendor: SMC EtherPower II 10/100
         timestamp: Sunday, June 4, 2000 9:38:53 -0600

From: arpwatch (Arpwatch)
To: root
Subject: new station (tigger)

          hostname: tigger
        ip address: 172.17.44.11
  ethernet address: 8:0:20:62:54:1b
   ethernet vendor: Sun
         timestamp: Sunday, June 4, 2000 9:38:53 -0600
^C
#
```

The other flags to `arpwatch` are given in Table 3–4. For further details, see the `arpwatch(8)` man page.

Table 3–4   arpwatch Flags

FLAG	DESCRIPTION
`-d`	Debug mode. Causes the `arpwatch` daemon to run in the foreground and redirects all output to the controlling terminal.
`-f file`	Uses the specified `file` as the file to which it will write all identified Ethernet/IP address pairs. The default, if configured without options, is `/usr/local/arp.dat` or the current working directory.

Table 3–4   arpwatch Flags *(Continued)*

FLAG	DESCRIPTION
`-i ifname`	Specifies that the interface, `ifname`, is to be watched. The default is `eth0`.
`-r file`	Causes `arpwatch` to get its packets from `file` instead of directly off the network. `file` must contain data in either `tcpdump(1)` or `pcapture(1)` format.

The `arpwatch` daemon not only provides useful administrative information but can also assist with security. Unknown `new activity`, `new station`, and `changed ethernet address` events could indicate a security violation and should always be investigated. For optimal coverage, run an `arpwatch` daemon on each local network.

A Related Protocol: RARP

The reverse address resolution protocol (RARP) gets its name from the fact that it operates in reverse to ARP. That is, where ARP takes a given IP address and gets a physical address, RARP utilizes a known physical address to get an IP address. Unlike ARP, however, RARP is not required functionality. RARP is used to support a client that does not know its IP address, somewhat like the dynamic host configuration protocol (DHCP) and `bootp`. DHCP is discussed in Chapter 10; `bootp` is an older protocol similar to DHCP. RARP is standardized by RFC 903.

The historical purpose of RARP is to support network clients that have no local storage for configuration files such as diskless clients and X terminals. Modern computing environments do not commonly use these types of nodes anymore—although some government installations continue to use diskless clients for security reasons. Another use of this utility is to support the JavaStation from Sun, which automatically boots using RARP. Supporting the JavaStation is covered in detail in the `JavaStation-HOWTO`. In order to take advantage of RARP with a PC client, the installed NIC in the client and the BIOS of the PC must support boot-time operations.

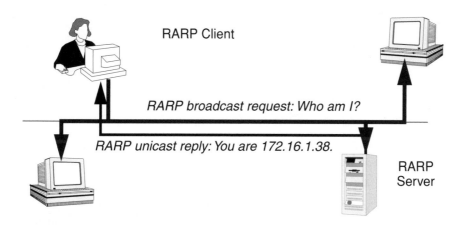

Figure 3–8   RARP Request and Reply

When such a system, called the *RARP client*, boots, it formulates a RARP request (using the same format as that for ARP as described in "ARP Request/ Reply" on page 58) and submits it to the NIC for signaling. Just as with ARP, the RARP request is a layer 2 broadcast. Unlike ARP, the only thing known to the RARP client is its own physical address. There must then be a server on the local network configured to reply to the request. This *RARP server* will reply with a unicast addressed packet with all the fields (described in "The Purpose of ARP" on page 56) supplied. Figure 3–8 illustrates the RARP request and reply.

Configuration of the server is fairly straightforward with Linux. RARP is supported in the kernel as a loadable module, but if you've never used it before you probably need to load it with the /sbin/insmod command.

```
[root@eeyore /root]# insmod rarp
```

Once you've got kernel support of RARP, just create an /etc/ethers file, each line of which is a physical address/IP address pair separated by a space. Example 3–14 shows a sample /etc/ethers file.

Example 3–14   Sample /etc/ethers File

```
[root@eeyore /root]# cat /etc/ethers
00:20:AF:DC:28:1F 172.16.1.25
00:60:94:B9:83:0A 172.16.1.38
00:08:19:03:31:49 172.16.1.114 temp
[root@eeyore /root]#
```

Now if you execute `rarp -f` it will read this file and store the entries in the kernel managed RARP cache. This cache can be viewed with `rarp -a` as shown in Example 3–15.

Example 3–15   Loading and Viewing the RARP Cache

```
[root@eeyore /root]# rarp -f
[root@eeyore /root]# rarp -a
IP address        HW type              HW address
172.16.1.114      10Mbps Ethernet      00:08:19:03:31:49
172.16.1.38       10Mbps Ethernet      00:60:94:b9:83:0a
172.16.1.25       10Mbps Ethernet      00:20:af:dc:28:1f
[root@eeyore /root]#
```

Recall from Table 3–2 on page 72 that `arp` can also use this file. Note that the last entry shown in Example 3–14 contains the trailing keyword `temp`. This keyword is meaningless to and fortunately ignored by the `rarp` command and so, `/etc/ethers` can be used for both RARP and ARP.

Once the RARP cache has the appropriate entries, the diskless clients can boot and successfully retrieve their IP addresses from the server. RARP provides no other functionality than this. Therefore, additional configuration is required for getting a remote boot image or other software as necessary to get the RARP client to do something beyond fetching its IP address. You can learn more about that in `Diskless-HOWTO` and `Diskless-root-NFS-HOWTO`.

Viewing Network Packets

Among the most useful classes of troubleshooting tools are network sniffers. These tools provide the network administrator with the ability to examine the network packets (or *traffic*) on the given communication medium. Unfortunately, these tools represent a double-edged sword—not only are they of assistance to administrators but also to bad guys who might be trying to get information (such as account names and passwords) about your environment. As an administrator, you can try to identify the illicit use of such tools with other utilities like `neped` and by keeping a close watch on what others are doing in your environment. Of course, if someone is using a sniffer on a public network, such as the Internet, there is little you can do except to make sure that the traffic generated from your environment is either not sensitive or is encrypted.

There are a great number of network sniffers available for Linux, both commercially and publicly available. For a decent listing of many of them, see

`http://linux.davecentral.com/netmon.html`

We will discuss two of them: `tcpdump` and Ethereal. The choice of describing `tcpdump` was motivated largely by the fact that it exists in, at least, all major Linux distributions.[6] The choice of describing Ethereal, as opposed to other publicly available utilities, was motived by the following:

- it is actively maintained and updates are released regularly
- there is an active mailing list and the developers pay attention to bug reports and wish lists
- it provides a reasonably easy-to-use graphical user interface (GUI)
- it includes a variety of features that make network troubleshooting easier
- it is robust

In this section, we provide a light introduction to `tcpdump` and Ethereal as well as additional reference information. Throughout the rest of this book we will describe additional features of these tools as appropriate.

tcpdump

The `tcpdump` utility is a very flexible network sniffer. It passively collects and reports the headers of all packets read by the specified NIC. These packets can then be filtered using the `tcpdump` boolean filtering syntax to reduce the overall amount of captured packets to just the packets of interest. You must have `root` privilege to run this tool.

Example 3–16 illustrates using `tcpdump` with the protocol filter `arp`. This filter restricts the packets reported by `tcpdump` to only those that are either ARP requests or replies. The `-t` flag suppresses the printing of timestamps (which we use here only for brevity).

---

6. At least it is included in Debian, Red Hat, SuSE, Caldera, and TurboLinux.

Example 3–16   Output of `tcpdump -t arp`

```
# tcpdump -t arp
User level filter, protocol ALL, datagram packet socket
tcpdump: listening on eth0
arp who-has topcat (Broadcast) tell sylvester
arp reply topcat (0:a0:cc:58:69:5) is-at 0:a0:cc:58:69:5 (0:e0:29:16:d0:68)
arp who-has topcat (Broadcast) tell roadrunner
arp reply topcat (0:a0:cc:58:69:5) is-at 0:a0:cc:58:69:5 (8:0:20:16:7:a8)

^C
#
```

In order to stop `tcpdump`, you must execute ctrl-C (`^C`). In this example, we see two ARP transactions. The first is between the hosts `topcat` and `sylvester`, and the second is between `topcat` and `roadrunner`. The ARP requests are identified by the `arp who-has` key phrase while the replies are identified by the `reply` key word. The output is nicely formatted as one line per record because the information is short enough to fit on one line. In cases in which you need to scan through the data, you can line buffer the output and write it to a file. For example,

```
# tcpdump -eln src topcat > dumpfile &
```

will cause `tcpdump` to capture the frame header (e flag), line buffer the output (l flag), suppress address to name translation (n flag), capture only those packets for which the source IP address matches that of `topcat` (`src topcat`), write all packets to the file `dumpfile` in the current working directory (`> dumpfile`), and background the process (`&`).

There are a great many additional flags and features to `tcpdump`. See the `tcpdump(1)` man page. Also, *TCP/IP Illustrated, Volume 1: The Protocols* as cited in "For Further Reading" on page 89 has a very good write-up on `tcpdump`.

Ethereal

We took a look at two Ethereal screenshots in "ARP Request/Reply" on page 58. You can obtain Ethereal from

```
http://www.ethereal.com/
```

Ethereal was originally written by Gerald Combs and has since been contributed to by many people. Ethereal is licensed under the GNU General Public License (GPL). It uses the GNU `configure` utility and as such is easy to build. The current version, as of this writing, is 0.8.8.

There are many options with which Ethereal can be invoked. See the `ethe-real(1) man` page for further details. Here, we invoke Ethereal with the `-m` option. This option specifies the font to be used for the collected data; it takes a font name as an argument. The font name must be one listed by `xlsfonts`. We also use the `-i` flag to specify the interface to which we want Ethereal to listen. Here, we specify `eth0`, which is the default.

```
# ethereal -m -adobe-helvetica-medium-r-normal--8-80-75-75-p-46-
iso8859-1 -i eth0&
```

This command will bring up the main Ethereal window shown in Figure 3–9.

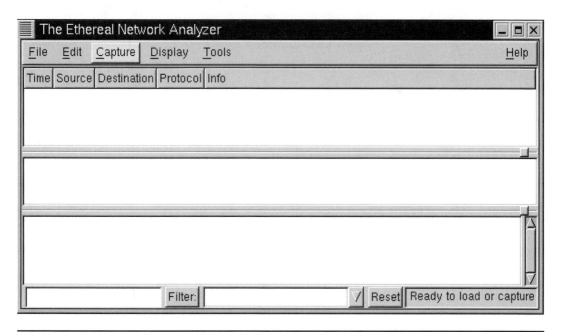

Figure 3–9   Main Ethereal Window

There is a lot you can do with configuring Ethereal and we describe the main features of the buttons on the top row in Table 3–5. Placing the cursor over the described button and then clicking on the left mouse button will open the drop down menu as described in the table.

Table 3–5   Button Functionality of the Main Ethereal Window

Button	Pull Down Menu	Functions
File	Open	Opens a captured file.
	Close	Closes a captured file.
	Save	Saves the currently captured packets to a file. A pop-up window will appear that allows you to specify the name of the file if you haven't previously saved it. It also allows you to specify the format in which it saves the data; for example, as Ethereal or `tcpdump`. Ethereal supports numerous formats.
	Save As	As above, except that the pop-up window always appears.
	Reload	Reloads a captured file.
	Print	Prints all currently captured packets. Careful! This could be a very large print job. This can also be set in Edit→Preferences.
	Print Packet	Submits the contents of the selected packet in the top pane of the main Ethereal window to the printer. This can also be set in Edit→Preferences.
	Quit	Quits Ethereal.
Edit	Find Frame	Allows for searching for strings in the currently captured packets.
	Go to Frame	Goes to the specified frame number.

Table 3–5   Button Functionality of the Main Ethereal Window *(Continued)*

Button	Pull Down Menu	Functions
	Preferences	Provides for the setting of preferences in four categories: Printing, Columns, TCP Streams, and GUI. The printing category provides for various printing options. The Columns category controls which columns get displayed in the top pane. There are many choices here. The TCP Streams category provides color choices for following TCP connections, and the GUI category permits the configuration of some aspects of the GUI.
	Filters	Creates and saves filters for future use. Uses the same syntax as `tcpdump`.
Capture	Start	Brings up the Capture Preferences window.
Display	Options	Provides for the modification of data display parameters such as the timestamp format and IPv4 type of service (TOS) field.
	Match Selected	Attempts to match the contents of the selected packet against the filter.
	Colorize Display	Permits the setting of various colors for the display.
	Collapse All	Collapses any expanded data in the middle pane.
	Expand All	Expands all data in the middle pane.
	Show Packet in New Window	Opens a separate window containing the contents of the selected packet.

Table 3–5   Button Functionality of the Main Ethereal Window *(Continued)*

BUTTON	PULL DOWN MENU	FUNCTIONS
Tools	Plugins	Allows for the dynamic configuration and loading of loadable modules. These modules would be used to further analyze the contents of the packets submitted to them.
	Follow TCP Stream	If you select a packet in the top window pane that is part of a TCP connection, you can then select this option which will bring up a window showing all of the data transmitted for that connection.
	Summary	Opens a separate window that displays summary information about the packets currently captured.
Help		Currently only an "About Ethereal" window pointing you to the manual page.

Let's see how we can get Ethereal to capture ARP packets as we did for `tcp-dump`. Left-mouse click on the Capture button and then click on "Start" and the pop-up window, as shown in Figure 3–10, will appear.

This figure provides options that we can specify with respect to the packets that are captured. At the top of the window, we see an entry that permits the choice of interfaces to which Ethereal listens. The "Count" entry dictates the number of packets to capture. Setting that field to 0 means that Ethereal will capture packets until you tell it to stop. The "Filter" entry allows you to enter a `tcpdump` type filter. Here we've specified `arp` as we did for `tcpdump`. Note that you can also specify filters, and save those filters, by selecting the Filters option under the Edit button as described in Table 3–5 on page 84. The "File" entry allows you to enter the name of a file to save captured packets to as did the Edit→Preferences→Printing option, described in Table 3–5. The "Capture length" entry permits you to specify the maximum number of octets per packet.

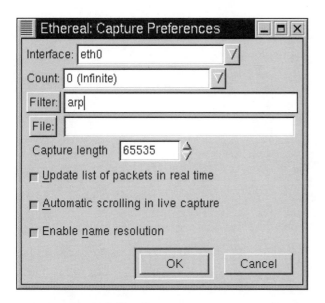

Figure 3–10   Ethereal Capture Preferences

The "Update list of packets in real time" checkbox causes packets to be reported through the Ethereal main window—if you do not select this option, then no packets are displayed in the Ethereal main window until you stop capturing packets. The "Automatic scrolling in live capture" checkbox causes the main window to scroll to the bottom, otherwise the display is statically located at the top (when packet capture began). The "Enable name resolution" checkbox causes addresses to be converted to names. Click start to begin capturing packets and the packet capture statistics window, which also serves as the "Stop" window, will appear, as shown in Figure 3–11. Clicking on the "Stop" button here will cause Ethereal to stop collecting packets.

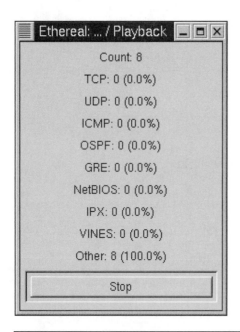

Figure 3–11   Ethereal Statistics and Stop Window

The captured packets will then be displayed in the main Ethereal window. Using our example with the `arp` filter, we get output that is quite similar to that of Example 3–16 on page 82. Clearly, Ethereal provides much more detail.

The main Ethereal window (Figures 3–9 and 3–12) is broken up into three major subwindows or *panes*. The top pane contains all of the packets in short form, with the information displayed being controlled by the choices made in the Edit→Preferences→Columns window as described in Table 3–5 on page 84. By selecting an entry in the top pane, the complete header information is then displayed in the middle pane, and both hexadecimal and ASCII interpretations are displayed in the bottom pane. Note that the middle pane contains information that can be expanded by clicking on the "+" sign. This can also be accomplished via Display→Expand All. Figure 3–12 displays the example.

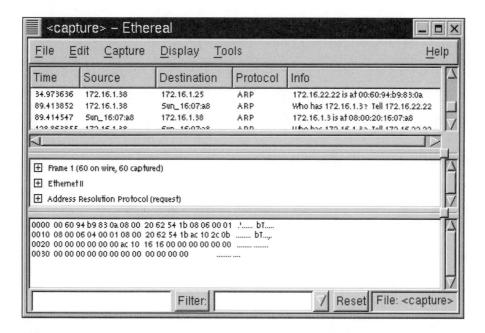

Figure 3–12   Ethereal Example Capture Session

We will revisit Ethereal and look at many of its other capabilities throughout this book.

Summary

We began this chapter by analyzing ARP. We noted that it is required functionality for IPv4 and we looked at ARP requests and replies. Next, we discussed `arpwatch`, a valuable tool for maintaining Ethernet/IP address pairs. Then we touched on RARP. We completed the chapter by discussing two network sniffers, `tcpdump` and Ethereal, which we will revisit later in this book.

For Further Reading

Books

A good reference for administrators and programmers working in the GNU environment (hint: if you are working with Linux, you ought to get this book).

Comer, Douglas E., *Internetworking with TCP/IP Vol I: Principals, Protocols, Architecture*, 3rd. ed., Englewood Cliffs, New Jersey, Prentice Hall, 1995.
Loukides, Mike, and Oram, Andy, *Programming with GNU Software*, Sebastopol, California, O'Reilly and Associates, 1997.
Stevens, W. Richard, *TCP/IP Illustrated, Volume 1: The Protocols*, Reading, Massachusetts, Addison-Wesley, 1994.

WWW and On-Line Resources

You can find the home page for many publicly available tools, including `arp-watch`, at

```
http://linux.davecentral.com/network.html
```

4

The Internet Layer: IPv4

The Internet layer of the TCP/IP model is, next to the Application layer, the layer of greatest concern to network administrators. It is at this layer that packets destined for networks other than local networks are processed. In fact, even packets with a local destination are initially processed by this layer (but, in that case, no *routing* is performed). In short, this is the layer that is responsible for getting packets from point A to point B—it must succeed in order for anything else to occur.

In this chapter we will explore the version 4 protocols of the TCP/IP Internet layer. We will take a look at the IPv4 header, ICMP, IPv4 addressing, variable length subnet masks (VLSM), `ifconfig`, and Linux NIC configuration files. But, there's more! The two chapters following this one and all the chapters in Part 3 deal with the TCP/IP Internet layer. So, sit back, relax, and enjoy the ride![1]

The Internet Protocol

The Internet layer is responsible for delivering packets on a global scale. That is, for all interconnected nodes and networks (or *internetwork* or *internet*) that have the capability and are permitted to communicate with each other, the Internet layer provides the path. In order to accommodate this internet, a protocol is used to formally set rules and implement the necessary capabilities. That protocol is IP.

---

1. Don't you just hate it when the pilot says that as you embark on a three hour flight?

IP implements a *best effort* delivery mechanism and through its subprotocol, ICMP,[2] reports certain error conditions when delivery cannot be made. Best effort simply means that given no failures and sufficient computing resources, the packet will be delivered. IP employs a *connectionless* delivery mechanism. This means that the packets processed by IP may get delayed, arrive out of order, or arrive more than once; furthermore, IP informs neither the receiver nor the sender of these events. It is up to higher layer protocols (such as TCP or an application) to determine what to do with out-of-order, duplicate, delayed, or missing packets. Thus, the TCP/IP Internet layer, as implemented through IP, provides an *unreliable* delivery mechanism. This just means that IP doesn't guarantee delivery—but then, neither does the phone company nor the postal service, although those services ordinarily work. IP usually works, too.

In order to accomplish its tasks, IP does two things. First, it provides a format for the data it processes; this is the datagram. Second, it defines a collection of rules that dictate the way in which all datagrams are processed. These rules include the process of routing which is what allows for internetworking or, more simply, getting packets from point A to point B.

IP is standardized by RFC 791. RFC 894 specifies the IP standard over Ethernet. Further refinements to IP are given in RFC 1122 and a number of other RFCs, some of which we mention later.

We begin our exploration of IP by looking at the datagram format. This will lead us into discussions about the rules by which the data is processed.

OH, BY THE WAY...

The terms Internet and internet (or internetwork) can be somewhat confusing. The Internet is the collection of nodes, LANs, and WANs that are interconnected and to which anyone with a computer and enough money can connect. The Internet layer refers specifically to layer 3 of the TCP/IP stack. On the previous page, we defined the general term internet which refers to any collection of interconnected nodes, LANs, and WANs. Thus, the Internet is a specific example of an internet.

---

2. ICMP can assist IP through its `redirect` message, however. This exception and ICMP, generally, is discussed later in this and subsequent chapters.

Two terms that enable distinctions between the Internet and an internal internet have come into common use. These terms are *intranet* and *extranet*. An intranet is an internal internet that is controlled and used exclusively by a specific organization. An extranet is the extension of an intranet to another organization's intranet, the two of which are interconnected by some means such as the Internet or leased telecommunications lines. Both intranets and extranets are special examples of internets.

Throughout this book, we will use the most appropriate term. Since most of our discussions are quite general, this often means that we will refer to internets.

IPv4 Datagram

The IPv4 datagram consists of a header and payload. The header is always at least 20 octets. The fields comprising the 20 octets are fixed in length and possible values. These fields are followed by an optional field that varies in length. The options field is always padded (with zeros) to ensure that it is a multiple of 32 bits (a *word* boundary). Following the options field is the payload—a TCP segment or UDP packet. The IPv4 datagram is given in Figure 4–1.

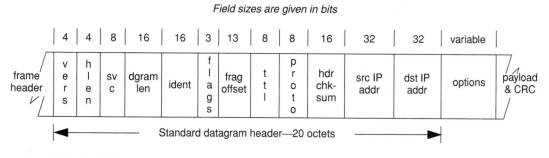

Figure 4–1   IPv4 Datagram Header

Table 4–1 provides a description of each of the fields.

Table 4–1   Datagram Header Field Descriptions

FIELD	DESCRIPTION
vers	Contains the IP version number. Either 4 or 6. (Although, if it is 6, the datagram format is different, see Chapter 5.)
hlen	The total length of the datagram header in 32-bit words. The minimum value is 5 (20 octets).
svc typ	Specifies how the datagram should be handled. This field includes the *precedence* and *type of service* (TOS) fields (see RFCs 791, 1122, and 1349), each four bits in length, or this field includes the 6-bit differentiated service (DS) field (see RFC 2474) and is discussed further in "TOS, Differentiated Services, and Integrated Services" on page 819.
dgram len	Contains the total length of the datagram in octets. Thus, in order to determine the size of the payload, hlen must be subtracted from dgram len. Since this field is 16 bits, the maximum total datagram size is limited to 65,535 octets (2^{16}).
ident	A unique integer defining the datagram. This value is used for fragment reassembly discussed in "Fragmentation and Path MTU Discovery" on page 96.
flags	The contents of this field is used for fragmentation. See "Fragmentation and Path MTU Discovery" on page 96.
frag offset	Contains a multiple of 8 octets or 0 to indicate the order for reassembly in the case of fragmentation. See "Fragmentation and Path MTU Discovery" on page 96.

Table 4–1   Datagram Header Field Descriptions *(Continued)*

FIELD	DESCRIPTION
`ttl`	Contains an integer that is used as a time-to-live value. This value is decremented by 1 by each router through which the datagram passes. When this value reaches 0, the router destroys the packet and generates an ICMP error message that gets sent to the sender of the datagram. In this way, datagrams cannot loop infinitely in a network. This value is maintained by the Linux kernel in `/proc/sys/net/ipv4/ip_default_ttl` and is 64 by default.
`proto`	Contains a code that indicates the type of data found in the payload. For instance, a value of 1 means ICMP, 6 means TCP, 17 means UDP, and so on. A listing of protocol numbers and assignments can be found in `/etc/protocols`. These numbers are controlled by the Internet Assigned Names Authority (IANA) and by the Internet Corporation for Assigned Names and Numbers (ICANN)—these organizations are discussed in "Assignment of Internet Addresses" on page 127.
`hdr chksum`	A 16-bit checksum of the datagram header. If the computed checksum does not match the checksum in this field, then the datagram is destroyed and *no* error message is generated—it is the responsibility of the upper layers to detect such an error. Notice that this checksum is *only* for the datagram header and does not cover the payload.
`src IP addr`	The IPv4 address of the sender. IPv4 addressing is discussed in "IPv4 Addressing" on page 108.
`dst IP addr`	The IPv4 address of the destination. This address is used, in particular, by IP to determine how to route the datagram. IPv4 addressing is discussed in "IPv4 Addressing" on page 108.
`options`	This field may or may not exist. If it does exist, it contains information appropriate to one of the supported options discussed in "Options Field" on page 98.

OH, BY THE WAY...

There is no real logical place to talk about the /etc/protocols file, so we introduce it here. The /etc/protocols file contains a listing of number to name assignment for values that can appear in the proto field of the IPv4 header. Most Linux distributions incorporate an RFC 1340 compliant copy of this file although authority for changes is currently in the hands of IANA and ICANN. Ordinarily, this file requires no attention. Perhaps its greatest benefit is that utilities like Ethereal will display the name associated with a protocol number using the data in /etc/protocols.

Fragmentation and Path MTU Discovery

Consider the scenario presented in Figure 4–2.

In this example, the host foghorn, connected to network B, is communicating with the host beauregard, connected to network C. In between networks B and C is network A, through which all packets must flow in order to reach either of the other two networks. Each of these networks employs a different MTU. The router R_1 routes packets between networks A and B, while the router R_2 routes packets between networks A and C.

Clearly, when beauregard sends packets to foghorn, beauregard simply needs to utilize its local datagram MTU of 1492 and send the packets on their way. Assuming that 1492 meets the minimum size requirements of each network, these packets will arrive at foghorn as they were originally encapsulated.

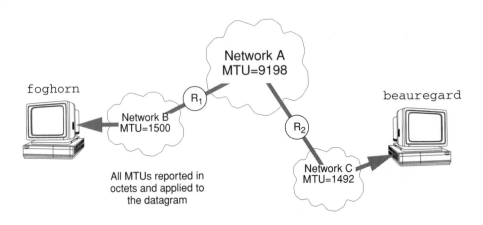

Figure 4–2   Packets Traversing Networks with Differing MTUs

On the other hand, when `foghorn` communicates with `beauregard`, it may encapsulate datagrams utilizing its MTU of 1500 octets, which will be too big for network C. There are two ways in which IP can handle this problem, *fragmentation* or *path MTU discovery* (PMTU).

Fragmentation is the earliest technique that resolved this problem. It essentially says that MTU size is a local problem. That is, when the 1500 octet packet arrives at the router (R_2), which interfaces between network A and C, it is responsible for fragmenting the packet into smaller packets that do not exceed the MTU limitations of network C. R_2 does this by utilizing the `flags`, `ident`, and `frag offset` fields of the IPv4 datagram.

The lower order two bits of the `flags` field control fragmentation. The first of these two bits is the *don't fragment* (DF) bit. If this bit is set, no fragmentation can occur. If fragmentation is needed and this bit is set, then the router requiring fragmentation will generate an ICMP error message to the sender and destroy the offending packet. Setting this bit is common practice for PMTU (discussed next), but its implementation was originally for debugging higher layer protocols and applications. In order for fragmentation to occur, this bit must be unset (set to 0). The second of these two bits is the *more fragments* bit. The purpose of this bit is to indicate to the destination system whether or not this fragment is the last—it is not the last if this bit is set (1) and it is the last if unset (0).

The `ident` field contains a unique identifier for the datagram. The fragmenting router will copy the value contained in this field to all fragments to assist in reassembly. The fragmenting router will also fill in the `frag offset` field with the offset from the beginning of the datagram in multiples of 8 octet increments, beginning with 0. This way, the destination system can order the packets properly for reassembly. Reassembly at the destination is time constrained. If all of the fragments to a particular packet do not arrive within the allotted time, then the fragments are destroyed. Thus, the loss of one fragment implies the loss of the entire packet.

Only the destination system will reassemble the fragments. So, for example, if there is a performance advantage to using the larger MTU on network A, there is no way for IP to assemble packets or reassemble packets to take advantage of that capability.

It turns out that fragmentation is a rather inefficient way of handling the problem posed in Figure 4–2. The alternative to fragmentation is PMTU, which is standardized for IPv4 by RFC 1191. It should be noted that IPv6 uses PMTU exclusively as is discussed in the next chapter.

PMTU utilizes the ICMP error message "fragmentation needed but don't fragment bit set" (for future reference, we'll call this message, ICMP-FN—ICMP messages are discussed in "ICMP" on page 104) capability. In Figure 4–2, whenever `foghorn` communicates to `beauregard`, the router, R_1, would be responsible for PMTU. It accomplishes this by sending a packet with the DF bit set utilizing the MTU of the network it is forwarding through to the destination. If no ICMP-FN messages are received, then R_1 proceeds by forwarding all packets utilizing that MTU. If it does receive such a message, it retrieves the smaller MTU from the ICMP-FN packet and then it encapsulates all packets utilizing the smaller MTU and always sets the DF bit. By always setting the DF bit, any changes in the networks traversed that result in a network requiring a smaller MTU will be reported with an ICMP-FN message and this process can be repeated. Thus, PMTU dynamically adjusts to changing network paths.

By default, the Linux kernel (versions 2.0.x and later) implements IPv4 PMTU. This means that Linux routers will use PMTU instead of fragmentation; however, Linux destinations still have the capability of reassembling fragmented packets.

You can turn off PMTU by writing a 1 into the file

```
/proc/sys/net/ipv4/ip_no_pmtu_disc
```

However, do not do this arbitrarily as it may cause performance problems with other routers.

Options Field

The options field is not required to exist in an IPv4 datagram. If it does not exist, then the datagram header is called *normal* and is exactly 20 octets. If it does exist, then special processing will take place. The option field varies in length, and depending on the option specified, can have different lengths at different instants in time. The option field *can contain multiple options*. Figure 4–3 illustrates an *example* option field of the IPv4 datagram. The option field varies and the information shown is of an option which causes an action. See Table 4–2 for further details.

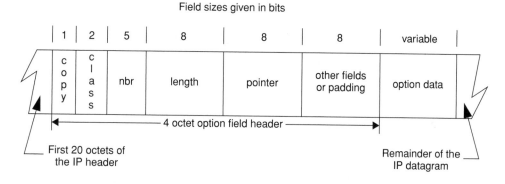

Figure 4–3   Option Field of the IPv4 Datagram

Notice that the option field has its own header. The information in this header dictates which option is employed for this datagram. The `class` and `nbr` fields dictate which option is being used. Table 4–2 serves to identify both the available options and the code fields within the options field header. We cover these fields first since it makes the definitions of some of the other fields clearer.

Table 4–2   Option Field Class and Number Field Meaning

CLASS FIELD[A]	NUMBER FIELD[B]	MEANING
0	0	End of option list indicator. This is used at the end of all options. Only uses the `copy`, `class`, and `nbr` fields.
0	1	A no operation (NOP) indicator. This type is often used between options, especially to align options on word (32 bit) boundaries. Only uses the `copy`, `class`, and `nbr` fields.
0	2	U. S. Department of Defense basic security. Uses the `copy`, `class`, `nbr`, and `length` fields. Uses a `security` field instead of the `pointer` and `other` fields. Option data contains another 56 bits in three formal fields. Only one option of this type can appear in a datagram. Standardized by RFC 1108. See this RFC and RFC 791 for further details.

Table 4–2   Option Field Class and Number Field Meaning *(Continued)*

CLASS FIELD[A]	NUMBER FIELD[B]	MEANING
0	3	Loose source routing. Allows for the sender to list router addresses through which the packet must traverse. The packet may also go through other routers. Uses the `copy`, `class`, `nbr`, `length`, and `pointer` fields. The `other` field is padded to meet the word boundary requirement. The list of addresses are written into the data portion of the option field by the sender.
0	7	Record the route that the datagram takes. This option uses the `copy`, `class`, `nbr`, `length`, and `pointer` fields. The `other` field is padded to meet the word boundary requirement. The data portion is initially empty. Each router through which this datagram passes will write its 32-bit IP address into the data portion of the field. We see an example of this option in "Recording the Route with `ping -R`" on page 102.
0	8	Stream identifier. Obsolete.
0	9	Strict source routing. Allows for the sender to list router addresses through which the packet must traverse. In this case, the datagram cannot use any other routers. Uses the `copy`, `class`, `nbr`, `length`, and `pointer` fields. The `other` field is padded to meet the word boundary requirement. The list of addresses are written into the data portion of the option field by the sender.

Table 4–2   Option Field Class and Number Field Meaning *(Continued)*

CLASS FIELD[a]	NUMBER FIELD[b]	MEANING
2	4	Internet timestamp. This option works similarly to the record route option. It causes each router to minimally record a timestamp as the datagram passes through it. Uses the `copy`, `class`, `nbr`, `length`, and `pointer` fields. The other field contains two 4-bit fields: `overflow` and `flags`. The `overflow` field contains a count of routers that could not write their timestamp due to a lack of space. The `flags` field has the following meanings for the given values: 0 record timestamps 1 record timestamp and IP address 3 the sender of the datagram has supplied a list of router addresses; the router will write its timestamp only if its address appears in the list

a.   Referenced as `class` in Figure 4–3. The values 1 and 3 are not currently used for this field.
b.   Referenced as `nbr` in Figure 4–3.

With the exception of the security option, the primary purpose of these options is for debugging and troubleshooting. It turns out that several clever people have figured out ways to utilize some of these options, particularly source routing, to compromise network sessions. See for example *Internet Security: Professional Reference*, *Hacker Proof*, or *Maximum Security* as cited in "For Further Reading" on page 145 for more details regarding this type of exploit. As a consequence of illicit activity, many sites on the Internet destroy all packets which have certain, or any, options set.

Now that we know what the options are and what they cause IP to do we can define the fields. Table 4–3 describes each of the option fields shown in Figure 4–3.

Table 4–3   Option Field Header Meanings

FIELD	DESCRIPTION
copy	This boolean field, if set, specifies that the option field in its entirety should be copied into all fragments. If not set, then the option field will only appear in the first fragment.
class	Specifies the category or class of the option. If 0, it is in the datagram or network control class. If 2, it is in the debugging and measurement class. The values 1 and 3 are reserved.
nbr	Specifies the IP option number. These values are defined in Table 4–2 on page 99.
length	The total length of the option field in octets.
pointer	Indicates the next available slot in the option data area to which data may be written.
other fields or padding	Consists of additional fields in the case of the security and timestamp options. Otherwise, it consists of zeros.
option data	Data as input by the sender or by intervening routers.

RECORDING THE ROUTE WITH PING -R   We can actually, very easily, take a look at an example that uses the record route option. The ping command (discussed in more detail in Chapter 6) can be executed with the -R flag which causes it to set the record route option. Example 4–1 illustrates the use of ping -R.

Example 4–1   Recording the Route with ping -R

```
[root@eeyore /root]# ping -R 198.29.75.75
PING 198.29.75.75 (198.29.75.75) from 172.16.22.22 : 56(124) bytes of data.
RR:    eeyore (172.16.22.22)
       daffy (172.16.44.11)
       ds1-golden (192.111.23.154)
       10.91.71.140
       10.82.35.202
       209.101.253.74
       207.251.150.193
       207.251.150.65
       209.101.251.150
^C
[root@eeyore /root]#
```

The output of `ping -R` provides us with a list of routers required to go from the source (`eeyore`, in this case) to the destination (`198.29.75.75`, in this example). If we run Ethereal while executing this command, we can see that the options field exists and contains the recorded routes. Figure 4–4 shows the Ethereal capture of one of the packets generated by Example 4–1.

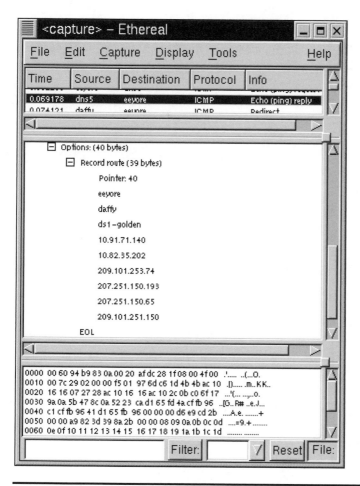

Figure 4–4   Ethereal Capture of a `ping -R` Packet

IPv4 Helper Protocols

Up to this point we have seen that IP establishes a format for the datagram and that the datagram carries information upon which IP makes decisions regarding the processing of that frame. We noted that ICMP handles error messaging. It turns out that ICMP is actually a subprotocol or helper protocol of IP. It is a required part of IP.

IGMP is another helper protocol of IP. Although a part of most TCP/IP implementations including Linux, it is, however, an optional protocol. We introduce these two protocols in the next two subsections.

ICMP

ICMP is the protocol that supports IP by generating error messages whenever certain error conditions in the datagram occur. ICMP also supports IP by handling certain types of queries. Thus, ICMP messages can be one of three classes: *errors*, *requests*, and *replies*.

It is important to note two things about ICMP error messaging.

- Not all datagram errors are reported by ICMP. For example, if the datagram header checksum is incorrect, IP simply destroys the packet and does not invoke ICMP. In such a case, it appears to the upper layers as if the packet never arrived. The upper layer protocols and/or applications are responsible for addressing this problem. Furthermore, ICMP will never generate an error message if the datagram
    - is a Network Interface layer broadcast such as an ARP request or multicast.
    - has a destination IP address that is either a broadcast or multicast address (see "IPv4 Addressing" on page 108).
    - has a source IP address that is a reserved address (see "IPv4 Addressing" on page 108).
    - is an ICMP error message (thus preventing infinite loops). Notice, however, that ICMP error messages can be generated for ICMP requests or replies.
    - is a fragment other than the first fragment.
- ICMP can only send error messages to the sender of the datagram. This is due to the fact that the only return address that is guaranteed to be in

the datagram is that of the sender. This means, in particular, that errors caused by intermediate routers are not deterministic through ICMP error messages and other tools (some of which are discussed in Chapter 9) must be used to analyze the network for such problems.

ICMP is standardized by RFC 792 and further refined by RFC 1122. Other RFCs associated with ICMP are cited in Table 4–4 on page 106. ICMP messages are formally defined by two values, the ICMP type and the ICMP code. These values are carried in a special header in the IP datagram that follows the IP header as is shown in Figure 4–5. Note that the ICMP header will contain type and code specific information in the lower order (rightmost) portion of the header. Also, the checksum is for the entire ICMP header.

Table 4–4 provides a brief description of each ICMP message based on the type and code fields. It also specifies the class of message; that is, whether it is an error, request, or reply message. The type field actually specifies a category of messages. Where appropriate, we define these categories in the table by specifying N/A in the code column. This is not a valid code nor a valid message; it is simply a way to identify the type category.

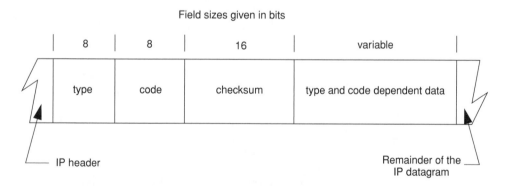

Figure 4–5   ICMP Header

Table 4–4   ICMP Message Descriptions

CLASS	type	code	DESCRIPTION
reply	0	0	Echo reply (pong).
error	3	N/A	Destination unreachable.
error	3	0	Network unreachable.
error	3	1	Host unreachable.
error	3	2	Protocol unreachable.
error	3	3	Port unreachable.
error	3	4	Fragmentation needed but DF bit set.
error	3	5	Source route failed.
error	3	6	Destination network unknown.
error	3	7	Destination host unknown.
error	3	8	Source host isolated (obsolete).
error	3	9	Communication with destination network is administratively prohibited.
error	3	10	Communication with destination host is administratively prohibited.
error	3	11	Network unreachable for this TOS.
error	3	12	Host unreachable for this TOS.
error	3	13	Communication administratively prohibited (see RFC 1812).
error	3	14	Host precedence violation (see RFC 1812).
error	3	15	Precedence cutoff in effect (see RFC 1812).
error	4	0	Source quench. Elementary flow control.
error	5	N/A	Redirect.

Table 4–4   ICMP Message Descriptions *(Continued)*

CLASS	type	code	DESCRIPTION
error	5	0	Redirect for network.
error	5	1	Redirect for host.
error	5	2	Redirect for network and TOS.
error	5	3	Redirect for host and TOS.
request	8	0	Echo request (ping).
reply	9	0	Router advertisement. This type of message is sent in the form of a broadcast or multicast (see RFC 1256).
request	10	0	Router solicitation. This type of message is sent in the form of a broadcast or multicast (see RFC 1256).
error	11	N/A	Time exceeded.
error	11	0	Time-to-live equals 0 during transit.
error	11	1	Time-to-live equals 0 during reassembly.
error	12	N/A	Parameter problem.
error	12	0	Catchall error. Pointer field indicates the error.
error	12	1	Required option missing. See RFC 1108.
error	12	2	Bad length.
request	13	0	Timestamp request.
reply	14	0	Timestamp reply.
request	15	0	Information request.
reply	16	0	Information reply.

Table 4–4   ICMP Message Descriptions *(Continued)*

CLASS	type	code	DESCRIPTION
request	17	0	Address mask request. See RFC 950.
reply	18	0	Address mask reply. See RFC 950.

There are a number of other ICMP `types` and `codes` that have been proposed for various purposes (see, for instance, RFC 1393 which describes ICMP support for the `traceroute`[3] program). Since these are not official standards, we do not list them here.

At various points throughout this text we describe different ICMP messages, their purpose, and behavior. For example, we have already considered the use of ICMP-FN (type=3, code=4) in "Fragmentation and Path MTU Discovery" on page 96.

IGMP

IGMP is the protocol responsible for handling multicast IP datagrams. The purpose of multicast datagrams is to allow for the configuration of groups of systems that can communicate with each other using multicast addresses. Multicast addresses are always associated with specific multicasting applications. We define multicast addresses in "Multicast Addresses" on page 111.

IPv4 Addressing

IP addresses are used to globally connect all nodes and networks within an internet. This is as true for the public Internet as it is for a private internal internet. All nodes that are *directly* connected to an internet must have a unique IP address within that internet. There are a number of ways, including proxy services and network address translation (discussed in Chapters 14 and 15), that allow for an *indirect* connection to a given internet. In order to move packets throughout an internet based on these global IP addresses, IP employs the *routing algorithm*. In order for us to have a discussion about routing, we must first understand IP addressing. We'll get to routing in Chapter 6.

---

3. The `traceroute` program is discussed in Chapter 9.

An IPv4 address is a 4-octet or 32-bit value. They are most commonly expressed in *dot decimal notation*. For example,

`172.16.22.22`

Each decimal value, separated by periods, is an eight bit value and therefore ranges from 0 to 255. These decimal values are sometimes called triplets, in that there are actually three decimal digits between the periods but, normally, leading zeros are not written. The address above could be expressed as `172.016.022.022`. Sometimes, IPv4 addresses are expressed in hexadecimal notation. For instance, the address above could also be represented as `0xAC101616`, which are four pairs of hexadecimal digits instead of four decimal triplets. IPv4 addresses can also be expressed as four sets of 8 binary values, although this type of representation is uncommon.

You can think of these addresses as having two components: the *network number* and the *host number*. Very much like a telephone number, the network number gets you to the "neighborhood" and the host number gets you to the node. Historically, IPv4 addresses have been defined in *classes*. These classes originally made strict definitions about which portion of the IPv4 address is the network number and which is the host number. These classes are given in Figure 4–6.

As depicted in Figure 4–6, a Class A address is defined as an address beginning with the decimal values 0 through and including 127 (0 and 127 are reserved, however, see "Reserved Addresses" on page 124) in the first (*leftmost* or *highest order*) octet. The highest order bit is always `0`. Class A addresses use the first octet as the network number and the last three octets as the host number. Class B addresses use the first two octets as the network number and the last two as the host number; the decimal range of the first octet is 128 through and including 191; the highest order two bits are always `10`. Class C addresses use the first three octets as the network number and the last octet as the host number; the decimal range of the first octet is 192 through and including 223; the highest order three bits are always `110`.

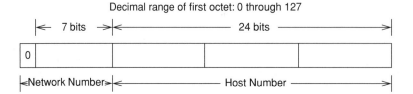

Class A

Decimal range of first octet: 0 through 127

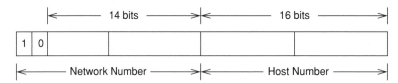

Class B

Decimal range of first octet: 128 through 191

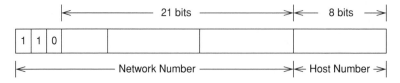

Class C

Decimal range of first octet: 192 through 223

Figure 4–6   IPv4 Class Definitions

These classes are characterized by the size of the networks they support. Class A networks (there are 126 of them) support the largest number of nodes at $2^{24} - 2 = 16,777,214$ per network. The reason for subtracting 2 in the previous equation is due to the fact that the address with all host bits (24 in this case) set to 0 is reserved for the network number and the address with all host bits set to 1 is reserved for the *broadcast address* (see "Reserved Addresses" on page 124). This is true for all IPv4 addresses. Class B networks consist of $2^{14} = 16,384$ possible networks and $2^{16}-2 = 16,534$ hosts per network. Class C networks include $2^{21} = 2,097,152$ possible networks each with $2^{8}-2 = 254$ hosts. For Internet use, the assignment of IP addresses is regulated. See "Assignment of Internet Addresses" on page 127. For internal use, the assignment of addresses is determined by the organization; however, if an organization is connected to the Internet, there are recommendations about which IPv4 addresses should be used; these are noted in "Reserved Addresses" on page 124.

Multicast Addresses

Class D (not shown in Figure 4–6) addresses are special addresses used for multicasting. The decimal range of the first octet is 224 through and including 239; the highest order four bits are always 1110. It should be noted that multicast addresses do not incorporate the concept of a network number.

At this point it is worth mentioning a few things about multicasting. The purpose of multicasting is to be able to communicate with a collection of nodes by sending packets to a single destination address. In order for this to work, nodes must join a multicast group, specified by the multicast address. Originally, IP had no support for multicasting and so IGMP was developed. IGMP provides the capability for nodes to join multicast groups and generate multicast destined packets. Routers must be able to forward multicast packets to networks that contain nodes which have joined multicast groups—IGMP supports this as well. In short, for any node to handle multicast packets properly it must use IGMP. Currently, IGMP version 1 and multicasting are standardized by RFC 1112. IGMP version 2 (with enhancements and IPv6 support) is standardized by RFC 2236.

Multicast addresses for IPv4 come in two forms, those that have been assigned by IANA (*permanent*) and those that are not assigned (*transient*). The IANA assignments can be found at

```
http://www.isi.edu/in-notes/iana/assignments/multicast-addresses
```

Permanent multicast addresses include a number of reserved addresses as well. For example, two of the permanent addresses are 224.0.0.1, which means *all nodes on the local network*, and 224.0.0.2, which means *all routers on the local network*. All multicast addresses in the 224.0.0.0 through 224.0.0.255 range are reserved as local, meaning that they are never routed. We explore example uses of multicasting in Chapters 11 and 12.

The Remaining IPv4 Address Space

The remaining addresses, the value of the first octet being 240 through and including 255, are reserved.

The strict class definitions made good sense back in 1981 when RFC 971 was officially published. The unexpected, dramatic growth of the Internet and the inherent limitations of these class definitions caused a rethinking of the definitions themselves that ultimately led to the introduction of greater flexibility in the way that these addresses are used.[4] The following sections reflect the current use and capabilities of IPv4 addresses today.

The Netmask

Given an IP address, IP can compute the network number of that address by applying the *logical AND* (&) of the IP *network mask* (netmask) of the address. The AND function is a binary operator and is defined in Table 4–5.

Table 4–5   Logical AND Binary Operator

&	0	1
0	0	0
1	0	1

The IP netmask is a 32-bit value that is selected specifically to define the network number. Given the class definitions in Figure 4–6, the default netmasks for each class are given in Table 4–6.

Table 4–6   Default Netmasks

CLASS	NETMASK
A	255.0.0.0
B	255.255.0.0
C	255.255.255.0

---

4. For a good collection of historical references about the growth of and changes in the Internet, see http://www.isoc.org/internet/history/.

For example, suppose that we assign a node the IP address of `172.16.22.22` and assign it the default netmask of `255.255.0.0`; the network number associated with this IP address can then be computed as shown in Figure 4–7.

Given the class definitions, the result in Figure 4–7 is not surprising. In fact, if we compare the network Class definitions shown in Figure 4–6 and the default netmasks given in Table 4–6, we can clearly see the pattern—wherever there is a 255 in the netmask, that octet is preserved as part of the network number when the netmask is logically ANDed to the IP address. Remember that the logical AND function is a binary operator, and so, wherever there are bits in the netmask set to 1 (255_{10} = 11111111_2), those bits will preserve whatever values are in the same bit location in the IP address. On the other hand, those bits in the netmask that are set to 0 will mask out (hence, the term netmask) the corresponding bits in the IP address, because 0 logically ANDed with 0 or 1 is always 0 (see Table 4–5).

Thus, all the bits that are set to 1 in the netmask dictate the network portion or network number of the IP address; and all the bits that are set to 0 in the netmask dictate the host portion or host number of the IP address.

It's very simple to determine, at a glance, what the network number is given an IP address when using default netmasks. For instance, if an IP address is `10.0.0.8`, then the network number is `10.0.0.0` when the default netmask of `255.0.0.0` is applied. We need not convert all the values to base 2 in order to determine this.

```
IPv4 Address ───────▶ 172.16.22.22₁₀ = 10101100 00010000 00010110 00010110₂
IPv4 Netmask ──────▶& 255.255.0.0₁₀  = 11111111 11111111 00000000 00000000₂
IPv4 Network Nbr ─▶ 172.16.0.0₁₀     = 10101100 00010000 00010110 00010110₂
```

Figure 4–7   Computing the Network Number

Subnetting

It turns out that we can change the netmask on a given system in order to change which portions of the IP address belong to the network and which to the host. So, why might we want to do this? Suppose that we are responsible for a growing network that has been assigned the IP network number 10.0.0.0. Figure 4–8 represents that network.

In Figure 4–8 we have used shaded areas to depict various forms of functionality—a group of human resources systems, an engineering group, and a sales group. In this depiction, each of the groups regularly intercommunicate with each other, but rarely between the other groups. Nonetheless, the current configuration has all of the groups using the same local network. As the number of nodes sharing the same media increases, this will result in performance degradations. There also may be security considerations among the different groups. For example, we might not

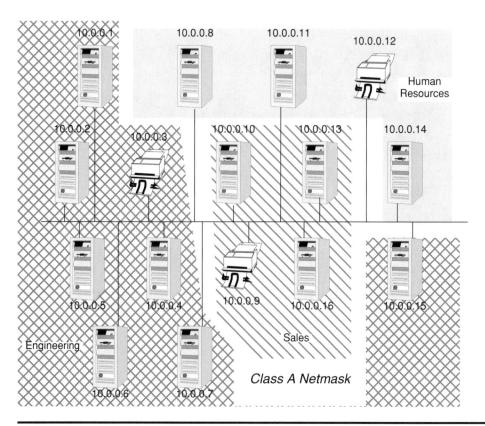

Figure 4–8   A Growing Local Network

want someone in engineering (running Ethereal or the like) to see all of the packets generated by systems in the human resources department; and we might not want the people in the sales department to be able to easily access systems in engineering. Furthermore, as an organization grows, there is often a need to break up networks into groupings that are easier to administrate.

While there are a number of ways to address these issues and reconfigure the network in Figure 4–8, one approach is to *subnet* the network. With respect to our example, we can break up the existing local network into three separate networks by changing our default netmask to a *subnetmask*, and changing some of the IP addresses. In doing this, we also must add routers[5] to the new environment to interconnect the new *subnetworks*. Figure 4–9 illustrates the new topology.

In our new scheme, we changed the default netmask from 255.0.0.0 (Class A) to 255.255.0.0 (Class B) and introduced a router (which could be a Linux system with three NICs). This makes our new network numbers 10.1.0.0 (for human resources), 10.2.0.0 (for sales), and 10.3.0.0 (for engineering). In other words, by changing the netmask to a Class B we made the second octet of the IP addresses a part of the network number—that is, we set the first 16 bits of the netmask to 1, making those bits part of the network number in the IP address. In essence, we changed our Class A network into a collection of Class B networks—or, more formally, *subnetworks*. At this point we need to make some definitions.

When we implement an IPv4 addressing scheme that utilizes the default netmasks, then the result is called a network. When we change the default netmask to one that increases the size (number of bits) of the network number (and therefore decreases the size in bits of the host number), the resulting networks are called subnetworks and the netmask used is called a *subnetmask*. More formally, the new component of the network number is called the *subnetwork number*. For example, the address 10.3.0.6 utilizing a subnetmask of 255.255.0.0 is broken down as follows: the network number is 10, the subnetwork number is 3, and the host number is 0.6. Generally, we will not make the subnetwork number

---

5. One of the benefits of using Linux is that adding routers to an environment often means simply getting enough Ethernet (or other layer 2 technology) cards for a PC. Of course, it won't perform as well as some of the dedicated blackbox routers from companies like Cisco, but it will do the job and in many cases performs well enough!

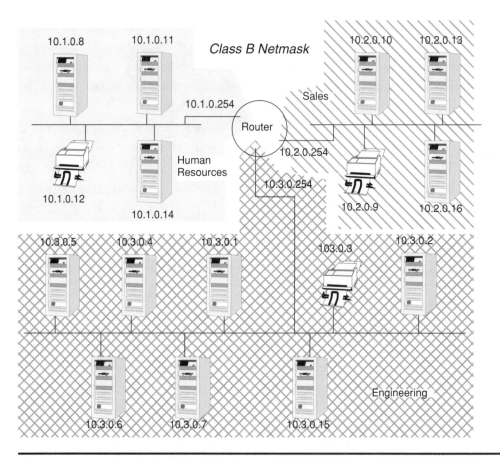

Figure 4–9 A Group of Subnetworks

distinction in our discussions and we will simply refer to the network number which includes the subnetwork number, if one exists.

On the other hand, if we were to change the default netmask to one that decreases the size of the network number (and therefore increases the size of the host number), the resulting networks are called *supernets* and the netmask used is called a *supernetmask*. Supernets and their purpose are described in "Route Aggregation and CIDR" on page 225.

In our example (Figures 4–8 and 4–9) it was pretty easy to see how the application of a Class B subnetmask on a Class A network could be used to solve our problem. In short, when we use octet-bounded netmasks it is easy to see what the network number will be and what we need to do to create more networks. But let's suppose that the network number you are currently using is 192.168.8.0, a

Class C network, and you have the subnetting requirement given in the foregoing example. Now it's not so easy to see how to create more networks. That's because we now have to choose a netmask that does not end on an octet boundary. Such a netmask is called a variable length subnetwork mask (VLSM—see "VLSM" on page 119). Now we need to cover broadcast addresses.

Broadcast Addresses

As with Ethernet addresses, there are three types of IPv4 addresses. They are *unicasts*, *multicasts*, and *broadcasts*. Unicasts are IPv4 addresses that can be assigned to a host. Multicasts are special group addresses and fall into Class D of the IPv4 addressing scheme (more about them in Chapters 11 and 12). A node must be appropriately configured in order for it to pay attention to a multicast address. Broadcast addresses are IPv4 addresses that are used to communicate to all nodes on a local network—that is, all of the nodes that have the same network number and are interconnected via the same communication medium. In point of fact, broadcast addresses are conceptually a special case of multicast addresses. In the case of a broadcast address, it is an address which includes all nodes in the local network as its group. A node must be configured to pay attention to a broadcast address. On Linux systems (and most other systems) this is the default behavior (we'll see how to disable and reenable this capability beginning with "ifconfig Syntax" on page 127).

By default, the broadcast address for a given local network is the network number followed by all host bits set to 1s (see RFCs 922 and 1122). For example, if the network number is 10.0.0.0, then the broadcast address is 10.255.255.255, because 10.0.0.0 is a Class A network and therefore the lower order 24 bits are reserved for the host number. Setting all 24 bits to 1s gives us this result. This type of broadcast is also known as a *net-directed broadcast*. The broadcast address is a reserved address that can only be specified as a destination address. It is an address to all nodes sharing the same physical medium and the same network number. In other words, it is an address that causes all nodes on the local network to deencapsulate the packet. The collection of all nodes that receive a given broadcast packet is called a *broadcast domain*. There are a number of other types of broadcast addresses and they are all discussed in "Reserved Addresses" on page 124.

So, how is the broadcast address computed? In order to understand that, we must define two more logical operators. These are the logical NOT (!) and the logical OR (|) binary operators. We define the logical NOT operator in Example 4–2:

Example 4–2   Logical NOT Binary Operator

```
!0 = 1
!1 = 0
```

and the logical OR operator in Table 4–7.

Table 4–7   Logical OR Binary Operator

|	0	1
0	0	1
1	1	1

The broadcast address of a given IPv4 address is then computed as follows:

```
IPv4 Address
| (! IPv4 Netmask)
IPv4 Broadcast
```

So, for example, the broadcast address for the IPv4 address 172.16.22.22 using the default Class B netmask can be computed as shown in Figure 4–10.

At this point, you may be wondering why make something so simple so hard with all those binary conversions? Good point! The next section should answer that question.

```
IPv4 Address ────▶172.16.22.22₁₀   = 10101100 00010000 00010110 00010110₂
IPv4 Netmask ─▶| (!255.255.0.0₁₀)  = 00000000 00000000 11111111 11111111₂
IPv4 Broadcast ──▶172.16.255.255₁₀ = 10101100 00010000 11111111 11111111₂
```

Figure 4–10   Computing the Broadcast Address

VLSM

VLSMs do not functionally differ from octet-bounded netmasks. It's just that we need to look at potential subnetmasks in base 2 (binary) instead of decimal. So, let's take the example given in Figure 4–8 and suppose that our network uses 198.168.8.0 as its network number. We have a lot less host addressing space (1 octet) to work with than we did with 10.0.0.0 (three octets), so we have to consider what the maximum number of nodes on a given subnetwork will be. Although it is often difficult to predict such things, let's just say that the maximum number of nodes on any given subnetwork will be 20. Recall that the way netmasks (and subnetmasks) work is that if a bit is set to 1 in a netmask or subnetmask, that bit is used for the network number, and if it is set to 0 that bit is used for the host number. In order to ensure that we can support at least 20 nodes per network, we need to choose a subnetmask that has enough bits set to 0. This is just an exercise in powers of two—that is, what is the smallest number of bits, n, that need to be zero so that $2^n - 2 \geq 20$? (Remember, we need to subtract 2 here because two addresses are reserved, the network address and the broadcast address.) The answer is $n = 5$, because

$$2^5 - 2 = 30 \geq 20$$

Now that we know the number of bits that need to be set to 0 in our new subnetmask, we can conclude that our subnetmask needs to be

$$11111111\ 11111111\ 11111111\ 11100000_2 = 255.255.255.224_{10}$$

OH, BY THE WAY...

In the original RFC that dealt with subnetmasks (RFC 922), it was recommended that *contiguous* subnetmasks be used. Contiguous subnetmasks are ones in which all the bits set to 1 (for the network) are in the highest order bits and all those set to 0 are in the lowest order (rightmost) bits. All of the subnetmasks that we use are contiguous (see, for example, Table 4–9 on page 124). RFC 922 left open the possibility of using *noncontiguous* subnetmasks. For example,

$$11111111\ 11111111\ 11111111\ 10101000_2 = 255.255.255.168_{10}$$

is a noncontiguous subnetmask. Imagine trying to keep track of which hosts belong to which network with this type of scheme! Fortunately, a number of RFCs standardized after RFC 922 make the use of this type of

**subnetmask illegal. Current Linux kernels, properly, do not permit the use
of noncontiguous subnetmasks.**

Good! So, now we know what subnetmask to use. The next problem is, given
this subnetmask, how do we know which addresses can be used for hosts? Also,
which addresses are going to be reserved for the network number and the broadcast address? The answer is, we've got to compute them! Let's consider the IP
address of 192.168.8.33 and the netmask of 255.255.255.224. Figure 4–11
shows the calculations necessary in order to compute the network number and
broadcast address in this case. Note that the broadcast, in this case, is called a
subnet-directed broadcast.

Rather than fill these pages with lots of binary calculations, the networks that
result from the use of the 255.255.255.224 netmask and the IP address of
192.168.8.x ($1 \le x \le 254$) together with the broadcast and host addresses are
provided in Table 4–8.

```
Address  ─────▶192.168.8.33₁₀     = 11000000 10101000 00001000 00100001₂
Netmask──────▶& 255.255.255.224₁₀ = 11111111 11111111 11111111 11100000₂
Network Nbr ──▶ 192.168.8.32₁₀     = 11000000 10101000 00001000 00100000₂


Address ─────▶ 192.168.8.33₁₀      = 11000000 10101000 00001000 00100001₂
Netmask─────▶| (!255.255.255.224₁₀) = 00000000 00000000 00000000 00011111₂
Broadcast ───▶ 192.168.8.63₁₀      = 11000000 10101000 00001000 00111111₂
```

Figure 4–11   Computing the Network Number and Broadcast Address

Table 4–8 Networks Arising from the Use of a 255.255.255.224 Netmask

NETWORK NUMBER	BROADCAST ADDRESS	HOST ADDRESSES
192.168.8.0	192.168.8.31	192.168.8.1 to 192.168.8.30
192.168.8.32	192.168.8.63	192.168.8.33 to 192.168.8.62
192.168.8.64	192.168.8.95	192.168.8.65 to 192.168.8.94
192.168.8.96	192.168.8.127	192.168.8.97 to 192.168.8.126
192.168.8.128	192.168.8.159	192.168.8.129 to 192.168.8.158
192.168.8.160	192.168.8.191	192.168.8.161 to 192.168.8.190
192.168.8.192	192.168.8.223	192.168.8.193 to 192.168.8.222
192.168.8.224	192.168.8.255	192.168.8.225 to 192.168.8.254

Great! We now know each network and range of available addresses so we can apply these schemes to our example. Figure 4–12 shows Figure 4–9 on page 116 revised to use the networks 192.168.8.32 (human resources), 192.168.8.64 (sales), and 192.168.8.96 (engineering). Note that we had to change the host portion of the IP addresses to support the new scheme.

Of course, this example may not suit your specific needs, so let's generalize the use of VLSM and then provide some utilities for computing subnetmasks, broadcast addresses, and network numbers.

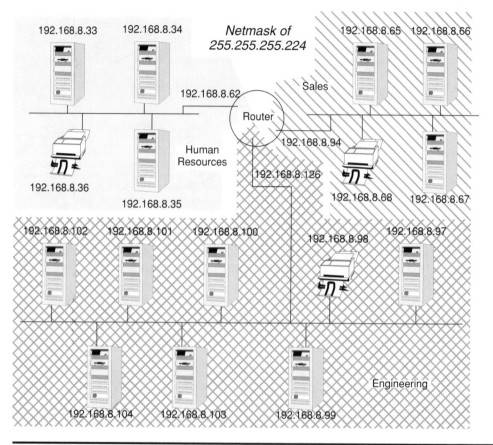

Figure 4-12   A Group of Subnetworks Using VLSM

Prefix Notation and Computing VLSMs

You can use VLSM subnetmasks in any octet that is used for the host number, so long as you keep the network number and host number bits contiguous, to create additional networks. In other words, you can use VLSM for subnetting purposes in the second octet of a Class A network, the third octet of a Class B network or subnetwork, or the fourth octet of a Class C network or subnetted network. In order to make the discussion of VLSM and the expression of subnetmasks easier, the notation, *address/n* where *address* is either an IP address or a portion of an IP address followed by zeros and *n* is the number of bits used for the network number, or as it is commonly called, the *prefix* is used. For example, 192.168.8.33/27 means that the IP address 192.168.8.33 uses the first 27 bits of the address as the network number or prefix; meaning that the subnetmask is 255.255.255.224. Similarly, we can express the use of the same subnetmask with 192.168.8.0/27, but in this case we are expressing it generally to the entire 192.168.8.0 network and we mean that 192.168.8.0 is subnetted according to Table 4–8. We will call this method of expressing a (sub)netmask, the *prefix notation*.

The prefix notation is actually quite useful in figuring out how many host addresses are in that network. For example, consider 172.16.0.0/20. This indicates that 20 bits are used for the network portion of the address. Since there are a total of 32 bits in an address, then 12 bits are used for the host portion of the address in this case. Thus, there are $2^{12}-2 = 4094$ host addresses available in this example.

Now suppose that we are given the address/prefix of 172.16.22.133/20. What's the network number and what's the broadcast address? One way of figuring that out is to convert all the values to binary and compute the answers as we have described earlier in this chapter. That's probably not too efficient and likely to lead to mistakes. The good news is, there's help!

There is an IPv4 address calculator available on the Internet at

```
http://www.agt.net/public/sparkman/netcalc.htm
```

This tool can compute network numbers and broadcast addresses given the (sub)netmask and IP address. Or, given an IP address and the number of hosts per subnetwork or number of subnetworks, it can compute the necessary subnetmask. It also includes short explanations about IPv4 addressing.

The Red Hat distribution includes the `ipcalc` program. This is a simple and flexible program that can compute IP addresses, network numbers, broadcast addresses, and netmasks for a single node. For instance, given 172.16.22.133/20, we can get the network number and broadcast address using `ipcalc`, as shown in Example 4–3.

Example 4–3   Using `ipcalc` to Compute the Network Number and Broadcast Address

```
[root@eeyore /root]# ipcalc --network --broadcast 172.16.22.133 255.255.240.0
BROADCAST=172.16.31.255
NETWORK=172.16.16.0
[root@eeyore /root]#
```

It is part of the `initscripts-5.00-1.i386.rpm` package.

A perl script, also called `ipcalc`, is available at

```
http://jodies.cx/ipcalc.pl
```

Its capabilities are more limited than the Red Hat `ipcalc`.

As a handy assistant, Table 4–9 provides a conversion chart for the variable length octet of a VLSM, showing decimal, binary, and prefix notation. It shows the prefix notation for each value depending upon the octet location of the variable length portion of the mask. For example, if we consider the variable length mask of `240`, then `/4` means `240.0.0.0` in decimal, `/12` means `255.240.0.0`, `/20` means `255.255.240.0`, and `/28` means `255.255.255.240`. The other entries have similar meaning.

Table 4–9   Conversion Chart for the Variable Length Octet of a VLSM Mask

DECIMAL	BINARY	PREFIX 1ST OCTET	PREFIX 2ND OCTET	PREFIX 3RD OCTET	PREFIX 4TH OCTET
0	00000000	/0[a]	/8	/16	/24
128	10000000	/1	/9	/17	/25
192	11000000	/2	/10	/18	/26
224	11100000	/3	/11	/19	/27
240	11110000	/4	/12	/20	/28
248	11111000	/5	/13	/21	/29
252	11111100	/6	/14	/22	/30
254	11111110	/7	/15	/23	/31[b]
255	11111111	/8	/16	/24	/32[c]

a. Special case for a default router entry.
b. Functional use of this subnetmask requires that the broadcast address be set to the network number.
c. Special case specifying a single host address.

Reserved Addresses

As we have noted throughout this chapter, there are certain IPv4 addresses that are reserved. Table 4–10 lists all of the reserved addresses and their purpose.

Limited Source

The IP address 0.0.0.0 is a special source only address (that is, it cannot appear in the destination IP address field of the Internet layer header) that is used

Table 4–10   IPv4 Reserved Addresses

ADDRESS	PURPOSE
0.0.0.0	Limited source.
255.255.255.255	Limited broadcast.
Network number followed by all host bits set to 1.	Net-directed broadcast.
Network number, followed by subnet number, followed by all host bits set to 1.	Subnet-directed broadcast.
127.x.x.x, where 0 ≤ x ≤ 255	Reserved for the software-only loopback (lo) interface.
10.0.0.0/8 172.16.0.0/12 192.168.0.0/16	RFCs 1597 and 1918 private addresses.

exclusively as the source address of a booting system that does not yet know its correct IP address. RARP, `bootp`, and DHCP boot-time operations can utilize this special address.

Broadcast Addresses

There are four different types of IPv4 broadcast addresses, three of which are noted in Table 4–10. They are the limited broadcast, the net-directed broadcast, the subnet-directed broadcast, and the *old* broadcast. All broadcast addresses can only be used as destination addresses in the Internet layer header.

The limited broadcast address is supposed to be read by only those nodes on the same (sub)network, that is, the nodes sharing the same network number. Often, this address is rewritten by applications to be the net- or subnet-directed broadcast.

The net-directed and subnet-directed broadcast addresses are used to send packets to all nodes on the network and subnetwork, respectively. Originally, net-directed broadcasts were supposed to be forwarded to all nodes on subnetworks of the network (see RFC 922). Most implementations, at best, optionally supported this capability. Linux does not support this option. Subsequent RFCs recommend against this, which is good since subnetworks are largely implemented as independent networks.

The old broadcast used all host bits set to 0 instead of 1. This type of broadcast appeared in the Berkeley Software Distribution (BSD) UNIX release in 1983 (prior to the standardization of broadcast addresses) and persisted in SunOS through version 4.x. While the use of this broadcast is nonstandard and Internet *illegal* (meaning that one or more standard RFCs prohibit its use), it can be supported if necessary by configuring an interface appropriately (discussed in "ifconfig Syntax" on page 127).

Another use of the old broadcast is for support of a 255.255.255.254 (/31) masked subnetwork. This subnetmask leaves only 1 bit for host numbers, meaning that there are two possible values (0 or 1). Given the standard requirement of one host address reserved for the network number and one for the broadcast address, there are no remaining addresses for hosts rendering this subnetmask useless. However, an interface can be configured so that it recognizes the network number as the broadcast address and then uses the remaining address for the lone host on the subnetwork. While this approach is Internet illegal, it can be utilized in an internal private network. Such configurations can be accomplished with the `ifconfig` command described in "ifconfig Syntax" on page 127.

Loopback

Any IPv4 address with 127 in the first octet is reserved for software only loopback addressing. The loopback is identified on Linux/UNIX systems as the `lo` interface. As noted earlier, it is used for testing and local network application support.

Private Addresses

IP addresses for use in the Internet are assigned and controlled by IANA and ICANN (discussed further in the next section). Internal or private (meaning nodes and networks not directly connected to the Internet) use of IP addresses, however, is not controlled by anybody. You can use any IP addressing scheme you like, so long as the use of those addresses are not exposed to the Internet.

RFC 1918 is a best current practice recommendation on internal, private IP address use. It suggests that organizations use the addresses shown in the last row of Table 4–10 for all internal addressing requirements. It also guarantees that these addresses will never be assigned as Internet addresses. While you are not obligated in any way to use these addresses internally, it is certainly considered as good netiquette!

Assignment of Internet Addresses

All Internet addresses are controlled by ICANN. This nonprofit corporation is in the process of assuming all responsibilities for the allocation of Internet address space, protocol parameter assignments, and DNS management. Formerly, IANA handled all of these responsibilities under contract with the U.S. government. As of this writing, the process of transferring responsibilities from IANA to ICANN is underway. During this interim period, both organizations are providing useful information at their web sites.

```
http://www.iana.org/
http://www.icann.org/
```

If you need to get a registered, Internet legal IP address, contact your Internet service provider (ISP) or visit one of the above sites.

Configuring NICs

At this point, armed with a good working knowledge of IP addresses, we can look at configuring NICs for participation in networks. Linux/UNIX operating systems provide a wonderfully flexible tool for that purpose. We introduced this tool in Chapter 2; it is the `ifconfig` program.

The `ifconfig` utility can be used to view the current configuration of a system's interfaces (with `ifconfig` or `ifconfig -a`); it can be used to modify the configuration of an interface and the interface's flags; it is used at boot-time to initially configure the system's interfaces based on a series of distribution dependent configuration files (discussed in "Start-up Scripts and NIC Configuration Files" on page 136). Let's take a look at some of its capabilities.

`ifconfig` Syntax

The `ifconfig` command has two different means of invocation, as presented below.

```
ifconfig [-a] [interface]
ifconfig interface arg [value] [arg value [arg value] ... ]
```

The first case causes `ifconfig` to display information about configured interfaces and is described in "Configured or Autodetected NIC" on page 42. The second case is used to modify the configuration of a NIC. In both cases `interface` means the name of the interface, like `eth0`, `eth1`, etc. The possible `arg` and `value` parameters to `ifconfig` are defined in Table 4–11, except for the point-to-point parameter and the IPv6 parameters.

Table 4–11   `ifconfig` Parameters

PARAMETER	DESCRIPTION
`up`	Causes the specified interface to receive and send packets.
`down`	Causes the specified interface to cease receiving and sending packets.
`[-]arp`	Without -, enables ARP on the interface. With -, disables ARP.
`[-]promisc`	Without -, enables promiscuous mode causing the interface to accept all packets even those not addressed to it. Normally, the interface will ignore packets with a destination physical address set to something other than its unicast address, any multicast addresses for which it is configured, or the broadcast address. With -, disables promiscuous mode.
`[-]allmulti`	Without -, causes the interface to accept all multicast packets, even those for which it is not configured to read. With -, disables all multicast receipt.
`metric n`	Specifies the metric n to be associated with this device, $0 \leq n \leq 15$. This metric is used in the routing table for routing information protocol (RIP) and is discussed beginning with Chapter 11.

Table 4–11 `ifconfig` Parameters *(Continued)*

PARAMETER	DESCRIPTION
`mtu` *n*	Specifies the MTU *n* to be used with this interface. *n* may be set to less than the MTU of the interface but not greater. This is useful in cases where PMTU is known and is less than the default MTU of this interface.
`dstaddr` *addr*	Used to set the remote address for a point-to-point link such as PPP. Deprecated in favor of `pointtopoint` below.
`netmask` *mask*	Specifies the netmask, *mask*, to be used with this interface.
`irq` *nbr*	Specifies the IRQ number, *nbr*, to be used with this interface. Not all drivers support this argument.
`io_addr` *addr*	Specifies the beginning *addr* I/O address range. Not all drivers support this argument.
`mem_start` *addr*	Specifies the starting *addr* for shared memory on cards that support it.
`media` *type*	Specifies the media *type* for cards that support different media types. For example, `media 10baseT`, will force a 10/100 autosensing card to always run at 10 Mbps. Not all drivers support this argument.
`[-]broadcast` *addr*	Without the *addr* value, `-broadcast` means to disable broadcast (no packets addressed to a broadcast will be received or sent) for the interface and `broadcast` means to enable broadcast. If used as `broadcast` *addr* (- cannot precede broadcast in this case), then the broadcast address is set to *addr*.
`[-]pointtopoint` *addr*	Used to enable point-to-point and set the remote address.

Table 4–11   `ifconfig` Parameters *(Continued)*

PARAMETER	DESCRIPTION
`hw` *class addr*	Sets the physical address *class* and *addr*. *class* must be a layer 2 technology supported by the card, `ether` is the default. *addr* must be an appropriate physical address. Not supported by all drivers.
`[inet]` *addr*	Sets the interfaces IPv4 address to *addr*. The `inet` keyword is optional.
`[-]multicast`	With -, sets the interface to ignore all multicast packets. Without -, enables the interface to receive and send multicast packets.
`txqueuelen` *length*	Sets the transmission queue length to *length* octets. Normally, this is only useful in reducing the size for slow links like 56k modems.
`[-]dynamic`	Disables (with -) or enables (without -) dynamic IP addressing. If enabled, whenever the interface goes down, the IP address, netmask, and broadcast fields are cleared. Used with autoconfiguration software such as DHCP often over a point-to-point link.

In the following sections, we'll look at utilizing some of these parameters.

Setting up an Interface

Let's suppose that we have an interface on a system that needs to be configured for a different IP address than its current configuration. This requirement might occur if, for instance, the system is moved from one location to another within the company. The following series of examples assumes that we need to set the IP address to `172.19.73.4/20`, thus the netmask is `255.255.240.0` (due to the /20 prefix), and, therefore, the broadcast address is `172.19.79.255`.

We can use `ifconfig` with the `inet` argument to specify the new IP address, the `netmask` argument to set the new netmask, and the `broadcast` argument to set the broadcast address. As noted in "Manipulating the ARP Cache" on page 67, we need to bring the interface down before modifying any of its parameters to avoid hanging the interface. Example 4–4 brings down eth0, sets the new values, brings the interface back up, and then displays the current interface configuration.

Example 4–4   Configuring an Interface with ifconfig

```
# ifconfig eth0 down
# ifconfig eth0 inet 172.19.73.4 netmask 255.255.240.0 broadcast 172.19.79.255
# ifconfig eth0
eth0    Link encap:Ethernet  HWaddr 00:60:94:B9:83:0A
        inet addr:172.19.73.4  Bcast:172.19.79.255  Mask:255.255.240.0
        UP BROADCAST RUNNING MULTICAST  MTU:1500  Metric:1
        RX packets:6219197 errors:0 dropped:0 overruns:0 frame:45
        TX packets:5951987 errors:0 dropped:0 overruns:0 carrier:0
        collisions:12995 txqueuelen:100
        Interrupt:14 Base address:0xb000
#
```

Notice that we do not need to use the up argument in order to bring the interface up after setting the new parameters—this is done automatically. The interface now reflects the new address, netmask, and broadcast address. At this point, with the NIC so configured, this interface needs to be connected to the 172.19.64.0/20 network—otherwise it won't be able to communicate with any other system.

WARNING

It may go without saying, but do *not* execute the steps shown in Example 4–4 over the network! Once the ifconfig eth0 down command is executed, you'll lose the network connection and be unable to continue. Always run ifconfig locally from the console or a terminal directly attached to the system.

Setting an interface using the ifconfig command only modifies the parameters in memory and will not survive reboots. Permanent changes are discussed in "Start-up Scripts and NIC Configuration Files" on page 136.

Next, let's take a look at the flags associated with the output of ifconfig.

ifconfig Flags

We actually looked at two of the flags associated with ifconfig already, the NOARP and the UP flags. In Example 4–4, the flags are UP BROADCAST RUNNING

MULTICAST. There are a number of other flags associated with `ifconfig` and we provide a listing and description of many of them in Table 4–12. These flags are actually defined in `/usr/include/net/if.h.`, but note that not all device drivers support all flags.

Table 4–12   Description of `ifconfig` Flags

FLAG	DESCRIPTION
UP	The interface is able to receive and send network packets. If the interface is not up, no flag will appear. An interface can be brought down with `ifconfig` *interface* `down`, where *interface* is the name of the interface, such as `eth0`. An interface can be brought up again with `ifconfig` *interface* `up`.
BROADCAST	The interface is able to receive and send broadcast packets from and to the broadcast address reported by `ifconfig`. The broadcast capability can be removed with `ifconfig` *interface* `-broadcast`, where *interface* is the name of the interface. Once again, `ifconfig` will report that it is not able to receive or send broadcasts with the absence of the BROADCAST flag. Turning broadcast back on is accomplished with `ifconfig interface broadcast`. This flag will appear by default.
RUNNING	This flag indicates that a device driver module is loaded into the kernel and associated with the specified device.
MULTICAST	As with broadcast, except for multicast packets. Disable multicasting with `ifconfig` *interface* `-multicast`; reenable with `ifconfig` *interface* `multicast`. This flag will appear by default.
NOARP	The presence of this flag indicates that ARP packets will neither be received nor sent. Set this flag with `ifconfig` *interface* `-arp`. Turn ARP back on with `ifconfig` *interface* `arp`. This flag will not appear by default.

Table 4–12   Description of `ifconfig` Flags *(Continued)*

FLAG	DESCRIPTION
PROMISC	The presence of this flag indicates that the interface has been put into promiscuous mode, meaning that all packets will be read by the interface, even those not addressed to it. Set this flag with `ifconfig interface` promisc; turn it off with `ifconfig interface` -promisc. Network sniffers operate by forcing the NIC into promiscuous mode. This flag will not appear by default.
ALLMULTI	As with MULTICAST, except that the parameter to `ifconfig` is allmulti. By default this flag does not appear. Note that if MULTICAST is enabled (i.e., the MULTICAST flag appears) then the ALLMULTI flag will not appear when ALLMULTI is enabled.

Configuring IP Aliases

Linux permits the configuration of more than one IP address to a physical interface. This can be useful for a variety of reasons. Perhaps you need to allow for two different networks to share the same medium because you are transitioning from one IP address scheme to another (for example, transitioning from IPv4 to IPv6—more about that in the next chapter). Or maybe you are utilizing the same medium for two purposes, for instance, a system that is attached to a stable network that also serves a lab or classroom environment that uses different addresses. Whatever the case, you can assign multiple addresses to a NIC by using IP *aliases*, also known as *logical interfaces*. It's really easy, too!

For purposes of this example, let's suppose that a system has the single interface, eth0, connected to a medium that is shared by two networks, 172.16.0.0/16 and 10.1.0.0/16. It is currently configured with the IP address 172.16.22.22 and therefore is participating in the 172.16.0.0 network. Suppose that 10.1.0.17 is an available address on the 10.1.0.0/16 network, then to add the interface to that network, we simply need to execute

```
# ifconfig eth0:0 inet 10.1.0.17 netmask 255.255.0.0 \
broadcast 10.1.255.255 up
```

With this command we have created an alias to eth0 which we have called
eth0:0. Example 4–5 illustrates the creation of the new aliased interface and
then displays the results with ifconfig.

Example 4–5   Creating an IP Alias

```
# ifconfig eth0:0 inet 10.1.0.17 netmask 255.255.0.0 \
  broadcast 10.1.255.255
# ifconfig
eth0      Link encap:Ethernet  HWaddr 00:60:94:B9:83:0A
          inet addr:172.16.22.22  Bcast:172.16.255.255  Mask:255.255.0.0
          UP BROADCAST RUNNING MULTICAST  MTU:1500  Metric:1
          RX packets:6526645 errors:0 dropped:0 overruns:0 frame:46
          TX packets:6241870 errors:0 dropped:0 overruns:0 carrier:0
          collisions:13428 txqueuelen:100
          Interrupt:14 Base address:0xb000

eth0:0    Link encap:Ethernet  HWaddr 00:60:94:B9:83:0A
          inet addr:10.1.0.17  Bcast:10.1.255.255  Mask:255.255.0.0
          UP BROADCAST RUNNING MULTICAST  MTU:1500  Metric:1
          Interrupt:14 Base address:0xb000

<...remaining output snipped...>
#
```

Notice that no statistics are displayed for the eth0:0 alias to eth0. All statistical information maintained by the kernel is only associated with the physical
device. In order to get statistical information about aliased interfaces you have to
configure IP accounting (discussed in Chapters 14 and 15). Note that HWaddr
reports the same address for both eth0 and eth0:0, which is consistent with the
fact that the two interfaces share the same physical device. Now that this system
has two interfaces it can act as a router between these two networks by enabling
IP *forwarding*, which is detailed in Chapter 6.

Any action applied to eth0 will also apply to its aliases. For instance, if you
execute ifconfig eth0 down, then all aliases of eth0 will be brought down as
well. This is true for flag settings also.

To remove the aliased interface, simply execute

```
# ifconfig eth0:0 down
```

and all reference to that interface will be deleted.

In our example, we have used the alias name eth0:0. An IP alias requires that
the physical interface name followed by the : exist in the alias name. What
comes after the : is zero or more characters up to a total of 16 characters, including the : and the physical interface name. So, for example, a valid alias name for

eth0 would be eth0: followed by up to an 11 character name. The following list represents a few possibilities.

```
eth0:a
eth0:T
eth0:17
eth0:10net
```

Be aware, however, that ifconfig only reports the first four characters after the :.

Other ifconfig Options and Details

Over the next several chapters we will revisit the ifconfig command and explore some of its other options and capabilities. For now, let's look at a few error conditions.

Suppose you have added a second NIC to the system, but have not yet configured it for recognition by the kernel as outlined in Chapter 2. Example 4–6 shows a typical error message when a NIC has yet to be assigned a kernel module (device driver).

Example 4–6   No Kernel Support Error Message

```
# ifconfig eth1
eth1: error fetching interface information: Device not found
#
```

The exact message you get will depend upon the version of the ifconfig command installed on your system.

Once you have added the necessary kernel module to support the new NIC (with modprobe or insmod), ifconfig will report that the interface exists, but it will have no parameters and will not be UP and RUNNING as shown in Example 4–7.

Example 4–7   Unconfigured NIC with Kernel Support

```
# ifconfig eth1
eth1       Link encap:Ethernet   HWaddr 00:50:BA:CA:23:25
           BROADCAST MULTICAST  MTU:1500  Metric:1
           RX packets:0 errors:0 dropped:0 overruns:0 frame:0
           TX packets:0 errors:0 dropped:0 overruns:0 carrier:0
           collisions:0 txqueuelen:100
           Interrupt:9 Base address:0xe000
#
```

At this point you can manually configure the new NIC. The next section describes how to cause configuration of the NIC to be repeated at each reboot by setting up the appropriate configuration files. Don't forget to add the necessary entries to `/etc/conf.modules` or `/etc/modules.conf` (as described in Chapter 2) to ensure that the driver gets loaded at each reboot.

Start-up Scripts and NIC Configuration Files

Understanding how to use the `ifconfig` command is very important and will come in handy. Ordinarily, though, you won't be manually configuring system interfaces with `ifconfig`, if for no other reason that it is extraordinarily tedious. Instead you'll want to configure your systems so that their NIC(s) are properly configured at each reboot. To that end, there are some configuration files that your system uses for NIC configuration purposes. These files are read at boot-time by the system start-up scripts.[6] Unfortunately, no two distributions are the same in this regard. Thus, the following sections will take you through the network configuration files and identify start-up scripts for each of the four distributions. Further details on each distribution's network related start-up scripts are described as appropriate in later chapters.

Red Hat 6.2

Red Hat uses `/etc/rc.d/init.d/network` as the master network start-up script. All network related functions are initiated from this script. This script looks for two types of configuration files. The first, `/etc/sysconfig/network`, is a high-level file that indicates whether or not networking is going to be used, what the hostname is, and what the default router (also called the gateway—we discuss default routers in Chapter 6) is, if any. A typical `/etc/sysconfig/network` file is shown in Example 4–8.

Example 4–8   Typical `/etc/sysconfig/network` File on Red Hat 6.2

```
[root@eeyore /root]# cat /etc/sysconfig/network
NETWORKING=yes
HOSTNAME=eeyore
GATEWAY=172.16.44.11
GATEWAYDEV=eth0
[root@eeyore /root]#
```

---

6. If you are unfamiliar with system start-up scripts, see, for example, *Linux Companion for System Administrators*, as cited in "For Further Reading" on page 145.

In this case, networking is turned on, the hostname is `eeyore`, and the default router is `172.16.44.11`, which can be reached through the `eth0` device. Most of the possible entries for the `/etc/sysconfig/network` file are given in Table 4–13. We provide notes about Caldera in this and the next table, since the two distributions share these files.

Table 4–13   Variables in Red Hat's `/etc/sysconfig/network` File

VARIABLE	DESCRIPTION
NETWORKING	Determines whether networking is to be configured. Can be yes or no.
IPFORWARDING	Caldera. If true (or yes), then IP forwarding is enabled and the system will route (forward) packets. Otherwise the system will not forward packets.
FORWARD_IPV4	Red Hat. Same meaning as IPFORWARDING. No longer used as of Red Hat 6.2; replaced by `/etc/sysctl.conf` which is discussed in Chapter 6.
HOSTNAME	The canonical hostname of this system. If the system has multiple interfaces, one name must be chosen as the canonical name.
DOMAINNAME	The DNS domainname.
GATEWAY	The IP address of the default router.
GATEWAYDEV	The device through which the default router can be reached. Use of this entry on systems other than routers will cause problems with RIP.
NISDOMAIN	The NIS domainname.
IF_LIST	Caldera. Accepts a quoted list of interface names. Used for searching for `ifcfg-`*ifname* files.

Table 4–13   Variables in Red Hat's `/etc/sysconfig/network` File *(Continued)*

VARIABLE	DESCRIPTION
SILENT	Red Hat. If `yes` or `true`, then if `routed` is started it is started with the `-q` flag. See "Using routed" on page 210.
EXPORT_GATEWAY	Red Hat. If `yes` or `true`, then if `routed` is started it is started with the `-g` flag. See "Using routed" on page 210.

The second file used for network start-up purposes is the NIC specific file, `/etc/sysconfig/network-scripts/ifcfg-`*ifname*, where *ifname* is the name of the interface, like `eth0`, `eth1`, etc. This file contains the configuration information for the named interface. The script, `/sbin/ifup`, actually parses this file and is called by `/etc/rc.d/init.d/network`. One such file must exist for each interface on the system. Aliases can also be set up through this mechanism by specifying the alias name in place of the interface name; for example, if the IP alias `eth0:0` exists, its configuration file would be called `/etc/sysconfig/network-scripts/ifcfg-eth0:0`. Example 4–9 illustrates such a file for an `eth0` NIC.

Example 4–9   A Typical `/etc/sysconfig/network-scripts/ifcfg-eth0` File

```
[root@eeyore /root]# cat /etc/sysconfig/network-scripts/ifcfg-eth0
DEVICE=eth0
BROADCAST=172.16.255.255
IPADDR=172.16.22.22
NETMASK=255.255.0.0
NETWORK=172.16.0.0
ONBOOT=yes
[root@eeyore /root]#
```

The meaning of the variables in Example 4–9 should be clear from the names used, but there are others not shown which may not be as clear at this point and so we describe most of them in Table 4–14.

Table 4–14   Variables in Red Hat's `ifcfg-ifname` Files

VARIABLE	DESCRIPTION
DEVICE	The name of the device.
IPADDR	The IP address.
NETMASK	The netmask.
NETWORK	The network number.
BROADCAST	The broadcast address.
BOOTPROTO	Red Hat. Specifies the method for obtaining IP information. Options are `dhcp`, `bootp`, or `none` (the default).
DYNAMIC	Caldera. Similar to `BOOTPROTO` above.
USERCTL	Red Hat. If yes, non-root users will be able to use `ifup` and `ifdown` on this interface. The default is no.
ONBOOT	If yes, the interface is configured at boot time. This is the default.
GATEWAY	Caldera. As defined in Table 4–13. Deprecated for Red Hat.
MACADDR	Red Hat. Specifies the physical address of the interface.

Other variables used in this and the `/etc/sysconfig/network` file are discussed at appropriate points in the book. These files can be configured through either the `linuxconf` or `netcfg` GUI interfaces in the Red Hat distribution.

Caldera 2.4

Caldera uses a scheme that is quite similar to Red Hat. In fact, we've noted Caldera specific entries in the tables above. It uses a single start-up script, `/etc/rc.d/init.d/network`, and the two files, `/etc/sysconfig/network` and `/etc/sysconfig/network-scripts/ifcfg-ifname`, where `ifname` is the name of the interface, such as `eth0`, `eth1`, etc. Example 4–10 shows an `/etc/sysconfig/network` file.

Example 4–10   Caldera's `/etc/sysconfig/network` File

```
[root@beauregard /root]# cat /etc/sysconfig/network
NETWORKING=yes
HOSTNAME=beauregard
IF_LIST='lo eth tr sl ppp'
[root@beauregard /root]#
```

The `IF_LIST` variable is Caldera specific and simply contains an ASCII string of valid interface types. This is used as a search list for `ifname` values. The other major difference between Red Hat and Caldera is that the GATEWAY variable for the default router appears in the `/etc/sysconfig/network-scripts/ifcfg-ifname` file instead of the `/etc/sysconfig/network` file.

You can use

```
#coas /usr/bin/coastool network.ether&
```

to bring up a GUI network management tool on Caldera. `coas` is a python shell used to invoke the python-based `coastool`. Caldera also offers a menu-driven utility, `lisa`. Otherwise, the description given in "Red Hat 6.2" on page 136 applies to Caldera.

Debian 2.1

The Debian distribution combines configuration and start-up script capabilities for basic network configuration into the single file `/etc/init.d/network`. Example 4–11 shows the file.

Example 4–11   Debian `/etc/init.d/network` File

```
foghorn:~# cat /etc/init.d/network
#! /bin/sh
ifconfig lo 127.0.0.1
route add -net 127.0.0.0
IPADDR=172.16.77.33
NETMASK=255.255.0.0
NETWORK=172.16.0.0
BROADCAST=172.16.255.255
GATEWAY=172.16.44.11
ifconfig eth0 ${IPADDR} netmask ${NETMASK} broadcast ${BROADCAST}
route add -net ${NETWORK}
[ "${GATEWAY}" ] && route add default gw ${GATEWAY} metric 1
foghorn:~#
```

The contents of this file are very straightforward. Don't worry about the router related entries; we discuss those in Chapter 6. The loopback interface is initially configured. Then, the environment variables IPADDR, NETMASK, NETWORK, and

BROADCAST are set. These variables are then supplied as arguments to the `ifconfig` command. This file is literally a shell script of the steps we took earlier in the chapter.

To add additional NIC or IP alias configuration information to this file, you can easily imitate the existing approach, just by using different variable names. For example, set the variables `IPADDR_1`, `NETMASK_1`, `NETWORK_1`, and `BROADCAST_1` to appropriate values and then add the line

```
ifconfig eth1 ${IPADDR_1} netmask ${NETMASK_1} \
broadcast ${BROADCAST_1}
```

to the end of the file and you'll have configured `eth1`. Of course, you'll also have to add the `route add -net ${NETWORK_1}`, but we'll get to that later.

SuSE 6.4

The SuSE distribution start-up scripts are located in `/sbin/init.d`, although there are links into `/etc/rc.d` and `/etc/rc.d/init.d`. The main networking start-up script is `/sbin/init.d/network`. Unlike the other distributions, SuSE uses a single configuration file for almost all system variables. That file is `/etc/rc.config`. We won't show the whole file here, just some of the pertinent network variables. These variables are *not* sequential as shown in Example 4–12.

Example 4–12   Pertinent Variables in `/etc/rc.config`

```
[root@topcat /root]# cat /etc/rc.config
<lots of output snipped>
FQHOSTNAME="topcat."
IFCONFIG_0="172.17.33.111 broadcast 172.17.255.255 netmask 255.255.0.0"
IPADDR_0="172.17.33.111"
NETCONFIG="_0"
NETDEV_0="eth0"
<remaining output snipped>
[root@topcat /root]#
```

Listed in Example 4–12 are the variables used to configure a NIC and set the hostname. The FQHOSTNAME variable sets the *fully qualified*[7] hostname of the system. The NETCONFIG parameter tells the system how many interfaces it has. In this case, the system has 1 interface indicated by the value `"_0"` supplied to NETCONFIG. This notation is used consistently for all the other variables: IFCONFIG_0,

---

7. Fully qualified means the hostname together with all its domain componenets. Here, there is no domainname. We discuss these DNS topics in Chapter 10.

IPADDR_0, and NETDEV_0 which specify the arguments to ifconfig, the IP address, and the device name for interface 0 (the first NIC), respectively.

Additional interfaces can be added by simply incrementing the code. For the second interface, the code to NETCONFIG would be "_1" and each of the other variables IFCONFIG_1, IPADDR_1, and NETDEV_1 would need to be set appropriately. IP aliases would be treated in the same way—simply increment the code appropriately.

We explore other variables in this and other files in the SuSE distribution throughout this book .

Hostname Resolution

Up to this point we haven't said anything about hostname resolution; that is, translating hostnames to IP addresses and vice-versa. Any time you use a hostname in order to reference a node on a network, your system must be able to translate that name into a valid IP address. This can be accomplished in several ways: through the file /etc/hosts, the network information service (NIS), DNS, or even LDAP. Your system determines which of these mechanisms to use and in what order to search for a resolution through the /etc/nsswitch.conf file. Example 4–13 illustrates the file.

Example 4–13   Sample /etc/nsswitch.conf File

```
[root@beauregard /root]# cat /etc/nsswitch.conf
# /etc/nsswitch.conf
#
# Name Service Switch configuration file.
#

passwd:      compat
shadow:      compat
group:       compat

hosts:       files nis dns
networks:    nis files dns

ethers:      nis files
protocols:   nis files
rpc:         nis files
services:    nis files
[root@beauregard /root]#
```

The syntax of this file is

```
service:option1 [option2] [option3]
```

where `service:` represents the information being sought. For example, `hosts:` indicates that the entry is for host lookups. The `option1`, `option2`, etc., list represents the sources to look up the information in the order given. For example, `host: files nis dns` means to look first in `/etc/hosts` (`files`), then, if the hostname is not resolved, query the NIS database, and if it's still not resolved, query DNS (both NIS and DNS are discussed in Chapter 10). The fields may be separated by tabs or spaces.

The `/etc/hosts` File

This now brings us to the `/etc/hosts` file. This is the simplest host resolution mechanism available. The `/etc/hosts` file contains a list of IP addresses, canonical hostnames, and hostname aliases, if any. Example 4–14 provides a sample `/etc/hosts` file.

Example 4–14   Sample `/etc/hosts` File

```
[root@eeyore /root]# cat /etc/hosts
127.0.0.1          localhost
10.13.1.1          beauregard
172.16.77.33       foghorn                          # C366
172.17.1.3         roadrunner          rr           # LX
172.16.1.3         wyle                             # LX le1
172.16.22.22       eeyore eeyore.corp.sgi.com  # IBM eth0
172.16.10.100      sgitux
172.17.1.254       sylvester                        # Gateway
172.16.1.254       underdog                         # Gateway
[root@eeyore /root]#
```

Each line in the file is a record. Each record consists of an IP address, followed by the canonical hostname, optionally followed by aliases and comments (preceded with #). Tabs or spaces can be used as separators. The use of this file allows us to reference the hostnames listed therein instead of their IP addresses. In this example, there are two entries, `roadrunner` and `eeyore`, with aliases. These hosts can be accessed by their hostname or alias; for instance, referencing `roadrunner` and `rr` will normally[8] yield the same result. Note that `eeyore.corp.sgi.com` is an example of a fully qualified DNS domain name. These are discussed in Chapter 10.

---

8. Some applications exclusively accept the canonical hostname.

Unresolvable Hostnames

Note that if a hostname is unresolvable, you will get an error message to that effect. For example, if DNS is being used, then attempting to communicate with the unresolvable hostname, `pyramid`, results in

```
# telnet pyramid
pyramid: No address associated with name
```

If DNS is not in use, the error message is slightly different.

```
# telnet pyramid
pyramid: Host name lookup failure
```

In either case, the meaning is that the system cannot resolve the hostname to an IP address and therefore encapsulation never takes place.

The solution is always to first check your spelling and then troubleshoot the resolution mechanism in use.

Summary

The Internet layer's fundamental responsibility is to move packets from point A to point B. In order to accomplish this task, a formal method of data formatting and processing is required. In the TCP/IP stack, that formal method, or ruleset, is embodied in the Internet Protocol. In this chapter, we introduced IP, ICMP, and IGMP. We presented the datagram header and defined its fields, then described IP addressing including VLSM. We described the `ifconfig` command and NIC boot-time configuration files for four Linux distributions. We concluded with an introduction to hostname to IP address resolution.

What's Next

In the next chapter, we cover the same ground for IPv6 as we did for IPv4 in this chapter. If you are not interested in IPv6, feel free to skip that chapter. In Chapter 6 we take a detailed look at routing, the real heart of IP.

For Further Reading

Anonymous, *Maximum Security: A Hacker's Guide to Protecting Your Internet Site and Network*, Indianapolis, Indiana, Sams.net, 1997.

Atkins, Derek, et al., *Internet Security: Professional Reference*, Indianapolis, Indiana, New Riders, 1996.

Comer, Douglas E., *Internetworking with TCP/IP Vol I: Principals, Protocols, Architecture*, 3d Ed., Englewood Cliffs, New Jersey, Prentice Hall, 1995.

Graham, Buck, *TCP/IP Addressing: Designing and Optimizing Your IP Addressing Scheme*, Orlando, Florida, AP Professional, 1997.

Hein, Jochen, *Linux Companion for System Administrators*, Reading, Massachusetts, Addison-Wesley, 1999.

Klander, Lars, *Hacker Proof: The Ultimate Guide to Network Security*, Las Vegas, Nevada, Jamsa Press, 1997.

Mancill, Tony, *Linux Routers: A Primer for Network Administrators*, Upper Saddle River, New Jersey, Prentice Hall PTR, 2000.

Maufer, Thomas A., *IP Fundamentals*, Upper Saddle River, New Jersey, Prentice Hall PTR, 1999.

Perlman, Radia, *Interconnections Second Edition: Bridges, Routers, Switches, and Internetworking Protocols*, Reading, Massachusetts, Addison-Wesley, 2000.

Stevens, W. Richard, *TCP/IP Illustrated, Volume 1: The Protocols*, Reading, Massachusetts, Addison-Wesley, 1994.

5

The Internet Layer: IPv6

In 1986 there were approximately 1,000 hosts connected to the Internet. As of July 1999 the estimate of connected hosts had risen to 56,218,000! The incredibly rapid growth of the Internet has really exercised the capabilities of the TCP/IP model. Amazingly, TCP/IP, and IP in particular, has held up very well. Nonetheless, given the rapid growth of the public Internet, in terms of the number of connected nodes, the types of applications being deployed, and the improvements in system and networking hardware, there are some fairly significant changes that need to be made to IP in order to continue supporting that growth. And all indications are that the growth will continue at its current pace.

In order to accommodate this growth, and to address the emerging needs of the Internet community, the IETF started work on developing a new IP called IP next generation (IPng), the final decision resulting in the standardization of IPv6[1] in 1996. Subsequent modifications, clarifications, and improvements continue to be made through standards track RFCs over the last few years—indeed, IPv6 is still an experiment. For a thorough treatment of the development of IPv6, see *IPv6: The New Internet Protocol* as cited in "For Further Reading" on page 172. As of this writing, RFC 2460 specifies the IPv6 protocol.

So what exactly does IPv6 provide that IPv4 did not? And how is it a benefit? We won't answer these questions in detail—that is left to works such as *IPv6:*

---

1. Version 5 of IP was reserved for a completely different experimental protocol described in RFC 1819. IPv5 was never standardized nor was IPv5 referenced in any RFC.

Clearly Explained as cited in "For Further Reading" on page 172. We do, however, provide the following list of major points.

- IPv6 specifies a 128 bit address, four times bigger than IPv4. This directly addresses the issue of IPv4 address exhaustion and accommodates more than one network per human being on the planet.
- IPv6 improves options capabilities in the header. IPv4 options are limited in scope, used in only exceptional cases, and often incur a significant performance hit when processing. IPv6 makes options an integral part of header processing as we'll see.
- IPv6 improves upon the IPv4 implementation of TOS. In IPv4 the TOS field is designed to provide a way to tell routers how to prioritize the processing of packets. While Linux implements TOS (described in Chapter 16), it is not a widely implemented IPv4 feature. IPv6 makes the processing of the type, quality, and priority of service much simpler and more flexible.
- IPv6 includes security enhancements over IPv4. While IP security is primarily being implemented through IPsec (see Chapter 14) for both IPv4 and IPv6, the IPv6 options make implementation easier and more efficient.
- IPv6 generally simplifies the header.

In short, IPv6 addresses the needs of a greater volume of Internet access in terms of hosts and networks and it also addresses router performance, bandwidth allocation, and security needs. Perhaps arguably not perfect, IPv6 nonetheless provides a lot of headroom for the future Internet. In any event, IPv6 is coming and we need to know how to deal with it.

For all intents and purposes, IPv6 provides exactly the same functionality that IPv4 does, namely: it provides a datagram format specification and a set of rules for processing the datagram. The difference between IPv6 and IPv4 is in the format specification and processing rules. In this chapter, we will cover the IPv6 and how it differs from IPv4. As we did with IPv4, we begin with the datagram format specification.

IPv6 Datagram

The IPv6 datagram, like the IPv4 datagram, consists of a header and the payload. Unlike the IPv4 header, the IPv6 header is always at least 40 octets. The fields comprising the 40 octets are fixed in length and possible values. Similar to IPv4, after the first 40 octets, IPv6 can carry optional fields that are each multiples of 8 octets (this improves overall processing performance). The IPv6 option fields are called *extension headers*. As with IPv4, these extension headers are optional and need not exist.

IPv6 is really an emerging standard. While the standard for the protocol itself (RFC 2460) has been published, there are many details that have yet to be completed. In this section, we provide information about IPv6 in its state at the time of this writing. It is unquestionably the case that by the time you read this, some of the missing pieces may be filled in and/or some elements of the protocol may have changed. Be sure to check the then prevailing RFCs.

The IPv6 header is depicted in Figure 5–1. It is useful for comparative purposes and for the discussion following this diagram to reference Figure 4–1 on page 93.

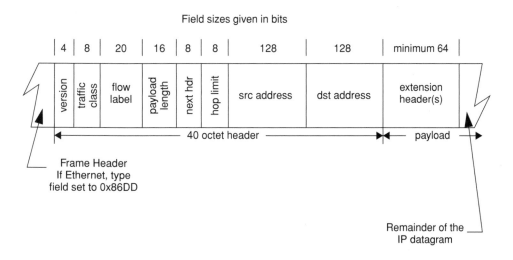

Figure 5–1   IPv6 Header

Table 5–1 provides a brief description of each field. A more detailed description follows for those fields requiring it.

Table 5–1　IPv6 Header Fields

FIELD	DESCRIPTION
version	The IP version number; 6 for IPv6.
traffic class	Currently in the experimental stages, this field supports TOS or differentiated service functionality. Formerly called the *priority* field. See "Traffic Class" on page 151.
flow label	Currently in the experimental stages, this field is used to request special handling by routers for series of packets in the same flow. See "Flow Label" on page 151.
payload length	Length of the IPv6 payload. This length field includes all extension headers. See "Payload Length" on page 151.
next hdr	Identifies the type of the header that follows the IPv6 header. The following header could be an extension header or it could be a higher layer protocol header. See "Next Header" on page 152.
hop limit	Decremented by 1 by each router that forwards the packet. See "Hop Limit" on page 152.
src address	IPv6 address of the sender. See "IPv6 Addressing" on page 158.
dst address	IPv6 address of the destination. See "IPv6 Addressing" on page 158.
extension header(s)	Optional fields providing a variety of possible services. See "Extension Headers" on page 153.

It should be apparent that the IPv6 header is more simplistic and less structured than the IPv4 header. This was one of the design goals—although for performance reasons and not for simplicity's sake alone. In the next few sections, we will take a more detailed look at each of the fields.

Traffic Class

The `traffic class` field is effectively the replacement to the TOS field in IPv4. The purpose of this field is to specify the way in which routers and other nodes handle packets with particular bit settings. The use of this field is still evolving and in particular is being defined to coincide with the use of the IPv4 TOS field. We discuss this topic further, largely as it relates to IPv4, and its current and potential application in Chapter 16.

Flow Label

In Chapter 4, we described IP as a connectionless protocol. This field has the potential of changing that definition somewhat. Historically, the utilization of packet switching worked fine for networking applications. The Internet explosion together with very high speed connections has brought us pseudo real-time applications such as interactive audio and video programs. These programs generate streams of data in which latencies (the time between the arrival of one packet and the next) must be small. In other words, if an FTP session receives packets out of order, it's no big deal, but if a video application gets packets representing a frame that should have been displayed before the current frame, that packet is now useless.

The `flow label` field is designed to address the issue by permitting the association of packets in a stream of packets. Each packet in the stream or flow will share the same label. This field together with the `traffic class` field has the potential of establishing connection-like capabilities through IP. These two fields also provide what is often called differentiated services. One protocol that attempts to provide differentiated services is the resource reservation protocol (RSVP—RFCs 2205 and 2750 are the primary specifications for RSVP). We mention this protocol, and differentiated services generally, in Chapter 16.

Currently, the informational RFCs that deal with this and the traffic class field as well as differentiated services generally are 1809, 1954, and 2430.

Payload Length

This field contains the payload length in octets. As depicted in Figure 5–1 on page 149, the payload includes any and all extension headers. Notice that, in

IPv4, in order for a payload length to be derived, the datagram header length must be subtracted from the total datagram length. The use of the `payload length` field in IPv6 makes that calculation unnecessary, saving processing time.

Next Header

This field effectively replaces the protocol field in the IPv4 header. It contains a protocol number found in the file `/etc/protocols` which is dictated by IANA and ICANN. New values have been specified for support of the available extension headers to IPv6. This field specifies what is next in the datagram—an extension header, higher protocol data, or no next header. We discuss these in "Extension Headers" on page 153.

Note that if the decimal value of this field is 59 that means there is no next header and IPv6 will ignore any data in the payload following the last octet of the header in which this code is specified.

Hop Limit

This field represents a replacement to the time-to-live field in the IPv4 header. As with IPv4, the value in the `hop limit` field of the IPv6 header is decremented by 1 by each router through which it passes. The major difference between the two fields is that where IPv4 *requires* the enforcement of the time-to-live field, IPv6 does not require the enforcement of the hop limit. This lack of requiring enforcement of the hop limit in IPv6 does not actually reflect a change in practice as implementations frequently ignore the requirement in IPv4.

When the value of the `hop limit` field reaches 0, the packet is destroyed and an ICMPv6 error message is transmitted to the sender of the packet.

NOTE

There are four fields in the IPv4 header that are not found in the IPv6 header. The IPv4 fields are: `ident`, `flags`, `frag offset`, and `hdr chksum`. The first three fields (`ident`, `flags`, and `frag offset`) deal with fragmentation which is not implemented in IPv6 (see "Fragmentation and PMTU" on page 155). The `hdr chksum` was dropped from IPv6 because checksums exist in higher layer protocols (TCP and UDP) and because

authentication extension headers can be used for the same purpose with greater security.

Extension Headers

Extension headers replace the IPv4 option field. This approach is far more efficient than its predecessor's because the next header field contains a protocol number that determines what type of header follows and the header is guaranteed to be a multiple of 8 octets. The IPv6 specification is quite general allowing for the future definition of extension headers. The extension headers currently defined and their protocol numbers (which must appear in the preceding header's next header field) are defined in Table 5–2. Multiple headers can exist, and if multiple headers are to exist in an IPv6 datagram, it is recommended that they exist in the following order:

- hop-by-hop options header
- destination options header
- routing header
- fragment header
- authentication header
- encapsulating security payload (ESP) header
- destination options header
- upper layer header and payload

Of these headers, *all* are processed by the destination node only, except for the hop-by-hop options header. The duplicate appearance in the list of the destination options header is not a mistake. The first destination options header is to be processed by the initial destination as specified in the IPv6 dst address field and any destinations listed in the routing header. The second destination options header is to be processed by the final destination which may not be revealed to intermediate routers in the presence of encryption. Not all of these extension headers need exist.

The following sections describe the purpose of the first four extension headers listed in Table 5–2 in more detail.

Table 5–2   Currently Supported IPv6 Extension Header Types

Protocol Number (Next Header Field)	Header	Description
0	hop-by-hop options	This option is processed by every node that routes the datagram and can contain additional instructions for the router including processing of additional extension headers. See "Hop-by-Hop" on page 155.
60	destination options	This option is to be processed by the destination node of the datagram. See "Destination" on page 155.
43	routing	This option supplies a list of destinations. Each destination is visited in order of listing until the final destination is reached. See "Routing" on page 155.
44	fragment	This option is used to specify that the datagram is fragmented. This option is not processed by intermediate routers. See "Fragmentation and PMTU" on page 155.
51	authentication	This option provides a method for computing a cryptographic checksum on the datagram. It is standardized by RFC 2402.
50	encapsulating security payload (ESP)	This option provides a method for encrypting the payload. This extension header, if it exists, is the last unencrypted portion of the datagram. It is standardized by RFC 2406.

Hop-by-Hop

The hop-by-hop options header is always processed by routers. Currently, only two options are defined. The jumbogram option (see RFC 2675) provides a mechanism for handling payloads that exceed 65,535 octets. The router alert option (see RFC 2711) is used to coerce routers to process additional information in the payload, such as RSVP control information.

Destination

This header carries information to be processed by the ultimate destination only. Currently, there are no specifications for this header.

Routing

The routing header contains a list of routers through which the packet must pass. It behaves in a way that is entirely similar to the loose source route and record route options of IPv4.

Fragmentation and PMTU

As we noted in Chapter 4, IPv6 does not permit fragmentation in the way that IPv4 does. Instead, it relies exclusively on PMTU (see RFC 1981) which functions very similarly to PMTU as described for IPv4 in "Fragmentation and PMTU" on page 155. The difference is that IPv6 has no need to set the DF bit since DF is the default in IPv6. So, an IPv6 node simply sends a packet based on the local MTU. If there is an MTU along the path that is smaller than the one used, the node requiring the smaller MTU will send an ICMPv6 (discussed in the next section) message to that effect with the required MTU. Instead of an ICMP-FN message (which does not exist in ICMPv6), however, the ICMPv6 message sent is "packet too big" (see Table 5–3).

Note that IPv6 imposes a *minimum* MTU of 1280 octets (see RFC 2460). That is, if a system cannot utilize an MTU of 1280, it cannot participate in IPv6. There are workarounds to this problem, however, such as embedding IPv6 inside IPv4 datagrams (usually through IP tunnels which are described in Chapter 16). Other than the differences cited, the PMTU functionality in IPv6 and IPv4 is identical.

Nonetheless, it may be necessary to fragment datagrams at the source (remember, IPv6 cannot fragment datagrams during routing). If this is the case, then the fragment header must be included in the datagram. The fragment header includes a flag to indicate whether or not more fragments are coming and an identification field to associate the correct fragments (quite similar to IPv4). The difference, once again, is that only the source and destination nodes are involved with fragmentation in IPv6.

ICMPv6

ICMPv6 provides nearly the same support role to IPv6 as did ICMPv4 to IPv4. The big difference with ICMPv6 is that it incorporates the ARP functionality in neighbor discovery (ND) messages which are described in "Neighbor Discovery" on page 170. Additionally, the number of ICMPv6 messages has been dramatically reduced, thus simplifying processing. As with ICMPv4, ICMPv6 never generates error messages under the following conditions:

- If the datagram is an ICMPv6 error message.
- If the datagram's destination IPv6 address is a multicast except for "packet too big" and "unrecognized IPv6 option encountered" messages.
- If the Network Interface destination physical address is a multicast or broadcast except for "packet too big" and "unrecognized IPv6 option encountered" messages.
- If the datagram's source address is anything other than a unicast.

Table 5–3 provides a brief description of each ICMP message based on the `type` and `code` fields. It also specifies the class of message, that is, whether it is an error, request, or reply message (request and reply messages are known as *informational* messages). The `type` field actually specifies a category of messages. Where appropriate, the categories are defined in the table by specifying N/A in the `code` column. Any row with N/A in the `code` column is not a valid `code` nor a valid message, it is simply a way to identify the `type` category. All messages are defined in RFC 2463 except where noted.

Table 5–3   ICMPv6 Message Descriptions

Class	type	code	Description
error	1	N/A	Destination unreachable
error	1	0	No route to destination

Table 5–3   ICMPv6 Message Descriptions *(Continued)*

CLASS	type	code	DESCRIPTION
error	1	1	Communication with destination is administratively prohibited
error	1	3	Address unreachable
error	1	4	Port unreachable
error	2	0	Packet too big.
error	3	N/A	Time exceeded
error	3	0	Hop limit exceeded in transmission
error	3	1	Fragment reassembly time exceeded
error	4	N/A	Parameter problem
error	4	0	Erroneous header field encountered
error	4	1	Unrecognized next header type encountered
error	4	2	Unrecognized IPv6 option encountered
request	128	0	Echo request (ping)
reply	128	0	Echo reply (pong)
request	133	0	Router solicitation (see RFC 2461)
reply	134	0	Router advertisement (see RFC 2461)
request	135	0	Neighbor request (see RFC 2461)
reply	136	0	Neighbor reply (see RFC 2461)
error	137	0	Redirect (see RFC 2461)

We discuss a number of these ICMPv6 messages in subsequent chapters.

IGMP and IPv6

Originally, when IPv6 was first published in 1996, IGMP was incorporated into ICMPv6. However, as IPv6 and ICMPv6 evolved, it was determined that IGMP should be kept separate. IGMP version 2 (IGMPv2) is now standardized by RFC 2236. IGMPv2 applies to both IPv4 and IPv6. We will look at some multicast implementations in Chapter 12.

IPv6 Addressing

The most obvious difference between IPv4 and IPv6 addresses is the size: 32 bits and 128 bits, respectively. There is a much bigger difference, however, in the way in which these addresses are defined. When we looked at IPv4 addresses in "IPv4 Addressing" on page 108, we saw that, originally, IPv4 addresses were broken out into classes. The growth of the Internet, and the expanded use of IP generally, forced a modification of those class definitions to include VLSM, and as we'll see in the next chapter, classless interdomain routing (CIDR). IPv6 addressing takes the concept embodied in VLSM and carries that into its address definitions. IPv6 addressing is currently defined by RFC 2373.

IPv6 Address Representation

We noted in Chapter 4 that the most common way of representing IPv4 addresses is in dot decimal notation. IPv6 addresses are most commonly expressed as 8 16-bit hexadecimal, or 8 hexadecimal quadruplet, values separated by colons. For example,

```
1. 2100:0:0:0:4D:31AC:12:45
2. 0:0:0:0:0:0:0:1
3. FF0C:0:0:0:36:0:0:1
4. CDCE:0:0:0:FA:0:0:0
5. 3FA:2:17:1EF2:AD:CB:200:11
```

are all valid IPv6 addresses. The designers of IPv6 included a convenient shorthand for representing addresses that have many zeros in them. Instead of writing out contiguous 16-bit zeros, a :: may be used instead. For instance, the examples 1 and 2 above can be written as

```
2100::4D:31AC:12:45
::1
```

respectively. But there are limitations to the use of the double colon notation. Only one string of contiguous zeros can be compressed. Thus, we can legally represent examples 3 and 4 as

```
FF0C::36:0:0:1 or FF0C:0:0:0:36::1
CDCE::FA:0:0:0 or CDCE:0:0:0:FA::
```

respectively. Note that we cannot simplify number 5 in the example because it has no contiguous 16-bit zeros.

IPv6 addresses can be thought of as having two major components: a network or subnetwork component and a host component. As we'll see in the next section, it is a little more complicated than that, but as with IPv4, we can use the prefix notation (see "Prefix Notation and Computing VLSMs" on page 122) to identify each part of the address. For example,

```
6. 2100:0:0:0:4D:31AC:12:45/64 or 2100::4D:31AC:12:45/64
7. 3FA:2:17:1EF2:AD:CB:200:11/60
```

represent that the bits significant for routing in the 6th example are the leftmost (highest order) 64 bits and in the 7th example are the leftmost 60 bits. This notation can be extended to the (sub)network number for 6 and 7 as

```
8. 2100::/64
9. 3FA:2:17:1EF0::/60
```

respectively. As with IPv4, the notation used in examples 8 and 9 represent the entire (sub)network.

The prefix notation actually hides a lot of detail in terms of what is actually done with the (sub)network portion of the address. Let's look at the types of addresses to see exactly how these bits are handled.

IPv6 Address Types and Definitions

RFC 2373 defines three address types for IPv6. They are unicast, multicast, and *anycast*. As with IPv4, there are also reserved addresses, some of which are for special purposes. We'll look at each type of address in the following sections. Table 5–4 represents the current address assignments for IPv6, based on the prefix (leftmost bits) value in binary.

Table 5–4   Allocation of IPv6 Address Space

Binary Prefix	Allocation	Fraction of Total Address Space	Notes
00000000	Reserved	1/256	Special addresses are allocated in this range. See "Special Addresses" on page 169.
00000001	Unassigned	1/256	
0000001	NSAP	1/128	For network service access point (NSAP) addresses. See "NSAP and IPX" on page 170.
0000010	IPX	1/128	For IPX addresses. See "NSAP and IPX" on page 170.
0000011 00001 0001	Unassigned	1/128 1/32 1/16	
001	Aggregable Global Unicast Addresses	1/8	See "Unicast Addresses" on page 161.
00111111 11111110	Experimental (See RFC 2471)	1/65536	See "Experimental Addresses" on page 169.

Table 5–4   Allocation of IPv6 Address Space (Continued)

BINARY PREFIX	ALLOCATION	FRACTION OF TOTAL ADDRESS SPACE	NOTES
010	Unassigned	1/8	
011		1/8	
100		1/8	
101		1/8	
111		1/8	
1110		1/16	
11110		1/32	
111110		1/64	
1111110		1/128	
11111110 0		1/512	
11111110 10	Link-Local Unicast Addresses	1/1024	See "Unicast Addresses" on page 161.
11111110 11	Site-Local Unicast Addresses	1/1024	See "Unicast Addresses" on page 161.
11111111	Multicast	1/256	See "Multicast Addresses" on page 165.

Unicast Addresses

An IPv6 unicast address is an address that is assigned to a specific, single interface. A packet sent to a unicast address is delivered to that interface. As with IPv4 addresses, an interface can have more than one unicast address associated with it.

As was mentioned earlier, the IPv6 unicast address can be simply thought of as having two parts: the subnetwork number and the host number. The prefix notation used with IPv6 addresses tells us explicitly how many highest order bits of the address belong to the subnetwork number (called the *subnet number*), or in other words, which part of the IPv6 address is used for routing. The prefix is the subnetwork mask and is applied in exactly the same way as described in "The Netmask" on page 112. The remaining bits are for the node number. The node number is called an *interface identifier* (interface ID). Thus, if the prefix is 60, then the leftmost 60 bits of the IPv6 address are the subnet number and all the remaining bits are the interface ID. But this simplistic view of IPv6 addresses assumes that the node has no routing responsibilities other than for itself. We discuss routing in Chapter 6 at which time the significance of the breakdown of IPv6 unicast addresses becomes clearer. In the meantime, we'll use analogies to describe the purpose behind the breakout of the subnetwork portion of each type of unicast address.

Aggregatable Global Unicast Addresses

The notion behind aggregatable global unicast (AGU) addresses is to provide a hierarchical addressing structure for ISPs. That is, a large ISP can obtain an AGU network block from ICANN and then in turn issue (for a fee, of course!) subnets of those AGU addresses to smaller ISPs or companies, who in turn can issue subnetted AGUs as needed. And so it could go until all bits of the subnet number had been consumed. Additionally, the scheme provides for the possibility for a *subscriber* (company or individual obtaining service from an ISP) to not have to change addresses whenever ISPs are changed or to use a single block of AGU addresses by subscribing to more than one ISP.

AGU addresses all begin with binary 001. This is called the format prefix (FP). RFC2373 further defines AGU addresses to utilize the highest order 64 bits (including the FP) for the subnet number and the lowest order 64 bits for the interface ID. Figure 5–2 illustrates the breakdown of these two components and the following subsections describe each field shown.

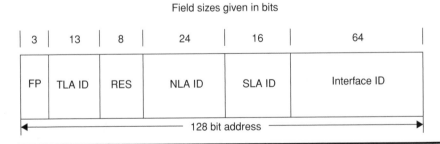

Figure sizes given in bits

3	13	8	24	16	64
FP	TLA ID	RES	NLA ID	SLA ID	Interface ID

◀──────────────── 128 bit address ────────────────▶

Figure 5–2   IPv6 AGU Address

FP   The FP formally identifies where in the IPv6 address space a given address resides. All AGU addresses belong to FP 001.

TLA ID   The top-level aggregation identifier (TLA ID). This field specifies the highest level routing information of the address. In particular, this means that in an IPv6 only environment (which the Internet will be one day), there is a maximum of 8,192 *default-free* routers at the top of the routing hierarchy. A default-free router is one that has no default router entry in its routing tables. The use of this IPv6 capability alone would substantially reduce the size of the routing tables in use today in the Internet's top-level routers. The role of this field does not have a direct analogy to IPv4.

RES   This field is reserved for future use.

NLA ID   The next-level aggregation identifier (NLA ID) is used as the next level routing information. This field will most likely be used by organizations that supply blocks of addresses to other organizations. At 24 bits, it is the largest of the network number fields providing the greatest flexibility for further subnetting. This field is somewhat analogous to a network number in IPv4.

SLA ID   The site-level aggregation identifier (SLA ID) provides the lowest level routing information. This field will be used for an organization's internal networking structure. At 16 bits of addressing space, there is a lot of flexibility in subnetting. This field is somewhat analogous to a subnetwork number in IPv4.

INTERFACE ID   The interface ID field holds the unique address for the interface. The interface ID must be unique within the *link* (what we've been calling the local network or local subnetwork). RFC 2373 interface IDs in AGU addresses will be in IEEE EUI-64 format. This format is similar to the 48-bit physical address format for Ethernet (and other layer 2) NICs. The EUI-64 format specifies that the first 24 bits of the address is the IEEE assigned vendor identification number (discussed in Chapter 2) and that the remaining 40 bits belong to the interface. You can learn more about this format at

`http://standards.ieee.org/regauth/oui/tutorials/EUI64.html`

This format paves the way to the day when all NICs ship with a unique interface ID burned into silicon on the card. In the interim, Appendix A of RFC 2373 provides a way of computing the Interface ID. This use of the interface ID has significant benefits in achieving autoconfiguration of an IP address which effectively can be used as a DHCP replacement.

Link-Local and Site-Local Unicast Addresses

As with IPv4, IPv6 reserves certain ranges of addresses for private use. These are link-local (LLU) and site-local unicast (SLU) addresses—these addresses will never be used in the Internet and, as with RFC 1918 (IPv4 private) addresses, routers are not supposed to forward them to the Internet.

LLU addresses are intended to be used with a single network link (a single local network). The format of these addresses is quite simple. The leading 10 bits are `1111111010`, followed by 54 bits of 0, followed by the 64 bit interface ID. There is no real equivalent type of address in IPv4.

The SLU addresses are intended to be used organizationally, and are very conceptually similar to RFC 1918 IPv4 addresses. These addresses incorporate a 16 bit subnet field as depicted in Figure 5–3.

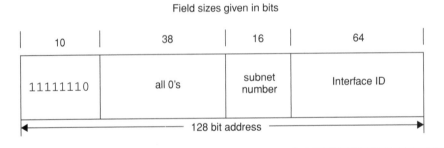

Field sizes given in bits

10	38	16	64
11111110	all 0's	subnet number	Interface ID

◀————————— 128 bit address —————————▶

Figure 5–3   IPv6 SLU Address

Multicast Addresses

An IPv6 multicast address is an identifier assigned to one or more interfaces. Any packet addressed to the multicast address will be delivered to all interfaces that have been configured for that address.

IPv6 reserves all addresses beginning with hex FF to be multicast addresses. As with IPv4, IPv6 multicast addresses can never be in the `src address` field of the IPv6 header (see Figure 5–1 on page 149). There are two types of multicast addresses: *permanent* and *transient*. A permanent multicast address (also referred to as a *well-known* multicast address) is one that has been assigned by a global Internet numbering authority (IANA and ICANN). The currently assigned permanent addresses are listed in Table 5–7. A transient multicast address is one that has not been assigned by IANA or ICANN. The format for IPv6 multicast addresses is given in Figure 5–4.

Note that the multicast format includes two fields, `flags` and `scope`. The first three bits of the `flags` field are reserved; the last bit, if 0, indicates a permanent multicast address and, if 1, a transient multicast address. The values of the scope field are given in Table 5–5. The group identifier (ID) must be unique within the type and scope.

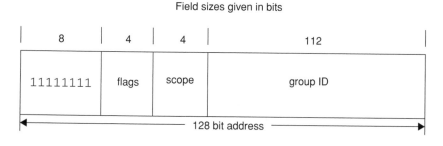

Figure sizes given in bits

8	4	4	112
11111111	flags	scope	group ID

128 bit address

Figure 5–4   IPv6 Multicast Address

Table 5–5   IPv6 Multicast Scope Field

HEX VALUE	MEANING
0 or F	Reserved.
3, 4, 6, 7, 9, A, B, C, or D	Unassigned.
1	Node-local scope, in other words, the system itself.
2	Link-local scope. The local (sub)network.
5	Site-local scope. All networks within the local site of an organization.
8	Organization-local scope. All networks within all sites of an organization.
E	Global scope. The Internet.

In order to understand the meanings of the scope values, let's consider an example. Let's suppose that we need to create a multicast group for all light-weight directory access protocol (LDAP) account servers in our organization. We'll choose hex 0008 as our group ID. Since there is no permanently assigned address for such use, we will need to set the flags field to hex 0001. The addresses we define are given in Table 5–6.

Table 5–6   Example Multicast Addresses and Meanings

ADDRESS	MEANING
FF12::8	All LDAP servers on the same link. This address will be used to pass messages to all LDAP servers on the same local network.
FF15::8	All LDAP servers at the same site. This address expands the systems that we're communicating with to include all LDAP servers within a given site. The determination of what is included at a site is usually dictated by administrative control and revealed through some domainname such as eng.acme.com.

Table 5–6   Example Multicast Addresses and Meanings *(Continued)*

ADDRESS	MEANING
`FF18::8`	All LDAP servers throughout our organization. This expands inclusion to our entire collection of sites as in the whole domain acme.com, which may have sites throughout the world.

Now that we have a sense of the purpose and meaning of the scope field, we can now define the permanent multicast addresses. They are given in Table 5–7.

Table 5–7   Permanent Multicast Addresses

MULTICAST ADDRESS	DEFINITION
`FF00:: through FF0F::`	Reserved.
`FF01::1`	All nodes multicast with node-local scope.
`FF02::1`	All nodes multicast with link-local scope.
`FF01::1`	All routers multicast with node-local scope.
`FF01::2`	All routers multicast with link-local scope.
`FF01::5`	All routers multicast with site-local scope.
`FF02::1:FFxx:xxxx`	Solicited-node address with site-local scope. Here, the six xs representing 24 bits in total must be replaced with the node's unicast or anycast lower order 24 bits. Each node *must* join this multicast group for *every* unicast or anycast address assigned to it.

The all nodes multicast addresses are used similarly to IPv4 broadcasts. The all routers multicast addresses are used to share routing information and will be discussed further in Chapters 11 and 12.

The solicited-node address is used for neighbor discovery (ND—discussed in "Neighbor Discovery" on page 170) and other similar purposes such as *stateless address autoconfiguration* (see RFC 2462).

But What about Broadcast Addresses?

You've probably noticed by now that IPv6 does not provide for a broadcast address. This is because broadcasts are a special case of multicasts. The IPv6 permanent multicast address, FF02::1, is effectively the equivalent of the IPv4 broadcast address. So, why did IPv4 define a broadcast address? The answer is that IPv4 broadcasts were defined before multicast address came into use. Had it been the other way around, broadcasts would never have been defined.

Anycast Addresses

An anycast address is a special type of unicast address. It must utilize one of the three format types for unicast addresses described in "Unicast Addresses" on page 161. Unlike a unicast address, however, it is not usually assigned to a specific interface; like a multicast it is normally assigned to many interfaces each on different nodes throughout a networked environment. A packet sent to an anycast address will be delivered to the *closest* interface configured with that address. The closest interface is determined by the routing tables of the sending node and the intermediate routers. Anycast addresses must never appear as an `src` `address` in the IPv6 header (see Figure 5–1 on page 149) and must only be assigned to routers. There is no IPv4 equivalent to anycast addresses except for one special case.

There is one very special anycast address. That address is the subnet number followed by all bits set to 0. Since anycast addresses use unicast format, this means that the interface ID is set to 0. This is the equivalent of the (sub)network number in IPv4 and is called the *subnet-router* anycast address. Any packet sent to this address will arrive at one router (the closest one) on the subnet link. In this way, applications can take advantage of the fact that subnetworks can be communicated with. For instance, consider a mobile node that wants to establish a connection with its home subnet for specific application support. Such an application can easily establish the connection by initially communicating with the subnet-router anycast.

Special Addresses

In addition to the subnet-router anycast, there are three special addresses defined for IPv6. They are the *unspecified* address, the loopback address, and IPv4 within IPv6 addresses.

The unspecified address is `0:0:0:0:0:0:0:0` or `::`. It is used by nodes at boot-time when they do not know their IP address and can only appear in the `src address` of the IPv6 header (see Figure 5–1). This address is analogous to the IPv4 limited source address described in "Limited Source" on page 124.

The loopback address for IPv6 is `0:0:0:0:0:0:0:1` or `::1`. This address can only be used for the loopback address and is entirely analogous to the IPv4 address `127.0.0.1`.

The folks who designed IPv6 knew that the transition from IPv4 to IPv6 would take time. Consequently, provision was made to support IPv4 addresses through the IPv6 scheme. There are two types of IPv4 in IPv6 address: *IPv4-compatible IPv6* and *IPv4-mapped IPv6* addresses.

IPv4-compatible IPv6 addresses are used on nodes that support IPv6. The syntax is

`0:0:0:0:0:0:x.x.x.x`

where x.x.x.x is the IPv4 address. For example, `0:0:0:0:0:0:172.16.22.22` or `::172.16.22.22` represent an IPv4-compatible address.

IPv4-mapped IPv6 addresses are used by IPv6 nodes to reference nodes that do not support IPv6. The syntax for these addresses is

`0:0:0:0:0:FFFF:x.x.x.x`

where x.x.x.x is once again the IPv4 address. As an example, `::FFFF:172.16.4.18` could be used on an IPv6 node to reference the IPv4 node `172.16.4.18`.

Experimental Addresses

RFC 2471 specifies that all addresses beginning with hex `3FFE` are reserved for experimental use and may be reclaimed at some point in the future. These addresses are being used in the primary IPv6 testbed known as the *6bone*. The 6bone is an IPv6 network backbone, the likes of which will one day take over the existing IPv4 Internet backbones. To learn more about or to begin participating in the 6bone visit

```
http://www.6bone.net/
```

NSAP and IPX

The designers of IPv6 incorporated the goal of interoperability. To that end, OSI NSAP and Novelle Netware IPX address allocations were adopted. NSAP addressing for IPv6 is defined in RFC 1888. IPX addressing has not yet been specified, likely due to the fact that the latest releases of Novelle Netware use TCP/IP as their native networking protocol.

Neighbor Discovery

Now that we have an initial understanding of IPv6 addresses, we can describe the IPv6 ARP replacement, Neighbor Discovery (ND). ND is standardized by RFC 2461.

In IPv4 we noted that there had to be a way to obtain a node's physical address. IPv4 uses a special protocol, ARP, to deal with this issue. IPv6, on the other hand, uses special ICMP messages to handle obtaining the necessary physical addresses. The reason for the change in the approach to this problem is largely due to the fact that other layer 2 technologies, such as ATM, cannot easily use broadcasts. The ICMP types and codes for ND are given in Table 5–3 on page 156.

As with ARP (see Chapter 3), whenever a node needs to communicate with another node it must obtain an appropriate physical address. If the destination node shares the same local link with the transmitting node, then the transmitting node needs the physical address of the destination node. Otherwise, the transmitting node needs the physical address of the router to which it will send the packet for forwarding on to its final destination.

In order to obtain the physical address of the next hop local destination, the transmitting node will send an ND solicitation using the solicited-node multicast address (see Table 5–7 on page 167) of the destination node or router. While this destination address is a multicast, it is a multicast address that is only used by the specific target node—thus, it incurs considerably less processing than an IPv4 ARP broadcast that must be deencapsulated up to layer 3 by all local nodes. The ND solicitation includes the physical address of the transmitting node. The recipient of the ND solicitation responds with a unicast ND advertisement including its physical address. As with ARP, both systems update their caches to reflect the IPv6/physical address pair. The ND discovered addresses are placed in the ARP cache on Linux systems.

The Current State of the Linux IPv6 Implementation

As of this writing, the implementation of IPv6 for Linux is still not mainstream. While the code supporting IPv6 and its associated infrastructure is much more stable than even six months ago, it is still in the experimental stages. Of the distributions we are covering, only the SuSE distribution ships with the IPv6 support compiled in the kernel—it's no wonder that most distributions don't ship prebuilt since code modifications to the IPv6 module and related components are still occurring on a highly regular basis.

If you'd like to experiment with IPv6 (and, perhaps, get connected to the 6bone as described in "Experimental Addresses" on page 169), the best place to start is with the `IPv6-HOWTO`, which can be found at

```
http://www.bieringer.de/linux/IPv6/IPv6-HOWTO/IPv6-HOWTO.html
```

This document contains many links (some of which are cited in "WWW Resources" on page 172) to IPv6 information and the source code necessary to build an IPv6 system that can be connected into the 6bone.

Throughout this book, we make references to the capabilities of IPv6 and its differences with IPv4 as appropriate.

Summary

In this chapter, we described the IPv6 datagram and its differences with IPv4. We discussed IPv6 addressing and defined the address assignments. We described ND and compared it to ARP. In closing, we pointed out that the Linux IPv6 implementation is still experimental.

For Further Reading

Listed below are books and WWW resources that provide further information about the topics discussed in this chapter.

Books

Huitema, Christian, *IPv6: The New Internet Protocol*, 2d Ed., Upper Saddle River, New Jersey, Prentice Hall PTR, 1998.

Loshin, Pete, *IPv6: Clearly Explained*, San Francisco, California, Morgan Kauffman, 1999.

WWW Resources

A good source of Linux IPv6 information can be found at the following two sites:

```
http://www.bieringer.de/linux/IPv6/
http://www.linuxhq.com/IPv6/
```

More general IPv6 information can be found at the following sites:

```
http://www.inner.net/~cmetz/ipv6
http://www.ipv6.org/
http://www.6bone.net/
```

Information about `radvd` can be found at:

```
http://www.terra.net/ipv6/radvd.html
```

6

The Internet Layer: Routing

Conceptually, routing is very simple. The initiating system, or sender, examines the destination IP address of the communication. If the destination IP address is not local (i.e., not destined to a system on the same local network), then the sending system looks up a router which is (hopefully) in the correct direction and sends the packets to that router. The router essentially does the same thing. Each router along the way repeats the process until the packets arrive at a router that has a local connection to the network to which the node with the destination address is attached. That's it. We're done! Well, not quite. While routing really is this simple, it rapidly becomes complex as (sub)networks grow and application bandwidth requirements increase. So, there are a lot of details we need to cover.

We approach the topic of routing through a series of examples, beginning with a simple one and then looking at increasingly complex scenarios. Throughout this process, we build a routing algorithm that we can then apply to all routing scenarios. We also point out the various RFCs that cover each of the routing related standards. In particular, we consider the topics of CIDR, RIP, router discovery, ICMP redirects, and some of the differences between IPv4 and IPv6.

A Simple Routing Example

Let's begin by considering the simple example shown in Figure 6-1. In this example, a user on the host `topcat` executes the `telnet` command to the host

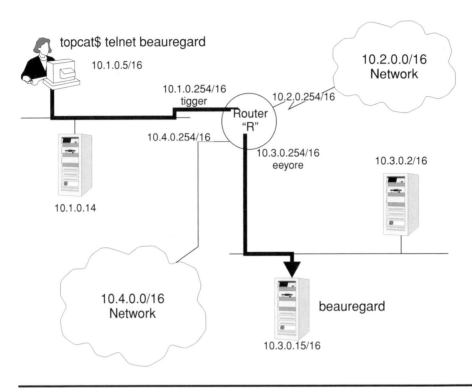

Figure 6–1   A Simple Routing Example

beauregard. This command will (hopefully) open a login session for the user on beauregard. In order for topcat to proceed, it must have the necessary information outlined in Chapter 3 in order to encapsulate the data for communication. The necessary information is: source and destination port numbers, source and destination IP addresses, and source and destination physical addresses. We won't worry about port numbers right now since they're covered in Chapter 8, so for the sake of this example, let's assume that the source and destination port numbers are available to topcat. The rest of the necessary information is obtained as follows. The source IP address is obtained from kernel memory which was read in at boot-time from the appropriate start-up script. The destination IP address is obtained from the command line and through hostname resolution. The source physical address is also obtained from kernel memory having been obtained by a start-up script at boot-time.

The destination physical address is obtained via ARP if using IPv4 addresses (as is the case in this example) or via ND if using IPv6. But wait! Which physical address is obtained in this case? Suppose, for the moment, that `topcat` is able to obtain `beauregard`'s physical address and then `topcat` encapsulates the packet and puts it on the wire. Remember, from Chapter 2, that the only packets a system will process are those that have a destination physical address to which the receiving host is configured to pay attention. These physical addresses are its unicast, the broadcast, multicast groups, if any, to which it belongs, and any addresses it is configured to proxy (but the only thing it will do with proxied addresses is respond to ARP requests). So, if `topcat` encapsulates a packet with `beauregard`'s physical address, no system on `topcat`'s shared media network will pay any attention to that packet whatsoever!

NOTE

The example in Figure 6–1 displays a router with four interfaces that we are generically referring to as R. The diagram also shows two hostnames for two of the interfaces (`tigger` at `10.1.0.254` and `eeyore` at `10.3.0.254`). Each interface is normally assigned a hostname, one of which is normally appointed the canonical name—usually the name assigned to the external interface (the one leading to the Internet) is appointed the canonical name of the system. There are some applications that attempt to verify a system's canonical name as we see in subsequent chapters. For purposes of this example, however, we simply refer to the router as R, in the hopes of avoiding confusion.

Thus, if `topcat` needs to encapsulate a packet that is destined to a system outside the local network, it must set the destination physical address to that of a system sharing the same physical medium and network number (i.e., another system on the local network). From Figure 6–1, it is pretty clear that `topcat` needs to send the packet to the router, R. But, how does it do that?

The answer is that each system makes a decision about the correct destination physical address by invoking the *routing algorithm*. We provide a complete and proper definition of the routing algorithm in "The Real Routing Algorithm" on page 826, but we start with a simple definition first in "A Simple Routing Algorithm" on page 193. After `topcat` gets the destination IP address (from the command line) and before it encapsulates the packet, it takes the IP address and applies the netmask (or prefix) for that destination address to get the network number (or prefix number) of the IP address. In this case, the netmask for the destination, beauregard, is the same as it is for the local network (but things can get more complex as we see later on). So, since beauregard's IP address is 10.2.0.15/16, this means that its netmask is 255.255.0.0 (due to the /16 prefix) and therefore its network number is 10.2.0.0. Once topcat has the destination network number, it looks for that number in its *routing table*. The routing table, which is detailed throughout this chapter, can be thought of very simply as a kernel memory cache that contains network number/router IP address pairs. In this case, when topcat looks up the network number 10.2.0.0, it will find 10.1.0.254 (R—see Figure 6–1) as the router that can reach beauregard. Once topcat knows that R is the router through which the packet(s) must travel, topcat encapsulates the packet, setting the destination physical address to that of R. This forces R to deencapsulate the packet to, at least, the Internet layer.

When R receives such a packet from topcat, it deencapsulates the frame because the destination physical address matches R's. It then reads the destination IP address from the datagram header and determines first that the address does not match its own, its broadcast, or any multicast groups to which it belongs. Because it has been explicitly configured to be a router, it will have *forwarding*[1] enabled. This means that when it receives a packet with a destination IP address for which it is not configured, it will execute the routing algorithm to determine how to send the packet on its way. In the case of Figure 6–1, R repeats the routing algorithm steps described above and reencapsulates the packet, but this time setting, or rewriting, the destination physical address to that of beauregard. It then sends the packet out its 10.2.0.254 interface because that is the interface that is connected to the same local network as beauregard.

Now, let's look at the routing tables.

Introducing Linux Routing Tables

In this section, we describe routing table management methods, introduce a number of commands to view and manipulate Linux routing tables, and make some definitions. We build on these initial discussions in the following sections

---

1. If forwarding were not enabled, all processing would cease and the packet(s) would be destroyed. A system with multiple NICs that has forwarding disabled is *not* a router.

and chapters. In other words, if you aren't familiar with the basics, it's a good idea to read this section!

Viewing the Linux Routing Table

At the heart of the routing algorithm is the routing table search. Our simple example of Figure 6–1 on page 174 indicates that, for the purposes of the `telnet` command invoked by a user on `topcat`, proper routing tables must exist for `top-cat` and `R` in order for the packets to reach `beauregard`. But `beauregard` must also have correct routing tables in order that it respond to the communications from `topcat`. We look at the routing tables for each of those systems and generally introduce the `/sbin/route` and `/bin/netstat -r` commands. We cover the complete syntax of the `route` command in "Statically Manipulating the Linux Routing Table" on page 184 and of the `netstat` command at various points throughout this book.

Viewing the routing table can be accomplished with either the `route` or `netstat` `-r` command. Each command produces a slightly different format. Example 6–1 shows the output of `route` on `topcat`.

Example 6–1   Output of the `route` Command on `topcat`

```
topcat:~ # route
Kernel IP routing table
Destination     Gateway         Genmask          Flags  Metric  Ref     Use Iface
topcat          *               255.255.255.255  UH     1       0         0 dummy0
10.1.0.0        *               255.255.0.0      U      0       0         0 eth0
loopback        *               255.0.0.0        U      0       0         0 lo
default         tigger          0.0.0.0          UG     0       0         0 eth0
```

The output of this command lists several fields per record (each line), each of which is described in Table 6–1. Notice that the first (leftmost) field contains the destination. This can be a network or a host. The second field contains the gateway or router that is used to reach the destination in the first field. The third field, `Genmask`, contains the netmask used for this record. This is often called the *route mask* or *route prefix*. The very last field is the interface used for this record, meaning that the indicated interface is the one through which the packet will be sent if the record containing it is used.

The `Flags` field contains flags specifying the state of the record. For example, the first entry contains the flags `UH`. This means that the interface is up (`U`) and that the record is a host to host (`H`) entry. The last entry utilizes the flags `UG`, meaning that the interface is up (`U`) and that the record specifies a gateway (`G`) or

router entry. This means that routing tables can have two different types of
records: host records and router records. A host record is one that can be used to
match a specific host destination, but no other system on its network. This type
of record is used for point-to-point, loopback, local host, and ICMP redirects
(discussed in "ICMP Redirects" on page 202). A router record is one that can be
used to match a destination network, subnetwork, or supernetwork. Router
records are much more common and, as we'll see, are generally preferable in
larger environments for performance reasons.

The Metric field contains a 16-bit value (ranges between 0 and 65,535) and
is used by some dynamic routing table protocols (see Chapter 11). The Linux
kernel does *not* use this field for any purpose whatsoever. The remaining fields,
Ref and Use, are described in Table 6–1. Note that the values of these two fields
are always 0 unless the -C option to the route command is given.

Table 6–1   Fields in the Output of the route Command

FIELD	DESCRIPTION
Destination	Contains the destination host or network number for the record. An entry of default or 0.0.0.0 indicates a default router record.
Gateway	Contains the gateway hostname or IP address to use for this record. An entry of * or 0.0.0.0 indicates that the destination is either to the local host or the local network.
Genmask	Contains the netmask used for this record. This entry is often called the route netmask or route prefix. A value of 255.255.255.255 in this field indicates that the record contains a host destination (instead of a network). An entry of 0.0.0.0 indicates that the record is for a default router.

Table 6–1   Fields in the Output of the `route` Command *(Continued)*

FIELD	DESCRIPTION

Flags	Contains flags that indicate the state and type of entry that this record contains. The possible flag values are:
	   U - the route is up and available
	   H - the gateway is a host
	   G - the gateway is a router
	   R - reinstated route (used by some routing table management daemons)
	   D - route dynamically entered by ICMP or a routing table management daemon
	   M - route dynamically modified by ICMP or a routing table management daemon
	   ! - rejected route

Metric	Contains a 16-bit value that can be used by routing table management daemons for best match determination. RIP uses the value in this field. The Linux kernel does *not* use this field when determining a match.
Ref	Contains the number of active references to this route. This field always contains the value of 0 unless you use the -c option to the `route` command.
Use	Contains the lookup count for this record. This field always contains the value of 0 unless you use the -c option to the `route` command.
Iface	Contains the name of the interface through which all packets are transmitted when this record is used.

Let's look at each of the records in Example 6–1 on page 177 in more detail. Consider the first record

```
topcat          *               255.255.255.255 UH    1      0       0 dummy0
```

This is a host record. The host `topcat` is running SuSE 6.4. SuSE systems set up the `dummy0` (first record) interface by default. The purpose of this interface is to support nonpermanent point-to-point links. You only need this interface if you are using PPP, SLIP, PLIP, or similar connection that is intermittent (that is, requires dial-up, or similar action, for connectivity). To disable this device, set SETUPDUMMYDEV=no in /etc/rc.config. The other distributions do not configure this device automatically. The flags indicate that this record is up and is a host entry. The destination is the local host itself, topcat. The gateway or router entry shows a * which means that the destination is handled by a local interface and no subsequent routing is necessary.

The second record

```
10.1.0.0         *              255.255.0.0    U    0    0        0 eth0
```

is for the local network. It is a network record. This record says that if the destination network number is 10.1.0.0, then the packet will be encapsulated with a local destination physical address (the Gateway value of *) and processed through the eth0 interface.

The third record

```
loopback         *              255.0.0.0      U    0    0        0 lo
```

is the loopback. It is also a network record. It handles any packets that have a destination IP network number of 127.0.0.0/8.

The fourth record

```
default       tigger           0.0.0.0         UG   0    0        0 eth0
```

is the default router entry. It, too, is a network record. The *default router* entry means, if no other entry in the table matches, then use this one. In particular, for topcat, this means that if the destination is other than the local network (10.1.0.0), the loopback, or topcat itself, then the packet will be sent to the router tigger (the 10.1.0.254 interface of R in Figure 6–1 on page 174).

The default router record is actually quite significant. If there were no default router record, then there would need to be a record for each network that topcat could reach. In the case of this example, that's really no big deal since there are only four networks. In particular, an alternate routing table for topcat would look like that given in Example 6–2.

Example 6–2   What topcat's Routing Table Would Look Like without a Default Router

```
topcat:~ # route
Kernel IP routing table
Destination     Gateway         Genmask         Flags Metric Ref    Use Iface
topcat          *               255.255.255.255 UH    1      0        0 dummy0
10.1.0.0        *               255.255.0.0     U     0      0        0 eth0
10.2.0.0        tigger          255.255.0.0     UG    0      0        0 eth0
10.3.0.0        tigger          255.255.0.0     UG    0      0        0 eth0
10.4.0.0        tigger          255.255.0.0     UG    0      0        0 eth0
loopback        *               255.0.0.0       U     0      0        0 lo
```

If this environment were connected to the Internet (as we consider in "An Intermediate Routing Example" on page 197), this type of routing table would be essentially impossible to build and maintain since it would require an entry for every possible network on the Internet. Even using CIDR (see "Route Aggregation and CIDR" on page 225), the absence of a default router entry would make this routing table ridiculously large. Fortunately, the type of routing table shown in Example 6–2 is unnecessary when a default router record is used.

You can suppress name translation when displaying the routing table by using `route -n`. This is likely to be the most common way that you view the routing tables since it makes troubleshooting and verification easier (you don't have to know what all the name translations are). Example 6–3 duplicates the output of Example 6–1 on page 177 but uses the `-n` argument to the route command.

Example 6–3   Output of the `route -n` Command on `topcat`

```
topcat:~ # route -n
Kernel IP routing table
Destination     Gateway         Genmask         Flags Metric Ref    Use Iface
10.1.0.5        0.0.0.0         255.255.255.255 UH    1      0        0 dummy0
10.1.0.0        0.0.0.0         255.255.0.0     U     0      0        0 eth0
127.0.0.0       0.0.0.0         255.0.0.0       U     0      0        0 lo
0.0.0.0         10.1.0.254      0.0.0.0         UG    0      0        0 eth0
topcat:~ #
```

Notice that the `*` translates to `0.0.0.0` in the `Gateway` field. These entries always mean that the destination is local (either the local host or the local network). Also, note that the `default` entry in the `Destination` field translates to `0.0.0.0`.

You can also view the routing table with the `netstat -r` command. Example 6–4 shows `netstat -nr` on `topcat` (the n option to `netstat` suppresses name translation).

Example 6–4   Output of the `netstat -nr` Command on `topcat`

```
topcat:~ # netstat -nr
Kernel IP routing table
Destination     Gateway         Genmask         Flags MSS Window  irtt Iface
10.1.0.5        0.0.0.0         255.255.255.255 UH    0 0         0 dummy0
10.1.0.0        0.0.0.0         255.255.0.0     U     0 0         0 eth0
127.0.0.0       0.0.0.0         255.0.0.0       U     0 0         0 lo
0.0.0.0         10.1.0.254      0.0.0.0         UG    0 0         0 eth0
topcat:~ #
```

The output of `netstat` is slightly different than that of `route`. The `Metric`, `Ref`, and `Use` fields are replaced with the `MSS`, `Window`, and `irtt` fields, respectively. The `MSS` field indicates the maximum segment size used by TCP, the

`Window` field indicates the TCP window size, and the `irtt` field indicates the TCP initial round trip time associated with this record.

NOTE

It turns out that the output format of `route -nr` can be duplicated by `netstat -enr`. Similarly, the output of `netstat -nr` can be duplicated by `route -enr`. If you'd like to see all of the fields produced by both `netstat -nr` and `route -n`, you can do so with `route -een`. This latter command outputs the entire contents of `/proc/net/route`, which you can view directly with `cat /proc/net/route`. Be advised, however, that the latter command will produce all values in hex.

Let's go on with our example from Figure 6–1 on page 174 by taking a look at the routing table for R. The router R is a Red Hat system with four interfaces, each of which is connected to a different network. Example 6–5 displays the output or `route -n` on R.

Example 6–5   Output of `route -n` on Router R

```
[root@dsl-golden /root]# route -n
Kernel IP routing table
Destination     Gateway         Genmask         Flags Metric Ref    Use Iface
10.1.0.254      0.0.0.0         255.255.255.255 UH    0      0        0 eth1
10.2.0.254      0.0.0.0         255.255.255.255 UH    0      0        0 eth2
10.3.0.254      0.0.0.0         255.255.255.255 UH    0      0        0 eth0
10.4.0.254      0.0.0.0         255.255.255.255 UH    0      0        0 eth3
10.1.0.0        10.1.0.254      255.255.0.0     UG    0      0        0 eth1
10.1.0.0        0.0.0.0         255.255.0.0     U     0      0        0 eth1
10.2.0.0        10.2.0.254      255.255.0.0     UG    0      0        0 eth2
10.2.0.0        0.0.0.0         255.255.0.0     U     0      0        0 eth2
10.3.0.0        10.3.0.254      255.255.0.0     UG    0      0        0 eth0
10.3.0.0        0.0.0.0         255.255.0.0     U     0      0        0 eth0
10.4.0.0        10.4.0.254      255.255.0.0     UG    0      0        0 eth3
10.4.0.0        0.0.0.0         255.255.0.0     U     0      0        0 eth3
127.0.0.0       0.0.0.0         255.0.0.0       U     0      0        0 lo
[root@dsl-golden /root]#
```

Based on our earlier description, the entries in this routing table should be clear. Each interface (the first four records in the table) has its own local host record indicating that communications to any one of the local interfaces will be handled via a local interface. There is a similar entry for topcat, as shown in Example 6–3, except, of course, topcat has only one interface. The next eight entries in Example 6–5 are records for each of the networks that R is connected to and, in this example, constitutes all of the networks in this internetwork.

Notice that the Red Hat table is more verbose than the SuSE table, and in fact more verbose than all of the other distributions we discuss in that its routing table contains two network records for each interface. Red Hat includes a gateway record for each interface. For instance, the pair of records

```
10.1.0.0        10.1.0.254      255.255.0.0     UG     0        0        0 eth1
10.1.0.0        0.0.0.0         255.255.0.0     U      0        0        0 eth1
```

would appear as the single record

```
10.1.0.0        0.0.0.0         255.255.0.0     U      0        0        0 eth1
```

on a SuSE 6.4, Debian 2.1, or Caldera 2.4 system. Functionally, the behavior is the same—which is to send or forward packets destined to any IP address with the network number `10.1.0.0/16` through the interface `eth1`. The only problem with this approach is that it roughly doubles the size of the routing table, and in environments in which there are many networks, this could have performance implications. The six entries that follow these two are identical except that they apply to `10.2.0.0/16`, `10.3.0.0/16`, and `10.4.0.0/16`, respectively.

The very last entry in Example 6–5 is for the loopback.

We need to mention at this point, that in order for R, which we earlier defined to be a Red Hat Linux system, to actually route packets it must have IP forwarding turned on. Turning on IP forwarding for Linux simply requires that `/proc/sys/net/ipv4/ip_forward` contains 1 (see "Configuring the Linux Router" on page 192). Thus, we can formally define a *router* to be any network node that has at least two different network connections, can execute the routing algorithm, and is configured to forward packets. By specifying two network connections in this definition, we mean two IP addresses for which the network numbers are distinct. There may only be one physical connection and the two IP addresses consist of one native address and one alias address assigned to the same interface. Any node that has at least two network connections but does not forward packets is not a router—very often such a nonforwarding node is called a *multihomed* node.

To complete our example, we need to look at the routing table on `beauregard`, a SuSE 6.4 system. This table must exist and have the correct entries in order for `beauregard` to respond to `topcat`. Example 6–6 shows us the table.

Example 6–6   Output of `route -n` on `beauregard`

```
[root@beauregard /root]# route -n
Kernel IP routing table
Destination     Gateway         Genmask         Flags Metric Ref    Use Iface
10.3.0.0        0.0.0.0         255.255.0.0     U     0      0        0 eth0
127.0.0.0       0.0.0.0         255.0.0.0       U     0      0        0 lo
0.0.0.0         10.3.0.254      0.0.0.0         UG    1      0        0 eth0
[root@beauregard /root]#
```

The routing table for `beauregard` is conceptually identical to the one for `topcat`. The main difference lies in the fact that `beauregard` is a SuSE system and it does not maintain the host record for the local host. The other difference, of course, is that `beauregard` is on a different network than `topcat`.

So, how do we maintain the routing table? The next two sections provide an initial answer to that question.

Routing Table Management Methods

There are two basic ways of managing the routing tables—*statically* and *dynamically*. Static routing table management consists of manually putting entries into or removing entries from the routing table and/or establishing configuration files that cause entries to be made at each reboot. Any entries made in this manner remain in the table permanently. This method is discussed in the next section.

Dynamic routing table management involves the use of daemons that automatically cause the updating of a host's or router's routing tables. There are two categories of dynamic routing table management daemons, *interior gateway protocols* (IGP) and *exterior gateway protocols* (EGP). The *routing information protocol* (RIP), router discovery and the *open shortest path first* (OSPF) protocol are examples of IGPs; the *border gateway protocol* (BGP) is an example of an EGP. These two categories of protocols are defined around the concept of an *autonomous system* (AS). The simplest definition of an autonomous system is that it is a collection of networks under a single administrative control. IGPs are protocols that operate within an AS while EGPs are protocols that operate between ASs. We discuss these topics in greater detail in Chapter 11.

For the remainder of this chapter, we consider static routing table management and two dynamic routing table management daemons: RIP and router discovery.

Statically Manipulating the Linux Routing Table

Now that we've looked at the routing tables we need to figure out how the entries get into the routing tables. In the previous section, we indicated that there are two ways for this to occur—statically or dynamically. In this section, we cover statically managing the routing tables.

The command used to add or delete entries into and from the routing table is the `route` command. The syntax of the `route` command is as follows: Viewing the routing table:

```
route[-CFvnee]
```

Adding entries to the routing table:

```
route[-v] [-A family] add [-net|-host] target [netmask nm] [gw
      router] [metric n] [mss m] [window w] [irtt i] [reject] [mod]
      [dyn] [reinstate] [[dev] ifname]
```

Deleting entries from the routing table:

```
route[-v] [-A family] del [-net|-host] target [netmask nm] [gw
      router] [metric n] [[dev] ifname]
```

Getting information from `route`:

```
route[-V] [-h]
```

Each argument and value available to route is defined in Table 6–2.

Table 6–2   `route` Command Arguments

Argument	Description
-C	Forces `route` to process the route cache for viewing by reading the file `/proc/net/rt_cache` instead of routing table stored in `/proc/net/route`. The route cache is discussed in greater detail in Chapter 16.
-F	Forces `route` to process the routing table by reading `/proc/net/route`. This is the default and this flag is rarely used.
-v	Provides more verbose output. Ineffective when viewing the routing table but does add some additional information when adding and deleting route entries.
-n	Suppresses name translation.

Table 6–2   `route` Command Arguments *(Continued)*

ARGUMENT	DESCRIPTION
`-e` and `-ee`	With `-e`, `netstat -r` format is used. With `-ee`, all fields from route and `netstat -r` are displayed. See the Note on page 182.
`-A` *family*	Specifies the address family, *family*, to be used. The default is `inet` for IPv4. Other families include `inet6` (IPv6), `ipx` (IPX), and `ddp` (Appletalk). Execute `route -h` for a complete list of supported families.
`add [-net|-host]` *target*	Adds the specified route to the routing table. If `-net` is used, then *target* must be a network number. If `-host` is used, then *target* must be an IP address. Minimally, the use of `add -net` also requires the `netmask` and `gw` arguments except for default router entries.
`del [-net|-host]` *target*	Deletes the specified route from the routing table. If `-net` is used, then *target* must be a network number. If `-host` is used, then *target* must be an IP address. Minimally, the use of `del -net` also requires the `netmask` and `gw` arguments except for default router entries.
`netmask` *nm*	Specifies the netmask, *nm*, for the route to be added or deleted.
`gw` *router*	Specifies the gateway (router), *router*, to be used with an `add` or `del`. It is important to note that this router must be reachable, meaning that its IP address must share the same network number as a local interface (or the one specified by `dev0`), or another route must already be in the table that can reach this router.

Table 6–2   `route` Command Arguments *(Continued)*

Argument	Description
`metric n`	Specifies the metric, *n*, to associate with the indicated route. This value can be used by dynamic routing table management daemons, but ordinarily is used only by RIP (see Chapter 11).
`mss m`	Sets the maximum segment size, *m*, for TCP connections that use this route. See Chapter 7.
`window w`	Sets the window size, *w*, for TCP connections that use this route. See Chapter 7.
`irtt i`	Sets the initial round trip time, *i*, for TCP connections that use this route. See Chapter 7.
`reject`	Sets up a blocking route that will force the use of, for example, a default route. Discussed in Chapter 16.
`mod`	Modifies a route. Used by routing table management daemons.
`dyn`	Dynamically a route. Used by routing table management daemons or ICMP. ICMP redirects use this mechanism introduced in "ICMP Redirects" on page 202. Further discussion can be found in Chapter 12.
`reinstate`	Reinstates a route. Used by routing table management daemons.
`[dev] ifname`	Specifies the device *ifname*, such as `eth0`, `eth1`, etc., to be used. If this argument is not specified, then the kernel will associate a device with the entry based on the current routing table. Note that the keyword `dev` must precede *ifname* only if *ifname* is not the last argument given in the route command.

Table 6–2   `route` Command Arguments *(Continued)*

ARGUMENT	DESCRIPTION
-V	Prints the version number of the `route` command and quits. All of the distributions which we discuss use version 1.96.
-h	Provides a usage message and quits.

We already explored viewing the routing table in "Viewing the Linux Routing Table" on page 177. Let's look at some simple examples of adding and deleting routing table entries. More complex examples are provided in later chapters.

Let's suppose that we are operating on the host `topcat`, `10.1.0.5/16`. Further suppose that there is a router, `s`, with two interfaces configured as `10.1.1.254/16` and `172.16.1.254/16`. You can add a route to the `172.16.0.0/16` network on `topcat` with the command shown in Example 6–7.

Example 6–7   Adding a Route to the Routing Table

```
topcat:~ # route add -net 172.16.0.0 netmask 255.255.0.0 gw 10.1.1.254
topcat:~ #
```

We left off the device specification since `topcat` has only one interface. Example 6–8 displays how the new routing table appears. The recently added entry is shown in **bold** for clarity.

Example 6–8   Routing Table on `topcat` after Adding a New Route

```
topcat:~ # route -n
Kernel IP routing table
Destination     Gateway         Genmask         Flags Metric Ref    Use Iface
10.1.0.5        0.0.0.0         255.255.255.255 UH    1      0        0 dummy0
10.1.0.0        0.0.0.0         255.255.0.0     U     0      0        0 eth0
172.16.0.0      10.1.1.254      255.255.0.0     UG    0      0        0 eth0
127.0.0.0       0.0.0.0         255.0.0.0       U     0      0        0 lo
0.0.0.0         10.1.0.254      0.0.0.0         UG    0      0        0 eth0
topcat:~ #
```

With this new entry, any packets destined to the `172.16.0.0/16` network will be sent there via `10.1.1.254`.

WARNING

A common mistake in adding entries to a routing table is to specify a non-reachable router after the gw argument. For instance, it is not uncommon to mistakenly attempt to enter the address 172.16.1.254 as the value to the gw argument instead of the correct command shown in Example 6–7. Doing so results in the error shown in Example 6–9.

Example 6–9   Incorrectly Adding a Routing Table Entry

```
topcat:~ # route add -net 172.16.0.0 netmask 255.255.0.0 gw 172.16.1.254
SIOCADDRT: Network is unreachable
topcat:~ #
```

Whenever you see an error message of this sort, carefully inspect the command that resulted in this error message, as it is most often an incorrect destination gateway.

The routing table entry added by the command shown in Example 6–7 is easily deleted with the command shown in Example 6–10.

Example 6–10   Deleting an Entry from the Routing Table

```
topcat:~ # route del -net 172.16.0.0 netmask 255.255.0.0 gw 10.1.1.254
topcat:~ #
```

Executing this command would return topcat's routing table to that shown in Example 6–3 on page 181.

WARNING

While it may well go without saying, be careful about deleting routing table entries. Deleting a route will disable connectivity to the destination unless there are other routes to the same destination in the table. Also, if you are operating on a host's or router's routing table over the network and delete the route in use, you will lose the connection unless there is another route in the table. Also, the system will allow you to delete all routes rendering the system effectively networkless. So, think before you delete!

NOTE

In all of the foregoing examples, we've used IP addresses instead of host-names. This is done primarily for clarity with network associations. You can certainly use hostnames so long as they are resolvable to IP addresses. Be aware that if you are in the process of adding static routes like these and that you are using a network oriented hostname resolution application, like NIS or DNS, you may not be able to resolve hostnames until the appropriate routes are added.

As a final example, Example 6–11 shows the addition of a default route to the routing table on the host `topcat`.

Example 6–11   Adding a Default Route

```
topcat:~ # route add -net default gw 10.1.0.254
topcat:~ #
```

Note that we supplied the value `default` to the `add -net` argument. We could have also used `0.0.0.0`. Deleting default routes proceeds similarly.

You probably don't want to have to manually add routes to every host and router in your environment by manually executing the `route` command for each one. Fortunately, you don't have to.

Making Static Routes Permanent

You can make static route entries permanent by configuring the appropriate files in the four distributions we're discussing. Placing entries in these files causes the routes to be added as if you manually executed the `route` command. The following sections describe adding static routes and static default routes to the appropriate files for the given distribution.

RED HAT 6.2   Red Hat systems can define a default router through the `GATEWAY` variable in `/etc/sysconfig/network` as described in "Red Hat 6.2" on page 136. Static routes are defined in `/etc/sysconfig/static-routes`. Default routes can also be placed in this file. The file is read by the `/etc/rc.d/init.d/network start-up` script. The syntax for the file is

```
ifname net|host target netmask nm gw router
```

Example 6–12 shows a simple `/etc/sysconfig/static-routes` file.

Example 6–12   Simple `/etc/sysconfig/static-routes` File

```
[root@tigger /root]# cat /etc/sysconfig/static-routes
eth1 net 172.16.0.0 netmask 255.255.0.0 gw 10.1.1.254
eth0 net 192.168.11.0 netmask 255.255.255.0 gw 10.3.1.254
[root@tigger /root]#
```

You can make changes to this file and then cycle the network start-up script with

```
# /etc/rc.d/init.d/network restart
```

CALDERA 2.4   Caldera also uses the GATEWAY variable for a default router entry, although in a different file than with Red Hat. It is described in "Caldera 2.4" on page 139. Caldera accommodates static routes through the file `/etc/sysconfig/network-scripts/ifcfg-routes`. This file contains actual route commands, so there is no syntax difference between the entries in this file and those on the command line. Simply put the commands in `/etc/sysconfig/network-scripts/ifcfg-routes` and make sure that the `/etc/sysconfig/network-scripts/ifcfg-routes` file is executable; then, whenever the `/etc/rc.d/init.d/network start-up` script is started, that file gets executed. The file will, therefore, also accommodate default route entries. You can create this file or make changes to it and then cycle the network script by executing

```
# /etc/rc.d/init.d/network restart
```

to have the changes take effect.

DEBIAN 2.1   Debian uses the file `/etc/init.d/network` for all interface and route configuration. See "Debian 2.1" on page 140. Thus, to add static routes permanently on a Debian system, enter the actual `route` commands in this file. It is its own script and is invoked by `/etc/rc.d/rcS` so, unlike the other distributions, it cannot be cycled without modification.

SUSE 6.4   The SuSE distribution uses a single file for both static and static default routes. The file is `/etc/route.conf` and it is read by the start-up script `/sbin/init.d/route`. The syntax for entries in `/etc/route.conf` is

```
destination gateway netmask interface
```

Example 6–13 illustrates a few simple entries in the `/etc/route.conf` file.

Example 6–13   Simple `/etc/route.conf` File on a SuSE System

```
topcat:~ # cat /etc/route.conf
172.16.0.0        10.1.1.254     255.255.0.0   eth0
default           10.1.0.254
topcat:~ #
```

Note that fields can be left out when unnecessary, as with the `default` entry in this case.

After creating or modifying this file, you can cause the changes to take effect by cycling the route script with

```
# /sbin/init.d/route restart
```

Configuring the Linux Router

In general, configuring a Linux system to be a router is a simple matter. It requires adding and configuring the necessary NICs as described in Chapters 2 and 4. Then it requires ensuring that the routing table is properly populated either by statically making the necessary entries as described in the foregoing sections, or by using dynamic routing table management daemons as described in subsequent sections and chapters. Then, IP forwarding must be turned on.

Turning on IP forwarding simply requires that the `/proc/net/sys/ipv4/ip_forward` kernel parameter be set to 1. This can be accomplished by executing

```
# echo 1 > /proc/net/sys/ipv4/ip_forward
```

or, on Red Hat 6.2, Caldera 2.4, and SuSE 6.4,

```
# /sbin/sysctl net.ipv4.ip_forward=1
```

The `sysctl` utility was introduced in kernel version 2.2.14. For more information about it, see the `sysctl(8)` man page.

Making IP forwarding permanent (i.e., survive reboots) on each of the four distributions is as follows.

For Red Hat 6.2, place the entry

```
net.ipv4.ip_forward = 1
```

in `/etc/sysctl.conf`. The `/etc/rc.d/init.d/network` start-up script sets the values in this file with `sysctl -p`.

For Caldera 2.4, set

```
IPFORWARDING=yes
```

in the `/etc/sysconfig/network` file.

For Debian 2.1, place

```
# echo 1 > /proc/net/sys/ipv4/ip_forward
```

in the file /etc/init.d/network.

For SuSE 6.4, set

```
IP_FORWARD=yes
```

in /etc/rc.config.

We've now completed our discussion of a simple routing example. Let's formalize this example by providing a simple routing algorithm and describing the routing process in the next two sections. Then, we move on to a slightly more complex example.

A Simple Routing Algorithm

Based on our discussion of how routing is accomplished in the previous section, we can formalize a simple, but accurate, routing algorithm. This routing algorithm is depicted as a flowchart in Figure 6–2. All network nodes that implement layer 3^2 of the TCP/IP model execute this algorithm whenever a network oriented application is invoked or a packet to be forwarded arrives.

The flowchart expresses the following procedure. It all begins when a sending host initiates a network-based application (like telnet) or a router receives a packet that needs to be forwarded. The netmask is applied to the destination IP address to compute the network number. The network number is then checked against the routing table. If it matches a local interface (a NIC or port on the system) network number, then the destination physical address of the destination is obtained via ARP (IPv4) or ND (IPv6); the packet is encapsulated and sent out the appropriate local interface.

If the search of the routing table for the destination network number does not find a local interface, then the packet must be sent to a router. At this point, the routing algorithm searches the table using a set of rules, often called *pruning* rules, to find the *best* match. In the example presented in this section, the best match and the default router are one and the same. If a match is found, then the matching record is used in its entirety—meaning that the destination physical address of the router and the local interface to send the packet through as indi-

---

2. Switches and repeaters, for example, do not implement layer 3 of the TCP/IP model.

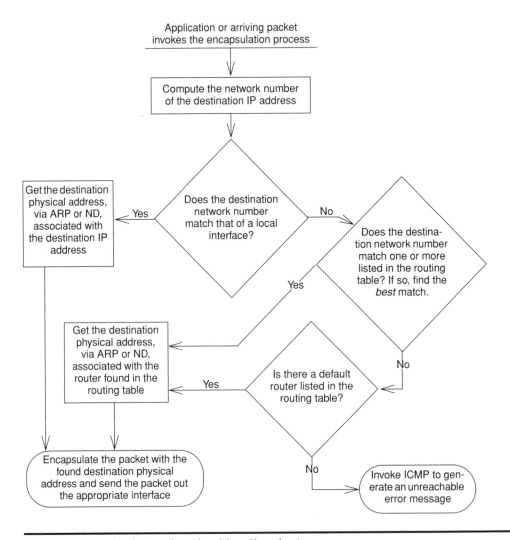

Figure 6–2   Simple Routing Algorithm Flowchart

cated in the record will be used. If no match is found, and there is a default router, then the record associated with the default router will be used. In either case, the packet is encapsulated with the destination physical address, obtained via ARP or ND, set to that of the router whose record matched in the routing table. The packet is sent out through the interface found in the matching record.

If no matches are found in the routing table and there is no default router, then ICMP is invoked and the process is terminated. ICMP will generate either a network unreachable or host unreachable[3] error message depending upon whether the lack of a proper routing table entry exists in the sender's routing table or an intermediate router's routing table, respectively.

   This depiction of the routing algorithm is perfectly adequate in many cases. We call it *simple* because we've left out the details of finding the best match. By default, the best match in the routing table is the *longest* match. The longest match is the entry in the routing table with the most number of matching left-most bits. For instance, suppose that the destination IP address is `10.15.4.76/16` and the routing table is as shown in Example 6–14. In this case, the best match is `10.0.0.0`, because it matches the leftmost 8 bits of the destination IP address. This is better than the only other match, which is the default.

Example 6–14   Simple Routing Table

```
topcat:~ # netstat -nr
Kernel IP routing table
Destination     Gateway         Genmask           Flags   MSS Window   irtt Iface
10.1.0.5        0.0.0.0         255.255.255.255   UH       0 0          0 dummy0
10.2.0.0        10.1.1.254      255.255.0.0       U        0 0          0 eth0
10.0.0.0        10.1.3.254      255.0.0.0         U        0 0          0 eth0
127.0.0.0       0.0.0.0         255.0.0.0         U        0 0          0 lo
0.0.0.0         10.1.0.254      0.0.0.0           UG       0 0          0 eth0
topcat:~ #
```

   There is a great deal more to pruning rules than what we've briefly described here. Pruning rules can be modified in Linux through the use of *routing policies*—we cover best match pruning rules and routing policies in Chapter 16.

The Routing Process

   Whenever an application initiates a network-based communication, it initiates the process of encapsulation from the Application layer of the TCP/IP stack. Whenever a router is involved in the process of forwarding packets, it deencapsulates the packet up to the Internet layer of the TCP/IP model and then reencapsulates it from that layer back down. Figure 6–3 illustrates this concept.

---

   3. See Table 4–4 on page 106 for ICMPv4 and Table 5–3 on page 156 for ICMPv6 types and codes.

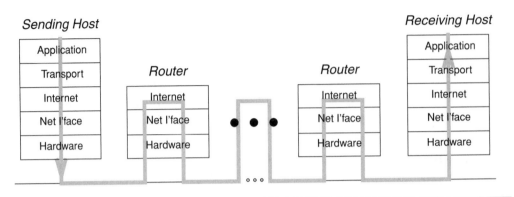

Figure 6–3   Encapsulation and Deencapsulation by Routers and Hosts

The sending host is always involved in only encapsulation, the receiving host exclusively in deencapsulation, and the routers, regardless of number, are only involved with deencapsulation and reencapsulation at the lower three layers of the TCP/IP stack. The only exception to this latter statement is when an *application proxy* is involved—we discuss this in Chapter 14.

It turns out that there is a command that can test layer 3 connectivity. That command is the /bin/ping command.

The ping Utility

You are probably already familiar with the /bin/ping command, and we introduced ping -R back in Chapter 3. This section simply serves to formalize the command. When invoked, ping (an application) causes encapsulation to occur via an ICMP echo-request message (ICMPv4 type=8 and code=0; ICMPv6 type=128 and code=0). The encapsulation, therefore, completely bypasses the Transport layer of the TCP/IP stack. This packet is then routed (if necessary) to its final destination where the destination system replies with an ICMP echo-reply message (ICMPv4 type=0 and code=0; ICMPv6 type=129 and code=0). Thus, a ping packet is only deencapsulated to the Internet layer of the TCP/IP stack by the destination system.[4] Given the way it works, ping is uniquely qualified to test connectivity to layer 3. This has a significant troubleshooting value, as we'll see in Chapter 9.

---

4. It could, therefore, be argued that ping is not a true peer-to-peer application.

You can `ping`, or attempt to `ping`, any node to which you are interconnected. For instance, Example 6–15 displays the use of `ping` by `topcat` to `beauregard`.

Example 6–15   A `ping` from `topcat` to `beauregard`

```
topcat:~ # ping beauregard
PING beauregard (10.3.0.15): 56 data bytes
64 bytes from 10.3.0.15: icmp_seq=0 ttl=254 time=1.521 ms
64 bytes from 10.3.0.15: icmp_seq=1 ttl=254 time=1.069 ms
64 bytes from 10.3.0.15: icmp_seq=2 ttl=254 time=1.028 ms
--- beauregard ping statistics ---
3 packets transmitted, 3 packets received, 0% packet loss
round-trip min/avg/max = 1.028/1.206/1.521 ms
^C
topcat:~ #
```

Note that the default use of `ping` causes it to send out packets once per second. To stop the `ping`, you must type ^C. You can avoid this by specifying the -c option. For example,

```
# ping -c 1 beauregard
```

would send one echo-request packet and wait for the one echo-reply, then quit. If no reply arrives, `ping` terminates with a message indicating that no response was received after 10 seconds.

The output of `ping` provides information about what has been received in response to a `ping`. In Example 6–15, we see that `ping` got three ICMP echo-reply responses, one for each echo-request. Each echo-reply was 64 octets (bytes) and the time-to-live (`ttl`) field was set to 254 (see Chapter 4 for a discussion of these fields). The time between the packet being sent and the response being received is recorded in the `time=` entry. This time is also known as the *round trip time* (RTT).

There are a lot of useful things that you can do with `ping`, many of which we discuss in Chapter 9.

An Intermediate Routing Example

In "A Simple Routing Example" on page 173, we looked at a really simple scenario and introduced the concept of routing. That scenario was simple for two basic reasons. First, each node in the environment only needed a default router in its routing table to reach all other networks. Second, it was a completely self-contained network in that there were exactly four networks that could be reached and no connection to the Internet. That example gave us the opportunity to describe the basics.

In this section, we'll look at a more complex example that is also arguably more realistic. We explore the routing tables for some of the hosts and routers in this new environment and we introduce an Internet connection. Figure 6–4 depicts the example.

In this example, we see the following systems. The router G is the Internet gateway. We have identified two of its interfaces: the external interface leading to the Internet is assigned the address of 192.29.75.251/27 and the interface assigned the address of 10.254.0.254/16 leading to router R. The external

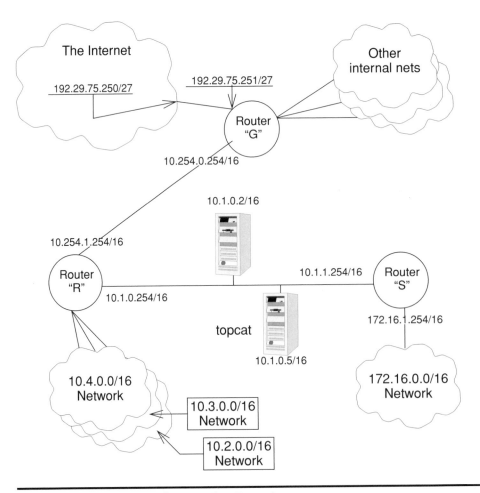

Figure 6–4   An Intermediate Routing Example

interface of G connects to a router (managed by an ISP) in the Internet through the address `192.29.75.250/27`. G is connected to some other internal networks that we won't worry about at this point. Router R is the same as it was in Figure 6–1 on page 174. There is another router attached to the `10.1.0.0/16` network called S with two interfaces: the one connected to the `10.1.0.0/16` network is assigned the address `10.1.1.254/16`; the other is assigned the address `172.16.1.254/16`. For the purpose of this example, we focus on the routers, labeled networks, and the host `topcat` (`10.1.0.5/16`).

Conceptually, the way packets should be routed in this environment is clear. Pick a source and a destination and then follow the lines to see which routers are needed. Let's see what the routing tables need to contain.

The `10.1.0.0/16, 10.2.0.0/16, 10.3.0.0/16,` and `172.16.0.0/16` networks are all *end* networks. That is, all of the hosts in such a network have only one router to use in order to communicate with any host on another network. In cases like that, it makes sense to configure a default router for each of those hosts as described in "Making Static Routes Permanent" on page 190. For these hosts, the default router entry, together with the local network and loopback entry, complete the table.

NOTE

The routing tables presented in this section are not intended to portray any particular distribution. They are illustrative and capture the essence of what the routing table would look like, in general.

Now, the router S is a little more complex, but still relatively simple. In order for S to be able to send packets everywhere, it needs to know about the two local networks to which it is attached and about the router R. The routing table here, then, could also be configured with a default router of R. We use this default entry because it leads to all other networks that can be reached by S. This default router entry, the two local network entries, and the loopback would complete the table for S. Its routing table would appear as in Example 6–16.

Example 6–16   Routing Table for the Router S

```
# route -n
Kernel IP routing table
Destination     Gateway         Genmask         Flags Metric Ref    Use Iface
10.1.0.0        0.0.0.0         255.255.0.0     U     0      0        0 eth0
172.16.0.0      0.0.0.0         255.255.0.0     U     0      0        0 eth1
127.0.0.0       0.0.0.0         255.0.0.0       U     0      0        0 lo
0.0.0.0         10.1.0.254      0.0.0.0         UG    1      0        0 eth0
#
```

The router R, in turn, is slightly more complex than S. In order for R to send and forward packets throughout this environment, it needs to know about its five local interfaces, the router S and the router G. The routing table for R, then, would consist of its five local networks, an entry with the destination of 172.16.0.0 with the router S (10.1.1.254), a default router of G (10.254.0.254 interface) and, of course, the loopback. In this case R cannot just have a default entry because in order to send or forward packets to the 172.16.0.0/16 network, R needs to send those packets to S. Its routing table is shown in Example 6–17.

Example 6–17   Routing Table for the Router R

```
# route -n
Kernel IP routing table
Destination     Gateway         Genmask         Flags Metric Ref    Use Iface
10.1.0.0        0.0.0.0         255.255.0.0     U     0      0        0 eth1
10.2.0.0        0.0.0.0         255.255.0.0     U     0      0        0 eth2
10.3.0.0        0.0.0.0         255.255.0.0     U     0      0        0 eth0
10.4.0.0        0.0.0.0         255.255.0.0     U     0      0        0 eth3
10.254.0.0      0.0.0.0         255.255.0.0     U     0      0        0 eth4
172.16.0.0      10.1.1.254      255.255.0.0     UG    0      0        0 eth1
127.0.0.0       0.0.0.0         255.0.0.0       U     0      0        0 lo
0.0.0.0         10.254.0.254    0.0.0.0         UG    1      0        0 eth1
#
```

The router, or gateway, G is the most complex of all. It will use a default router of 192.29.75.250, which is the IP address of a router that is managed by an ISP. That default router entry will allow G to send and forward all packets to all networks on the Internet. G will additionally need a number of other entries in its routing table so that it can send or forward packets to every network in the internal environment. Disregarding the "other nets" in Figure 6–4, the routing table on G will appear as in Example 6–18.

Example 6–18   Routing Table for the Router G

```
# route -n
Kernel IP routing table
Destination     Gateway          Genmask            Flags Metric Ref    Use Iface
10.254.0.0      0.0.0.0          255.255.0.0        U     0      0        0 eth1
192.29.75.248   0.0.0.0          255.255.255.248 U     0      0        0 eth0
10.1.0.0        10.254.1.254     255.255.0.0        UG    0      0        0 eth1
10.2.0.0        10.254.1.254     255.255.0.0        UG    0      0        0 eth1
10.3.0.0        10.254.1.254     255.255.0.0        UG    0      0        0 eth1
10.4.0.0        10.254.1.254     255.255.0.0        UG    0      0        0 eth1
172.16.0.0      10.254.1.254     255.255.0.0        UG    0      0        0 eth1
127.0.0.0       0.0.0.0          255.0.0.0          U     0      0        0 lo
0.0.0.0         192.29.75.250    0.0.0.0            UG    1      0        0 eth0
#
```

As can be seen, this table has a large number of gateway entries. It could be statically managed through the configuration files as described in "Making Static Routes Permanent" on page 190. But as an environment grows, this can become tedious, and as we see in "Multiple Routes" on page 205, statically managed tables cannot dynamically identify routers that are down nor find alternate routes. The use of dynamic routing table daemons to maintain routing tables provides both convenience and the ability to recover from down routers. We begin looking at those shortly.

Now, consider the host topcat. It is not a router and therefore does no packet forwarding. However, its routing tables need to tell it how to get to every network in the local environment and on the Internet. This can be accomplished with the entries shown in Example 6–19.

Example 6–19   Routing Table for topcat

```
# route -n
Kernel IP routing table
Destination     Gateway          Genmask            Flags Metric Ref    Use Iface
10.1.0.0        0.0.0.0          255.255.0.0        U     0      0        0 eth0
172.16.0.0      10.1.1.254       255.255.0.0        UG    0      0        0 eth0
127.0.0.0       0.0.0.0          255.0.0.0          U     0      0        0 lo
0.0.0.0         10.1.0.254       0.0.0.0            UG    1      0        0 eth0
#
```

Take note of the fact that in *all* of the foregoing routing table examples, for every gateway entry (the G flag is present), the Gateway field *always* contains a local destination consistent with the Iface field. Noting this fact will assist tremendously in understanding the network layout of an environment and in troubleshooting network problems.

ICMP Redirects

Now, just *suppose* that the routing table on topcat appears as shown in Example 6–20.

Example 6–20   Deficient Routing Table for topcat

```
# route -n
Kernel IP routing table
Destination    Gateway      Genmask        Flags Metric Ref    Use Iface
10.1.0.0       0.0.0.0      255.255.0.0    U     0      0        0 eth0
127.0.0.0      0.0.0.0      255.0.0.0      U     0      0        0 lo
0.0.0.0        10.1.0.254   0.0.0.0        UG    1      0        0 eth0
#
```

This routing table is deficient for topcat because it does not specify the correct route for the 172.16.0.0/16 network. Nonetheless, if the routing table for R (10.1.0.254) is correct, users on topcat will still be able to get to the 172.16.0.0/16 network because ICMP will generate a redirect message and tell topcat how to get there. Figure 6–5 illustrates the process.

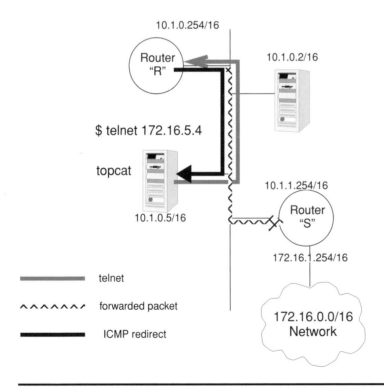

Figure 6–5   An ICMP Redirect

It works like this. Say a user on `topcat` executes `telnet 172.16.5.4` (of course, the user will probably use the hostname). The kernel executes the routing algorithm and determines that `172.16.5.4` is not local and needs to be sent to a router. So, the kernel checks the routing table (actually, I've been lying to you, it really checks the *routing cache*—keep reading, we'll get to it) and discovers that the only route is to the default router `10.1.0.254`. Consequently, the kernel encapsulates the packet and sends it off to `10.1.0.254` (R).

Now, R gets the packet and deencapsulates it to layer 3 of the TCP/IP stack. It determines that the packet needs to be forwarded and executes the routing algorithm. It finds that it needs to send the packet to S, which happens to be on the same network as `topcat`. This causes R to forward the packet to S and generate an ICMP redirect message to topcat.

R really should not have to forward every such packet back to S for `topcat`. So, when `topcat` gets the ICMP redirect, the kernel adds a host entry to its routing cache (*not* the routing table—the routing table remains unchanged). We can view the routing cache with `route -Cn` (see Table 6–2 on page 185). Example 6–21 shows the routing cache on `topcat` after the redirect occurs. The redirect is in **bold**.

Example 6–21   Routing Cache on topcat after an ICMP Redirect

```
# route -Cn
Kernel IP routing cache
Source          Destination     Gateway         Flags Metric Ref    Use Iface
10.1.0.254      10.1.0.5        10.1.0.5        il    0      0        1 lo
10.1.0.254      10.1.255.255    10.1.255.255    ibl   0      0        1 lo
10.1.0.5        172.16.5.4      10.1.1.254      i     0      0        1 eth0
10.1.0.5        10.1.0.5        10.1.0.5        l     0      4        3 lo
10.13.1.1       10.1.0.5        10.1.0.5        l     0      0       12 lo
10.1.0.5        172.16.5.4      10.1.0.254            0      0        0 eth0
#
```

The first thing that is obvious in the routing cache is that it contains only host entries. The kernel maintains this list of all routes that are currently in use on a per host basis. Whenever the routing algorithm is invoked, the kernel looks for the best route in the routing cache first, then it searches the routing table, if necessary. Since the routing cache is empty initially, all entries in the routing cache are derived from the routing table. Furthermore, changes to the routing table (whether dynamic or static) cause the kernel to update the cache. Since ICMP is an internal kernel function, it directly modifies the routing cache. Since ICMP updates are temporary, as are all routing cache entries, there is no need for the kernel to update the routing table with an ICMP redirect. All routing cache entries, ICMP redirects included, are subject to timeout. After an entry has not been used for about 300 seconds (controlled by `/proc/sys/net/ipv4/route/gc_timeout`), it is dropped from the cache.

The next thing that is striking about the routing cache is that the flags are different. These flags are internally used by the kernel for the rapid processing of the entries. For example, the b flag means broadcast. So, if the kernel is searching for a route that is not a broadcast, it can disregard all entries flagged with b. You can interpret the flags by comparing the output of `route -Cn` with `/proc/net/rt_cache`, which lists the flags in hex. Then look at the constants beginning with `RTCF_` defined in `/usr/src/linux/in_route.h` (kernel versions 2.2.12 through 2.2.14 for sure—the contents and names of header files [files ending in `.h`] routinely change) and compare the hex values to determine which flag is used.

It also has some odd looking entries like the first entry in the table

```
10.1.0.254      10.1.0.5        10.1.0.5        il    0    0    1 lo
```

where `10.1.0.254` is the source, `10.1.0.5` is both the destination and gateway, and the interface is `lo`. These types of entries are used in conjunction with existing communications, or communications that terminated less than 300 seconds ago. Needless to say, this cache gets very large very quickly on systems that are actively engaged in network communications.

ICMP redirects are very helpful; however, they should not be relied upon generally. A routing table should cover all routes that could be used. Depending upon ICMP redirects causes additional network overhead (two extra network communications on the same link). Furthermore, ICMP redirects only cause *host* route entries to be added to the routing table, not network route entries. Thus, if `topcat` next communicated with `172.16.5.5`, a new redirect would be sent. Each additional host communicated with on the `172.16.0.0/16` network would cause another redirect. This causes extraneous network traffic and fills up the offending host's routing cache. ICMP redirects are almost always an indication that the initiating host's routing tables need to be corrected.

You can see ICMP redirects with Ethereal. Set the filter to `icmp` (or to capture only redirects, set the filter to `icmp[0] = 5`) in the Start window to filter out all packets except ICMP and then start capturing. Figure 6–6 shows an example.

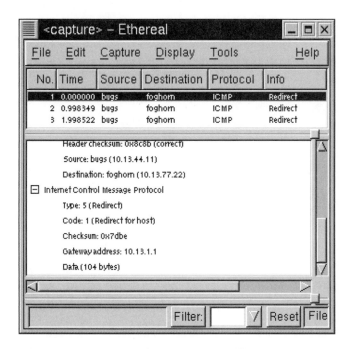

Figure 6–6   Ethereal Capture of ICMP Redirects

Note that the contents of the ICMP messages includes the correct router to use (`Gateway address: 10.13.1.1`, in this case).

Multiple Routes

One of the problems with the example in Figure 6–4 on page 198 is that each router represents a single point of failure for at least one network. For example, if the router S fails, then the `172.16.0.0/16` network cannot be reached. While this may be acceptable in certain environments, it may become desirable or even necessary to incorporate redundant paths. Figure 6–7 provides an example that provides redundancy for a number of internal networks. In this example, the routers R and S now serve the same purpose.

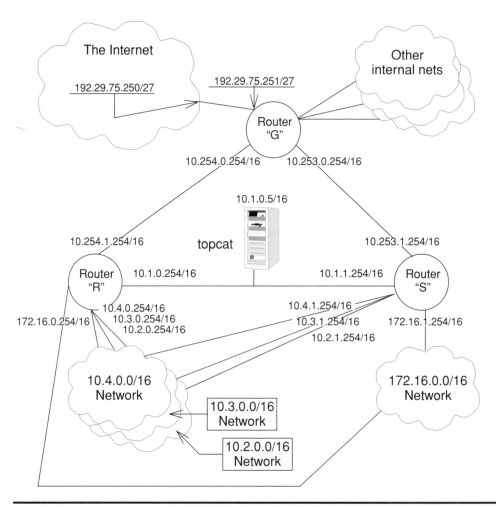

Figure 6–7   An Intermediate Routing Example with Redundancy

The problem with Figure 6–7 is that up to this point we have only been using static entries in our routing table. In particular, if one of the two routers, R or S, ceases to function, there is no way for any of the network nodes to determine that fact dynamically. Even if you were to add the redundant routes statically to all the routing tables on the hosts in this environment, only the last static entries made would ever be used. In short, you would be faced with having to manually reconfigure all of the node's routing tables, effectively defeating the purpose of introducing redundant routes. The solution is to use a dynamic routing table daemon to manage the tables automatically.

Introducing Dynamic Routing Table Management

In "Routing Table Management Methods" on page 184 we mentioned that there are two different types of routing table management protocols, IGPs and EGPs. In this section, we consider two IGPs, RIP and router discovery.

Routing table management daemons, in general, have the following attributes:

- They can dynamically read and update the routing table (*not* the routing cache) of a system or a router to reflect available routes.
- They can assist the kernel in identifying the best route.
- They are application layer programs and therefore often use either broadcasts or multicasts to local networks in order to effect their communications.

There are a number of different routing table management daemons ranging from simple and limited in capabilities to complex and extraordinarily flexible. Part of the decision about which one to use entails an assessment of the administrative effort involved. By considering RIP and router discovery, we are looking at the two simplest and least flexible protocols. In chapters 12 and 13, we consider more complex protocols. Throughout our discussions, we point out the advantages and disadvantages of each protocol.

RIP

The routing information protocol (RIP) is currently standardized by RFC 2453 as RIP version 2 (RIPv2). RIPv1 is standardized by RFC 1058 and still enjoys a certain amount of use. RIP is implemented through an Application layer daemon and communicates over the network using UDP as its Transport layer protocol. The primary advantage of RIP (either version) is that it is very simple. It is easy to understand and easy to implement and manage. With that simplicity, however, are some limitations, as we see in this section.

While there are a number of differences between RIPv1 and RIPv2, the most significant differences are as follows:

- RIPv1 does not propagate route masks with its updates while RIPv2 does. Thus, all routes that it propagates assume that either the default netmask (based on address classes discussed in Chapter 4) is used or that the receiving system will use the mask associated with the interface on

which the RIP packets are received. This severely limits the usefulness of RIPv1 on a wide scale.
- RIPv1 cannot include anything other than itself in its advertisements. RIPv2 can include entries in its updates that lead to non-RIP routers.
- RIPv2 can include an authentication string in its packets to make spoofing[5] RIP updates harder.
- RIPv2 incorporates route tags that can be used to identify routes advertised by RIP that came from another dynamic routing table management protocol.

It turns out that there are two widely available daemons that can be used to implement RIP on a Linux system. They are `routed` and `gated`. The `routed` daemon only implements RIPv1 and is discussed later in this section. The `gated` daemon can implement either RIPv1 or RIPv2 (except for the route tag functionality) and is introduced in Chapter 11.

RIP is known as a *distance-vector* protocol. This means that it propagates routing information based on the shortest distance to a destination. The best route, as far as RIP is concerned, is the one with the smallest metric. The metric is a value between 0 and 15 inclusive and is carried in the `metric` field of the routing table (the kernel ignores this field, only the RIP daemon pays attention to it). Generally, this metric is a *hop count*—a count of the routers between sender and receiver. To see how this works, consider Figure 6–8.

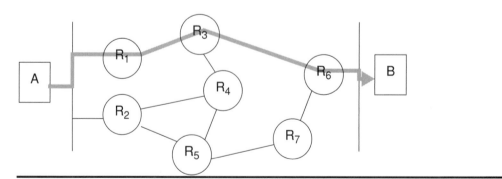

Figure 6–8   Routers, RIP, and Hop Counts

---

5. Spoofing means to deliberately generate a packet that has false information in it, usually for illicit purposes.

Suppose that A wishes to communicate with B. A sends its packets to R_1 for forwarding. R_1, and all of the other routers shown in Figure 6–8 use RIP. R_1 looks up the destination network number of B and finds the entry to R_3. It reencapsulates the packets and sends them on to R_3, which in turn sends them to R_6, and then R_6 finally delivers the packet to B. Note that other paths could have been chosen. For example, A to R_2 to R_5 to R_7 to R_6 to B. But that route, and indeed any other route, would take more hops. Thus, due to the use of RIP, the former route is chosen. Another way of saying this is, the distance from A to B through R_1, R_3, and R_6 is 3. The distance from A to B through R_2, R_5, R_7, and R_6 is 4. Since 3 is less than 4, that route is chosen. Note that RIP chooses these routes and then updates the routing tables accordingly.

The above computation assumes that the metric associated with each hop is 1. The metric can be artificially increased to make a particular route less desirable to RIP. For example, if the metric associated with R_1 were set to 3, which can be set with the `metric` flag to the `route` command, then A would always use R_2—because the path through R_1, R_3, and R_6 would then have a cost of 3+1+1=5 which is greater than 4. The only case in which A would use R_1, once its metric has been set to 3, would be if R_2 was unavailable *and* A had received an update to that effect.

RIP enforces an upper limit of 15 in its distance metric. Any route that has a total metric of 15, also called *infinity*, is unreachable.

RIP, as implemented through a daemon, can run in two different modes: listen-only and broadcast. Normally, routers run RIP in broadcast mode (they listen to broadcasts from other routers, too) and non-routers run RIP in listen-only mode. Each router running RIP will broadcast (sending the packets with a destination IP address of the IP broadcast for the given network) its then current tables to all of its local networks every 30 seconds—these are called *response* packets. The only exception to the use of broadcasts is in the case of a point-to-point connection, in which case a unicast is used to send the response packet. Listening nodes receive the responses and apply the information it contains in the following way.

- Add each entry to the routing table that is not currently in the routing table and the metric is not infinite.
- Update existing routing table entries if the entries are for the same router that the RIP broadcast is from.

- Update an entry if it hasn't been updated for 90 seconds.
- Update an entry if the new route has a smaller metric to the destination.

All routes accepted as either a new entry or an updated entry are dynamically placed in the routing table. All entries managed by RIP are assigned a three minute timeout. At the end of that time, if it hasn't been updated by a RIP response, then its metric is set to infinity and the record is marked for deletion. This infinite route is maintained in the table for 60 seconds so that, if in broadcast mode, it can be propagated out to other hosts and routers, advising them of the lost route.

All systems using a RIP daemon will send out a broadcast packet at start-up send to each of its local networks seeking RIP routing tables from all those systems running RIP in broadcast mode. This type of packet is called a *request* and is used to initially populate a system's routing tables.

RIP can be implemented on Linux systems through one of two daemons: `gated` or `routed`. All major Linux distributions ship with `routed`; it is somewhat easier to configure than `gated`. Unfortunately, `routed` implements RIPv1. It nonetheless has certain applicability.

USING ROUTED   The `/usr/sbin/routed` daemon is quite simple to use. When started, it runs in listen-only mode if it finds one interface, and in broadcast mode if it finds two or more interfaces on the system. This default behavior can be overridden with appropriate flags. The flags are described in Table 6–3.

Table 6–3   The Flags of `routed`

FLAGS	DESCRIPTION
-d	Sends debug output to `syslog` selector `daemon.debug`.
-g	Causes a router to include itself as a default in its broadcasts.
-s	Run in broadcast mode even if the system is not a router.
-q	Run in listen mode even if the system is a router.
-t	Writes all RIP packets sent and received to standard out.

The `routed` daemon is normally started through a start-up script, but it can be invoked manually. The Red Hat start-up script for routed is `/etc/rc.d/init.d/`

routed. For Red Hat, you must additionally execute `chkconfig routed on`, to get `routed` to start at each reboot. Caldera does not include a start-up script for `routed`, so you would have to create your own or add the `routed` invocation to another start-up script. The Debian start-up script for routed is `/etc/init.d/netstd_init` and for SuSE it is `/sbin/init.d/routed`.

There is one configuration file associated with `routed`, the `/etc/gateways` file. This file can be used to provide routes to `routed` that it would not get via RIP. For example, it is unlikely that RIP would be run in broadcast mode on G in Figure 6–7 on page 206 because other dynamic routing table protocols or static entries would be used for that Internet gateway. Thus, all those networks defined as "other networks" would not have routes advertised to the routers R and S. In such a case, the `/etc/gateways` file could be used on R and S to add those routes. Suppose that the "other networks" included `192.168.1.0/16`, `192.168.2.0/16`, and `192.168.3.0/16`. Then the `/etc/gateways` file would appear as shown in Example 6–22 for R.

Example 6–22   /etc/gateways File for R

```
# cat /etc/gateways
net 192.168.1.0 gateway 10.254.0.254 metric 1 passive
net 192.168.2.0 gateway 10.254.0.254 metric 1 passive
net 192.168.3.0 gateway 10.254.0.254 metric 1 passive
#
```

Here, the syntax of the file is:

```
net | host destination gateway router metric value passive | active | external
```

This syntax is quite similar to that of the `route` command itself. The initial keyword must be either `net` or `host` indicating that the record is for a network or host destination and the argument, *destination*, following the `net` or `host` keyword must be a network number for `net` or host IP address for `host`. The `gateway` keyword requires *router* to be the IP address of a router; the `metric` keyword requires a metric value ($0 \leq$ metric ≤ 15). The final keyword can be either `passive`, `active`, or `external`. The keyword `passive` means that the entry is to be permanent and not subject to the normal three minute RIP nonuse timeout. The `active` keyword is used to add an entry that is subject to RIP nonuse timeouts. The `external` keyword is used to add an entry that is not included in any RIP updates sent out by this system.

WARNING

The only way to add entries to `routed` for propagation via RIP is to use the `/etc/gateways` file and then only entries marked `passive` or `active` will be propagated. Added routes to the routing table with the `route` command will not be propagated by `routed`.

The only necessary difference in Example 6–22 for this file to be applicable to `s` would be to change the address following the `gateway` keyword to `10.253.0.254`.

RUNNING ROUTED **IN FIGURE 6–7**   Now that we have some details about how to implement RIPv1 with `routed`, let's see how it can be applied to the example given in Figure 6–7 on page 206 (once again, we ignore the "other nets" in the example).

Our goal in using RIPv1 in this example is to allow our environment to dynamically take advantage of the fact that there is redundancy in the routing environment. It also has the side effect of providing the routing tables without any static management—so, we can take advantage of that, too. Let's also suppose that the ISP has told us that our service would be summarily cut off if we broadcast RIP packets from G through the `192.29.75.251/27` interface. Therefore, we cannot run `routed` in broadcast mode on G because `routed` cannot selectively broadcast to specific interfaces (`gated`, however, can be selective about which interfaces it broadcasts and reads as we see in Chapter 11). Given our goals, we can run `routed` on the routers R and S in broadcast mode and run `routed` on all other systems in listen mode. This includes running RIP in listen mode on G (our ISP told us we couldn't broadcast, they didn't say anything about listening!) which will allow G to become aware of failures of either R or S.

To accomplish these goals, we run `routed` in the following way for each of the systems in the environment described by Figure 6–7. On the routers R and S, `routed` needs to be invoked with

```
routed -g
```

Using the `-g` option causes both R and S to advertise themselves as default routers. The routers R and S will need a default router of their own. In both cases, the default router is G. R and S can be configured with a static default router as described in "Making Static Routes Permanent" on page 190 or an entry of the form

```
net 0.0.0.0 gateway 10.254.0.254 metric 1 passive
```

in the `/etc/gateways` file for the router R. For the router S, the entry would be

```
net 0.0.0.0 gateway 10.253.0.254 metric 1 passive
```

in the `/etc/gateways` file.

On every other system in the environment (ignoring the "other nets"), we simply need to invoke

```
routed
```

and those nodes will listen-only. All of these systems should *not* have a statically defined default router or gateway because R and S will be broadcasting themselves as default routers.

On the Internet gateway, G, we cannot run `routed` because the two routers R and S will be broadcasting themselves as default routers. G cannot use them as default routers since it must use `192.29.75.250/27` as its default router, not only for itself but also for all the other hosts in the environment. Effectively, this example presses beyond the capabilities of the routed daemon. If we know nothing else, the only solution is to install static routes on G and then accept the fact that G will be unable to automatically receive availability information about R or S. This may well be an unacceptable solution. Fortunately, `gated` can solve this problem. G can listen to the RIP broadcasts using `gated` because `gated` allows for a more selective use of received RIP routes. We discuss `gated` in Chapter 11 and, in particular, address the specifics of this example in "One More Thing…" on page 545. For the purposes of this example, assume that G is listening to the RIP broadcasts with `gated`.

Each of these invocations can be placed in the appropriate start-up script together with the appropriate variable settings (for Red Hat, see "Red Hat 6.2" on page 136) as described in "Using routed" on page 210.

ROUTING TABLES FOR R AND S USING `routed`   Once these configuration changes have been made, R and S will have nearly identical routing tables. With the exception of G, each of the hosts in the environment depicted by Figure 6–7 will all share very similar routing tables.

Example 6–23 shows the routing table for the Red Hat 6.2 router R.

Example 6–24 displays the routing table for the Caldera 2.4 router S.

Example 6–23   Routing Table on the Red Hat Router R

```
# route -n
Kernel IP routing table
Destination     Gateway         Genmask             Flags Metric Ref    Use Iface
172.16.0.254    0.0.0.0         255.255.255.255 UH      0      0      0 eth1
10.1.0.254      0.0.0.0         255.255.255.255 UH      0      0      0 eth2
10.2.0.254      0.0.0.0         255.255.255.255 UH      0      0      0 eth3
10.3.0.254      0.0.0.0         255.255.255.255 UH      0      0      0 eth4
10.4.0.254      0.0.0.0         255.255.255.255 UH      0      0      0 eth5
10.254.0.254    0.0.0.0         255.255.255.255 UH      0      0      0 eth0
172.16.0.0      172.16.0.254    255.255.0.0     UG      0      0      0 eth1
172.16.0.0      0.0.0.0         255.255.0.0     U       0      0      0 eth1
10.1.0.0        10.1.0.254      255.255.0.0     UG      0      0      0 eth2
10.1.0.0        0.0.0.0         255.255.0.0     U       0      0      0 eth2
10.2.0.0        10.2.0.254      255.255.0.0     UG      0      0      0 eth3
10.2.0.0        0.0.0.0         255.255.0.0     U       0      0      0 eth3
10.3.0.0        10.3.0.254      255.255.0.0     UG      0      0      0 eth4
10.3.0.0        0.0.0.0         255.255.0.0     U       0      0      0 eth4
10.4.0.0        10.4.0.254      255.255.0.0     UG      0      0      0 eth5
10.4.0.0        0.0.0.0         255.255.0.0     U       0      0      0 eth5
10.254.0.0      10.254.0.254    255.255.0.0     UG      0      0      0 eth0
10.254.0.0      0.0.0.0         255.255.0.0     U       0      0      0 eth0
127.0.0.0       0.0.0.0         255.0.0.0       U       0      0      0 lo
0.0.0.0         10.254.0.254    0.0.0.0         UG      0      0      0 eth0
#
```

Example 6–24   Routing Table on the Caldera Router S

```
# route -n
Kernel IP routing table
Destination     Gateway         Genmask             Flags Metric Ref    Use Iface
172.16.1.254    0.0.0.0         255.255.0.0     U       0      0      0 eth1
10.1.1.254      0.0.0.0         255.255.0.0     U       0      0      0 eth2
10.2.1.254      0.0.0.0         255.255.0.0     U       0      0      0 eth3
10.3.1.254      0.0.0.0         255.255.0.0     U       0      0      0 eth4
10.4.1.254      0.0.0.0         255.255.0.0     U       0      0      0 eth5
10.253.1.254    0.0.0.0         255.255.0.0     U       0      0      0 eth0
127.0.0.0       0.0.0.0         255.0.0.0       U       0      0      0 lo
0.0.0.0         10.253.0.254    0.0.0.0         UG      0      0      0 eth0
#
```

Although the two routing tables in Examples 6–23 and 6–24 show a remarkable difference, the do not functionally differ. Once again, we simply see the differences in distribution implementations—Red Hat systems are much more verbose with their routing tables and include more entries that you would otherwise only see in the routing cache.

These two routers will broadcast their entire table to each local network every 30 seconds. Figure 6–9 shows a typical RIP broadcast packet and focuses specifically on the contents to the packet which includes the routing table entries. The packet shown was generated by 10.1.0.254 (R) and, in particular, the contents of the RIP packet is displayed in the lower pane. Due to size constraints, only

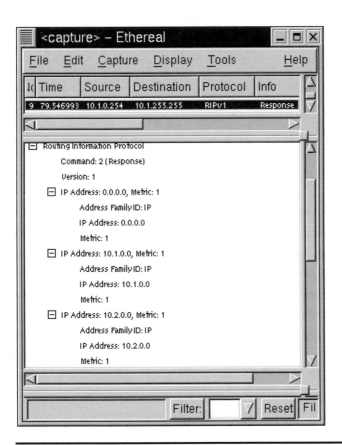

Figure 6–9 Contents of a RIPv1 Packet

the default router entry (IP Address: 0.0.0.0) and the first two network entries (10.1.0.0 and 10.2.0.0) are shown. If we were able to see the entire pane, we would also see the 10.3.0.0, 10.4.0.0, and 172.16.0.0 entries. Note that the RIPv1 packet carries no gateway entry since the gateway is always the sending router. Also notice that no netmask is included—the fact that the 10.x.0.0 networks are treated as networks is due to the interfaces on R being configured with the 255.255.0.0 subnetmask.

HOST ROUTING TABLES USING routed Now, let's take a look at some example routing tables in this environment.

Example 6–25 displays a typical routing table for a Debian host with the IP address 10.3.10.15/16.

Example 6–25   Routing Table in a `routed` Environment for a Debian Host

```
# route -n
Kernel IP routing table
Destination     Gateway          Genmask             Flags Metric Ref    Use Iface
10.3.10.15      0.0.0.0          255.255.255.255 U        0      0        0 eth0
10.3.0.0        10.3.10.15       255.255.0.0         UG       0      0        0 eth0
172.16.0.0      10.3.1.254       255.255.0.0         UG       1      0        0 eth0
10.1.0.0        10.3.1.254       255.255.0.0         UG       1      0        0 eth0
10.2.0.0        10.3.1.254       255.255.0.0         UG       1      0        0 eth0
10.4.0.0        10.3.1.254       255.255.0.0         UG       1      0        0 eth0
127.0.0.0       0.0.0.0          255.0.0.0           U        0      0        0 lo
0.0.0.0         10.3.1.254       0.0.0.0             UG       1      0        0 eth0
#
```

Example 6–26 shows a typical routing table for a Red Hat host on the `10.2.0.0/16` network—in this case, it is the routing table for a Red Hat 6.2 system with the IP address `10.2.22.22`.

Example 6–26   Routing Table in a `routed` Environment for a Red Hat Host

```
# route -n
Kernel IP routing table
Destination     Gateway          Genmask             Flags Metric Ref    Use Iface
10.2.22.22      0.0.0.0          255.255.255.255 UH       0      0        0 eth0
10.2.0.0        10.2.22.22       255.255.0.0         UG       0      0        0 eth0
10.2.0.0        0.0.0.0          255.255.0.0         U        0      0        0 eth0
172.16.0.0      10.2.1.254       255.255.0.0         UG       1      0        0 eth0
10.1.0.0        10.2.1.254       255.255.0.0         UG       1      0        0 eth0
10.3.0.0        10.2.1.254       255.255.0.0         UG       1      0        0 eth0
10.4.0.0        10.2.1.254       255.255.0.0         UG       1      0        0 eth0
127.0.0.0       0.0.0.0          255.0.0.0           U        0      0        0 lo
0.0.0.0         10.2.1.254       0.0.0.0             UG       1      0        0 eth0
#
```

Note that in Examples 6–25 and 6–26 there are entries for each network known to the environment. This is due to the fact that the RIP routers R and S are broadcasting information about all of the local interfaces that they have in addition to offering themselves as default routers. Once again, the Red Hat routing table is much more verbose. In both cases, the routing tables shown will be built at the time `routed` first runs on each system. When `routed` is invoked, it issues a RIP request. It will build the routing tables from the first response it receives when there are duplicate routes, as in this case, to the same destinations.

If the router S goes down, both systems will behave similarly. Given that both systems are currently using S for all their routes, once S goes down, both systems will begin reporting destination unreachable messages for all network communications. Within 30 seconds, R will broadcast its routes and both systems will update their tables with the available entries and resume normal network operations. It does work and, although it takes a bit to explain, it really is very simple to administrate.

At this point, we need to consider an anomalous situation. Suppose that the Red Hat system described by Example 6–26 is using S as its router. In the midst of some network activity, S goes down and the system recovers its network connectivity as soon as it gets a RIP response from R. Then S comes back and issues a RIP response before the Red Hat system can expire the routes provided by S (recall that after a route has been set to infinity, there is a 60 second delay before the records are expired). When S issues this RIP response, the Red Hat system dutifully updates the entries, thus maintaining two sets of entries, as shown in Example 6–27. The Red Hat inuse routes would be evident from the routing cache and in any event, whenever a system has two different routes to the same destination with the same metric, the first entry found is used. The first entry found is always the last entry added. In essence, under these circumstances, the duplicate entries remain until one of the routers goes down long enough for the records to expire or the system's network script is cycled (such as with a reboot).

Example 6–27   Routing Table with Multiple Routes to the Same Destination

```
# route -n
Kernel IP routing table
Destination     Gateway         Genmask           Flags Metric Ref   Use Iface
10.2.22.22      0.0.0.0         255.255.255.255   UH    0      0       0 eth0
10.2.0.0        10.2.22.22      255.255.0.0       UG    0      0       0 eth0
10.2.0.0        0.0.0.0         255.255.0.0       U     0      0       0 eth0
172.16.0.0      10.2.0.254      255.255.0.0       UG    1      0       0 eth0
172.16.0.0      10.2.1.254      255.255.0.0       UG    1      0       0 eth0
10.1.0.0        10.2.0.254      255.255.0.0       UG    1      0       0 eth0
10.1.0.0        10.2.1.254      255.255.0.0       UG    1      0       0 eth0
10.3.0.0        10.2.0.254      255.255.0.0       UG    1      0       0 eth0
10.3.0.0        10.2.1.254      255.255.0.0       UG    1      0       0 eth0
10.4.0.0        10.2.0.254      255.255.0.0       UG    1      0       0 eth0
10.4.0.0        10.2.1.254      255.255.0.0       UG    1      0       0 eth0
127.0.0.0       0.0.0.0         255.0.0.0         U     0      0       0 lo
0.0.0.0         10.2.0.254      0.0.0.0           UG    1      0       0 eth0
0.0.0.0         10.2.1.254      0.0.0.0           UG    1      0       0 eth0
#
```

Now that we've seen some example routing tables built dynamically by RIP, we can take a closer look at our example. Notice that all the non-router systems in Figure 6–7 on page 206 really only need a default router. And, if one router goes down, they need to know about the other default router so that they can continue communicating throughout the network. The entries that we've looked at, for the hosts in particular, contain a lot more information than they need.

There are ways to accomplish maintaining a default router dynamically so that the redundancy providing multiple routers, such as R and S, can be utilized. One way is with router discovery, which we discuss in "Router Discovery" on page 219.

ROUTING TABLE FOR G   The routing requirements for G in this example are quite straightforward. Ignoring "Other internal nets," G simply needs to forward all outbound traffic to the Internet and all inbound traffic to either R or S. But if G is to take advantage of the redundancy offered by R and S, it must run a dynamic routing table protocol. RIPv1 is not a good choice for this purpose (we look at better choices in Chapter 11), but suppose that G is running gated (as stipulated previously) in listen mode. Its routing table would appear something similar to that shown in Example 6–28.

Example 6–28   Routing Table for G for the Example Given in Figure 6–7

```
# route -n
Kernel IP routing table
Destination     Gateway         Genmask            Flags Metric Ref   Use Iface
192.29.75.248   192.29.75.251   255.255.255.248 UG    0      0       0 eth0
10.253.0.0      10.253.0.254    255.255.0.0     UG    0      0       0 eth1
10.254.0.0      10.254.0.254    255.255.0.0     UG    0      0       0 eth2
172.16.0.0      10.254.1.254    255.255.0.0     UG    1      0       0 eth1
10.1.0.0        10.254.1.254    255.255.0.0     UG    1      0       0 eth1
10.2.0.0        10.254.1.254    255.255.0.0     UG    1      0       0 eth1
10.3.0.0        10.254.1.254    255.255.0.0     UG    1      0       0 eth1
10.4.0.0        10.254.1.254    255.255.0.0     UG    1      0       0 eth1
127.0.0.0       0.0.0.0         255.0.0.0       U     0      0       0 lo
0.0.0.0         192.29.75.250   0.0.0.0         UG    1      0       0 eth0
#
```

At this point in time, G is using R for all of its internal routes. Notice that there are five distinct routes that all go to R. Clearly, this routing table is overly complex given the simple task at hand for G. We initially discuss simplifying this routing table in "A More Complex Routing Example" on page 225.

THE RIPQUERY UTILITY   If RIP is running on a system, either via routed or gated, there is a handy troubleshooting tool, ripquery. The ripquery utility generates a RIP request to the specified host. If that host is running RIP, it will reply with its routing table. Example 6–29 illustrates the use of ripquery. The -n option suppresses name translation.

Example 6–29 Output of `ripquery -n`

```
# ripquery -n 172.16.2.22
84 bytes from 172.16.2.22 version 1:
        0.0.0.0              metric  1
        10.1.0.0             metric  2
        10.2.0.0             metric  2
        10.3.0.0             metric  2
        10.4.0.0             metric  2
        172.16.0.0           metric  1
#
```

There are a number of other options to the `ripquery` command and we explore them further in Chapter 11. Also, see the `ripquery (8)` man page.

Router Discovery

Router discovery is implemented through ICMP and is standardized by RFC 1256 for IPv4 and by RFC 2461 for IPv6. It is designed specifically to address the issue of making default routers available in an automated way. Unlike RIP, it does not propagate routing tables, it only causes the advertisements of routers themselves for use as defaults. Also, unlike RIP, router discovery uses multicasting for its communication instead of broadcasts.

With router discovery, hosts and routers play distinct roles. A host implementing router discovery attempts to find a router, usually at boot-time, by sending requests, called *solicitations*, to the all routers multicast address (224.0.0.2 for IPv4; FF01::2 for IPv6). The router, if appropriately configured, will reply to this with a response, known as an *advertisement*, to the all nodes multicast (224.0.0.1 for IPv4; FF02::1 for IPv6). Routers will, additionally, advertise periodically and hosts can use each advertisement to update their routing tables.

ROUTER DISCOVERY AND FIGURE 6–7 For the purposes of the example contained in Figure 6–7 on page 206, router discovery would be an improvement. In short, all the hosts in that environment only require default routers and the ability to change the router in use if one goes down. Router discovery can take care of both of these issues. Furthermore, in this case, it would also mean that the routing tables on each host would be smaller—containing, at most, two default entries in addition to the local interface and loopback entries. The routing tables on the hosts are smaller because the router discovery routers are sending smaller packets—they only contain the one default router entry—which implies, directly, a reduction in network traffic. Additionally, the frequency with which router discovery advertisements are generated by routers can be controlled; it is not fixed at every 30 seconds as with RIP.

Using router discovery in that example would allow R and S to run routed in broadcast mode without the -g argument (so they wouldn't advertise a default router) and G could run routed in listen mode (routed -s would be invoked on G—the -s argument would be required in that case because G has two or more interfaces).

LIMITED USE OF ROUTER DISCOVERY   Router discovery is not always a good choice, though. Hosts using router discovery always use as their default router the one sent in the last advertisement on the local network. Consider Figure 6–10. In this example, the routers G, R, and S are as they were previously. Two new routers, X and Y, appear, each leading to distinct networks that have been added and neither leading to the Internet. Suppose that R, S, X, and Y are all providing router discovery advertisements. The host topcat receives these advertisements and updates its routing table with each new advertisement. Thus, at any given moment in time, topcat may have a default router of any one of the four routers directly attached to its local network.

The problem with that approach is that regardless of which router is the current default on topcat, the possibility of ICMP redirects exists. For example, suppose that the default router on topcat is currently X. Then some user comes along, runs Netscape, and starts browsing Web pages throughout the Internet. Because the current default router is X, each Web page access to a unique IP address will generate an ICMP redirect. The routing cache on topcat will begin to fill up with these ICMP redirects. This will continue until topcat gets a new advertisement from R or S. Then all will be well until the next advertisement from X or Y.

If only one user is doing this sort of thing, it's probably no big deal. On the other hand, if the described activity on topcat is multiplied by many users on many different hosts, then router discovery is no longer providing any kind of benefit because of the large number of ICMP redirects that will be generated (see "ICMP Redirects" on page 202).

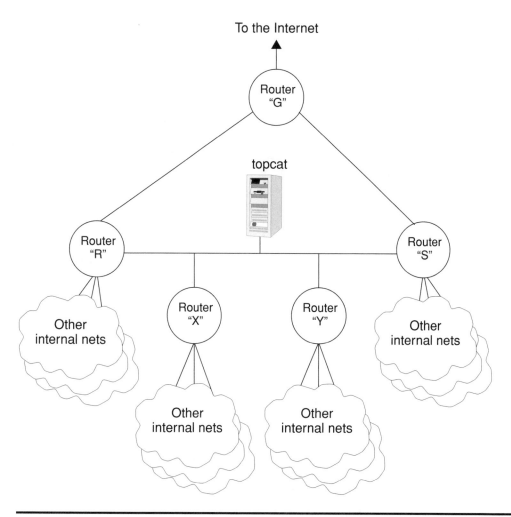

Figure 6–10   Internetwork Requiring Multiple Routing Table Management Methods

There are a couple of solutions to the problem posed by Figure 6–10. One approach is to allow R and S to advertise themselves as default routers and have X and Y use RIP to broadcast their routing tables *except* for the default router. The hosts, for example, topcat, would then have to listen for both router discovery advertisements and RIP broadcasts. Its tables would be built by a combination of the two protocols.

Another solution would be to use static routing table entries for the networks routed to by X and Y, and let R and S advertise by router discovery. This approach has the advantage of less network traffic, but the disadvantage of manually managing a lot of routing tables. Beginning with Chapter 11, we'll have a look at other possible solutions to this type of problem.

NOTE

Static routing table files can be managed in an automated way through the use of utilities such as `rdist` and `rsync`. These utilities can maintain a file on one host as a master, identify changes, and distribute the file to a list of hosts on a regular basis. They are useful tools for maintaining consistency in certain files throughout a network. They *cannot* dynamically update the routing table. If you use either of these utilities, it is important to realize that they ought to be used with the Secure Shell (SSH) to overcome their security flaws. See the `rsync(1)`, `rdist(1)`, and `rdist(8)` man pages for more information. For further details about SSH, see for example, `http://www.openssh.com/`.

Router discovery can be implemented in Linux using `gated`. Red Hat is shipping a daemon called `rdisc` with their 6.2 version of the software, but it only supports generating solicitations by hosts and not advertisements by routers. Consequently, we will discuss the actual implementation of router discovery with `gated` and `rdisc` in Chapter 11.

RIP Advantages and Disadvantages

The primary advantage of RIP is that it is simple to implement and maintain. It provides the basic functionality necessary in an environment where it is desirable to dynamically propagate changes in a routing environment. But RIP has its limitations, and we list the major ones here.

- RIP broadcasts its routing tables every 30 seconds. This has the advantage of imposing a limited period of time for which unavailable routes are maintained. It has the disadvantage of generating a lot of network traffic that all nodes on the local network must fully deencapsulate. This is particularly an issue when routing tables get large.
- RIP's notion of best route is limited to the single metric value. In smaller internetworks, this is rarely a problem, but as we'll see in the next section and in later chapters, even moderately large environments may suffer from this limited distance-vector approach.

- In a heavily subnetted environment, RIPv1 may not be a viable solution at all. In such cases, RIPv2 must be implemented, which at this point means that `gated` must be used. While configuring `gated` for RIPv2 is reasonably straightforward, as we see in Chapter 11, if you are going to the trouble of configuring `gated` for RIPv2, it may be desirable to use another protocol.

- Both RIPv1 and RIPv2 suffer from a number of potential problems associated with the algorithm they implement. One such problem is called *counting to infinity.* This type of problem occurs when links or routers go down and routing tables are not updated properly due to update synchronization issues similar to that depicted by Example 6–27 on page 217. In any event, such a scenario can cause routers to broadcast that they have routes to destinations that they do not and, consequently, packets are forwarded in a routing loop until the time-to-live is exceeded (the number of hops until the packet is destroyed). For a thorough treatment of this topic see *Routing in the Internet* or *Interconnections* as cited in "For Further Reading" on page 233. While problems like this tend to be rare, they almost always require manual intervention to correct.

Router Discovery Advantages and Disadvantages

Router discovery is a very simple mechanism for propagating available routers to the networks to which the routers are connected. As such, the scope of this protocol is limited to providing hosts (or possibly limited scope routers) with default routers. Its primary disadvantage is described in "Router Discovery" on page 219 and its potential for introducing large numbers of ICMP redirects.

Another disadvantage is the frequency with which routers advertise their existence. As we see in Chapter 11, `gated` causes routers using router discovery to advertise every 10 minutes by default. Fortunately, this frequency can be modified to a shorter period of time—of course, the trade-off is that more frequent advertisements means more network traffic. Whatever the time delta, if a host's default router goes down it must wait for an advertisement from another router before it can resume normal network communications.

When used under the proper circumstances, router discovery provides a simple and convenient method for maintaining default router availability to hosts.

Some Basic Routing Table Construction Guidelines

It is difficult to predict every conceivable network topology. It is equally difficult to predict the requirements and limitations of every possible environment. We provide some basic suggestions here regarding the construction and maintenance of routing tables, generally. Be sure to adjust them appropriately for your environment.

- When determining routing table needs, consider hosts and routers separately.
- If hosts are connected to a network that has a single router, use static default routers.
- If hosts are connected to a network that has multiple routers for the purpose of redundancy, consider using router discovery.
- If hosts are connected to a network that has multiple routers that lead to different networks, consider using RIP or, depending on complexity, another protocol (discussed in Chapter 11).
- If hosts are connected to a network that has multiple routers that lead to different networks and incorporate redundancy, consider utilizing router discovery and RIP (or another protocol) appropriately.
- Routers that are connected to single point of failure environments are probably best configured with static routes unless there is a requirement that they use RIP because of the needs of the rest of the environment.
- Routers that are connected to environments with multiple redundant paths need to use a dynamic routing table management protocol. The decision about which one to use depends upon many things, including the complexity of the environment, the administrative overhead of the protocol, and the protocol(s) being used by other routers. Chapter 11 provides additional information that will help clarify this process.

The most important point to carry into any routing strategy is to keep things as simple as possible. We reconsider this list for more complex environments in Chapter 11.

A Note about Hostnames

We haven't used hostnames much in this chapter, largely for clarity in the examples. All of the commands discussed accept hostnames instead of IP addresses as long as those hostnames are resolvable (see "Hostname Resolution" on page 142). Generally speaking, however, hostnames should be avoided in the configuration of your routing tables to avoid problems that arise when hostname resolution mechanisms, like NIS and DNS, are temporarily unavailable. Troubleshooting is also always easier when considering addresses as opposed to names.

A More Complex Routing Example

In "Routing Table for G" on page 218 we pointed out that the routing table for G is unnecessarily complex. That was true because G's routing table contained references to every network in the environment. It would be much simpler if the routing table for G had routes based on groups of addresses. This can be accomplished via route aggregation and/or through the use of CIDR. CIDR is standardized by RFC 1519.

Route Aggregation and CIDR

Consider Figure 6–11. In this example, G is, once again, the Internet gateway. It is then connected to four routers, that are in turn connected to multiple networks (which may contain other routers). It is apparent from this diagram that G really only needs to know that any packet whose destination IP address has a 10 in the first octet goes to R, 172.16-172.31 in the first two octets goes to S, 192.168.0-192.168.127 in the first three octets goes to X, and 192.168.128-192.168.255 goes to Y. Everything else goes to the Internet. So how do we tell G to operate this way? The answer is to utilize CIDR or, in other words, set the route mask appropriately.

　　We actually already know how to do this based on our discussion of VLSM (see Chapter 4). In short, we need to specify the networks in the following way: 10.0.0.0/8, 172.16.0.0/12 (recall that 172.16.0.0/12 is the supernetwork address representing all networks 172.16.0.0/16 through 172.31.0/16 inclusive), 192.16.0.0/17, and 192.168.128.0/17. The last three networks are examples of supernets. Example 6–30 displays a routing table for G that would accomplish this.

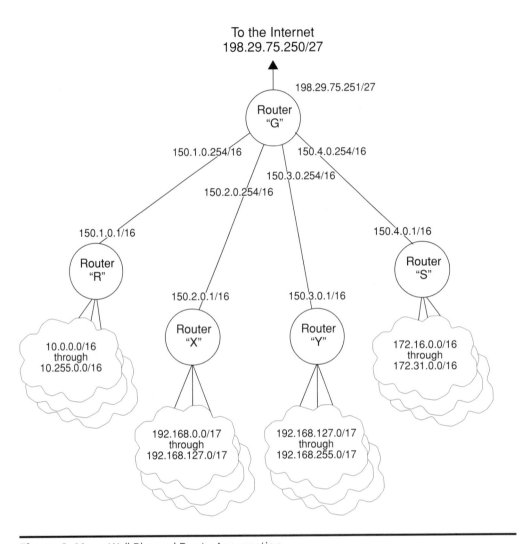

Figure 6–11   Well Planned Route Aggregation

Example 6–30   Routing Table on G for a Well Planned Aggregated Network

```
# route -n
Kernel IP routing table
Destination     Gateway          Genmask            Flags Metric Ref   Use Iface
198.29.75.248   198.29.75.251    255.255.255.248 UG    0      0       0 eth0
150.1.0.0       150.1.0.254      255.255.0.0     UG    0      0       0 eth1
150.2.0.0       150.2.0.254      255.255.0.0     UG    0      0       0 eth2
150.3.0.0       150.3.0.254      255.255.0.0     UG    0      0       0 eth3
150.4.0.0       150.4.0.254      255.255.0.0     UG    0      0       0 eth4
172.16.0.0      150.4.0.1        255.240.0.0     UG    1      0       0 eth4
10.0.0.0        150.1.0.1        255.0.0.0       UG    1      0       0 eth1
192.168.0.0     150.2.0.1        255.255.128.0   UG    1      0       0 eth2
192.168.128.0   150.3.0.1        255.255.128.0   UG    1      0       0 eth3
127.0.0.0       0.0.0.0          255.0.0.0       U     0      0       0 lo
0.0.0.0         198.29.75.250    0.0.0.0         UG    1      0       0 eth0
#
```

Example 6–30 is a Red Hat-like table (we've left out some of the local interface entries for simplicity). Essentially, what we have done with this routing table is aggregate the routes. That is, we've taken the enumerated routes `10.0.0.0/16`, `10.1.0.0/16`, `10.2.0.0/16`, etc., and created one route for `10.0.0.0/8` because all of the packets destined to `10.x.x.x` ($0 \le x \le 255$) go to R as far as G is concerned.

Notice that the route mask entries in Example 6–30 match the prefix notation in Figure 6–11. That is

/8 is `255.0.0.0`

/12 is `255.240.0.0`

/17 is `255.255.128.0`

/27 is `255.255.255.248`

The `192.168.0.0/17`, `192.168.128.0/17`, and `172.16.0.0/12` entries are formally known as CIDR entries. They are also examples of aggregated routes. The entry for `10.0.0.0/8` is not formally a CIDR entry as it is a class A address, but it is an aggregated route. Essentially, we are simply using the route mask as a shorthand way to reference groups of networks.

The important thing to bear in mind is that CIDR (and routing aggregation, generally) is routing based on the route mask, not on any concept of the (sub)network number. In other words, if an entry for `10.0.0.0/8` (route mask `255.0.0.0`) exists in the table, then that means that routing decisions for this entry are made based on the first 8 bits of the destination IP address—if those first 8 bits match decimal 10 (and it's the best match), then this route will be used. It doesn't matter whether or not the actual destination IP address uses the same netmask. The only time the inuse (sub)netmask really matters is at routers that actually have an interface into the network using that (sub)netmask. Furthermore, it should be clear from our examples that, in general, the route mask can be set to any legal value—that is prefix /1 through prefix /254.

At this point, you are probably thinking that Figure 6–11 is so well planned that it's the planning that allows for aggregating the routes. This is true. Route aggregation and CIDR, to be effectively used, require good planning. If your environment is not well planned, then aggregate what you can. Consider, for example, Figure 6–12.

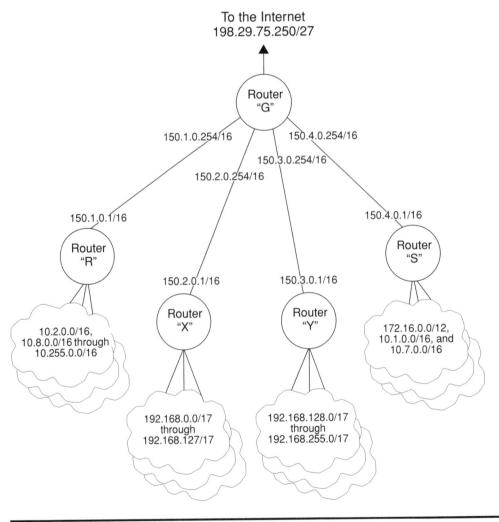

Figure 6–12   Not So Well Planned Route Aggregation

Based on Figure 6–12, the routing tables for G won't be as nice as they were for Figure 6–11. But, we can aggregate some of the routes. Example 6–31 shows the routing table for G as depicted in Figure 6–12. The additions over Example 6–30 are shown in **bold**.

Example 6–31   Routing Table on G for a Not So Well Planned Aggregated Network

```
# route -n
Kernel IP routing table
Destination     Gateway         Genmask          Flags Metric Ref   Use Iface
198.29.75.248   198.29.75.251   255.255.255.248  UG    0      0       0 eth0
150.1.0.0       150.1.0.254     255.255.0.0      UG    0      0       0 eth1
150.2.0.0       150.2.0.254     255.255.0.0      UG    0      0       0 eth2
150.3.0.0       150.3.0.254     255.255.0.0      UG    0      0       0 eth3
150.4.0.0       150.4.0.254     255.255.0.0      UG    0      0       0 eth4
172.16.0.0      150.4.0.1       255.240.0.0      UG    1      0       0 eth4
10.1.0.0        150.4.0.1       255.255.0.0      UG    1      0       0 eth4
10.7.0.0        150.4.0.1       255.255.0.0      UG    1      0       0 eth4
10.0.0.0        150.1.0.1       255.0.0.0        UG    1      0       0 eth1
192.168.0.0     150.2.0.1       255.255.128.0    UG    1      0       0 eth2
192.168.128.0   150.3.0.1       255.255.128.0    UG    1      0       0 eth3
127.0.0.0       0.0.0.0         255.0.0.0        U     0      0       0 lo
0.0.0.0         198.29.75.250   0.0.0.0          UG    1      0       0 eth0
#
```

Note that some of the entries in Example 6–31 are simply more general than others. How does the kernel know which one to use? The answer is that part of the routing algorithm (simply depicted in Figure 6–2 on page 194) is to select the best route. Part of what is meant by best route is the match of the most route masked bits, also known as the *longest* match. So, for example, if G gets a packet with the destination IP address of 10.1.3.17, it will forward that packet to S, not R, because more bits of the route mask match that record. It would be similarly true for any packet destined to 10.7.x.y (x != 1 | 7, $0 \le x, y \le 255$).

All of the routes shown in Examples 6–30 and 6–31 can be added manually using the route command. In Chapter 11, we consider ways of configuring and automating CIDR and route aggregation. We also consider taking advantage of redundancy (for example, suppose routers R, S, X, and Y are interconnected) through automatic updating.

Multicast Routing

We briefly touched on multicasting in the previous two chapters and saw the use of multicast addresses in this chapter with router discovery. With respect to router discovery, only link-local (addresses that will not get routed) multicast addresses are used. For the most part, those are the only types of multicast addresses that we consider in this book. In this section, we consider multicasting from an overview perspective and touch on multicast routing. The details of multicasting implementation are left to other documents.

Linux Multicast Support

The Linux 2.2.x kernels provide multicast sending and receiving support by default. This support is fully IGMPv1 (RFC 1112) compliant and mostly IGMPv2 (RFC 2236) compliant.

If your system does not have multicasting turned on, you will need to rebuild the kernel to support it. See the `Multicast-HOWTO` document for details.

Multicast Applications

All nodes participate in the `224.0.0.1` multicast group. This is the all nodes link-local scope multicast address. You can verify that the nodes in your network are participating in this group with `ping`. Example 6–32 illustrates `ping` `224.0.0.1` from a host on the `172.16.0.0/16` network. The results are that all hosts reply to this `ping` just as if you had `ping`ed the IPv4 broadcast address.

Example 6–32   Using `ping 224.0.0.1`

```
# ping 224.0.0.1
PING 224.0.0.1 (224.0.0.1) from 172.16.22.22 : 56(84) bytes of data.
64 bytes from eeyore (172.16.22.22): icmp_seq=0 ttl=255 time=0.3 ms
64 bytes from 172.16.1.1: icmp_seq=0 ttl=255 time=2.8 ms
64 bytes from wyle (172.16.1.3): icmp_seq=0 ttl=255 time=5052.1 ms
64 bytes from underdog (172.16.1.254): icmp_seq=0 ttl=255 time=5052.7 ms
64 bytes from daffy (172.16.44.11): icmp_seq=0 ttl=255 time=5053.1 ms
64 bytes from beaver (172.16.88.22): icmp_seq=0 ttl=255 time=5053.4 ms
^C
#
```

All other multicast addresses must be *joined*. That is, an application must inform the kernel that the kernel needs to pay attention to a particular multicast address. For example, when a router discovery daemon (like `gated`) is run on a router, then the daemon causes the interfaces on the router to join the `224.0.0.2` all routers group.

Other applications work similarly. When you invoke a multicast application it will cause the kernel to join the appropriate multicast group. There are many multicast applications available on Linux; you can get a list of them, together with links to the source code, at

```
http://www.cs.washington.edu/homes/esler/multicast/#apps
```

Routing Multicast Packets

Routing multicast packets uses the multicast routing algorithm as specified in RFCs 1112 and 2236. This algorithm can be implemented by running the `mrouted` daemon. The `mrouted` daemon is available in source code form from

```
ftp://ftp.parc.xerox.com/pub/net-research/ipmulti/
```

Multicast routing entries are placed in the routing table and the kernel uses them to forward multicast packets to hosts and other routers. Your kernel must be built with IP multicast routing turned on (normally it is turned off).

There are a number of multicast routing table daemons that can be used to propagate multicast routes. For a good discussion of these topics, see *Multicast Networking and Applications* as cited in "For Further Reading" on page 233.

What about IPv6?

IPv6 routing is entirely similar to IPv4 routing when using routing aggregation and CIDR. Routers and nodes simply apply the route mask (the IPv6 prefix) to the destination IPv6 address and check their tables for a match.

There is a bit more formality in the prefix for IPv6 than in IPv4. Recall that we defined unicast and anycast addresses in Chapter 5 and, in particular, defined the components to those IPv6 addresses in "Unicast Addresses" on page 161. The TLA ID, NLA ID, and SLA ID comprise a routing hierarchy in that each of those identifiers is utilized by routers at different levels—TLA ID being the highest and SLA ID the lowest. This approach has the effect of reducing the size of the routing table for each router, somewhat like routing aggregation as we saw in "Route Aggregation and CIDR" on page 225. Reducing the size of the routing table in large, networked environments, such as the Internet, is very important for efficient packet forwarding.

Default Free Routers

In any internetwork, and the Internet is no exception, there must be a router or collection of routers that do not have a default router entry—such a router is called *default free*. Think of these routers as being at the very top of a hierarchy. They must know how to get everywhere else in the hierarchy.

Consider it this way. Suppose that G in Figure 6–12 on page 228 did not have a connection to the Internet. Then it would have no default router and, in particular, it would have to be able to route packets to all connected networks or generate an error message whenever a requested destination did not have a route.

The routing tables for G are of reasonable size because of CIDR and route aggregation—clearly, they would be much larger in the absence of those techniques. Now, consider the Internet with hundreds of thousands of interconnected networks. Its default free routers have very large tables, even with the use of route aggregation and CIDR! The larger the routing table, the more time it takes for a system to search for a match. And this search must be conducted for each packet requiring forwarding!

One of the most significant advantages of IPv6 is that, once deployed, it places an upper limit of 8,192 unicast (or anycast) routing table entries in the default free routers. This is due to the 13-bit size of the TLA ID field (see Chapter 5). This is one of the most significant reasons for migrating to IPv6 in the Internet.

Summary

We covered a lot of material in this chapter. We defined and described routing, routing tables, and the routing algorithm. We defined and looked at the purpose of a default router, described managing the routing tables statically, and introduced the notion of managing the routing tables dynamically through exploring RIPv1 and router discovery.

Yet, all we've really done in this chapter is describe the basics of how a packet gets from point A to point B. There are many more nuances of how that occurs and much of that is discussed in Chapters 11 through 16. But we haven't even begun to discuss what is done with a packet once it arrives at its destination! That's covered beginning with the next chapter.

For Further Reading

Listed below are books and WWW resources that provide further information about the topics discussed in this chapter.

Books

Comer, Douglas E., *Internetworking with TCP/IP Vol I: Principals, Protocols, Architecture*, 3d. Ed., Englewood Cliffs, New Jersey, Prentice Hall, 1995.

Huitema, Christian, *Routing in the Internet*, 2d ed, Upper Saddle River, New Jersey, Prentice Hall PTR, 1999.

Mancill, Tony, *Linux Routers: A Primer for Network Administrators*, Upper Saddle River, New Jersey, Prentice Hall, 2000.

Miller, C. Kenneth, *Multicast Networking and Applications*, Reading, Massachusetts, Addison-Wesley, 1999.

Perlman, Radia, *Interconnections Second Edition: Bridges, Routers, Switches, and Internetworking Protocols*, Reading, Massachusetts, Addison-Wesley, 2000.

Stevens, W. Richard, *TCP/IP Illustrated, Volume 1: The Protocols*, Reading, Massachusetts, Addison-Wesley, 1994.

WWW Resources

You can get a good deal of information about multicasting as well as a number of links to other multicast sites by visiting

```
http://www.cs.washington.edu/homes/esler/multicast/
```

You can get the `mrouted` daemon for multicasting at

```
ftp://ftp.parc.xerox.com/pub/net-research/ipmulti/
```

7

The Transport Layer

The previous six chapters fundamentally describe how packets, transmitted over some medium, move from host A to host B. This and the next chapter describe what is done with packets once they arrive at their destination and how data is encoded for transmission to an ultimate application.

The Transport layer of the TCP/IP stack is responsible for end-to-end connectivity—that is, getting packets to and from the appropriate application. This is accomplished through the use of one of two distinct protocols, UDP or TCP, each of which behaves very differently. There isn't much administrative work to be done at this layer, but understanding what this layer does and how it does it is very important for successful administration of other layers, particularly the Application layer. In this chapter we describe the two protocols, UDP and TCP, their headers and functionality, and some of the kernel tunable parameters that can be set to modify their default behavior.

The Protocols

TCP and UDP are very different in the way they transport data. TCP is a *stateful*, *connection-oriented* protocol, whereas UDP is *stateless* and *connectionless*. The notion of *state* in a protocol is analogous to that of memory. A protocol is said to be stateful if it maintains information about what has been done and what needs to be done next. The concept of connection is analogous to the attachment of a cable to its endpoints. A protocol is said to be connection-oriented if it implements a method to ensure that the endpoints are "attached;" normally, this is accomplished by way of a special type of communication called *acknowledgments*.

A protocol that is both stateful and connection-oriented is said to be *reliable*. This simply means that the protocol is designed to detect communication failures and provide error messaging—it does not mean that applications using the protocol are fail-proof! Protocols that are not stateful and connection-oriented are called *unreliable*. This does not mean that the protocol doesn't work, it simply means that the protocol cannot detect error conditions, cannot assure the delivery of packets, and therefore requires the application to provide that functionality. TCP is an example of a reliable protocol. UDP and IP are examples of unreliable protocols.

Perhaps the best way to describe the two protocols within the transport layer is by way of analogy. TCP is like a telephone call. Suppose that Joe calls Mary. He picks up the phone, inputs Mary's number, hears a ring (as does Mary, presumably), and then Mary picks up the phone, answering by saying "Hello." When Mary says "Hello," she is issuing an implicit acknowledgment of the communication. Upon hearing Mary, Joe responds with something like "Hi, Mary! This is Joe." By responding to Mary's initial "Hello," Joe is implicitly acknowledging the receipt of Mary's communication. Once the acknowledgments have been exchanged, the communication is in a connected, *synchronized* state.

As Joe and Mary proceed with their conversation, they continue to supply acknowledgments (implicitly) by having a coherent discussion. These acknowledgments are used to maintain the connection. Suppose that at one point Joe doesn't hear Mary clearly and says, "What did you say?" At this point, the conversation is *desynchronized*—that is, some data was lost and it has to be retransmitted. Because Joe and Mary maintain state (they're human and have memory), Mary does not need to repeat the entire conversation, she only needs to repeat the last sentence or two. Once she does so, the communication can resynchronize and continue as before. Conceptually, this is how TCP works.

UDP, on the other hand, is like a letter sent by way of the postal service. The letter is written, put in an envelope with an address and stamp on it, and then dropped in a mailbox. There is no connection established in this process. Either the letter reaches its destination or it does not. In fact, we never know whether it reaches its destination or not through this communication method—we only become aware of its arrival (or nonarrival) by virtue of another, distinct communication from one of the two parties involved. There is also no state maintenance in this process—if the letter does not arrive, it must be retransmitted in its entirety. In essence, use of this type of protocol requires that an application (the people involved in sending and receiving the letter in our analogy) preside over receipt of the communication, detection of errors, and initiating other communications to inform the other party of the status of the communication. From our discussion, it should be clear that these two protocols are quite different in the way that they work. This means that the applications which use them must also behave differently. With some applications, the choice of TCP or UDP can be controlled; with most, it cannot. Understanding the behavior of these two protocols significantly enhances the understanding of the various applications that use them. Consequently, we revisit the topic of this chapter at various later points throughout this book.

Service Ports

In order that the Transport layer carry out its purpose (that of getting a packet to the correct application) it writes both a source and destination *port* number in the Transport layer header. This is true for both UDP and TCP (as we see later in this chapter). The port number is not a physical port on the systems involved, but rather a virtual number that gets associated with a particular application or process—these applications or processes are generally known as *services*. Generally, port numbers fall into one of three categories, as defined by IANA/ICANN, and are described in Table 7–1.

We explore the specifics of port number use and meaning in Chapter 8. For the purposes of our discussions in this chapter, we simply need to know that they are used in the Transport layer header to assure delivery to the correct application. We also need to make the following two definitions. The combination of the four items: the source and destination IP addresses from the IP header and the source and destination port numbers from the Transport layer header is called a *socket*.[1] If the Transport layer protocol is TCP, then the socket uniquely identifies a *connection*.

---

1. This definition is made in RFC 793. The term *socket* is perhaps more commonly associated with the Berkeley derived programming interface.

Table 7–1   Port Number Ranges as Assigned by IANA/ICANN

RANGE OF PORT NUMBERS	NAME	DESCRIPTION
0 through 1023	Well known, privileged	Port numbers in this range are assigned to specific services and processes. Processes that bind to ports in this range must have root privilege. The concept of binding to a port is further described in "Services and Ports" on page 267. If used, these ports remain in use while a system is up and running.
1024 through 49151	Registered ports	Port numbers in this range can be registered to a particular service, but there is no root privilege requirement. Use of these ports may be for the duration of system up-time or may be dynamic as described below.
49152 through 65535	Dynamic or private ports	Port numbers in this range are generally allocated dynamically for use during the lifespan of a process.

Now that we have a conceptual overview of the behavior of UDP and TCP, we can describe the details of the two protocols.

User Datagram Protocol

UDP provides no reliability whatsoever. It accepts messages from the Application layer, encapsulates them (into UDP packets), and then passes them on to the Internet layer. UDP does not guarantee delivery and, in fact, has no way to determine whether or not delivery is successful. UDP also does nothing about sequencing of packets—it is quite possible that UDP packets arrive out of order. It is entirely up to the application that uses UDP as its Transport layer protocol to deal with reliability issues. The advantage of this approach is that it reduces overhead both in processing and in consumption of space within the datagram.

Included among the applications that use UDP are DNS (for certain communications), NIS, DHCP, and real-time applications like RealAudio.

UDP is formally standardized by RFC 768. Its simplicity is clear from the RFC (only three pages) and its header. The standard UDP header is only 8 octets. UDP provides an optional checksum that increases the header size by 12 octets, for a maximum size of 20 octets. Figure 7–1 depicts the UDP packet.

The description of the fields shown in Figure 7–1 are clear except for MBZ and Proto. The field labeled MBZ is an 8-bit field that must be zero. The field labeled Proto contains the protocol value for UDP (17). This number is controlled by IANA and ICANN. The "Optional UDP Pseudo Header" only exists when a checksum is computed. The checksum field exists in the formal UDP header but may or may not contain a checksum—computation of the checksum is optional and dictated by the implementation of the application using UDP. Following the UDP header is the data from the Application layer identified as app.data.

Ignoring the "optional" portion of the UDP header for the moment, we see that the UDP header includes the source port number followed by the destination port number. The source port number field in the UDP header can contain the port number of the sending process for the purpose of addressing replies. This field can contain the value of 0, indicating that replies are not forthcoming.

Following the destination port number field is the UDP length field, which consists of the length in octets of the UDP header and application data and, finally, by the UDP checksum. If the checksum is 0, then no checksum is included; otherwise, a non-zero value indicates that the field carries the checksum value of the UDP pseudo header (marked optional in Figure 7–1), the UDP header, and the message.

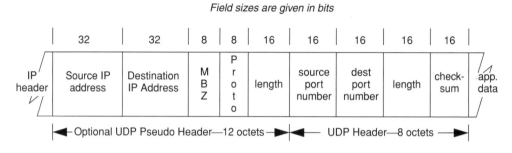

Figure 7–1   UDP Header

Note that the section marked "optional" is the portion of the header that is used only when UDP checksums are enabled. This "optional" portion of the UDP packet is called the *pseudo header*. The information contained within the pseudo header is partially redundant in that it includes the source and destination IP addresses (which already exist within the Internet layer header). The IP addresses within the pseudo header are used to double check that the UDP packet is at the correct host and is also used together with the rest of the pseudo header, the UDP header, and the message for computation of the checksum. Additionally carried in the pseudo header is a protocol number which is 17 for UDP (and found in the file /etc/protocols). The UDP length field in the pseudo header is identical to the UDP length field in the UDP header. If the optional checksum is computed by the sender, then the message will be padded with zeros, if necessary, to ensure that the UDP packet aligns on a 16-bit (2 octet) boundary. Whether or not the optional checksum is computed is driven by the application and cannot be controlled administratively unless the application provides a mechanism to do so.

It is important to note that the application data (data from the Application layer) encapsulated by UDP is not fragmented by UDP. Whatever the size of the data from the Application layer is sent unchanged to the Internet layer by UDP as long as it does not exceed the maximum UDP message size of 65,535 octets. If the message size exceeds the maximum, UDP generates an error and discontinues processing.

As we can see from this brief description, UDP is quite simple. Next, we take a look at TCP, which turns out to be rather complex. Then, we finish the chapter with a short discussion of considering situations under which UDP and TCP are most appropriate.

Transmission Control Protocol

TCP is standardized by RFC 793 with several corrections and clarifications included in RFC 1122. Other RFCs are associated with specific features of TCP and are mentioned when those features are discussed. TCP provides a stateful, connection-oriented, and, therefore, reliable transport mechanism. Where UDP is simple, TCP is complex because it provides these capabilities. TCP provides reliability by incorporating the following capabilities.

- The Application layer sends data to TCP in a stream. Unlike UDP, the application does not need to break up the data into chunks because TCP takes the stream of data and breaks it up into segments for submission to the internet layer.
- Because TCP relies on the lower layers for transmission and the lower layers can be unreliable (as is the case for IP), TCP utilizes *sequence* numbers to order the segments of a stream. Thus, the receiving node can use the sequence numbers to properly order the segments. Duplicate segments can also be identified and discarded in this way.
- TCP expects an acknowledgment for each segment or group of segments. If an acknowledgment is not received within a timeout period, the segment or segments are retransmitted.
- TCP generates a checksum on the header and data. If a recipient receives a segment for which the checksum is incorrect, it discards the segment. The recipient depends upon the sender timeout for retransmission.
- TCP provides flow control. Each end of the communication initially, and perhaps during the communication session, negotiates a maximum amount of data to be sent at one time.
- Each end of a TCP communication can also buffer segments for processing.
- TCP pays no attention to the contents of the data stream. It only reliably transmits the stream.

In the following sections, we consider these capabilities in further detail; however, see either *TCP/IP Illustrated, Volume 1* or *Internetworking with TCP/IP, Volume 1* as referenced in "For Further Reading" on page 264 as well as the appropriate RFCs for definitive details. Let's begin with the TCP header.

The TCP Header

The TCP header is a minimum of 20 octets. If options are used it can be much larger. Figure 7–2 depicts the TCP header.

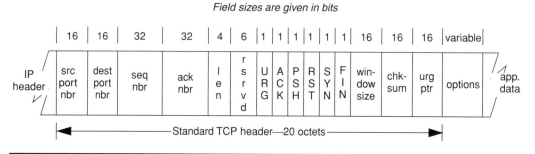

Figure 7–2　TCP Header

The fields shown in Figure 7–2 are defined in Table 7–2.

Table 7–2　Fields of the TCP Header

FIELD	DESCRIPTION
src port nbr	The source port number.
dest port nbr	The destination port number.
seq nbr	The sequence number.
ack nbr	The acknowledgment number. This field is only valid if the ACK bit is set.
len	The length in 32-bit increments of the TCP header. For example, if the length of the TCP header is 20 octets, this field will carry a value of 5.
rsrvd	An unused, reserved field.
URG	The urgent flag. This indicates that the urg ptr field contains valid data.
ACK	The acknowledgment flag. Indicates that a valid acknowledgment is present in the ack nbr field.

Table 7–2   Fields of the TCP Header *(Continued)*

FIELD	DESCRIPTION
PSH	The push flag. This flag tells the recipient to get this data to the application as soon as possible.
RST	The reset flag. This flag indicates that the connection needs to be abnormally terminated.
SYN	The synchronize flag. This flag indicates that sequence numbers need to be synchronized in order to establish or reestablish a connection.
FIN	The finish flag. This flag indicates that the sender has completed sending all data in the stream and is ready to terminate the connection.
window size	Contains the amount of data, in octets, that the receiver is willing to accept. Since this is a 16-bit field, the maximum that can be specified is 65,535 octets. The window scaling option can compensate for this limitation and is described in "TCP Options" on page 244.
chksum	Contains the checksum of the TCP segment (header and data).
urg ptr	This field is only used when the URG flag is set. It contains an offset which, when added to the sequence number, yields the sequence number of the last chunk of urgent data. An example of urgent data is a ctrl-C in a telnet session.
options	The options field can contain one or more options. There are a variety of available options, some of which are discussed in "TCP Options" on page 244.

The TCP header consists of identification and control information. The source and destination ports carried in the header ensure that the TCP segment reaches the correct application and/or is associated with the correct connection. The seq nbr field holds the sequence number which is used to identify where the segment fits in the overall data stream from the sender. The acknowledgment number in the ack nbr field, when used, is the sequence number of the next segment expected by the sender. The `len` and `rsrvd` fields are fully described in Table 7–2.

The TCP bit flags, URG, ACK, PSH, RST, SYN, and FIN, are used for controlling the connection. If a flag field contains a value of 1, then the flag is set; if 0, it is not set. They are briefly described in Table 7–2 and further detailed throughout the rest of this chapter. The `window size` field is defined in the table and is addressed again at various points in this chapter. The `urg ptr` field is also defined in Table 7–2. We discuss some of the TCP options next.

TCP Options

RFC 793, the original RFC for TCP, specifies three valid options. Other options have been proposed over the years with three of them enjoying common use and full support by Linux kernel series 2.2.x. Options are defined by an octal value (the leftmost 8 bits of the options field) known as a *kind*. These six options are defined in Table 7–3, which lists the kind value, the RFC(s) that standardize them, and the option name and description.

Table 7–3   TCP Header Option Kinds

KIND	RFC(S)	OPTION NAME AND DESCRIPTION
0x0	793	End of options list indicator. This is used at the end of all options in the options field to indicate that the list is complete.
0x1	793	No operation (NOP). This can be used to separate options. It is not required and may be used to align word boundaries between options.
0x2	793	Maximum segment size (MSS). This option is used to advertise the largest segment (TCP header and data) that will be accepted by the sender. This option is only set in a segment in which the SYN flag is set. This option is followed by a length field that indicates the number of octets contained in the payload of the option.

Table 7–3   TCP Header Option Kinds *(Continued)*

KIND	RFC(S)	OPTION NAME AND DESCRIPTION
0x3	1072, 1185, 1323	Window scale. This option carries a scaling factor for the window size. It can only be sent in a segment with the SYN flag set. Both sender and receiver must be able to utilize scaling, even if the scale factor used is different. The scale factor must be a power of 2 and is applied directly to the window size specified in the TCP header to create a larger window size. This option is commonly used in high speed networks such as Gigabit Ethernet.
0x4 and 0x5	1072, 2018	Selective acknowledgment (SACK). This option is used to acknowledge those segments that have been received, making it easier to identify which segments within a stream were not received and therefore which must be retransmitted. A kind value of 0x4 is used in conjunction with a SYN segment to indicate that the SACK option is available—this is called the SACK-Permitted option. A kind value of 0x5 indicates that the SACK option contains a selective acknowledgment—this option is called the TCP SACK option. This option is discussed further in "The Sliding Window, Flow Control, and SACK" on page 252.
0x8	1323	Timestamp. This option is used to add a timestamp to each segment. In this way, segments with identical sequence numbers can be differentiated; for example, if a segment is seriously delayed and contains a sequence number that fits within a current session to which it does not belong, the timestamp can be used to determine its invalidity with respect to the existing session. There are two possible timestamps included as four octet values each. The first is called *TSval* and is the current value of the clock on the system of the sender; the second is called *TSecr* and is only valid (nonzero) if the ACK flag is set. It contains the value of TSval of the segment being acknowledged.

Now that the TCP header and options are defined, we consider the operation of TCP in the next several sections, beginning with the *opening three-way handshake*.

Initial Connection Three-Way Handshake

When a TCP connection is initiated, it is done so by a user or process invoking an application that is built over TCP. Examples include telnet and FTP. So, for example, when a user on the host `pyramid` executes

```
foghorn% telnet dsl-golden
```

that user is causing a TCP connection to be established between two systems, `foghorn` and `dsl-golden`. In this case, the system `foghorn` is called the *client* and the system `dsl-golden` is called the *server* (the client/server model is discussed in Chapter 8). After the user executes the telnet command above, that user expects to see a login prompt such as that shown in Example 7–1. Line numbers are added for clarity.

Example 7–1   Login Prompt via `telnet` Application

```
1 Trying 192.111.23.154...
2 Connected to dsl-golden.
3 Escape character is '^]'.
4
5 Red Hat Linux release 6.1 (Cartman)
6 Kernel 2.2.12-20 on an i586
7 login:
```

Note that at line 1 of Example 7–1, the `telnet` application tells us that it is trying to connect to the IP address of `dsl-golden`. The next thing we see is line 2 telling us that the connection has been established. There is a lot that goes on between these two lines that are not reported by the telnet application. In particular, TCP goes through a process known as the *three-way handshake* to establish the connection. Let's take a look at that process.

When the `telnet` command (or any other application that uses TCP) is invoked, the TCP three-way handshake procedure is initiated and is depicted in Figure 7–3. The first TCP segment of the three-way handshake is a segment sent by the client to the server with the SYN flag set, an initial sequence number, A, (shown as SN=A, in the diagram), and an advertisement of available options. The sequence number is arbitrarily chosen. Upon sending this segment,

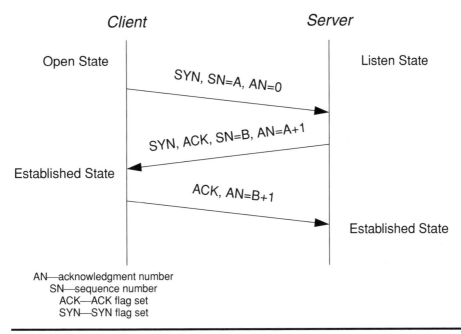

Client   Server

Open State   Listen State

SYN, SN=A, AN=0

SYN, ACK, SN=B, AN=A+1

Established State

ACK, AN=B+1

Established State

AN—acknowledgment number
SN—sequence number
ACK—ACK flag set
SYN—SYN flag set

Figure 7–3   TCP Three-Way Opening Handshake

the client starts a timer. If the timer times out before the client gets a response to the first segment, it will retransmit the segment. There is no acknowledgment in this initial segment (indicated by AN=0 and the absence of ACK). This segment is frequently called a *SYN segment* or *SYN packet*.

Once the server receives the SYN segment, it responds by sending a *SYN/ACK segment* (sometimes also called a *SYN/ACK packet*). The SYN/ACK segment has both the SYN and ACK flags set. The server sends an arbitrarily chosen sequence number, B (indicated by SN=B in Figure 7–3), and increments by 1 the sequence number sent by the client and uses this value as the acknowledgment number (indicated as AN=A+1 in the diagram). In this way, the server is telling the client that the next sequence number it expects is "A+1." Also, since the server sends its own sequence number to the client, two distinct sequence number series are maintained; thus, TCP can accommodate full duplex communications without confusion. Once the server sends the SYN/ACK segment, it starts a timer which upon expiration will cause the server to retransmit the packet.

Upon receipt of the SYN/ACK segment from the server, the client enters the "established state." This means that the client has successfully connected with the server. The client responds to the SYN/ACK segment by sending an acknowledgment packet to the server with the acknowledgment number set and the sequence number received from the server incremented by 1 (shown as AN=B+1 in the diagram). Again, this acknowledgment number also serves the purpose of informing the server that "B+1" is the next sequence number the client expects. Once the server receives this acknowledgment, the server enters the established state. At this point, line 2 of Example 7–1 on page 246 is displayed on the client.

We explore these packets further by looking at the output captured by Ethereal. Figure 7–4 shows Ethereal having captured the three-way handshake. In the upper pane of the Ethereal window, the first SYN segment is highlighted, showing some of its details in the middle pane and the contents of the packet in

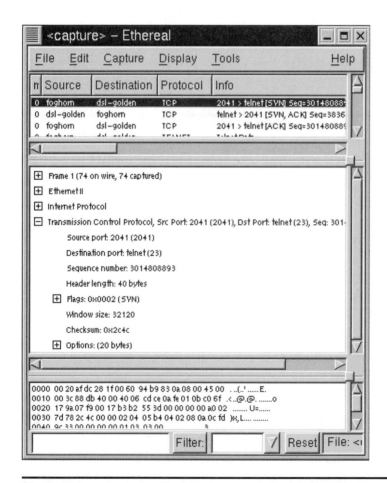

Figure 7–4   Capturing the TCP Three-Way Handshake with Ethereal

the lower pane. In the upper pane, the second and third packets of the three-way handshake are also visible. This screen capture is shown for illustrative purposes throughout the remainder of the chapter; we will largely focus on the middle pane of Ethereal so that we can examine the details contained in the TCP header. We look at the details in the TCP header using Ethereal to view each of the three packets of the three-way handshake in Figures 7–5, 7–6, and 7–7.

Figure 7–5 shows the SYN segment transmitted by the client (part 1 of the three-way handshake). The sequence number selected by the client is 3014808893. Note

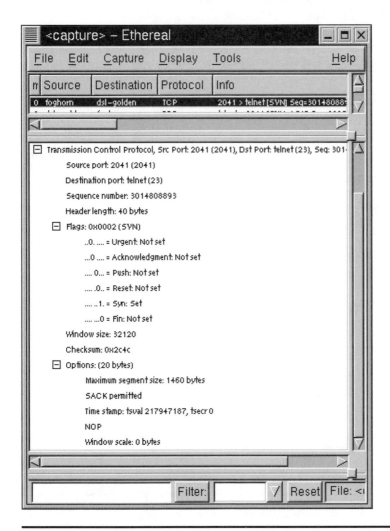

Figure 7–5   Part 1 of the Three-Way Handshake: The SYN Segment

that Ethereal reports that only the SYN flag is set. The window size is set to 32120 octets. Under "Options: (20 bytes)," notice that the client is advertising a maximum segment size of 1460 octets, it allows SACK, but does not provide a scaling factor for increasing the window size (but the option is turned on). The `tsval` option contains a timestamp, but the `tsecr` field is 0 because this segment does not have the ACK flag set. The "NOP" is used to pad out the field to a word boundary.

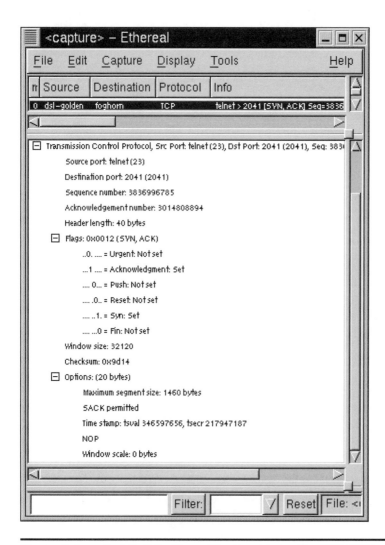

Figure 7–6   Part 2 of the Three-Way Handshake: The SYN/ACK Segment

Figure 7–6 shows an Ethereal capture of part 2 of the three-way handshake: the SYN/ACK segment. As expected, both the SYN and ACK flags are set. The arbitrary sequence number chosen by this server is 3836996785. Note that the acknowledgment number here is 3014808894, which is one more than the sequence number of the initial SYN segment (see Figure 7–5). The server also advertises its window size (not scale factor, but scaling is supported), its MSS, and that it allows SACK. Note in the "Timestamp" field, it writes its timestamp in `tsval` and because the ACK flag is set, it sets `tsecr` to the value previously received (compare this to `tsval` in Figure 7–5).

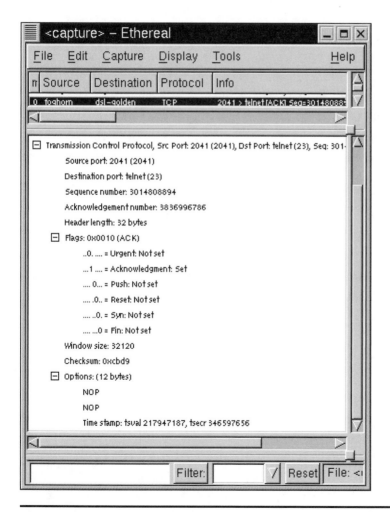

Figure 7–7   Part 3 of the Three-Way Handshake: The Client ACK

Figure 7–7 shows the Ethereal capture of part 3 of the three-way handshake. This is the acknowledgment from the client. Compare the sequence number here with that of the acknowledgment number shown in Figure 7–6 to see that they match as expected. Further note that the acknowledgment number here reflects an increment of 1 over the SYN/ACK segment sent by the server—again this represents the sequence number that the client expects to see in the next segment from the server. Only the ACK flag is set and therefore the `tsecr` field contains the `tsval` from the SYN/ACK segment (compare to Figure 7–6).

Continuing Communications

Once the three-way handshake is successfully completed, the client and server will exchange segments containing data. Initially, the data carried is usually authentication information for login purposes. Once the application login (if it uses one) is established, the client and server can exchange data such as an `ls` command through a `telnet` session or a `get` command through an FTP session. These communications proceed through the send and acknowledge process similar to that described for the three-way handshake. The difference between acknowledgment requirements of the initial three-way handshake and ongoing communications is essentially that the initial three-way handshake requires an ACK segment prior to proceeding to the next step, whereas most post connection operations do not (for example, the formal close operation, described in "Closing a Connection" on page 255, requires a particular sequence of that similar to the initial three-way handshake). TCP utilizes a *sliding window* mechanism to reduce delays and also to assist in flow control as described in the next section.

TCP also implements a keep-alive mechanism. If no data is exchanged between two ends of a TCP connection for, by default, three hours, then the two ends will exchange ACK segments to verify that each node is still up and running. Many applications will timeout prior to this three-hour limit. The three-hour time period between keep-alives is controlled by a tunable kernel parameter and is discussed in "TCP Tunable Kernel Parameters" on page 261.

The Sliding Window, Flow Control, and SACK

Under normal operation, TCP expects an acknowledgment for each segment sent. Our description of the initial three-way handshake emphasized this mechanism. During post connection communications, however, if every sent segment required an acknowledgment before the next segment could be sent, then substantial network delays would be incurred. Consequently, TCP implements a sliding window scheme to address this issue.

The basic sliding window mechanism works as follows. Suppose that a sender knows that the window size for the recipient is 16384 octets, based on the most recent window size advertisement in an acknowledgment segment from the recipient. The sender will then send enough segments to fill this window before it must receive an acknowledgment for the first segment. Suppose that all of the segments will be 1460 octets in size; then the sender will transmit 11 segments before it expects an acknowledgment for the first of the 11 segments. Figure 7–8 illustrates.

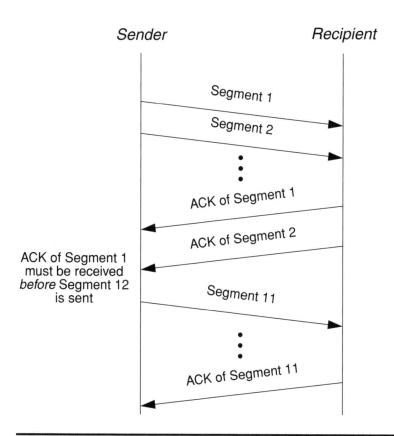

Figure 7–8   Window Size Acknowledgments

Once the ACK of the first segment has been received, the window *slides* one segment—that is, the ACK for the second segment must be received before the thirteenth segment will be sent. And on it goes; the window slides for each ACK received. On the other hand, each ACK from the recipient will contain a window size in the header. This window size can vary (usually depending on the available buffer size of the receiving system). Thus, if the sender gets an ACK with a smaller window size, it will adjust the number of segments that fit in the window accordingly and suspend sending segments until the ACKs have caught up. This offers one form of flow control. The window size can also be increased by the recipient, in which case the sender will increase the number of segments it sends before expecting an ACK.

The sliding window scheme is very useful but doesn't address two basic issues. First, it is possible that one of the segments isn't received by the recipient. Second, it is possible that due to network congestion (that is, a reduction in the capacity of the network not directly related to the communicating nodes, such as a router becoming too busy to handle the rate of flow of traffic), the rate of transmission needs to decrease in order to avoid a lot of retransmissions. The first issue can be handled by regular TCP ACKs or by SACKs and is discussed in the next section.

The second potential problem is handled by a number of algorithms described in RFC 2581 and largely based on round trip times (RTT) measured over the segment sent to ACK received events. In part, TCP uses RTTs to determine what timeouts to use before retransmitting a given segment. In this way, TCP can dynamically slow its retransmission rate in response to a congested network and control the overall flow rate of segments. The algorithms used to implement this capability are fairly complex. The details of these algorithms are standardized by RFC 2581, although current series 2.2.x kernels are compliant with its predecessor, RFC 2001. The references cited in "For Further Reading" on page 264 also provide a more detailed discussion of this issue.

Acknowledgments and Selective Acknowledgments

Consider the example given in Figure 7–8 on page 253. Suppose that of the eleven segments, segments 3 and 4 do not arrive at the recipient node, but the remaining segments do arrive. When the recipient receives segment 2, it sends an acknowledgment with an acknowledgment number matching the sequence number of segment 3. It does this because it expects that to be the next sequence number. When segment 5 arrives, the recipient sends an acknowledgment with an acknowledgment number that still matches the sequence number of segment 3. The same is true for all subsequent segments that the recipient receives. This is due to the fact that the recipient is still expecting to receive segment 3. TCP only provides a way to positively acknowledge what has been received; there is no way to indicate what has not been received. This type of acknowledgment is known as *cumulative*.

At this point the sender will either need to retransmit segment 3 and 4 or, if the lost packets cannot be determined by the sender (which is often the case), retransmit segments 3 through 11 inclusive. Clearly, the latter scenario of having to retransmit segments that have already been received is inefficient. The solution to this problem is to use selective acknowledgments via the SACK option. This option can only be used if both sender and recipient support the option and advertised that fact in the initial three-way handshake.

If the SACK option is available (as it is in series 2.2.x Linux kernels), then a recipient can positively acknowledge the precise segments that have been received by putting this information in the SACK option field. This option is particularly useful for systems experiencing large throughput or using large window sizes. SACK is standardized by RFC 2018. Additionally, there are extensions to the basic SACK mechanism recently proposed in RFC 2883.

The RST Flag

Normally, when a TCP connection closes, an orderly disconnection process proceeds as described in the next section. However, abnormal conditions, such as a link going down temporarily, can cause two nodes to enter an unstable state. The TCP RST flag is used to terminate a connection when an abnormal situation arises. When one node sends an RST segment to the other node, the recipient passes the reset event to the application. Most applications will then flush all buffers and immediately terminate the connection.

Closing a Connection

When a TCP application terminates or receives a termination command, TCP goes through a formal closure process known as the *four-way handshake*. This procedure is illustrated in Figure 7–9. Initially, the application receives a termination signal from a user or process. Either side of the connection can initiate

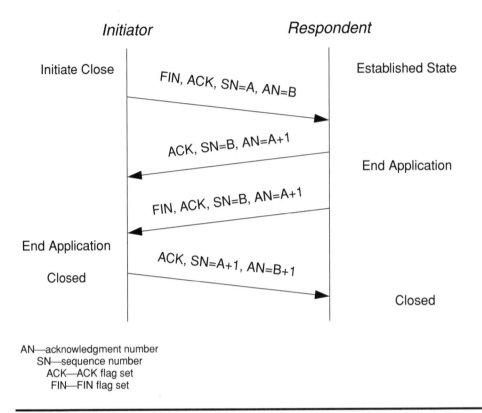

Figure 7–9   TCP Four-Way Handshake

the close (hence, "Initiator" in Figure 7–9). The application then sends an initial segment with the FIN and ACK flags set. As with other TCP communications, the sequence number has been incremented by 1 since the last segment was sent (shown as "SN=A" in Figure 7–9), and the acknowledgment number is set to what the client expects as the next sequence number from the server (shown as "AN=B" in the diagram). The server responds by acknowledging the FIN segment with a single ACK segment. Then, the server sends a termination signal to the application and sends a FIN segment. Finally, the client acknowledges the FIN segment from the server to complete the close. The sequence and acknowledgment numbers are incremented as previously described.

As with the initial three-way handshake, we look at each of the four segments in the four-way handshake by examining the middle pane of the Ethereal capture in Figures 7–10, 7–11, 7–12, and 7–13.

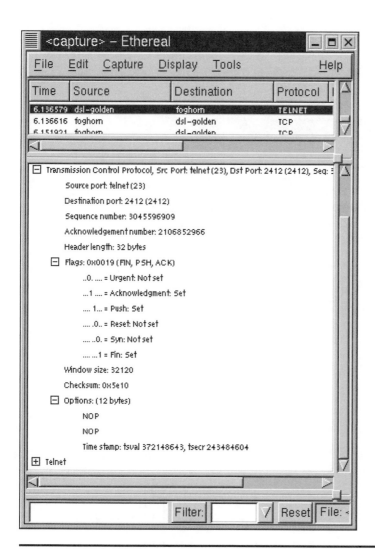

Figure 7–10   Part 1 of the Four-Way Handshake: The Initial FIN Segment

Figure 7–10 displays the details of the initial FIN segment sent by the initiator of the closing of the connection. Note that the PSH flag is set in addition to the FIN and ACK flags. The PSH flag indicates that this segment should be processed as soon as possible.

Figure 7–11 shows the ACK of the prior FIN. Note that the sequence and acknowledgment numbers are set as expected based on the FIN segment in Figure 7–10.

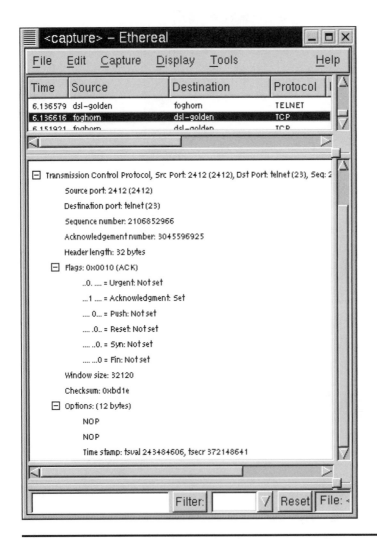

Figure 7–11   Part 2 of the Four-Way Handshake: The First ACK Segment

Figure 7–12 depicts the second FIN segment. Note that the acknowledgment number is the same as the prior ACK. This is due to the fact that this system still expects that to be the sequence number of the next segment from the initiator.

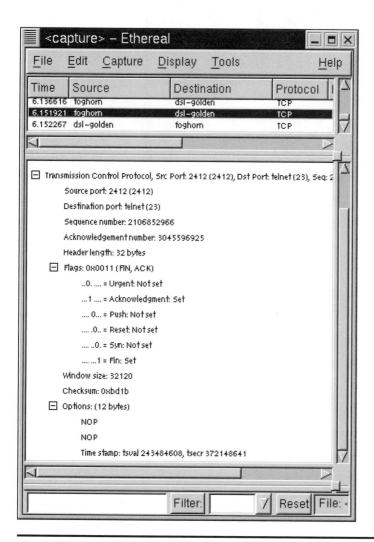

Figure 7–12   Part 3 of the Four-Way Handshake: The Second FIN Segment

Figure 7–13 shows the final acknowledgment.

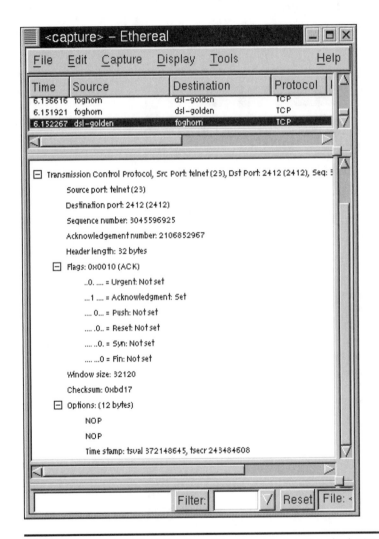

Figure 7–13   Part 4 of the Four-Way Handshake: The Final ACK Segment

TCP Tunable Kernel Parameters

The Linux kernel incorporates a number of kernel parameters that can be modified to change the behavior of TCP. Prior to this section, we have discussed the default behavior of the Linux 2.2.x series kernel. These parameters, like all dynamically tunable kernel parameters, are maintained in the /proc filesystem. For the TCP parameters, they are all found in /proc/sys/net/ipv4/. The values contained in the files within this directory can be manipulated directly or through the use of the sysctl(2) and/or sysctl(8) interface. Table 7–4 lists the most significant kernel tunable parameters associated with TCP, their function, and potential reasons for modifying them, where appropriate.

Table 7–4   TCP Kernel Tunable Parameters

FILE IN /PROC/SYS/NET/IPV4	DESCRIPTION
tcp_fin_timeout	Specifies the number of seconds to wait for the final FIN segment in a four-way close operation. The default is 180 seconds.
tcp_keepalive_probes	Maximum TCP keep-alive probes to send before dropping the connection. The default is 9.
tcp_keepalive_time	Specifies the number of seconds after no data has been transmitted over a connection before a keep-alive ACK segment is sent. The default is 10800 seconds (three hours).
tcp_sack	Enables the RFC 2018 SACK option. Enabled by default (file contains "1"). This is a performance enhancing option that under normal operations should be enabled. To disable: cat "0" > /proc/sys/net/ipv4/tcp_sack.

Table 7–4   TCP Kernel Tunable Parameters *(Continued)*

FILE IN /PROC/SYS/NET/IPV4	DESCRIPTION
`tcp_stdurg`	By default, most TCP implementations are not compliant with the RFC 793 definition of the urgent pointer. Most implementations set the urgent pointer to the first octet of data after the urgent data while RFC 793 specifies that it should point to the last octet of urgent data. This parameter is disabled by default. It can be enabled with `cat "1" > /proc/sys/net/ipv4/tcp_stdurg,` but this will lead to problems with interoperability with other operating systems that do not have this functionality.

`tcp_timestamps`	Enables the RFC 1323 timestamp option. This parameter is enabled by default and is useful in that it provides additional information for segment identification (see "TCP Options" on page 244). On the other hand, turning this option off can lead to significant performance improvements on heavily used servers like web servers. To disable:
	`cat "0" > /proc/sys/net/ipv4/`
	`tcp_timestamps.`

`tcp_window_scaling`	Enables the RFC 1323 window scaling option. This option is enabled by default. It provides performance enhancements to high speed and low latency links. To disable:
	`cat "0" > /proc/sys/net/ipv4/`
	`tcp_window_scaling.`

Table 7–4   TCP Kernel Tunable Parameters *(Continued)*

FILE IN /PROC/SYS/NET/IPV4	DESCRIPTION
`tcp_retries1`	Specifies the number of retries made in answer to a SYN or SYN/ACK segment before failing. The default is 7. This option has potential security ramifications with respect to DoS attacks. See the next section for further information.
`tcp_retries2`	Specifies the number of retries made in an established connection before forcibly terminating the connection. The default is 15.
`tcp_syn_retries`	Specifies the number of times an initial SYN segment is sent to a remote host in an attempt to establish a connection before giving up. The default is 10.

TCP Security Issues

There are a great many security issues associated with TCP, including SYN flooding (sending large numbers of SYN segments to a node and ignoring the SYN/ACK responses), falsifying TCP communications, and hijacking TCP connections. Discussing these issues requires at least a good portion of a book and fortunately these types of attacks are reasonably well documented. The following three books each provide a good discussion of this topic.

Anonymous, *Maximum Security: A Hacker's Guide to Protecting Your Internet Site and Network*, Indianapolis, Indiana, Sams.net, 1997.

Atkins, Derek, et al., *Internet Security: Professional Reference*, Indianapolis, Indiana, New Riders, 1996.

Klander, Lars, *Hacker Proof: The Ultimate Guide to Network Security*, Las Vegas, Nevada, Jamsa Press, 1997.

A very good resource for security issues in general is

```
http://www.securityfocus.org/
```

which among other things is the home of the Bugtraq mailing list.

Use of TCP versus UDP

The implementation differences between TCP and UDP should make it fairly clear under what circumstances each should be used. Generally, any application that is time critical or one that makes use of short communications (a few packets or less) benefit from the lack of overhead implemented with UDP—in short, UDP is faster for these types of applications. Although faster, using UDP means that some packets will be lost and that must be accounted for by applications that use UDP. Real-time applications that provide audio and video over the Internet are common examples of UDP.

TCP, on the other hand, is used by applications for which the delivery of data is critical. Most interactive sessions, such as `telnet`, `ftp`, and `rlogin`, use TCP. Whenever data delivery time frames are of little or no importance, TCP is often the proper solution.

There are some applications that can make use of both protocols. Usually, such use is for different purposes. For example, both NIS and DNS are designed to use UDP and TCP. In both cases the default behavior is to use UDP for short communications and TCP for longer data transfers. NFSv3 and NFSv4 (see Chapter 10) give the administrator the ability to select which underlying protocol is used. In the case of NFS, the purpose of making the choice of UDP or TCP selectable is to permit the administrator to fine tune the performance of NFS under a variety of different circumstances.

Summary

In addition to describing the purpose of the Transport layer, this chapter takes an introductory look at the two Transport layer protocols UDP and TCP. We established the fact that these two protocols differ greatly and pave the way for our discussions of the applications that use them in subsequent chapters.

For Further Reading

Comer, Douglas E., *Internetworking with TCP/IP Vol I: Principals, Protocols, Architecture*, 3d ed., Englewood Cliffs, New Jersey, Prentice Hall, 1995.
Stevens, W. Richard, *TCP/IP Illustrated, Volume 1: The Protocols*, Reading, Massachusetts, Addison-Wesley, 1994.

8

The Application Layer

Applications within the Application layer of the TCP/IP stack are programs that take advantage of the functionality of the lower four layers of the stack. As we have seen in the previous chapters, the lower four layers deal with identifying the appropriate application, routing to the appropriate end location, and generating the proper signals. All of the functionality in these lower four layers is managed internally by the kernel, kernel modules, and/or device drivers, as well as the requisite hardware. Applications, on the other hand, are managed outside the kernel by user processes.

In this chapter, we describe the enabling aspects of the Application layer, including inetd, xinetd, and the portmapper. Additionally, we consider the TCP_wrappers utility which is used to enhance the security of a networked system. We also look at the general way in which network application behave. To this end, our discussion begins with the client-server model.

The Client-Server Model

The client-server model is a generic representation of the way in which many network oriented applications operate.[1] A *server* is any application that provides

---

1. Some network applications, such as routed and router discovery, can and often issue broadcast and/or multicast messages which require no response and, therefore, such types of communications do not fall into the client-server model. On the other hand, both routed and router discovery, as is discussed in Chapter 11, can operate in query-response mode, in which case the client-server model applies.

some resource, called a *service*. Normally, the service is made available over a network. Almost all servers are run as daemon processes.[2] A *client* is any application which issues a request for a service provided by a server. It is not uncommon to generally refer to the node on which one or more server applications run as simply a server. Often, systems that predominantly run a particular server are called that specific server type. For instance, a system that predominantly provides FTP services is called an FTP server. Similarly, the node running one or more client applications is often referred to as a client. Normally, the use of these terms is clear from the context in which it is discussed.

The *client-server model*, then, describes the interaction between a client and a server. Essentially, the interaction is as follows: A client makes a request of the server and waits for a response. A server, upon receiving the request, responds to the client request. The server application, or a program acting on its behalf, must always be running and waiting for a client request—it is also said that the server is *listening*. Applications that operate in this way are known as *client-server applications*. Often, the server component is referred to as the *server-side*; the client component as the *client-side*. For example, FTP is a client-server application. The server-side application is `in.ftpd` and the client-side application is `ftp`.

A server application processes client requests in one of two ways. The first way is known as *direct* or *iterative*. A direct server application runs all of the time listening to a particular port number. When a client request arrives at that port number, the server processes the request and then responds to the client. The server then resumes listening. Server applications of this type include `gated`, `routed`, and router discovery. Figure 8–1 depicts this type of server.

The other type of server application is called *indirect* or *concurrent*. An indirect server application, upon receiving a client request, starts an independent server application that supplies the requested service (based on port number) to satisfy the client's request. The indirect server application, after starting the second server application, resumes listening for client requests. This second server application runs as long as is necessary to process the client's request. Once completed, the second server application terminates. An example of an indirect server is `inetd` or `xinetd`, also known as internet *superservers*. These servers can invoke such applications as `telnet`, FTP, and SSH. Figure 8–2 illustrates the indirect server.

---

2. A daemon process is a process that runs in the background and answers requests.

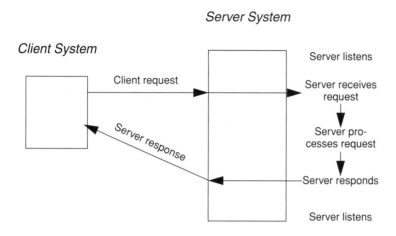

Figure 8–1   Direct Server

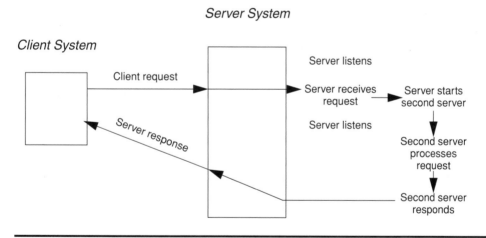

Figure 8–2   Indirect Server

Services and Ports

We introduced port numbers in Chapter 7, and in particular defined the purpose of port number ranges in Table 7–1 on page 238. Here, let's take a closer look at the relationship of port numbers to the services they represent. We begin by repeating Table 7–1 here as Table 8–1.

When a server application is started on a system it *binds* to at least one port. One way of describing this is, when the server application starts, it becomes a

Table 8–1   Port Number Ranges as Assigned by IANA/ICANN

RANGE OF PORT NUMBERS	NAME	DESCRIPTION
0 through 1023	Well known, privileged	Port numbers in this range are assigned to specific services and processes that bind to ports in this range must have root privilege. The concept of binding to a port is further described in this section. If used, these ports remain in use while a system is up and running.
1024 through 49151	Registered ports	Port numbers in this range can be registered to a particular service, but there is no root privilege requirement. Use of these ports may be for the duration of system up-time or may be dynamic—that is, used for the duration of the running of the application (or process).
49152 through 65535	Dynamic or private ports	Port numbers in this range are generally allocated dynamically for use during the lifespan of a process.

user process on the system and is assigned a unique process identifier (PID) by the kernel. The kernel also associates the application's socket (and protocol) with the PID. In this way, any incoming client requests to the application's port number is passed to the process with the associated PID by the Transport layer. Another way of describing this mechanism is to say that the server listens to the port number (or numbers) to which it is bound. Note that the indirect servers, inetd and xinetd, bind to many ports, as we see in the next section.

Any server that binds to a privileged port (0 through 1023) must run as root. Servers that bind to other ports (1024 and up) can run as any user for the purpose of binding to the port. Client applications normally utilize unprivileged ports for the purpose of establishing a socket or connection (see Chapter 7 for definitions of socket and connection). Usually, there is no client requirement for a specific port as long as it is unique on its system. Client port numbers are also only used for the duration of the session with the server. Once the session terminates, the client releases the port number. These types of port numbers are called *dynamic* or *ephemeral*. Note that certain client applications, such as `rlogin` and SSH, utilize privileged dynamic ports by default.

The Linux operating system associates port numbers with services in the `/etc/services` file. Example 8–1 shows a portion of a typical `/etc/services` file on a Linux system.

Example 8–1   A Portion of the `/etc/services` File

```
<lots of the file removed>
ftp-data    20/tcp
ftp         21/tcp
fsp         21/udp      fspd
ssh         22/tcp                  # SSH Remote Login Protocol
ssh         22/udp                  # SSH Remote Login Protocol
telnet      23/tcp
domain      53/tcp      nameserver# name-domain server
domain      53/udp      nameserver
<lots of the file removed>
```

Each line in the `/etc/services` file constitutes a record. The syntax of each record is

```
service_name    port_number/protocol    alias_name
```

where `service_name` is the name of the service, `port_number` is the port number associated with the service, `protocol` is a valid protocol listed in `/etc/protocols` (and is normally either `tcp` or `udp`), and `alias_name` is another name by which the service is known. Multiple aliases can appear in a white-space (spaces or tabs) separated list. Comments can appear at the end of any record by preceding it with `#`.

Notice that there are often two entries for a particular service—one for UDP and one for TCP. IANA/ICANN, the authority for registered port numbers in the `/etc/services` file, specifically states that a given service that can operate over either protocol be assigned the same port number. For instance, Example 8–1 shows two entries for the service `domain`. This is the DNS service. Certain DNS client-side requests use UDP while others use TCP. The DNS server-side will operate over the protocol requested by the client or return an error message.

NOTE

It is very important to note that just because a service record appears in `/etc/services` does not mean that the service is available! Either the server application supporting that service must be running as a direct server, or an indirect server must be running that knows how to start a server to support the given service. Although records in `/etc/services` are required (for instance, with `inetd`), generally, the `/etc/services` file can be thought of as a convenient database for associating names to port numbers.

Indirect Servers: `inetd`, `xinetd`, and `portmap`

While some services are provided by a server daemon that runs all the time (such as `named` and `gated`), many commonly used services are invoked only when requested. The vast majority of these services are started by either `inetd` or `xinetd`. There are a few common applications that are started and/or controlled by the `portmap` daemon (also called the *portmapper*). The portmapper is responsible for client-server applications that use the remote procedure call (RPC) library, originally developed by Sun Microsystems. We explore the configuration of these daemons throughout the remainder of this chapter. In this section, we take a conceptual look at how these daemons operate.

The `inetd` and `xinetd` Daemons

From the user perspective, the `inetd` and `xinetd` daemons provide the same functionality. Each daemon, when started (usually at boot-time), reads a configuration file (`/etc/inetd.conf` for `inetd` and `/etc/xinetd.conf` for `xinetd`) that lists all of the services and their associated server daemons. For each service found in the configuration file, the daemon will bind to the associated port and listen for requests on that port. When a request to one of the bound ports arrives, `inetd` or `xinetd` (whichever one has bound to the port) invokes the server found in the configuration file for that port number.

Let's consider an example in which a server `topcat` is running `inetd`. The client `beauregard` requests the service `telnet` (port 23) from `topcat`. Figure 8–3 illustrates.

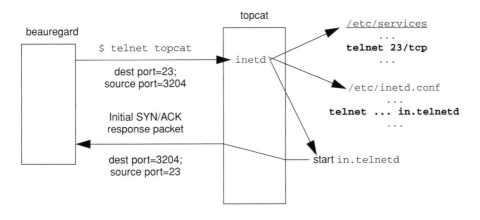

Figure 8–3   inetd Flow of Events

In this example, a user on beauregard executes the client-side application telnet to the host topcat. The telnet client uses port 23 as the destination port and is assigned an available port (by the kernel) for its source port (3204 in this case). The source port will be used for the duration of the connection. The initial request is received by the inetd daemon on topcat. The inetd daemon depends on two configuration files, /etc/services and /etc/inetd.conf. The /etc/services file tells inetd which service is associated with port 23 (telnet), and the /etc/inetd.conf file tells inetd that the in.telnetd daemon is the server-side program for the telnet service. Once inetd identifies that in.telnetd is the server, it starts one copy of that service. Note that many copies of in.telnetd can run simultaneously. The in.telnetd daemon then proceeds with the TCP three-way handshake (see Chapter 7). It may be obvious, but notice nonetheless, that the destination and source port numbers reverse depending upon which system is sending packets.

Historically, inetd has provided the superserver service for Linux and UNIX. The xinetd daemon provides similar functionality with greater flexibility and more security. xinetd ships with SuSE 6.4 and is the default superserver for Red Hat 7.0. It is likely that xinetd will eventually replace inetd as the superserver in all Linux distributions.

Both inetd and xinetd are discussed in more detail later in this chapter.

The `portmap` Daemon and RPC

RPC-based client-server applications are characterized by the following basic features.

1. All data is converted to the external data representation (XDR) format before transmission over the network. It is converted to the system's native format upon receipt.

   All RPC applications communicate by transmitting data into XDR. XDR is a data formatting language much like ASCII or extended binary coded decimal interchange code (EBCDIC). RFC 1831 standardizes the RPC message format using XDR, and RFC 1832 standardizes XDR.

2. RPC server-side daemons do not have fixed port numbers assigned to them.

   When an RPC server-side daemon starts, it is assigned an available port number. Some RPC servers request a specific port number (such as `nfsd` which expects to use port `2049`). Port numbers are allocated for both TCP and UDP—in general, RPC programs can use either UDP or TCP. Once the running server has its port number, it registers this information with the portmapper. Note that `inetd` or `xinetd` will register the port number for any RPC programs that it is configured to manage. The portmapper, normally the `portmap` daemon on Linux (but may be replaced by the functionally similar `rpcbind` daemon), must be running prior to any other RPC programs being started. The Linux `portmap` daemon currently implements RPC version 2 as specified by RFC 1831.

3. Each RPC program is uniquely defined by a program and version number. The program number to RPC server association is given in the `/etc/rpc` file. An excerpt of this file is given in Example 8–2.

Example 8–2   An Excerpt from `/etc/rpc`

```
portmapper     100000        portmap sunrpc rpcbind
rstatd         100001        rstat rup perfmeter rstat_svc
rusersd        100002        rusers
nfs            100003        nfsprog
ypserv         100004        ypprog
mountd         100005        mount showmount
ypbind         100007
walld          100008        rwall shutdown
yppasswdd      100009        yppasswd
```

The syntax of `/etc/rpc` is

```
RPC_server     program_number     alias(es)
```

where `RPC_server` is the name of the server-side daemon, `program_number` is the assigned number for this application (see RFC 1831 for program number assignments), and `alias(es)` is zero or more nicknames for the service in a space separated list. The three fields in this file are tab separated. It should be noted that very few RPC programs are enabled by default on Linux systems. The most commonly used are NFS and NIS.

Each RPC program also has a version number. Version numbers are used to differentiate different versions of the same client-server program, for example, NFS versions 2, 3, and 4. Version numbers are not contained in `/etc/rpc`, but can be determined with the `rpcinfo` program described in "The `rpcinfo` Command" on page 276.

Note that whenever the `/etc/rpc` file is modified, then either the portmapper daemon must be stopped and started directly or

```
# killall -HUP inetd
```

must be executed. This latter command causes all configuration files, including `/etc/services`, `/etc/rpc`, `/etc/protocols`, and `/etc/inetd.conf`, to be reread by `inetd` and made available to applications such as the portmapper.

OH, BY THE WAY...

The `kill` and `killall` commands are really misnamed. They should be called signal and signalall, because they cause signals to be sent to processes. We'll just discuss `kill` since these two commands operate identically (except for the fact that `kill` requires a process identifier to which it will send the signal, while `killall` requires a process name and will send the signal to all processes of that name).

When you issue the `kill` command, you are causing the specified process to be sent a signal. Different signals mean different things. You can obtain a list of signals by executing `kill -1`; this list is also found in `/usr/include/linux/signal.h`. If you do not specify the signal, such as HUP, on the command line, the default signal, TERM, will be sent. These signals are not sent directly to the process, however. Rather, the kernel looks up the given process and interrupts it, passing it the specified signal. If the process' interrupt handler accommodates the received signal, then it will execute the appropriate code; for example, if it received a HUP signal and has been programmed to deal with that signal, it will reread its configuration file. If it is not programmed to deal with a given signal, or it receives the default TERM signal, it will release all of its allocated resources, terminate all subprocesses (called children), and then terminate itself.

Many of you may be in the habit of issuing kill -KILL or, equivalently, kill -9 for every process you wish to terminate. This is a bad habit. Stop it! Always try kill -TERM (or just kill, since the default signal is TERM) first! Here's why. When you issue kill -9, the kernel does not interrupt the process. Instead, it releases all of the processe's resources and then terminates the specified process. If the process had any children, they become zombie processes, which appear as defunct when you look at the output of ps. The good news is that an internal kernel mechanism, known as the reaper (hey, *I* didn't make these names up!), will eventually release the resources of any zombie processes it finds and reassign them to be children of the process init (process id = 1), thus minimizing the impact of zombie processes. The bad news is that zombie processes are not removed until the next reboot.

This isn't to say that you should never use kill -9. Just use it as a last resort.

All applications that are written using the RPC library depend upon either the portmap daemon or the rpcbind daemon. While there are some differences between these two programs, they are functionally equivalent and most Linux distributions ship with the portmap daemon. The portmapper binds to port 111. While we have described the portmapper as an indirect server, it behaves somewhat differently than inetd and xinetd. Note that item 2 above indicates that each RPC server when started, or inetd/xinetd if these daemons find an RPC entry in their configuration files, registers the port number with the portmapper. The portmapper maintains the list of registered RPC programs in memory. Since the portmapper contains the list of port numbers for the RPC servers, the RPC client first communicates with the portmapper running on the server to get the port number of the application with which it wants to communicate. Once the RPC client knows the port number, it communicates directly to that port. In this way, the portmapper directs the client request to the appropriate port number. For example, if the root user on beaver executes the mount command in order to mount an NFS resource from foghorn-2, an initial communication is made to the portmapper on foghorn-2 to get the port number of the mountd RPC server-side program and then a following communication is made directly to the mountd daemon. This is illustrated in Figure 8–4. Note that beaver allocates reserved port numbers for these communications due to the fact that the client-side mount program requests them and it is being run by root.

Figure 8–5 depicts the same events described in Figure 8–4 but through an Ethereal capture session. Note that beaver issues the GETPORT request of fog-horn-2 to get the port number for mountd. Next, beaver issues the mount request to foghorn-2 at the port number received from the previous communication. After that, beaver initiates a session with an nfsd daemon on foghorn-2 to complete the mount operation. Thus, mountd is also a type of indirect server.

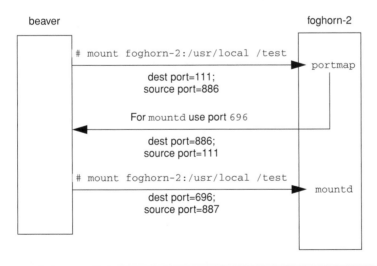

Figure 8–4   Portmapper and RPC Program Flow of Events

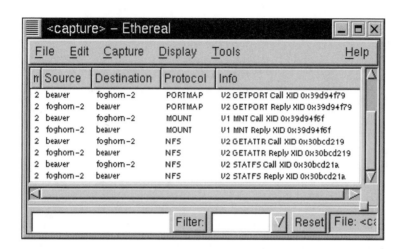

Figure 8–5   Initial `mount` Request Handoffs

NFS is covered in Chapter 10.

THE `rpcinfo` **COMMAND**   The `rpcinfo` command can be used to query a running `portmap` daemon on either the local system or a remote system. The syntax for this command is given in Example 8–3.

Example 8–3   Syntax of the `rpcinfo` Command

```
rpcinfo [ -n portnum ] -u host prognum [ versnum ]
rpcinfo [ -n portnum ] -t host prognum [ versnum ]
rpcinfo -p [ host ]
rpcinfo -b prognum versnum
rpcinfo -d prognum versnum
```

Each of the flags and arguments to `rpcinfo` are given in Table 8–2.

Table 8–2   Flags and Arguments of `rpcinfo`

FLAG/ARGUMENT	DESCRIPTION
`-n portnum`	An optional parameter that specifies the port number for the query.
`-u host prognum [versnum]`	Query the RPC server specified by `prognum` and optionally `versnum` running on the indicated `host` using UDP. An error message is returned if the server is not running.

Table 8–2   Flags and Arguments of `rpcinfo` *(Continued)*

FLAG/ARGUMENT	DESCRIPTION
`-t` *host prognum* [*versnum*]	Same as above except TCP is used.
`-p` [*host*]	Query the portmapper to get a list of registered servers.
`-b` *prognum versnum*	Issue a broadcast request to all servers specified by *prognum* and *versnum* using UDP.
`-d` *prognum versnum*	Delete the server indicated by *prognum* and *versnum* from the portmapper's registration list. Once this is done, the program can only be reregistered by killing and starting either the RPC server or the `portmap` daemon.

It is important to note that, as with all RPC programs, `rpcinfo` must query the `portmap` daemon (to get the server port number) before querying the RPC server.

The most common way of using the `rpcinfo` command is to use the `-p` flag to determine which RPC programs have registered with the `portmap` daemon. Example 8–4 illustrates the use of `rpcinfo -p` on a local system.

Example 8–4   Output of `rpcinfo -p` on a Local System

```
[root@foghorn /root]# rpcinfo -p
   program vers proto   port
    100000    2   tcp    111  portmapper
    100000    2   udp    111  portmapper
    100021    1   udp   1024  nlockmgr
    100021    3   udp   1024  nlockmgr
    100021    1   tcp   1024  nlockmgr
    100021    3   tcp   1024  nlockmgr
    100024    1   udp    621  status
    100024    1   tcp    623  status
    100011    1   udp    688  rquotad
    100011    2   udp    688  rquotad
    100005    1   udp    696  mountd
    100005    1   tcp    698  mountd
    100005    2   udp    701  mountd
    100005    2   tcp    703  mountd
    100003    2   udp   2049  nfs
[root@foghorn /root]#
```

The output of this command is quite straightforward, showing the program number, version number, port number, and RPC server name for each program registered with the `portmap` daemon. In this case, except for the portmapper entry itself, the only programs registered are NFS programs. For clarity of this example, note that the `rquotad`, `mountd`, and `nfs` entries reflect daemons used to support the NFS server-side. The remaining programs (`nlockmgr` and `status`) are used for file locking and synchronization.

Example 8–5 shows the use of `rpcinfo` to query the portmapper of a remote host (`beauregard`, in this case). Note that `beauregard` is not running NFS server-side daemons.

Example 8–5   Using `rpcinfo -p` to Query a Remote Host's Portmapper

```
[root@foghorn /root]# rpcinfo -p beauregard
   program vers proto   port
    100000    2   tcp    111  portmapper
    100000    2   udp    111  portmapper
    100021    1   udp   1024  nlockmgr
    100021    3   udp   1024  nlockmgr
    100021    1   tcp   1024  nlockmgr
    100021    3   tcp   1024  nlockmgr
    100024    1   udp    656  status
    100024    1   tcp    658  status
[root@foghorn /root]#
```

As noted in Table 8–2, we can query specific servers using specific protocols. Example 8–6 illustrates using UDP to query the NFS server.

Example 8–6   Successful UDP Query with `rpcinfo`

```
[root@foghorn /root]# rpcinfo -u foghorn 100003
program 100003 version 2 ready and waiting
[root@foghorn /root]#
```

When a server is not available, an error message is generated. Example 8–7 shows querying a host that is not running the NFS server.

Example 8–7   Unsuccessful UDP Query with `rpcinfo`

```
[root@foghorn /root]# rpcinfo -u beauregard 100003
rpcinfo: RPC: Program not registered
program 100003 is not available
[root@foghorn /root]#
```

If the `portmap` daemon is not running on a queried system, a timeout error message will be returned.

It turns out that access control over the `portmap` daemon can be implemented. This allows an administrator to restrict access to the portmapper and therefore the services that register with the portmapper. Since the restrictions apply to the `portmap` daemon, any access restrictions would also apply to `rpcinfo` queries. Access control over the portmapper is described in "Implementing Portmapper Access Control" on page 308.

Start-up Scripts for `inetd`, `xinetd`, and `portmap`

In order to support the services managed by the indirect servers `inetd` or `xinetd` and `portmap`, those daemons must be running all of the time. This is accomplished by system start-up scripts. Table 8–3 lists the start-up scripts for each daemon based on the four distributions that we have been discussing.

Table 8–3   Start-up Scripts

DISTRIBUTION	START-UP SCRIPT FOR `inetd` OR `xinetd`[A]	START-UP SCRIPT FOR `portmap`
Caldera 2.3	`/etc/rc.d/init.d/inet`	`/etc/rc.d/init.d/portmap`
Debian 2.1	`/etc/init.d/netbase`	`/etc/init.d/netbase`
Red Hat 6.2	`/etc/rc.d/init.d/inet`	`/etc/rc.d/init.d/portmap`
SuSE 6.4	`/etc/rc.d/init.d/inetd` `/etc/rc.d/init.d/xinetd`	`/etc/rc.d/init.d/rpc`

a. Since most distributions do not yet ship with `xinetd` as the default superserver, it is assumed that it will (or certainly could) be started from the same script as `inetd`.

The `/etc/inetd.conf` Configuration File

The `/etc/inetd.conf` file is read by `inetd` when `inetd` starts. This is the main configuration file for `inetd`. Example 8–8 provides a listing of the file as found on Red Hat 6.2 systems. Note that most of the entries contain `/usr/sbin/tcpd`. This causes the TCP_wrappers daemon to be invoked and is discussed in "TCP_Wrappers" on page 282.

Example 8–8   Default /etc/inetd.conf File in Red Hat Distributions

```
# inetd.conf        This file describes the services that will be available
#                   through the INETD TCP/IP super server.  To re-configure
#                   the running INETD process, edit this file, then send the
#                   INETD process a SIGHUP signal.
#
# Version:          @(#)/etc/inetd.conf    3.10     05/27/93
#
# Authors:          Original taken from BSD UNIX 4.3/TAHOE.
#                   Fred N. van Kempen, <waltje@uwalt.nl.mugnet.org>
#
# Modified for Debian Linux by Ian A. Murdock <imurdock@shell.portal.com>
#
# Modified for RHS Linux by Marc Ewing <marc@redhat.com>
#
# <service_name> <sock_type> <proto> <flags> <user> <server_path> <args>
#
# Echo, discard, daytime, and chargen are used primarily for testing.
#
# To re-read this file after changes, just do a 'killall -HUP inetd'
#
#echo    stream  tcp     nowait  root      internal
#echo    dgram   udp     wait    root      internal
#discard         stream  tcp     nowait  root      internal
#discard         dgram   udp     wait    root      internal
#daytime         stream  tcp     nowait  root      internal
#daytime         dgram   udp     wait    root      internal
#chargen         stream  tcp     nowait  root      internal
#chargen         dgram   udp     wait    root      internal
#time    stream  tcp     nowait  root      internal
#time    dgram   udp     wait    root      internal
#
# These are standard services.
#
ftp      stream  tcp     nowait  root      /usr/sbin/tcpd  in.ftpd -l -a
telnet   stream  tcp     nowait  root      /usr/sbin/tcpd  in.telnetd
#
# Shell, login, exec, comsat and talk are BSD protocols.
#
shell    stream  tcp     nowait  root      /usr/sbin/tcpd  in.rshd
login    stream  tcp     nowait  root      /usr/sbin/tcpd  in.rlogind
#exec    stream  tcp     nowait  root      /usr/sbin/tcpd  in.rexecd
#comsat  dgram   udp     wait    root      /usr/sbin/tcpd  in.comsat
#talk    dgram   udp     wait    root      /usr/sbin/tcpd  in.talkd
#ntalk   dgram   udp     wait    root      /usr/sbin/tcpd  in.ntalkd
#dtalk   stream  tcp     waut    nobody    /usr/sbin/tcpd  in.dtalkd
#
# Pop and imap mail services et al
#
#pop-2   stream  tcp     nowait  root      /usr/sbin/tcpd ipop2d
pop-3    stream  tcp     nowait  root      /usr/sbin/tcpd ipop3d
#imap    stream  tcp     nowait  root      /usr/sbin/tcpd imapd
#
# The Internet UUCP service.
#
#uucp    stream  tcp     nowait  uucp      /usr/sbin/tcpd  /usr/lib/uucp/uucico    -l
#
# Tftp service is provided primarily for booting.  Most sites
# run this only on machines acting as "boot servers." Do not uncomment
# this unless you *need* it.
#
#tftp    dgram   udp     wait    root      /usr/sbin/tcpd  in.tftpd
#bootps  dgram   udp     wait    root      /usr/sbin/tcpd  bootpd
#
# Finger, systat and netstat give out user information which may be
```

Example 8–8   Default /etc/inetd.conf File in Red Hat Distributions *(Continued)*

```
# valuable to potential "system crackers."  Many sites choose to disable
# some or all of these services to improve security.
#
#finger stream  tcp       nowait   root     /usr/sbin/tcpd  in.fingerd
#cfinger stream tcp       nowait   root     /usr/sbin/tcpd  in.cfingerd
#systat stream  tcp       nowait   guest    /usr/sbin/tcpd  /bin/ps -auwwx
#netstat         stream  tcp      nowait  guest   /usr/sbin/tcpd /bin/netstat    -f inet
#
# Authentication
#
auth   stream  tcp       nowait     nobody     /usr/sbin/in.identd in.identd -l -e -o
#
# End of inetd.conf

linuxconf stream tcp wait root /bin/linuxconf linuxconf --http
#swat       stream  tcp      nowait.400      root /usr/sbin/swat swat
```

The syntax for the /etc/inetd.conf file is

service type protocol wait-state owner[.group] path invocation

where each of the fields are tab separated and are described in Table 8–4.

Table 8–4   Fields in an /etc/inetd.conf Record

FIELD	DESCRIPTION
service	The name of the service as it appears in the /etc/services file.
type	The type of data delivery service used. There are three types: stream—the stream service provided by TCP dgram—the packet service provided by UDP raw—data transmitted directly by IP (no Transport layer involved)
protocol	The name of the protocol used as it appears in the /etc/ protocols file.
wait-state	This field takes a value of either wait or nowait. wait means that inetd must wait until the server releases its socket before honoring new requests. nowait means that inetd can begin listening for new requests on the associated port immediately. Services for which multiple, simultaneous sockets can exist (like ftp, telnet, and rlogin) use the nowait state.
owner[.group]	The *owner* is the UID under which the server runs. It may optionally contain .*group* to additionally specify the GID.

Table 8–4   Fields in an `/etc/inetd.conf` Record *(Continued)*

FIELD	DESCRIPTION
`path`	Specifies the absolute path name of the server program. Note that most of the services are invoked via `tcpd`. This is discussed in the next section.
`invocation`	Specifies the server program name and any flags and/or arguments with which it is to be invoked.

If a service is invoked through `inetd`, support for that service can be removed. Simply comment out or remove the appropriate entry from `/etc/inetd.conf` and then inform `inetd` of the changes. For example, suppose that you want to disallow `rlogin` requests from all clients. Edit the `/etc/inetd.conf` file and change the entry

```
login   stream  tcp    nowait  root   /usr/sbin/tcpd  in.rlogind
```

to the following, by simply adding the "#" comment character at the beginning of the line.

```
#login   stream  tcp    nowait  root   /usr/sbin/tcpd  in.rlogind
```

Then inform `inetd` of the change by executing

```
# killall -HUP inetd
```

Now, `inetd` will refuse all requests for `in.rlogind`. To enable a service, simply uncomment the entry (or create a new one) and `killall -HUP inetd`.

TCP_Wrappers[3]

Almost all of the services provided through `inetd` are invoked through TCP_wrappers by way of the TCP_wrappers daemon, `tcpd`. TCP_wrappers is included with most (if not all) Linux distributions and it runs on most flavors of UNIX. TCP_wrappers was written and continues to be maintained by Wietse Venema and is currently at version 7.6.

The TCP_wrappers mechanism provides access control list restrictions and logging for all service requests to the service it wraps. It may be used for either

---

3. Much of the remainder of this chapter is derived from Chapter 10 of *Linux System Security: The Administrator's Guide to Open Source Security Tools*, courtesy Prentice Hall, Inc.

UDP or TCP services so long as the services are invoked through a central dae-mon process such as inetd. This requirement is based on the nature of the TCP_wrappers daemon (tcpd), which must be invoked prior to the server dae-mon itself. Note that for most of the services in Example 8–8 on page 280 (some of which are commented out and therefore not available), the sixth field is /usr/sbin/tcpd instead of the server daemon, and that the seventh field specifies the server daemon. This seventh field becomes an argument to tcpd. Therefore, when a service with such an entry like in.telnetd is requested by a client, inetd will invoke tcpd to process the request and then, if successful, tcpd will invoke in.telned.

Basically, whenever a client requests a service, it will either be invoked through inetd, through the portmap daemon (RPC services only), or a server daemon will already be running. Server daemons which are run all the time (such as named) will be invoked at boot time through a start-up script or started manually. Otherwise, in order for a service to be available on a server, you will find an entry in /etc/inetd for management by inetd or in /etc/rpc for RPC services managed by portmap.

This means that the functionality provided by tcpd is separate from any ser-vice being requested. Therefore, to get similar functionality into a daemon which is always bound to a port, such as portmap, named, or sendmail, the bound daemon would have to be rewritten for that purpose. The portmap dae-mon used with Linux was rewritten to take advantage of TCP_wrappers access control (discussed in "Access Control and the Portmapper" on page 308), and fortunately, most daemons like named and sendmail have their own access con-trol mechanism built in. Figure 8–6 provides an overview of the flow of an initial request to a server, in the presence of TCP_wrappers.

As is shown in Figure 8–6, TCP_wrappers performs a few simple, but very important, tasks. It checks the access control list to determine whether a con-nection should be allowed and submits a log entry to syslogd. If the access list allows the service, tcpd invokes the appropriate daemon which then proceeds with its own authentication mechanism (if applicable) and may write its own message to syslogd.

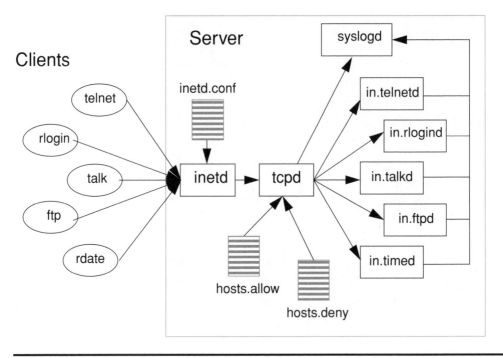

Figure 8–6   TCP_Wrappers Intercepts and Filters Requests

Access Control with TCP_Wrappers

TCP_wrappers implements access control through the use of two files, /etc/
hosts.allow and /etc/hosts.deny. As you might have guessed, the /etc/
hosts.allow file is an allow list, while the /etc/hosts.deny file is a deny list.
They share the same syntax and both offer features which make them considerably more utilitarian than simple allow and deny lists. Let's have a look.

A very simple /etc/hosts.allow file is shown in Example 8–9. Note that
the first record of each line in this file (except those comment lines beginning
with #) is a reference to a daemon like in.ftpd or in.telnetd. This daemon
name must identically match the last record of a line in /etc/inetd.conf (the
daemon invocation line) in order for tcpd to utilize the entries in this file.

Example 8–9   Simple /etc/hosts.allow File

```
# wrapper allow list
in.ftpd: 172.17.,139.6.77.0/255.255.255.0
in.telnetd: .eng.sprocket.com
in.fingerd: nomad,topcat,otter,foghorn,\
            c58608-a,underdog
```

In this example, we are allowing access to `in.ftpd` from any system in the `172.17.0.0` network and any system from the `139.6.77.0` subnetwork. For `telnet` access, we are accepting any host in the `eng.sprocket.com` subdomain. Lastly, we will only respond to `finger` requests from the list of hosts shown. In Example 8–10, we show a trivial companion `/etc/hosts.deny` file to the allow file shown in Example 8–9. The file in Example 8–10 has the effect of denying everything which is not explicitly allowed in Example 8–9.

Example 8–10   Simple `/etc/hosts.deny` File

```
# wrapper deny list
# deny everything
ALL: ALL
```

These two files taken together constitute the complete set of restrictions imposed on all services which are invoked through `tcpd`.

Note that blank lines and lines beginning with `#`, appearing in either the deny or allow file, are ignored by `tcpd`. Also, as displayed in the last two lines of Example 8–9, a `\` character acts to continue a line by escaping the newline. The general syntax of an entry (also called a *rule*) in either file is of the form

```
daemon[,daemon,...] : client[,client,...] [: option : option ...]
```

NOTE

The availability of the options requires the use of the compile time flag "`-DPROCESS_OPTIONS`". You can learn about this and other compile-time options by reviewing the README file that ships with the TCP_wrappers distribution. By default, this option is used on all of the Linux distributions that we have discussed. If this option is not chosen, then the syntax of the entries becomes

```
daemon[,daemon,...] : client[,client,...] [: shell_command]
```

where `shell_command` may be any single shell command.

Here, `daemon` must match a daemon name exactly as it appears in `/etc/inetd.conf`, and that daemon must be invoked through `tcpd`. Multiple daemons may be listed on the same line and separated by commas. After the daemon list a colon must appear, followed by a `client` or, optionally, a comma separated list of clients. The clients may be specified in a variety of forms as described in Table 8–5.

Table 8–5   Specifying the Clients in Allow and Deny Files

CLIENT SYNTAX	DESCRIPTION
`hostname`	Specifies the hostname or IP address of the client system. If using the hostname, it must be resolvable to an IP address through `/etc/hosts`, NIS, or DNS.
`.domain`	Use of this syntax assumes DNS. Any hostname which resolves to `hostname.domain` is granted access. For example, if `.domain` is `.acme.com`, then any host in the DNS domain `acme.com` is a match.
`net_number.`	This syntax matches the portions of the IP address shown. For example, if `net_number.` is `87.3.`, then any system whose IP address begins with `87.3.` will match regardless of the netmask being used.
`@netgroup`	The leading `@` indicates that a netgroup is specified causing a match for every host in the netgroup. Netgroups can only be used to match clients.
`net_number/netmask`	This syntax provides for specifying subnetworks. For example, `144.20.16.0/255.255.240.0`, will match all of the addresses, `144.20.16.0` through and including `144.20.31.255`.

If a colon appears after the client list, it indicates that one or more optional keywords follow each option being delimited by a colon. Again, these options are only available if PROCESS_OPTIONS are turned on at compile-time. The options are listed in Table 8–6.

It turns out that many of the options described in Table 8–6 may utilize information collected by `tcpd`. This is accomplished through a defined set of variables, listed in Table 8–7. The information is carried in letters which may be expanded with a preceding `%`, such as `%a` for client IP address and `%d` for the daemon name.

Table 8–6   Extending Capabilities in Allow and Deny Files

OPTIONAL KEYWORD	DESCRIPTION
`nice value`	Sets the `nice value` for the process.
`keepalive`	Causes the server to periodically send a message to the client. If the client does not respond, the connection is considered broken and will be terminated. Only for use with TCP services.
`linger seconds`	Specifies the number of `seconds` after the termination of a connection during which the server will attempt to send undelivered data.
`severity facility.level`	Allows for the relocation of log messages through `syslogd`. Normally, the Red Hat 6.2/7.0 implementation will log to `authpriv.info`. By using this option, you may change both the facility and level, such as with `severity local0.warn`. If you change the facility, then you may also need to make an appropriate entry in `/etc/syslog.conf` for this change to have an effect. Use of this option does not require the facility, but it does require the level.
`allow` `deny`	These options permit maintaining both allow and deny rules in the same file. If used, one of these two mutually exclusive options must appear last in the rule. See "Condensing TCP_Wrappers Rules into One File" on page 300 for examples.
`spawn shell_command`	Executes the specified `shell_command` as a child process. See "Using `spawn`" on page 296 for examples.
`twist shell_command`	Executes the specified `shell_command` as a replacement process to the process specified as the last field in the `/etc/inetd.conf` file. See "Using `twist`" on page 298 for examples.

Table 8–6   Extending Capabilities in Allow and Deny Files *(Continued)*

OPTIONAL KEYWORD	DESCRIPTION
`rfc931 seconds`	Causes the server to execute a call to the client in order to obtain the username invoking the request. The client must be running `identd` or similar RFC 931 or RFC 1413 compliant daemon. A timeout for the call may be specified in `seconds`; the default is 10 seconds. This option does not apply to UDP services.
`banners dir`	Specifies the fully qualified directory, `dir`, in which `tcpd` will search for a file of the same name as the wrapped daemon, the contents of which will be displayed prior to the `login` prompt. See "Using banners" on page 291 for examples. This option is only available for certain TCP services. Services such as `in.rshd` in remote execution mode will not work with banners.
`setenv var value`	Allows for the establishment or modification of a shell environment variable (`var`); usually this option is followed by a `spawn` or `twist` option.
`umask value`	Sets the umask for any operations in a rule; `value` must be in octal.
`user username.group`	Causes the privileges within the rule to be set to the specified `username` and optionally the specified `group`.

Table 8–7   Variable Expansions in Allow and Deny Files

VARIABLE	EXPANSION
%a	Client IP address.
%A	Server IP address.
%c	Becomes `user@host`, `user@IPaddress`, `hostname`, or `IPaddress`, depending upon what is available.
%d	The name of the daemon.
%h	The client hostname or IP address, if hostname is unavailable.
%H	The server hostname or IP address, if hostname is unavailable.
%n	The client hostname. Resolves to unknown if host is `unknown` and to `paranoid` if a reverse DNS lookup was performed and the hostname provided by DNS does not match the hostname claimed by the client.
%N	The server hostname.
%p	The process identifier (PID) of the daemon.
%s	Becomes daemon name, `daemon@host`, or `daemon@IPaddress`, depending upon available information. See "Distinguishing Source Interfaces for Multihomed Servers" on page 301, for example use of the `daemon@host` pattern.
%u	The client username. Resolves to unknown if not known. Use of this variable will cause `tcpd` to attempt an RFC 931 call.
%%	Resolves to %.

There are also a number of wildcard characters available for use in these files, such as ALL (see the last line of Example 8–10). These are described in Table 8–8.

Table 8–8   Wildcards in Allow and Deny Files

WILDCARD	DESCRIPTION
ALL	Matches everything.
LOCAL	Matches any hostname which does not contain a ". " character.
KNOWN	Matches any user whose username is known. Matches any host whose hostname and IP address are known. Examples are given in "Using `twist`" on page 298 and subsequent sections.
UNKNOWN	Matches any user whose username is `unknown`. Matches any host whose hostname or IP address are not known. Examples are given in "Using `twist`" on page 298 and subsequent sections.
PARANOID	Matches any host for which there is a hostname/IP address mismatch based on a reverse DNS lookup of the IP address. If the compile-time option, `-DPARANOID`, is used, all such connection attempts are automatically dropped and this option does not control access.
EXCEPT	This keyword is actually an operator which may appear in either daemon lists or client lists. Examples are given in "Using `spawn`" on page 296 and following sections.

NOTE

The `tcpd` stops when it finds the first daemon, client match. In short, it will grant access when it finds a matching pair in `/etc/hosts.allow`; access will be denied if a matching pair is found in `/etc/hosts.deny`, otherwise, access will be *allowed*. Therefore, make sure that you configure the deny file appropriately since the default behavior is to allow access unless directed to the contrary. On the other hand, if neither file exists, then all wrapped daemons will deny access. Thus, you may turn off access to all wrapped services simply by re-naming the allow and deny files. The only exception to these rules is that the `localhost` is always granted access.

As we can see, the TCP_wrappers access control files syntax gives us a lot of flexibility. Let's take a look at what we can do with this syntax in some more complex examples.

Using banners

Suppose that you want to display a message to anyone connecting to your system *before* they attempt to login. You may accomplish this very simply by using the banners option in either the allow or deny file or both. Example 8–11 provides an example entry for in.telnetd in the /etc/hosts.allow file.

Example 8–11   banners Entry for in.telnetd

```
# wrapper allow file
in.ftpd: 172.17.,139.6.77.0/255.255.255.0
in.telnetd: .eng.sprocket.com: banners /etc/security/banners/allow
in.fingerd: nomad,topcat,otter,foghorn,\
        c58608-a,underdog
```

The in.telnetd entry with the banners option, in this case, will cause tcpd to look for the file

/etc/security/banners/allow/in.telnetd

and display its contents prior to posting the login prompt. You will need to create this file, which you may do manually or use the Banners.Makefile as described in "Using Banners.Makefile" on page 293. If the contents of this file appears as shown in Example 8–12,

Example 8–12   Sample Allow Banner File

```
# in.telnetd allow message
Welcome to %H.
You are logging in from %c.
Remember all activity on this system is recorded.
If you don't like this policy leave now!
```

then when Mary logs in from underdog.eng.sprocket.com, she sees the message displayed in Example 8–13.

Example 8–13   Banner Displayed upon Connection

```
underdog$ telnet topcat
Trying 172.17.33.111...
Connected to topcat.
Escape character is '^]'.
Welcome to topcat.eng.sprocket.com.
You are logging in from underdog.eng.sprocket.com.
Remember all activity on this system is recorded.
If you don't like this policy leave now!

Red Hat Linux release 6.2 (Zoot)
Kernel 2.2.14-5.0 on an i686
login:
```

Notice that the message appears prior to the `login` prompt. Notice also that `%c`, in `/etc/security/banners/allow/in.telnetd` as shown in Example 8–12, expands to `underdog.eng.sprocket.com`, and `%H` expands to `topcat.eng.sprocket.com`, as defined in Table 8–7 on page 289. Recall that `%c` expands to the information available to the server, `topcat` in this case, and note in particular that no user name appears. If we modify Example 8–11 on page 291, as given in Example 8–14 below,

Example 8–14   Modified banners Entry for `in.telnetd`

```
# wrapper allow file
in.ftpd: 172.17.,139.6.77.0/255.255.255.0
in.telnetd: .eng.sprocket.com: rfc931: \
          banners /etc/security/banners/allow
in.fingerd: nomad,topcat,otter,foghorn,\
          c58608-a,underdog
```

then the line from Example 8–13,

```
You are logging in from underdog.eng.sprocket.com.
```

becomes

```
You are logging in from mary@underdog.eng.sprocket.com.
```

because the option, `rfc931`, caused `tcpd` to issue a call to `identd` on the client, `underdog`, and obtain the username, `mary`. If `identd` were not running on `underdog`, or was running but declined to supply the username information, the `rfc931` call would simply add no new information. It is important to note that if a rule references `%u`, it will implicitly make the `rfc931` call.

The log entry generated by the successful `telnet` connection by Mary would appear as follows in `/var/log/secure` (or whatever log file is specified by facility `authpriv` in `/etc/syslog.conf`):

```
Apr 11 09:23:24 topcat in.telnetd[3632]: connect from
underdog.eng.sprocket.com
```

The information contained in this line includes the following from left to right: date and time (`Apr 11 09:23:24`), server hostname (`topcat`), daemon name (`in.telnetd`), PID in brackets (`3632`), success (`connect`) or failure (`refused connect`), and the client hostname (`underdog.eng.sprocket.com`).

Using deny `banners` works identically, except that the option would appear in the `/etc/hosts.deny` file. Also, make sure that you specify a different directory for the deny message. An example deny banner is given in the following section.

USING `Banners.Makefile` It turns out that there is a handy `Makefile` that you can use to create these banner files. This file ships with the TCP_wrappers distribution. If you cannot find it using locate on your system, you may need to install the appropriate source to get a copy. For convenience, Example 8–15 reproduces the file.

Example 8–15   The `Banners.Makefile` File

```
# @(#) Banners.Makefile 1.3 97/02/12 02:13:18
#
# Install this file as the Makefile in your directory with banner files.
# It will convert a prototype banner text to a form that is suitable for
# the ftp, telnet, rlogin, and other services.
#
# You'll have to comment out the IN definition below if your daemon
# names don't start with 'in.'.
#
# The prototype text should live in the banners directory, as a file with
# the name "prototype". In the prototype text you can use %<character>
# sequences as described in the hosts_access.5 manual page ('nroff -man'
# format).  The sequences will be expanded while the banner message is
# sent to the client. For example:
#
#Hello %u@%h, what brings you here?
#
# Expands to: Hello username@hostname, what brings you here? Note: the
# use of %u forces a client username lookup.
#
# In order to use banners, build the tcp wrapper with -DPROCESS_OPTIONS
# and use hosts.allow rules like this:
#
#daemons ... : clients ... : banners /some/directory ...
#
# Of course, nothing prevents you from using multiple banner directories.
# For example, one banner directory for clients that are granted service,
# one banner directory for rejected clients, and one banner directory for
# clients with a hostname problem.
#
SHELL= /bin/sh
IN= in.
BANNERS= $(IN)telnetd $(IN)ftpd $(IN)rlogind # $(IN)fingerd $(IN)rshd

all:$(BANNERS)

$(IN)telnetd: prototype
cp prototype $@
chmod 644 $@

$(IN)ftpd: prototype
sed 's/^/220-/' prototype > $@
chmod 644 $@

$(IN)rlogind: prototype nul
( ./nul ; cat prototype ) > $@
chmod 644 $@

# Other services: banners may interfere with normal operation
# so they should probably be used only when refusing service.
# In particular, banners don't work with standard rsh daemons.
# You would have to use an rshd that has built-in tcp wrapper
# support, for example the rshd that is part of the logdaemon
# utilities.
```

Example 8–15   The Banners.Makefile File *(Continued)*

```
$(IN)fingerd: prototype
cp prototype $@
chmod 644 $@

$(IN)rshd: prototype nul
( ./nul ; cat prototype ) > $@
chmod 644 $@

# In case no /dev/zero available, let's hope they have at least
# a C compiler of some sort.

# Other services: banners may interfere with normal operation
# so they should probably be used only when refusing service.
# In particular, banners don't work with standard rsh daemons.
# You would have to use an rshd that has built-in tcp wrapper
# support, for example the rshd that is part of the logdaemon
# utilities.

$(IN)fingerd: prototype
cp prototype $@
chmod 644 $@

$(IN)rshd: prototype nul
( ./nul ; cat prototype ) > $@
chmod 644 $@

# In case no /dev/zero available, let's hope they have at least
# a C compiler of some sort.

nul:
echo 'main() { write(1,"",1); return(0); }' >nul.c
$(CC) $(CFLAGS) -s -o nul nul.c
rm -f nul.c
```

In any case, copy `Banners.Makefile` to your `banners` directory. We'll use `/etc/security/banners/allow` for the allow messages and `/etc/security/banners/deny` for the deny messages in our examples. Example 8–16 depicts the necessary steps to effect this copy.

Example 8–16   Copying `Banners.Makefile`

```
# cd /usr/doc/tcp_wrappers-7.6/
# cp Banners.Makefile /etc/security/banners/allow/Makefile
# cp Banners.Makefile /etc/security/banners/deny/Makefile
```

Note that we changed the name of the file from `Banners.Makefile` to `Makefile`. This will save typing when we execute `make`, since `make` expects its `Makefile` to be named `Makefile`, `makefile`, or `GNUmakefile`. If it is not one of those names; for example, if it were `Banners.Makefile`, you would need to execute `make -f Banners.Makefile`.

All you have to do is create a file called `prototype`, in each of the two directories, which contains the desired message. For example, in the directory `/etc/`

security/banners/deny, we might create a prototype file which looks like the one shown in Example 8–17.

Example 8–17   Sample Deny prototype File

```
# Deny Prototype
Hello, %u@%h trying to connect to %d.
What are you doing here? You aren't authorized and
I'm afraid I've logged this attempt. Do it again and
I'll have to tell your mother.
```

Once you have written the prototype, you can execute make in the appropriate directory as exhibited in Example 8–18.

Example 8–18   Output of make and ls in /etc/security/banners/deny

```
# make
cp prototype in.telnetd
chmod 644 in.telnetd
sed 's/^/220-/' prototype > in.ftpd
chmod 644 in.ftpd
echo 'main() { write(1,"",1); return(0); }' >nul.c
cc  -s -o nul nul.c
rm -f nul.c
( ./nul ; cat prototype ) > in.rlogind
chmod 644 in.rlogind
# ls
Makefile    in.ftpd    in.rlogind  in.telnetd  nul        prototype
```

Note that the ls output shows that the Makefile caused three banner files, in.ftpd, in.rlogind, and in.telnetd, to be generated. The Makefile is also set up to create messages for finger and rsh (however, the banner will not be displayed if rsh is used for remote execution). Example 8–19 shows how to make the message for in.fingerd.

Example 8–19   Creating the Deny Message for in.fingerd

```
# make in.fingerd
cp prototype in.fingerd
chmod 644 in.fingerd
#
```

If we add an appropriate entry to the /etc/hosts.deny file, for example,

```
in.fingerd: ALL: banners /etc/security/banners/deny
```

then whenever an unauthorized (not found in the /etc/hosts.allow file) finger attempt is made, the message will be displayed.

Now let's see what happens when Joe attempts to `finger` the user `mary` on `topcat`. The outcome is shown in Example 8–20.

Example 8–20   Unauthorized `finger` Attempt

```
$ finger mary@topcat.eng.sprocket.com
[topcat.eng.sprocket.com]

Hello joe@sly.no.good.org trying to connect to in.fingerd.
What are you doing here? You are not authorized and
I'm afraid I've logged this attempt. Do it again and
I'll have to tell your mother.
```

The log generated by this failed attempt would appear as

```
Apr 11 13:56:04 topcat in.fingerd[3907]: refused connect from
sly.no.good.org
```

in the `/var/log/secure` file.

If you wish to have distinct messages for each daemon you will need to either manually modify each file or create a customized script/`Makefile` to do it for you. You may also create additional directories as needed utilizing different messages for different circumstances. For example, you may wish to create special messages for clients which resolve to UNKNOWN (see Table 8–8 on page 290). One way to accomplish this is to place the following entry in your `/etc/hosts.deny` file,

```
ALL: UNKNOWN: banners /etc/security/banners/unknown
```

then, any client that connects to this server and for which the server cannot determine either the hostname or the IP address (either of which may be due to network problems, such as the DNS server not responding) will be denied access and a suitable message may be displayed.

As noted in Table 8–6 on page 287, `banners` may not be used with UDP services nor with certain TCP services such as `in.rshd` and `in.talkd`.

Using `spawn`

The `spawn` option allows you to specify any shell command within a given rule. This includes any custom shell script or program. Let's take a look at some examples.

The TCP_wrappers package includes a special finger program, `safe_finger`, which implements numerous safety mechanisms to protect against finger servers including: limiting the amount of data it will accept, limiting the line length it will accept, and implementing a hard timeout limit. The `safe_finger` program accepts the same arguments as `finger`. The purpose of using finger from TCP_wrappers is to obtain more information about whoever is trying to establish a connection to your system. If the connecting client provides a response to the safe_finger probe, then you can use this information in many ways. Example 8–21 displays a sample entry in the `/etc/hosts.deny` file. It uses `safe_finger` and then pipes the result to a mail message which gets sent to `root`. This procedure of querying the client based on an incoming request from that client is called a *booby-trap* in the TCP_wrappers documentation.

Example 8–21   Sample Use of `EXCEPT` and `safe_finger`

```
# hosts.deny
ALL EXCEPT in.fingerd: ALL: spawn (/usr/sbin/safe_finger  -lp @%h | \
     /bin/mail -s "Connect attempt from %h using %d" root) &: \
     banners /etc/security/banners/deny
```

WARNING

Be careful about using `ALL` in conjunction with shell commands such as `/usr/sbin/safe_finger`. In addition to the potential `finger` loop problem described in the next paragraph, it may be that the invocation of a shell command may not work as expected with certain services. For example, the `ALL` entry in Example 8–21 will capture incoming `portmap` requests (see the section "Access Control and the Portmapper" on page 308), by default, on Red Hat 6.2/7.0 systems. Given this rule, a `portmap` request which is denied will cause the generation of the e-mail, but will benignly fail the `safe_finger`. Other commands may not be so friendly, so make sure that you test things out before you go live!

The `-l` flag used with `safe_finger` forces formatting of the response to one user per line, making it easier to subsequently parse; the `-p` flag suppresses plan and project information. Notice that we will not respond to incoming `finger` attempts (`EXCEPT in.fingerd`) with our `safe_finger`; this avoids potential infinite `finger` loops in the case that the client system responds to `finger` queries with a `finger` of its own! Now that we have this file set up, when Joe attempts unauthorized access, say, via `rlogin` or `ftp` or `telnet`, then he will get the same deny message as shown in Example 8–20 on page 296; additionally, `root` on the server (`topcat` in this case) will get an e-mail message similar to that shown in Example 8–22.

Example 8–22   Email Generated by Example 8–21 Entry

```
From root  Sun Apr 11 05:16:31 1999
Date: Sun, 11 Apr 1999 05:16:31 -0600
From: root <root@topcat>
To: root@topcat
Subject: Connect attempt from sly.no.good.org using in.telnetd

[sly.no.good.org]
Login: root                              Name: root
Directory: /root                         Shell: /bin/bash
On since Sat Apr 10 20:51 (MDT) on tty1     18 hours 57 minutes idle
     (messages off)
On since Sat Apr 10 20:52 (MDT) on ttyp0 from :0.0
    17 hours idle
On since Sat Apr 10 21:47 (MDT) on ttyp1 from :0.0
    13 minutes 30 seconds idle
Mail last read Sun Apr 11 04:04 1999 (MDT)

Login: joe                               Name: Joseph James
Directory: /home/joe                     Shell: /bin/bash
On since Sun Apr 11 15:47 (MDT) on ttyp2 from topcat
    1 second idle
No mail.
```

As you can see, a lot of information can be obtained through `finger` (which is one reason why it is suggested that `in.fingerd` be turned off). Since `spawn` allows for any shell command, there are a variety of actions that may be taken based on the rules provided. For example, we might replace the invocation of `/bin/mail` in Example 8–21 with a different command, such as a script which keeps count of the number of times a particular user makes unauthorized connection attempts, and when it reaches a threshold (like three such attempts) an action is performed, such as generating a page to the administrator or shutting down a particular service. In fact, such a script does exist in the public domain; it is called `swatch`, and you can learn more about it in *Linux System Security* as cited in "For Further Reading" on page 344. It can be obtained from

```
ftp://coast.cs.purdue.edu/pub/tools/unix/logutils/swatch
```

Using `twist`

The `twist` option causes a specified daemon or command to be invoked instead of the daemon indicated in `/etc/inetd.conf`. For example, if `/etc/inetd.conf` has an entry like

```
ftp stream  tcp    nowait  root    /usr/sbin/tcpd  in.ftpd -a -l
```

then, normally, whenever a successful request for `ftp` is encountered, `/usr/sbin/in.ftpd -l -a` will be invoked. Suppose that you have configured an anonymous `ftp` environment for internal use. Further suppose that your internal Security Policy requires all systems to run `identd`, but further specifies that internal access to `ftp` servers, like the one in this example, is critical to productivity. To satisfy this criteria, you may implement TCP_wrappers to take different actions based on whether a given user is identifiable, and as we see in Example 8–23, invoke different daemons based on the availability of a particular user identity. As indicated in Table 8–8 on page 290, `tcpd` will report KNOWN if a user's identity is known and UNKNOWN if not.

Example 8–23   Sample `/etc/hosts.allow` Using `twist`

```
# hosts.allow
in.ftpd: KNOWN@KNOWN

in.ftpd: UNKNOWN@KNOWN: banners \
   /etc/security/banners/unknown: spawn (/bin/echo "Policy Violation!" \
   | /bin/mail -s "%h isn't running identd!" root@%H,root@%h)&: \
   twist PATH=/usr/sbin/extra;exec in.ftpd -i -o -l

in.ftpd: PARANOID: banners /etc/security/banners/paranoid: \
   spawn (/bin/echo "%n reported when %u@%h connected using %d" | \
   /bin/mail -s "Alert! Hostname Lookup Failure!" root@%H)& :deny

in.ftpd: ALL: deny
```

Notice the use of `@KNOWN` in both `in.ftpd` rules. Recall from Table 8–8 on page 290 that in the case of client lists, this will match only if both the hostname and IP address are known, so a result of UNKNOWN for a hostname may mean that hostname resolution services are not working properly. The presence of this option forces a reverse lookup (regardless of compile-time options). Further in Example 8–23, we see entries in an `/etc/hosts.allow` file which distinguishes between known and unknown users in the following way. By virtue of the fact that the entry KNOWN@KNOWN appears, whenever an incoming `ftp` request occurs, `tcpd` will generate an RFC 931 call (regardless of compile-time options) to get the incoming username. If it is successful, then the rule matches and `in.ftpd -a -l` is invoked from the compile-time daemon source directory (`/usr/sbin` in the case of Red Hat 6.2/7.0). Note that the `-l` flag to `in.ftpd` causes `in.ftpd` to log the connection and the `-a` flag causes `in.ftpd` to check the `/etc/ftpaccess` file. See the `ftpd(8)` man page for more information.

On the other hand, if the request to the client for the username fails, the username will resolve to UNKNOWN. In such a case, the connection is still allowed, however, a special banner is displayed (presumably notifying the user that identd is not running on the client) and email is sent to both root on the server (root@%H) and root on the client (root@%h) notifying the administrator that a Security Policy violation has occurred. Finally, we see the use of the twist option in this case, which causes /usr/sbin/extra/in.ftpd -i -o -l to be invoked instead of /usr/sbin/in.ftpd -a -l. The use of PATH=/usr/sbin/extra (it is used in this example simply to illustrate the capability) causes the change in the directory path and is only required if the daemon you wish to invoke is not in /usr/sbin (Red Hat 6.2/7.0 default). Note that the -i and -o flags to in.ftpd cause the logging of uploaded and downloaded files, respectively, to /var/log/xferlog, by default.

Next, in Example 8–23, if the client resolves to PARANOID (because the reverse lookup of IP address to hostname disagrees with forward lookup of hostname to IP address), a special message is displayed to the client, email is sent to root notifying the administrator of the problem, and access is then denied with the deny keyword. In an internal environment, such as the case of this example, it is quite likely that PARANOID reports are indicative of networking troubles; nonetheless, such reports should always be thoroughly investigated. The use of PARANOID in these files assumes that the -DPARANOID option was *not* chosen at compile-time (as is the case with Red Hat 6.2/7.0). Finally, the last line of the example denies ftp access under any other circumstance.

It is worth noting the appearance of entries in the log file based on the different entries in Example 8–23.

Condensing TCP_Wrappers Rules into One File

In the previous section, we saw the use of the deny option in an /etc/hosts.allow file. Use of this option, and the allow option, will permit you to build a single file for access control. This approach may well be a convenience under circumstances in which the rules are relatively straightforward. More complex rule sets, such as those configured for major server systems, may be organized more easily in a typical two-file system.

Example 8–24 presents a simple example of a one-file access control list. In this case, /etc/hosts.allow is used.

Example 8–24   A Single File Access Control List

```
# hosts.allow file
# Internal systems only allow telnet and ftp
in.ftpd: KNOWN@LOCAL: banners /etc/security/banners/allow
in.telnetd: KNOWN@LOCAL: banners /etc/security/banners/allow
ALL: ALL: banners /etc/security/banners/deny: deny
```

Note the use of the keyword LOCAL. This will match any host which does not have a "." in its name. Since this is an allow file, the behavior is to allow matched entries. The last entry overrides this behavior with the deny keyword. You could accomplish the same thing in a deny file, using the allow keyword as appropriate. Whether you use the deny or allow keyword, it must appear last in the rule.

Another use of these keywords is to keep complex rule sets in one file as in Example 8–23 on page 299. In that case, all of the rules regarding in.ftpd are maintained in one location, making it easier to understand and troubleshoot.

Distinguishing Source Interfaces for Multihomed Servers

It may be that you are putting together a single ftp server with multiple network interfaces. In such a case, you can use TCP_wrappers to direct daemon invocation based on the destination IP address (described as server endpoint patterns in the TCP_wrappers documentation) used in the requesting packets. Example 8–25 gives us a very simple example.

Example 8–25   Sample Allow Entries Using Server Endpoint Patterns

```
# hosts.allow
# ftp server entries
in.ftpd@24.1.11.113: ALL EXCEPT .evil.com:twist in.ftpd
in.ftpd@24.2.8.118: ALL EXCEPT .evil.com:twist in.wuftpd
```

In this example, we use the form daemon@IPaddress; however, any client form, as described in Table 8–5 on page 286, may be used instead of the IP address. This is one way to cause an incoming ftp request to be serviced based on destination IP addresses.

NOTE

You cannot use EXCEPT with network numbers in client lists. For example, 172.17. EXCEPT 172.17.1.3 will not have the desired behavior.

Putting It All Together

Building the `hosts.allow` and `hosts.deny` files takes some consideration. You will probably end up with a variety of configurations depending upon the use of a given system. Typical desktop systems will likely have very simple access control lists, server systems will have somewhat more complex lists, and systems exposed to untrusted networks, such as the Internet, may have highly specialized lists.

Perhaps the best approach to determining the prototypical list for a given type of system is to consider what it does. Make a list of services that the system needs to provide and, very importantly, an associated list of clients. If you aren't sure whether a service is to be provided, deny it (unless your Security Policy indicates otherwise). You can always go back and add it later.

As an example, let's suppose that we have an internal server which provides `ftp`, time, and POP3 services to the internal networks. All POP3 services are localized on two networks, `172.17.0.0` and `172.18.0.0`; all other networks use `sendmail`. Further assume that in this environment, there are engineering test networks, `172.19.0.0` through and including `172.19.15.255`, which do not utilize the time services but do utilize `ftp`. For simplicity, suppose that all networks in this environment begin with `172` in the first octet of the IP address. Every system runs `identd`, except the PC and MAC clients, which live on either the `172.17.0.0` or `172.18.0.0` networks. Example 8–26 provides an allow file which matches these criteria.

Example 8–26   Working Allow File

```
# hosts.allow
in.ftpd: KNOWN@KNOWN, UNKNOWN@172.17., UNKNOWN@172.18.

in.ftpd: UNKNOWN@KNOWN: banners \
  /etc/security/banners/unknown: spawn (/bin/echo "Policy Violation!" \
  | /bin/mail -s "%h isn't running identd!" root@%H,root@%h)&

in.ftpd: PARANOID: banners /etc/security/banners/unknown: \
  spawn (/bin/echo "%n reported when %u@%h connected using %d" | \
  /bin/mail -s "Alert! Hostname Lookup Failure!" root@%H)& :deny

in.timed: 172.19.0.0/255.255.240.0; deny

in.timed: KNOWN

ipop3d: 172.17., 172.18.

ALL: ALL: deny
```

Remember that `tcpd` stops when it reaches the first match, so order in this file is important. Also, notice that we do not use the form KNOWN@KNOWN for `in.timed`. This is because a username query to the client will not work with `in.timed`. The remaining entries are quite similar to those previously discussed. We provide more activity around `ftp` as it is more likely to be used to compromise the system.

You may wish to additionally create an `/etc/hosts.deny` file which contains the single line

```
ALL: ALL
```

for clarity, although it is not necessary because of the final line in Example 8–26.

In Example 8–27, we view three log entries which were generated by attempted access to the server, `topcat`, using the `/etc/hosts.allow` file shown in Example 8–26.

Example 8–27   Sample Log Entries

```
Apr 11 14:03:57 topcat in.ftpd[3947]: connect from mary@underdog
Apr 11 14:04:29 topcat in.ftpd[3948]: connect from roadrunner
Apr 12 12:38:04 topcat in.timed[819]: refused connect from 172.19.1.3
```

The first two lines reflect granted access to `ftp`; however, notice in the second case there is no username. This means that the line containing `mary@underdog` matched the first `in.ftpd` rule in Example 8–26, while the line containing `roadrunner` matched the second `in.ftpd` rule. The last line in Example 8–27 occurs because of the first `in.timed` rule in Example 8–26. A more useful way to check the rules is discussed in "TCP_Wrappers Utility Programs" on page 305.

While there is certainly tremendous value in building access control lists for the purpose of controlling access, it is not the only thing that may be done with TCP_wrappers. Consider the case of a DMZ or Firewall system. One approach to establishing an early warning system on such systems is to leave many of the ports most likely to be attacked open in `/etc/inetd.conf` and booby-trap them. For example, you might not comment-out references to `in.rlogind` and `in.ftpd` in `/etc/inetd.conf`; you would create an `/etc/hosts.deny` file, which looks something like that in Example 8–28.

Example 8–28   Use of Deny File As an Early Warning Mechanism

```
# hosts.deny
# Nobody should ever try to connect via these services
# So let's find out as much as we can and log, log, log

in.rlogind: ALL: severity local5.warn: spawn (/usr/sbin/safe_finger \
   -lp @%h | logger -p local5.warn; /bin/echo "%u attempted %d from \
   %h" | /bin/mail -s "Someone's Knocking!" root)&

in.ftpd: ALL: severity local5.warn: spawn (/usr/sbin/safe_finger \
   -lp @%h | logger -p local5.warn; /bin/echo "%u attempted %d from \
   %h" | /bin/mail -s "Someone's Knocking!" root)&
```

Notice that we do not use the standard facility and level for these entries, instead we use `local5` (arbitrarily chosen, but should not be used for anything else). This way, you can configure `/etc/syslog.conf` (see the `syslog.conf(5)` man page) to cause log messages generated by activity associated with this deny file to a separate file and then process it with a utility such as `logcheck` or `swatch`.[4] You must watch these files carefully, however, since if someone perpetrates a denial of service attack against a system configured in this way and the perpetrator uses spoofed, but valid, IP addresses, this system will `finger` a lot of innocent sites! You may decide, therefore, not to use the `safe_finger` request as shown in Example 8–28, but use the log files alone, as they may prove their value in identifying a potential attack.

OH, BY THE WAY...

If you don't know what daemon name to specify in an allow or deny list, you can put an allow ALL daemons rule in the file temporarily (and in a contained, trusted environment), then issue a request from a client to the server. TCP_wrappers will generate a log entry which will include the name of the daemon it expects to see in the access control rules. Use this information to modify your rules accordingly.

---

4. The `logcheck` and `swatch` utilities can be used to filter log files to obtain important messages. You can learn more about these tools in *Linux System Security* as cited in "For Further Reading" on page 344.

TCP_Wrappers Utility Programs

The TCP_wrappers distribution includes three utility programs. They are `tcp-dchk`, `tcpdmatch`, and `try-from`. These utilities exist for the purpose of testing your TCP_wrappers configuration.

USING `tcpdchk`   The `tcpdchk` utility provides syntax checking of the `/etc/hosts.allow` and `/etc/hosts.deny` files against the `/etc/inetd.conf` file. This is a good utility to run when you first implement `/etc/hosts.allow` and `/etc/hosts.deny` and subsequently when you make changes to those files.

There are four flags associated with this utility. They are described in Table 8–9.

Table 8–9   Flags of `tcpdchk`

FLAG	DESCRIPTION
`-a`	Displays additional information whenever access is granted without an explicit `allow` keyword.
`-v`	Verbose. Normally, `tcpdchk` only outputs warnings and errors.
`-d`	Uses the `hosts.allow` and `hosts.deny` files in the current working directory. Useful for debugging.
`-i` *filename*	Uses the specified *filename* instead of `/etc/inetd.conf`

Example 8–29 illustrates the use of `tcpdchk`.

Example 8–29   Sample `tcpdchk` Output

```
# tcpdchk -av
>>> Rule /etc/hosts.allow line 10:
daemons:  in.ftpd
clients:  KNOWN@.eng.sprocket.com
warning: /etc/hosts.allow, line 10: implicit "allow" at end of rule
access:   granted

>>> Rule /etc/hosts.allow line 11:
daemons:  in.ftpd
clients:  UNKNOWN@.eng.sprocket.com
warning: /etc/hosts.allow, line 11: implicit "allow" at end of rule
access:   granted

>>> Rule /etc/hosts.allow line 12:
```

Example 8–29   Sample `tcpdchk` Output *(Continued)*

```
daemons:  in.ftpd
clients:  PARANOID
option:   deny
access:   denied
...
<lots of output snipped>
...
>>> Rule /etc/hosts.allow line 15:
daemons:  ALL
clients:  LOCAL
option:   banners /etc/security/banners/allow
warning:  /etc/hosts.allow, line 15: implicit "allow" at end of rule
access:   granted

>>> Rule /etc/hosts.deny line 9:
daemons:  ALL
clients:  ALL
option:   banners /etc/security/banners/deny
access:   denied
#
```

USING `tcpdmatch`   The `tcpdmatch` utility takes a daemon/client pair as input and checks the rules for a match. It then provides a resolution, either denying or granting access. Example 8–30 exhibits its typical use.

Example 8–30   Sample `tcpdmatch` Output

```
# tcpdmatch in.ftpd underdog
client:   hostname underdog.eng.sprocket.com
client:   address  172.17.55.124
server:   process  in.ftpd
matched:  /etc/hosts.allow line 11
access:   granted
#
```

As you add rules, this is a very useful tool to check anything you add. It is also an excellent utility for determining the behavior of the various keywords and options described in this text.

USING `try-from`   The `try-from` utility tests the hostname and username lookup mechanism. You may use `rsh` to test it, which requires running `in.rshd`, setting up the appropriate allow entry in `/etc/hosts.allow` (or `/etchosts.deny` with the `allow` option), and creating an entry in `/etc/hosts.equiv` or in the appropriate `$HOME/.rhosts` file on the server. Just be sure to close that hole after your tests! Once done, you may execute `try-from` as in Example 8–31.

Example 8–31   Using `try-from`

```
$ rsh topcat /usr/sbin/try-from
client address   (%a): 172.17.55.124
client hostname  (%n): underdog.eng.sprocket.com
client username  (%u): mary
client info      (%c): mary@underdog.eng.sprocket.com
server address   (%A): 172.17.33.111
server hostname  (%N): topcat.eng.sprocket.com
server process   (%d): try-from
server info      (%s): try-from@topcat.eng.sprocket.com
$
```

Notice that the values of the variables captured by `tcpd` are listed. See Table 8–7 on page 289 for a description of these variables.

TCP_Wrappers Vulnerabilities

The TCP_wrappers program itself is very mature and, thanks to the continuing attention of its author and many users throughout the world, bugs are identified and fixed quickly. The vulnerabilities associated with its use come from the other programs it depends on, such as DNS and `identd`.

There are all sorts of things that can occur which will cause a breach of the security provided by TCP_wrappers. If a system which is granted access by the wrappers is compromised, for example, then there are no defenses. If DNS names and IP addresses are spoofed, it will be impossible for TCP_wrappers to detect a PARANOID condition. Denial of service attacks can fill up the log files. The `identd` daemon on a remote system may be configured to provide false information. In short, there are no guarantees.

The TCP_wrappers package does provide a fair amount of logging of connection activity and it also forces would-be bad guys to do a lot more work to compromise a system using the wrappers. In any event, this should not be your only tool nor your only line of defense. In particular, any system which is exposed to an untrusted external network, such as the Internet, should be additionally configured with `ipchains`. Internal systems which are critical should take advantage of `ipchains` as well. See Chapter 14 for a detailed look at the use of `ipchains`.

Access Control and the Portmapper

We introduced the portmapper in "The `portmap` Daemon and RPC" on page 272. The purpose of this section is to describe the enhanced Portmapper Version 4[5] (current version in Linux) access control and logging capabilities. Like TCP_wrappers, this version of the Portmapper was written and continues to be maintained by Wietse Venema.

Implementing Portmapper Access Control

Implementing access control for the `portmap` daemon is similar to that of TCP_wrappers. The capabilities described here assume that TCP_wrappers is installed and, in particular, it depends upon the `libwrap.a` library, which is a part of TCP_wrappers.

The portmapper uses the same `/etc/hosts.allow` and `/etc/hosts.deny` files for access control as TCP_wrappers. It also automatically authorizes the `localhost`. The options for the `portmap` daemon, however, reflect a subset of that available to TCP_wrappers. Therefore, in Table 8–10, we list the type of option followed by a list of available capabilities for that option when used in conjunction with the portmapper. It may be useful to cross-reference the information contained in this table with Table 8–5 on page 286, Table 8–6 on page 287, Table 8–7 on page 289, and Table 8–8 on page 290.

Table 8–10   Available Syntax and Options for the Portmapper

SYNTAX TYPE	AVAILABILITY FOR `portmap`
Client specification	`IP address`, `net_number.`, or `net_number/netmask`. Note that hostnames *cannot* be used.
Extended options	`allow`, `deny`, `spawn`, `setenv`, and `umask`.
Variable expansion	`%a`, `%c`, `%d`, `%p`, and `%s`. Note that the server IP address is *not* available and that `%d` and `%s` expand identically.
Wildcard	`ALL`

---

5. Some System V.4 based UNIX systems, such as Solaris 2.x, use `rpcbind` instead of `port-map`. Wietse Venema also maintains an enhanced version of `rpcbind` for those systems.

While this list clearly represents a reduction in functionality, it does preserve the ability to use the important `spawn` option and, of course, to limit access based on IP addressing. Other than these restrictions, the syntax for the portmapper is identical.

In Example 8–32, we see a representative sample of the use of a `portmap` entry in `/etc/hosts.allow`.

Example 8–32   Sample Entries for the Portmapper

```
# hosts.allow
portmap: 172.19.0.0/255.255.240.0: deny

# Many PC's still don't broadcast properly
portmap: 255.255.255.255, 0.0.0.0: spawn (/usr/sbin/safe_finger \
   -lp @%a | logger -p local5.warn)&

# Allow the rest of our internal network
portmap: 172.17.

# Deny everybody else
portmap: ALL: deny
```

In this instance, we deny `portmap` services to the subnetwork of addresses from `172.19.0.0` through and including `172.19.15.255`. We allow the (illegal) broadcast addresses used by many PCs for NFS and other `portmap`-based services, but we make a special log entry for such requests so that we can detect when a potential attack occurs from those addresses. Next, all other IP addresses beginning with `172.17` are allowed. Everything else is denied. Now let's take a look at the log entries.

The `portmap` Log Entries

It turns out that the `portmap` daemon is ordinarily silent about its activity. Only failed requests will generate a log message, by default. In some cases, this may be sufficient; however, ordinarily more detail is desired. In order to increase logging to incorporate both unsuccessful and successful connections, you simply need to invoke `portmap -v`, instead of `portmap`. In Example 8–33, we see a series of log entries generated by `portmap -v` (line wraps are due to formatting constraints).

Example 8–33   Sample Log Output from `portmap -v`

```
Apr 12 10:50:24 topcat portmap[6112]: connect from 172.17.55.124 to getport(mountd)
Apr 12 10:51:03 topcat portmap[6113]: connect from 172.17.1.3 to getport(mountd)
Apr 12 11:01:15 topcat portmap[6193]: connect from 172.17.1.3 to getport(nlockmgr)
Apr 12 11:01:15 topcat portmap[6194]: connect from 172.17.1.3 to getport(nfs)
Apr 12 11:02:08 topcat portmap[6199]: connect from 172.17.1.3 to getport(mountd)
Apr 12 11:06:12 topcat portmap[6214]: connect from 172.17.1.3 to getport(mountd)
Apr 12 14:55:53 topcat portmap[6624]: connect from 172.17.1.3 to dump()
Apr 12 14:58:15 topcat portmap[6640]: connect from 172.17.1.3 to dump()
Apr 12 14:59:27 topcat portmap[6657]: connect from 172.17.1.3 to getport(sprayd)
Apr 12 14:59:27 topcat portmap[6662]: connect from 172.17.1.3 to getport(sprayd)
Apr 12 15:13:38 topcat portmap[6724]: connect from 172.17.55.124 to callit(rstatd)
Apr 12 21:28:24 topcat portmap[7089]: connect from 172.19.7.38 to dump(): request
from unauthorized host
```

There is only one unsuccessful attempt (last line of Example 8–33) shown in this example; all of the other entries exist because of the -v flag to portmap. The fields in each record of the log file are given in Table 8–11.

Table 8–11   Log Records Generated by the Portmapper

RECORD	DESCRIPTION
Date and Time	Date and timestamp, such as `Apr 12 15:13:38`.
Server	Hostname of the server, such as `topcat`.
Daemon Name	Name of the daemon, as with other TCP_wrappers entries. For the portmapper, it will always be `portmap`.
[PID]	Process identifier used for this session, such as `[6724]`
`connect from IP Address`	The IP address of the client.
`to` Type of Call	The type of call may be one of: null: a null call. set: register a program, usually effected by `killall -HUP inetd` after `/etc/rpc` has been modified. unset: unregister a program, such as with `rpcinfo -d`. getport: get the port number for the RPC program. dump: get all registered RPC programs, normally the result of `rpcinfo -p`.

Table 8–11   Log Records Generated by the Portmapper *(Continued)*

RECORD	DESCRIPTION
(Program Name)	The name of the RPC program, such as (mountd) for the NFS mount daemon.
Message	A message explaining the reason for rejection. No messages are generated for successful calls.

It should be noted that when a host is denied by rule in /etc/hosts.allow or /etc/hosts.deny, or generally when an error condition occurs, the client will only see an error message of the type, Program Not Registered, because the portmapper does not pass back the specific error condition. However, more specific error messages will be logged on the server by both the portmapper and the requested service (if the error condition was not caused by a deny rule). Normal error messages will be generated by daemons after a client request has been passed to it by the portmapper.

Gracefully Terminating and Recovering the Portmapper

Since the portmapper is very dynamic in terms of allocating ports and invoking services, it is important to gracefully terminate and restart it whenever it becomes necessary to do so. The two programs, pmap_dump and pmap_set, which come with portmapper version 4, provide this functionality.

Whenever you need to terminate the portmapper, do so by executing the steps outlined in Example 8–34 to ensure that the state of processes under its control are maintained.

Example 8–34   Gracefully Terminating and Restarting portmap

```
# pmap_dump > /root/pmaptable
# killall portmap
# /sbin/portmap
# pmap_set < /root/pmaptable
# rm -f /root/pmaptable
```

The use of the file /root/pmaptable in this example is somewhat arbitrary. The choice of the /root directory is based largely on the fact that its permissions prohibit world access, providing some protection against unauthorized modification of the table. The name of the table itself is completely arbitrary. The steps outlined in Example 8–34 can also be enscripted.

Portmapper Vulnerabilities

As outlined in "TCP_Wrappers Vulnerabilities" on page 307, the principal vulnerabilities associated with the portmapper have to do with its dependencies. Since the portmapper mainly relies upon IP addresses for its access control, there is no protection against spoofed addresses (which needs to be taken care of by `ipchains`; see Chapter 14). Furthermore, the portmapper cannot protect against services which it does not control after the initial invocation, such as `rpc.mountd`.

Of course, there is always the possibility that a vulnerability in the portmapper itself will be identified, so be sure to regularly read the appropriate newsgroups, such as `comp.unix.security`, and subscribe to the pertinent email lists, like `bugtraq` (see `http://www.securityfocus.org/` for more information about `bugtraq`).

Replacing `inetd` with `xinetd`

Up to this point, we have discussed using the existing `inetd` and portmapper utilities with TCP_wrappers to provide some protection against unauthorized access and to provide additional logging. The latter being a reasonably effective early warning mechanism. There is an alternative to this approach. You can implement `xinetd`, a complete replacement for `inetd`. In fact, `xinetd` is the default super server daemon as of Red Hat 7.0 and it ships as an alternative beginning with SuSE 6.4.

The Extended Internet Services Daemon, `xinetd`, provides many of the capabilities seen with TCP_wrappers and adds some capabilities not incorporated into those utilities. The `xinetd` daemon also supports TCP_wrappers. There are some disadvantages, however, which make for an additional bit of work. Let's examine this daemon.

WARNING

The configuration of `xinetd` is quite different than that of `inetd`. Also, the additional features of `xinetd` make for more complex configuration entries. This means that, at least initially, you may make mistakes in configuring `xinetd`. **These mistakes could have severe security ramifications. Therefore, take the necessary time to learn about and extensively test** `xinetd` **configurations.**

Advantages of `xinetd`

The `xinetd` provides access control in a way that is quite similar to TCP_wrappers or the portmapper. It additionally affords the following functionality.

- Access control for TCP, UDP, and RPC services
- Access limitations based on time
- Extensive logging capabilities for both successful and unsuccessful connections
- Implements RFC 1413 username retrievals
- Provides for hard reconfiguration by killing services that are no longer allowed
- Provides numerous mechanisms to prevent denial of service attacks
  - Limits may be placed on the number of daemons of a given type which may concurrently run
  - An overall limit of processes forked by `xinetd` may be imposed
  - Limits on log file sizes may be imposed
- Provides a compile-time option to include `libwrap`, the TCP_wrappers library
  - Causes `/etc/hosts.allow` and `/etc/hosts.deny` access control checks in addition to `xinetd` access control checks
- Provides for the invocation of `tcpd`
  - All TCP_wrappers functionality is available
- Services may be bound to specific interfaces
- Services may be forwarded (proxied) to another system
- Supports IPv6

All these features will be discussed in detail in the sections that follow.

Disadvantages of `xinetd`

In spite of its capabilities, there is a downside.

- The configuration file, `/etc/xinetd.conf`, is incompatible with `/etc/inetd.conf`
  - However, a conversion utility, `itox`, is included with the distribution
- Timeouts and other problems occur for RPC services, especially on busy systems
  - However, `xinetd` and `portmap` may coexist allowing RPC through the portmapper

Each of these issues will be discussed subsequently.

It should be noted that `xinetd` does not consult the `/etc/services` file for service configuration. It is only used by `xinetd` to determine which services are "listed."

Obtaining `xinetd`

The `xinetd` daemon was originally written by Panagiotis Tsirigotis. Rob Braun has made numerous enhancements and currently maintains it. The latest version, as of this writing, is 2.1.8.8p3. You may obtain either a `gzipped`, `tar` archive of the source or RPM packages of both the source and i386 executables from

```
http://synack.net/xinetd/
```

As noted earlier, `xinetd` ships with SuSE 6.4 and later as well as Red Hat 7.0 and later. The Debian package is available at

```
http://www.debian.org/Packages/stable/net/xinetd.html
```

It is likely that, by the time you read this, the `xinetd` software will already be installed on your system.

Next, we discuss the syntax of the `xinetd` configuration file and the flags associated with the `xinetd` daemon. After that, we will look at some examples and log messages.

NOTE

There is a `xinetd` version 2.2.1 which is *not* newer than, nor does it incorporate, the additional functionality described for `xinetd` version 2.1.8.8p3. The last update for `xinetd` 2.2.1, found at `ftp://coast.cs.purdue.edu/`

`pub/tools/unix/xinetd/`, was April 1997, and it does not appear as if anyone is actively working on that version. The folks who put together `xinetd` 2.2.1 used version numbering, which conflicts with the copyright (see the `COPYRIGHT` file in the distribution). Rob Braun has adhered to the version numbering described in the copyright; hence, the discrepancy in version numbers. Version 2.1.8.8p3 of `xinetd` described herein continued to be actively worked on at the time of this publication.

WARNING

While it is entirely possible to simultaneously run `inetd`, `xinetd`, and `portmap`, they must not have equivalent service configurations. For example, if both `inetd` and `xinetd` have configuration entries for `telnet`, then only one of the two daemons will service the request. Normally, this behavior is benign and will simply generate log messages which indicate that `inetd` or `xinetd` (whichever one started last at boot-time) could not bind to a particular port (`23` for `telnet`), as it was already in use. Problems can occur, however, especially if the `flags = REUSE` (see Table 8–12 on page 317) option is specified for `xinetd`. This will make the socket available for binding even if `inetd` is already bound to it, which may in turn allow usually unauthorized connections. In short, if you are using a combination of two or all three daemons, `inetd`, `xinetd`, and `portmap`, make sure that they serve daemons exclusively.

The `xinetd` Configuration File

The `xinetd` configuration file is by default `/etc/xinetd.conf`. Its syntax is quite different than, and incompatible with, `/etc/inetd.conf`. Essentially, it combines the functionality of `/etc/inetd.conf`, `/etc/hosts.allow`, and `/etc/hosts.deny` into one file. Each entry in `/etc/xinetd.conf` is of the form,

```
service service_name
{
attribute operator value value ...
...
}
```

where `service` is a required keyword and the braces must surround the list of attributes.

The *service_name* is arbitrary, but normally chosen to conform with the standard network services. Additional and completely non-standard services may be added, so long as they are invoked through a network request including network requests from the localhost itself.

There are a number of *attributes* available. These are described in Table 8–12 on page 317. We will also describe the required attributes and rules of attribute usage later in this section.

The *operator* may be one of "=", "+=", or "-=". All attributes may use "=" which has the effect of assigning one or more values. Some attributes may use the forms, "+=" and/or "-=", which have the effect of adding to an existing list of values or removing from an existing list of values, respectively. The attributes which may use these latter forms are noted in Table 8–12.

The *values* are the parameters set to the given attribute.

Before we look at Table 8–12, let's consider a simple example. In Example 8–35, we see a partial /etc/xinetd.conf file.

Example 8–35   Partial /etc/xinetd.conf File

```
service ftp
{
        socket_type     = stream
        protocol        = tcp
        wait            = no
        user            = root
        server          = /usr/sbin/in.ftpd
        server_args     = -l -a
}

service telnet
{
        socket_type     = stream
        protocol        = tcp
        wait            = no
        user            = root
        server          = /usr/sbin/in.telnetd
}
```

Notice that, in spite of the formatting differences, the information contained in these records is identical to what is found in /etc/inetd.conf. The reason that these two entries look so similar to /etc/inetd.conf is because they were generated from /etc/inetd.conf with the itox utility which simply converts /etc/inetd.conf entries to the proper syntax for xinetd. In this case, the attributes (everything inside the braces and to the left of the = symbol) are very straightforward in their meaning, as are the associated values (everything inside the braces and to the right of the = symbol).

The easiest way to initially create the `/etc/xinetd.conf` file is with the `itox` utility. The syntax for its use is, very simply (this example assumes that the current working directory is the `xinetd` build directory),

```
# xinetd/itox -daemon_dir /usr/sbin </etc/inetd.conf >/etc/
xinetd.conf
```

The option `-daemon_dir /usr/sbin` to `itox` specifies the actual location of the daemons, which would not be deterministic from `/etc/inetd.conf` if TCP_wrappers is implemented. Once done, you may start adding attributes and values which restrict access and increase logging. Be sure to modify the `/etc/xinetd.conf` to take advantage of the features of `xinetd`, otherwise, if you just convert `/etc/inetd.conf` to `/etc/xinetd.conf`, `xinetd` will behave identically to `inetd`.

Table 8–12 details the attributes and values which may be used in `/etc/xinetd.conf`.

Table 8–12   Extended Internet Services Daemon Attributes

ATTRIBUTE	DESCRIPTION AND ALLOWED VALUE
`socket_type`	The type of TCP/IP socket used. Acceptable values are `stream` (TCP), `dgram` (UDP), `raw`, and `seqpacket` (reliable, sequential datagrams).
`protocol`	Specifies the protocol used by the service. Must be an entry in `/etc/protocols`. If not specified, the default protocol for the service is used.
`server`	Daemon to invoke. Must be absolutely qualified.
`server_args`	Specifies the flags to be passed to the daemon.
`port`	Port number associated with the service. If listed in `/etc/services`, it must match.

Table 8–12   Extended Internet Services Daemon Attributes *(Continued)*

ATTRIBUTE	DESCRIPTION AND ALLOWED VALUE
`wait`	There are two possible values for this attribute. If `yes`, then `xinetd` will start the requested daemon and cease to handle requests for this service until the daemon terminates. This is a single threaded service. If `no`, then `xinetd` will start a daemon for each request, regardless of the state of previously started daemons. This is a multithreaded service.
`user` *username*	Sets the UID for the daemon. The *username* specified must exist in `/etc/passwd`. This attribute is ineffective if the effective UID of `xinetd` is not 0.
`group` *groupname*	Sets the GID for the daemon. The *groupname* specified must exist in `/etc/group`. This attribute is ineffective if the effective UID of `xinetd` is not 0.
`groups`	Accepts either the YES or NO value. If YES, then the specified server daemon runs with the group privileges associated with the effective UID of the server. If NO, it does not.
`nice`	Specifies the `nice` value for the daemon.
`id`	Used to uniquely identify a service when redundancy exists. For example, `echo` provides both `dgram` and `streams` services. Setting `id=echo_dgram` and `id=echo_stream`, respectively, would uniquely identify these two services. If not specified, `id` assumes the value specified by the `service` keyword.
`type`	May take one or more of the following values, RPC (for RPC services), INTERNAL (for services handled by `xinetd`, like `echo`), or UNLISTED (a service not listed in a standard system file such as `/etc/rpc` or `/etc/services`).

Table 8–12   Extended Internet Services Daemon Attributes *(Continued)*

ATTRIBUTE	DESCRIPTION AND ALLOWED VALUE
`access_times`	Sets the time intervals for when the service is available. Format is `hh:mm-hh:mm`; for example, `08:00-18:00` means the service is available from 8 a.m. through 6 p.m.
`banner file`	Accepts an absolutely qualified `file`, the contents of which are displayed to the client whenever a connection is made. This banner is displayed regardless of access control.
`banner_success file`	Accepts an absolutely qualified `file`, the contents of which are displayed to the client whenever a connection is granted.
`banner_fail file`	Accepts an absolutely qualified `file`, the contents of which are displayed to the client whenever a connection is denied.
`flags`	One or more of the following options may be specified: REUSE: Sets the TCP/IP socket to be reusable. This is particularly valuable when `xinetd` is terminated and restarted. See the section, "Signals Available for Use with xinetd" on page 342, for further details. INTERCEPT: Intercepts packets destined to single threaded daemons and performs an access check. Cannot be used with INTERNAL services. NORETRY: Do not retry `fork` if it fails. IDONLY: Accept connections only if the client returns the UID to an RFC1413 call. The USERID value must be set for `log_on_success` and/or `log_on_failure` attributes for this value to take effect. Only available for multithreaded, stream services. NAMEINARGS: Allows for the first argument in the `server_args` attribute to be a fully qualified path to a daemon, allowing for the use of TCP_wrappers (very cool!). NODELAY: Causes the `TCP_NODELAY` flag to be set on the socket. Applies only to TCP services.

Table 8–12   Extended Internet Services Daemon Attributes *(Continued)*

ATTRIBUTE	DESCRIPTION AND ALLOWED VALUE
`rpc_version`	Specifies the RPC version number or numbers for the service. Multiple version numbers are specified in a range, for example, `2-3`.
`rpc_number`	Specifies the RPC program number if it does not exist in `/etc/rpc`.
`env`	A space-separated list of VAR=VALUE, where VAR is a shell environment variable and VALUE is its setting. These values will be passed to the service daemon upon invocation together with `xinetd`'s environment. This attribute supports the "+=" operator in addition to "=".
`passenv`	A space-separated list of environment variables from `xinetd`'s environment which are passed to the service daemon upon invocation. Setting no value causes no variables to be passed. This attribute supports all operators.
`only_from`	A space-separated list of allowed clients. The syntax for clients is given in Table 8–13. If this attribute is specified without a value, it acts to deny access to the service. This attribute supports all operators.
`no_access`	A space-separated list of denied clients. The syntax for clients is given in Table 8–13. This attribute supports all operators.
`instances`	Accepts an integer greater than or equal to 1 or UNLIMITED. Sets the maximum number of concurrent running daemons. UNLIMITED means no limit is imposed by `xinetd`.

Table 8–12   Extended Internet Services Daemon Attributes *(Continued)*

ATTRIBUTE	DESCRIPTION AND ALLOWED VALUE
`per_source`	Accepts an integer greater than or equal to 1 or `UNLIMITED`. Specifies the maximum number of concurrent running daemons of this service per source IP address. `UNLIMITED` means no limit is imposed by `xinetd`.
`cps nbr wait`	This attribute limits the rate of incoming connections. The first argument, `nbr`, specifies the maximum number of connections per second. If the maximum rate is exceeded, the second argument, `wait`, specifies the number of seconds that the service will be disabled.
`max_load load`	This attribute specifies a floating point value, `load`, which is the load average of the service averaged over a minute. If the load value is exceeded, the service will stop accepting connections until the load drops below this value.
`log_type`	By default, `xinetd` logs to `syslogd daemon.info`. There are two available values: `SYSLOG facility [level]`: Sets the facility to one of `daemon`, `auth`, `user`, or `local0-7`. Setting the `level` is optional. All levels are accepted. `FILE file [soft [hard]]`: Specifies the indicated `file` for logging instead of `syslog`. The limits, `soft` and `hard` are, optionally, specified in kbytes. Once the `soft` limit is reached, `xinetd` logs a message to that effect. Once the hard limit is reached, `xinetd` stops logging all services which use this file. If no `hard` limit is specified, it becomes `soft` plus 1%, but cannot exceed 20k by default. The default `soft` limit is 5k.
`redirect`	This attribute assumes the syntax, `redirect = IPaddress port`. It has the effect of redirecting a TCP service to another system. The `server` attribute is ignored if this attribute is used.

Table 8–12   Extended Internet Services Daemon Attributes *(Continued)*

ATTRIBUTE	DESCRIPTION AND ALLOWED VALUE
`bind`	Binds a service to a specific interface. Syntax is `bind = IPaddress`. This allows hosts with multiple interfaces (physical or logical), for example, to permit specific services (or ports) on one interface but not the other.
`log_on_success`	Specifies the information to be logged on success. Possible values are: PID: PID of the daemon. If a new daemon is not forked, PID is 0. HOST: client host IP address. USERID: captures UID of the client user through an RFC1413 call. Only available for multithreaded, stream services. EXIT: logs daemon termination and status. DURATION: logs duration of session. By default, nothing is logged. This attribute supports all operators.
`log_on_failure`	Specifies the information to be logged on failure. A message indicating the nature of the error is always logged. Possible values are: ATTEMPT: Records a failed attempt. All other values imply this one. HOST: client host IP address. USERID: captures UID of the client user through an RFC1413 call. Only available for multithreaded, stream services. RECORD: records additional client information such as local user, remote user, and terminal type. By default, nothing is logged. This attribute supports all operators.

Table 8–12   Extended Internet Services Daemon Attributes *(Continued)*

ATTRIBUTE	DESCRIPTION AND ALLOWED VALUE
`disabled`	Only available for use with the special `defaults` entry (see "The `defaults` Entry" on page 325). Accepts a space-separated list of services which are unavailable. It has the same effect as commenting out the service entry in the `/etc/xinetd.conf` file.

There are certainly a large number of attributes. We will take a look at some examples in "Configuration Examples" on page 332, which will clarify many of these attributes.

Table 8–12 on page 317 provides the syntax for `only_from` and `no_access` lists. In Table 8–13, we provide the syntax for specifying hostnames, IP addresses, and networks.

Table 8–13   Access Control List Syntax for `/etc/xinetd.conf`

SYNTAX	DESCRIPTION
`hostname`	A resolvable hostname. All IP addresses associated with the hostname will be used.
`IPaddress`	The standard IP address in dot decimal form.
`net_name`	A network name from `/etc/networks`.

`x.x.x.0`
`x.x.0.0`
`x.0.0.0`
`0.0.0.0`
	The `0` is treated as a wildcard. For example, an entry like `88.3.92.0` would match all addresses beginning with `88.3.92.0` through and including `88.3.92.255`. The `0.0.0.0` entry matches all addresses.

Table 8–13   Access Control List Syntax for `/etc/xinetd.conf` *(Continued)*

Syntax	Description

`x.x.x.{a, b, ...}`
`x.x.{a, b, ...}`
`x.{a, b, ...}`
	Specifies lists of hosts. For example, `172.19.32.{1, 56, 59}` means the list of IP addresses `172.19.32.1`, `172.19.32.56`, and `172.19.32.59`.

`IPaddress/netmask`	Defines the network, or subnetwork, to match. For example, `172.19.16.0/20` matches all addresses in the range `172.19.16.0` through and including `172.19.31.255`.

Now that we've seen the basic attributes, let's have a look at which ones are required and how to go about using them.

Required Attributes

Certain attributes must be specified for every service. Some services need more attributes than others because they are "unlisted" (not in `/etc/services` nor `/etc/rpc`). Table 8–14 lists the attributes which are required.

Table 8–14   Required Attributes

Attribute	Required By
`socket_type`	all services
`wait`	all services
`user`	services listed in `/etc/services` or `/etc/rpc`
`server`	non-internal services
`port`	non-RPC services which are not in `/etc/services`
`protocol`	all RPC services and all other services not in `/etc/services`
`rpc_version`	all RPC services
`rpc_number`	any RPC service which is not listed in `/etc/rpc`

Special xinetd Services

There are four special entries which may be specified in the `/etc/xinetd.conf` file. They are: `defaults`, `servers`, `services`, and `xadmin`. The `defaults` entry is not a service and must not have a preceding `service` keyword (otherwise, it will be treated as a service called `defaults`). Each of these is described in the next four sections.

THE defaults ENTRY   The purpose of the `defaults` entry in the `/etc/xinetd.conf` file is to specify default values for all services in the file. These default values may be overridden or modified by each service entry. The attributes which may be specified in the `defaults` entry are listed in Table 8–15. This table also indicates the acceptable modification behavior in subsequent service entries.

Table 8–15   Attributes Available to `defaults`

ATTRIBUTE	SERVICE MODIFICATION
log_on_success log_on_failure only_from no_access passenv	May be overridden with the "=" operator or modified with either the "+=" or "-=" operators.
instances log_type	May be overridden with the "=" operator.
disabled	Service may be commented out, but the `disabled` attribute may not be used within a service entry.

The modification behaviors cited in the *Service Modification* column of Table 8–15 are clarified in "Configuration Examples" on page 332.

Example 8–36 provides an example `defaults` entry as it might appear in `/etc/xinetd.conf`.

Example 8–36   Sample `defaults` Entry in `/etc/xinetd.conf`

```
defaults
{
        log_type          = SYSLOG local4 info
        log_on_success    = PID HOST EXIT DURATION
        log_on_failure    = HOST
        instances         = 8
         disabled          = in.tftpd in.rexecd
}
```

Here, we see that for all services, log messages will be sent to the `syslogd` daemon via the `local4.info` selector. Successful connections to services will cause the PID, client IP address, termination status, and time of connection to be logged. Unsuccessful connection attempts will have the client IP address logged. The maximum number of instances for any one service is set to eight. The two services, `in.tftpd` and `in.rexecd`, are disabled.

The use of the `defaults` entry essentially offers a shortcut for establishing certain attributes throughout the file being applied to all services which do not set these attributes otherwise.

NOTE

If you do not have a `defaults` entry in your `/etc/xinetd.conf` file and subsequently decide to add one, you must terminate and restart `xinetd` in order for the `defaults` to take effect. This is also true for any new service you may add to `/etc/xinetd.conf`. This may be accomplished by

```
# killall -TERM xinetd
# /usr/sbin/xinetd
```

or you can enscript this capability. It may well be that your distribution includes a start-up script that will provide this functionality.

THE `servers` ENTRY   The purpose of the `servers` special service is to provide a list of daemons, together with pertinent information about those daemons, currently running on the server. In other words, it provides a list of active connections. This is a useful mechanism for troubleshooting as well as for examining the state of `xinetd`. Example 8–37 displays a sample `servers` entry in the `/etc/xinetd.conf` file. Notice that this service is of INTERNAL, UNLISTED type, which means that it is an internal function of `xinetd` and is not listed in `/etc/services`. The port number used is completely arbitrary.

Example 8–37   Sample `servers` Entry

```
service servers
{
        type                 = INTERNAL UNLISTED
        socket_type          = stream
        protocol             = tcp
        port                 = 9997
        wait                 = no
        only_from            = 172.17.33.111
        wait                 = no
}
```

Note that this service is available only from the specific IP address, `172.17.33.111`, which should be the IP address of the server itself. This disallows any other host from obtaining this information from this server. The security ramification here is, very simply, that if this information were allowed to be read by others on other systems, it could well lead to an exploit based on the knowledge of what daemons are currently running. It is, perhaps, ill-advised to run this server at all, except for debugging purposes, since any user on `172.17.33.111` is able to obtain this information by executing `telnet 172.17.33.111 9997`, as shown in Example 8–38 (line numbers added for clarity).

Example 8–38   Example Output of `servers` Service

```
 1  $ telnet topcat 9997
 2  Trying 172.17.33.111...
 3  Connected to topcat.
 4  Escape character is '^]'.
 5  telnet server
 6  pid = 5931
 7  start_time = Sat Apr 17 10:32:15 1999
 8  Connection info:
 9          state = CLOSED
10          service = telnet
11          descriptor = 20
12          flags = 9
13          remote_address = 10.48.3.2,39958
14          Alternative services =
15  log_remote_user = YES
16  writes_to_log = YES
17
18  ftp server
19  pid = 5960
20  start_time = Sat Apr 17 10:49:06 1999
21  Connection info:
22          state = CLOSED
23          service = ftp
24          descriptor = 20
25          flags = 9
```

Example 8-38   Example Output of `servers` Service *(Continued)*

```
26          remote_address = 172.17.55.124,2320
27          Alternative services =
28 log_remote_user = YES
29 writes_to_log = YES
30
31 telnet server
32 pid = 5961
33 start_time = Sat Apr 17 10:49:20 1999
34 Connection info:
35          state = CLOSED
36          service = telnet
37          descriptor = 20
38          flags = 9
39          remote_address = 172.17.1.3,35461
40          Alternative services =
41 log_remote_user = YES
42 writes_to_log = YES
43
44 Connection closed by foreign host.
45 $
```

Note that `xinetd` simply provides the information and exits, providing no inter-active connection. The output shown in Example 8–38 tells us that there are two running `telnet` daemons (lines 5 and 31, respectively), one with the PID of `5931`, the other with the PID of `5961` (lines 6 and 32, respectively). There is one `ftp` daemon (line 18) running with the PID of `5960` (line 19). For each running daemon, some connection information, together with logging information, is provided. Probably not the sort of information you want floating around and, in general, for security reasons, you may want this turned off except perhaps on tightly secured systems. To turn it off, make sure that no entry of the type shown in Example 8–37 is present in your `/etc/xinetd.conf` file.

THE `services` ENTRY   The purpose of the `services` special entry is to provide a list of available services. As with the `servers` special entry, this is a useful troubleshooting utility, but for the same security reasons as cited above, it should probably also be left off. Nonetheless, let's see how it works.

Example 8–39 illustrates a sample `services` entry in the `/etc/xinetd.conf` file. Once again, the choice of port numbers is arbitrary, and notice that access is limited to `topcat`, which is the hostname of the server itself.

Example 8–39   Sample `services` Entry in `/etc/xinetd.conf`

```
service services
{
        type               = INTERNAL UNLISTED
        socket_type        = stream
        protocol           = tcp
        port               = 8099
        wait               = no
        only_from          = topcat
}
```

As with the `servers` service, any user may execute `telnet topcat 8099`, and obtain the output from the `services` service, so long as that user is logged in to `topcat`. Example 8–40 provides the details.

Example 8–40   Output from a Query to the `services` Internal Service

```
$ telnet topcat 8099
Trying 172.17.33.111...
Connected to topcat.
Escape character is '^]'.
servers tcp 9997
services tcp 8099
ftp tcp 21
telnet tcp 23
shell tcp 514
login tcp 513
talk udp 517
ntalk udp 518
pop-2 tcp 109
pop-3 tcp 110
imap tcp 143
linuxconf tcp 98
Connection closed by foreign host.
$
```

Note that `xinetd` simply provides the information and exits, providing no interactive connection.

THE `xadmin` **ENTRY**   This special service entry provides an interactive way of obtaining the information provided by the special services, `servers` and `services`. An example `/etc/xinetd.conf` entry is given in Example 8–41 (again, the choice of port numbers is arbitrary).

Example 8–41   The xadmin Entry

```
service xadmin
{
        type            = INTERNAL UNLISTED
        socket_type     = stream
        protocol        = tcp
        port            = 9967
        wait            = no
        only_from       = topcat
}
```

Much like the services and servers services, there is no password or other protection for this service. So, make sure that you use an only_from entry of the type shown here, allowing requests from the server itself only.

As with the previous two special service types, you need only telnet to the port listed. In this case, telnet topcat 9967. Unlike the previous two services, xadmin does provide an interactive environment. As of this writing, there are five commands which may be executed once you have connected to the xadmin server. They are: help, show run, show avail, bye, and exit. The help command displays the other commands together with a brief usage message. The bye and exit commands both close the connection. The show run and show avail commands provide the information provided by servers and services, respectively. Example 8–42 shows the use of each of these commands.

Example 8–42   Using the xadmin Service

```
$ telnet topcat 9967
Trying 172.17.33.111...
Connected to topcat.
Escape character is '^]'.
> help
xinetd admin help:
show run   :    shows information about running services
show avail:     shows what services are currently available
bye, exit :     exits the admin shell
> show run
Running services:
service  run retry attempts descriptor
telnet server
pid = 5931
start_time = Sat Apr 17 10:32:15 1999
Connection info:
        state = CLOSED
        service = telnet
        descriptor = 20
        flags = 9
        remote_address = 10.48.3.2,39958
        Alternative services =
log_remote_user = YES
writes_to_log = YES
```

Example 8–42 Using the `xadmin` Service *(Continued)*

```
telnet server
pid = 5961
start_time = Sat Apr 17 10:49:20 1999
Connection info:
        state = CLOSED
        service = telnet
        descriptor = 20
        flags = 9
        remote_address = 172.17.1.3,35461
        Alternative services =
log_remote_user = YES
writes_to_log = YES

xadmin server
pid = 0
start_time = Wed Dec 31 17:00:00 1969
Connection info:
        state = OPEN
        service = xadmin
        descriptor = 20
        flags = 9
        remote_address = 172.17.33.111,17165
        Alternative services =
log_remote_user = NO
writes_to_log = NO

> show avail
Available services:
servers
xadmin
services
ftp
telnet
telnet
shell
login
talk
ntalk
pop-2
pop-3
imap
finger
auth
linuxconf
> bye
bye bye
Connection closed by foreign host.
$
```

Once again, notice that a non-root user can access this service; therefore, exercise caution in making this special service available for the reasons outlined at the end of "The `servers` Entry" on page 326.

WARNING

As pointed out in the previous sections, the special services, `servers`, `services`, and `xadmin` produce information which may be used to compromise your system. You probably don't need these services running all the time—perhaps just when you are debugging. In any event, if you do run these services, make sure that you configure access control using either `access_from` or `no_access` or both. Also, use the `bind` attribute for these services to further restrict access. Using `bind` is discussed in "Using the `bind` Attribute" on page 336

Configuration Examples

In this section, we will take a look at a number of different configuration examples, the behavior associated with them, and the log messages which they generate.

ACCESS CONTROL   We'll begin with a simple access control example. In Example 8–43, we see a `login` service entry for the server, `topcat`, which allows access from any system whose IP address begins with `172` except for those whose address begins with `172.19`.

Example 8–43   Sample `login` Service Entry in `/etc/xinetd.conf`

```
defaults
{
        log_type        = SYSLOG local4 info
        log_on_success  = PID HOST EXIT DURATION
        log_on_failure  = HOST
        instances       = 8
}
service login
{
        socket_type     = stream
        protocol        = tcp
        wait            = no
        user            = root
        flags           = REUSE
        only_from       = 172.0.0.0
        no_access       = 172.19.0.0
        log_on_success  += USERID
        log_on_failure  += USERID
        server          = /usr/sbin/in.ftpd
        server_args     = -l -a
}
```

We include the `defaults` section in this example for clarity. Given this entry for the `login` service, which is invoked through an `rlogin` command from the client, let's examine a successful and unsuccessful attempt and the logs they generate.

Suppose that the host, `underdog`, has the IP address `172.18.5.9`. Then, when Mary executes `rlogin` to `topcat`, she would be granted access. The successful login is shown in Example 8–44.

Example 8–44   Successful `rlogin` Attempt

```
[mary@underdog]$ rlogin topcat
Password:
Last login: Wed Apr 14 17:45:02 from roadrunner
[mary@topcat]$
```

While Example 8–44 is not terribly exciting, let's look at the log entries generated by Mary's action. This is shown in Example 8–45.

Example 8–45   Log Entries Associated with Example 8–44

```
Apr 15 11:01:46 topcat xinetd[1402]: START: login pid=1439 from=172.18.5.9
Apr 15 11:01:46 topcat xinetd[1439]: USERID: login OTHER :mary
...
<lots of unrelated output snipped>
...
Apr 15 11:39:31 topcat xinetd[1402]: EXIT: login status=1 pid=1439 duration=2265(sec)
```

The last entry in Example 8–45 reflects the exit condition when Mary logs out. You can always trace the exit of a session by PID so long as you specify that the PID is to be logged in `/etc/inetd.conf`, as in Example 8–43. The log entries are as follows. Every `xinetd` log entry records the date and timestamp, followed by the server hostname, then `xinetd`, followed by the PID of `xinetd` in brackets. The first record of Example 8–45 begins with the START keyword indicating the initiation of the session; next, the daemon invoked is identified (`login`), then the PID of the invoked daemon and, lastly, the client address.

The second entry begins with the USERID keyword indicating that an RFC 1413 call was issued successfully. It is followed by the service name (login), the remote system's response to the RFC 1413 call (OTHER is this case) and, finally, the remote username (`mary`).

These log entries are relatively straightforward, but Table 8–16 provides a list of explanations regarding the keywords (such as START, USERID, and EXIT) and the information which follows that keyword.

Table 8–16   Description of `xinetd` Log Entries

LOG KEYWORD	FORMAT AND DESCRIPTION
`START`	`START: service_id [pid=PID] [from=IPaddress]` This entry is recorded whenever a service has started. The `service_id` is the name of the service as specified by the `id` attribute (recall that if this attribute is not explicitly set, it assumes the value of the service argument; see Table 8–12 on page 317), the `PID` is the process identifier of the invoked daemon, or 0 if no daemon is invoked (only recorded if `PID` is specified to `log_on_success`), and the `IPaddress` is the client's IP address (only recorded if HOST is `log_on_success`).
`EXIT`	`EXIT: service_id [type=s] [pid=PID] [duration=#(sec)]` This entry is recorded when a daemon terminates, only if `EXIT` is specified to `log_on_success`. The `service_id` and `PID` entries are as before. The `type` entry will record the exit status or signal which caused termination. The duration captures the duration of the session in seconds and requires the DURATION option to `log_on_success`.
`FAIL`	`FAIL: service_id reason [from=IPaddress]` This entry is generated whenever a failed attempt occurred and at least one value is specified to the `log_on_failure` attribute. The `service_id` is as before. The `reason` is a simple word or phrase explaining the cause of failure. The `IPaddress` is the client's and the HOST value to `log_on_failure` must be set for this to appear.
`DATA`	`DATA: service_id data` Only recorded when the RECORD value to `log_on_failure` occurs. The `service_id` is as before. The `data` recorded depends upon the service, but normally includes the remote username if available and status information.
`USERID`	`USERID: service-id text` This information is only recorded when the `USERID` value is specified to `log_on_success` or `log_on_failure` or both. The `service_id` is as before. The `text` includes the client's response to the RFC1413 call and, in particular, the remote username.

Table 8–16   Description of `xinetd` Log Entries *(Continued)*

LOG KEYWORD	FORMAT AND DESCRIPTION
NOID	NOID: service_id IPaddress reason This entry will only appear if the IDONLY value is set to the `flags` attribute and the USERID value is set to at least one of `log_on_success` or `log_on_failure`. The `service_id` is as before. The IPaddress given is the client's. The reason is a failure status.

Now, let's suppose that `joe` attempts to use `rlogin` from the host `sly.no.good.org` (IP address, `19.152.1.5`). Example 8–46 displays the result of his attempt.

Example 8–46   Failed `rlogin` Attempts from Unauthorized Host

```
sly.no.good.org$ rlogin topcat
topcat: Connection reset by peer
sly.no.good.org$ rlogin -l paul topcat
topcat: Connection reset by peer
sly.no.good.org$ rlogin -l mary topcat
topcat: Connection reset by peer
sly.no.good.org$
```

It seems that Joe is getting a little frustrated. Or maybe he's trying to break in (nah, couldn't be!). Let's take a look at the log entries generated by these three attempts in Example 8–47.

Example 8–47   Log Entries Associated with Example 8–46

```
Apr 15 12:08:40 topcat xinetd[1402]: FAIL: login address from=19.152.1.5
Apr 15 12:08:52 topcat xinetd[1402]: FAIL: login address from=19.152.1.5
Apr 15 12:12:49 topcat xinetd[1402]: FAIL: login address from=19.152.1.5
```

Notice that the log entries do not include the remote username, even though we have specifically requested that information by virtue of the `log_on_failure` attribute in Example 8–43 on page 332. This is because the remote host, `sly.no.good.org`, is not running `identd` or a similar daemon (maybe Joe *is* up to something!). Because the host, `sly.no.good.org`, is not in the `only_from` list in Example 8–43 on page 332, even if we added the entry, "`flags = IDONLY`", to the `login` service entry, it would not record the fact that `sly.no.good.org` is not running `identd`. Such a log record will only occur if the host is allowed.

One last log entry to examine. Note that the attribute `instances` is set to 8 in Example 8–43 on page 332. What happens to the ninth login session? When the ninth user attempts to `rlogin` to `topcat`, that user will see the following error message:

```
rcmd: topcat: Address already in use
```

and the log entry recorded on `topcat` for this event will be

```
Apr 15 13:37:33 topcat xinetd[1402]: FAIL: login service_limit
from=172.17.55.124
```

Comparing this record to the description given in Table 8–16, the `FAIL` keyword is followed by the service, then an explanation for the failure (`service_limit` in this case) and, lastly, the client address.

USING THE `bind` **ATTRIBUTE** The `bind` attribute allows for associating a particular service with a specific interface's IP address. Suppose we have an internal `ftp` server which supplies read-only resources for company employees via anonymous `ftp`. Further suppose that this `ftp` server has two interfaces, one which attaches to the corporate environment and the other which connects to a private internal network which is generally only accessible to employees who work in that particular group. While there are a number of things that need to be done to secure this server, (`ipchains` being one; see Chapter 14), we will only consider the requirement to provide two different `ftp` services based on interfaces in this example. Example 8–48 shows two `ftp` service entries in `/etc/xinetd.conf` which would implement the desired functionality. Again, the `defaults` section is provided for completeness.

Example 8–48   Binding Services to Specific Addresses

```
defaults
{
        log_type         = SYSLOG local4 info
        log_on_success   = PID HOST EXIT DURATION
        log_on_failure   = HOST
        instances        = 8
}
service ftp
{
        id               = ftp
        socket_type      = stream
        protocol         = tcp
        wait             = no
        user             = root
        only_from        = 172.17.0.0 172.19.0.0/20
        bind             = 172.17.1.1 # widget
```

Example 8–48 Binding Services to Specific Addresses *(Continued)*

```
        log_on_success  += USERID
        log_on_failure  += USERID
        server          = /usr/sbin/in.ftpd
        server_args     = -l -a
}

service ftp
{
        id                = ftp_chroot
        socket_type       = stream
        protocol          = tcp
        wait              = no
        user              = root
        bind              = 24.170.1.218 # widget-srvr
        log_on_success  += USERID
        log_on_failure  += USERID
        access_times      = 8:30-11:30 13:00-18:00
        log_on_success  += USERID
        log_on_failure  += USERID
        server            = /usr/sbin/anon/in.aftpd
}
```

Notice that we have two `ftp` service entries, each with a unique `id` attribute (see Table 8–12 on page 317). There is no limit to the number of services with the same name so long as each has a unique identifier. In this case, we set the `id` attribute to `ftp` for the internal `ftp` server and `ftp_chroot` for the external anonymous server. Note that in the latter case the daemon invoked is `/usr/sbin/anon/in.aftpd` (this is the effective equivalent to `twist` for TCP_wrappers), which is different than the former service.

The use of `bind` in each case will only allow packets destined to that interface to invoke the indicated daemon. Thus, we can reach the anonymous server by executing `ftp widget-srvr`. Since there are no access controls for that service, everyone has access. However, access is only granted between 8:30 a.m. through 11:30 a.m. and 1 p.m. through 6 p.m., due to the `access_times` attribute.

On the other hand, executing `ftp widget` will only be successful if the first two octets of the client IP address begin with `172.17` or the request comes from an address in the range `172.19.0.0` through `172.19.15.255`, because of the `only_from` attribute.

USING THE `redirect` ATTRIBUTE The `redirect` attribute provides a method for proxying a service through a server. In other words, the user may `telnet` to a particular server running `xinetd`, and that server would open another connection to a different system. We can accomplish this with the entries in `/etc/xinetd.conf` shown in Example 8–49. Here we are using `tel-net` as the example, but it could be used with any TCP service.

Example 8–49   Use Of `redirect` and `bind` in `/etc/xinetd.conf`

```
service telnet
{
        socket_type      = stream
        wait             = no
        flags       = REUSE
        user             = root
        bind        = 172.17.33.111
        server           = /usr/sbin/in.telnetd
        log_on_success   = PID HOST EXIT DURATION USERID
        log_on_failure   = RECORD HOST
}

service telnet
{
        socket_type      = stream
        protocol         = tcp
        wait             = no
        flags       = REUSE
        user             = root
        bind        = 201.171.99.99
        redirect    = 172.17.1.1 23
        log_on_success   = PID HOST EXIT DURATION USERID
        log_on_failure   = RECORD HOST
}
```

The REUSE value to the flag attribute is essential. Notice the use of the `bind` attribute. It has the following effect. If the command `telnet 172.17.33.111` (or `topcat`, in this case) is used, then the connection will be made to the server itself (`topcat`). If, on the other hand, the command `telnet 201.171.99.99` is used, then the connection will be forwarded to the host `172.17.1.1` (`foghorn`) at port 23 (the `telnet` port). Example 8–50 shows the effect of the latter command.

Example 8–50   The Effect of `redirect`

```
$ telnet 201.171.99.99
Trying 201.171.99.99...
Connected to 201.171.99.99.
Escape character is '^]'.

UNIX(r) System V Release 4.0 (foghorn)

login:
```

While the redirect mechanism may be quite useful, be cautious about implementing it. Make sure that logging occurs both at the proxy server and the end system. Another, arguably more secure, method for implementing proxies is through the netfilter utility discussed in Chapter 15. However, the xinetd implementation may be convenient in tightly controlled internal networks.

INCORPORATING TCP_WRAPPERS   Including TCP_wrappers functionality in /etc/xinetd.conf is so simple that, except for the significant functionality it represents, it is anticlimatic. All of the capabilities of TCP_wrappers may be incorporated through xinetd, just as they were through inetd. Example 8–51 displays a sample /etc/xinetd.conf file which uses TCP_wrappers for many of its services. Wherever /usr/sbin/tcpd is set as the value for the attribute server, that service will be wrapped. Notice also that such entries *always* have the server_args attribute set to the daemon to be invoked (fully qualified path). This is required!

Example 8–51   Using TCP_wrappers in /etc/xinetd.conf

```
defaults
{
        log_type        = SYSLOG local4 info
        log_on_success  = PID HOST EXIT DURATION
        log_on_failure  = HOST
        instances       = 8
}

service xadmin
{
        type            = INTERNAL UNLISTED
        flags           = REUSE
        socket_type     = stream
        protocol        = tcp
        port            = 9967
        wait            = no
        only_from       = topcat
}


service ftp
{
        id              = ftp
        socket_type     = stream
        protocol        = tcp
        wait            = no
        user            = root
        only_from       = 172.17.0.0
        log_on_success  += USERID
        log_on_failure  += USERID
        access_times    = 8:00-16:30
        server          = /usr/sbin/tcpd
        server_args     = /usr/sbin/in.ftpd -l -a
}
```

Example 8–51   Using TCP_wrappers in `/etc/xinetd.conf` *(Continued)*

```
service telnet
{
        socket_type     = stream
        wait            = no
        flags           = NAMEINARGS REUSE
        user            = root
        bind            = 172.17.33.111
        server          = /usr/sbin/tcpd
        server_args     = /usr/sbin/in.telnetd
        log_on_success  = PID HOST EXIT DURATION USERID
        log_on_failure  = RECORD HOST
}

service telnet
{
        socket_type     = stream
        protocol        = tcp
        wait            = no
        flags           = REUSE
        user            = root
        bind            = 201.171.99.99
        redirect        = 172.17.1.1 23
        log_on_success  = PID HOST EXIT DURATION USERID
        log_on_failure  = RECORD HOST
}
...
<remainder of file snipped>
...
```

Note that `xinetd` can be (and ordinarily is) compiled with `libwrap`, the TCP_wrappers library that provides support for the use of `/etc/hosts.allow` and `/etc/hosts.deny`. Whether you compile with `libwrap` or not, the above configuration file will behave as expected. Compiling with `libwrap` has the effect of incorporating only the access restrictions (not the options) found in `/etc/hosts.allow` and `/etc/hosts.deny`. What is shown in Example 8–51 provides the entire set of features, `banners`, `spawn`, `twist`, etc., of TCP_wrappers. All of the detail described about TCP_wrappers, beginning with the section "TCP_Wrappers" on page 282, now applies here.

The `xinetd` Daemon

The `xinetd` daemon accepts a number of arguments. These arguments may be overridden by attributes in the special service `default`, or individual attribute entries in one or more services. However, all parameters given here, or their defaults, control the behavior of `xinetd` itself. For example, if the `filelog` flag is specified to `xinetd`, then it will log all state transformation messages there, even though the `/etc/xinetd.conf` file specifies other log locations for service-related messages. The available arguments are listed in Table 8–17.

Table 8–17   Flags of `xinetd`

FLAG	DESCRIPTION
`-d`	Debug mode. Output may be used with a debugger, like `gdb`.
`-syslog` *`facility`*	Specifies the `syslogd` facility. One of `daemon`, `auth`, `user`, `local0-7`.
`-filelog` *`file`*	Specifies the *`file`* to which logs are written instead of `syslog`. Must be absolutely qualified.
`-f` *`config_file`*	Specifies the configuration file. Must be absolutely qualified. Default is `/etc/xinetd.conf`.
`-pid`	Causes the PID to be written to standard error.
`-loop` *`rate`*	Specifies the number of daemons forked per second. Default is 10. You may wish to change this for faster machines.
`-reuse`	Sets the TCP socket to be reusable, which means that other daemons may be started while previous instances are running. You have more specific control over services when using this with the `flags` attribute (see Table 8–12 on page 317).
`-limit` *`numproc`*	Limits the total number of concurrently running processes started by `xinetd` to *`numprocs`*.
`-logprocs` *`limit`*	Limits the number of concurrent RFC 1413 requests to *`limit`*.
`-shutdownprocs` *`limit`*	When the RECORD value to the `log_on_failure` attribute is used, `xinetd` forks a service called shutdown to collect information when the service terminates. This option limits the total number of concurrently running shutdown processes to `limit`.
`-cc` *`interval`*	Forces `xinetd` to run a consistency check on its internal state every *`interval`* seconds. May manually be accomplished with `killall -IOT xinetd`.

It should be noted that all status information reported by xinetd, such as reconfiguration notices, always appear in the log file specified by the -syslog or -filelog flags (syslog selector daemon.info, by default), regardless of the settings, through defaults or otherwise, in /etc/xinetd.conf. Also, if you want to capture the PID of xinetd in a file, you may do so with

```
xinetd -pid 2> /var/run/xinetd.pid
```

Signals Available for Use with xinetd

The xinetd daemon also takes special actions based upon certain signals being sent. Table 8–18 describes the functionality of each of the signals it accepts.

Table 8–18   The xinetd Signals

SIGNAL	ACTION
SIGUSR1	Soft reconfiguration. Rereads /etc/xinetd.conf and adjusts accordingly.
SIGUSR2	Hard reconfiguration. Rereads /etc/xinetd.conf and kills all daemons which no longer match the criteria set forth in the configuration file. For example, if a client is connected to the server and that client is added to the no_access list, then this signal will terminate the client's session.
SIGQUIT	Terminates xinetd *without* terminating any of the daemons it forked.
SIGTERM	Terminates all of the daemons forked by xinetd, then terminates xinetd.
SIGHUP	Dumps xinetd state information to /var/run/xinetd.dump.
SIGIOT	Checks for corruption of internal databases and reports the result.

Note that you must terminate xinetd with the SIGTERM (or more simply, TERM) signal whenever you add new services or a defaults entry, or whenever one of the following attributes is changed on any service: protocol, socket_type, type, or wait. Whenever you issue a soft or hard reconfiguration signal to xinetd, a log entry of the type shown in Example 8–52 will be written. This particular example is the result of a hard reconfiguration.

Example 8–52   Log Record for a Hard Reconfiguration of `xinetd`

```
Apr 15 14:42:31 topcat xinetd[1402]: Starting hard reconfiguration
Apr 15 14:42:31 topcat xinetd[1402]: readjusting service servers
Apr 15 14:42:31 topcat xinetd[1402]: readjusting service services
Apr 15 14:42:31 topcat xinetd[1402]: readjusting service telnet
Apr 15 14:42:31 topcat xinetd[1402]: readjusting service shell
Apr 15 14:42:31 topcat xinetd[1402]: readjusting service login
Apr 15 14:42:31 topcat xinetd[1402]: readjusting service talk
Apr 15 14:42:31 topcat xinetd[1402]: readjusting service ntalk
Apr 15 14:42:31 topcat xinetd[1402]: readjusting service pop-2
Apr 15 14:42:31 topcat xinetd[1402]: readjusting service pop-3
Apr 15 14:42:31 topcat xinetd[1402]: readjusting service imap
Apr 15 14:42:31 topcat xinetd[1402]: readjusting service linuxconf
Apr 15 14:42:31 topcat xinetd[1402]: readjusting service ftp
Apr 15 14:42:31 topcat xinetd[1402]: Reconfigured: new=1 old=12 dropped=1 (services)
```

Note that one service was terminated as a result of this hard reconfiguration.

NOTE

As of this writing, the most reliable way to ensure that a modified `/etc/xinetd.conf` file is read is to stop and restart the `xinetd` daemon. It is best to terminate `xinetd` with a `SIGTERM` signal. As described in this section, sending `xinetd` a `SIGTERM` causes it to terminate (with a `SIGKILL` or signal number 9) every daemon under its control. Sometimes there is a delay before `xinetd`'s children terminate, which means that if you kill and immediately restart `xinetd`, it may not be able to bind to all ports (an error message to this effect will be entered in the log file for `xinetd`, *not* the log file(s) specified for the services). Thus, if you write a script, it is a good idea to use a command like `sleep 3` between the stopping and starting `xinetd`. You may completely obviate this problem by using the `flags = REUSE` attribute and value for TCP services, such as `telnet` and `ftp`, or by specifying the `-reuse` option to `xinetd` itself.

Which One Should I Use?

The principal disadvantages to `xinetd` were identified in "Disadvantages of `xinetd`" on page 314. One of the significant benefits of `xinetd` for any systems exposed to an untrusted network, such as the Internet, is its ability to limit the number of daemons running and the amounts of log data it accepts. This can make the perpetration of a denial of service attack against such a protected system much more difficult. Additionally, its ability to bind services to a particular interface and proxy services to another host are useful features for some systems exposed to the Internet. Generally, its ability to invoke `tcpd` and logging make it useful for all systems. Further, since `xinetd` is likely to replace `inetd` in all Linux distributions, it should be preferred.

Since `xinetd`, `inetd`, and `portmap` may coexist peacefully (so long as they don't try to simultaneously provide the same services; see the warning on 315), there may be some cases where it is advantageous to use a combination of these tools.

Summary

This chapter covers the TCP/IP Application layer and the client-server model conceptually. The notion of direct versus indirect servers is introduced and the indirect servers, `inetd`, `xinetd`, and `portmap` are covered in detail. The TCP_wrappers utility is also covered in detail.

For Further Reading

Comer, Douglas E., *Internetworking with TCP/IP Vol I: Principals, Protocols, Architecture*, 3rd. ed., Englewood Cliffs, Prentice Hall, 1995.

Klander, Lars, *Hacker Proof*, Las Vegas, Nevada, Jamsa Press, 1997.

Mann, Scott, and Ellen L. Mitchell, *Linux System Security: The Administrator's Guide to Open Source Security Tools*, Upper Saddle River, New Jersey, Prentice Hall, 2000.

Miller, Mark A., *Troubleshooting TCP/IP*, 3d ed., Foster City, California, IDG Books, 1999.

Stevens, W. Richard, *TCP/IP Illustrated, Volume 1: The Protocols*, Reading, Massachusetts, Addison-Wesley, 1994.

9

Troubleshooting and Monitoring

Troubleshooting can be a big part of a network administrator's job. And a big part of troubleshooting a network is monitoring that network. Most network-related problems can be categorized in one of two ways: either something doesn't work at all or it doesn't work as well as expected. The former problem is most commonly reflective of something that is not functioning correctly, while the latter is most often a performance-related issue (which is sometime due to the fact that something is broken).

In this chapter, we first consider a troubleshooting process. It provides a way to approach troubleshooting functional problems on a network, but can also be used to isolate performance bottlenecks. Subsequently, we survey a variety of network monitoring tools.

Troubleshooting Tips

Generally speaking, troubleshooting is the technique of identifying problems or faults in a given environment and correcting them. Finding and correcting problems that are network oriented can be simple or difficult. The simplicity or difficulty lies both in the nature of the problem and the level of experience of the administrator. The more experience an administrator has, the more likely that administrator will find and resolve problems quickly. However, even the most experienced administrators will run into issues that are difficult to resolve. This is particularly true of networked environments that continue to grow and for which many network applications must be run. The following guidelines can be used to assist the inexperienced administrator to gain valuable experience and remind experienced administrators of a basic practice.

- Keep notes
- Use Ethereal regularly
- Read system log files routinely
- Monitor the network
- Know your applications

These guidelines should be practiced regularly to maintain the knowledge of the environment being administered. Keeping notes, in particular about trouble-shooting activities, can make future problem resolutions easy and fast. In addition to following these guidelines, we provide one approach for general troubleshooting in the next few sections.

Splitting the Stack with `ping`

The `ping` utility is described in Chapter 6. There, we noted that `ping` uses the ICMP echo-request and echo-reply messages to verify reachability. In particular, `ping` completely bypasses the Transport layer on the client-side and has no Application layer or Transport layer presence on the server-side. This makes `ping` uniquely qualified for splitting the stack—that is, it can be used to verify or not verify proper operation of the lower three layers of the TCP/IP stack. `ping` does not perfectly determine connectivity, however, as there could be a firewall or filtering switch that blocks communication. Nonetheless, `ping` is a very useful tool for troubleshooting purposes in that it can provide information about whether or not two nodes are reachable via the lower three layers of the stack. In short, if there is a general connectivity problem on the network, `ping` can guide the administrator as to where to look for the problem.

Suppose that two hosts, A and B, are unable to communicate using some application. Further suppose that there are no firewalls between A and B. Figure 9–1 describes a flowchart that provides a general approach to trouble-shooting network problems.

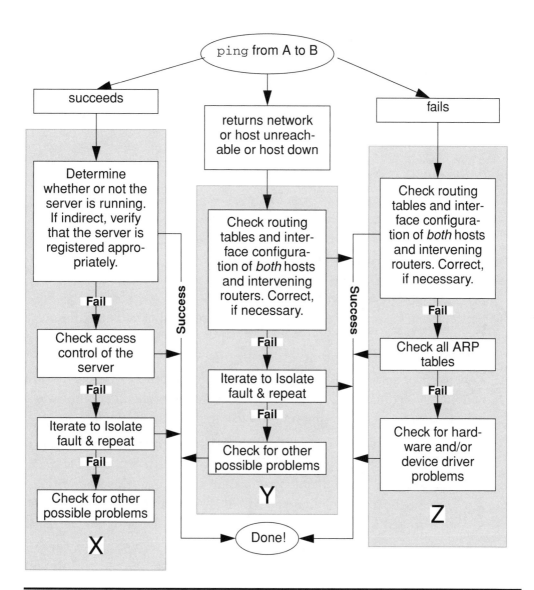

Figure 9–1   Troubleshooting Flowchart

This flowchart, together with the discussion provided in the following sub-sections, provides a reasonable process for minimally narrowing down the source of any problems arising on your network. In the following discussions we will refer to the shaded areas as *columns*. Thus, for example, column X refers to the portion of the flowchart that follows from a successful ping.

Name Resolution

Whenever you approach troubleshooting, make sure that you test the problem using both IP addresses and hostnames. If it works with the IP address but not the hostname, then the problem is hostname resolution (check /etc/hosts, NIS, and/or DNS). This is a common problem when, for example, host A can ping host B, but not the other way around.

Firewalls

Firewalls can often be the legitimate cause of communication failures. Many firewalls are configured to ignore ICMP echo-requests, but will permit certain other applications. On the other hand, a firewall may be configured to pass through ICMP echo-replies but not permit the application that you are trying to use. Always verify that things are working correctly on each side of a firewall before troubleshooting communications that must go through the firewall. In particular, make sure that the firewall can be reached from both sides.

General ping Failures

Whenever ping fails (either column Y or Z in Figure 9–1), there are a number of actions you can take to either quickly resolve the problem or eliminate a number of possibilities. Assuming no firewalls, these actions include:

- Check the NIC link lights. If these lights aren't on, there's a good possibility that there is some problem with the NIC or the cable being used. Always replace the cable with a known working cable first. If this doesn't solve the problem, then you will likely need to replace the NIC.
- Check the link lights on the repeaters and/or switches. If the light(s) associated with the systems in question are not on (but they are working on the NICs), then either the cable, specific port, repeater, or switch can be bad. Replace the cable with a known working cable. If that doesn't resolve the problem, then use a different port on the repeater or switch. If that fails, but other systems can successfully use the ports you've tested, then the problem is elsewhere (continue on to the next bullet item). If no other systems can use the repeater or switch, then replace the repeater or switch.

- Issue `ping 127.0.0.1`. If this fails, then the host on which this command was executed does not have networking enabled, does not have the TCP/IP stack installed, or that software is corrupt. Review the first four chapters of this book for verification of this problem.
- Use `ifconfig` to verify the NIC configuration. See "`ifconfig`" on page 360 and Chapter 4 for more details about `ifconfig`.
- Use `traceroute` in an effort to isolate the routing problem. See "`traceroute`" on page 357 for more details. Once you've isolated the routing problem, use the `route` command (see "`route`" on page 361) to gather information about the routing tables and/or repeat these steps as necessary from the newly isolated host.

These steps offer a collection of activities that you are likely to get into the habit of walking through every time you identify a `ping` failure. The order given here is not critical except where it makes logical sense (for instance if `ping 127.0.0.1` fails, trying to use `traceroute` is silly). You may also find that checking for hardware problems is something you do after checking software. The following sections provide some additional detail for each general type of failure.

`ping` **Failures with Error Messages**

If `ping` from A to B fails and no firewalls are involved (either column Y or Z in Figure 9–1), this indicates that the problem is at layer 3 or below. If `ping` reports that the host or network is unreachable, then there is a routing table problem either locally on A or at an intermediate router between A and B. If `ping` reports that host B is down when, in fact, host B is up and running, then there is either a routing table problem on B or somewhere between A and B, or the interface on B is misconfigured. In all cases, thoroughly check all routing tables and the output of `ifconfig` (or `ip link`—see Chapter 16) on A and B for accuracy. Also, verify that there are no ARP cache problems.

If all of these checks do not result in success, try iterating the problem as described in "Isolating the Problem" on page 352.

`ping` **Failure Due to Timeout**

If `ping` simply times out and no firewalls are involved (column Z of Figure 9–1), then there could be a routing table problem on B or an intermediate router. B must have a route back to A in order for the ICMP echo-reply message to reach A. If the routing tables are correct everywhere, but `ping` still times out or reports any error messages, then the interface configuration on each of A and B must be carefully checked with the `ifconfig` (or `ip link`) command. Also, verify that each intermediate Linux router has IP forwarding enabled (see Chapter 6). This is a common cause of `ping` failure without any messages.

Closely inspect the output of `ifconfig` for an improper netmask, broadcast, or IP address setting. Also, make sure that the interface is configurable (if not, then there is a device driver problem) and is marked UP. If all of this is correct, verify that ARP is working properly by checking the ARP caches on each system involved. If the problem still persists, then the problem is likely a bad cable, Ethernet card, repeater port, repeater, switch port, switch, router port, or router.

When tracking down a hardware problem, it is important to isolate the problem as much as possible as described in "Isolating the Problem" on page 352 prior to checking hardware. Once you've got the problem located to a particular system, repeater, router, or switch, then go through the process of replacing each component one item at a time. For instance, if you've isolated the problem to a particular host and switch, begin by replacing the cable between the host and switch. If that doesn't resolve the problem, try a different port on the switch. Then try a different switch and then a different Ethernet card in the system. There are a number of tools that can help identify which component or components are the source of the problem. Many of these are discussed in "Network Monitoring and Troubleshooting Utilities" on page 353.

`ping` Succeeds but Problem Persists

If `ping` is successful from A to B, but the application still fails (and, again, no firewall is involved), then the most likely source of the problem is the server application on B. This conclusion assumes that `ping` works using hostnames, which verifies that name resolution is working properly and that the lower three layers are configured and operating properly. It is still possible that DNS is causing the problem if the application in question does reverse lookups and the reverse lookup is failing (see Chapter 10 for a discussion of DNS). Application problems, generally, fall into one of two categories depending upon whether the application utilizes a direct or indirect server.

If the application provides a direct server, then troubleshooting focuses on that server. Determine whether the server is running and whether there are any access control rules, then read through the log files for any tips on what might be going on. If none of these checks resolve the issue, using Ethereal or a similar network sniffer can often provide additional information that can lead to problem resolution. If you still cannot resolve the issue, start making queries about the problem. If the application was supplied by a commercial vendor, make the queries to that vendor. If the application is in the public domain, post the queries to the appropriate newsgroup or email list. For each of the network applications that are described in later chapters of this book, you will find some troubleshooting tips that may assist you if one of those applications is causing you trouble.

If the application utilizes an indirect server, there are a number of issues to consider in addition to those described in the preceding paragraph. The indirect server needs to be running and it must also know about the actual server it is going to invoke. We noted this in our discussions of `inetd`, `xinetd`, and the `portmap` in Chapter 8. Make sure that the indirect server is both running and configured correctly for the application you are investigating. Additionally, indirect servers on Linux often use access control such as `libwrap` (the library used to implement TCP_wrappers) and the use of `/etc/hosts.allow` and `/etc/hosts.deny`. Checking the log files for these utilities often provides useful clues as to what the problem might be.

Whether an application is implemented via a direct or indirect server, one issue that may cause problems is the TTL set by the application. Normally, `ping` sets the TTL value to 255. Thus, it is possible that an application that sets the TTL to a smaller value could fail because the number of hops to the destination exceeds the application's TTL. Such a problem will result in ICMP unreachable and/or hop limit exceed error messages. You can actually attempt to verify this type of problem by determining the number of hops with `ping -R` or `traceroute` (described in "`traceroute`" on page 357) and attempt to duplicate it with `ping -t ttl` (described in "ping" on page 354). If the problem turns out to be a low hop limit imposed by the application, you will need to determine how to modify the limit. If that cannot be done, an alternative, but often costly, solution might be to implement a tunnel which is described in "Tunneling" on page 814.

Isolating the Problem

The entire process described in this section and depicted in Figure 9–1 on page 347 is one which attempts to isolate the problem. To further the likely success of this approach, it can be very useful to walk through the connections. For example, if something is not working from host A to host B, check to see if it works from another host on the same local network as B. If the problem persists at this point, you've isolated the issue to a local network and perhaps even the particular host B (although there could still be other problems elsewhere). If, on the other hand, it works locally, then try from a host that is one network closer to host A. At this point, either the problem exhibits itself or it doesn't and the process outlined above can be repeated. Once the problem shows itself, you've isolated at least the network circumstances under which the fault exists. When you've isolated the problem within those constraints, you can apply the technique of this section from that point. Figure 9–2 illustrates this iterative approach. It depicts successful communications from intermediate hosts 1 and 2, but a broken communication from intermediate host 3, which in this case is one network closer to B from A.

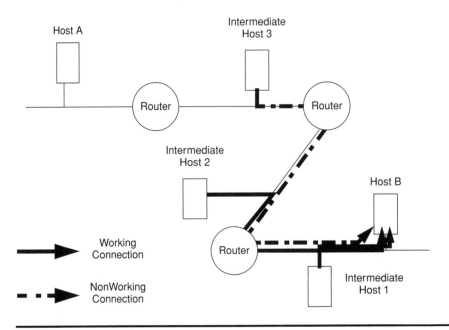

Figure 9–2   Iteration to Problem Isolation

If the problem still persists, the fault may be with some other aspect of the environment. Some possibilities are described in the next section.

Other Possible Problems

There are a number of other possible problems that can cause communication issues. These can be categorized into three basic areas: the kernel, performance issues, and user space applications.

In addition to device driver issues previously noted in this section, kernel configuration issues can cause communication problems. Make sure that networking is enabled in the kernel (which it will be by default). If a system is acting as a router, ensure that IP forwarding is enabled (`echo "1" > /proc/sys/net/ipv4/ip_forward`). Additionally, if you have modified any kernel parameters, you may need to recover those changes to get networking operational again and then make each parameter change individually until networking breaks to isolate the problem.

Performance problems can also cause network failures. In the next section, we describe a number of network monitoring and troubleshooting utilities that can help isolate problems generally and performance problems specifically.

We already noted in "`ping` Succeeds but Problem Persists" on page 350 that applications outside of the kernel (user space applications) and, in particular, servers, can be the cause of communication problems. While it may be easy in some cases to isolate user space server problems, in other cases it is the interaction of the various servers that cause the problem. For example, suppose that there is a problem with electronic mail. Often, electronic mail depends on a number of applications such as `sendmail`, DNS, and `procmail`. Perhaps each individual application works properly on its own, but the interrelationship is dysfunctional due to some configuration problem. Identifying these types of problems is often difficult and time consuming.

Network Monitoring and Troubleshooting Utilities

There are a large number of network monitoring and troubleshooting utilities available for Linux systems. Many of these are publicly available and some are part of your distribution. In this section, we cover a number of these tools and point to resources where still others can be found. In each case, we relate where the tool fits with respect to the discussion in the previous section. We also explore, in each appropriate case, performance-related information that can be obtained from the given tool.

Bear in mind that in many cases not only are these tools useful for trouble-shooting, monitoring, and performance tuning, but also for learning about TCP/IP in general.

ping

We previously looked at the `ping` utility, specifically the route record option (`ping -R`) in Chapter 4 and an introductory overview in Chapter 6. In the latter section, we noted that the `ping` command bypasses the Transport layer on the client and utilizes ICMP messages to communicate. Here, we consider this useful utility in a bit more detail. Table 9–1 lists the standard flags to `ping`.

Table 9–1   `ping` Options

OPTION	DESCRIPTION
-D	Sets the don't fragment bit. Not available in all distributions.
-L	Disables the loopback so that the local host does not receive the echo-requests. Useful for the pinging of multicast and broadcast addresses.
-R	Record route.
-d	Sets the SO_DEBUG option on the socket.
-f	Flood packets. Outputs packets as fast as they come back or 100 times per second, whichever is more. For each echo-request, a "." is printed, while for each echo-reply, a backspace is executed. Thus, the number of periods reflects the number of dropped packets. Use this option with great caution as it can seriously reduce network performance. Limit the use of this option to test networks only.
-n	Suppresses address to name translation.
-q	Quiet operation. Suppresses all but the summary messages.

Table 9–1 ping Options *(Continued)*

OPTION	DESCRIPTION
`-r`	Causes ping to ignore the routing table and attempts to transmit on the local network to reach the destination. If the destination host is not on the local network, an error is returned.
`-v`	Verbose output. All ICMP packets are reported.
`-c count`	Stops after sending count echo-request and receiving the echo-reply messages.
`-I iface`	Specifies the interface through which to transmit packets. For use with unicast and multicast addresses.
`-i wait`	Wait wait seconds between sending each packet. The default is 1 second. Cannot be used with `-f`.
`-l preload`	Causes ping to send preload number of packets as quickly as possible. Once complete, ping resumes its normal behavior.
`-p pattern`	Specifies a 16-bit pattern to be included in the data portion of the packet. This option can be useful for identifying bit patterns that cause problems in a given environment.
`-s size`	Specifies that size data octets are to be sent. The default is 56 octets. If the -D, -T, or -t (to a unicast destination) flags are used, then size includes the 8 octet header.
`-t ttl`	Specifies the TTL value to put into the header. Default is 255.
`-w maxwait`	Specifies that maxwait seconds is the longest amount of time that the sending system will wait for a reply before sending another packet. Default is 10 seconds.
`-T tos` `-T tstamp`	Depending upon distribution, the `-T` option either takes a TOS value or a timestamp indicator. See the ping(8) man page for further details.

There are a variety of different things that can be done with the ping command. Of the more significant options are the delays you can incur. These can become quite important in getting sufficient information. For instance,

Example 9–1 illustrates the use of `ping` with the record route option and limiting the number of packets sent to 5. Nothing appears to be wrong with the output, except that only 1 of 5 packets was responded to.

Example 9–1   Packets Lost Due to `ping` Impatience

```
[root@foghorn /root]# ping -R -c 5 clubted.csd.sgi.com
PING fddi-clubted.csd.sgi.com (150.166.9.128) from 10.254.1.11 : 56(124) bytes of data.
64 bytes from fddi-clubted.csd.sgi.com (150.166.9.128): icmp_seq=0 ttl=245 time=89.0 ms
RR: foghorn (10.254.1.11)
dsl-golden (192.111.23.154)
10.91.71.140
10.82.35.202
209.101.253.74

--- fddi-clubted.csd.sgi.com ping statistics ---
5 packets transmitted, 1 packets received, 80% packet loss
round-trip min/avg/max = 89.0/89.0/89.0 ms
[root@foghorn /root]#
```

Example 9–2 shows the output of the same command as before except that now we've forced `ping` to be more patient and only send packets out every 10 seconds (-i 10). Notice that a lot more information about the recorded route is now available, and that all 5 packets were responded to. Quite often, causing `ping` and other testing utilities to be more patient will result in a greater amount of information being returned. Always take the extra time and be more patient.

Example 9–2   Significant Additional Information Due to Increase in Wait Time

```
[root@foghorn /root]# ping -R -c 5 -i 10 clubted.csd.sgi.com
PING fddi-clubted.csd.sgi.com (150.166.9.128) from 10.254.1.11 : 56(124) bytes of data.
64 bytes from fddi-clubted.csd.sgi.com (150.166.9.128): icmp_seq=0 ttl=245 time=418.5 ms
RR: foghorn (10.254.1.11)
dsl-golden (192.111.23.154)
10.91.71.140
10.82.35.202
209.101.253.74
207.251.150.193
207.251.150.65
209-101-251-150.pao-e100.cust.gw.epoch.net (209.101.251.150)
rhythmsgate.corp.sgi.com (169.238.216.138)

64 bytes from fddi-clubted.csd.sgi.com (150.166.9.128): icmp_seq=1 ttl=245
time=16347.4 ms(same route)
64 bytes from fddi-clubted.csd.sgi.com (150.166.9.128): icmp_seq=2 ttl=245
time=6431.4 ms(same route)
64 bytes from fddi-clubted.csd.sgi.com (150.166.9.128): icmp_seq=3 ttl=245 time=87.3
ms(same route)
64 bytes from fddi-clubted.csd.sgi.com (150.166.9.128): icmp_seq=4 ttl=245 time=89.1
ms(same route)

--- fddi-clubted.csd.sgi.com ping statistics ---
5 packets transmitted, 5 packets received, 0% packet loss
round-trip min/avg/max = 87.3/4674.7/16347.4 ms
[root@foghorn /root]#
```

In the next example, we deliberately incur an error (by using a small TTL) to show the additional output generated by -v. Example 9–3 shows the use of ping to the same destination as before, but this time limiting the number of packets to 2 and setting the TTL to 10. Note that the -v option causes the header information of the ICMP "Time to live exceeded" packets to be displayed.

Example 9–3   ping and the -v Option

```
[root@foghorn /root]# ping -v -t 10 -c 2 -i 5 clubted.csd.sgi.com
PING fddi-clubted.csd.sgi.com (150.166.9.128) from 10.254.1.11 : 56(84) bytes of data.
ping: packet too short (56 bytes) from 150.166.200.5
From b1-dco-cisco2-200.corp.sgi.com (150.166.200.5): Time to live exceeded
Vr HL TOS  Len   ID Flg  off TTL Pro  cks      Src      Dst Data
 4  5  00 5400 fc19   0 0000  01  01 7ef3 10.254.1.11  150.166.9.128
ping: packet too short (56 bytes) from 150.166.200.5
From b1-dco-cisco2-200.corp.sgi.com (150.166.200.5): Time to live exceeded
Vr HL TOS  Len   ID Flg  off TTL Pro  cks      Src      Dst Data
 4  5  00 5400 ff19   0 0000  01  01 7bf3 10.254.1.11  150.166.9.128

--- fddi-clubted.csd.sgi.com ping statistics ---
2 packets transmitted, 0 packets received, +2 errors, 100% packet loss
[root@foghorn /root]#
```

Now compare Example 9–4, which does not use -v, with that above.

Example 9–4   ping Output Sans -v

```
[root@foghorn /root]# ping -c 2 -t 10 -i 5 clubted.csd.sgi.com
PING fddi-clubted.csd.sgi.com (150.166.9.128) from 10.254.1.11 : 56(84) bytes of data.
From b1-dco-cisco2-200.corp.sgi.com (150.166.200.5): Time to live exceeded
From b1-dco-cisco2-200.corp.sgi.com (150.166.200.5): Time to live exceeded

--- fddi-clubted.csd.sgi.com ping statistics ---
2 packets transmitted, 0 packets received, +2 errors, 100% packet loss
[root@foghorn /root]#
```

Once again we see that the optional flags on ping can be quite useful. Take some time to understand what they do and when they can help you.

traceroute

The traceroute program is somewhat similar to ping -R in terms of the end result. Where ping -R uses the record route option in the IP header, traceroute sets the TTL of the IP header to a small value attempting to elicit an ICMP time-exceeded (error type 11) message. Also, unlike ping -R, traceroute utilizes UDP as the Transport layer protocol. traceroute is a part of all major Linux distributions.

The traceroute program works by sending UDP packets with small TTL values. It begins by setting the TTL to 1 and increments it by 1 until it reaches the destination or the maximum of 30 (which can be changed with the -m flag; see Table 9–3 on page 360). As these packets are sent out, `traceroute` waits for an ICMP time-exceeded message or a timeout, whichever occurs first. If a time-exceeded message is received, `traceroute` reports the IP address of the intervening router and RTT in milliseconds (ms), otherwise it reports ∗ , meaning that it got no response. By default, `traceroute` sends out three packets, each with a different TTL, to each hop. Example 9–5 illustrates a simple use of `traceroute`.

Example 9–5   Simple `traceroute` Example

```
[root@foghorn /root]# traceroute fleby.csd.sgi.com
traceroute to fleby.csd.sgi.com (150.166.93.138), 30 hops max, 38 byte packets
 1  golden-1 (10.254.1.1)  0.777 ms  0.758 ms  0.517 ms
 2  10.91.71.140 (10.91.71.140)  2.045 ms  2.114 ms  1.981 ms
 3  10.82.35.202 (10.82.35.202)  19.600 ms  20.135 ms  19.655 ms
 4  10.82.32.1 (10.82.32.1)  20.023 ms  19.928 ms  19.949 ms
 5  207.251.150.193 (207.251.150.193)  20.344 ms  23.147 ms  19.909 ms
 6  209.212.174.97 (209.212.174.97)  70.382 ms  71.299 ms  70.264 ms
 7  207.251.150.66 (207.251.150.66)  75.406 ms  73.122 ms  68.749 ms
 8  rgate-hssi.corp.sgi.com (191.82.174.112)  72.383 ms  71.316 ms  70.240 ms
 9  wangate.corp.sgi.com (155.16.198.2)  70.547 ms  71.169 ms  70.767 ms
10  router200.corp.sgi.com (150.166.200.1)  72.833 ms  72.589 ms  72.380 ms
11  router141.corp.sgi.com (150.166.141.1)  71.271 ms  70.804 ms  70.492 ms
12  fleby.csd.sgi.com (150.166.93.138)  73.447 ms  73.100 ms  73.395 ms
[root@foghorn /root]#
```

Each line represents a packet sent out by `traceroute`. The leftmost column contains the packet number followed by the router name (or IP address, if the name is unavailable) and IP address in parentheses. Following the address information are three times in milliseconds for each of the three traceroute packets sent to that router. In Example 9–5, `traceroute` was successful in receiving responses from all routers. This is not always the case and is noted in `traceroute` output, according to Table 9–2.

Table 9–2   Output Codes for `traceroute`

CODE	DESCRIPTION
∗	No response received.
!	TTL of received packet is less than or equal to 1.
!F	Indicates that an ICMP-FN message was received. If this occurs, then there is likely a problem with the router that generated this message.

Table 9–2   Output Codes for `traceroute` *(Continued)*

CODE	DESCRIPTION
`!H`	Indicates that an ICMP destination host unreachable message was received.
`!N`	Indicates that an ICMP destination network unreachable message was received.
`!P`	Indicates that an ICMP destination protocol unreachable message was received.
`!S`	Indicates that the source route option failed. If this occurs, then there is likely a problem with the router that generated this message.
`!X`	Indicates that an ICMP administratively disabled message was received.
`!<N>`	Indicates that an ICMP message of code *N* was received. See Chapter 4 for ICMP message codes and types.

Since `traceroute` output can provide a lot of information about connectivity throughout a network, it is a very handy debugging tool. For example, the ICMP error codes that it reports can be of great assistance in determining which router is causing a problem. Thus, `traceroute` can be used in a similar way to `ping` as described in "Troubleshooting Tips" on page 345. Most often, you will find the need to use both `traceroute` and `ping` for the purpose of isolating problems in larger networks. Sometimes, the default behavior of `traceroute` does not produce as much information as it otherwise could. The `traceroute` program has a large number of options; a few significant options are described in Table 9–3 (see the `traceroute(8)` man page for complete details).

ARP Tools

The `arpwatch` utility is described in Chapter 3. Maintaining current `arpwatch` log files for each network can provide valuable information about hardware location and allocation of IP addresses.

Another useful tool is `arping`. This utility uses ARP packets to "ping" other hosts on the local network. It is simple to use and has as one of its primary ben-

Table 9–3   Options to `traceroute`

OPTION	DESCRIPTION
`-p port`	By default, when `traceroute` begins sending packets, it uses a destination port of 33434 (known as the base port). Each subsequent packet increments the port number by 1. The incrementing of ports is done in the event that the port is in use or blocked at the destination. Often, `traceroute` will report a `!P` under such circumstances. If all such ports are in use, the base port can be changed with this option.
`-f ttl`	Specifies that the initial TTL of the first packet is `ttl` instead of the default value of 1.
`-q queries`	Sets the number of queries for each TTL value to `queries` instead of the default value of 3.
`-m maxhops`	Specifies the maximum TTL value to `maxhops` instead of the default value of 30.
`-w wait`	Sets the wait time for a response to a packet to `wait` seconds instead of the default value of 5 seconds.

efits the ability to detect duplicate addresses. It is available on some distributions and also at

    http://synscan.nss.nu/programs.php

Be sure to bear in mind that ARP packets do not cross routers. Thus, this tool is limited to testing local networks only.

`ifconfig`

We previously covered the `ifconfig` command in Chapter 4 in some detail. From the troubleshooting perspective, `ifconfig` is useful in that it reports existing configurations of a system's network interface(s). Once you've identified problems at layer 3 and below, use `ifconfig` to verify the correct configuration of all affected interfaces.

We also noted earlier that `ifconfig` does report statistical information which can be useful in determining performance-related issues. All of the statistics that `ifconfig` can report are also reportable by `netstat` and are discussed in "`netstat`" on page 361.

There are other commands, including `ip link` and `ip address`, which can effectively replace the `ifconfig` command. These commands are discussed in Chapter 16.

route

This utility is described in great detail in Chapter 6. It is an extremely valuable troubleshooting utility as it always reflects the state of the routing knowledge of the given system. Whenever you determine that there are routing table problems, pay close attention to the data returned by the `route` command.

Additional routing table utilities include `rtquery` (see Chapter 11) for RIP environments and `ospf_monitor` (see Chapter 12) for OSPF environments. Additional troubleshooting tips for dynamic routing table daemons, such as `routed` and `gated`, are described beginning with Chapter 11.

Advanced routing capabilities, such as routing policies and traffic control, can also contribute to troubleshooting complexity. See Chapter 16 for further details.

netstat

The `netstat` command is one of the most useful commands for analyzing network activity. It offers information that can both aid troubleshooting, at layers 2 and above, and assist network performance analysis. This tool is briefly described in Chapter 2. Let's take a more detailed look at it.

The `netstat` command can be used to display the following types of information.

- Network connections
- Routing tables
- Interface statistics
- Masquerade connections
- Network statistics
- Multicast group memberships

Each type of information is controlled by a flag to `netstat`. Most of the flags are described in Table 9–4 and each is associated with one of the types listed above. See `netstat(8)` for further details.

Table 9–4   `netstat` Operational Flags

FLAG	TYPE OF INFORMATION	DESCRIPTION
`no flag`	network connections	Prints information about all active sockets.
`-a`	network connections	Prints information about all active sockets and listening servers.
`-l`	network connections	Prints information about all listening servers.
`-t|-u|-w`	network connections	These options show active TCP (`-t`), UDP (`-u`), and raw (`-w`) sockets.
`-A family`	network connections	Prints all active connections of the specified protocol `family`. Available families are `inet`, `unix`, `ipx`, `ax25`, `netrom`, and `ddp`. These options can also be specified in other ways. See the `netstat(8)` man page for details.
`-r[C]`	routing table/cache	Displays the routing table (`-r`) or the routing cache (`-rC`).
`-i [iface]`	interface statistics	Displays statistical information about all interfaces. If a specific interface, `iface`, is specified, then statistics for only that `iface` are listed.
`-M`	masquerade connections	Lists active masqueraded connections. See Chapter 14.
`-s`	network statistics	Displays a summary of statistical information about each protocol.

Table 9–4   `netstat` Operational Flags *(Continued)*

FLAG	TYPE OF INFORMATION	DESCRIPTION
`-g`	multicast memberships	Prints the list of multicast address groups for which this host is a member.
`-v`	N/A	Prints the `netstat` version and quits.
`-h`	N/A	Prints the `netstat` usage message and quits.

The behavior of `netstat` can be further modified with an option. Most of the options are specific to network connections. In all cases, where an option has no impact on the output of `netstat`, it is silently ignored. The options to `netstat` are listed in Table 9–5.

Table 9–5   `netstat` Options

OPTION	DESCRIPTION
`-e`	Causes `netstat` to print extended information. The type of information varies with the flags used.
`-v`	Causes `netstat` to be more verbose and include some debugging information. The exact type of information varies with the flags used.
`-p`	Causes `netstat` to display the process identifier associated with established sockets.
`-n`	Suppresses name translations.
`-c`	Puts `netstat` into continuous mode. If used, `netstat` will refresh its output every second until interrupted.
`-o`	Causes `netstat` to add timer data about established sockets.

Over the next several sections, we consider a series of examples based on the different types of information (except for routing table output which is discussed in Chapter 6) produced by `netstat`.

Network Connections

The netstat command can provide a lot of useful information about active connections and available servers on a system. This detail provided can help troubleshoot problems, analyze performance issues, and identify potential security problems. Let's see what it can do.

The netstat -a command lists all active and available sockets. Example 9–6 illustrates.

Example 9–6   Output of netstat -a

```
[root@beauregard /root]# netstat -a
Active Internet connections (servers and established)
Proto Recv-Q Send-Q Local Address           Foreign Address         State
tcp        0    138 beauregard:telnet        foghorn:4588            ESTABLISHED
tcp        0      0 beauregard-1:1030        eeyore:telnet           ESTABLISHED
tcp        0      0 beauregard:telnet        foghorn:2324            ESTABLISHED
tcp        0      0 *:smtp                   *:*                     LISTEN
tcp        0      0 *:printer                *:*                     LISTEN
tcp        0      0 *:linuxconf              *:*                     LISTEN
tcp        0      0 *:finger                 *:*                     LISTEN
tcp        0      0 *:login                  *:*                     LISTEN
tcp        0      0 *:shell                  *:*                     LISTEN
tcp        0      0 *:telnet                 *:*                     LISTEN
tcp        0      0 *:ftp                    *:*                     LISTEN
tcp        0      0 *:auth                   *:*                     LISTEN
tcp        0      0 *:658                    *:*                     LISTEN
tcp        0      0 *:1024                   *:*                     LISTEN
tcp        0      0 *:sunrpc                 *:*                     LISTEN
udp        0      0 *:ntalk                  *:*
udp        0      0 *:talk                   *:*
udp        0      0 *:656                    *:*
udp        0      0 *:1024                   *:*
udp        0      0 *:sunrpc                 *:*
raw        0      0 *:ospf                   *:*                     7
raw        0      0 *:icmp                   *:*                     7
raw        0      0 *:icmp                   *:*                     7
raw        0      0 *:tcp                    *:*                     7
Active UNIX domain sockets (servers and established)
Proto RefCnt Flags       Type       State         I-Node Path
unix  0      [ ACC ]     STREAM     LISTENING     696    /tmp/.font-unix/fs-1
unix  10     [ ]         DGRAM                    485    /dev/log
unix  0      [ ACC ]     STREAM     LISTENING     638    /dev/gpmctl
unix  0      [ ACC ]     STREAM     LISTENING     579    /dev/printer
unix  0      [ ]         DGRAM                    90193
unix  0      [ ]         DGRAM                    72639
unix  0      [ ]         DGRAM                    2316
unix  0      [ ]         DGRAM                    799
unix  0      [ ]         DGRAM                    747
unix  0      [ ]         DGRAM                    700
unix  0      [ ]         DGRAM                    625
unix  0      [ ]         DGRAM                    573
unix  0      [ ]         DGRAM                    508
unix  0      [ ]         DGRAM                    495
[root@beauregard /root]#
```

The netstat -a command lists both internet sockets (identified as Active Internet connections in Example 9–6) and UNIX domain sockets. UNIX `domain sockets` are primarily used for local connections. Each type of socket has slightly different output.

OUTPUT FOR `Active Internet connections`.   The output headers here are `Proto`, `Recv-Q`, `Send-Q`, `Local Address`, `Foreign Address`, and `State`. The `Proto` field lists the protocol family for the entry which can be: `tcp` for TCP sockets, `udp` for UDP sockets, or `raw` for sockets that do not use the Transport layer such as ICMP and OSPF.

The `Recv-Q` field lists a count in octets of data not yet received by the user space program connected to this socket. The `Send-Q` field lists a count in octets of data not yet acknowledged by the remote system connected to this socket.

The `Local Address` field contains the local hostname or IP address, followed by a colon, and then followed by the port number associated with the socket. The `Foreign Address` field contains the same information for the remote host. When there is no connection, an * is reported as the local IP address, the remote (foreign) IP address, and the remote port.

The `State` field displays the current state of the socket. For `raw` and `udp` sockets, this field is often blank since there is often no state associated with them. Table 9–6 lists the possible `State` values and their meanings.

Table 9–6   `State` Values and Meanings

VALUE	DESCRIPTION
`ESTABLISHED`	The socket currently has an established connection.
`SYN_SENT`	The socket is attempting to establish a connection with the specified foreign address.
`SYN_RECV`	The socket has received a connection request from the specified foreign address.
`FIN_WAIT1`	The socket is closed and the connection is in the process of terminating.
`FIN_WAIT2`	The connection is closed and the socket is awaiting a termination message from the specified foreign address.

Table 9–6   `State` Values and Meanings *(Continued)*

VALUE	DESCRIPTION
TIME_WAIT	The socket is handling the final packets after a termination message.
CLOSED	The socket is closed and not in use.
CLOSE_WAIT	The foreign address has terminated and is waiting for the socket to close.
LAST_ACK	The foreign address has terminated, the socket is closed and is waiting for the last acknowledgment from the foreign address.
LISTEN	The socket is listening for incoming connection request.
CLOSING	Both local and foreign sockets are closed but not all of the data has been sent.
UNKNOWN	The socket is in an unknown state.

OUTPUT FOR `UNIX domain sockets`.   The output headers here are `Proto`, `RefCnt`, `Flags`, `Type`, `State`, `I-Node`, and `Path`. The `Proto` field specifies the UNIX domain protocol family which is normally `unix`. The `RefCnt` field lists the number of processes associated with the socket. The `Flags` field displays the flag(s) set on the socket. Most flags are for internal use, but if `ACC` appears here it means that the process associated with the socket is waiting for a connection.

The `Type` field lists the type of data access for the socket. The available types are listed in Table 9–7.

Table 9–7   UNIX Domain Socket Data Access Types

TYPE	DESCRIPTION
DGRAM	Indicates that the data access method is connectionless.
STREAM	Indicates that the data access method is connection-oriented.
RAW	Indicates that the socket is used in the absence of a data access method (no Transport layer protocol).

Table 9–7   UNIX Domain Socket Data Access Types *(Continued)*

Type	Description
RDM	Indicates that the data access method is reliable, that is, connection-oriented and stateful.
SEQPACKET	Indicates that the data access method is sequential.
PACKET	Indicates that an interface accesses the socket directly.
UNKNOWN	Indicates that the data access method is unknown.

The State field displays the state of the socket. If no value is shown in the State field, it indicates that the socket is not currently in use. These states are listed in Table 9–8.

Table 9–8   UNIX Domain Socket State Values

Value	Description
FREE	The socket is not allocated for use.
LISTENING	The socket is listening for a connection request.
CONNECTING	The socket is in the process of establishing a connection.
DISCONNECTING	The socket is in the process of terminating a connection.
CONNECTED	The socket is in an established state.
UNKNOWN	The socket is in an unknown state.

The I-Node field lists an index value in memory associated with the socket. The Path field lists the path name(s) by which process(es) attach to the socket.

While the basic information supplied by netstat -a is quite useful, significant additional information can be obtained by also using the -p option. This option displays the PID, program name, and, for UNIX socket domains, the process owner associated with each connected socket. Example 9–7 illustrates. Note that the lines wrap due to formatting constraints.

Note that for internet connections, the PID/Program name field is added to the output. This field lists the PID and the program name separated by a "/".

Example 9–7   Output of `netstat -ap`

```
[root@beauregard /root]# netstat -ap
(Not all processes could be identified, non-owned process info
 will not be shown, you would have to be root to see it all.)
Active Internet connections (servers and established)
Proto Recv-Q Send-Q Local Address          Foreign Address      State
PID/Program name
tcp    0      283    beauregard:telnet      foghorn:4588         ESTABLISHED
22574/in.telnetd: f
tcp    0      0      beauregard-1:1030      eeyore:telnet        ESTABLISHED
12066/telnet
tcp    0      0      beauregard:telnet      foghorn:2324         ESTABLISHED
12014/in.telnetd: f
tcp    0      0  *:smtp             *:*                LISTEN       708/sendmail: accep
tcp    0      0  *:printer          *:*                LISTEN       660/
tcp    0      0  *:linuxconf        *:*                LISTEN       646/inetd
tcp    0      0  *:finger           *:*                LISTEN       646/inetd
tcp    0      0  *:login            *:*                LISTEN       646/inetd
tcp    0      0  *:shell            *:*                LISTEN       646/inetd
tcp    0      0  *:telnet           *:*                LISTEN       646/inetd
tcp    0      0  *:ftp              *:*                LISTEN       646/inetd
tcp    0      0  *:auth             *:*                LISTEN       596/
tcp    0      0  *:658              *:*                LISTEN       479/
tcp    0      0  *:1024             *:*                LISTEN       -
tcp    0      0  *:sunrpc           *:*                LISTEN       454/
udp    0      0  *:ntalk            *:*                             646/inetd
udp    0      0  *:talk             *:*                             646/inetd
udp    0      0  *:656              *:*                             479/
udp    0      0  *:1024             *:*                             -
udp    0      0  *:sunrpc           *:*                             454/
raw    0      0  *:ospf             *:*                7             913/
raw    0      0  *:icmp             *:*                7             913/
raw    0      0  *:icmp             *:*                7             -
raw    0      0  *:tcp              *:*                7             -
Active UNIX domain sockets (servers and established)
Proto RefCnt Flags      Type     State       I-Node PID/Program name   Path
unix  0      [ ACC ]    STREAM   LISTENING   696    807/xfs             /tmp/.font-unix/fs-1
unix  10     [ ]        DGRAM                485    573/syslogd         /dev/log
unix  0      [ ACC ]    STREAM   LISTENING   638    723/gpm             /dev/gpmctl
unix  0      [ ACC ]    STREAM   LISTENING   579    660/               /dev/printer
unix  0      [ ]        DGRAM                90193  22575/login -- sdm
unix  0      [ ]        DGRAM                72639  12015/login -- sdm
unix  0      [ ]        DGRAM                2316   646/inetd
unix  0      [ ]        DGRAM                799    913/
unix  0      [ ]        DGRAM                747    847/
unix  0      [ ]        DGRAM                700    807/xfs
unix  0      [ ]        DGRAM                625    708/sendmail: accep
unix  0      [ ]        DGRAM                573    660/
unix  0      [ ]        DGRAM                508    596/
unix  0      [ ]        DGRAM                495    582/
[root@beauregard /root]#
```

For UNIX domain sockets, this same field is added. Note that, where applicable, the process owner is listed to the right of the program name (after `--`) in this field for UNIX domain sockets.

Very often, the use of the `-a` flag provides too much information. Using the other, less inclusive flags can help focus in on specific socket information. For instance, Example 9–8 shows the use of `netstat -t`, which only lists TCP connections.

Example 9–8   Output of `netstat -t`

```
[root@beauregard /root]# netstat -t
Active Internet connections (w/o servers)
Proto Recv-Q Send-Q Local Address          Foreign Address        State
tcp        0    126 beauregard:telnet      foghorn:4588           ESTABLISHED
tcp        0      0 beauregard-1:1030      eeyore:telnet          ESTABLISHED
tcp        0      0 beauregard:telnet      foghorn:2324           ESTABLISHED
[root@beauregard /root]#
```

As another illustration of simplifying the output of `netstat`, the `-A unix` flag is used in Example 9–9.

Example 9–9   Output of `netstat -A unix`

```
[root@beauregard /root]# netstat -A unix
Active UNIX domain sockets (w/o servers)
Proto RefCnt Flags       Type       State       I-Node Path
unix  10     [ ]         DGRAM                  485    /dev/log
unix  0      [ ]         DGRAM                  90193
unix  0      [ ]         DGRAM                  72639
unix  0      [ ]         DGRAM                  2316
unix  0      [ ]         DGRAM                  799
unix  0      [ ]         DGRAM                  747
unix  0      [ ]         DGRAM                  700
unix  0      [ ]         DGRAM                  625
unix  0      [ ]         DGRAM                  573
unix  0      [ ]         DGRAM                  508
unix  0      [ ]         DGRAM                  495
[root@beauregard /root]#
```

You can also always pipe the output of `netstat` to `grep` to reduce the information. Example 9–10 shows the use of `netstat -a|grep telnet`.

Example 9–10   Filtering `netstat -a` Output with `grep`

```
[root@beauregard /]# netstat -a|grep telnet
tcp        0      0 beauregard:telnet      foghorn:4588           ESTABLISHED
tcp        0      2 beauregard:telnet      foghorn:2324           ESTABLISHED
tcp        0      0 *:telnet               *:*                    LISTEN
[root@beauregard /]#
```

The one type of network connections that are not displayed by `netstat -a` are masqueraded connections (see Chapter 14 for a discussion of masquerading). These can only be viewed with `netstat -M`. Example 9–11 illustrates its use.

Example 9–11   Output of `netstat -M`

```
[root@golden /root]# netstat -M
IP masquerading entries
prot    expire source          destination      ports
udp    0:05.69 beaver          odin.corp.sgi.com 1026 -> domain (62658)
tcp   59:53.65 foghorn         momserv.denver    6451 -> ftp (62661)
tcp   55:05.08 wyle            momserv.denver    6395 -> imap2 (62539)
tcp    1:21.85 beaver          shell.sgi.com     6450 -> ftp (62660)
tcp   58:55.78 beaver          clubted.csd.sgi.com 6449 -> telnet (62659)
[root@golden /root]#
```

The netstat -M command displays five fields of information. The prot field lists the protocol family. The expire field lists application specific timing information, which is often a timeout associated with the application. The source field lists the real source host or IP address of the connection which is not exposed outside of the masquerading system. The destination column lists the destination host or IP address associated with the connection. Finally, the ports field lists the source port and destination port, with an arrow in between, associated with the connection. Note that this command only yields useful results on a host that is providing masquerading services.

Interface Statistics

The netstat -i command is used to display statistical information about each interface on a system. Example 9–12 illustrates.

Example 9–12   Output of netstat -i

```
[root@beauregard /]# netstat -i
Kernel Interface table
Iface   MTU Met    RX-OK RX-ERR RX-DRP RX-OVR    TX-OK TX-ERR TX-DRP TX-OVR Flg
eth0    1500   0   702004      0      0      0   352321      0      0      0 BRU
eth1    1500   0    60516      0      0      0   340584      0      0      0 BRU
eth2    1500   0        0      0      0      0   331777      0      0      0 BRU
lo      3924   0       77      0      0      0       77      0      0      0 LRU
[root@beauregard /]#
```

The output columns of this command are quite straightforward. The Iface column displays the interface for the output record. The MTU field displays the MTU and the Met field displays the metric associated with the interface. The RX-OK and TX-OK columns list the number of packets received and transmitted, respectively.

The RX-ERR column lists the number of bad packets received. A bad packet is one which could not be interpreted. A large value (20% of the value in RX-OK or more) can indicate that a node on the network is transmitting a lot of garbage. This could be due to a bad port on a hub (repeater, switch, or router), a bad Ethernet card, or a bad cable. If you are still using transceivers (a device that connects via cables between the interface card and the rest of the network), a bad transceiver can also generate bad packets. High numbers of receive errors can also be due to duplicate IP address use in the environment. The TX-ERR column displays the number of bad packets sent. This column also includes the number of collisions associated with the interface. Normally, large values here are due to high collision rates which generally reflect a large volume of network traffic. Recall from Chapter 2 that the number of collisions can more easily be viewed with `ifconfig`. If collision rates sustain a high rate (3% to 5% for 10 Mbps Ethernet, for instance), it is indicative of the need to analyze network use.[1] This may ultimately involve, among other things, reorganizing which hosts attach to which networks, incorporating subnetworks and/or switches, implementing full duplex Ethernet and/or higher speed Ethernet, and restructuring application use.

A large value (greater than about 20%) in the `TX-ERR` column can also be due to the hardware problems noted above (except for transceivers), except that such values would indicate a hardware problem locally. Please note that the percentages quoted in this and the prior paragraph are rough estimates only; to get accurate, safe operating ranges for a given system requires profiling the behavior of the system over a period of time.

The `RX-DRP` and `TX-DRP` fields list packets that were destroyed prior to receipt or transmission, respectively. The `RX-OVR` and `TX-OVR` fields show the number of packets that generated software overflow conditions. High counts in these fields only occur on major servers and systems configured as routers and generally reflect the inability of the system to keep up with all of the networking activity.

The `Flg` field lists the flags that are set on the interface. This is the same information that is available from `ifconfig`; compare these with the `ifconfig` flags described in Chapter 4. Table 9–9 lists the flags that can be displayed in this field and their associated meanings.

Table 9–9   Flags in the `Flg` Field of `netstat -i`

FLAG	DESCRIPTION
B	Specifies that broadcasts are enabled.
L	Indicates that this device is a loopback.
M	Indicates that the device is in promiscuous mode.
O	Specifies that ARP is disabled.
P	Indicates that the interface is a point-to-point link.

---

1. The collision rate on a system is different than the collision rate on a network. The `netstat -i` command yields data that estimates the collision rate for the specific system, since not all collisions on the network are captured by each system. To obtain an estimate of the collision rate of a given network, various systems must be sampled.

Table 9–9   Flags in the `Flg` Field of `netstat -i` *(Continued)*

FLAG	DESCRIPTION
R	Indicates that the interface is running.
U	Indicates that the interface is up.

Note that `netstat -i` only displays information for interfaces marked UP. To see all interfaces you must use `netstat -ai`.

Network Statistics

A summary of network statistics can be displayed with `netstat -s` as shown in Example 9–13.

Example 9–13   Output of `netstat -s`

```
[root@beauregard /]# netstat -s
Ip:
    755194 total packets received
    6 forwarded
    0 incoming packets discarded
    722927 incoming packets delivered
    1021691 requests sent out
Icmp:
    54 ICMP messages received
    0 input ICMP message failed.
    ICMP input histogram:
        destination unreachable: 4
        echo requests: 29
        echo replies: 21
    31 ICMP messages sent
    0 ICMP messages failed
    ICMP output histogram:
        destination unreachable: 2
        echo replies: 29
Tcp:
    10 active connections openings
    0 passive connection openings
    4 failed connection attempts
    0 connection resets received
    2 connections established
    18222 segments received
    14371 segments send out
    2 segments retransmited
    0 bad segments received.
    0 resets sent
Udp:
    22 packets received
    0 packets to unknown port received.
    0 packet receive errors
    19 packets sent

[root@beauregard /]#
```

The output is very simple and is broken up based on the IP, ICMP, TCP, and UDP protocols.

Multicast Group Connections

The `netstat -g` command is used to list all active multicast memberships for each interface. Example 9–14 illustrates.

Example 9–14   Output of `netstat -g`

```
[root@beauregard /]# netstat -g
IPv6/IPv4 Group Memberships
Interface        RefCnt Group
---------------- ------ --------------------
lo               1      all-systems.mcast.net
eth0             1      ospf-dsig.mcast.net
eth0             1      ospf-all.mcast.net
eth0             1      all-systems.mcast.net
eth1             1      ospf-dsig.mcast.net
eth1             1      ospf-all.mcast.net
eth1             1      all-systems.mcast.net
eth2             1      ospf-dsig.mcast.net
eth2             1      ospf-all.mcast.net
eth2             1      all-systems.mcast.net
[root@beauregard /]#
```

The `Interface` column lists the interface, the `RefCnt` lists the number of processes that are using the multicast group, and the `Group` column lists the multicast address. See Chapter 12 for details about the specific OSPF multicast groups.

As a final note about `netstat`, Table 9–10 lists many of the files in `/proc` that are queried by `netstat` for the data it outputs.

Table 9–10   Files in `/proc/net` Used by `netstat`

FILE IN /proc/net	DESCRIPTION
dev	Devices information
raw	Raw sockets
tcp	TCP sockets
udp	UDP sockets
igmp	Multicast data
unix	UNIX domain sockets

Table 9–10   Files in `/proc/net` Used by `netstat` *(Continued)*

FILE IN `/proc/net`	DESCRIPTION
route	Routing table
rt_cache	Routing table cache
ip_masquerade	Masqueraded connections

socklist

The `socklist` command is a simple perl script that outputs basic information about active sockets. In particular, for each active socket, the PID, port number, and server name are provided. While not as detailed as `netstat`, it does provide a quick way to check what is happening on the system. Example 9–15 illustrates.

Example 9–15   Output of `socklist`

```
[root@beauregard /]# socklist
type   port      inode    uid      pid   fd   name
tcp     23       72630      0    12014    2   in.telnetd
tcp     25         626      0      708    4   sendmail
tcp    515         581      0      660    6   lpd
tcp     98         564      0      646   13   inetd
tcp     79         563      0      646   12   inetd
tcp    513         560      0      646    9   inetd
tcp    514         559      0      646    6   inetd
tcp     23         558      0      646    5   inetd
tcp     21         557      0      646    4   inetd
tcp    113         511      0      603    4   identd
tcp    658         413      0      479    1   rpc.statd
tcp   1024         390      0        0    0
tcp    111         373      0      454    4   portmap
udp    518         562      0      646   11   inetd
udp    517         561      0      646   10   inetd
udp    656         410      0      479    0   rpc.statd
udp   1024         387      0        0    0
udp    111         372      0      454    3   portmap
raw     89         806      0      913    7   gated
raw      1         805      0      913    6   gated
raw      1           0      0        0    0
raw      6           0      0        0    0
[root@beauregard /]#
```

This command is a useful companion to `netstat` in that it can be used to quickly identify available services that can then be analyzed in more detail with `netstat`.

Netcat

The Netcat utility, implemented through the `nc` command, provides a method for testing TCP and UDP connectivity. Although largely useful for resolving programming issues, it can also be used to troubleshoot Application layer configuration problems and use loose source routing to check networking paths. It can also act as a rudimentary *port scanner*. A port scanner is a tool that attempts to determine which ports on a remote system are open, closed, and/or blocked. There are other, more sophisticated port scanners and we mention two of them later in this section. All of these capabilities make Netcat one of the most useful learning tools for the understanding of TCP/IP generally and the discovery of complex network topologies. It is particularly useful for learning purposes when used in conjunction with Ethereal.

One of Netcat's primary features is that it is easy to implement in a script. It ships with most Linux distributions and can also be found at

```
http://www.10pht.com/~weld/netcat/
```

Both UNIX and Windows 95/98/NT versions are available. Additionally, a number of sample scripts are included. The `nc` command accepts a number of flags. These are listed in Table 9–11.

Table 9–11   Flags of the `nc` Command

FLAG	DESCRIPTION
`-g router`	Specifies that `router` is to be included as a hop along a loose source routed path. This option can be specified multiple times for each such router.
`-i seconds`	Specifies the delay time in seconds between transmission or receipt of each line of text. Also sets the delay between connecting to different ports.
`-l`	Puts `nc` in listen mode like a server. Any hostname specifications here act to restrict incoming connection attempts to those hosts only.
`-n`	Suppresses name translation. In particular, no DNS lookups and no translation of port numbers to port names (and vice-versa) are performed.

Table 9–11   Flags of the `nc` Command *(Continued)*

FLAG	DESCRIPTION
`-o file`	Specifies that a hexadecimal log of all data transferred be written to `file`. Each line of data in `file` will be preceded by < for all received data and > for all transmitted data.
`-p port`	Specifies the source port used by `nc`. By default, `nc` gets an available, unprivileged port.
`-r`	Specifies that source and/or destination ports should be chosen somewhat randomly instead of sequentially within a range or as assigned by the system.
`-s host`	Specifies the source `host` interface to use. Can either be a hostname or IP address. It must be configured on the system.
`-u`	Use UDP. By default, TCP is used.
`-v`	Causes `nc` to be verbose. Multiple `-v` flags can be specified to increase amount of additional output.
`-w timeout`	Specifies the number of seconds before `nc` drops the connection attempt.
`-z`	Specifies port scan mode. Causes `nc` to scan listening daemons without sending any data for them.
`-h`	Displays a help message and quits.

There are two other flags that only become available by setting special compile-time options. The first flag is `-e`. It effectively allows `nc` to act as if it were an indirect server like `inetd`. It is not compiled by default due to the serious security vulnerability it introduces. The other flag is `-t`. This flag allows `nc` to script telnet sessions and can be used to modify data streams. In order to learn more about these flags and their associated compile-time options, see the README file that comes with the Netcat distribution. This file can also be viewed at

```
http://www.l0pht.com/~weld/netcat/readme.html
```

The general syntax for the `nc` command is

```
nc [-flag(s)] [hostname] [port[-port] [port[-port]] ...]
```

where *flags* are as defined in Example 9–15, *hostname* is the remote hostname or IP address (it must be an IP address if the -n flag is used), and *port* is the destination port name or number (again, if -n is used it must be a number). Ports can also be specified in a range, such as `10-30`, a space-separated list, or a combination thereof.

In its simplest form, `nc` is used to connect to an open port on another system. This behavior is similar to `telnet`. Example 9–16 shows this functionality by connecting to a remote `sendmail` port. Note that once connected, all data submitted to standard input is sent to the remote system and standard output receives all responses. In the example, **bold** entries are typed in locally. Here, an `ehlo` is sent eliciting the standard `sendmail` greeting and list of capabilities in response.

Example 9–16   Using `nc` to Connect to a Remote `sendmail` Port

```
[root@foghorn /root]# nc beauregard mail
220 localhost.localdomain ESMTP Sendmail 8.9.3/8.9.3; Sat, 4 Nov 2000 04:34:50 -0700
ehlo .
250-localhost.localdomain Hello IDENT:root@foghorn [10.254.1.11], pleased to meet you
250-EXPN
250-VERB
250-8BITMIME
250-SIZE
250-DSN
250-ONEX
250-ETRN
250-XUSR
250 HELP
Ctrl-C
punt!
[root@foghorn /root]#
```

Using the `-z` flag of `nc`, Netcat can perform a port scan to determine which ports are open. This can be quite valuable in determining whether other hosts see the same open ports as are reported locally. Example 9–17 provides a simple illustration. In this case, all ports between `20` and `25` inclusive on the host `beauregard` are probed to see if they are open. Between each probe is a five-second delay.

Example 9–17   Port Scanning with `nc`

```
[root@foghorn /root]# nc -v -w 5 -z beauregard 20-25
beauregard [10.254.1.10] 25 (smtp) open
beauregard [10.254.1.10] 23 (telnet) open
beauregard [10.254.1.10] 21 (ftp) open
[root@foghorn /root]#
```

There are other, more sophisticated port scanners available. Two that are worth investigating are `nmap` and `hping`. Of the two, `nmap` probably has more active users and is more actively worked on, but `hping` has some useful features that make it noteworthy. The home page for `nmap` is

```
http://www.insecure.org/nmap/
```

The home page for `hping` is

```
http://www.kyuzz.org/antirez/
```

Netcat also provides a multipurpose client-server application. You can accomplish this by running `nc` in listen mode on one system (the server) and connect to it via `nc` on another system. There are many uses for interconnecting `nc` in this way and lots of examples are provided in the Netcat distribution and described in the README. One example use is to stress test the environment. A very simple way to do this is to start an `nc` server on one system, feeding it lots of irrelevant data.

```
[root@foghorn /root]# yes xxxxxxxxxxx | nc -v -v -l -p 5555 > /dev/null
```

Here, the `yes` command repeats the string xxxxxxxxxxx until killed. This repeated pattern is piped into the `nc` server, with standard out (all received packets) redirected to `/dev/null`. Meanwhile, on another system, a client can be started to send lots of irrelevant data.

```
[root@beauregard /root]# yes yyyyyyyyyyy | nc foghorn 5555 > /dev/null
```

At this point, each side is sending the other repetitious strings until one or the other is killed. Because of the use of `-v -v` on the server side, an accounting of packets sent and received will be output when the connection is terminated. Example 9–18 shows this behavior after the above two commands have been executing for a while.

Example 9–18   Termination of nc Server

```
[root@foghorn data]# yes xxxxxxxxxxx | nc -v -v -l -p 5555 > /dev/null
listening on [any] 5555 ...
connect to [10.254.1.11] from beauregard [10.254.1.10] 1044
 sent 3264512, rcvd 3219744

[root@foghorn data]#
```

The `nc` command is quite flexible and capable. It can act as an `rsh` or `rlogin` client for debugging and security testing. It can be used to test log servers (systems that run `syslogd -r`). And it can be used to test `ipchains` and/or `ipta-`

`bles` rule sets. Check out the README file and add-on scripts and programs that come with the Netcat package for more details.

Ethereal

Ethereal is initially described in Chapter 3 and examples of its use are given throughout this book. This tool is an extremely valuable troubleshooting and learning tool. Whenever a network-related problem is not easily and quickly resolved, this tool should be used in conjunction with one or more of the other tools described here. Take the time to become very familiar with it.

`iptraf`

`iptraf` is a curses-based network traffic monitor. It can display information including current TCP connections with packet and byte counts and other protocol (UDP, ICMP, OSPF, etc.) packet and byte counts; all counts can be displayed on a per interface basis or on a per port basis, and packet counts by size or IP address. It ships with most distributions as optional software or it can be obtained in compiled form for Linux 2.2.x kernels from

```
http://cebu.mozcom.com/riker/iptraf/
```

Be sure to peruse the README and INSTALL files that come with the `iptraf` software. Also included are an `iptraf(8)` man page and documentation in HTML; be sure to read through these resources as well.

`iptraf` is a very simple program to use. Although it can be invoked with flags, the flags serve to put `iptraf` into a particular display screen, any of which can also be reached through the `iptraf` interactive mechanism. To invoke `iptraf` in interactive mode, simply execute `iptraf`. Figure 9–3 shows the initial window displayed after executing `iptraf` in a shell.

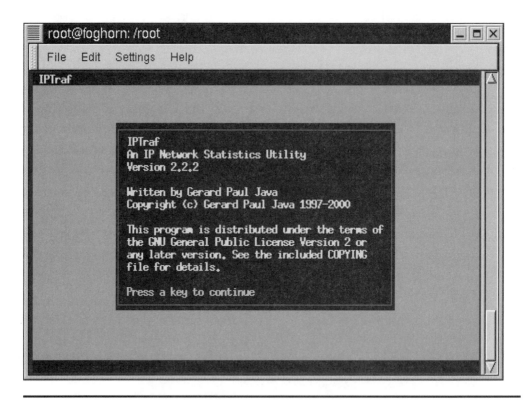

Figure 9–3   `iptraf` Initial Window

After the initial window appears, press any key to reach the main menu. This is shown in Figure 9–4. Navigating through this menu, and all submenus, is accomplished by using the Up or Down arrow keys to highlight (or in some cases, a > will appear to the left of the selection as an equivalent indicator) a selection. Once you've highlighted the selection of your choice, a carriage return (press the Enter key) will invoke the choice.

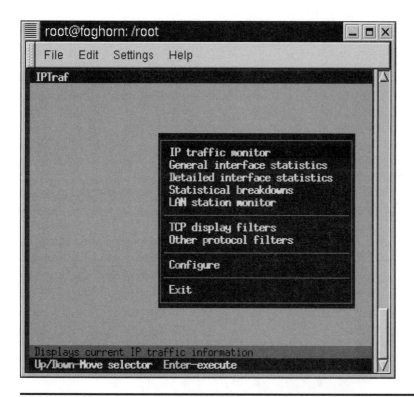

Figure 9–4   `iptraf` Main Menu

The `iptraf` main menu lists the options to choose to obtain an active monitoring window. The available selections invoke submenus that provide a variety of different information displays. These are described below. Note that after you have selected one of these options and cause another window to be displayed, you can always return to this menu by typing X in the window.

IP traffic monitor

This selection invokes a real-time traffic monitor of all packets and TCP connections for a given interface. Once you've selected this option from the menu, a submenu will pop up requesting which interfaces you'd like to monitor. This menu is shown in Figure 9–5 and, as you can see, it allows for the selection of any specific interface or all interfaces.

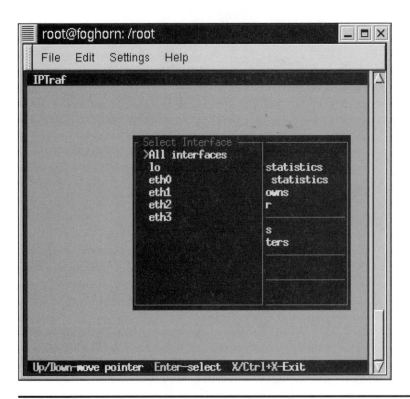

Figure 9–5   `iptraf` Select Interface Submenu

Whether you select `All interfaces` or a specific interface, the next window will appear the same and differ only with respect to what `iptraf` records. Figure 9–6 displays the window as it would appear if you select `All interfaces`.

The upper pane of this window contains the current TCP connection details, while the lower pane displays packets in real-time. Use `w` to toggle which pane is active. A pane must be active in order to scroll through its contents. Scrolling is accomplished by using the Page Up and Page Down keys.

The upper pane provides basic statistics and detail about existing TCP connections. The column headers are as follows. The leftmost column contains the

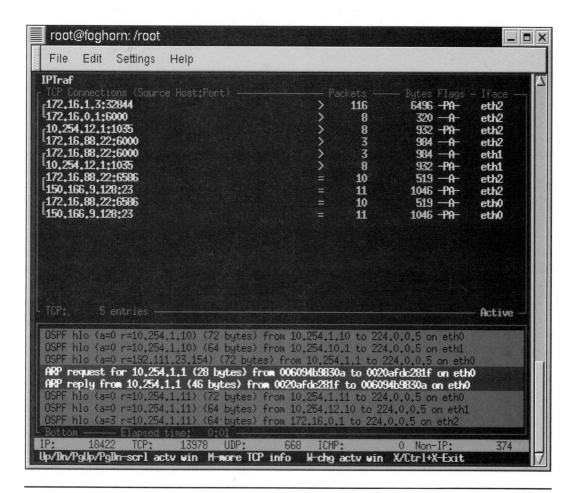

Figure 9–6   `iptraf` IP Traffic Monitor

source address:port, and the line below it, linked with the bracket, lists the destination address:port. The next column indicates the direction of the statistics followed by the packet and byte counts. These two columns can be changed to show the last packet size and current TCP window size by typing M on the keyboard. Another M will change it back. The next column displays the flags associated with the latest TCP packet. The meanings of these flags are listed in Table 9–12 (see Chapter 7 for further details regarding TCP bit fields). The last column displays the interface for which the statistics apply.

Table 9–12   TCP Flags in `IP traffic monitor`

Flag	Meaning
S	The synchronize bit is set.
A	The acknowledgment bit is set.
P	The push bit is set.
U	The urgent bit is set.
RESET	The reset bit is set.
DONE	The connection is in a half-closed state.
CLOSED	The connection has completed its four-way close handshake.
–	No flags set.

The lower pane lists summary information about packets passing through the given interface(s). Below the lower pane is a summary line of number of packets collected for each different protocol type.

General interface statistics

Selecting the General interface statistics option brings up a window that summarizes IP traffic and data rates on a per interface basis. Figure 9–7 displays this window.

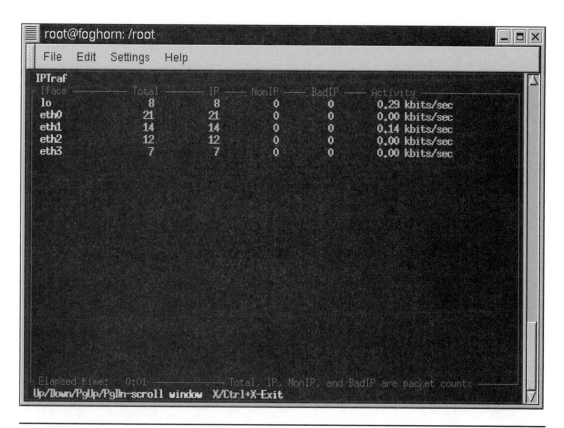

Figure 9–7   iptraf General Interface Statistics

Detailed interface statistics

This selection is similar to the General interface statistics, except that a specific interface must be selected, via a menu similar to that shown in Figure 9–5 which appears upon choosing this option. Once you've selected an interface, the window shown in Figure 9–8 appears. The information provided in this window is self-explanatory.

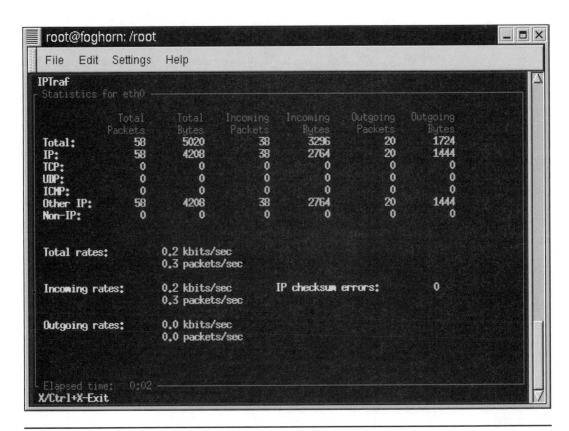

Figure 9–8   iptraf Detailed interface statistics

Statistical breakdowns

This selection produces one of two displays for viewing summary information of traffic over a specific interface. Once you've selected this option, you will see a submenu soliciting your choice of statistical summary detail. This submenu is shown in Figure 9–9. Regardless of which of the two choices you make, a window similar to that shown in Figure 9–5 will pop up asking for an interface. The two possible choices are `By packet size` or `By TCP/UDP port`. Both are similar in terms of their output, except for the different way of organizing the statistics. Figure 9–10 shows the `By packet size` window. Its output is, once again, self explanatory.

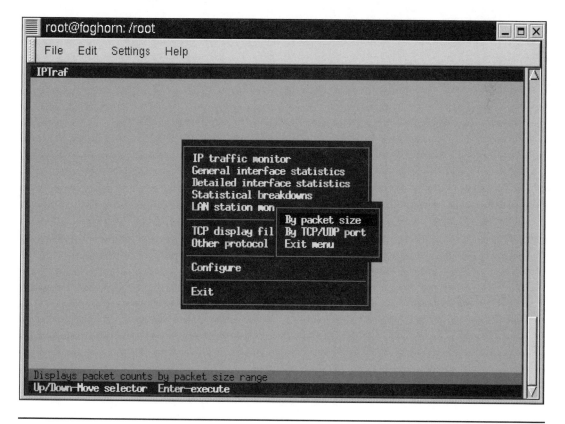

Figure 9–9   `iptraf` Statistical breakdowns Submenu

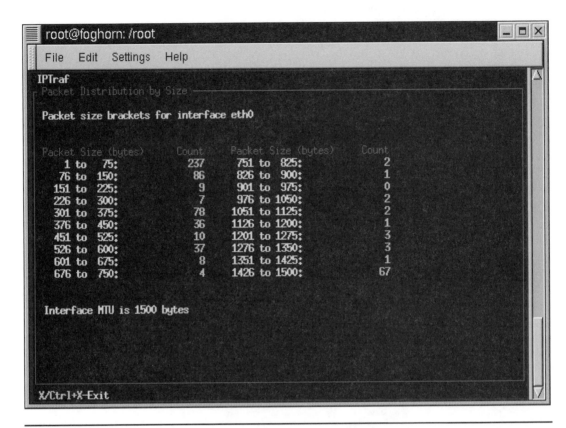

Figure 9–10   `iptraf` Packet Distribution Window

LAN station monitor

The LAN station monitor discovers MAC addresses and displays statistics on the number of incoming and outgoing packets. It also includes statistics for incoming and outgoing kilobits per second for each discovered station. Once again, prior to seeing the actual LAN station monitor window, a submenu similar to that shown in Figure 9–5 pops up first. Once you select an interface choice, the window similar to that shown in Figure 9–11 (which captures information about all interfaces) appears.

The columns of output here are quite straightforward. IP In and IP Out are counts of packets received and transmitted, respectively, on the specified interface. BytesIn and BytesOut capture the number of octets received and transmitted while InRate and OutRate captures the rate of traffic through the interface in kbps.

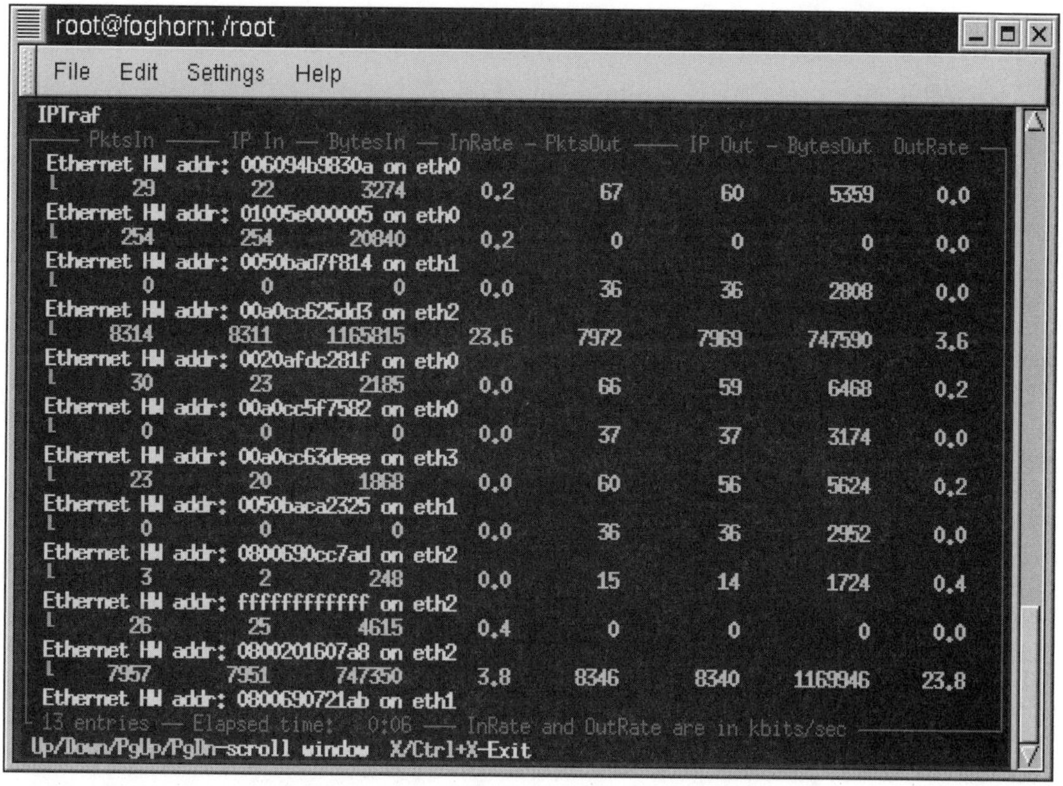

Figure 9–11   `iptraf` LAN Station Window

Display Filters and Configuration

There are two types of display filters: `TCP display filters` and `Other protocol display filters`. These can be used to filter what is displayed based on a variety of information such as IP addresses and port numbers. Much like with Ethereal, this allows you to focus your analysis on a particular type of traffic.

Additionally, configuration of `iptraf` can be specified through the `Configuration` selection on the main menu. All configuration changes are stored in `/var/local/iptraf/iptraf.cfg`. Configuration options include: setting up log files to store captured information, setting up color parameters for display purposes, and setting up additional port definitions. See the HTML documentation for details.

Simple Network Management Protocol (SNMP)

Arguably, the best way to manage and troubleshoot a network is through a network monitoring system of some sort. In brief, network management is generally performed by utilizing systems that collect information about the systems in a networked environment. The systems that collect information are called *consoles* or *management servers*. The consoles are able to collect information because each node in a given networked environment is running an *agent*. The agent is a program that monitors vital system activity and makes that information available to one or more consoles.

The simple network management protocol (SNMP) provides the infrastructure for a network-oriented management system. Almost all Linux distributions ship with the major components necessary to implement a network management mechanism using SNMP. One example of the use of SNMP is the publicly available Multi Router Traffic Grapher (MRTG). MRTG can monitor traffic on various networks from a central location.

Not all network management tools utilize SNMP. The `ntop` utility can provide information about a networked environment from a central location in a similar fashion to MRTG. These tools and SNMP implementations on Linux are covered in good detail in *Red Hat Linux Network Management Tools* as cited in "For Further Reading" on page 392. Obtaining these and other tools is discussed in the next section.

Other Tools

There are a variety of useful utilities for monitoring, troubleshooting, and assessing the security of a networked environment. We mention many of them in Table 9–13.

Table 9–13   List of Network Tools

TOOL	AVAILABILITY	DESCRIPTION
Big Brother	http://bb4.com/ Free for personal use only.	A web-based system and network monitor. Very flexible and scalable.
cheops-ng	http://cheops-ng.sourceforge.net/ GPL	A networking mapping and monitoring tool with an HP OpenView-like look and feel.
ipac	http://www.comlink.apc.org/~moritz/ ipac.html GPL	A simple utility that collects, summarizes, and displays IP accounting data.
MRTG	http://ee-staff.ethz.ch/~oetiker/webtools/ mrtg/mrtg.html GPL	A tool that monitors traffic on networks.
RRDtool	http://ee-staff.ethz.ch/~oetiker/webtools/ rrdtool/ GPL	The graphing and data storage component to MRTG.
NetSaint	http://netsaint.linuxbox.com/ GPL	A host and service network monitoring program.

Table 9–13   List of Network Tools *(Continued)*

TOOL	AVAILABILITY	DESCRIPTION
SARA	http://www-arc.com/sara/index.shtml Free-use license	The security auditor's research assistant (SARA) is the modern follow on to SATAN. It is also a great troubleshooting and learning tool.
Others	http://linux.davecentral.com/	A great collection of Linux tools, in general.

Summary

In this chapter, we provided one approach to troubleshooting network problems generally. The focus of that process was to eliminate possible problems with the use of `ping` and to identify the location of the problem through iteration. Additionally, this chapter presents a survey of some of the many tools that can be used to monitor, troubleshoot, and analyze the security of a networked environment.

For Further Reading

Maxwell, Steve, *Red Hat Linux Network Management Tools*, New York, New York, McGraw Hill, 2000.

Miller, Mark A., *Managing Internetworks with SNMP*, 3d ed., Foster City, California, IDG Books, 1999.

Miller, Mark A., *Troubleshooting TCP/IP*, 3d ed., Foster City, California, IDG Books, 1999.

Perkins, David, and Evan McGinnis, *Understanding SNMP MIBs*, Upper Saddle River, New Jersey, Prentice Hall, 1997.

Spurgeon, Charles E., *Ethernet: The Definitive Guide*, Sebastopol, California, O'Reilly and Associates, 2000.

10

Network Applications

Network applications are programs which use the network services and protocols to perform various functions over the network. These functions may include, but are not limited to, hostname-IP address resolution, dynamic management of network configuration for systems, various protocols and methods for file and printer sharing, centralization of system and network management, management of directory services, configuration and delivery of electronic mail, terminal services, moving files between systems, and many other services.

This chapter will concentrate on showing an overview of some of the more popular network applications. These will include Domain Name Services, Dynamic Host Configuration Protocol, Network File Systems, Samba, Network Information Systems, Lightweight Directory Access Protocol, and electronic mail.

Domain Name Service

Perhaps the single most deployed application throughout the Internet and a great many private networks is the domain name system (DNS). DNS, very simply, provides a way to translate names of systems to IP addresses and back again. This capability is accomplished by way of a hierarchical naming structure which is served by a decentralized organization of systems running DNS software that can resolve names and addresses. DNS is very simple, very powerful, and used almost everywhere.

DNS came into use in the mid-1980s as a direct result of the growth of the Internet. In particular, prior to the implementation of DNS, all nodes connected to the Internet had to have a hosts file (called `hosts.txt`) with all of the IP addresses and hostnames within the Internet. Managing and maintaining this file became so unwieldy that DNS emerged to overcome the limitations of a static database.

Anyone who has browsed the Internet has used DNS names. We have mentioned many of them throughout this book as part of Web page addresses. For example, the Web site

```
http://www.sgi.com/
```

includes the DNS name `www.sgi.com`. This name can be translated by some DNS server or servers into an IP address. Once the IP address is obtained, then the Web page can be reached by virtue of the TCP/IP stack, as described in Chapters 1 through 8.

DNS names are hierarchical with the naming hierarchy proceeding right to left; that is, the rightmost name is the highest part of the name. The names are delimited by the "." character. Thus, the example `www.sgi.com` reflects the highest level name `com` and the next level name `sgi.com`. These two names represent *domains*. A DNS domain is the collection of all nodes that share the DNS name. In this case, `com` is the *top-level* domain (TLD) and `sgi.com` is a *subdomain* of the `com` domain. Moreover, `com` is an example of a reserved TLD. Reserved TLDs are ones that are managed by the authorities responsible for maintaining Internet names and numbers. This authority is vested in IANA and ICANN and their designees. Companies, such as SGI, or individuals who wish to maintain a presence in the Internet can obtain a registered subdomain, like `sgi.com`, from the appropriate authority (and, of course, by paying the appropriate fee). All registered subdomain names within the Internet are a subdomain of some TLD.

The TLDs are divided into two categories, generic TLDs and country code TLDs (ccTLDs). Generic TLDs include such names as `com`, `net`, and `org`. ccTLDs include names such as `jp`, `de`, and `uk`. ccTLDs are assigned to specific countries. You can obtain a list of ccTLDs and their definitions at

```
http://www.iana.org/cctld/cctld-whois.htm
```

You can also get information about the various generic TLDs at either the IANA or ICANN Web sites

```
http://www.iana.org/
http://www.icann.org/
```

To clarify some of the information regarding generic TLDs, Table 10–1 lists the current generic TLDs and their purpose.

Table 10–1   Generic TLDs

TLD	AVAILABILITY	PURPOSE
com	All	Originally intended to identify commercial companies. Subdomains of this domain are now available to individuals and businesses worldwide.
net	All	Originally intended to identify commercial ISPs. Subdomains of this domain are now available to individuals and businesses worldwide.
org	All	Originally intended to identify commercial ISPs. Subdomains of this domain are now available to individuals and businesses worldwide.
gov	Restricted	Reserved for the United States government.
edu	Restricted	Reserved for four year degree granting colleges and universities within the United States.
mil	Restricted	Reserved for the United States military.
int	Restricted	Reserved for organizations created by international treaty.
aero	Restricted	Reserved for the air transport industry. This TLD is new as of November 2000. See the ICANN Web site for further details.
biz	Restricted	Reserved for business use. This TLD is new as of November 2000. See the ICANN Web site for further details.
coop	Restricted	Reserved for nonprofit cooperatives. This TLD is new as of November 2000. See the ICANN Web site for further details.

Table 10–1   Generic TLDs *(Continued)*

TLD	AVAILABILITY	PURPOSE
info	All	Available to individuals, businesses, governments, and other organizations worldwide. This TLD is new as of November 2000. See the ICANN Web site for further details.
museum	Restricted	Reserved for museums. This TLD is new as of November 2000. See the ICANN Web site for further details.
name	Restricted	Reserved for individual use. This TLD is new as of November 2000. See the ICANN Web site for further details.
pro	Restricted	Reserved for professional organizations, but apparently limited to accountants, lawyers, and physicians. This TLD is new as of November 2000. See the ICANN Web site for further details.

It should be noted that the use of these TLDs is controlled within the Internet; however, there is nothing prohibiting their use in networks that are not exposed to the Internet. Internal use, for example, of unregistered subdomain or domain names is entirely acceptable so long as the translation of the unregistered names is not necessary within the Internet. We will explore the creation of internal DNS domains and subdomains later in this chapter.

DNS Domain Name Hierarchy

The easiest way to understand DNS naming is to look at some pictures. Figure 10–1 depicts a piece of the hierarchy as it is implemented in the Internet. This hierarchy is also referred to as the DNS *tree*.

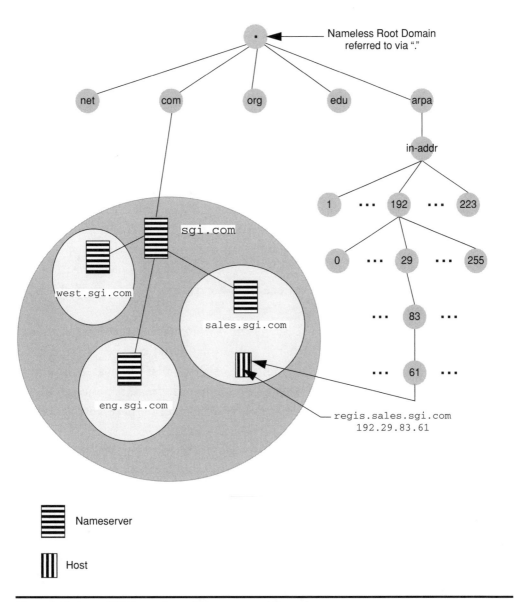

Figure 10–1   DNS Domain and Nameserver Hierarchy

In the figure, shaded circles are used to represent Internet domains, and circles with dots in them are used to represent internal domains. In this context, the internal domains all fall within `sgi.com` and the only significance is that the internal domains are managed by those who manage `sgi.com`. The shaded circles are also known as *nodes* of the DNS tree. Each node also constitutes a *level*. DNS supports a maximum of 127 levels.

Notice that there are *nameservers* shown in some cases. A DNS nameserver is a system that is running the software and is capable of answering DNS *queries*. One such software package is the Berkeley Internet Name Daemon (BIND). It is the most commonly used package on UNIX/Linux systems.

A DNS query is a request to translate a name to an address or vice-versa. We discuss DNS nameservers and queries in detail a bit later in this section. For now, note that each DNS domain must have at least one *primary* or *master* server. A DNS master server is one which is responsible for accurately maintaining name and address translation records for a collection of nodes. These records are stored, modified, and maintained on the master, making it *authoritative* for those records. A DNS master server can be the master server for more than one domain. Consequently, the collection of records for which the master is authoritative is known as its *zone of authority*.

At the very top of Figure 10–1, the *nameless root* domain is depicted. This highest-level domain must exist in any implementation of DNS and can be referenced by ".". This domain, like all others, must have at least one master nameserver. In practice, the Internet-managed domains, including the root domain and the TLDs, require a number of master nameservers as well as other types of nameservers to provide continuous and correct services.

Underneath the com TLD is the sgi.com domain. Within the sgi.com domain are a few example subdomains of sgi.com. Note that one nameserver is depicted for each domain. The lines interconnecting the nameservers are not topological network designations but rather reflect the ability of the nameservers to communicate with each other. Although not shown, the same would be true for the nameservers of the TLDs and root domain. In essence, this diagram depicts the network topologic independence of DNS; that is, DNS domains do not need to consider physical network layouts in order for DNS to be functional—although it may be prudent to do so for performance reasons.

Now, consider the host

```
regis.sales.sgi.com.
```

This name is known as a fully qualified domain name (FQDN). Strictly speaking, the trailing period (rightmost period) or *dot* in the name is part of the FQDN, although it is more often left off. FQDNs with the trailing dot are *abso-*

lute names. Recall that these names are hierarchically significant from right to left. In this case, com is the TLD, sgi.com is a subdomain of com, and sales.sgi.com is a subdomain of sgi.com. regis is a host in the sales.sgi.com domain and is referred to simply as regis within that domain. Throughout sgi.com and its subdomains it is referred to as regis.sales. Elsewhere, the hostname must be fully qualified in order for resolution to be successful (although there are shortcuts that can be implemented in the /etc/resolv.conf file; see the resolver(5) man page for more details).

The host regis.sales.sgi.com has been assigned the IP address of 192.29.83.61. DNS maintains records for hosts to address translations for systems such as this. The translation from FQDN to IP address is known as a *forward* translation. DNS must also be able to translate in the opposite way, that is, it must be able to translate an IP address into an FQDN. Such translations are called *reverse* translations. In order to accomplish this, DNS uses the special TLD in-addr.arpa. In short, all IPv4 (we discuss IPv6 later) addresses fall under this TLD. In particular, the reverse FQDN for regis.sales.sgi.com is

    61.83.29.192.in-addr.arpa.

Bear in mind that these names are hierarchically significant from right to left; hopefully, making the reverse appearance somewhat tolerable. Fortunately, outside of the configuration files required on DNS master servers, these reverse FQDNs are rarely used.

DNS Names

Formally, DNS names are comprised of a series of *labels* between delimeters. A label is a string of characters between dots (which are the delimeters). For instance, the DNS domain name sales.sgi.com has three labels, sales, sgi, and com. According to RFC 1035, labels are a maximum of 63 octets and there is a maximum of 127 levels. Each label represents a level. Thus, the maximum length of a DNS name is $(63 \times 127) + 126 = 8127$ octets. Note that in this equation the 126 represents the number of dots (each label is separated from the next by a dot). An absolute name, then, would have to include the trailing dot and therefore would have a maximum possible length of 8128 octets. In any event, it is unlikely that you will ever run into any of the maximum limits either on a label or an entire FQDN.

Beginning with BIND version 4.9.4, all hostnames are checked for compliance with RFC 952 (*DOD*[1] *Internet Host Table Specification*). In particular, this RFC limits hostnames to include only ASCII alphanumeric values, that is, the letters a through z, A through Z, and the numbers 0 through 9. Additionally, minus or dash symbols ("-") are permitted. In particular, note that underscores ("_") are *not* permitted. These limitations have been extended to apply to FQDNs even though RFC 952 was written prior to the universal adoption of DNS. RFC 952 checking can be disabled on the client side with the no-check-names option in the /etc/resolv.conf file. RFC 952 checking can be disabled on servers using the check-names option.

At this point, we now have a sense of DNS naming, an understanding of the domain hierarchy imposed by DNS, and know that each domain must have at least one nameserver. So, the next question is, how does a DNS query get resolved? Figure 10–2 depicts the process.

This figure depicts the process of resolving an FQDN into an IP address. The process begins with the execution of the command

```
regis$ ftp ftp.rs.internic.net
```

by a user on the system regis.sales.sgi.com. As is described in the first eight chapters, in order for the ftp command to cause encapsulation to begin, the IP address of ftp.rs.internic.net must be obtained. The process of obtaining the IP address for the FQDN is started by the ftp command itself, which programmatically calls the gethostbyname(3) routine. This routine attempts to resolve the name through a variety of methods based on the configuration of the /etc/nsswitch.conf file (see Table 10–3 on page 404 and the nsswitch.conf(5) man page). If one of the methods is DNS, then gethostbyname invokes the DNS resolver[2] to initiate a query to a DNS nameserver.

In Figure 10–2, this initial query is the arrow marked 1. When regis.sales.sgi.com needs to resolve the FQDN ftp.rs.internic.net, it sends a DNS query to that effect to ns.sales.sgi.com, which is a nameserver for the sales.sgi.com domain. This type of request is called a *recursive* request. Recursive requests require the nameserver (for sales.sgi.com, in this case) to either return an IP address (the answer) or an error message.

---

1. Department of Defense.
2. The DNS resolver is actually a collection of routines used for handling DNS queries and responses. See the resolver(3) man page.

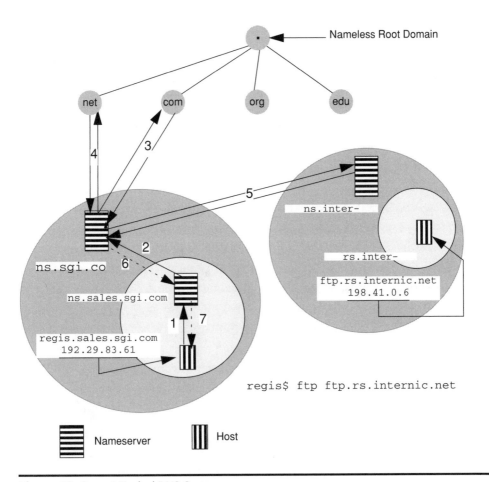

Figure 10–2 A Typical DNS Query

When the `ns.sales.sgi.com` gets the request, it will search its *database* and *cache* for an answer. Each DNS sever may have a database of hosts and may also have a collection of recently received host/address pairs in a DNS cache. We consider both of these repositories later in this chapter. If `ns.sales.sgi.com` cannot find an answer, it will ask another server. Step 2 in Figure 10–2 illustrates the recursive query made by `ns.sales.sgi.com` to the nameserver `ns.sgi.com` which serves `sgi.com`.

The namesever `ns.sgi.com` repeats the process by first looking in its database and cache and then by initiating a query to another nameserver. In this case, however, `ns.sgi.com` issues an *iterative* query to a nameserver in the `com` domain (see step 3 in Figure 10–2). An iterative query is one that causes the responding server to either provide the answer (if it has it) or provide a reference to another server that might have it. Iterative queries are predominant throughout the Internet for performance reasons. For example, step 3 in Figure 10–2 depicts `ns.sgi.com` querying a nameserver in the `com` domain and getting an answer suggesting that a nameserver in the `net` domain be queried (step 4). The nameserver in the net domain responds by suggesting that `ns.sgi.com` contact the nameserver `ns.internic.net`, which it does (step 5). In this example, `ns.internic.net` supplies the IP address for `ftp.rs.internic.net`. Then, `ns.sgi.com` sends this answer to `ns.sales.sgi.com` (step 6). Finally, `ns.sales.sgi.com` answers the original request by passing this information back to `regis.sales.sgi.com`. Note that each server involved with this process will store the answer it obtained in *cache* (a buffer area in memory) for some period of time so that subsequent use will not incur the costs associated with the lookup process. Thus, whenever a server attempts to resolve a query it looks both in its database and cache.

Note that if `ns.internic.net` is the authoritative server for `ftp.rs.internic.net`, then the answer it gives is called an *authoritative answer*. Any time an answer comes from another server, for example, because that information is cached, the answer is called *non-authoritative*. The vast majority of DNS answers in the Internet are non-authoritative, since obtaining authoritative answers often require additional processing time and network bandwidth.

Now that we have a reasonable theoretical overview of how DNS operates, let's explore a bit more of the operational details. The next section covers the different types of DNS servers and their requisite configuration files.

DNS Server Types and Configuration Files

There are a number of different server types in DNS, each of which is generically referred to as a DNS nameserver. Previously, we defined the DNS master server. Table 10–2 enhances that definition and provides definitions for the other two server types, *slave* and *caching*, and for a DNS *client*. There are many configuration variations which lead to the use of other names for DNS servers, such as *forwarding* servers and *norecursion* servers, however, all DNS servers are one of the three types listed in Table 10–2. The variations of DNS servers are covered at various points throughout this chapter.

Table 10–2 Major DNS System Types

DNS TYPE	DESCRIPTION
Master Server	The DNS master server is the system that contains the database of official hostname/address pairs and other pertinent information about the systems it serves. It is the system that can provide authoritative answers about the systems within its database, also known as its zone of authority. Every DNS domain is served by at least one master server. A master server for the nameless root domain is known as a *root master server*.
Slave Server	A slave server is identical to a master server except that the zone of authority database is not maintained by the slave but rather obtained from the master. Slave servers act to back-up the master when it is down and as additional systems for handling DNS queries, thus improving performance. Slave servers are not required, but are often desirable. Slave servers are also known as *secondary* servers.
Caching Server	A caching server is one which has no database of its own and does not obtain one from another server. Caching servers simply make queries on behalf of clients and cache all of the answers. Over time, caching servers build a rich repository of DNS data. Caching servers are used for performance reasons.
Client	A DNS client is any system that participates in a DNS environment. Clients make queries but provide no answers. Normally, clients do not run any daemons, however, bear in mind that all servers are also clients. Also, it is entirely possible to set up a caching server that only answers queries generated by itself—this can be quite useful on large, multiuser systems.

Each DNS server, regardless of type, must run the BIND daemon `named`. The `named` daemon, upon invocation, reads a configuration file (`/etc/ named.conf`, by default) and then runs in the background listening for DNS queries on port 53 (by default). There are a number of commands and scripts associated with `named` and that are part of the BIND software; these are discussed in the next section.

The `/etc/named.conf` file is the master configuration file for `named`. Effectively, it tells `named` where to get the rest of its configuration information. Normally, the additional configuration information is contained in one of three different types of files. These files can have any name, so it is easier to refer to them by type based on content. These files, and other DNS files, are listed and described in Table 10–3.

Table 10–3   Common DNS Files

FILE	DESCRIPTION
`/etc/ nsswitch.conf`	This file determines which service to use for resolution of common system resouces such as hostnames, user accounts, and network services. This file must indicate that DNS is one way to resolve hostnames, otherwise, BIND will not be invoked for most applications.
`/etc/named.conf`	This file is the master file for BIND servers.
hints file	This file contains a list of DNS servers; the server on which the file exists can iteratively query whenever a name cannot be resolved locally. DNS servers can also be configured to forward queries to specific servers recursively.
zone file	This file contains the hostname to IP address resolution database.
reverse zone file	This file contains the IP address to hostname resolution database.
reverse loopback file	This file contains the necessary records for resolution of `127.0.0.1` to the loopback `localhost`. It is a reverse zone file.
`/etc/resolv.conf`	This file contains information, including the IP addresses of nameservers, used for the creation and submission of DNS queries.

As it sometimes becomes confusing as to which file is required for which server, Table 10–4 provides a handy cross reference that associates the files with the different server types. The details of the syntax of the files used by DNS can be found in the references cited in "BIND Software" below.

Table 10–4   DNS File Requirements per DNS System Type

	MASTER SERVER	SLAVE SERVER	CACHING SERVER	CLIENT
`/etc/nsswitch.conf`	required	required	required	required
`/etc/named.conf`	required	required	required	none
HINTS FILE OR FORWARDERS	required	required	required	none
ZONE FILE	required	copied from master	none	none
REVERSE ZONE FILE	required	copied from master	none	none
REVERSE LOOPBACK FILE	required	required	required	none
`/etc/resolv.conf`	recommended	recommended	recommended	required

BIND Software

BIND software implements DNS as it is described in various RFCs. The primary DNS RFCs are 1034 (concepts and facilities) and 1035 (implementation and specification). There are many other RFCs that address various enhancements to these RFCs, hence, DNS and, where appropriate, those RFCs are referenced later in this chapter.

At the time of this writing, there are a number of versions of BIND in common use. Version 8.2.x is predominant in current Linux releases. BIND 9.0.1 is the latest release. Some other UNIX operating systems are still shipping BIND 4.9.x. Although inconsistent, there are no versions of BIND between 4.9.x and

8.x. You can learn more about the various BIND versions, as well as obtain various versions, at

```
http://www.isc.org/products/BIND/
```

Although basic documentation, including man pages, is available at the above site, there is extensive additional documentation at

```
http://www.dns.net/dnsrd/
http://www.nominum.com/
```

WARNING

There is a major security vulnerability in all BIND versions prior to 4.9.7 and 8.2.2p5. Make sure that if you configure BIND for production use that you are using these versions or later. For full details visit `http://www.isc.org/products/BIND/bind-security.html`.

For additional information, including copies of the various RFCs and sample configuration files, look in the `/usr/doc/bind-x.x.x` directory (the `x.x.x` indicates whatever the current version happens to be). For further information on DNS see the following references and Web sites:

```
http://www.dns.net/dnsrd/
http://www.linuxdoc.org/HOWTO/DNS-HOWTO.html
```

Albitz, Paul, and Cricket Liu, *DNS and BIND*, 3d ed., Sebastopol, California, O'Reilly & Associates, Inc., 1998.

Hunt, Craig, *Linux DNS Server Administration*, Sybex, Inc., July, 2000.

Dynamic Host Configuration Protocol

Many users do not understand the technical aspects of networking. For those users, configuring TCP/IP is too complex. Dynamic Host Configuration Protocol (DHCP) is a network application that allows you to centralize the configuration for users who want to connect to the network. It also simplifies the network support and maintenance. The ability to control the configuration of every system in your department or on your network and point your clients to your other servers from one central location simplifies the difficult task of managing a network.

DHCP is one of the most useful protocols available in Linux. It turns out that this protocol is also available for use by other UNIX systems as well as Windows systems. DHCP is very helpful for a number of situations in which network administrators tend to find themselves. The two most common are those of mobile systems and too few IP addresses. Mobile systems may be computers which are attaching to your network from various locations within the network (even different subnets). The second situation is one where the company or group has more computers than it has IP addresses. Suppose you have 253 IP addresses and 500 computers and not all of your computers need to be on the network at all times. This is an ideal situation for DHCP. A third time that DHCP might be helpful is when you are on a network that needs to control and manage network addresses and parameters on each system from a central location, thus relieving the user of the complexity of this task.

DHCP is an extension of the Bootstrap (bootp) protocol. bootp was the first configuration protocol to be able to provide comprehensive information to a client to allow it to configure itself for TCP/IP use. bootp was designed to deliver this information to a client regardless of whether the client knows its IP address. DHCP performs the same task and allows much more (such as dynamic allocation of IP addresses).

The DHCP protocol is defined by RFC 2131 "Dynamic Host Configuration Protocol." The bootp protocol is defined in RFC 951. Additional information about the interoperation between DHCP and bootp can be found in RFC 1534. Extensions and options are given in RFC 2132.

The DHCP environment consists of DHCP *servers*, *clients*, and *relay agents*. DHCP servers are hosts with static IP addresses which supply IP configuration information to DHCP clients. DHCP clients are hosts which are not initially configured with any IP information (such as IP address, netmask, or any other network parameters). DHCP relay agents simply forward DHCP messages between DHCP clients and DHCP servers.

The communications between the DHCP server and client will initially be broadcast. The client uses broadcast to initiate contact with a DHCP server. After the client has been sent an IP address, all communication which follows is unicast traffic.

Because the DHCP client uses broadcast to initiate DHCP communications, the DHCP server is required to either be on the same physical network or have DHCP relay agents on the intervening routers. A host or router with interfaces which directly connect to the client's subnet is usually where you want to run the DHCP relay agent. Many routers, such as Cisco or NorTel, have the relay capability already built into their operating systems. Figure 10–3 shows a typical DHCP environment.

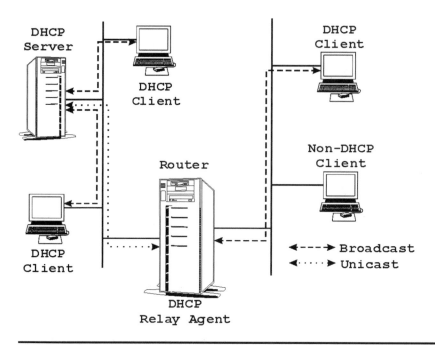

Figure 10–3   Typical DHCP Environment

DHCP has three methods which it uses for allocation of IP addresses. The three methods are manual, automatic, and dynamic allocation. Manual allocation is where the client's IP address is specifically set by defining it in the configuration file. In other words, the client machine is assigned a specific IP address. The connection between the IP address and the client is usually based on either the host name or the MAC address (the physical address) of the system. This allocation is permanent and is not reused by the server. The automatic allocation method assigns the client system an IP address from a pool of IP addresses. This assignment is permanent and the IP address is not reused. The last method, dynamic allocation, is the most commonly used. This is where the server assigns an IP address to the client from a pool of IP addresses on a temporary basis. The IP address is loaned out or "leased" to the client for a previously defined period of time. When the lease time is up, the client must relinquish the IP address (some versions of DHCP, most notably Windows versions, do not want to return their IP addresses when their leases are up; this can cause problems later on) or request an extension on the lease. When the client does relinquish the IP address, it can be added back to the pool of IP addresses and reused by another client requesting an IP address. Table 10–5 shows the relationship between the three allocation methods.

Table 10–5   DHCP Allocation Methods

METHOD	DESCRIPTION	TIME-LENGTH
Manual	Uses fixed IP addresses for clients	Permanent
Automatic	Uses pool of IP addresses for clients	Permanent
Dynamic	Uses pool of IP addresses for clients	Temporary

A DHCP client which has no IP parameters negotiates with DHCP servers on its local network for those parameters. If there are no DHCP servers on the local network, then there must be a DHCP relay agent on the local network to relay the negotiation request to a DHCP server. The negotiation process is depicted in Figure 10–4.

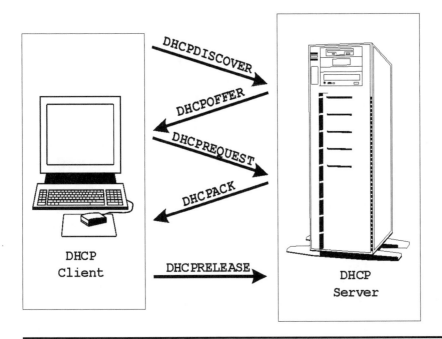

Figure 10–4   DHCP Handshaking

When a DHCP client boots up and has no recognizable IP parameters, it sends out a DHCPDISCOVER broadcast. The client usually delays sending out this broadcast for some time period (a random time between one and ten seconds is used) to avoid clashing with other clients which may have started up at the same time (an occurrence which is not unusual after, for example, a power failure).

The DHCPDISCOVER broadcast is encapsulated within a UDP packet with its destination port number set to 67. It uses a broadcast address of 255.255.255.255. As previously stated, if there is no DHCP server on the local network, then there must be a DHCP relay agent to forward the DHCP-DISCOVER to a DHCP server on another subnetwork. DHCP relay agents will be discussed later in this chapter and more information may be found in RFC 1542.

After sending out the DHCPDISCOVER broadcast, the DHCP client waits some period of time (the amount of time is implementation dependent) for DHCPOFFER messages from any DHCP servers which may be configured to respond to it. The client will then select one of the responses (DHCPOFFER) that it receives. The DHCPOFFER message contains the network layer information needed by the client (such as IP address, etc.) along with a predefined lease time (if the offer is a temporary one). The client then sends a DHCPRE-QUEST message to the DHCP server that it chooses. The DHCP server will verify that the information is still valid and then must respond to the client with a DHCPACK as a confirmation. The DHCPACK message from the server may also contain a full set of configuration parameters (additional information) for the client. The client must also verify the validity of the information (making sure that the information is not already in use by some other client), usually by issuing an ARP broadcast to the network.

Once the DHCPACK from the server is accepted, the client can then begin using network services and is considered to be bound. At this point the client starts three timers, T1, T2, and T3. T1 is the lease renewal timer and is defined as the default amount of time given to an address lease. T2 is the rebinding timer and is basically a timeout to wait for the original server to respond to a lease renewal request. T3 is the maximum duration of the lease. T3 is returned as part of the DHCPACK from the DHCP server. Values for T1 and T2 may be configured at the DHCP server. If they are not set, then default values based on T3 are used (T1=0.5×T3 and T2=0.875×T3).

At time T1 the client will begin the process of renewing the lease (assuming it still needs the IP information). The client will attempt to negotiate a renewal (technically, a new lease) from the original DHCP server. The client will wait through the end of T2 for a response from the original DHCP server.

At time T2 the client will consider that the original DHCP server is no longer available and will attempt to contact any DHCP server to renew or extend its lease. The client will send a DHCPREQUEST broadcast on the network. If some DHCP server responds with a DHCPACK message, then the client will consider its lease renewed and restart all the timers again. If no DHCP server responds, then the lease expires and the client must surrender the IP address and stop any network processing using that IP address.

Obviously, the client doesn't have to wait for the expiration of the lease (T3) to surrender the IP address. An IP address can be voluntarily released by simply canceling its lease. This generally happens when a client is gracefully shut down, but can be done manually also. When the client is shut down, it sends a DHCPRELEASE message to the DHCP server which cancels its lease. This makes the surrendered IP address now available to another DHCP client.

There are three additional messages which may be used for various pieces of the DHCP negotiation process. They are the DHCPNAK (from server to client), the DHCPDECLINE (from client to server), and the DHCPINFORM (from client to server).

The DHCPNAK message is used by the server. After the server receives the client's DHCPREQUEST message, it has to verify whether the information requested is valid. If for any reason it is not (perhaps the address is incorrect or maybe the lease has expired), the server will send a DHCPNAK to the client to deny its request. This requires the client to start over by broadcasting a new DHCPDISCOVER message.

The DHCPDECLINE may be used after the client receives the DHCPOFFER from the DHCP server. If the client determines that the information is already in use by another client, then the client must send a DHCPDECLINE message to the server to decline the server's offer. The client must then start over again by broadcasting a new DHCPDISCOVER message.

Once the client has been assigned an IP address it can't use a DHCPDISCOVER or DHCPREQUEST message to obtain any configuration parameters.

The client may want to request additional configuration information from the server and therefore must use the DHCPINFORM message to accomplish this.

The first obstacle in using DHCP is to make sure that the software is installed. Most of the Linux versions in use have RPM available so DHCP can be installed using the appropriate RPM file (see versions note). The exception to this is the Debian distribution where you have to use the Debian package manager.

After you install the `dhcpd` software, there are three steps that you must complete to get the DHCP server up and running. First, you must configure the server software in order for clients to be able to use it. Second, you must create the leases file. Finally, you must start the server software itself.

All configuration is done through the `/etc/dhcpd.conf` file. This file is read by `dhcpd` (the DHCP daemon) and contains information concerning which subnets and hosts it will respond to and what configuration information it will supply to them. The `/etc/dhcpd.conf` file is an ASCII text file that is easily readable and should be well commented.

The configuration file contains two different types of data. It begins with a global section, which defines parameters, and information, which applies to all clients or controls the behavior of `dhcp`, such as leasing information and options which will be passed to all clients. These options might include subnet-masks, routers, broadcast-addresses, and many other network-related items which might be needed by the clients.

Following the global section might be the definitions of subnets or other groups. These are called declarations and are used for defining the scope of service for the server and the topology of the network. Each of these declarations sections may also have parameters and options which are specific to that subgroup. Declarations which describe network topology are usually either shared-network or subnet statements. Other statements which may appear here are the host and group statements. For still more information concerning DHCP options see the `dhcpd.conf(5)` and `dhcpd-options(5)` man pages.

Once the configuration file has been created, you must create the `/var/state/dhcp/dhcpd.leases` file. This file is used to store a database of the address leases which it has assigned. Every time a lease is acquired, renewed, or released, this lease information is added to the end of the file. Prior to starting the server itself, you must create an empty `dhcpd.leases` file. This will ensure that the `dhcpd` daemon will start correctly.

This file is rewritten periodically to prevent it from growing too large. This is accomplished by creating a temporary copy of the lease file into which all known leases are dumped, then renaming the original lease file to `/var/state/dhcp/dhcpd.leases~`. After this is completed, the temporary lease file is moved to `/var/state/dhcp/dhcpd.leases`.

If the DHCP server dies for some reason or the system crashes between the time that the old lease file has been renamed and the new lease file has been moved into place, the DHCP server will not start because there is no `/var/state/dhcp/dhcpd.leases` file. If this happens, do not create an empty leases file. Instead, move the `/var/state/dhcp/dhcpd.leases~` file to the `/var/state/dhcp/dhcpd.leases` file. In other words, simply restore the original file from the old file. Then start the `dhcpd` daemon. This will restart the daemon with a valid lease file and guarantee a minimum of lost lease information.

The `dhcpd` daemon writes the leases file as ASCII text. This makes it easily readable so that if you want to see what leases have been assigned, you may do so. The entries in the file consist of a keyword lease followed by the IP address and this information is then followed by a set of statements which give additional details about the lease.

When it starts up, the `dhcpd` daemon reads the `/etc/dhcpd.conf` file and stores the list of available IP addresses for each subnet in memory. It then sits and waits for a client to request an IP address using the DHCP protocol. The `dhcpd` daemon then allocates an IP address for the client. Each client is also assigned a lease. This lease expires after a particular amount of time which is defined by the DHCP administrator (the default is one day). If a client wishes to continue using the IP address assigned to it, they must renew the lease prior to its expiration. Once the lease expires, the client is no longer permitted to use the assigned IP address.

The `dhcpd` daemon keeps track of leases in the `/var/state/dhcp/dhcpd.leases` file. This allows it to keep track of the leases across system reboots, crashes, and server restarts. Prior to granting a lease to a client, the `dhcpd` daemon records the lease in the `dhcpd.leases` file and flushes the buffer to disk. This is done to ensure that `dhcpd` will not lose information about a lease if the system goes down for some reason.

The DHCP daemon is started with the `dhcpd` command. This command may include command line options for debugging, quiet operation, or several others. For more information on the dhcpd command see the dhcpd(8) man page. You might also check the /usr/doc/dhcpd-x.x directory.

The DHCP relay agent is designed to listen for DHCP boot requests and forward them to a DHCP server. It is important to remember that the DHCP client uses the limited broadcast address so this means that the DHCP relay agent must be on the same physical network as the DHCP client. The relay agent, however, does not have to be on the same physical network as the DHCP server. It knows the IP address of the DHCP server and therefore can use that to forward the request to the DHCP server. The DHCP server will then send the DHCP reply packet back to the DHCP relay agent. The DHCP relay agent is then responsible for broadcasting the reply packet on the local network so that the client can retrieve it.

The DHCP relay agent program, dhcprelay, is included as part of the DHCP server software package (except in the Debian distribution). It is located in the /usr/sbin directory. This program may be started manually as in the case of the DHCP server program. However, as was the previous case, there are a number of other methods of starting the DHCP relay agent (such as adding the command to the /etc/rc.d/rc.local file, etc.). The most common method is to start the program from the command line (although this may be in a script of some type).

The DHCP relay agent will listen for DHCP requests on all interfaces attached to the host or on those interfaces specified on the command line. When a query is received by the relay agent, it will forward it to the list of DHCP servers which were specified on the command line. At least one DHCP server must be specified on the command line.

Now is the point at which we set up clients to use the DHCP server or relay agents which have previously been created. The easiest way to create a DHCP client is during the installation. Most versions of Linux will attempt to determine whether or not your system has a network interface card. If the installation program finds one, it will give you the option to configure the interface either by static assignment or through a DHCP server.

The DHCP client's job is basically to get the host information from a DHCP server and configure the network interface of the machine which it runs on. It will also try to renew leases when needed. There are basically three different clients available for use in Linux to configure a system as a DHCP client. Red Hat includes the older dhcpcd and the faster, simpler pump programs. SuSE has the newer dhclient program. It turns out that Caldera includes both dhcpcd and dhclient daemons.

The older of the three client programs is the dhcpcd daemon. It appears to be the most robust of the client daemons. This is mainly because of the number of options that it has available. The dhcpcd command is located in the /sbin directory.

There are also a number of files which are associated with the dhcpcd daemon. Some of these are created at the time the daemon is started. Some of these files are stored in the /etc/dhcpc directory. The /etc/dhcpc/dhcpcd-*interface*.info file is where dhcpcd saves the host information. The *interface* in the filename is really supposed to be the actual network interface name which is being used by dhcpcd (such as eth0). The /etc/dhcpc/dhcpcd-*interface*.exe is a special file that dhcpcd will attempt to execute whenever it detects a change in the IP address. The /etc/resolv.conf file is created by dhcpcd and is used to store the DNS and domain name options. If an /etc/resolv.conf already exists, then it is renamed /etc/resolv.conf.sv and is restored when dhcpcd exits. The /var/run/dhcpcd-*interface*.pid file contains the process id of the currently running dhcpcd. Finally, the /etc/dhcpc/dhcpcd-*interface*.cache file contains previously assigned IP addresses along with a few other things.

Another client program, dhclient, reads the /etc/dhclient.conf file on startup. This file contains configuration instructions for the DHCP client. Following this, the client gets a list of all of the network interfaces recognized on the system. For each interface (either all or the ones specified on the command line or configuration file) the client will attempt to configure the interface using the DHCP protocol.

The DHCP client will also keep a list of leases it has been assigned in the /etc/dhclient.leases file. This allows it to keep track of leases across system reboots and server restarts. After reading the /etc/dhclient.conf file, the client will read the /etc/dhclient.leases file. This is done to refresh the client's memory about what leases it has had assigned to it. This file is rotated in a similar fashion to the leases file that the DHCP server maintains. We will look at the /etc/dhclient.leases file in more detail later.

The old leases are also maintained so that if the DHCP server is not available when dhclient is first invoked dhclient will have a backup plan. The dhclient can try to use old leases (from the `/etc/dhclient.leases` file) that have not yet expired. These are tested and if determined to be valid may be used until either they expire or the DHCP server becomes available.

Another situation which may arise here is what to do if a mobile host system needs to access a network where no DHCP server exists. In this case, the system may be preloaded with a lease for a fixed address (in the `/etc/dhclient.conf` file) on that network. After all attempts to connect with a DHCP server have been exhausted, `dhclient` can try to validate the static lease. If this is successful, the client can use the lease until it is restarted.

The `/etc/dhclient.conf` file is a free-form ASCII text file. It may contain tabs, newlines, and keywords that are case-insensitive. Comments are, as always, encouraged and can be placed anywhere in the file (except within quotes). Comments begin with a # character and end at the end of the line.

The `/etc/dhclient.conf` file is used to configure the behavior of the client in a number of ways including: protocol timing, information requested from the server, information required of the server, defaults to use if information from the server is lacking, values which may be used to override that which is obtained from the server, or values to augment information from the server. This file may also be used to define static information used on networks that don't have a DHCP server.

The one key thing to remember about the `/etc/dhclient.conf` file is that it only needs to exist. You don't have to use it to configure `dhclient`. In most cases, `dhclient` will work fine with just an empty `/etc/dhclient.conf` file. However, if you want to change the default settings for the DHCP client, that capability exists.

For additional information on DHCP, check out the following references and Web sites:

Kercheval, Berry, *DHCP: A Guide to Dynamic TCP/IP Network Configuration*, Prentice Hall, Upper Saddle River, New Jersey, 1999.
Siyan, Karanjit S., *Inside TCP/IP*, 3d ed., New Riders Publishing, Indianapolis, Indiana, 1997.

```
http://www.linuxdoc.org/HOWTO/mini/DHCP/index.html
http://www.dhcp.org
```

Remote Filesystems

Many environments are made up of distributed filesystems which are located on multiple systems throughout the network. These filesystems may be remotely accessed by one or more hosts within the network, allowing users to access their files from any system as though they were part of the local file structure. The next few sections will look at some of the methods for mounting and using remote filesystems. These methods include the Network File System (NFS), the Andrew File System (AFS), and the Novell Netware File System.

Network File System

The advent of distributed computing has resulted in a requirement for sharing disk resources. Network File System (NFS) is one solution for this requirement. NFS was originally created by Sun Microsystems and is a standard on most UNIX systems.

NFS is basically a client/server application. It allows clients to access directories that are on a server. This is done in a manner which is transparent to the user so that remote directories appear as local directories. When a client attaches a remote directory to a local filesystem it is called *mounting* a directory. A server which is offering to share a directory is said to be *exporting* that directory. Figure 10–5 shows an NFS server which is sharing or exporting four directories: /usr/share/data, /usr/catman, /usr/people, and /home/staff. These exported directories are mounted on Client1, Client2, Client3, and Client4 at the following local mount points: /usr/data (read-write), /home (read-only), /usr/catman (read-only), and /usr/people (read-write).

The local directory on Client1, for example, allows the remote directory on the NFS server to appear as part of the local directory tree. Figure 10–6 shows the relationship of the server directory tree to the local directory tree. In this example, the directory /home/staff on the NFS server is being exported and mounted locally at the /people/staff directory on the client. This means that bill's directory on the server /home/staff/bill would be accessed as /people/staff/bill on the client.

NFSv2 runs on top of UDP and IP and is a remote procedure call (RPC) protocol. I/O calls from programs needing NFS files are intercepted by NFS and sent to the remote server for processing. This is known as a remote procedure call.

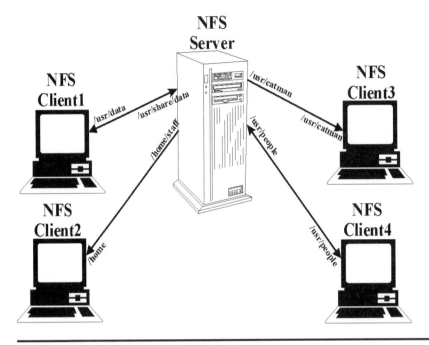

Figure 10–5   NFS Client-Server Model

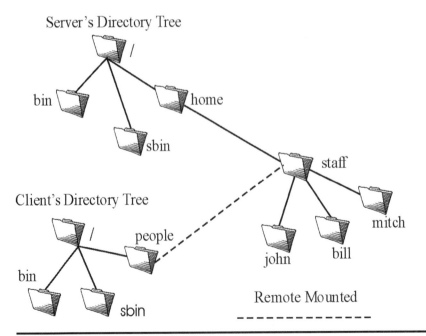

Figure 10–6   NFS Mounted Directory Structure

NFS uses the External Data Representation (XDR) protocol at the presentation layer. XDR was developed by Sun Microsystems for use with NFS and NIS. XDR uses a fixed byte ordering for everything which is transmitted over the network called the canonical form (which is actually the byte ordering for Motorola and SPARC processors). Any system which uses NFS will convert its data bytes to canonical form prior to transmission and will assume that any data received from the network is in canonical form and convert it to local form, if necessary.

There are currently two versions of NFS, NFSv2 and NFSv3. Version 2.2.X of the Linux kernel currently only supports NFSv2. Support for NFSv3 should be available in the next kernel version (2.4.X). There are four major differences between the two versions: file handle size, transport layer limitations, UDP block size, and performance. These differences are illustrated in Table 10–6.

Table 10–6   NFSv2 and NFSv3 Differences

ITEM	NFSv2	NFSv3	NOTES
File handle size	Fixed array of 32 bytes	Variable-length array of up to 64 bytes	Reduces local storage and network bandwidth requirements on some systems.
Transport layer issue	Only UDP	UDP or TCP	NFSv2 must maintain state information and connection. NFSv3 gives choice of mounting using TCP or UDP.
UDP block size	8k bytes maximum	64k bytes maximum	Both still allow independent read and write block size specification in increments of 512 bytes.
Performance	Uses `readdir` and `getattr` for file attributes	Uses `readdirplus` for file attributes	NFSv3 requires only one network request for directory and attributes.

A newer version of NFS, NFSv4, is currently in development. It is also expected to be supported in the next kernel version. NFSv4 is actually a remote filesystem protocol which is derived from the previous two versions. It will support traditional file access as well as integrated support for file locking and strong security, something which is somewhat lacking in the previous two versions. We will discuss NFSv4 later in this section.

The RFC for all versions of NFS is available online at `http://www.ietf.org`. NFSv2 is defined in RFC 1094 while NFSv3 is defined in RFC 1813. Both of these are stored in the `/rfc` directory at the above address. NFSv4 is an ongoing definition and is found in the `/internet-drafts` directory.

Most versions of Linux include NFS with the basic distribution. For newer versions of the software you can check at the `http://nfs.sourceforge.net` Web site. There is a FAQ there, as well as a number of links which include the NFS ftp server which has the latest versions of the NFS software and various patches available for downloading as tarred-zipped (`.tar.gz`) files.

There are six daemons associated with the current version of NFS in Linux. These daemons include `status`, `rquotad`, `mountd`, `nfs`, `nlockmgr`, and `automount`. All of the software required for these is contained in one package, `nfs-utils`. Since all but one of the major versions of Linux can utilize RPM files, we will refer to that package. As of this writing, the current version of this package is `nfs-utils-0.1.9.1-1.rpm`.

The status (`rpc.statd`) daemon is responsible for the status monitor. This reports crashes and reboots to the lock manager. This is necessary in order to allow file locks to be properly reset if any NFS client ungracefully reboots. Usually, there are two copies of the `rpc.statd` daemon running so that both TCP and UDP traffic can be monitored. This daemon runs on both the client and the server.

The `rqoutad` (`rpc.quotad`) daemon is for the remote quota server. This allows enforcement of the filesystem quotas for NFS mounted filesystems. This allows the system to extend the control of disk space usage for users to NFS users. This daemon runs only on the server.

The `mountd` (`rpc.mountd`) daemon is used to field NFS client systems mount requests. This program checks things like whether or not a filesystem is actually exported or whether a client is allowed to mount a particular filesystem that it requests. It also schedules all the `nfsd` daemons. This daemon only runs on the server.

The `nfsd` (`rpc.nfsd`) daemon is designed to handle most of the user-level interface to the NFS kernel module. The kernel module (`nfsd.o`) does most of the real work involving NFS file I/O.

The lock manager (`rpc.lockd`) daemon is the NFS lock manager. Its purpose is to handle file-lock requests from NFS clients. File locking is necessary to keep multiple sources from writing to a file at the same time. This daemon runs on both the server and the client.

The automount (`amd`) daemon is there to handle automatic NFS mount requests. These are requests from the non-root users to mount NFS filesystems.

If NFS is installed and running on the system you should see a number of copies of the `nfsd` daemon running on the system. The `ps` command illustrates in Example 10–1. The number of copies of `nfsd` that are run is controlled in the NFS start-up script.

Example 10–1   `ps -ef|grep nfs`

```
$ ps -ef | grep nfs
root     1115    1       0 17:31 ?        00:00:00 rpc.mountd -no-nfs-version 3
root     1124    1       0 17:31 pts/0 00:00:00 [nfsd]
root     1125    1       0 17:31 pts/0 00:00:00 [nfsd]
root     1126    1       0 17:31 pts/0 00:00:00 [nfsd]
root     1127    1       0 17:31 pts/0 00:00:00 [nfsd]
root     1128    1       0 17:31 pts/0 00:00:00 [nfsd]
root     1129    1       0 17:31 pts/0 00:00:00 [nfsd]
root     1130    1       0 17:31 pts/0 00:00:00 [nfsd]
root     1131    1       0 17:31 pts/0 00:00:00 [nfsd]
root     1215 1149       0 18:36 pts/0 00:00:00 grep nfs
$
```

If NFS is not currently running, then you will have to start the daemons manually. There usually are one or more scripts which will start up or shut down all the daemons necessary for use by NFS.

Assuming that we have installed the necessary software for NFS to perform, let's look at what else is necessary to configure an NFS server. An NFS server is a host which allows other hosts (clients) to utilize certain resources. In other words, the server serves up directories and files for other hosts. It might be interesting to note here that a host can be both an NFS server and client at the same time, but more on that later.

In order to do its job, the NFS server must first define what resources it will serve up. This is done through the `/etc/exports` file. This file is used to control a number of issues including which files and directories are exported, which cli-

ents are allowed to access them, and how these clients can access the data which
is exported. The general format of the /etc/exports file is

```
directory [host(option,option,...)]. . .
```

The directory is the name of the resource (directory or file) being exported.
This must be a full path designation. The directory name may be followed by an
option host or hosts with or without options. When no optional (host or
options) information follows the directory, all clients are allowed read-write
access to the resource. In Linux, you can also export subdirectories of directories
that are already exported.

The host specification refers to the hostname which is allowed access to the
resource. If there is no host specification, then access to the resource is given to
all clients. Some valid host specifications include individual hostnames or IP
addresses (such as maureen.gcp.org or 148.114.64.1), domain wildcards
(such as *.gcp.org for all hosts in the gcp.org domain), and IP address/
address mask pairs (such as 148.114.64.0/255.255.255.0 for all hosts whose
address starts with 148.114.64).

The option specification is used to define the type of access allowed. If you
specify the option without a hostname, then the access defined is given to all clients. If the option is specified with a hostname, then the access defined is given
to that host. You can have multiple instances of hosts and/or host-option lists.

A sample /etc/exports file is shown in Example 10–2. It includes several
entries showing the various methods and options which may be allowed in the
file. The first line of the file shows that directory /maureen can be accessed only
by the host whose IP address is 148.114.64.10. The directory /maureen will
be both readable and writeable by that host. The second line shows that directory /usr/local may be accessed by the host named nanoo.gcp.org but it is
read-only. The directory /maureen may be accessed by a non-secure port from
nanoo.gcp.org and if root is the one that accesses it, the UID will be set to 99
(anonymous). The third line shows that directory /home may be accessed by two
hosts (maureen and gnome). Note the whitespace separation between the two
host designations. In this case, host maureen will have only read access to the
directory while host gnome will have both read and write access, but any access
by root will change the UID to 500. The fourth line allows read-write access to
the /usr/doc directory by host taz but will remap UIDs 0 through 15 and 25
through 98 to anonymous. The fifth line shows directory /usr/public being

accessible to all hosts, but with read-only privileges. The last line in the file has directory `/home/joe` read-write accessible to all hosts whose IP address starts with `148.114.50` and all hosts that are members of the `gcp.org` domain (for this domain all `root` access is remapped to anonymous). For more information about the `/etc/exports` file, see the `man` page for `exports(5)` as well as the resources listed at the end of this section.

Example 10–2   Sample `/etc/exports` File

```
/maureen      148.114.64.10(rw)
/usr/local    nanoo.gcp.org(ro, insecure, root_squash)
/home         maureen(ro) gnome(rw, root_squash,anonuid=500)
/usr/doc      taz(squash_uids=0-15, 25-98)
/usr/public   (ro)
/home/joe     148.114.50.0/255.255.255.0(rw) \
              *gcp.org(rw, root_squash)
```

Once you have defined which directories to export, it is necessary to run the `/usr/sbin/exportfs` command. Note that some versions of Linux may not have an `exportfs` command. If this is the case, such as in some versions of Caldera, then you must recycle to NFS script to read the `/etc/exports` file. This reads the entries in `/etc/exports` file and creates the `/var/lib/nfs/xtab` file. The `xtab` file contains information about what files and directories are currently exported. The `xtab` file is created and maintained by the system and should not be edited. To accomplish this you use the `exportfs` command with the `-a` option on the command line. The `-a` option tells `exportfs` to process all entries in the `/etc/exports` file.

```
# exportfs -a
```

You can also use the `exportfs` command to manually export a directory which is not listed in the `/etc/exports` file. This is done by adding the information about the directory you wish to export on the command line. Shown below is the `exportfs` command that exports the directory `/home/mitch` to `nanoo` with read-only privileges. Note that the options are identified on the command line by a preceding "-o". Also note that resources exported on the fly like this are added to the `xtab` file by the system.

```
# exportfs nanoo:/home/mitch -o ro
```

Additionally, the `exportfs` command can be used to unexport a resource (make it no longer available). This is done by using the `-u` option on the com-

mand line and listing the resource to be unexported. The directory /home/mitch
which was previously exported to host nanoo can be unexported as follows:

```
# exportfs -u nanoo:/home/mitch
```

The -u and -a options can also be combined (-ua) to unexport all currently
exported directories. For more information on the exportfs command, see the
man page for exportfs(8).

One other file which probably needs to be mentioned here is the /var/lib/
nfs/rmtab file. This file contains a list of locally exported NFS directories currently remote mounted and the remote hosts (clients) on which they are
mounted. This file is also dynamically created and maintained by the system and
therefore should not be edited.

Now that we have seen how to configure an NFS server, let's look at the other
side of the coin—configuring an NFS client. The NFS client is a host which
will remotely mount a resource from an NFS server. The first step in setting up
the client is to determine what resources are available on the server. We can do
this using the showmount command with the -e command line option.
Example 10–3 shows a sample showmount command to see what resources are
available on the server fubar.

Example 10–3   Output of the showmount Command

```
# showmount -e fubar
Export list for fubar:

/maureen      148.114.64.10
/usr/local    nanoo.gcp.org
/home         maureen,gnome
/usr/doc      taz
/usr/public   (everyone)
/home/joe     148.114.50.0/255.255.255.0,*.gcp.org
#
```

The output from the showmount command indicates which directories on the
server fubar are accessible or mountable and by what clients. For example, the
first line shows that the host whose IP address is 148.114.64.10 can mount
directory /maureen.

Now that you know what resources are available, you can go through the process of mounting them locally so that you can actually use them. You must use
the mount command to do this. You must also be root. The mount command,
by itself is reasonably smart. It can generally figure out what kind of filesystem

you are trying to mount and mount that for you. This means that most of the time all that you have to do to mount a remote resource is to supply the hostname and remote directory along with the local mount point to the mount command. The following example will result in the directory /usr/public being mounted locally as the directory /local/public.

```
#mount   fubar:/usr/public    /local/public
```

This example assumes that the local directory /local/public already exists. You can make sure that the mount command recognizes that the resource that you want to mount is an NFS resource by using the -t option of the mount command.

```
#mount -t nfs fubar:/usr/public    /local/public
```

You might find it necessary to use additional security on the mount itself. If so, check the mount(8) man page. There are a number of options which can be very useful for better network security when using NFS mounts. You can control things such as whether to permit execution of files from the NFS filesystem or whether to limit the filesystem to read-only.

Unmounting an NFS filesystem is done through the umount command. An NFS filesystem can be unmounted by specifying either the remote filesystem name or the local mount point on the command line with the umount command. To unmount the previously mounted resource from fubar, execute

```
# umount fubar:/usr/public
```

or

```
# umount /local/public
```

Generally, people will want to mount an NFS resource everytime the system is booted up. This can be done by putting the NFS mount entries in the /etc/fstab file. This file is processed as part of the start-up scripts for the system. The basic syntax for these entries is similar to that of the standard fstab entry. The major difference is the format of the resource to be mounted and the file type which will now be nfs. The general syntax is

```
Resource_to_be_mounted local_mount_point fs_type    options 0 0
```

The *Resource_to_be_mounted* is the NFS filesystem to mount. It must have both the hostname and the directory separated by a colon (:). The hostname may be an actual resolvable hostname or an IP address. The directory must be a fully qualified directory. You may also mount a subdirectory of an exported directory.

The `local_mount_point` is a fully qualified directory name on the client. This directory must exist. It will be the access point in the client's filesystem hierarchy. In other words, this is the local directory path through which you will be able to access the remote system.

The `fs_type` is the filesystem type. When using NFS resources, this will always be `nfs`.

The `options` parameter is a list of comma-separated options. Some of the more common ones are shown in Table 10–7. See the `mount(8)`, `nfs(5)`, and `fstab(5)` man pages for more information on options. The last two fields are shown as zeros. These are not used by NFS, but must always exist as they are a required part of the `fstab` syntax. See `fstab(5)` for more details.

Table 10–7   NFS Client-Side Options

OPTION	DESCRIPTION
`defaults`	Uses the default options: `rw`, `suid`, `dev`, `exec`, `auto`, `nouser`, and `async`
`hard`	This option indicates that a major timeout during an NFS file operation will cause the error message "server not responding" to be sent to `syslogd`. The system will continue retrying indefinitely. This is the default.
`soft`	This option indicates that a major timeout during an NFS file operation will cause an I/O error to be reported to the calling program and the termination of the request.
`intr`	This option indicates that signals such as those sent via kill or ^C will be allowed to interrupt an NFS file operation if the filesystem has a major timeout and is hard mounted. This is *not* the default.
`rsize=n` `wsize=n`	This option is used to specify read and write sizes in bytes. The default is 4096 bytes.

Table 10–7   NFS Client-Side Options *(Continued)*

OPTION	DESCRIPTION
`timeo=n`	This option indicates the value (in tenths of a second) to wait before sending the first retransmission after a timeout. The default is 7 (0.7 seconds). This option only applies when the `udp` option (which is the default) is used.
`retrans=n`	This option is used to specify the number of retransmissions before a major timeout is declared. The default is 3.
`retry=n`	This option indicates the number of minutes to retry an NFS mount operation. The default is 10,000 or roughly one week.
`tcp`	This option indicates to use the Transmission Control Protocol as the Transport layer protocol.
`udp`	This option indicates to use the User Datagram Protocol as the Transport layer protocol. This is the default.

Example 10–4 shows a sample `/etc/fstab` file. The last two lines are NFS filesystem mount requests. The first one will mount the directory `/home/bob` from host `fubar` to a local directory `/home/bob/fubar`. It uses the `defaults` so the directory will be read-write, assuming that `fubar` has given the client that privilege.

Example 10–4   The `/etc/fstab` File

```
/dev/hda1          /boot             ext2    defaults1 1
/dev/hda2          /home             ext2    defaults1 2
<other entries....>
fubar:/home/bob    /home/bob/fubar   nfs     defaults0 0
nanoo:/usr/doc     /usr/doc          nfs     ro,tcp0 0
```

The last line will mount the directory `/usr/doc` from host `nanoo` to a local directory `/usr/doc`. The resource will be mounted read-only and is requested to use TCP. This is useful for congested networks or networks where NFS is used a lot. Both local directories must already exist.

Using the entries in the `/etc/fstab` file, the NFS resources will be mounted whenever the client is booted up. If you are adding new NFS entries into the file, you can mount them without rebooting the system by using the `mount` command with the -a option. The `mount` command also results in the creation and/ or updating of the `/etc/mtab` file. The `/etc/mtab` file contains a list of currently mounted resources (local and remote). You can also remount or mount only the NFS resources listed in the `/etc/fstab` file using the `mount` command with the -t and -a options, as in

```
# mount -t nfs -a
```

Unmounting NFS resources works, as we have seen previously, using the `umount` command. You can also unmount all the NFS resources currently mounted with

```
# umount -t nfs -a
```

Using the -a option alone will unmount all resources currently mounted (in the `/etc/mtab` file). The last option for unmounting works as before. You can unmount a currently mounted resource (listed in `/etc/mtab`) by using the `umount` command with either the resource name or local mount point on the command line. For example

```
# umount fubar:/home/bob
```

or

```
# umount /home/bob/fubar
```

When using NFS, sometimes it is easier to allow mounting and unmounting to be done automatically so that the system administrator is not required to be involved or so that a regular user can mount the remote filesystem. Automounting will handle this task. The automounter can be configured to mount a filesystem when a user attempts to access the filesystem. This allows filesystems to be mounted only when they are needed. Automounting automatically unmounts a filesystem after it has not been used for a while (usually about 5 minutes). The automounter is also useful for removable devices such as floppy drives and CD-ROMs.

Two different automounters are shipped with Linux, `amd` and `autofs`. The `amd` is an automounter daemon and works in a manner similar to the original automounter under SunOS.[3] The `amd` is not part of the kernel and is run in user space. The `amd` uses the NFS system and all automount traffic is routed through

---

3. Sun Microsystem's operating system based on BSD UNIX. SunOS is still used by some companies even though Sun began the process of phasing it out in favor of Solaris (based on SVr4 UNIX) in 1992.

NFS. `autofs` is the newer of the two automounters (and is similar to `autofs` found in Solaris). It is supported in the 2.2.X kernel code as a filesystem type. This allows the kernel's filesystem code to keep track of the automount mount points and treat all of the filesystems as a normal filesystem. `autofs` uses simpler code, has better reliability, is much faster than `amd`, and, arguably, is much easier to configure.

For more information concerning the two automounters see the following Web sites:

```
http://www.Linux-Consulting.com/Amd_AutoFS/autofs.html
http://www.linuxhq.com/issue24/nielson.html
http://www.cs.columbia.edu/~ezk/am-utils
http://www.linuxdoc.org/HOWTO/mini/Automount.html
```

Although it hasn't been completed yet, NFSv4 is currently in design and development. A number of interesting features have been proposed to be included in this version. These new features are expected to emphasize the following areas: 1) improved access and better internet performance, 2) better security, 3) improved interoperability, and 4) extensibility.

The first improvement for access and performance is the development of the NFS protocol which doesn't require the portmapper or mount protocols. This would mean connection to a server may be made by a single TCP connection, allowing packets to be passed through firewalls and proxies easier.

Currently, the file locking is managed by a separate NFS Lock Manager. The file lock manager is not registered on a fixed port so it also is difficult to pass through firewalls and proxies. NFSv4 is expected to include the definition of file locking operations as part of the NFS protocol. In addition, file locking will need to support both UNIX and DOS/Windows systems.

Another feature expected to be included is a mechanism to allow multiple procedure calls which are combined into a single call and response. One example might be a protocol which would generate a `LOOKUP`/`ACCESS`/`GETATTR` call from a `file_open()` call. This would have the effect of reducing round trip latency (the time it takes to receive a reply to an RPC call) and improving overall performance.

Additional performance might be gained in NFSv4 through the use of efficient file data caching. The inclusion of a redirection capability built into the protocol would assist with NFS clients using a proxy cache server to access NFS servers worldwide.

NFSv2 and NFSv3 have a requirement that file handles cannot change. It has been suggested that NFSv4 might include a special classification of file handle known as volatile. This would let the server designate a file handle in a special manner if its indefinite validity could not be guaranteed. The client might then be able to associate pathname information with the file handle guaranteeing that if the file handle is lost or unuseable in any way, a new one could be obtained. This capability would support high-availability clusters and replica configuration.

Most NFS servers tend to be set up behind firewalls or simply on internal networks. Security is usually lacking because the majority of the use is by "trusted" users. This freedom or lackadaisical attitude can't be used for NFS servers which exist beyond the firewall, especially if sensitive data is involved. NFSv4 should include a mechanism which allows NFS to query and/or negotiate the security to be used for a particular directory structure, rather than depending on the somewhat lacking user authentication scheme currently in use.

NFS claims to be a platform-independent protocol. However, it clearly favors UNIX. This can easily be seen, for example, by examining the coded structures used for file attributes. They are UNIX-like file attributes.

NFSv4 needs to include a file attribute model which allows dynamic definition and expansion of file attributes. Instead of using a fixed set of attributes for files, NFS could receive the list of attributes needed by the client and set or read them accordingly. NFSv4 could then support a larger, more versatile set of file attributes required by different systems.

An additional item to be addressed by NFSv4 is the representation of file ownership. The current method of using UID or GID is insufficient for clients and servers in different domains (where the same UID or GID might be assigned to different usernames or groups). One suggestion is the use of a string, similar to an email address, to represent users and groups. If mapping of a user or group representation into a string didn't work, the unmapped string could still be viewed or used directly.

Another challenge facing NFSv4 is the ability to support an access control list (ACL) attribute which supports many ACL models. At a minimum, it will need to be compatible with both UNIX (POSIX style) and NT ACL models.

One of the goals of NFSv4 is to be a true Internet protocol that will span multiple languages. In order to accomplish this, NFSv4 must find a way to name files while still preserving character sets. One suggestion for doing this is to include the use of a character set tag to be provided for each file. Another suggestion is to encode everything using Unicode.

The final NFSv4 feature to be addressed is with respect to extensibility. NFSv4 requires the ability to add new features without completely overhauling the protocol. This could be done through the IETF since they already have a process in place for standardizing incremental changes to standards.

NFS has been around for a long time as a file-sharing protocol. It is rich with features and is easy to use. However, it tends to be slow, somewhat overburdened with overhead (RPC), and not very secure. It is in the process of being revamped so that it will remain in use for a very long time. Later in this section, we will look at an alternative to NFS called Samba.

For additional information on NFS, check out the following references and Web sites:

Stern, Hal, *Managing NFS and NIS*, Sebastopol, California, O'Reilly & Associates, Inc., 1992.

```
http://nfs.sourceforge.net/
http://www.linuxdoc.org/HOWTO/NFS-HOWTO/index.html
```

Samba

Mixed environment networks are common in many workplaces. The combination of Windows-based and UNIX-type systems exist for numerous reasons. The ability for all of these systems to easily coexist resides in numerous software packages like pc-NFS, which essentially brings the UNIX capability to the Windows environment. The principal software package that brings Windows style file and resource sharing to the UNIX/Linux environment is Samba.

Samba is a software suite that allows Windows computers to act as clients to UNIX/Linux systems, as well as allowing the reverse. These clients can share files and also use other resources on the UNIX/Linux servers (such as printers, CD-ROMs, etc.). It is interesting to note that Samba can also allow other UNIX/Linux systems to act as clients for each other, thus allowing one protocol to be used for file sharing for both Windows and non-Windows systems. Samba runs on virtually all platforms. Figure 10–7 illustrates.

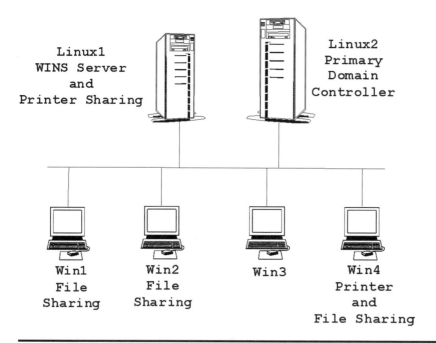

Figure 10–7   Samba Environment with Linux

Samba uses the Server Message Block (SMB) protocol which is based on Network Basic Input Output System (NetBIOS). NetBIOS is the same pseudo-protocol used for printer and file sharing by Windows-based systems. Samba also allows UNIX/Linux systems to perform many of the functions that Windows systems usually handle (such as WINS server, Primary Domain Controller, etc.). All resources are defined in terms of shares, short for shared resources, which may be directories or other resources such as printers or CD-ROMs.

SMB was first defined in 1987 in a Microsoft/Intel document titled, "Microsoft Networks/OpenNET-FILE SHARING Protocol." It was implemented as Samba in 1992 by Andrew Tridgell to allow DOS computers to link to non-DEC servers by running DEC Pathworks. It was further developed into `smbserver`, an SMB protocol server. In 1994, the name was changed to Samba. Samba development had literally followed in the footsteps of Microsoft. As features have been added to NT, they have shown up in the next Samba release, including enhancements to the protocol, changing it to the Common Internet File System (CIFS). Samba's popularity has been linked directly to Linux.

The way that Samba works is fairly standard for network type daemons. Whenever a client requests a session, a new copy of the server is created for that session. During the session, all connections made by the client are serviced by that session's copy of the server. Once the connections for that session are closed, the copy of the server associated with it is terminated.

When you install the software for Samba, it includes two daemons that the server uses, a number of client and utility programs, some configuration files, and a number of documentation files. The key parts of the server are the nmbd and smbd daemons.

The nmbd daemon is used by the server to be able to understand and reply to NetBIOS over IP name service requests. These are the same types of requests which are generated by SMB/CIFS (Win95/98/NT) clients. nmbd also allows the server to participate in the browsing protocols that are used by the "Network Neighborhood" view used by Windows. In addition, nmbd listens for requests from other SMB/CIFS clients who want to know its NetBIOS name. Other functions provided by nmbd include serving as a Windows Internet Name Server (WINS) and a WINS proxy by relaying broadcast queries from clients that don't understand the WINS protocol.

The smbd daemon is responsible for providing file sharing and printing services to SMB clients. It does so using the SMB/CIFS protocol. This is actually compatible with LanManager, all Windows clients, MSCLIENT 3.0 for DOS, OS/2, DAVE for Macs, and smbfs, which runs on Linux systems. It will also work with other UNIX versions of Samba.

The smbd and nmbd daemons can be started directly or by a script (we will see this later). Only root can run these daemons. The binaries for these daemons are generally located in the /usr/sbin directory.

The syntax for nmbd is:

```
nmbd [-D] [-a] [-o] [-h] [-V] [-H lmhosts-file]
[-d debuglevel][-l log-file-basename]
[-n primary-NetBIOS-name] [-p port-number]
[-s configuration-file] [-i NetBIOS-scope]
```

The options to the nmbd daemon are given in Table 10–8.

Table 10–8   Flags to nmbd

FLAG	DESCRIPTION
-D	This parameter is used to indicate that nmbd is to operate as a daemon. By default, it does not operate as a daemon. It can also be run from inetd, but this is generaly not recommended.
-a	This parameter is used to specify that each new connection will append log messages to the log file. This is the default behavior.
-o	This parameter is used to specify that the log files will be overwritten, when opened. This overrides the default behavior in the previous parameter.
-h	This parameter requests that nmbd print the usage or help information.
-V	This parameter is used to tell nmbd to print its version number.
-H *lmhosts-file*	This parameter is used to specify a file name to be searched instead of the /etc/lmhosts file. This is a file similar to the /etc/hosts file in most versions of UNIX except that it has NetBIOS hostnames and IP addresses in it. This file is used by nmbd to resolve NetBIOS name queries needed by the server only. It is not used to answer any name queries. See the lmhosts man page for additional information.

Table 10–8   Flags to nmbd *(Continued)*

FLAG	DESCRIPTION
-d *debuglevel*	This parameter is an integer number ranging from zero to ten. The default value is zero. The value of this parameter determines the level of output from the nmbd server to the log file. The higher the value, the more detailed the output is. Level one is generally reasonable for most servers. Levels above one generate large amounts of output and are good for problem resolution. Using a level above three is usually discouraged for anyone except developers as it generates extremely large amounts of cryptic log data. Specifying this parameter on the command line will override any log level parameter specified in the smb.conf file.
-l *log-file-basename*	This parameter is used to specify a path and base file name for the nmbd log file. The actual log file name is created by appending ".nmb" to the basename specified on the command line.
-n *primary-NetBIOS-name*	This parameter is used to allow you to override the NetBIOS name that the Samba server uses for itself. Using this parameter on the command line will override any NetBIOS name parameter specified in the smb.conf file.
-p *port-number*	This parameter is used to change the default UDP port number used by nmbd to respond to name queries. This number must be a positive integer value. The default is 137. You should be very cautious about changing this.
-s *configuration-file*	This parameter is used to change the configuration file name which nmbd will use to get configuration details. The default is /etc/smb.conf.
-i *NetBIOS-scope*	This parameter is used to specify the NetBIOS scope that nmbd will use to communicate with when generating NetBIOS names. This particular parameter is not used very much.

The most common method of starting up `nmbd` is

```
# /usr/sbin/nmbd -D
```

This will start `nmbd` in daemon mode and is the exact same method used in the system start-up scripts that we will look at later in this section.

A couple of notes need to be mentioned here concerning signals sent to `nmbd`. The first concerns the proper way to terminate the daemon. `nmbd` should be terminated by sending a SIGTERM to the process. This can be done using the `killall` program in the following manner:

```
# killall nmbd
```

Do not use the SIGKILL signal to terminate the process. This may leave the name database used by `nmbd` in an inconsistent state. The second note is about using the SIGHUP signal. The `nmbd` daemon will accept this signal and then dump out its namelists into the file `namelist.debug`. It will also dump out its server database to the file `log.nmb`. The SIGHUP signal can be sent to the daemon as follows:

```
# killall -HUP nmbd
```

Finally, the SIGUSR1 and SIGUSR2 signals can be used to raise and lower the debug level of the `nmbd` daemon. SIGUSR1 raises the level by one, SIGUSR2 lowers the level by one. The higher the level, the more information sent to the log files. These signals can be sent using the `killall` command. For example:

```
# killall -USR1 nmbd
# killall -USR2 nmbd
```

This use of signals allows the system administrator to diagnose problems on the fly without disturbing the operation of the server by getting more debug information only when it is needed.

The second big component to the Samba server is the `smbd` daemon. This daemon is responsible for providing the file sharing and printing services. It is the key component of the server and does most of the work. `smbd` reads the configuration file once every minute, assuming that it changes. A reread can be forced by sending a SIGHUP to `smbd`. An important note here is that rereading the configuration file does not affect any connections to already established Samba services. In order for changes to the configuration to affect those users, they would have to disconnect and reconnect or the `smbd` daemon would have to be killed and restarted.

The syntax for the `smbd` daemon is

```
smbd [-D] [-a] [-o] [-P] [-h] [-V]
[-d debuglevel][-l log-file-basename]
[-p port-number] [-O socket-options]
 [-s configuration-file] [-i NetBIOS-scope]
```

Many of the options for `smbd` are the same as the usage for `nmbd`. For those that are the same, you can refer to the previous section where they are defined. All of the remaining options are described in Table 10–9.

Table 10–9   Flags to `smbd`

FLAG	DESCRIPTION
-P	This parameter is called the passive option. It causes `smbd` to refrain from sending out any network traffic. This is primarily used for debugging by developers.
-O *socket-options*	This parameter can be used to tune options which will help the performance of Samba on your network. This should only be used if Samba is suspected to be the bottleneck. The default for this parameter is TCP_NODELAY. For more information on this parameter, see the "socket options" section in the `smb.conf man` page.

The most common method for starting `smbd` is similar to that of `nmbd`:

```
# /usr/sbin/smbd -D
```

Again, this will start the Samba server program in daemon mode, which is the preferred method.

The third major component of the server is the configuration file. If this file is not correct, Samba will not work properly. This file is the key to a smoothly-performing Samba. By default, it is stored in `/etc/smb.conf`. Most of the distributions have a sample configuration file that you can use with little or no changes and that can be up and running with a small amount of effort.

The configuration file consists of a group of sections. The file is line based, meaning that each line will be interpreted as either a comment, a section name, or a parameter. You can use the line continuation character (\) to continue a line over several physical lines. The section and parameter names are not case sensitive and only the first equal sign in a parameter declaration is significant. Generally, whitespace is ignored in most cases, except when it is within a parameter value, then it is kept exactly as it is found. Any line which begins with a semicolon (;) or hash character (#) is considered a comment and ignored. Values following the equals sign in a parameter will either be a string (no quotes are necessary), a numeric value, or a Boolean value.

Each section in the configuration file is known as a share and usually describes a shared resource. A share is a resource to which access is being given. In addition, the share may have other attributes associated with it, such as what access rights are granted to users, housekeeping options, who can access the share, and many others. The beginning of the share section is indicated by the share name being on a line, enclosed by square brackets. Everything after that line up to the next share name is considered to be attributes of the share. There are three predefined shares—global, homes, and printers.

The exception to the share rule is the [global] section which defines parameters or attributes of Samba. These may be items which don't apply to specific shares or may override items in specific shares. In fact, the [global] statement is not required. Samba interprets anything from the beginning of the file to the first share name (in square brackets) to be global parameters.

There are over 200 options which can be specified in the smb.conf file. For more information concerning these other options and how they may be used, see the man page for smb.conf(5), as well as the additional documentation in the /usr/doc/samba-X.X.X directory.

Creating the configuration file is the first step to configuring the Samba server. Once this has been done, you can test the configuration with the testparm command. This program does a sanity check on the smb.conf file and lets you know whether the information is configured correctly (syntactically, of course). Use of the testparm program is given in Example 10–5.

Example 10–5   Output of the testparm Program

```
# testparm
Load smb config files from /etc/smb.conf
Processing section "[homes]"
Processing section "[printers]"
Loaded services file OK.
Press enter to see a dump of your service definitions.
```

At the end of Example 10–5 the testparm program waits for you to press the enter key. Once pressed, the output will appear as in Example 10–6.

Example 10–6   Continuing Output of `testparm`

```
# Global parameters
[global]
workgroup = GNOMES
netbios name =
netbios aliases =
server string = Samba Server
interfaces =
bind interfaces only = No
security = USER
encrypt passwords = No
update encrypted = No
allow trusted domains = Yes
hosts equiv =

<... lots of output snipped ...>

[printers]
comment = All Printers
path = /var/spool/samba
print ok = Yes
browseable = No
```

The output of `testparm` shows what the default parameters (`[global]` sections) were in `smb.conf`, as well as showing the settings for the `[home]` and `[printers]` sections. It would also show any other `share` definitions that you have defined. These parameters and settings were explained above in the section on the configuration file.

Once the `smb.conf` file has been completed and tested, you can use the various scripts to start and stop the server. All of these scripts may be used with start and stop options. Many of these scripts have additional features which allow you to restart the server (stop and then start) in one command and also find out the status of the server. The location and names of the scripts for each distribution are given in Table 10–10.

Table 10–10   Samba Start-up Script Location by Distribution

DISTRIBUTION	SCRIPT
Red Hat	/etc/rc.d/init.d/smb
Caldera	/etc/rc.d/init.d/samba
SuSE	/sbin/init.d/smb
Debian	/etc/init.d/samba

Typically, starting Samba simply requires submitting a start argument to the start-up script. For instance, on Red Hat

```
# /etc/rc.d/init.d/smb start
```

will start the necessary daemons. This script starts both the smbd and nmbd daemons for the Samba server. At this point the Samba server should be successfully up and running.

It turns out that Samba essentially comes out of the box ready to go. Just make sure that you have the default smb.conf file (which in most cases will be in the /etc directory). The one change that you may have to make to this file is to the line which defines the workgroup name. The default for this is

```
workgroup=mygroup
```

You may need to change mygroup to the name of the workgroup which you want your computer to be a part of. For example, the workgroup which I use on my network is called gnomes. So, in my smb.conf file I would change the line to:

```
workgroup=gnomes
```

The only thing left to do is to start the Samba server itself. As usual, there are a number of ways to do this. We will look at them in detail later, but they all basically boil down to the same thing—starting a number of daemons. The daemons can be started manually with

```
# /usr/sbin/smbd
# /usr/sbin/nmbd
```

This will start both daemons necessary for the operation of Samba (and duplicates the effort of the /etc/rc.d/init.d/smb script shown above). At this point, Samba is up and running and can be used to share data. By default, the home directories and printers on the system are configured. You will also have to create Samba passwords for each user that you wish to be able to use the Samba server. Each user must exist in the /etc/passwd file. After this has been done, then you create a Samba password for them using the /etc/smbpasswd command:

```
# smbpasswd -a username
```

Adding a Samba password for user krell to the smbpasswd file would be done with the following:

```
# smbpasswd -a krell
```

This system will prompt you for the password to be used and also request that you confirm it by retyping the password (similar to the way the passwd command works). User `krell` should now be able to mount his home directory using the SMB protocol.

As for the client, once the software has been installed, using Samba is only a matter of finding out what resources are available to you and then accessing them. You can find out which resources are available to you and use them both with the same program, `smbclient`. To find out what resources you can use, execute

```
$ smbclient -L hostname -U username
```

where hostname is the name of the Samba server system and username is the name of the user to login as. The hostname can be an IP address or a resolvable name. The username must exist in both the `/etc/passwd` and `/etc/smbpasswd` files. An example might be:

```
$ smbclient -L nanoo -U krell
```

to see the shares for user `krell` on the Samba server `nanoo`. This will result in the Samba server requesting the user's password. The user will then be presented with a list of shares available to that user as well as some additional information as illustrated in Example 10–7.

Example 10–7   Output from `smbclient`

```
    Domain=[GNOMES]  OS=[Unix]  Server=[Samba 2.0.6]

Sharename       Type        Comment
---------------------------------------------------
IPC$            IPC         IPC Service (Samba Server)
lp              Printer
krell           Disk        Home Directories

Server          Comment
---------------------------
BREA
NANOO           Samba Server

Workgroup       Master
----------------------
GNOMES          BREA
```

The above example shows that on the Samba server `nanoo` the Samba service is available to user `krell` along with the `krell` home directory and the printer `lp`. It also shows that the workgroup name is GNOMES and that BREA is the master browser. You can also see all public shares by using the same command with the following options:

```
smbclient -NL hostname
```

For instance

```
$ smbclient -NL brea
```

where `brea` is the name of the host you want to look at. Using this form is somewhat more limiting in that you only see shares which are browseable (available to all). This form of the command does not prompt you for a password. The output will look similar to the above command but will only show those shares which are available to all users. The above example requests a listing of public shares on the system `brea`.

Once you have determined the share that you wish to use, you can do so with the `smbclient` command. This form of the command is

```
smbclient //servername/sharename -U username
```

where `servername` is the resolvable name of the server which has the share on it, sharename is the access name of the share on the server, and username is the name of the user to log in as (this can be left off and Samba will default to the current username). The server will prompt you for your password and then print out the Domain name, operating system type, and the server type followed by the `smbclient` prompt. An example might look like

```
$ smbclient //nanoo/krell -U krell
```

to request access to the `krell` share on server `nanoo`. After entering your password at the prompt, you will see something like

```
Domain=[GNOMES]  OS=[Unix]   Server=[Samba 2.0.6]
smb: \>
```

to indicate that you are in the `smbclient` program connected to the share that you requested. This is an `ftp` like interface that allows you to look at the files in the shared directories as well as moving files back and forth between systems. You can type `exit` at the prompt to release the share. For more information on `smbclient`, check the `man` page for `smbclient(1)`.

Samba is a full-featured program which will allow heterogeneous systems to coexist on a single network. It is expected to get bigger and better as time and expertise expands it. Samba is here to stay. For more information regarding Samba, check out the following references and Web sites:

```
http://www.linuxdoc.org/HOWTO/SMB-HOWTO.html
http://www.samba.org
```

Litt, Steve et al., *Samba Unleashed*, Sams Publishing, April, 2000.

Other Remote Filesystems

Another remote filesystem used in Linux is the Andrew File System (AFS). AFS differs in structure and maintenance from NFS while achieving the same result for the user, a remote filesystem which looks like part of the standard UNIX/Linux file hierarchy. AFS is a distributed filesystem that allows users to share or access files in a heterogeneous distributed environment. One of its features is that the files can be stored on many different systems, while being available to users all over the network environment.

AFS uses file server machines to store files. These machines provide delivery services and file storage, as well as other, more specific services to the rest of the machines on the network. Any machine that is not a file server machine is a client machine. Client machines provide power for computational servers, general purpose tools, and access to the files in the AFS system. Clients are usually the largest number of systems in the network.

AFS servers provide a set of specialized services called server processes. These processes handle AFS services such as handling file requests, tracking file locations, and security. Table 10–11 shows a list of the server processes and their purpose.

Table 10–11   AFS Server Machine Processes

AFS PROCESS	DESCRIPTION
File Server	This process is used to deliver data files from the file server machine to any client which requests it. It also stores files on the server after any updates.
Basic OverSeer Server	This process is used to oversee the other AFS processes on the server machine.
Authentication Server	This process is used to verify logins and provide a facility for identification of server/client pairs (as in mutual authentication). It also maintains the Authentication Database.
Protection Server	This process is used to help users control who is allowed access to their directories and files. It also maintains the Protection Database.

Table 10–11 AFS Server Machine Processes *(Continued)*

AFS PROCESS	DESCRIPTION
Volume Server	This process is used for various types of volume manipulation. It is also used to assist in load balancing between servers.
Volume Location Server	This process is used to maintain the Volume Location Database. This is important for transparent file access by users.
Update Server	This process is used to propagate updates to server process and configuration information changes to the file server machines. It is necessary for maintaining stable system performance among the server machines.
Backup Server	This process is used to maintain the Backup Database.

Each administratively independent site which runs AFS is called a cell. Each cell has its own system administrator who makes decisions about how the configuration of that cell will be set up. Each cell will, for example, determine the number of server machines and clients, where it wants its files stored, and how to allocate client machines for users.

AFS lets cells organize their local file areas into a global file space. These are designed in a way to allow file access for users to appear transparent. All a user needs to know to access a file is the pathname of the file (not its actual location). This means that every user sees the collection of files in exactly the same fashion, thus providing a uniform namespace.

In AFS, files are grouped into volumes which may be distributed over multiple machines all within a uniform namespace. A volume is a container of files which are related and limited to a single partition. Volumes correspond to a directory within the file space. The actual location of the volume is transparent to the user; it is just part of the file hierarchy.

AFS provides security by making clients and servers prove their identities to each other prior to allowing any information to be exhanged. This mutual authentication procedure uses Kerberos authentication which requires the demonstration of the knowledge of a piece of secret information known only by the server and the client. This guarantees the servers will only give information to clients which are authorized to have it and that clients will get information only from servers which are known to be trusted.

AFS also supports the use of ACLs to allow users to deny or grant permission to directories. An ACL lets the user specify a user name with specific types of permissions. This allows seven different permissions which can be specified, along with as many as 20 different users or groups in an ACL.

For more information concerning AFS see the following Web sites:

```
http://www.homepages.uel.ac.uk/5291n/afs/afsmain.html
http://consult.cern.ch/service/afs
http://www.cs.cmu.edu/afs/andrew.cmu.edu/usr/shadow/www/afs.html
http://wwwinfo.cern.ch/pdp/ose/linux/afs
```

Two other filesystems are also supported in Linux, Novell's Netware and Apple's Appletalk. The Novell Netware File System is really a network operating system. It is based on the Internet Packet Exchange/Sequenced Packet Exchange (IPX/SPX) protocols. The IPX/SPX protocol has an advantage over protocols such as NetBIOS because it is routable. Features of Netware include Novell Directory Services (NDS), security services, database services, messaging services, print services, and loadable modules.

Linux can share Netware resources through the use of the Netware Core Protocol File System (NCPFS). There are clients for mounting and unmounting Netware File Servers. This is done through the use of the `ncpmount` and `ncpumount` commands. For more information on Linux and Netware, see the `man` pages for the above commands and check out the following Web sites:

```
http://www.linuxdoc.org/HOWTO/IPX-HOWTO.html
http://www.novell.com
```

The Netatalk daemon is used to implement the Appletalk protocol in Linux. It provides support for file sharing, printing, routing, and allows Linux systems to access Mac machines on an Appletalk network as well as letting Mac machines access Linux systems as though they were Appletalk servers.

The Appletalk support in Linux includes a number of programs and daemons. The Netatalk daemon is called `atalkd`. It supplies routing and configuration services. The `papd` daemon is used to let Mac systems spool jobs to Linux printers. The `pap` program is used to allow Linux systems to print to Appletalk printers. The `apfd` is the interface daemon for the Linux filesystem, while the `npblkup` program shows a list of all the Appletalk objects found on the network.

Netatalk requires kernel-level support for Appletalk's Datagram Delivery Protocol (DDP). If this is not included in the kernel, you can recompile the kernel and include this support or you can include it as a loadable module.

For information about Netatalk, see the `man` pages for the various commands and check out the following Web pages:

```
http://www.anders.com/projects/netatalk
http://www.umich.edu/~rsug/netatalk
http://www.umich.edu/~rsug/netatalk/faq.html
```

Network Information Service

One of the biggest problems that you run into when you have a distributed computing system is maintaining the separate copies of configuration files on each system on the network. These configuration files (`/etc/passwd`, `/etc/hosts`, `/etc/group`, etc.) must be kept up to date so that the configuration of the network and its systems is consistent. This consistency can be difficult to maintain if the network is very large because every time a new computer is added to the network or a change is made in the configuration, the changed files must be propagated to all the systems on the network. This can be a large task if the network is made up of hundreds or thousands of computers. It is easy to see that the number of mistakes that can be made will grow with the increase in the network size because of the increased number of places that must be updated.

The Network Information Service (NIS[4]) was designed to help address the problems of distributed computing. NIS is a distributed database system which uses a centralized management concept to propagate the configuration information to all the systems which are part of the network. It does this by replacing the common configuration files with database files. These database files are maintained on a central server (called the *master*) so that they don't have to be managed on each host in the network. The systems on the network using NIS simply retrieve any information needed from the databases on the master server. If a system is added to the network, all that is necessary is to modify the appropriate configuration file on the master server and let NIS propagate the information to the rest of the network. This is much easier than changing the configuration files on all of the hosts on the network.

---

4. NIS was formerly Yellow Pages (YP).

NIS uses a client-server model. The NIS server is a system which stores NIS databases called maps. NIS clients are systems the request information the servers get from these maps. A server can be either a master or a *slave*. The master is the only owner of the map data and is always considered to be true and correct. The master is also responsible for maintaining the maps and distributing them to the slave servers. When a map is changed on the master server, it is then distributed to any slave servers. Slave servers provide redundancy of maps and offloading of client requests. Slave servers are not required but even in modestly sized environments can benefit from them. Clients will see any changes propagated when they query the server for information from updated maps.

NIS is divided into groups called domains. An NIS domain consists of all systems that share a single set of NIS database files. The domain is given a name and includes one master server, one or more clients and, possibly, one or more slave servers. Figure 10–8 shows a typical NIS domain.

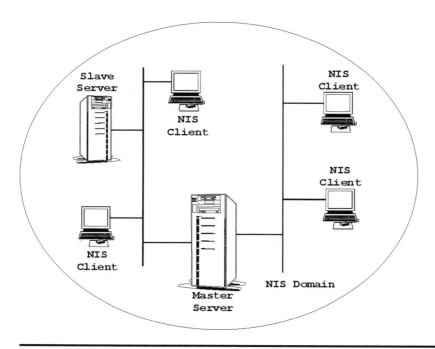

Figure 10–8 Typical NIS Domain

The master server maintains the single database created from the original ASCII configuration files. It also maintains the original ASCII files. The maps are created in a special format which allows fast keyword searches. This format is called the Database Management (DBM) format. The master also responds to NIS queries from clients for things such as login requests and hostname lookups. These are done through the `ypserv` daemon. The master is the sole system for maintaining the password information. It does this through the `rpc.yppasswdd` daemon. There can be only one master server in a domain.

Once the master is set up and running, clients and slave servers can be configured. Once a client is configured a user can login and use NIS for authentication. Thus, when a user logs on, the password authorization will be handled by the NIS master server. This allows a user to log on and have access to the NIS domain services from any host in the NIS domain. When an application requests a host address from the NIS `/etc/hosts` file, that information will be supplied from the hosts map file on the master server.

Slave servers can also respond to NIS queries. The DBM maps are propagated to the slave servers in order to allow them to do so. The slave server does not store a copy of the original ASCII configuration files. The main purpose of a slave server is to offload some of the queries and to back up or replace the master in case the master crashes or goes down for some reason. There may be any number of slave servers in an NIS domain.

Creating an NIS domain is a simple three-step process. First, you create the NIS master server. There can be exactly one master server per NIS domain. The master must run the `ypserv`, `rpc.passwdd`, and `ypbind` daemons. It may also run the `rpc.ypxfrd` daemon to propagate the maps to the slave servers. Second, any slave servers must be configured. The slaves will run `ypserv` and `ypbind` and possibly `rpc.ypxfrd`. Third, any clients must be configured. NIS clients will need to run `ypbind`. All systems which will participate in an NIS domain have to set their domain name to be the same domain name as the master server. This can be done using the `domainname` command.

```
# domainname gcp.org
```

This example shows the domain name being set to `gcp.org`. The setting shown here must be placed in a start-up script in order to survive reboots. Also, all participants in an NIS domain must properly configure the `/etc/nsswitch.conf` file (see Example 10–11 on page 456).

The first step in setting up an NIS master is to determine which configuration files you want NIS to centrally manage on the master. A list of the files the NIS can manage under Linux is listed in Table 10–12. The list contains the files which are standard configuration files. NIS allows you to add non-standard configuration files to the database set also.

Table 10–12   Configuration Files Converted to NIS Maps by Default

FILENAME	USAGE
/etc/group	This file is used to define the groups to which users belong.
/etc/passwd	This file is used to define user account information.
/etc/shadow	This file is used to store the hashed passwords and password aging information for users listed in the /etc/passwd file.
/etc/gshadow	This file is used to store hashed passwords and group administrators associated with groups in the /etc/group file.
/etc/aliases	This file is used to store user aliases which are used by mail. These aliases can allow mail sent to a particular user to be redirected to a different user or group of users.
/etc/ethers	This file is used by RARP to map Ethernet (MAC) addresses to IP numbers. It is generally used for ARP proxies.
/etc/bootparams	This file is used for entries which may be needed to start diskless clients.
/etc/hosts	This file is used to translate hostnames to IP numbers.
/etc/networks	This file is used for translation of network numbers to names (generally, to make them more readable).
/etc/protocols	This file is used to identify numbers that are associated with different Internet protocols.
/etc/rpc	This file is used to identify support Remote Procedure Call (RPC) protocols. It contains protocol names and their associated program numbers and any aliases.

Table 10–12   Configuration Files Converted to NIS Maps by Default *(Continued)*

Filename	Usage
`/etc/services`	This file is used to identify port numbers and protocols that are associated with the supported network services.
`/etc/netgroup`	This file is used to define users (usually associated with a particular host and domain) for permission checking when performing remote mounts, remote logins, and remote shells.

For more information on these files check out their respective man pages. Also, different distributions of Linux may have other standard configuration files. All of these files may not be relevant to your systems, so you need to determine which ones will be useful for you. The most commonly used are passwd, group, hosts, aliases, rpc, and services.

Once you have determined the configuration files that you want to use, you will need to convert these to map files for storage on the master server. The process for doing this varies between the different distributions, but it generally involves the use of a make or script file. For example, using the Red Hat or SuSE distributions, you will have to edit the /var/yp/Makefile and define the configuration you want to use. This file, some of which is shown in Example 10–8, lets you determine which configuration files to convert as well as allowing you to configure a large number of other parameters for NIS, such as the directory to store the map files in, the minimum UID number to be stored in the password maps, and many others.

Example 10–8   A Sample /var/yp/Makefile

```
#
# Makefile for the NIS databases
#
# This Makefile should only be run on the NIS master server of a domain.
# All updated maps will be pushed to all NIS slave servers listed in the
# /var/yp/ypservers file. Please make sure that the hostnames of all
# NIS servers in your domain are listed in /var/yp/ypservers.
#
# This Makefile can be modified to support more NIS maps if desired.
#

# Set the following variable to "-b" to have NIS servers use the domain
# name resolver for hosts not in the current domain. This is only needed,
# if you have SunOS slave YP server, which gets here maps from this
# server. The NYS YP server will ignore the YP_INTERDOMAIN key.
```

Example 10–8   A Sample `/var/yp/Makefile` *(Continued)*

```
#B=-b
B=

# If we have only one server, we don't have to push the maps to the
# slave servers (NOPUSH=true). If you have slave servers, change this
# to "NOPUSH=false" and put all hostnames of your slave servers in the file
# /var/yp/ypservers.
NOPUSH=true

# We do not put password entries with lower UIDs (the root and system
# entries) in the NIS password database, for security. MINUID is the
# lowest uid that will be included in the password maps.
# MINGID is the lowest gid that will be included in the group maps.
MINUID=500
MINGID=500

# Should we merge the passwd file with the shadow file ?
# MERGE_PASSWD=true|false
MERGE_PASSWD=true

# Should we merge the group file with the gshadow file ?
# MERGE_GROUP=true|false
MERGE_GROUP=true

# These are commands which this Makefile needs to properly rebuild the
# NIS databases. Don't change these unless you have a good reason.
AWK = /usr/bin/gawk
MAKE = /usr/bin/gmake
UMASK = umask 066

#
# These are the source directories for the NIS files; normally
# that is /etc but you may want to move the source for the password
# and group files to (for example) /var/yp/ypfiles. The directory
# for passwd, group and shadow is defined by YPPWDDIR, the rest is
# taken from YPSRCDIR.
#
YPSRCDIR = /etc
YPPWDDIR = /etc
YPBINDIR = /usr/lib/yp
YPSBINDIR = /usr/sbin
YPDIR = /var/yp
YPMAPDIR = $(YPDIR)/$(DOMAIN)

# These are the files from which the NIS databases are built. You may edit
# these to taste in the event that you wish to keep your NIS source files
# seperate from your NIS server's actual configuration files.
#
GROUP     = $(YPPWDDIR)/group
PASSWD    = $(YPPWDDIR)/passwd
SHADOW    = $(YPPWDDIR)/shadow
GSHADOW   = $(YPPWDDIR)/gshadow
ADJUNCT   = $(YPPWDDIR)/passwd.adjunct
#ALIASES    = $(YPSRCDIR)/aliases # aliases could be in /etc or /etc/mail
ALIASES    = /etc/aliases
ETHERS    = $(YPSRCDIR)/ethers   # ethernet addresses (for rarpd)
BOOTPARAMS = $(YPSRCDIR)/bootparams # for booting Sun boxes (bootparamd)
```

Example 10–8   A Sample `/var/yp/Makefile` *(Continued)*

```
HOSTS     = $(YPSRCDIR)/hosts
NETWORKS  = $(YPSRCDIR)/networks
PRINTCAP  = $(YPSRCDIR)/printcap
PROTOCOLS  = $(YPSRCDIR)/protocols
PUBLICKEYS = $(YPSRCDIR)/publickey
RPC   = $(YPSRCDIR)/rpc
SERVICES  = $(YPSRCDIR)/services
NETGROUP  = $(YPSRCDIR)/netgroup
NETID  = $(YPSRCDIR)/netid
AMD_HOME  = $(YPSRCDIR)/amd.home
AUTO_MASTER = $(YPSRCDIR)/auto.master
AUTO_HOME  = $(YPSRCDIR)/auto.home

YPSERVERS = $(YPDIR)/ypservers# List of all NIS servers for a domain

target: Makefile
@test ! -d $(LOCALDOMAIN) && mkdir $(LOCALDOMAIN) ; \
cd $(LOCALDOMAIN) ; \
$(NOPUSH) || $(MAKE) -f ../Makefile ypservers; \
$(MAKE) -f ../Makefile all

# If you don't want some of these maps built, feel free to comment
# them out from this list.

all: passwd group hosts rpc services netid protocols netgrp mail \
# shadow publickey # networks ethers bootparams printcap \
# amd.home auto.master auto.home passwd.adjunct
```

```
< rest of file, not shown>
```

You will note that this file uses `passwd`, `group`, `hosts`, `rpc`, `services`, `netid`, `protocols`, `netgrp`, and `mail` as defaults for maps. Note that on some systems the `Makefile` is in the `/var/nis` directory. For more information about the `/var/yp/Makefile` file see the NIS-HOWTO.

Once the `/var/yp/Makefile` file has been edited the maps are created by running the `ypinit` command. To initialize the master server you would use the `-m` option

```
# ypinit -m
```

This command will prompt you to notify it of the names of any NIS servers that you know of. You should respond with the name of the master server and any slave servers which you are aware of (you will be prompted for each of these). This input will be confirmed and then the `ypinit` command will run the `/var/yp/Makefile` to actually create the database files.

Using the Caldera distribution, the process is slightly different. First, you have to create an NIS directory in `/etc/nis` to store the shared files that you want to use. This directory will have the same name as the NIS domain that you are creating. For example, if the NIS domain name is gcp.org, then the directory that you need to create would be called /etc/nis/gcp.org. Once the directory has been created you will need to copy any files that you wish to be shared (maps) into the /etc/nis/gcp.org directory. If there are certain files which change a lot, such as /etc/passwd, /etc/shadow, and /etc/group, these should be made accessible by using symbolic links instead of copying. Once these files or links have been created, you will run the /etc/nis/nis_update command to create the map files.

Once the master server has been configured and the maps created, you will want to start the server software running. Prior to actually starting the NIS server software, ypserv, there are two configuration files which you may wish to edit, /var/yp/securenets and /etc/ypserv.conf.

The /var/yp/securenets file is used to determine which clients are valid for the server to respond to. If you choose to specify nothing in this file, then you are allowing access to the server for anyone. This is the default behavior for this file. However, using this default is dangerous and can lead to compromise of your server or entire NIS domain. It is always better to configure this file properly. Example 10–9 shows a typical /var/yp/securenets file.

Example 10–9   Sample /var/yp/securenets File

```
#
# securenets This file defines the access rights to your NIS
#           server
#           for NIS clients. This file contains netmask/network
#           pairs. A clients IP address needs to match with at least
#           one of those.
#
#           One can use the word "host" instead of a netmask of
#           255.255.255.255. Only IP addresses are allowed in this
#           file, not hostnames.
#
# Always allow access for localhost
255.0.0.0127.0.0.0
# Add valid networks and hosts here
255.0.0.0    10.0.0.0      # allow 10.0.0.0 network
255.255.255.0148.114.64.0 # allow 148.114.64.0 network
255.255.255.255172.16.10.4 # allow this particular host
# This line gives access to everybody. PLEASE ADJUST!
# uncomment the line below to allow the world access to this server
#  and domain
#0.0.0.0     0.0.0.0
```

This particular example shows that networks `10.0.0.0` and `148.114.64.0`, along with host `172.16.10.4`, are allowed access to the server. Note that the last line of the file with all zeros has been commented out to override the default behavior of allowing everyone access.

The `/etc/ypserv.conf` file is the configuration file for the `ypserv` daemon. It also may be used to control the behavior of the `rpc.ypxfrd` daemon if that daemon is being used. A sample `/etc/ypserv.conf` file is shown in Example 10–10. This is the default `/etc/ypserv.conf` file. It is self document-ing. For more information on this file, see the man page for `ypserv.conf(5)`.

Example 10–10   A Sample `/etc/ypserv.conf` File

```
#
# ypserv.conf In this file you can set certain options for the NIS
#        server,
#        and you can deny or restrict access to certain maps based
#        on the originating host.
#
#        See ypserv.conf(5) for a description of the syntax.
#

# Some options for ypserv. These things are all not needed, if
# you have a Linux net.

dns: no

# The following, when uncommented, will give you shadow like passwords.
# Note that it will not work if you have slave NIS servers in your
# network that do not run the same server as you.

# Host          : Map         : Security  : Passwd_mangle
#
# *             : passwd.byname  : port     : yes
# *             : passwd.byuid   : port     : yes

# Not everybody should see the shadow passwords, not secure, since
# under MSDOG everbody is root and can access ports < 1024 !!!
*               : shadow.byname  : port     : yes
*               : passwd.adjunct.byname : port : yes

# If you comment out the next rule, ypserv and rpc.ypxfrd will
# look for YP_SECURE and YP_AUTHDES in the maps. This will make
# the security check a little bit slower, but you only have to
# change the keys on the master server, not the configuration files
# on each NIS server.
# If you have maps with YP_SECURE or YP_AUTHDES, you should create
# a rule for them above, that's much faster.
*               : *           : none
```

The next decision to make for the master server is whether or not to run the `rpc.ypxfrd` daemon. This daemon is used to improve performance in map delivery when the size of the maps becomes large. It is only run on the master server.

The normal method of map delivery is to use the `yppush` utility which is executed whenever the maps are created using the `/var/yp/Makefile`. The `yppush` utility checks the map files to see if they are out of date. If so, then `yppush` will transfer the new maps to the slave servers that it was told about in the `ypinit` configuration. A problem may arise if, for some reason, the `yppush` is unable to transfer the maps (for example, if a slave is down). To solve this problem, the slave server can use `ypxfr` (which runs on the slave) to transfer the maps to itself. The `ypxfr` utility can be run from a `cron` script, as needed. It will contact the `rpc.ypxfrd` daemon running on the master to download the maps. The main difference between the `yppush` and `ypxfr` utilities is that the `yppush` requires that the map file already exist on the slave, where the `ypxfr` utility will retrieve the map whether it already exists on the slave or not. In reality, `yppush` actually does a remote `ypxfr` if the slave's copy of the map is out-of-date.

If you wish to use `rpc.ypxfrd` on the master, you must either start it manually or place it in a start-up script to start it at boot-time (check your distribution to determine whether or not `rpc.ypxfrd` is already in an existing script). This daemon should be started prior to the start of the master/slave server daemon, `ypserv`. To start the server daemon, execute

```
# ypserv
```

or use the appropriate start-up script.

Following the `ypserv` command you should start the `rpc.yppasswdd` and `ypbind` daemons for handling NIS passwords and make the NIS master a client of itself. You can start these from the command line or from a script. Fortunately, most distributions of Linux have a script for these daemons which already exists. For Red Hat Linux, use the following scripts:

```
# /etc/rc.d/init.d/ypserv start
# /etc/rc.d/init.d/yppasswdd start
# /etc/rc.d/init.d/ypbind start
```

On a Caldera system you use

```
# /etc/rc.d/init.d/nis-server start
# /etc/rc.d/init.d/nis-client start
```

The SuSE version of NIS also has the `ypxfrd` script, so you use

```
# /sbin/init.d/ypxfrd start
# /sbin/init.d/ypserv start
# /sbin/init.d/yppasswdd start
# /sbin/init.d/ypbind start
```

Assuming that you have set the domain name as we saw previously, the master server should be up and running, ready to respond to NIS requests. The `/etc/nsswitch.conf` file tells the system where to look for database files. The order of locations to search is listed out beside each database name. Generally, the locations will be either `nis`, `nisplus` (the followon to NIS[5]), `files` (on the local host), or `dns`. An example of the `/etc/nsswitch.conf` file is shown in Example 10–11.

Example 10–11   Sample `/etc/nsswitch.conf` File

```
#
# /etc/nsswitch.conf
#
# An example Name Service Switch config file. This file should be
# sorted with the most-used services at the beginning.
#
# The entry '[NOTFOUND=return]' means that the search for an
# entry should stop if the search in the previous entry turned
# up nothing. Note that if the search failed due to some other reason
# (like no NIS server responding) then the search continues with the
# next entry.
#
# Legal entries are:
#
#nisplus or nis+Use NIS+ (NIS version 3)
#nis or ypUse NIS (NIS version 2), also called YP
#dnsUse DNS (Domain Name Service)
#filesUse the local files
#dbUse the local database (.db) files
#compatUse NIS on compat mode
#hesiodUse Hesiod for user lookups
#[NOTFOUND=return]Stop searching if not found so far
#
passwd:     files nisplus nis
shadow:     files nisplus nis
group:      files nisplus nis

hosts:    files nisplus nis dns
bootparams: nisplus [NOTFOUND=return] files

ethers:     files
netmasks:   files
networks:   files
```

---

5. NIS+ is effectively a dead product. Currently, the more capable replacement for NIS is LDAP.

Example 10–11   Sample `/etc/nsswitch.conf` File *(Continued)*

```
protocols: files
rpc:       files
services:   files

netgroup:  nisplus

publickey: nisplus

automount: files nisplus
aliases:   files nisplus
```

For more information about the `/etc/nsswitch.conf` file, see the `man` page for `nsswitch.conf(5)`.

Configuring an NIS slave server is similar to that of the NIS master, only easier. As with the master, you must set the domain name, configure the `/etc/ypserv`, `/var/yp/securenets`, and the `/etc/nsswitch.conf` files. These are done in the same manner as before. Then start the proper daemons as before, in the case of the slave server, `ypserv` and `ypbind`.

The slave server doesn't store copies of the original ASCII configuration files. It only stores copies of the maps from the master. The last thing to do is to run the `ypinit` command for the slave. This must be done using the `-s` option and specifying the name or IP address of the NIS master server. This option tells the slave to request the copies of the maps from the master. The command initializing the slave server and identifying the master server named `nanoo` is

```
# ypinit -s nanoo
```

The last consideration for the slave server is how to control the map transfers from the master. NIS includes three scripts which can be used by `cron` to automate map transfers. These scripts are `ypxfr_1perhour`, `ypxfr_1perday`, and `ypxfr_2perday` which are used to transfer certain maps as necessary (such as `passwd`, `shadow`, and `publickey` once per hour). There are five different ways to transfer maps from the master to the slave server. You can manually invoke the `ypxfr` utility on the slave, use custom scripts with `cron` on the slave, manually run `yppush` from the master server, use custom scripts with `cron` from the master, or some combination of these methods. The important thing is that you have some sort of method to ensure that maps get propagated to the slaves.

Configuring NIS clients is the easiest part of the NIS process. First, you have to set the NIS domain name, as we have previously seen. Second, you must properly configure the `/etc/nsswitch.conf` file. The last task to be done prior to starting up the client daemon `ypbind` is to edit the client configuration file `/etc/yp.conf`. A typical `/etc/yp.conf` file is shown in Example 10–12.

Example 10–12   Sample `/etc/yp.conf` File

```
# /etc/yp.conf - ypbind configuration file
# Valid entries are
#
#domain NISDOMAIN server HOSTNAME
#    Use server HOSTNAME for the domain NISDOMAIN.
#
#domain NISDOMAIN broadcast
#    Use broadcast on the local net for domain NISDOMAIN
#
#ypserver HOSTNAME
#    Use server HOSTNAME for the local domain. The
#    IP-address of server must be listed in /etc/hosts.
#
ypserver 148.114.64.1
ypserver 148.114.64.10
```

This file is used to control the behavior of the client daemon. You are allowed to specify domains and/or servers in this file. This file is well documented. The above example shows two servers defined for the local domain (which is defined here by domainname). The servers may be defined by IP address or hostname as long as the hostname is resolvable. For more information concerning the `yp.conf` file, see the NIS-HOWTO.

Once the `yp.conf` file is properly configured, you can start up the client daemon, `ypbind`. This can be done, as we have seen before, using the start-up scripts. When `ypbind` starts, it checks the `yp.conf` file for any server listings using the `ypserver` keyword. It will attempt to bind to the servers it finds in the order listed. If this fails, the client will broadcast a request to the local network. When `ypbind` gets a response from a server, the client will attempt to bind to that server. Any subsequent NIS requests will be directed at that server until the server no longer responds. For more information on `ypbind` see the `man` page for `ypbind(8)`.

At this point you have a fully functioning NIS domain with a master server, zero or more slave servers, and one or more clients. There are a few utility programs which can be very helpful in maintaining and using NIS. These include the `ypset`, `ypcat`, `ypmatch`, `ypwhich`, and `yppasswd` commands.

The `ypset` command is used to bind the NIS client to a particular server. This command is useful if a master goes down or if you want to bind to a different domain or server. The example below shows the `ypset` command being used to bind the client to the server `nanoo`.

```
# ypset nanoo
```

The `ypcat` command is used just like the `cat` command except that it only works with NIS maps. You can specify the map by nickname (such as `passwd`) or by the actual map name (such as `passwd.byname`). Example 10–13 shows `ypcat` being used to display the contents of the hosts map.

Example 10–13   Output of `ypcat hosts`

```
$ ypcat hosts
10.62.92.51   timberwolves
10.62.92.236  dhcp-130-62-92-236
10.62.154.60  diskhog dh
10.62.241.37  ernest
10.166.166.65 anvil
<...remaining output snipped...>
```

The `ypmatch` command is used to search for specific keys within a map file. You must specify both the key you are searching for and the map file to search in. The result will be the line that matches that key in the file (if it exists). Example 10–14 illustrates a `ypmatch` command to find the record for `krell` in the `passwd.byname` map.

Example 10–14   Using `ypmatch`

```
$ ypmatch krell passwd.byname
krell:hb3x5g0kN/8fE:38482:10:Mitch Krell,,,,,,,/home/krell:/bin/bash
$
```

The `ypwhich` command is used to show which server the client is currently bound to. Example 10–15 shows that the client is currently bound to the NIS master named `maureen`.

Example 10–15   The `ypwhich` Command

```
# ypwhich
maureen
#
```

Once NIS is controlling your network environment, users can no longer change their passwords with the `passwd` command. The `yppasswd` command is used for this. This command allows users and administrators to change passwords which will be propagated up to the master. This command works just like the `passwd` command except that it doesn't change the password locally. The password is changed on the master.

NIS is useful for small to modestly sized networks. It is very simple to implement and maintain. However, NIS is not well suited for large environments and generally has the following drawbacks:

- All NIS traffic traverses the network in clear text, including passwords.
- Updates are propagated by sending entire maps, even if only a few bytes are changed.
- There is no synchronization mechanism between masters and slaves.

These limitations can be overcome through the implementation of the lightweight directory access protocol (LDAP). LDAP, however, is somewhat more difficult to implement and maintain. The simplicity of NIS, despite its limitations, ensures that it is likely to enjoy continued use for some time to come.

For more information regarding NIS, check out the following books and Web sites:

```
http://www.securiteam.com/unixfocus/
RedHat_andSuSE_release_an_updated_ypserv_package.html
http://www.kernel.org/pub/linux/utils/net/NIS
http://www.linuxdoc.org/HOWTO/NIS-HOWTO/index.html
```

Stern, Hal, *Managing NFS and NIS*, Sebastopol, California, O'Reilly & Associates, Inc., April, 1992.

Lightweight Directory Access Protocol

The Lightweight Directory Access Protocol (LDAP) was developed to provide a simple client interface for directories which comply with the X.500 directory standard. It was developed at the University of Michigan to address the problem of a lack of resources for directory clients which were mostly PCs and Macintosh systems. The X.500 directory specifications were used to define the attribute names and hierarchical structure of LDAP. Although LDAP doesn't actually specify a directory structure, it does provide a protocol which can be used to interact with any X.500-like attribute-based, hierarchical directory structure.

Many of the large network developers have adopted LDAP as the official Internet access protocol. The current version is LDAPv3, which is compatible with the previous version and includes specifications for allowing LDAP to be used with both non-X.500 and standalone directories. LDAP is defined in RFC 1777 and is being touted as the "new NIS" or "NIS replacement."

The LDAP directory services is based on the basic client-server model. The data which makes up an LDAP directory tree is stored on one or more LDAP servers. An LDAP client connects to one of the LDAP servers and requests information. The server will attempt to respond with the information or tell the client where that information may be retrieved from (usually another LDAP server). All of the LDAP servers see the same view of the directory tree.

The LDAP process involves the use of two programs. The LDAP server daemon is called `slapd`. It is the stand-alone daemon and listens for connections on port 389. The LDAP client can be one of many programs or applications. Three LDAP clients which are included in Linux are `ldapsearch`, `ldapdelete`, and `ldapmodify`. The `ldapsearch` utility is used to open a connection to an LDAP server and perform searches of the directory using various filters. The `ldapdelete` program is used to delete one or more entries from the directory. The `ldapmodify` command is used to add to or modify records in the directory. For more information on the syntax and usage of these commands see their `man` pages.

LDAP is designed to be simpler and use less resources on client systems. Because it was designed to interact with other types of directories, it is easier to build directory access capabilities into more applications.

For more information on LDAP check out the following Web sites:

```
http://www.linuxdoc.org/HOWTO/LDAP-HOWTO.html
http://www.ldap.org
http://www.umich.edu/~dirsvcs/ldap/index.html
```

Electronic Mail

Electronic mail (email) works a lot like paper mail in that it is sent through the United States Postal Service (USPS). Suppose, for example, that you write a letter to a friend. You live in a suburb of Denver and your friend lives in a suburb of Philadelphia. You address the envelope for the letter, affix the appropriate postage, and drop the letter in a local mailbox. At some point, a USPS employee collects your letter from the mailbox and takes it to the local suburban post office. At that location, the letter is sorted as either being destined to the local zip code or somewhere else. All letters, including the one to your friend in Philadelphia, goes to the major sorting post office in Denver (we'll call this a *mail relay* station). At the mail relay in Denver, your letter to a suburb of Philadelphia is sent (or routed) to that suburb's nearest mail relay (probably in Philadelphia). Once it arrives at the Philadelphia mail relay, it is then routed to the appropriate suburban post office which in turn sends it out for delivery via postal carrier.

Email works much the same way. At your workstation, you compose an email message using a *mail user agent* (MUA) program. MUA programs include Netscape, Outlook, `/usr/bin/mail`, and `procmail`. Once you complete writing the message and submit it for processing, the MUA submits the message to a *mail transfer agent* (MTA). MTAs include such programs as `sendmail`, `qmail`, `postfix`, and IMAP. The MTA creates an envelope for the message and determines how to forward the message to its destination, usually by obtaining mail exchanger (MX) DNS records for the destination domain. An MX record contains the IP address of a mail relay or *gateway* system which will then forward it on to its ultimate destination. Mail relay and gateway systems act in much the same way as the USPS mail relays described above. Once the message arrives at its destination, the MTA passes the message to a *mail delivery agent* (MDA) to put the message in the user's mailbox. Most MUAs are also MDAs. Some MTAs can be configured to act as MDAs.

Figure 10–9 illustrates the concepts of MUA, MDA, and MTA.

The details of implementing and maintaining electronic mail in a networked environment is a topic unto itself. Further details can be found in the references cited below.

```
http://www.sendmail.org/
http://www.sendmail.com/
http://www.qmail.org/
http://www.inter7.com/qmailadmin/
```
(administrative front end to *qmail*)

Costales, Brian, *sendmail*, 2nd ed., Sebastopol, California, O'Reilly & Associates, 1997.

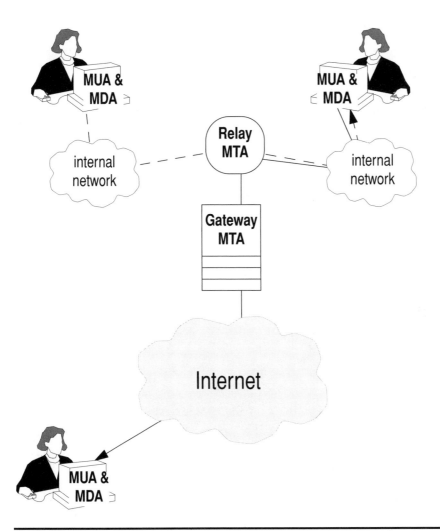

Figure 10–9   Electronic Mail Environment

X Window System

X Windows is used as a generic display server. It uses a client–server-based process to allow local and remote-based program (clients) to request services from the X Windows server. The X Windows software runs on the local machine and serves up resources to the clients. These services are performed on the local machine's screen (such as creating windows and displaying images). This eliminates the need for each program to have to worry about the details of creating a display. Using X Windows makes the graphics and display details device independent and therefore hides the details of the hardware.

X Windows provides a programmer interface (APIs) to allow easy access to the display. It also has the ability to create various objects on the screen (lines, images, etc). Linux provides a number of programs for configuring X Windows to run on Linux-based systems. The two most popular are Xconfigurator and XF86Setup. For more information on these program, see the `man` pages for `Xconfigurator(1X)` and `XF86Setup(1)`.

X Windows was developed at MIT as part of the Athena project. It is a portable, windowing system which is totally independent of the Linux kernel. It has been ported to numerous versions of UNIX/Linux and is fairly easy to install and configure. For more information on X Windows, check out the following Web sites:

```
http://www.xfree86.org/
http://www.linuxdoc.org/XFree86-HOWTO/index.html
/usr/doc/XFree86-doc-X.X.X/
http://www.linuxdoc.org/HOWTO/mini/Remote-X-Apps.html
```

Summary

There are a number of useful and sometimes necessary network applications available for Linux. We have looked at some of the more common ones, DNS, DHCP, NFS, Samba, NIS, and email. There are many, many more available to make networking in Linux easier or more useful, depending on the system's specific needs.

New, better, and more efficient programs for networking in Linux are being developed every day. If you have a specific need for some network application, all that you have to do is take a few minutes and search out on the Internet for a Linux version. If it doesn't exist yet, wait a bit and try again. Software develops quickly in the Linux venue.

11

Introducing Dynamic Routing Table Management

Initially, the Internet was connected together through a collection of routers. Each router had a complete routing table for all of the interconnected networks within the Internet. The routers exchanged information using a distance vector protocol called the gateway-to-gateway protocol (GGP). As the Internet grew, it became apparent that this simple approach was not feasible. Over time, three distinct elements addressing routing in the Internet (and, therefore, any large internetwork) emerged.

- Autonomous systems (ASes)
- CIDR, route aggregation, and IPv6
- Ongoing development of IGPs and EGPs

In previous chapters, we addressed CIDR, route aggregation, and IPv6. In Chapter 6, we mentioned AS, and in this chapter we refine its definition and consider AS use.

This chapter describes interior gateway protocols (IGPs) and exterior gateway protocols (EGPs) and using the `gated` daemon that implements them. We begin with a very brief conceptual introduction to the protocol types. We next take a look at the basics of the `gated` daemon. There's a lot of detail there, but it will make for good reference material later on. Next, we cover the conceptual details of RIP and router discovery. Then, we consider implementing RIP and router discovery with `gated` by way of an example. The example begins in "A Routing Example" on page 531 and if this is your first read of this topic, you will likely prefer reading through the example first. Most of the details of the flags and options used become clear from use and you can always flip to the earlier sections to fill in the details.

If you are not familiar with the concepts associated with IGPs, EGPs, and ASes, you would do well to refer to *Routing in the Internet* and/or *Interconnections* as cited in "For Further Reading" on page 546. Both of these books are excellent and provide an outstanding foundation for the detailed implementation discussion of RIP, router discovery, OSPF, and BGP which is the focus of this and the next two chapters.

Autonomous Systems

We provided a very simple definition of AS in Chapter 6, largely so that we could define IGPs and EGPs. There, we said that an AS is a collection of networks under a single administrative control. More precisely, an AS is a collection of prefix numbers (network numbers and subnetwork numbers) that appear to be collectively managed by a single, well-defined *routing policy*. A routing policy is a set of rules that dictates how routing decisions are made. Very often routing policies are implemented through the use of an IGP or BGP—the configuration of which specifies the policy—as the protocols used cause routing tables on systems and routers to be updated in particular ways. It turns out that in Linux you can also impose routing policies on a per system or per router basis to augment or override IGP or BGP policies. We discuss this Linux capability in Chapter 16.

Note that in our definition of an AS, the routing policy needs to *appear* to be a single, well-defined set of routing rules. The point of that is to the rest of the world, and other ASes in particular, the routing policy must be consistent. In point of fact, the inside of an AS may have many routing policies—static tables may be used in some cases and IGPs such as RIP and OSPF in other cases. ASes must be able to share information about routes among each other and that information must be consistent and well-defined regardless of how packets are handled inside of any given AS. In large part, these details are handled by EGPs, which are used to share information between ASes.

Within the Internet, ASes are formal entities. Each AS is assigned a unique 16-bit autonomous system number (ASN) by the appropriate Internet authorities (IANA and ICANN). These ASNs are used whenever routing information is exchanged between ASes. We'll have a look at them later in this chapter.

As we mentioned in Chapter 6, there are two classes of dynamic routing table management protocols. IGPs, which operate inside an AS, and EGPs, which operate between ASes. Table 11–1 provides a list of some protocols, identifies for each protocol whether it is an IGP or EGP, lists the protocol type (discussed in the next section), and provides resources for further information.

Table 11–1   IGPs and EGPs

Protocol	Category	Type	Description
router discovery	IGP	N/A	ICMP-based protocol for obtaining default routers. See "Router Discovery" on page 525.
RIP	IGP	distance vector	Routing information protocol. See Chapter 6 and "RIP" on page 509.
IGRP	IGP	distance vector	Interior gateway routing protocol. Also, enhanced IGRP (EIGRP). A Cisco proprietary protocol. See `http:/www.cisco.com/univercd/` `cd/td/doc/cisntwk/ito_doc/` `igrp.htm` and `../en_igrp.htm`.
IS-IS	IGP	link state	Intermediate system to intermediate system. See *Interconnections* as cited in "For Further Reading" on page 546.
OSPF	IGP	link state	Open shortest path first. See "OSPF Overview" on page 548
GGP	EGP	distance vector	Gateway-to-gateway protocol. See RFC 823. Obsolete.

Table 11–1   IGPs and EGPs *(Continued)*

PROTOCOL	CATEGORY	TYPE	DESCRIPTION
EGP	EGP	distance vector	Exterior gateways protocol. See RFC 904. This protocol has been largely, if not completely, replaced by BGP.
BGP	EGP	path vector	Border gateway protocol. See Chapter 13.

In the next section, we'll take a brief tour of the different protocol types.

Protocol Types

The many routing table protocols generally fall into one of the three types: distance vector, link state, and path vector, although there are variations and exceptions (like router discovery). Each of these types of protocols has applicability for specific types of implementations. We discuss each in the following sections.

Distance Vector Protocols

We covered the basics of distance vector protocols, generally, when we examined RIP in the previous chapter. Protocols in this family work by advertising routes using a simple hop count metric that is used to determine the best (the one with the lowest metric) route. As we noted previously, protocols in this family suffer from counting to infinity problems that can cause packets to loop between routers until the time-to-live field in the packet is exhausted.

Link State Protocols

Link state protocols operate by sharing entire maps of the network that are updated regularly. The instant a link goes down, a new map is propagated throughout the environment. Additionally, best routes can be determined from a variety of metrics like cost of service, performance, or securest route. Multiple metrics can be weighted and used in an overall scheme to derive a best route.

All of this means that looping cannot occur and that routers always have an accurate and reliable map of the networked environment. The downside to link state protocols is that they are memory and CPU intensive relative to distance vector protocols.

IS-IS and OSPF are the most commonly used protocols in this family. We consider OSPF in detail in "OSPF Overview" on page 548.

Path Vector Protocols

Path vector protocols are sort of a marriage between distance vector and link state protocols. The idea is to propagate accurate routing information that is accurate and complete like a link state protocol to avoid looping problems, but which does not incur the overhead of a link state protocol. This is accomplished largely by using an approach that looks a lot like source routing (see Table 4–2 on page 99).

The most commonly implemented path vector protocol is BGP. This protocol is discussed in Chapter 13.

The gated **Daemon**

The `gated` daemon is truly a marvelous program. Its purpose is to provide routing information through one or more dynamic routing table protocols. It supports many dynamic routing table protocols utilizing a single syntax. It can be implemented on hosts or routers, each of which can be configured to participate in one or more IGPs and/or EGPs. It maintains a database of routes, called a routing information base (RIB), that are obtained through one or more protocols, assigns preferences to each route, and updates the kernel routing table based on this information. Given its flexibility, there is also a fair amount of complexity as we see beginning with "The `/etc/gated.conf` Configuration File" on page 476. Collectively, the `gated` daemon and all of its utilities is called *GateD*.

It is currently maintained by NextHop Technologies, Inc. (NextHop) which provides both publicly available and commercial versions. The publicly available version supports the GateD *unicast* protocols. The name "unicast" is used to indicate that the multicast capabilities are not included. The included protocols are:

- RIPv1 and RIPv2 (RFC 2453 compliant)
- Router discovery
- OSPF (RFC 1583 compliant with RFC 2178 MD5 calculations)
- IS-IS

- EGP
- BGPv3 and v4 (RFC 1771 compliant but many additional features such as communities and confederations are not supported in the publicly available version)

NextHop also offers to members, for a fee, multicast protocols (these include a variety of protocols for multicast routing) and IPv6 protocols (like RIPng and OSPFv6). The commercial versions of `gated` additionally support current and future enhancements to protocols like BGP. For complete information about the various NextHop offerings, visit their Web page.

```
http://www.nexthop.com/
```

Licensing is only required for the nonpublic versions and can be obtained from NextHop.

Our discussions will focus on public version 3.6 of `gated`. As of this writing, only the Red Hat distribution includes `gated` as a standard part of the distribution (it's at version 3.5.11 in Red Hat 6.2 and 3.6 in Red Hat 7.0). Thus, the next section covers obtaining, compiling, and installing `gated`.

Obtaining, Compiling, and Installing `gated`

You can obtain the `gated` version 3.6 public release from the NextHop source code page.

```
http://www.nexthop.com/products/public/public.shtml
```

At this site, you'll also find a prerelease version 3.6 that includes IPv6 support. When you select the download hyperlink for version 3.6, you'll get `gated-pub.tar.gz`. Put it in a working directory for extracting and compilation.

Unfortunately, the 3.6 version does not include the `man` pages. You need to obtain the 3.5.11 version at the same site to get the `man` pages, or obtain the `gated-3.5.11-1.i386.rpm` Red Hat package which will have them as well as a `gated` binary. The Red Hat package can be obtained from the Red Hat primary distribution CD, `ftp://ftp.redhat.com/`, or one of its mirrors. You'll find a list of mirrors at

```
http://www.redhat.com/download/mirror.html.
```

A more general and non Red Hat specific source for RPMs is `http://rufus.w3.org/`. Fortunately, the `man` pages are not that critical as the better source of documentation is in the manual set that is available at

`http://www.nexthop.com/techinfo/manuals/manuals.shtml`

These manuals are fairly comprehensive. They cover everything from installation to configuration to troubleshooting. It is well worth the time to read through them, especially if you are going to use OSPF, IS-IS, or BGP. They are available in HTML and (mostly) PDF formats.

Once you have obtained downloaded `gated-pub.tar.gz` into a working directory, extract its contents and go into the `gated-public-3_6` directory created by the extraction. Then execute the following commands:

```
# ./configure --prefix=/usr
# make depend
# make
# make install
```

Note that we set the prefix to `/usr`. This has the effect of installing the `gated` daemon in `/usr/sbin` instead of the default `/usr/local/sbin` directory. Use of the `--prefix=/usr` is really a matter of preference, but we'll assume it for purposes of our discussion. By default, `gated` will be built to accommodate all of the protocols it supports—this fact is not altogether clear from the documentation. Check `./configure --help` to view the available options which, in particular, shows how to disable support for protocols that you do not need. Note that `gated` will not listen for a particular protocol's communications unless so configured in `/etc/gated.conf`; thus, disabling a protocol or two here only completely removes that component from the binary. This makes the binary smaller and makes it impossible to run the disabled protocols.

Oddly, the `make install` as shown above will not install the `gdc` (a `gated` helper utility described in "The `gdc` Helper Utility" on page 503) binary. You must do this manually from the `gated-public-3_6` directory with

```
# install -m 755 src/gdc/gdc /usr/bin/gdc
```

If you want to get the 3.5.11 `man` pages, retrieve `gated-3-5-11.tar.gz` from the GateD source code page cited above and extract the files from the tar image. This creates the `gated-3-5-11` subdirectory in your working directory. Enter this directory and install the `man` pages.

```
# cd gated-3-5-11
# make install-man
```

The man pages from version 3.5.11 do not map directly to version 3.6, but they are close. As noted, our discussions will focus on version 3.6, so between this document and the version 3.5.11 documentation, you will be able to derive the differences. The differences are also documented at[1]

```
http://www.gated.org/gated-web/code/doc/info/source/
source.html#public
```

The only downside to using gated in larger environments is that it needs to be installed on all platforms for which the protocols it supports are required. In the cases of hosts using RIP or router discovery exclusively, routed or rdisc, respectively, can be used instead of gated. But for all other protocols, gated, or some other daemon supporting that protocol, must be used. This means that the daemon has to be installed on each such machine, which can be a daunting task.

The best solution to this type of problem is to compile the source for each target platform. This will give you a binary for each system. You can then propagate this binary to all the systems throughout your environment through a variety of means, such as rsync, NFS, or Samba. You can also create a Debian or Red Hat package and then install that package on each system, perhaps automating the process with scripts or programs. You can deal with the /etc/ gated.conf file similarly.

In any event, outside of gated and rdisc on Red Hat, there is no daemon that supports anything other than RIP on any of the four distributions of which we speak. Therefore, if you need to use something other than RIP, you will have to install an appropriate daemon. Ah...there's no rest for the weary admin.

The gated Daemon

This section is one of those "cart before the horse" issues. We need to mention the command line operations of gated, but we can't really describe them well until we use them. So, we list the flags, describe the behavior of the signals, and note the various files here with a light description, detailing them as appropriate in the following sections.

---

1. The previous home for gated was http://www.gated.org/ where a lot of good information still remains.

The `gated` daemon can be invoked directly from the command line. When invoked, `gated` looks for a `/etc/gated.conf` configuration file by default. If compiled, as shown in "Obtaining, Compiling, and Installing gated" on page 470, then `gated` runs RIP. For example, assuming that there is no `/etc/gated.conf` configuration file,

```
# gated
```

causes `gated` to daemonize (go to the background) and run as if it were configured to run RIP in much the same way as `routed` (if two or more interfaces exist, it will run in broadcast mode, otherwise it runs in listen-only mode). This feature can be turned off by using

```
# ./configure --disable-ripon
```

when building `gated`. Running `gated` manually is probably not the way you'll want to normally start the daemon, so we provide an example script in "An Example Start-up Script for gated" on page 507.

WARNING

> Before you try to run `gated`, make sure that any other daemon that implements an IGP or EGP, like `routed`, is *not* running. If another daemon is running, `gated` will silently fail and log an error message via `syslog` to facility `daemon` which normally means it will be written to `/var/log/messages`.

The `gated` daemon accepts a number of option flags. We describe them in Table 11–2.

Table 11–2   Flags to `gated`

FLAG	DESCRIPTION
-c	Causes `gated` to check the syntax of the configuration file `/etc/gated.conf` or that specified by the `-f` flag. If there are no errors in the configuration file, then `gated` dumps its data to `/var/tmp/gated_dump` and exists. If there are syntax errors in the configuration file, then `gated` reports them to standard error and exits.
-C	Similar to `-c` except that `gated` simply returns 0 if the configuration file syntax was correct and 1 otherwise.

Table 11–2   Flags to `gated` *(Continued)*

FLAG	DESCRIPTION
`-n`	Specifies that `gated` will not modify the routing table. Used for testing purposes only.
`-N`	Causes `gated` to run in the foreground and not daemonize.
`-t`*options* [*trace_file*]	Specifies a comma separated list of trace options as listed by *options*. Very valuable for debugging, `gated` will trace all of the events specified and write them to `trace_file` or standard out if no file is specified.
`-f` *config_file*	Specifies the configuration file *config_file* to use. If this flag is not specified, then `/etc/gated.conf` is assumed.
`-v`	Causes `gated` to print its version information and quit.

The `gated` daemon also accepts a variety of signals. We list them in Table 11–3.

Table 11–3   Signals Recognized by `gated`

SIGNAL	ACTION
`SIGHUP`	Causes `gated` to reread its configuration file. `gated` retains its state in the event that the configuration file has syntax errors and, if such is the case, continues to use the old syntax file and writes an error message to `syslog`. OSPF must be shut down and restarted in the case of an error free configuration file which may have an adverse effect on routing by the system. Use this signal with caution.
`SIGINT`	Causes `gated` to dump its state data to `/var/tmp/gated_dump`.
`SIGTERM`	Gracefully terminates `gated`. All routes in the routing table populated by `gated` will be removed except those with the `retain` option in the configuration file (see Table 11–14 on page 496). All static routes added with the `route` command are unaffected.

Table 11–3   Signals Recognized by gated *(Continued)*

SIGNAL	ACTION
SIGKILL	Terminates gated unceremoniously. All routing table entries populated by gated are removed except for those identified as exterior in the configuration file (see, for instance, "A Note About OSPF External Routes" on page 571).
SIGUSR1	Toggles tracing. Causes gated to cease writing to the trace file if it is currently doing so or restart writing to the trace file if it is not. The trace file must be specified, either at the command line or in the configuration file (see "The traceoptions Statement" on page 484). If no trace file is specified, this signal has no effect.
SIGUSR2	Causes gated to reread the kernel interface list for new interfaces.

Finally, the gated daemon uses and/or creates a number of files. These are given in Table 11–4.

Table 11–4   Files Utilized by gated

FILE	PURPOSE
/etc/gated.conf	The default gated configuration file. Discussed in "The /etc/gated.conf Configuration File" on page 476.
/var/tmp/gated_dump	gated writes its current database on receipt of a SIGINT signal.
/var/run/gated.pid	Contains the process identifier (PID) of the currently running gated daemon.
/var/run/gated.version	Contains the version number of the currently running gated daemon.
/var/log/messages	The gated daemon writes all of its log messages to syslog facility daemon. Normally, those messages will get written to this file, but check your /etc/syslog.conf file to be sure.

Note that `gated` writes all of its messages to `syslog` via the `daemon` facility. By default, it logs everything at level `info` and above. The level can be controlled in the `/etc/gated.conf` file as described subsequently. By default, all of the Linux distributions we are discussing send `daemon` messages to `/var/log/messages`. See the `syslog.conf(5)` man page for further details regarding `syslog` configuration.

The `/etc/gated.conf` Configuration File

The `gated` configuration file dictates what `gated` will do. It can be very simple, it can be very complex, or it can be somewhere in between. The full range of configuration options that can be placed in this file is overwhelming. Consequently, we introduce the file's syntax and basic directives in this section. More detailed examples for use with RIP, router discovery, OSPF, and BGP will follow.

The configuration file, `/etc/gated.conf` by default, consists of a series of statements terminated by a semicolon (`;`). Each statement is one of the following types: directive, trace, option, interface, definition, protocol, static, or control. Of these types, options, interface, definition, protocol, static, and control can have multiple statements associated with them called *groupings* or *stanzas*. Stanzas are collected together between an open brace (`{`) and a close brace (`}`). The other two statement types, directive and trace, have no direct applicability to routing and are used to control `gated` behavior.

One syntactical note. Because of the use of the `;` and `{ }`, line continuation characters are unnecessary. Carriage returns can appear anywhere since the gated parser looks for the appropriate closing symbol (either `;` or `}` as appropriate). This makes it easy to create very readable configuration files.

The `/etc/gated.conf` file uses two forms for comments. Everything following a `#` to the end-of-line is ignored by the parser. It also supports C-style comment syntax—that is, everything between `/*` and `*/` is ignored by the parser.

In Table 11–5, we list many of the major statements together with their types and a brief description.

Table 11–5   `gated` Configuration File Statement Types

STATEMENT	TYPE	DESCRIPTION
`%directory`	directive	Sets the directory for include files.
`%include`	directive	Includes a file into `/etc/gated.conf` at the point at which it appears in `/etc/gated.conf`. If only a file name is specified, then the directory specified by `%directory` is assumed.
`options`	option	Specifies a list of options.
`interfaces`	interface	Identifies system interfaces.
`autonomoussystem`	definition	Sets the autonomous system number.
`routerid`	definition	Defines the originating router protocol.
`martians`	definition	Defines invalid destination addresses such as RFC 1918 private addresses.
`import`	control	Defines routes to import from specific protocols.
`export`	control	Defines routes to export from specific protocols.
`aggregate`	control	Specifies routes to aggregated.
`generate`	control	Similar to route aggregation, except that route is generated instead of specified.
`traceoptions`	control	Specifies the events to trace.
`static`	static	Specifies a static route, much as if the `route` command had been used.
`kernel`	protocol	Specifies kernel interface options.
`icmp`	protocol	Specifies the processing of ICMP packets.
`redirect`	protocol	Specifies the handling of ICMP redirects.
`routerdiscovery`	protocol	Enables router discovery.
`rip`	protocol	Enables RIP.

Table 11–5   `gated` Configuration File Statement Types *(Continued)*

STATEMENT	TYPE	DESCRIPTION
`isis`	protocol	Enables IS-IS.
`ospf`	protocol	Enables OSPF.
`egp`	protocol	Enables EGP.
`bgp`	protocol	Enables BGP.
`snmp`	protocol	Enables the SNMP agent.

There are many other statements that can appear in the configuration file, some of these deal with multicasting, others are specific to a particular protocol. Beginning with "A Routing Example" on page 531, we look at examples using these and protocol-specific statements.

Ordering in the `/etc/gated.conf` file is very important. Statements should appear in the following order based on statement type.

1. directive
2. option
3. interface
4. definition
5. protocol
6. static
7. control

The following sections describe the `gated` global and generally applicable statements, options, and parameters.

`gated` Preferences

Whenever `gated` receives routes to the same destination from different protocols, preferences can be used to determine which is the best route. Preferences can be set based on network interfaces, protocols, or specific routers. Thus, the `preference` option can be specified within a variety of different statements.

Preference values range from 0 to 255 with lower values being more preferable. These values are arbitrary, but permit the establishment of a routing policy among protocols within `gated`. It is important to note that the use of preferences has no effect whatsoever on a particular protocol's decision about best route—it only distinguishes from the best routes of various protocols or interfaces. The default preference values for many types of routes are provided in Table 11–6.

Table 11–6   Default preference Values Used by gated

PREFERENCE FOR	MODIFIABLE WITHIN THE STANZA OF	VALUE
Directly connected networks	interface	0
OSPF routes	ospf	10
Internally generated default for BGP/EGP	gendefault	20
ICMP redirects	redirect	30
Static routes in /etc/gated.conf	static	60
RIP routes	rip	100
Point-to-point interfaces	various statements	110
Routes to interfaces that are down	interfaces	120
Aggregated routes	aggregate or generate	130
OSPF AS external routes	ospf	150
BGP routes	bgp	170

The BGP protocol additionally permits the use of a preference2 value which is used for tie-breakers. The preference2 value has a default of 0 and must be configured to be of any use.

We explore the use of preference throughout this chapter.

The gated interfaces Statement

The interfaces statement can be used to define certain options for an interface or interface list. The interfaces statement is global in scope and should not be confused with the interface statement which is used within a stanza to set options for a particular statement. The general form of the interfaces statement is given in Example 11–1.

Example 11–1   The `interfaces` Statement

```
interfaces {
    options [strictinterfaces] [scaninterval time] ;
    interface iface_list [preference pref] [down preference pref]
        [passive] [simplex] [reject] [blackhole] [AS asn] ;
    define address [broadcast address | pointtopoint address]
        [netmask mask] [multicast] ;
} ;
```

Each of the available parameters for this statement are given in Table 11–7.

Table 11–7   Parameters to the `interfaces` Statement

PARAMETER	ARGUMENTS	DESCRIPTION
`options`		Permits configuration of global options associated with interfaces.
	`strictinterfaces`	Causes `gated` to fail at startup if an interface is referenced in the `/etc/gated.conf` file, but is not configured on the system or is not identified by a `define` parameter. By default, `gated` issues a warning message if this occurs.
	`scaninterval time`	Specifies the `time` in seconds that `gated` checks the kernel interface list. Default is 15 seconds. Rechecking this list may also be accomplished by sending a `SIGUSR2` signal to `gated`.

Table 11–7   Parameters to the `interfaces` Statement *(Continued)*

PARAMETER	ARGUMENTS	DESCRIPTION
`interface iface_list`		Specifies a list of one or more space-separated interfaces. The list can be interface name(s) (`eth0`, `eth1`, `ppp0`, etc.) or interface name wildcard(s) (e.g., `eth`, meaning all Ethernet interfaces on the system; `tr`, meaning all token ring interfaces, etc.), IP addresses, fully qualified DNS hostnames, or `all`, meaning all interfaces on the system.
	`preference pref`	Sets the preference for routes to this interface. The default is 0. See "gated Preferences" on page 478.
	`down preference pref`	Sets the preference for the interface when gated believes it to be dysfunctional, but the kernel does not report it as down. Default is 120. See "gated Preferences" on page 478.
	`passive`	Prevents gated from changing the preference to this interface if gated believes it is down.
	`simplex`	Specifies that the interface cannot read its own broadcasts through a physical interface, but rather reads them through the loopback.

Table 11–7   Parameters to the `interfaces` Statement *(Continued)*

PARAMETER	ARGUMENTS	DESCRIPTION
	`reject`	Specifies that this address will be used to insert reject routes into the routing table. See, for example, Table 11–14 on page 496 for a description of reject routes.
	`blackhole`	As above, except for blackholes. See, for example, Table 11–14 on page 496 for a description of blackhole routes.
	`AS asn`	Specifies the ASN, `asn`, assigned to this interface.
`define address`		The define statement is used to specify interfaces that might not be up and running when `gated` starts, such as point-to-point interfaces. Each such `address` must have its own `define` statement. If the `define` statement is for a point-to-point link, then the `address` specified here is the *remote* address.
	`broadcast address | pointtopoint address`	Specifies that the address above is either a broadcast capable interface using the indicated broadcast `address`, or that it is a point-to-point interface using the indicated `address` as the *local* address.

Table 11–7   Parameters to the `interfaces` Statement *(Continued)*

PARAMETER	ARGUMENTS	DESCRIPTION
	`netmask mask`	Specifies the (sub)netmask to be used for this address.
	`multicast`	Specifies that the interface is capable of sending and receiving multicast packets.

There's a lot of information contained in these syntax definitions, so let's look at a couple examples to make it clearer.

Suppose that the system you are configuring has two point-to-point interfaces, `ppp0` and `slip0`. Example 11–2 illustrates defining these interfaces so that `gated` won't complain when it starts up and doesn't find these interfaces.

Example 11–2   Use of the `interfaces` Stanza

```
interfaces {
    interface ppp0 slip0 passive ;
/* Definition for the ppp0 interface. First address is remote,
    second address is local. */
    define 151.16.3.88 pointtopoint 151.16.3.89 multicast ;
# Definition for the slip0 interface. First address is remote.
    define 193.43.7.15 pointtopoint 193.43.7.17 ;
} ;
```

Note that we use the `passive` keyword here for both `ppp0` and `slip0`. In this case, we don't want `gated` to reduce the preference of the routes just because the point-to-point interfaces are down. The two definition statements set the addresses for the two point-to-point links. Notice in this case that the `ppp0` interface is supporting multicast, while the `slip0` interface is not.

Suppose that you have IP aliases configured for a particular interface—perhaps for testing purposes. You'd like to force packets destined to the aliased networks to use RIP (it could be any protocol; we specify RIP here only to establish to what value we need to set the preference in order that it is less desirable than the protocol route) routes instead of the local interface. You can accomplish this using `preference` as shown in Example 11–3.

Example 11–3   Using `preference` in an `interfaces` Stanza

```
interfaces {
# These are the aliases on eth0---we don't want packets going
# out eth0 for these destinations
    interface 128.50.3.2 128.51.3.2 preference 110 ;
} ;
```

Using IP addresses as arguments to the `interface` statement is the only way to distinguish aliases to an interface. Here, we set these preferences to 110 to make them less than the default RIP preference of 100 (see Table 11–6 on page 479).

While the `interfaces` statement is global in scope, it turns out that we can make use of the `interface` argument within other types of stanzas, like `rip`, `ospf`, `routerdiscovery`, and `bgp`. We'll see examples of such use later in this chapter.

The `traceoptions` Statement

The `gated` daemon provides a flexible and powerful mechanism for tracing its activity. This capability is very useful for troubleshooting and security audits. It is implemented through the `traceoptions` statement. The `traceoptions` statement can appear globally and/or within stanzas. Specific `traceoptions` inherit higher level `traceoptions` (such as globally defined ones) unless the `traceoptions` specifies an option to override the higher level option. The general form of a `traceoptions` statement is given in Example 11–4.

Example 11–4   `traceoptions` Form in `/etc/gated.conf`

```
traceoptions [none] | ["trace_file" [replace]
    [size filesize [k|m] files max] ] [nostamp]
    trace_options [except trace_options] ;
```

The arguments accepted by `traceoptions` is given in Table 11–8.

Table 11–8   Arguments to the `traceoptions` Statement

ARGUMENT	DESCRIPTION
`none`	Indicates that no tracing is to be done. Cannot be used with any other arguments.
`"trace_file"` [replace]	Indicates the name of the file to which all tracing information is written. If not an absolute name, then the directory from which `gated` was started is used. Normally, each time `gated` restarts tracing (such as when restarted or `gated` receives a `SIGHUP`), it appends new information to the end of this file. Using the `replace` keyword causes the file to be overwritten at each restart. The filename must be a quoted string. If no `trace_file` is specified, all trace output is sent to standard error. Therefore, it is advisable to specify a trace file at least once.
`size filesize` [k|m] `files max`	`size` specifies the maximum `filesize` of the trace file in kilobytes (KB) or megabytes (MB). When a file reaches its `size` limit, the old file(s) are copied to `trace_file.0`, `trace_file.1`, etc. The default file size is 10 KB. `files` specifies the maximum number of files, `max`, that are created. The default and minimum is 2.

Table 11–8   Arguments to the `traceoptions` Statement *(Continued)*

Argument	Description
`nostamp`	Do not prefix each entry in the *trace_file* with a timestamp.
trace_options [except *trace_options*]	A space-separated list of trace options as defined in Table 11–9. If `except` is used, then the space-separated list of trace options following the `except` keyword are excluded from the output.

Note that if you specify a *trace_file* by using `traceoptions` globally, all subsequent traces will be written to that file unless you specify a different file in the protocol-specific `traceoptions` statement in that statement's stanza. Specifying a trace file in a stanza will cause that file to be used for the specific trace options associated with that `traceoptions` statement only. Failure to specify a trace file causes all traces to be sent to standard error, therefore, you should specify at least one global trace file or a trace file for each distinct stanza in which you want tracing performed.

The complete list of available options to `traceoptions` is given in Table 11–9, which also identifies the scope of the option—*global* means that it must be specified outside of any stanzas, *protocol* means that it must be specified within a stanza or as part of a protocol statement.

Table 11–9   Trace Options Available to `traceoptions`

Option	Scope	Description
`parse`	global	Traces the activity of the parser. Normally used for source code debugging.
`adv`	global	Traces the allocation and freeing of policy blocks. Used for source code debugging.

Table 11–9   Trace Options Available to `traceoptions` *(Continued)*

OPTION	SCOPE	DESCRIPTION
symbols	global	Traces the symbols read from the kernel at start-up. While this option is available here, it should never be used. If you want to look at the kernel symbol table as read by gated, use the -t symbols option to gated (see Table 11–2 on page 473).
iflist	global	Traces the reading of the kernel interface list. This trace (like the above) will not be effected on startup, only on receipt of a SIGHUP or SIGUSR2. To get a trace at startup, you must use the -t iflist option to gated.
all	global or protocol	Causes all of the following trace options to be turned on (but none that appear before this one in this table).
general	global or protocol	Traces normal and route as defined below.
normal	global or protocol	Specifies that normal protocol communications are to be traced. Abnormal communications are always traced.
route	global or protocol	Specifies that routing table changes by the protocol in which this option appears are to be traced.
state	global or protocol	Traces state transitions by the protocol(s).
policy	global or protocol	Traces the application of user-specified policies to routes being imported and exported.

Table 11–9   Trace Options Available to `traceoptions` *(Continued)*

OPTION	SCOPE	DESCRIPTION
`task`	global or protocol	Traces system interface and route determination processing.
`timer`	global or protocol	Traces timer usage for those specifications that impose time restrictions.
`[detail] [send|recv] packets`	global or protocol	The `packets` option traces all packets for the protocol for which the option appears. Each packet generates about two lines of information. Using `detail packets` increases the amount of information per packet substantially. Using `send packets` or `recv packets` will trace outbound or inbound packets, respectively. You can get more detail with `detail send packets` or `detail recv packets`.

There are other protocol-specific trace options. Not all protocols support all options. We consider a variety of `traceoptions` examples throughout this chapter.

The `%directory` and `%include` Statements

The `%directory` statement is used exclusively to identify the directory in which include files are to be found. Include files are indicated by the `%include` statement and can be placed anywhere within the `/etc/gated.conf` file. Example 11–5 illustrates.

Example 11–5   Use of `%directory` and `%include`

```
# GateD config file
%directory /etc/gated
interfaces {
    %include interfaces
} ;
%include traceoptions
<remainder of file snipped>
```

In this case, all include files are found in `/etc/gated`. The file `interfaces` is included right after the `interfaces` statement and found in the directory `/etc/gated`. Similarly, the file `traceoptions` is incorporated at the end of the `interfaces` stanza. Note that neither `%directory` nor `%include` have a trailing `;`. These statements terminate with a newline (carriage return).

The Global `options` Statement

We already saw the use of an `options` statement in "The `gated` interfaces Statement" on page 479. That `options` statement was peculiar to the `interfaces` statement. Many protocol statements will have their own `options` statement. There is also the global `options` statement. That statement must appear before any other configuration statements in the `/etc/gated.conf` file.

The general form of the global options statement is given in Example 11–6.

Example 11–6   Global `options` Form

```
options [nosend] [noresolv]
    [gendefault [preference pref] [gateway gwopts]]
    [syslog [upto] level] [mark time] ;
```

The available global options are described in Table 11–10.

Table 11–10   Global Options

OPTION	DESCRIPTION
`nosend`	Causes `gated` to send no packets. This option does not apply to BGP. This option is useful for testing.
`noresolv`	Suppresses the use of DNS to resolve hostnames. If there is insufficient routing information to resolve DNS names, `gated` will deadlock and require a restart. It is always best to eliminate or at least minimize hostname resolution in the `/etc/gated.conf` file.
`gendefault [preference pref]` `[gateway gwopts]`	Used for BGP default route generation. This option is discussed in Chapter 13.

Table 11–10   Global Options *(Continued)*

OPTION	DESCRIPTION
`syslog [upto]` *`level`*	Specifies the `syslog` *`level`* for `gated` messages to be written (to facility `daemon`). By default, `gated` logs level `info` and above which is equivalent to `syslog upto info`. Using `syslog info` would only capture `syslog` events at level `info`.
`mark` *`time`*	Causes `gated` to write a timestamp to the global trace file every *`time`* seconds. The timestamp is followed by the keyword `MARK`. Trace files specified in the stanza of a statement will not get this mark.

Definition Type Statements

There are three general configuration statements that fall into the category of definition statements. They are: `autonomoussystem`, `routerid`, and `martians`. The `autonomoussystem` and `routerid` statements are associated with BGP and OSPF and will be discussed later.

The `martians` statement, however, has general applicability. It describes addresses that are not to be routed or it permits addresses to be routed that otherwise would not be. Example 11–7 shows the form of a `martians` statement.

Example 11–7   Form for `martians` Statement

```
martians {
    host address [allow] ;
    network [mask mask | masklen number] [allow] ;
    default [allow] ;
} ;
```

Even though the specification for `martians` looks fairly simple, there is a fair amount of detail in the way in which network ranges can be specified. To illustrate the use of the `martians` statement, however, we provide Example 11–8.

Example 11–8   Sample Use of the `martians` Statement

```
martians {
    host 128.0.0.5 ;
    192.0.0.0 masklen 24 allow ;
    222.18.16.0 mask 255.255.255.0 ;
} ;
```

In this example, the system using this configuration entry will refuse to route the host 128.0.0.5 and the network 222.18.16.0/24. It will, on the other hand, route for the 192.0.0.0/24 network.

This capability is very important, especially for gateway routers to the Internet. Using the `martians` statement, you can configure your Internet gateway to refuse to route private addresses.

The `gated` software sets up certain martians by default. These are listed in Table 11–11. In order to use any of these addresses, you must use an entry like the third line of Example 11–8.

Table 11–11   Addresses That `gated` Will Not Route

MARTIAN NETWORK	NOTES
0.0.0.0/8	This address is a source-only address. See Chapter 4.
127.0.0.0/8	This network is reserved for loopbacks. See Chapter 4.
128.0.0.0/16	This network has been reserved by IANA.
192.0.0.0/24	This network has been reserved by IANA.
192.255.0.0/16	This range of networks has been reserved by IANA.
223.255.255.0/24	This network has been reserved by IANA.
255.255.240.0/17	This range of addresses is at the upper end of the reserved range of addresses.

Route Filtering

Numerous different statements, including `martians`, `static`, `aggregate`, `generate`, `import`, and `export`, can utilize the special `gated` syntax for filtering routes. We modestly introduced a part of this syntax in the previous section. This section describes that syntax, examples of which we consider later on. Note that this syntax is not a statement in itself, rather it needs to be part of a statement.

The general form of a filter is

```
network [mask mask | masklen len] [exact | refines | between low and
high]
```

where each of the parameters are given in Table 11–12.

Table 11–12   Parameters to the `network` Keyword

PARAMETER	DESCRIPTION
`network`	The network number in decimal dotted notation.
`mask mask`	Specifies the route mask in decimal dotted notation, `mask`. Either this or `masklen` may be used, but not both in the same filter.
`masklen len`	Specifies the route mask in prefix notation (without the preceding /). For example, `masklen 8` is the same as `mask 255.0.0.0`. Either this or `mask` may be used, but not both in the same filter.
`exact`	Specifies that the masked network must identically match the destination network number. This form is not used for CIDR or route aggregation.
`refines`	Specifies that the mask of the destination is longer (more network bits) than this route mask. This is the classical route aggregation syntax.
`between low and high`	Specifies that the mask of the destination must be at least as long as the `low` route mask but no longer than the `high` route mask.

Additionally, there are three special filtering keywords. They are:

```
all
default
host host
```

The `all` keyword matches anything. It can also be specified by

```
0.0.0.0 masklen 0
```

The default keyword matches the default route and can alternatively be specified by

```
0.0.0.0 mask 0.0.0.0 exact
```

The host keyword is used to match the specific *host*. It can equivalently be matched with

```
host masklen 32 exact
```

where *host* must be replaced with the IP address or hostname in question.

gated **Handling of ICMP**

The gated daemon can really only deal with two types of ICMP messages: router discovery (discussed in "Configuring gated for Router Discovery" on page 527) and redirects. On the other hand, gated can trace *all* ICMP communications. If you need to control the kernel handling of ICMP messages in general, the Linux *ipchains* utility is the tool that you need. You can learn more about ipchains by referencing *Linux System Security* and/or *Linux Routers* as cited in "For Further Reading" on page 546. We also cover some aspects of ipchains in Chapter 14.

The gated daemon supports two statements, other than routerdiscovery, for the handling of ICMP communications. They are the icmp and redirect statements.

The icmp statement is used only for tracing packets. The form for the icmp statement is given in Example 11–9. Note that all of the options described in "The traceoptions Statement" on page 484 related to the specification of a trace file apply here, even though not shown.

Example 11–9   Form of the icmp Stanza

```
icmp {
    traceoptions [[detail [send | recv]] packets] | [redirect]
        [routerdiscovery] [info] [error] ;
} ;
```

Either packets is used as the option or one or more of redirect, routerdiscovery, info, and/or error. Table 11–13 lists the trace options.

Table 11–13   Trace Options for `icmp`

TRACE OPTION	DESCRIPTION
`packets`	Traces all ICMP packets. Can be modified with `detail`, `send`, and `recv` as described in "The `traceoptions` Statement" on page 484.
`redirect`	Traces only ICMP redirects.
`routerdiscovery`	Traces only routerdiscovery messages.
`info`	Traces only ICMP requests and replies. See Chapter 4.
`error`	Traces only ICMP error messages. See Chapter 4.

You can also use the `except` keyword (described in "The `traceoptions` Statement" on page 484).

The `redirect` statement in `gated` controls whether or not *received* ICMP redirects are maintained in the kernel's routing table. Since `gated` operates at the Application layer of the TCP/IP stack, it is likely that ICMP redirects will be inserted into the routing cache by the kernel before `gated` has a chance to reject them (if so configured). Furthermore, `gated` can do *nothing* about ICMP messages sent by the system on which `gated` is running. If you need more finely grained control than this, you must use `ipchains`. By default, `gated` removes redirects when actively participating in RIP, OSPF, or IS-IS.

If these caveats are acceptable in your environment, then `gated` can be used to implement an ICMP redirect policy. Example 11–10 displays the form of the `redirect` statement.

Example 11–10   Form of the `redirect` Stanza

```
redirect on | off [ {
    preference pref ;
    interface iface_list [noredirects | redirects] ;
    trustedgateways router_list ;
    traceoptions options ;
} ] ;
```

We have already described most of the options in this stanza in previous sections, so we'll just highlight the `icmp` specific details. The `interface` option is used to specify whether or not redirects are to be accepted on the specified interface(s). The `trustedgateways` option takes a space separated list of systems from which ICMP redirects are accepted; all others are ignored. By default, `gated` accepts all redirect messages.

Static Routes with `gated`

Perhaps the simplest of all the protocol-type statements supported by `gated` is the very important `static` statement. Using `static` is the way to get static routes into the routing table when running `gated`. Functionally, it is similar to using the `route` command and/or placing static routes in an appropriate configuration file (see Chapter 6).

The form of the static statement is given in Example 11–11.

Example 11–11   The `static` Stanza

```
static {
    host host | default | network [mask mask | masklen len]
            gateway router [interface iface_list] [preference pref]
                    [retain] [reject] [blackhole] [noinstall] ;
    network [mask mask | masklen len]
            interface iface [preference pref]
                    [retain] [reject] [blackhole] [noinstall] ;
} ;
```

Each `static` stanza can contain two different forms of entries. The `gateway` form and the `interface` form. The `gateway` form is used to identify a specific *router* for the static route. It can be refined for exclusive association to specific interfaces with the `interface` option. The `interface` form is used to associate a particular route with a specific interface. This latter form of `interface` only accepts one interface per *network* entry. It can be used to set the route to the local interface and to support multiple addresses on one interface (i.e., aliases).

The `host`, `default`, and *network* filters are described in "Route Filtering" on page 491. The `interface` option, subject to the restriction identified in the previous paragraph, is described in "The gated interfaces Statement" on page 479. The remaining options available within the `static` stanza are described in Table 11–14.

Table 11–14   Available Options Within the `static` Stanza

Option	Description
`gateway router`	Specifies the `router` to which packets are to be forwarded with this route.
`preference pref`	Specifies the preference value, `pref`, of the static route. Used only for comparison of other routes learned via other protocols. The default for static routes is 60. See "`gated` Preferences" on page 478.
`retain`	When `gated` terminates, it removes all the routes from the routing table that it placed there. If `retain` is used, then it will not remove the route at termination.
`reject`	This keyword specifies that the route is not to be used. Any packets attempting to use this route will get an ICMP unreachable message. This type of route will have an `!` in the flags column of the routing table.
`blackhole`	This keyword has the identical effect of `reject` except that no ICMP unreachable messages are generated.
`noinstall`	Ordinarily, `gated` puts the route with the lowest preference in the routing table. Using this option prevents `gated` from installing this route in the kernel's routing table, but permits it to be advertised to other hosts and routers.

Let's look at an example to help clarify the `static` stanza. Example 11–12 illustrates an entry that specifies a default route to be installed in the kernel's routing table and also identifies two addresses for the `eth1` interface. Notice that for the 10.16.0.0 network, routing is disabled with the `reject` keyword. This means that the local system can send packets to this network but will not forward packets from other systems to this network.

Example 11–12   A Sample `static` Stanza

```
static {
    default gateway 192.111.23.153 interface eth0 retain ;
    10.16.0.0 masklen 16 interface eth1 retain reject ;
    10.254.1.0 masklen 24 interface eth1 retain ;
} ;
```

We explore other examples of the static stanza beginning in "A Routing Example" on page 531.

Import and Export Policies

The gated daemon provides extensive and flexible control over which routes learned from other systems are to be used and/or repropagated to other systems. gated permits the specification of import and export policies with the import and export statements, respectively. These statements are not required to cause the various protocols to do what they are supposed to do. For instance, RIP routers automatically propagate routes that they learn from other RIP routers—no import or export statements are required. However, RIP routers won't propagate static routes or routes from other protocols and that is where these statements come into play. These statements are protocol-specific and therefore we leave the details of protocol-specific implementations to later sections. Here, we look at some simple examples and generally define the syntax.

The use of the import statement specifies which routes are learned from other systems, learned from other protocols, or learned from specific static entries that are to be installed in the RIB. Example 11–13 illustrates a simple example that causes all ICMP redirects to be imported into the RIB (thus, overriding the default behavior whenever RIP, OSPF, or IS-IS is used).

Example 11–13   A Simple import Stanza

```
import proto redirect {
    all ;
} ;
```

There are many variations and options to using the import statement and we consider a few of them later on in this and the next chapter. Note that all route importation can only be controlled by the source of the routes being imported. Route exportation, on the other hand, can be controlled by both source and destination.

The export statement is used to tell gated which routes are to be exported via a particular protocol. For instance, if RIP is running on a router and you need it to propagate static routes via RIP, this can be accomplished with the export statement. Example 11–14 illustrates.

Example 11–14　　A Sample export Stanza

```
rip on {
    interface all version 2 broadcast ;
    trustedgateways 10.254.1.10 10.254.2.10 ;
} ;
static {
    146.18.0.0 masklen 16 exact retain ;
} ;
export proto rip {
    proto static {
        148.18.0.0 masklen 16 metric 2 ;
    } ;
} ;
```

So, what's going on in this example? The rip stanza specifies that this system is running RIP version 2 in broadcast mode to all of its interfaces. It will only accept rip communications from the two routers listed after the trustedgateways option. The rip stanza is more completely described in "Configuring gated for RIPv1 and RIPv2" on page 513.

After the rip stanza is a static stanza (see "Static Routes with gated" on page 495). It adds the static route shown to the local system's routing table. Since it is a static entry, it will not be propagated by RIP by default. Therefore, the export statement is used to put it into the RIB for export purposes and it will be advertised by RIP.

Generally, the export statement takes the form illustrated in Example 11–15.

Example 11–15　　General Form of an export Statement

```
export proto protospecifics restrict ;
export proto protospecifics {
    export_list ;
} ;
```

Here, protospecifics represents syntax specific to the protocol to which the routes are being exported. The specifics of the different protocols are discussed in conjunction with the more general discussion of a given protocol. The export_list represents the sources of those routes.

The first form of the export statement given in Example 11–15 is used to prevent routes from being advertised via the indicated protocol. This is the purpose of the restrict keyword. The second form of the export statement provides for the enumeration of the source of routes in the form of export_list, which can be one or more of the possible statements as shown in Example 11–16.

Example 11–16   Statements for *export_list*

```
proto bgp as ASN restrict ;
proto bgp as ASN [metric MED] {
    route_filter [restrict | metric MED] ;
} ;
proto rip [interface iface_list | gateway gateways] restrict ;
proto rip [interface iface_list | gateway gateways] [metric metric] {
    route_filter [restrict | metric metric] ;
} ;
proto ospf | ospfase restrict ;
proto ospf | ospfase [metric metric] {
    route_filter [restrict | metric metric] ;
} ;
proto proto | all aspath aspath_regexpr origin [any | igp |
    egp | incomplete] restrict ;
proto proto | all aspath aspath_regexpr origin [any | igp |
    egp | incomplete] [metric metric] {
        route_filter [restrict | metric metric] ;
} ;
proto proto | all tag tag restrict ;
proto proto | all tag tag [metric metric] {
    route_filter [restrict | metric metric] ;
} ;
proto direct | static | kernel [interface iface_list] restrict ;
proto direct | static | kernel [interface iface_list] [metric metric] {
    route_filter [restrict | metric metric] ;
} ;
proto default | aggregate restrict ;
proto default | aggregate [metric metric] {
        route_filter [restrict | metric metric] ;
} ;
```

Many of these statements will be described and/or examples will be given
when the pertinent protocol is described. It is worth pointing out here, however,
that each of the statements can utilize the restrict keyword. Whenever that
keyword is used, it has the effect of prohibiting the specified route or routes
from being exported by the indicated protocol. It is important to bear in mind
(and therefore is worth repeating) that the syntax described in Example 11–16 is
used to specify the source of routing information for exportation via the export
statement given in Example 11–15.

Route Aggregation with gated

Routing aggregation and CIDR are described in Chapter 6. We saw that using
aggregation can reduce the number of routing table entries and thereby reduce
the search time for a specific route. Routing aggregation can also reduce the
amount of information passed between routers. By default, gated performs no
routing aggregation. However, it can be configured to aggregate routes with
either the aggregate or generate statements.

The `aggregate` statement provides a way of creating a more general route based on information received from other routers. The `aggregate` statement is essentially a limited scope aggregation in that it will only route packets to the aggregate route if the packet being forwarded matches one of the contributing routes to the aggregate. Additionally, the aggregated route created by the aggregate statement is *never* used by the router on which it is configured. Thus, the `aggregate` statement, for it to be of any use, is always followed by an `export` statement that exports the aggregated route.

Consider Figure 11–1.

Suppose that on the router, A, you want to use an aggregate route for `192.168.0.0/16`. Suppose further that the only routes learned by B from other routers are `192.168.4.0/24`, `192.168.7.0/24`, and `192.168.12.0/24` because

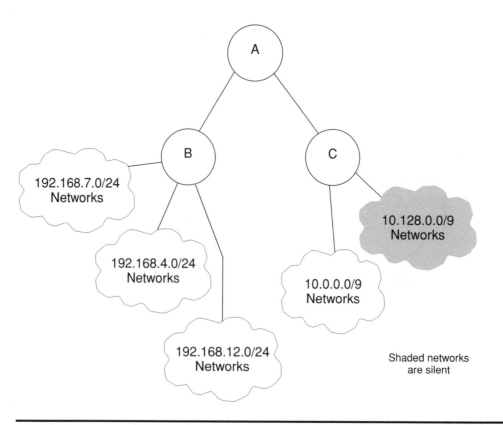

Figure 11–1   Different Route Aggregation with `aggregate` and `generate`

they are all that exist. Clearly, from the diagram, A simply needs to route any-thing to these networks via an aggregate of, for example, `192.168.0.0/16`. If B uses the `aggregate` statement to create the aggregate `192.168.0.0/16` route and export it (via some protocol like RIP or OSPF), A will forward all packets destined for `192.168.0.0` to B. B, however, will only forward the packet if the packet to be forwarded matches one of the components of the aggregate (`192.168.4.0/24`, `192.168.7.0/24`, and `192.168.12.0/24`, in this case) because B *does not actually use* the aggregate. If B receives a packet with a desti-nation of `192.168.44.8/24`, B will generate an ICMP unreachable message even though the routing table on A shows the aggregate `192.168.0.0/16` entry. The reason for this type of route aggregation is to prevent the propagation of packets that loop until the time-to-live field expires. For example, if `192.168.44.0/24` doesn't exist (which it doesn't in this example) and A for-wards the packet based on the aggregate `192.168.0.0/16`, it will go to B. Sup-pose B has the same aggregate and also has a default router entry for A. Since there is no `192.168.44.0/24` network, B will send the packet back to A due to its default router entry. We examine an example use of `aggregate` in "A Rout-ing Example" on page 531.

On the other hand, you may have good reason to create an aggregate route similar to one that could be created with the `route` command (see Chapter 6 for discussions about the `route` command) or with the `static` statement in `/etc/gated.conf`. Perhaps there are numerous routes that are not propagated, but they exist nonetheless. For instance, Figure 11–1 shows the collection of net-works `10.128.0.0/9` in gray, indicating that no routes are propagated from this network and therefore not propagated by C to A. Perhaps this is due to the fact that these networks are experimental and are up and down a lot. In any event, if you want to make routing in this environment available to and from them via an aggregate route, something other than the `aggregate` statement must be used. The `gated` daemon provides this capability with the `generate` statement. In this case, you can also use a static aggregate route that you would then export from C.

Note that you can create default routes using `aggregate` and `generate`. Ordinarily, creating a default route in this way is only done by routers on an AS border or an OSPF or BGP backbone—it is not a general purpose substitute for a default router. Aggregated routes created with either the `aggregate` or `gen-erate` statements will *not*, by default, be propagated. Only through an `export` statement will these routes be included in any type of communication to other routers or hosts.

The form for the `aggregate` and `generate` stanzas are identical and provided in Example 11–17.

Example 11–17   Form for the `aggregate` and `generate` Stanzas

```
aggregate | generate default | route_filter [preference pref] [brief] {
    proto [all | protocol ]
            [as asn | tag tag | aspath aspathexp ] restrict ;
    proto [all | protocol ]
            [as asn | tag tag | aspath aspathexp ] {
                route_filter ;
                [route_filter] ;
                [ ... ] ;
    } ;
    [preference pref {
        route_filter [restrict | preference pref] ;
    } ; ]
] } ;
```

Here, `route_filter` means the use of a *network* filter statement as described in "Route Filtering" on page 491. The `brief`, `as`, and `aspath` options are used by BGP (see Chapter 13 for further details about BGP). The `tag` option is used for route filtering in `import` and `export` statements (see "Importing and Exporting BGP Routes" on page 637). Either of these statements create an aggregate route either for a `default` or for the specified `route_filter`. The aggregated route is created from routes learned via the specified protocols following the `proto` keyword, which could be the special word `all`, meaning create the aggregate from all protocols. Multiple `proto` stanzas can also be specified. The `restrict` keyword means that the route matching the `route_filter` is not to be used in creating the aggregate. The `preference` value is used to determine, given multiple routes to the same destination, which one should be used for the purposes of the aggregate.

It should be noted that the protocol value following the `proto` keyword can take some special values besides the routing table protocol (like `rip`, `ospf`, or `bgp`). These special keywords are `static`, `direct`, `kernel`, and `aggregate`. The use of `static` is for routes that have been defined with the `static` statement. The use of `direct` is for local interface IP addresses. The use of `kernel` is for routes that have been installed with the `route` command. And, finally, you can actually add existing aggregate routes to an aggregate by specifying `proto aggregate`. We look at examples utilizing these statements later in this chapter and then again in the next two chapters.

The gdc Helper Utility

The gdc utility is a front-end tool that makes controlling gated easier. It provides a simple command line interface for sending signals to gated. It also provides syntax checking of new or modified configuration files and the changing of which configuration file is used. It further permits the use of a special group, gdmaint, if gdc is installed with set user identifier (SUID) to root. Configuring gdc in that way permits any user in the gdmaint group to control gated with gdc.

The gdc utility takes both flags and commands. The flags are listed in Table 11–15.

Table 11–15   gdc Flags

FLAGS	DESCRIPTION
-d	Debug mode.
-n	Runs without modifying the routing table. Used for debugging and on multihomed systems.
-q	Runs in quiet mode. All messages to standard output are suppressed and all errors are written to syslog. Useful for use in scripts.
-t seconds	Specifies the time in seconds that gdc waits for gated to complete start-up or termination. If this option is not specified, gdc waits 10 seconds by default.
-p path_to_bin	Specifies the fully qualified name of the gated binary, path_to_bin. For example, -p /usr/sbin/gated.
-l path_to_pidfile	Specifies the fully qualified name of the PID file, path_to_pidfile. For example, -p /var/run/ gated.pid
-c size	Sets the maximum size in bytes of the core file. If gdc COREDUMP is used, then the core file cannot exceed this size.

Table 11–15   gdc Flags *(Continued)*

Flags	Description
-m *size*	Sets the maximum *size* in bytes of the data segment used by gated. Useful on systems that have small default segment sizes. Only an issue on systems with little memory for its purpose.
-s *size*	Sets the maximum *size* in bytes of the stack allocated for gated. Useful on systems that impose small defaults. Only an issue on systems with little memory for its purpose.
-f *size*	Sets the maximum *size* of the dump file (usually /var/tmp/gated_dump) produced by gated.

Most of the commands to gdc are described in Table 11–16.

Table 11–16   gdc Commands

Command	Action
COREDUMP	Causes gated to terminate and dump core.
dump	Causes gated to write its current state information to /var/tmp/gated_dump. Same as sending gated a SIGINT.
interface	Causes gated to reread the kernel interface list for new interfaces. Same as sending gated a SIGUSR2.
term	Gracefully terminates gated. Same as sending gated a SIGTERM.
KILL	Ungraceful termination. Same as sending gated a SIGKILL.
reconfig	Causes gated to reread its configuration file. Same as sending gated a SIGHUP.
toggletrace	Turns tracing on if tracing is currently off and off if currently on. Same as sending gated a SIGUSR1.

Table 11–16   gdc Commands *(Continued)*

COMMAND	ACTION
checkconf	Checks /etc/gated.conf for syntax errors. Reports whether or not an error occurred to standard error. Writes actual errors to /var/tmp/gated_parse.
checknew	Like checkconf except that it reads /etc/gated.conf+. In this way, modifications can be placed in a file other than the configuration file.
newconf	Moves /etc/gated.conf- (if it exists) to /etc/gated.conf--, /etc/gated.conf to /etc/gated.conf-, and /etc/gated.conf+ to /etc/gated.conf. Fails if /etc/gated.conf+ does not exist or is of zero size, but will perform this operation *even if* syntax errors exist in /etc/gated.conf+.
backout	Reverses the operation of newconf above unless /etc/gated.conf- doesn't exist or is of zero size, or /etc/gated.conf+ exists and is not of zero size.
BACKOUT	Forces a backout even if /etc/gated.conf+ exists and is of nonzero size.
modeconf	Sets all configuration files to permissions 0664, owner root, group owner gdmaint. This operation permits users in the gdmaint group to execute gdc commands.
createconf	Creates an empty /etc/gated.conf+ file, if it does not exist, and sets permissions 0664, owner root, group owner gdmaint.
running	Determines if gated is running by reading the PID from /var/run/gated.pid and verifying that the PID is an active process. Exits with 0 if gated is running; nonzero return otherwise.

Table 11–16   gdc Commands *(Continued)*

COMMAND	ACTION
start	Starts gated. An error is returned if gated is already running. gdc waits 10 seconds or the number of seconds specified by -t for gated to write its PID to /var/run/gated.pid. If gated fails to do this within the specified time frame, gdc returns a nonzero status and writes an error message to standard error. If gated returns an error status, then so does gdc. Otherwise, a zero exit status is returned.
stop	Stops gated gracefully, if possible, ungracefully otherwise. gdc does this by sending a SIGTERM and waiting the specified delay (as specified by -t or 10 seconds by default) for gated to terminate. If gated does not terminate two seconds after sending the signal, gdc posts a message to standard error indicating that gated has yet to terminate. If gated does not terminate the first time, a second SIGTERM is sent. If it fails the second time, gdc sends a SIGKILL. gdc and returns an exit code of 0 once it detects that gated has terminated; a nonzero return code otherwise or if gated is not running.
restart	Executes gdc stop and then gdc start.
rmcore	Removes any existing gated core files.
rmdump	Removes /var/tmp/gated_dump.
rmparse	Removes any /var/tmp/gated_parse files.

Let's consider some example uses of gdc. Example 11–18 shows a successful gdc start. It also illustrates the use of the -p flag.

Example 11–18   Starting gated with gdc

```
# gdc -p /usr/sbin/gated start
gated started, pid 12974
#
```

We can stop gated with gdc stop. We use -t 8 to specify a time delay of eight seconds. Notice that gdc only waits six seconds after issuing the second SIGTERM. Example 11–19 illustrates.

Example 11–19   Stopping gated with gdc

```
# gdc -t 8 stop
gated signalled but still running, waiting 6 seconds more
gated terminated
#
```

To illustrate the behavior of gdc restart, we execute it when gated is not running. Example 11–20 shows the results.

Example 11–20   Using gdc restart

```
# gdc -p /usr/sbin/gated restart
gated not currently running
gated started, pid 12983
#
```

Now, verify that gated is running with gdc running, as shown in Example 11–21.

Example 11–21   Verify That gated is Running with gdc running

```
# gdc running
gated is running (pid 12983)
#
```

Throughout the remainder of this chapter we explore the other uses of gdc, beginning with the next section.

An Example Start-up Script for gated

In Example 11–22, we provide a sample start-up script for gated. This script is derived from that provided with Red Hat 6.2. You can use this or something similar to control sending any available signal to gated. This script does so by using the gdc front-end. Of course, you will also want to link[2] this script to the appropriate directories and names within the /etc/rc.d start-up infrastructure for automatic shutdown and start-up during reboots.

---

2. This is not necessary with Red Hat if you use the chkconfig utility. This script provides the necessary information for chkconfig. See the chkconfig(8) man page for further details.

Example 11–22   Sample `gated` Start-up Script

```sh
#!/bin/sh
#
# gated        This script is used to start/stop the gated routing
#              daemon
#
# chkconfig: - 32 75
# description: Starts and stops gated (routing daemon). GateD is a modular \
#      software program consisting of core services, a routing database, \
#      and protocol modules supporting multiple routing protocols (RIP \
#      versions 1 and 2, DCN HELLO, OSPF version 2, EGP version 2 and BGP \
#      version 2 through 4)
# processname: gated
# pidfile: /var/run/gated.pid
# config: /etc/gated.conf

# Source function library.
. /etc/rc.d/init.d/functions

# Source networking configuration.
. /etc/sysconfig/network

# Check that networking is up.
[ ${NETWORKING} = "no" ] && exit 0

gdc=/usr/bin/gdc

[ -f /etc/gated.conf ] || exit 0
[ -f $gdc ] || exit 0

PATH=$PATH:/usr/bin:/usr/sbin

RETVAL=0

# See how we were called.
case "$1" in
  start)
        echo -n "Starting gated: "
        daemon gated
        RETVAL=$?
        [ $RETVAL -eq 0 ] && touch /var/lock/subsys/gated
        echo
        ;;
  stop)
        # Stop daemons.
        echo -n "Shutting down gated: "
        $gdc stop
        RETVAL=$?
        if [ $RETVAL -eq 0 ] ; then
                echo "gated done"
        rm -f /var/lock/subsys/gated
        else
                echo
        fi
        ;;
  status)
        $gdc running
        RETVAL=$?
```

Example 11–22   Sample `gated` Start-up Script *(Continued)*

```
        ;;
  reload)
        $gdc reconfig
        RETVAL=$?
        ;;
  restart)
        $gdc restart
        RETVAL=$?
        ;;
  toggle)
        $gdc toggletrace
        RETVAL=$?
        ;;
  dump)
        $gdc dump
        RETVAL=$?
        ;;
  *)
        echo "Usage: $0 {start|stop|status|reload|restart|toggle|dump}"
        exit 1
esac

exit $RETVAL
```

If you aren't using Red Hat, you will need to adjust the beginning portion of this script to suit your distribution. The action of this script based on the arguments given is very straightforward. If given the `start` argument, it starts the daemon using the `daemon` function. The `daemon` function is defined in the Red Hat file `/etc/rc.d/init.d/daemon` and simply checks for a nice value to use (which would be 0 in this case). If you aren't using Red Hat, just remove `daemon` and you probably also want to remove `touch /var/lock/subsys/gated`. You can adjust these items to suit your distribution.

The `stop` argument invokes `gdc stop` (described in "The `gdc` Helper Utility" on page 503). If you aren't using Red Hat, adjust the remaining portion of this case statement as needed. The remaining arguments are a straightforward invocation of the `gdc` command.

RIP

RIP is generally described in "RIP" on page 207. The differences between RIPv1 and RIPv2 are noted there as well. The `gated` daemon can be configured to support either RIPv1 or RIPv2 or both. In order to get a good understanding of the configuration options to `gated`, let's first look at RIPv1 and RIPv2 in more detail.

RIPv1 and RIPv2

It helps to look at the format of RIPv1 and RIPv2 messages (requests and responses) to clarify the options to `gated` for these two protocol versions. So, that's what we'll do.

The format of the RIPv1 message is shown in Figure 11–2. The message has two parts, the RIP Header and the Route. Only one Route is shown, but there may be many others (as indicated by "Other Routes" in the figure)—in fact, there may be up to 24 additional routes.

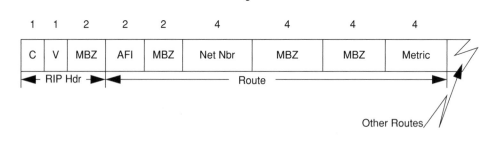

Figure 11–2   RIPv1 Message Format

The fields shown in the RIP Header and Route portion of the RIP message are described in Table 11–17.

Table 11–17   Fields of the RIPv1 Message

FIELD	DESCRIPTION
C	The RIPv1 command. A value of 1 means that this is a request. A value of 2 means that this is a response. This field can also carry a value of 5, which is an undocumented request commonly known as a *poll*. This particular type of request was initially developed by Sun. It can be used by `gated` and the `ripquery` command.
V	The RIP version. It must be 1.
MBZ	All fields with this indicator must be zero.

Table 11–17   Fields of the RIPv1 Message *(Continued)*

FIELD	DESCRIPTION
AFI	Address family identifier. A value of 2 indicates that the addresses contained in each route are IP addresses.
Net Nbr	The destination network number or IP address for the route.
Metric	The metric associated with the route. This value can be 1 through and including 16; however, 16 means infinity and the destination is not reachable.

A RIP request, then, will have a value of 1 set in the c field. The most common sort of request is the broadcast request for an entire routing table. That type of request will have 0 in the AFI field, 16 in the Metric field, and zeros elsewhere. All other requests will have an enumerated list of routes by setting the appropriate value in the Net Nbr field. The system receiving the request will put the metric associated with the route in the Metric field. If there is no route, it puts 16 in the Metric field. Once complete, it sends the response back to the requesting system. The special value of 0.0.0.0 in the Net Nbr field is used to indicate a default route. If the requesting system sends out the request using a source port of 520 (RIP's port—see Chapter 7 for a discussion of port numbers), then only systems running in broadcast mode will answer. If the source port is other than 520, then even systems running in listen-only mode will answer.

The format of the RIPv2 message is shown in Figure 11–3.

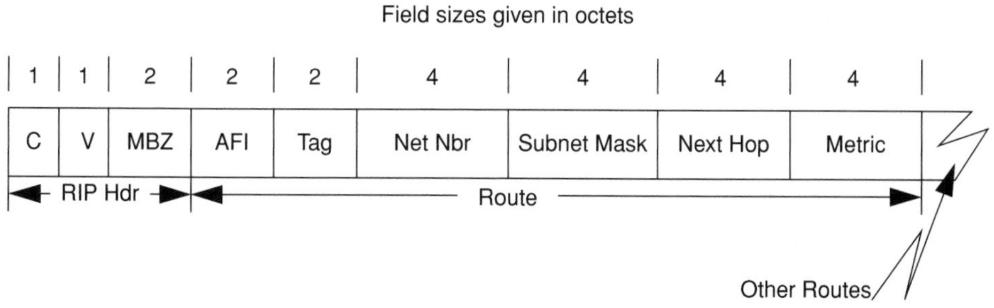

Field sizes given in octets

Figure 11–3   RIPv2 Message Format

Note that the only difference in the RIPv2 message is that the two fields in the Route portion of the packet that were MBZ fields in Figure 11–2 for RIPv1 are used by RIPv2 for the Subnet Mask field and Next Hop fields, respectively. The Subnet Mask field carries the route mask to be applied to the address carried in the Net Nbr field. The Next Hop field contains the IP address of a router that can be locally reached. The purpose of this field is to advertise routers that are external to RIPv2—that is, they are not running RIP.

The other MBZ field in the Route portion of the message from RIPv1 is consumed by the Tag field in RIPv2. This field carries a route tag that indicates from which protocol the associated route came from if not from RIP. The primary purpose of this field is to synchronize routes with BGP and, if used for that purpose, will contain the ASN of the router from which the route was obtained. This field is ignored by gated. But gated does permit the use of a similar field (see "Importing and Exporting BGP Routes" on page 637).

The command (C) field is identical to RIPv1 in RIPv2. The version (V) field carries a 2. All remaining fields are identical.

Recall that the other difference between RIPv1 and RIPv2 is that RIPv2 offers authentication. Authentication is accomplished by replacing the first Route entry in a RIPv2 message with special authentication fields. Figure 11–4 shows these special fields.

Notice that the AFI field carries the special value 0xffff. This indicates that the Route is really an authentication message. The Auth Type field specifies the type of authentication used—currently, either a simple password or an MD5 hashed password. The MD5 hashed password scheme for RIPv2 is defined in RFC 2082. The Authentication field carries the password (whichever type).

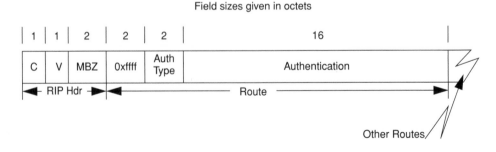

Figure 11–4   RIPv2 Authentication Format

The most secure way of implementing this method is to require authentication all the time. This means that a system or router running RIPv2 securely will never pay any attention to RIPv1 messages and won't respond to queries from utilities like `ripquery` without the correct password. On the other hand, RIPv1 systems can listen to RIPv2 "secure" messages because RIPv1 will ignore a message with the AFI field set to anything but 2, and we can configure `gated` to cause it to ignore those fields that must be zero. We will look at implementing this capability with `gated` in "RIP Authentication with `gated`" on page 518.

Configuring `gated` for RIPv1 and RIPv2

We considered implementing RIPv1 using `routed` in Chapter 6. In this section we look at implementing RIPv1 and RIPv2 with `gated`.

The form for a `rip` stanza in `/etc/gated.conf` is given in Example 11–23.

Example 11–23   The `rip` Stanza

```
rip on | off [ {
    broadcast | nobroadcast ;
    nocheckzero ;
    preference pref ;
    defaultmetric metric ;
    query authentication none | simple pw | md5* pw ;
    interface iface_list [noripin | ripin] [noripout | ripout]
        [metricin metric] [metricout metric]
        [version 1 | 2 [multicast | broadcast] ]
        [ [secondary] authentication [none | simple pw |
            md5 md5_stanza ] ;
    trustedgateways list ;
    sourcegateways list ;
    traceoptions options ;
} ] ;
```

*. Although specified here and in the `gated` documentation, this option does not currently work. See "RIP Authentication with `gated`" on page 518.

Although the RIP protocol statement used by `gated` seems rather simple, there is quite a lot of detail to cover, especially with respect to the authentication components. So, we'll cover the authentication component separately in "RIP Authentication with `gated`" on page 518.

When `gated` is compiled (see "Obtaining, Compiling, and Installing `gated`" on page 470), it turns on RIP by default. So, even if your `/etc/gated.conf` file has no `rip` stanza, `gated` will behave as if

```
rip on ;
```

were in the `/etc/gated.conf` file. This causes RIP to behave in listen-only mode if there is only one interface, and in broadcast (or multicast, if the interfaces support it) mode if there are two or more interfaces. Thus, if you don't want your system to use RIP and you are running a default compiled `gated`, then you must put

```
rip off ;
```

in the `/etc/gated.conf` file. This is the only protocol that `gated` treats in this way.

Table 11–18 lists the statements within the `rip` stanza and provides a description of each.

Table 11–18   RIP Stanza Statements

STATEMENT	DESCRIPTION
`broadcast|nobroadcast`	By default, RIP will run in broadcast mode if two or more interfaces are present and listen-only mode otherwise. You can control this behavior with these statements. Using `broadcast` forces the system to run RIP in broadcast mode regardless of the number of interfaces. Using `nobroadcast` forces the system to run RIP in listen-only mode.
`nocheckzero`	Normally, RIPv1 will ignore any messages that have something other than 0 in the MBZ fields (see Figure 11–2 on page 510). By using this statement, RIPv1 will accept such messages and in particular RIPv2 messages that use these fields for other purposes (see Figure 11–3 on page 511). Note that it only makes sense to use this option if an interface is operating in RIPv1 mode (see Table 11–19 on page 516).
`preference pref`	Sets the preference of all routes learned via RIP. The default is 100. See "`gated` Preferences" on page 478. This value can be overridden by the use of `preference` in an `import` statement.

Table 11–18   RIP Stanza Statements *(Continued)*

STATEMENT	DESCRIPTION
`defaultmetric` *`metric`*	The value of `metric` set by the `defaultmetric` statement is used whenever RIP broadcasts routes learned from other protocols. This value can be overridden by one set in an `export` statement.
`query authentication`	This controls the authentication requirement for all RIP requests including poll requests generated by `ripquery` (RIP poll requests are defined in Table 11–17 on page 510). In other words, this statement only applies to RIP messages in which the c field, as described in "RIPv1 and RIPv2" on page 510, is set to 1 or 5. The default authentication requirement is `none`, meaning that no authentication is performed. This option is discussed in detail in "RIP Authentication with `gated`" on page 518.
`interface` *`iface_list`*	This statement sets specific options to each interface or groups of interfaces specified by *`iface_list`*. The syntax for *`iface_list`* are those described in Table 11–7 on page 480.
`trustedgateways` *`list`*	Specifies a space-separated *`list`* of hostnames or IP addresses from which RIP will accept updates. If this option is specified, then updates will only be accepted from routers in the list. If this option is not specified, then updates will be accepted from any routers.

Table 11–18   RIP Stanza Statements *(Continued)*

STATEMENT	DESCRIPTION
sourcegateways *list*	Specifies a space-separated *list* of hostnames or IP addresses to which gated will *unicast* RIP updates. This overrides the any noripout specifications (described in Table 11–19). This option is useful for configuring a router that does not broadcast or multicast RIP but needs to propagate certain RIP routes to other RIP routers.
traceoptions *options*	Specifies the trace *options* in a space-separated list. RIP supports all of the trace options described in "The traceoptions Statement" on page 484. Additionally, RIP supports the following trace options: packets (traces all packets), request (traces request packets only), and response (traces response packets only). Each of these options can be modified with the detail, send, and recv keywords.

The gated implementation of RIP supports multiple interface statements within the rip stanza (as shown in Example 11–23) so that different interfaces, or groups of interfaces, can be treated differently. The interface statement within the RIP protocol supports a number of options which are described in Table 11–19.

Table 11–19   Options to the interface Statement in the rip Stanza

OPTION	DESCRIPTION
noripin | ripin	Specifies whether or not the interface(s) will listen to RIP messages. noripin means they won't, ripin means they will.

Table 11–19   Options to the `interface` Statement in the `rip` Stanza *(Continued)*

OPTION	DESCRIPTION
`noripout` | `ripout`	Specifies whether or not the interface(s) will send (via broadcast or multicast) RIP messages. `noripout` means they won't, `ripout` means they will.
`metricin` *metric*	Specifies the absolute *metric* associated with all RIP routes learned on this interface(s). If not specified, the hop count is used. Use of this option is to make routes from other interfaces specified by RIP more desirable.
`metricout` *metric*	Specifies the *metric* to be added to routes that are sent out this interface(s). The default is zero. The purpose of this metric is to make other RIP routes more desirable than this one.
`version 1` | `2 [multicast` | `broadcast]`	Specifies the version of RIP used for outbound packets on this interface(s). The default is 1, meaning that RIPv1 packets are sent. Specifying version 2 causes all outbound packets to use RIPv2 format and multicast. If multicast is unavailable or broadcast is specified, then RIPv1 compatible RIPv2 packets are sent.

Table 11–19   Options to the `interface` Statement in the `rip` Stanza *(Continued)*

OPTION	DESCRIPTION
`[secondary] authentication [none | simple pw | md5 md5_stanza ]`	This `authentication` statement applies to the specified interface(s) and only to RIP messages for which the `c` field, as described in "RIPv1 and RIPv2" on page 510, is set to 2. If other than `none`, all inbound RIP messages are authenticated with the specified scheme and all outbound messages are generated with the specified scheme. Two authentication methods can be specified per interface: primary and secondary. The secondary method must be specified with the `secondary` keyword. Outbound RIP messages are always processed with the primary method, while inbound packets are checked against both methods. RIP authentication is detailed in the next section. If no authentication is specified, then `none` is assumed.

We explore uses of the `rip` stanza beginning in "A Routing Example" on page 531.

RIP Authentication with `gated`

The RIP authentication message format is described in "RIPv1 and RIPv2" on page 510. The `gated` daemon utilizes this format for two purposes.

- authenticating `ripquery` poll requests and host or router requests
- authenticating RIP exchanges between routers—that is, response messages

The former authentication is controlled by the `query authentication` statement within the `rip` stanza. The later authentication is controlled on an interface list basis as part of the `interface` statement using the `authentication` option. The formats of these two authentication statements are somewhat different (see Example 11–23 on page 513). We already defined the `none` option to mean that no authentication is to be performed. In an environment in which you are not concerned about users reading the routing tables of systems and/or you are not concerned about routing table interchanges among the routers, use `none`.

On the other hand, if you are concerned about which users are viewing the routing tables in the environment, you need to configure `query authentica-tion` appropriately. Additionally, if you are worried about inappropriate data being introduced into the routing tables of one or more of your systems, and particularly the routers, then using the `authentication` option to the `inter-face` statement can help. Although the `gated` documentation suggests that the `md5` option can be used with `query authentication`, use of this option as of this writing does not work.

WARNING

The documentation for the syntax of the `query authentication md5` statement is incorrect. It suggests that the format of this statement is the same as that for the `authentication` statement, which is not true. The correct syntax is `query authentication md5` *pw*, where *pw* is an 8 octet value in decimal dotted notation, an 8 octet hex value preceeded by 0x, or an 8 octet quoted string. Unfortunately, while this syntax is acceptable, it does not work at the time of this writing. This is very unfortunate because a simple password traverses the network in the clear and can therefore be sniffed. Thus, without MD5 capabilities, the security offered by this mechanism is minimal.

The use of `simple` allows for the use of a simple cleartext password *pw*. It is supported by both statements, `query authentication` and `authentication`, and both statements use the same syntax for `simple` authentication. The value of *pw* can be 8 one-octet decimal digits (each digit must be between 0 and 255) separated by periods (*decimal dotted notation*), a one- to 8-octet hexadecimal string preceded by `0x`, or a one- to 8-character quoted string. Whatever the *pw*, it is passed in the RIPv2 authentication message in the clear and can therefore be easily captured with a network sniffer. Because of this, it makes a poor choice of authentication but is useful in trusted environments in which you want to restrict from which routers a particular host or router updates its routing tables (although this can be handled with the `trustedgateways` and `sourcegateways` statements).

The use of `md5` permits much greater security. It is only functional for the `authentication` statement, as of this writing. Instead of passing a password in the clear, the use of `md5` causes `gated` to compute the MD5 cryptographic hash[3] (MD5 hash) of the RIP message using the given password. It then includes this in the `Authentication` field of the message (see Figure 11–4 on page 512) and sends it over the network. The recipient, who also has the password (this shared password is often called *shared key*), receives the packet and computes the MD5 hash. If the computed hash matches the one carried in the `Authentication` field, then the message is accepted and the routes are accepted. If the MD5 hash values don't match, then the message is ignored.

There is nothing in this scheme that prevents the use of a network sniffer from capturing all of the information contained in the messages. All this MD5 authentication scheme does is provide a way to prevent tampering of the message or spoofing of messages. The only realistic way to tamper or spoof MD5 authenticated messages is to obtain the shared password. How to prevent *that* from occurring is an entirely different topic. See, for example, *Linux System Security* as cited in "For Further Reading" on page 546.

The `md5` option utilizes its own stanza, the form for which is shown in Example 11–24. Note that the form shown here *cannot* be used by itself! It must be preceded with the `authenticate` statement as part of an `interface` statement.

---

3. A cryptographic hash is a checksum which has been computed using a cryptographic one-way hash function (or message digest) such as the RSA Data Security, Inc. Message Digest 5 (MD5) algorithm. If you are unfamiliar with these types of functions and/or cryptography in general, read the outstanding book *Network Security: Private Communications in a Public World* as cited in "For Further Reading" on page 546.

Example 11–24 Form of the md5 Option

```
md5 [ password | {
     key pw id idn [ {
             [start-generate time ; ]
             [stop-generate time ; ]
             [start-accept time ; ]
             [stop-accept time ; ]
     } ] ;
     key pw id idn [ {
             [start-generate time ; ]
             [stop-generate time ; ]
             [start-accept time ; ]
             [stop-accept time ; ]
     } ] ;
<other similar entries may appear each with distinct idn values>
} ] ;
```

Note that the md5 stanza supports multiple key entries. Each such entry contains information about a particular password for a particular identification number. The meanings of the entries shown in Example 11–24 are described in Table 11–20.

Table 11–20 Description of md5 Stanza Authentication Parameters for RIP

PARAMETER	DESCRIPTION
password	If there's only the MD5 key, then it becomes part of the query authentication or authentication statement; for example, query authentication md5 "secret01".
key pw	The key keyword is used to indicate that what follows is the password or cryptographic key, pw. As with the pw parameter to the simple option, this pw can be a one- to 8-octet decimal value in decimal dotted notation, a one- to 8-octet hexadecimal value prefixed with 0x, or a one- to 8-character string in quotes. The pw and idn must identically match on all systems participating in this scheme.
id idn	The id keyword is used to indicate that an identification number, idn follows, where $1 \leq idn \leq 255$.

Table 11–20   Description of md5 Stanza Authentication Parameters for RIP *(Continued)*

PARAMETER	DESCRIPTION
start-generate *time*	This indicates the date and time at which this key starts being used for generating authentication messages. *time* is specified in YYYY/MM/DD HH:MM format; for example, start-generate 2000/06/30 18:30. The default is to always generate the key.
stop-generate *time*	This indicates the date and time at which this key stops being used for generating authentication messages. *time* is as described for start-generate above.
start-accept *time*	This indicates the date and time at which this key starts being used verifying incoming authentication messages. *time* is as described for start-generate above. If not specified, the key will always be accepted.
stop-accept *time*	This indicates the date and time at which this key stops being used verifying incoming authentication messages. *time* is as described for start-generate above.

Let's consider an example of each type of authentication to help clarify these descriptions. First, we consider a query authentication statement using simple authentication. Example 11–25 shows a configuration file for a router with the simple query authentication enabled. Note that the password is "foobie01."

Example 11–25   Sample rip Stanza with simple query authentication

```
rip on {
        interface 10.254.11.10 10.254.12.10 ripin ripout version 2 ;
        interface 172.16.0.1 172.17.0.1 noripin noripout ;
        query authentication simple "foobie01" ;
        trustedgateways 10.254.11.1 10.254.12.1 ;
        traceoptions "/var/log/gated.trace" request ;
} ;
```

Notice that within the rip stanza we are tracing requests to the file /var/log/gated.trace. That way we can see what this system is doing with the authentication.

Now, if we attempt to use `ripquery` to get the routing table on `foghorn` without the password, it fails. There are no error messages to standard out in this case, as shown in Example 11–26.

Example 11–26   Failed `ripquery` Attempt

```
[root@foghorn /root]# ripquery foghorn
[root@foghorn /root]#
```

The trace file, pertinent portion displayed in Example 11–27, shows what happened.

Example 11–27   Authentication Failure As Reported in the Trace File

```
Jul  4 19:52:44 rip_recv: ignoring RIP Poll packet from 10.254.11.10+1048 -
authentication failure
```

NOTE

The error message given in Example 11–27 will always appear when a system restarts its RIP daemon (`gated` or otherwise) because there is no way to set up `gated` to supply the password sought by `query authentication`. This actually is no real problem as `foghorn` (in this case) will gratuitously advertise its table within 30 seconds.

Supplying the password to the `ripquery` command, however, results in success, as shown in Example 11–28.

Example 11–28   Authenticated and Successful `ripquery`

```
[root@foghorn /root]# ripquery -a foobie01 foghorn
184 bytes from foghorn(10.254.11.10) version 2:
    10.254.12.0/255.255.255.0     router 10.254.11.1      metric  4  tag 0000
  192.168.255.0/255.255.255.0     router 10.254.11.1      metric  2  tag 0000
  192.168.4.0/255.255.255.0       router 10.254.11.1      metric  2  tag 0000
  10.254.10.0/255.255.255.0       router 10.254.11.1      metric  2  tag 0000
   10.254.1.0/255.255.255.0       router 10.254.11.1      metric  2  tag 0000
   10.254.2.0/255.255.255.0       router 10.254.11.10     metric  2  tag 0000
  10.254.11.0/255.255.255.0       router 10.254.11.10     metric  4  tag 0000
  10.254.13.0/255.255.255.0       router 10.254.11.10     metric  2  tag 0000
[root@foghorn /root]#
```

The related portion of the trace file is shown in Example 11–29. Notice that the password is very unsecurely recorded there.

Example 11–29   Record of Successful `ripquery` in Trace File

```
Jul  4 19:51:30 RIP RECV 10.254.11.10 vers 2, cmd Poll, length 44
     Authentication: foobie01
     routing table request
RIP RECV end of packet
```

Now, let's consider the use of authentication on a per interface basis using MD5. Example 11–30 shows the `/etc/gated.conf` file for the router `foghorn`.

Example 11–30   Sample `/etc/gated.conf` on `foghorn` with MD5 Authentication

```
rip on {
        interface 10.254.11.10 10.254.12.10 ripin ripout version 2
             authentication md5 key "bletch01" id 1 ;
        interface 172.16.0.1 172.17.0.1 noripin noripout ;
        trustedgateways 10.254.11.1 10.254.12.1 ;
        traceoptions "/var/log/gated.trace" request response ;
} ;
```

Example 11–31 shows the `/etc/gated.conf` file for the router `beauregard`.

Example 11–31   Sample `/etc/gated.conf` on `beauregard` with MD5 Authentication

```
rip on {
        interface 192.168.4.100 noripin noripout ;
        interface 10.254.11.1 ripin ripout version 2
             authentication md5 key "bletch01" id 1 ;
        interface all ripin ripout version 1 ;
        trustedgateways 10.254.1.1 10.254.10.10 10.254.11.10 ;
} ;
```

It is *very* important to note that the above two examples specify an authentication scheme between *only* the two routers involved. This is ensured by the fact that it is specified on an interface basis.

Both of these configuration files contain an MD5 authentication entry with the same password *and* the same `id` value. The trace file reveals in Example 11–32 that the exchange between the two routers is authenticated. Note that using MD5 causes the recording of the password to be suppressed and replaced with `???`.

Example 11–32   Trace of a Successful MD5 `response` and `request` Authentication

```
Jul  4 20:35:59 RIP SENT 10.254.12.10 -> 224.0.0.9+520 vers 2, cmd Response, length
104
        Authentication: MD5 Digest: ???
                172.17/255.255        router 10.254.12.10    metric  1 tag 0000
                172.16/255.255        router 10.254.12.10    metric  1 tag 0000
            10.254.11/255.255.255     router 10.254.12.10    metric  1 tag 0000
        Invalid family: 65535
RIP SENT end of packet
Jul  4 20:35:59
Jul  4 20:35:59 RIP RECV 10.254.11.10 vers 2, cmd Response, length 104
        Authentication: MD5 Digest: ???
                172.17/255.255        router 10.254.11.10    metric  1 tag 0000
                172.16/255.255        router 10.254.11.10    metric  1 tag 0000
            10.254.12/255.255.255     router 10.254.11.10    metric  1 tag 0000
        Invalid family: 65535
RIP RECV end of packet
```

Router Discovery

We introduced router discovery in "Router Discovery" on page 219. There, we noted that IPv4 router discovery is defined by RFC 1256 and that it uses special ICMP types and codes. We further noted that router discovery has two distinct roles. Advertisements by routers carry default router information. Hosts (non-routers) utilize this information to place a default router in their routing table. Hosts also issue solicitations to obtain a default router when they boot. Let's formalize that discussion by considering the details of router discovery advertisements and solicitations.

Figure 11–5 depicts the form of a router discovery advertisement.

The router discovery advertisement consists of three parts as shown in Figure 11–5. The ICMP header (ICMP Hdr), the advertisement header (Adv Hdr), and one or more default routes (Default Route).

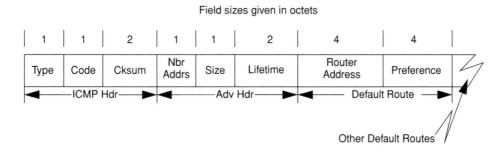

Figure 11–5   Router Discovery Advertisement

The ICMP header contains the `Type` field set to 9 and the `Code` field set to 0 (see Chapter 4 for ICMPv4 types and codes). The `Cksum` field contains the ICMP checksum.

The advertisement header consists of the three fields `Nbr Addrs`, `Size`, and `Lifetime`. The `Nbr Addrs` field contains the number of default routes in the advertisement. The `Size` field is the number of 32-bit words consumed for each default router entry—all default route entries are always two 32-bit words. The `Lifetime` field contains the number of seconds for which the default routes in the advertisement should be considered valid.

The Default Route portion of the advertisement contains the four octet IP address (`Router Address`) of the default router followed by a four octet `Preference` value. The preference value is a signed, 32-bit two's complement. The higher the preference, the more desirable this route is over other default routes being advertised to this local network. There may be other default routes in the advertisement, each containing the router's IP address followed by the preference.

All router advertisements are sent to the `224.0.0.1` (all nodes multicast—see "Multicast Addresses" on page 111) unless the router does not support multicasting, in which case it is sent to the local broadcast address for the interface through which the router is sending the advertisements. `gated` can be configured to issue advertisements via multicast or broadcast.

Figure 11–6 depicts the form of a router discovery solicitation.

The router solicitation is very simple. It is an ICMP packet with an ICMP type of 10 and code of 0. All router solicitations are sent to 224.0.0.2 (the all routers multicast—see "Multicast Addresses" on page 111). If the system does not support multicasting, then it will send the solicitation to the local broadcast address. `gated` can be configured to send solicitations via multicast or broadcast.

Field sizes given in octets

1	1	2	4
Type	Code	Cksum	Reserved

◀—ICMP Hdr—▶

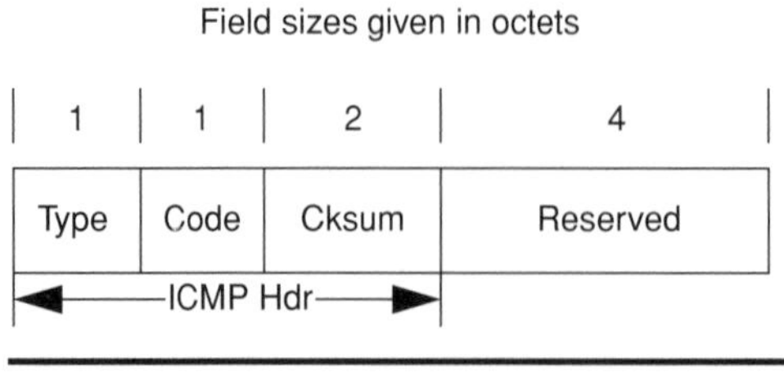

Figure 11–6   Router Discovery Solicitation

Hosts will listen for router discovery advertisements and update their routing tables with each advertisement received based on the preference level of the route. If preference levels of two default routes are identical, then the host will always use the latest advertisement.

Keep in mind that a system can act as either a router discovery router (also called a *server*) or host (also called a *client*), but not both.

Configuring `gated` for Router Discovery

Configuring `gated` to support router discovery is rather straightforward. There are two forms, server and client. We'll consider the server form first.

The Router Discovery Server

The general form for a router discovery server in `/etc/gated.conf` is given in Example 11–33.

Example 11–33   Syntax for Router Discover Server in `/etc/gated.conf`

```
routerdiscovery server on|off [ {
        traceoptions options ;
        interface iface_list [maxadvinterval time] [minadvinterval time]
            [lifetime time] ;
        address address_list [advertise | ignore] [broadcast | multicast]
            [ineligible] [preference level] ;
} ] ;
```

Simply turning on router discovery on a router using the default values for all interfaces uses

```
routerdiscovery server on ;
```

You can control the behavior of router discovery with respect to each interface by using the `interface` option. You can make sure that router discovery is off by using the `off` argument instead of `on`. `off` is the default.

Each of the options within the `routerdiscovery server` stanza are described in Table 11–21.

Table 11–21   Options for Router Discovery Server

OPTION	SUBOPTIONS	DESCRIPTION
`traceoptions options`	N/A	Router discovery only supports the `state` option.
`interface iface_list`		Unlike the interface keyword for all other `gated` applications, for router discovery this argument takes a space-separated list of device names. For example, replace `iface_list` with `eth0 eth1 eth2`. You cannot specify alias interfaces, but you can control the advertisement using the `address` keyword.
	`maxadvinterval time`	The maximum `time` in seconds between router advertisements. Default is 600. Minimum allowable value is 4 seconds.
	`minadvinterval time`	The minimum `time` in seconds allowed between unsolicited router advertisements. The default is `0.75 x maxiadvinterval` The minimum allowable time is 3 seconds.
	`lifetime time`	The life `time` of the default route in seconds. Default is `3 x maxadvinterval` This value maps directly into the Lifetime field as shown in Figure 11–5 on page 525.

Table 11–21 Options for Router Discovery Server *(Continued)*

OPTION	SUBOPTIONS	DESCRIPTION
address *address_list*		Specifies a space-separated list of IP addresses *address_list*. These addresses must be associated with an interface on the router.
	advertise | ignore	Advertise (advertise) or don't advertise (ignore) this address. The default is advertise.
	broadcast | multicast	Generate router advertisements via broadcast or multicast. multicast is the default.
	ineligible	Sets the preference of this address to 0x80000000, thus making it ineligible as a default route. The route is still advertised. This is useful for hosts to determine that the route is still available and that it can be used in an ICMP redirect.
	preference *level*	Sets the preference *level* for the address. This is used in the Preference field of the advertisement. See Figure 11–5 on page 525.

Router Discovery Client

The general form for a router discovery client in `/etc/gated.conf` is given in Example 11–34.

Example 11–34   Syntax for Router Discovery Client in `/etc/gated.conf`

```
routerdiscovery client on|off [ {
        traceoptions options ;
        preference preference ;
        interface iface_list [enable | disable | multicast]
              [quiet | solicit] ;
} ] ;
```

Simply turning on router discovery on a host using the default values for all interfaces uses

```
        routerdiscovery client on ;
```

You can control the behavior of router discovery with respect to each interface by using the `interface` option. You can make sure that router discovery is off by using the `off` argument instead of `on`. `off` is the default.

Each of the options within the `routerdiscovery client` stanza are described in Table 11–22.

Table 11–22   Options for Router Discovery Client

OPTION	SUBOPTIONS	DESCRIPTION
`traceoptions options`	N/A	Router discovery only supports the `state` option.
`preference preference`	N/A	Sets the `gated` preference for this protocol as described in "`gated` Preferences" on page 478.
`interface iface_list`		Unlike the interface keyword for all other `gated` applications, for router discovery this argument takes a space-separated list of device names. For example, replace `iface_list` with `eth0 eth1 eth2`. You cannot specify alias interfaces.

Table 11–22 Options for Router Discovery Client *(Continued)*

Option	SubOptions	Description
	`enable|disable|multicast`	`enable`, the default, specifies that client router discovery should be performed on this interface. `disable` specifies that router discovery will not be performed on the specified interface. `multicast` specifies that solicitations can use multicasting only—if the interface does not support multicasting, it will not solicit, but it will still listen for advertisements.
	`quiet|solicit`	`quiet` specifies that this interface is to listen to advertisements and never generate solicitations. `solicit` causes three solicitations to be generated through this interface and it is the default.

We look at setting up both router discovery servers and clients in "Implementing RIP and Router Discovery with `gated`—An Example" on page 535.

A Routing Example

Throughout the remainder of this chapter, we consider implementing RIP and router discovery using `gated` to correctly populate routing tables for both hosts and routers. To that end, we utilize the example shown in Figure 11–7 to explain the operations of each of the different protocols. Where appropriate, we introduce variations of this example and different examples to make certain points; however, for the most part, this is the example with which we work.

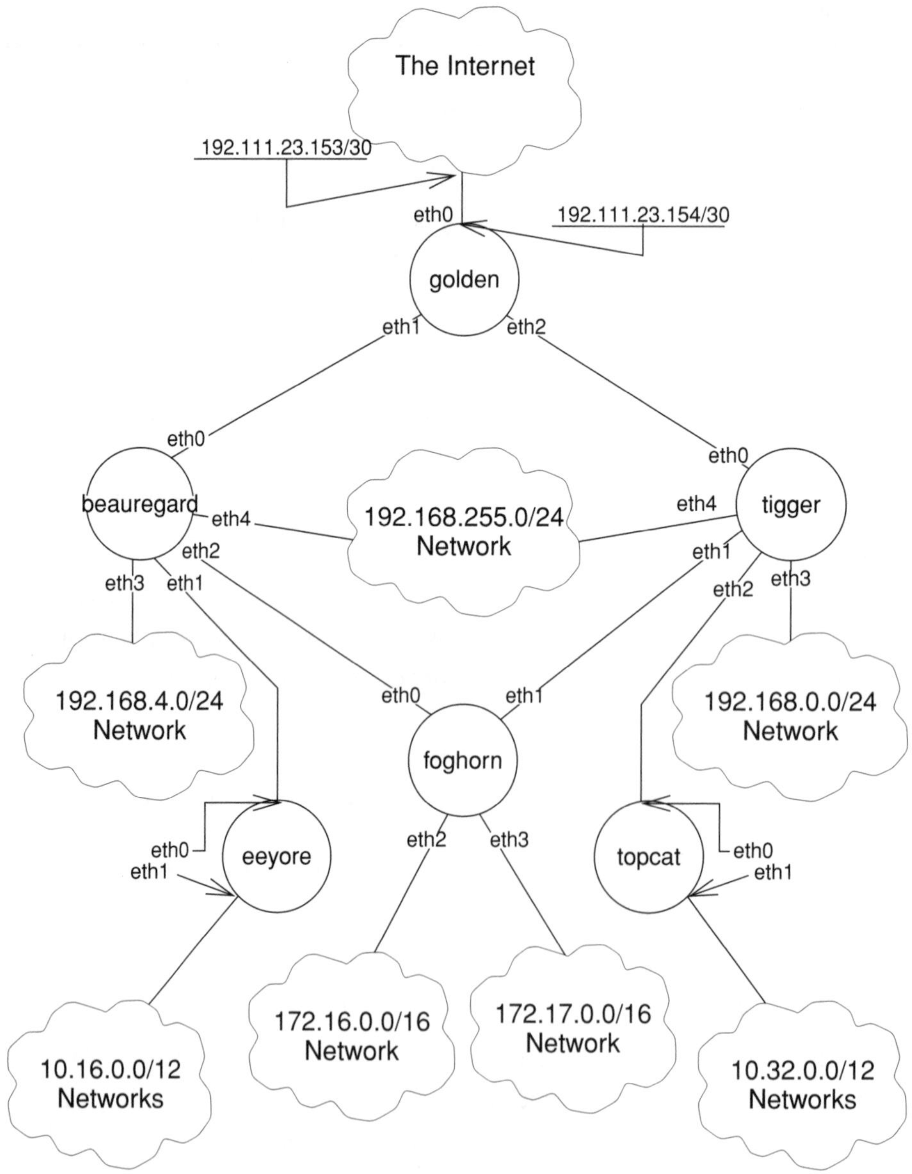

Figure 11–7   A Routing Example

To make this diagram clearer, the interfaces are labeled with device names instead of addresses. In this diagram, circles represent routers and clouds represent networks. Each router has been assigned a canonical name (shown in each circle). Table 11–23 serves to identify each router/interface/address triplet. It also shows the canonical name together with the name for each address.

Table 11–23   Figure 11–7 Canonical Name to Address Associations

CANONICAL NAME	INTERFACE NAME	HOST NAME	IP ADDRESS
golden	eth0	golden	192.111.23.154/30
	eth1	golden-1	10.254.1.1/24
	eth2	golden-2	10.254.2.1/24
beauregard	eth0	beauregard	10.254.1.10/24
	eth1	beauregard-1	10.254.10.1/24
	eth2	beauregard-2	10.254.11.1/24
	eth3	beauregard-3	192.168.4.100/24
	eth4	beauregard-4	192.168.255.100/24
tigger	eth0	tigger	10.254.2.10/24
	eth1	tigger-1	10.254.12.1/24
	eth2	tigger-2	10.254.13.1/24
	eth3	tigger-3	192.168.0.200/24
	eth4	tigger-4	192.168.255.200/24
eeyore	eth0	eeyore	10.254.10.10/24
	eth1	eeyore-1	10.16.0.1/16
foghorn	eth0	foghorn	10.254.11.10/24
	eth1	foghorn-1	10.254.12.10/24
	eth2	foghorn-2	172.16.0.1/16
	eth3	foghorn-3	172,17,0,1/16
topcat	eth0	topcat	10.254.13.10/24
	eth1	topcat-1	10.32.0.1/16

Each network is assigned a network number, or range of network numbers, using prefix notation. Table 11–24 provides a listing of the networks shown in Figure 11–7.

Table 11–24   Figure 11–7 Network Descriptions

NETWORK DESCRIPTION	MEANING, USE, AND/OR PURPOSE
Other Networks and the Internet	Indicates the connection to the Internet and other networks within the organization. We revisit this part of the example in the next two chapters.
`10.254.1.0/24`	This network connects the two routers `golden` and `beauregard`.
`10.254.2.0/24`	This network connects the two routers `golden` and `tigger`.
`10.254.10.0/24`	This network connects the two routers `beauregard` and `eeyore`.
`10.254.11.0/24`	This network connects the two routers `beauregard` and `foghorn`.
`10.254.12.0/24`	This network connects the two routers `tigger` and `foghorn`.
`10.254.13.0/24`	This network connects the two routers `tigger` and `topcat`.
`192.168.0.0/24`	This is the Class C network `192.168.0.0/24`.
`192.168.4.0/24`	This is the Class C network `192.168.4.0/24`.
`192.168.255.0/24`	This is the Class C network `192.168.255.0/24`.
`10.16.0.0/12`	This represents the collection of networks `10.16.0.0/16` through and including `10.31.0.0/16`.
`10.32.0.0/12`	This represents the collection of networks `10.32.0.0/16` through and including `10.47.0.0/16`.

Table 11–24   Figure 11–7 Network Descriptions *(Continued)*

NETWORK DESCRIPTION	MEANING, USE, AND/OR PURPOSE
172.16.0.0/16	This is the Class B network 172.16.0.0/16.
172.17.0.0/16	This is the Class B network 172.16.0.0/16

Implementing RIP and Router Discovery with gated— An Example

Now, let's consider the example in Figure 11–7 and see how that environment can be configured to dynamically maintain routing tables using RIP and router discovery. Our goals are as follows:

- Make sure that each routing table is populated with routing tables that allow each system to connect to all the others shown in Figure 11–7.
- Whenever there are redundant routers for hosts, we need to automate the failover process—that is, make sure that the hosts automatically obtain the new routes from the router that did not fail.
- The router tigger is slower than the router beauregard. Thus, where possible, we want our configuration to choose beauregard over tigger.
- Keep things as simple as possible to minimize administrative headaches.

Given these goals, the following sections detail the gated configuration necessary for each router and for the hosts. As these sections show, the majority of the configuration effort is focused on the routers, with little effort expended for the hosts. That is as it should be.

Configuring golden

From the diagram in Figure 11–7, it is clear that golden has one way to the Internet and it needs to provide this service to all routers. Since it acts as the only gateway to the Internet, we can handle access to the Internet using static default routes. There's no reason to include this external route in a dynamic mechanism because there is no benefit to doing that. If there were other gateways, then we'd include the Internet access points in our dynamic scheme—we consider that possibility in the examples in the next two chapters.

The other routes that `golden` needs to know about are those that interconnect the internal networks. These routes need to be propagated by `beauregard`
and `tigger`. Thus, we need to cause `golden` to pay attention to the broadcasts
of `beauregard` and `tigger` in order that it get routing information about the
internal environment. We use RIPv2 for this purpose. Furthermore, since `tig-
ger` is slower than `beauregard`, we use the `gated` `preference` value to force
`gated` to choose `beauregard` over `tigger` when that makes sense.

Notice also, from Figure 11–7, that we can aggregate some routes for `golden`
in order to reduce its routing table. This isn't, strictly speaking, necessary since
this example does not represent a large environment and `golden` does not have a
hierarchically higher router to pass this information up to (the real beneficiary of
aggregate routes), but we provide two `generate` statements as an illustrative
example.

The `/etc/gated.conf` file for `golden` is shown in Example 11–35. The line
numbers shown to the left are for clarity and are not actually part of the file.

Example 11–35   `/etc/gated.conf` for `golden`

```
 1 options mark 300;
 2 rip on {
 3         interface 192.111.23.154 noripin noripout ;
 4         interface eth1 eth2 ripin ripout version 2 broadcast ;
 5         trustedgateways 10.254.1.10 10.254.2.10 ;
 6 } ;
 7 static {
 8         default gateway 192.111.23.153 interface eth0 retain ;
 9 } ;
10 generate 10.16.0.0 masklen 20 preference 90 {
11         proto rip {
12                 10.16.0.0 masklen 20 refines ;
13         } ;
14 } ;
15 generate 10.32.0.0 masklen 20 preference 90 {
16   proto rip {
17                 10.32.0.0 masklen 20 refines ;
18         } ;
19 } ;
20 import proto rip gateway 10.254.1.10 preference 95 {
21                 all ;
22 } ;
23 traceoptions "/var/log/gated.log" replace size 100k files 4 route ;
```

Let's analyze Example 11–35. The configuration file opens with an `options`
`mark 300` option statement at line 1. This has the effect of writing a timestamp

into the `/var/log/gated.log` file every 5 minutes. The `/var/log/gated.log` file is defined by the `traceoptions` control statement (at line 23) which also writes all routing table updates to that file due to the `route` option. The file can reach a maximum of 100 KB before `gated` rotates it and 4 old logs are retained due to the `size 100k files 4` option.

The first stanza is the `rip` protocol statement at line 2. This turns RIP on and then specifies within the stanza (at line 3) that no RIP requests or responses are to be read or sent to the `192.111.23.154` interface (`eth0`) which leads to the Internet. The other two interfaces, however, are used both for receiving and sending of RIP information using RIPv2 broadcasts (line 4). The `trust-edgeways` entry (line 5) causes `golden` to only accept RIP responses from `10.254.1.10` (`beauregard`) and `10.254.2.10` (`tigger`).

The next stanza begins at line 7 and is a `static` protocol statement. In this case, it is used to specifically add the static default route to the Internet. This route will not be advertised via RIP because it is not included in any `export` statements for RIP. Notice that the `retain` keyword is included in the static default route entry (line 8). This causes the default route to remain in the routing table (together with all direct, local interface routes which were added at boot-time with the `route` command—see Chapter 6) even when `gated` terminates.

The next two stanzas at lines 10 and 15 are `generate` control statements. These two statements generate aggregate routes for the `10.16.0.0/20` and `10.32.0.0/20` destinations, respectively. Note that we set the `preference` value to `90` so that these routes are preferred over any RIP routes learned (RIP default preference is `100`—see "`gated` Preferences" on page 478).

The last stanza begins at line 20. It is an `import` control statement. Its only purpose is to set the preference for all RIP routes learned from `10.254.1.10` (`beauregard`) to `95`. It does this because the default preference for RIP is 100 and the preference for the two aggregate routes is 90. Therefore, `golden` will always prefer routes through `beauregard` over `tigger` (one of the goals listed at the beginning of this section), yet still prefer the aggregates when they apply. The beauty of using the `gated` preference is that it doesn't have anything to do with the protocol metrics. The substantially more difficult alternative would have been to set higher metrics on every route broadcast by `tigger` that is also broadcast by `beauregard`.

Notice that the ordering of this file follows the requirements given in the statement type list on 536. In this example, an `option` statement (line 1) is followed by `protocol` statements (lines 2 and 7), and then by `control` statements (lines 10, 15, 20, and 23).

Use of the `/etc/gated.conf` file shown in Example 11–35 on `golden` causes the routing table shown in Example 11–36 to be generated.

Example 11–36   Routing Table on `golden`

```
[root@golden /root]# route -n
Kernel IP routing table
Destination     Gateway          Genmask          Flags Metric Ref    Use Iface
127.0.0.1       0.0.0.0          255.255.255.255 UH    0      0        0 lo
192.111.23.152  0.0.0.0          255.255.255.252 U     0      0        0 eth0
10.254.10.0     10.254.1.10      255.255.255.0   UG    0      0        0 eth1
10.254.11.0     10.254.1.10      255.255.255.0   UG    0      0        0 eth1
192.168.4.0     10.254.1.10      255.255.255.0   UG    0      0        0 eth1
192.168.0.0     10.254.2.10      255.255.255.0   UG    0      0        0 eth1
10.254.12.0     10.254.2.10      255.255.255.0   UG    0      0        0 eth2
10.254.13.0     10.254.2.10      255.255.255.0   UG    0      0        0 eth2
10.16.0.0       10.254.1.10      255.255.240.0   UG    0      0        0 eth1
10.32.0.0       10.254.2.10      255.255.240.0   UG    0      0        0 eth2
10.254.2.0      0.0.0.0          255.255.255.0   U     0      0        0 eth2
10.254.1.0      0.0.0.0          255.255.255.0   U     0      0        0 eth1
192.168.255.0   10.254.1.10      255.255.255.0   UG    0      0        0 eth1
172.16.0.0      10.254.1.10      255.240.0.0     UG    0      0        0 eth1
127.0.0.0       -                255.0.0.0       !     0      -        0 -
0.0.0.0         192.111.23.153   0.0.0.0         UG    0      0        0 eth0
[root@golden /root]#
```

The routing table should be clear from Example 11–35, Figure 11–7, and our analyses of routing tables in Chapter 6. Note that the aggregated routes for `10.16.0.0/20` and `10.32.0.0/20` appear with the correct route mask of `255.255.240.0`. Further, there is an aggregate route for `172.16.0.0/12` (route mask of `255.240.0.0`) which has been propagated to this router by routers lower in the hierarchy (`beauregard`, `tigger`, and `foghorn`). We look at the creation of this aggregate in "Configuring `foghorn`" on page 541. Also, notice that `gated` installs a reject route (`!` in the `Flags` column) for `127.0.0.0`, as that is one of the default `martians` (see "Definition Type Statements" on page 490).

Configuring `beauregard` and `tigger`

The `gated` configuration files for `beauregard` and `tigger` are nearly identical. In both cases, they need to run RIPv2 to get the routing tables from `golden` and to propagate them to each of the five networks to which they are attached. They both need to act as router discovery servers for the `192.168.255.0/24` network so that hosts on that network can dynamically obtain a default router. They also need to advertise router discovery information to foghorn because it is attached to each of them. The only difference between these two routers is that tigger is slower than beauregard, so we will give beauregard a higher router discovery preference (not a gated preference—"Configuring gated for Router Discovery" on page 527).

The /etc/gated.conf file for beauregard is given in Example 11–37. Once again, the line numbers to the left are for discussion purposes and won't actually appear in the file.

Example 11–37   /etc/gated.conf on beauregard

```
1  rip on {
2      interface 192.168.4.100 ripin noripout version 2 broadcast ;
3      interface all ripin ripout version 2 broadcast ;
4      trustedgateways 10.254.1.1 10.254.10.10 10.254.11.10 ;
5  } ;
6  routerdiscovery server on {
7      address 10.254.11.1 advertise multicast preference 100 ;
8      address 192.168.255.100 advertise multicast preference 100 ;
9      address 10.254.1.10 ignore ;
10 } ;
11 static {
12     default gateway 10.254.1.1 interface eth0 retain ;
13 } ;
```

This file opens with a rip stanza. It specifies, at line 2, that beauregard will listen only to RIPv2 on its interface to the 192.168.4.0/24 network, but it won't broadcast. This is because at line 6 router discovery is turned on and therefore a default route will be advertised to that network. That network needs no other routes to reach the rest of the environment.

Line 3 specifies that RIPv2 operates in broadcast mode to all other interfaces. Line 4 specifies that golden (10.254.1.1), foghorn (10.254.11.10), and eeyore (10.254.10.10) are the only routers from which RIP responses will be received.

Router discovery server advertisements are sent to the 10.254.11.0/24 and 19.168.255.0/24 networks with the router discovery preference of 100 (lines 7 and 8) to make beauregard a more desirable default router than tigger. Router discover advertisements are also sent, by default, to the 192.168.4.0/24 and 10.16.0.0/16 networks. Router advertisements are not sent to golden (line 9) since it won't use them.

Finally, `beauregard` has a default router entry pointing to `golden` in the static stanza at line 11.

The `/etc/gated.conf` file for `tigger` would be the same except that no preference value would be assigned to the router discover entries and, of course, the entries would need to reflect the correct addresses and interfaces.

The routing table for `beauregard` is shown in Example 11–38. Notice the addition of the multicast entry `224.0.0.2`. This entry is due to the fact that `beauregard` is running router discover and in so doing has joined the all routers multicast group (which for IPv4 is `224.0.0.2`), and `gated` has added the route for that address. It is worth mentioning that there is no aggregation of routes for the `10.16.0.0/20` or `10.32.0.0./20` networks. That's because aggregation was only performed on `golden` and `golden` is not broadcasting the aggregate route (that would require an `export` statement and, in any event, only the `10.32.0.0/20` aggregated would be of use to `beauregard`). Thus, in this routing table, we see the entries for the specific `10.16.0.0/16`, `10.17.0.0/16`, `10.23.0.0./16`, and `10.32.0.0/16` networks. Also, notice that the aggregate route for `172.16.0.0/12` exists here as well. This route was propagated by `foghorn` as we'll see in the next section. The rest of the table is as expected for this example. The routing table for `tigger` would be similar.

Example 11–38   Routing Table on `beauregard`

```
[root@beauregard /root]# route -n
Kernel IP routing table
Destination     Gateway         Genmask          Flags Metric Ref    Use Iface
224.0.0.2       127.0.0.1       255.255.255.255  UGH   0      0        0 lo
127.0.0.1       0.0.0.0         255.255.255.255  UH    0      0        0 lo
10.254.10.0     10.254.10.1     255.255.255.0    UG    0      0        0 eth1
10.254.10.0     0.0.0.0         255.255.255.0    U     0      0        0 eth1
10.254.11.0     10.254.11.1     255.255.255.0    UG    0      0        0 eth2
10.254.11.0     0.0.0.0         255.255.255.0    U     0      0        0 eth2
192.168.4.0     0.0.0.0         255.255.255.0    U     0      0        0 eth1
10.254.12.0     10.254.11.10    255.255.255.0    UG    0      0        0 eth2
10.254.13.0     10.254.11.10    255.255.255.0    UG    0      0        0 eth2
10.254.2.0      10.254.1.1      255.255.255.0    UG    0      0        0 eth0
10.254.1.0      10.254.1.10     255.255.255.0    UG    0      0        0 eth0
10.254.1.0      0.0.0.0         255.255.255.0    U     0      0        0 eth0
192.168.255.0   0.0.0.0         255.255.255.0    U     0      0        0 eth2
172.16.0.0      10.254.11.10    255.240.0.0      UG    0      0        0 eth2
10.16.0.0       10.254.10.10    255.255.0.0      UG    0      0        0 eth1
10.17.0.0       10.254.10.10    255.255.0.0      UG    0      0        0 eth1
10.23.0.0       10.254.10.10    255.255.0.0      UG    0      0        0 eth1
10.32.0.0       10.254.1.1      255.255.0.0      UG    0      0        0 eth0
10.32.0.0       10.254.1.1      255.255.0.0      UG    0      0        0 eth0
127.0.0.0       -               255.0.0.0        !     0      -        0 -
0.0.0.0         10.254.1.1      0.0.0.0          UG    0      0        0 eth0
[root@beauregard /root]#
```

Configuring `foghorn`

The router `foghorn` needs to run RIPv2 in broadcast mode to all networks except `172.16.0.0/16` and `172.17.0.0/16`. Those networks can accept router discovery or simply (as in this case) configure a static default router pointing to `foghorn`. So `foghorn` won't run router discover in server mode, but it will run it in client mode to get the advertisements from `beauregard` and `tigger`, thereby taking advantage of that redundancy. Since no useful router discovery information can be obtained from the interfaces `eth2` and `eth3`, we'll disable it on those interfaces.

We'll also aggregate the routes to `172.16.0.0/16` and `172.17.0.0/16` using an `aggregate` statement and then `export` the aggregate to RIP. As with the `generate` example for `golden`, this really isn't necessary given the limited scope and size of our example, but it serves to illustrate the capability. Note that the `aggregate` statement aggregates the routes using `proto direct` and `proto rip` (they are the two contributing protocols). We use `proto direct` because the networks are directly attached to two of `foghorn`'s interfaces. We use `proto rip` for illustrative purposes; if there were additional `172.16.0.0/12` networks attached, but not directly, `foghorn` would discovery them via RIP broadcasts and add them to the aggregate. After the `aggregate` statement we include an `export` statement to ensure that the aggregate gets broadcast via RIP. Note that the routing table (see below) for `foghorn` does not include the aggregate as described in "Route Aggregation with `gated`" on page 499.

The `/etc/gated.conf` file for `foghorn` is given in Example 11–39

Example 11–39   `/etc/gated.conf` on foghorn

```
rip on {
     interface 10.254.11.10 10.254.12.10  ripin ripout version 2 broadcast ;
     interface 172.16.0.1 172.17.0.1 noripin noripout ;
     trustedgateways 10.254.11.1 10.254.12.1 ;
} ;
routerdiscovery client on {
     interface eth2 eth3 disable ;
} ;
aggregate 172.16.0.0 masklen 12 preference 90 {
     proto rip {
          172.16.0.0 masklen 12 refines ;
     } ;
     proto direct {
          172.16.0.0 masklen 16 exact ;
          172.17.0.0 masklen 16 exact ;
     } ;
} ;
```

Example 11–39   `/etc/gated.conf` on `foghorn` *(Continued)*

```
export proto rip {
    proto aggregate {
           172.16.0.0 masklen 12 ;
    } ;
} ;
```

The routing table on `foghorn` appears as in Example 11–40.

Example 11–40   Routing Table on `foghorn`

```
[root@foghorn /root]# route -n
Kernel IP routing table
Destination     Gateway          Genmask          Flags Metric Ref    Use Iface
127.0.0.1       0.0.0.0          255.255.255.255  UH    0      0        0 lo
10.254.10.0     10.254.11.1      255.255.255.0    UG    0      0        0 eth0
10.254.11.0     10.254.11.10     255.255.255.0    UG    0      0        0 eth0
10.254.11.0     0.0.0.0          255.255.255.0    U     0      0        0 eth0
192.168.4.0     10.254.11.1      255.255.255.0    UG    0      0        0 eth0
10.254.12.0     10.254.12.10     255.255.255.0    UG    0      0        0 eth1
10.254.12.0     0.0.0.0          255.255.255.0    U     0      0        0 eth1
10.254.13.0     10.254.12.1      255.255.255.0    UG    0      0        0 eth1
10.254.2.0      10.254.12.1      255.255.255.0    UG    0      0        0 eth1
10.254.1.0      10.254.11.1      255.255.255.0    UG    0      0        0 eth0
10.32.0.0       10.254.12.1      255.255.0.0      UG    0      0        0 eth1
10.35.0.0       10.254.12.1      255.255.0.0      UG    0      0        0 eth1
10.16.0.0       10.254.11.1      255.255.0.0      UG    0      0        0 eth0
10.17.0.0       10.254.11.1      255.255.0.0      UG    0      0        0 eth0
10.23.0.0       10.254.11.1      255.255.0.0      UG    0      0        0 eth0
192.168.255.0   10.254.11.1      255.255.255.0    UG    0      0        0 eth0
172.16.0.0      172.16.0.1       255.255.0.0      UG    0      0        0 eth2
172.16.0.0      0.0.0.0          255.255.0.0      U     0      0        0 eth2
172.17.0.0      172.17.0.1       255.255.0.0      UG    0      0        0 eth3
172.17.0.0      0.0.0.0          255.255.0.0      U     0      0        0 eth3
127.0.0.0       -                255.0.0.0        !     0      -        0 -
0.0.0.0         10.254.11.1      0.0.0.0          UG    0      0        0 eth0
[root@foghorn /root]#
```

Configuring `topcat` and `eeyore`

The routers `topcat` and `eeyore` are fairly simple to configure. They each have
only one way to the rest of the environment (so we'll set up static default routes)
and they each have connections to an indeterminate (Figure 11–7 on page 532
doesn't precisely show them) number of networks `10.32.0.0/20` and
`10.16.0.0/20`, respectively. Even though there are these many networks, `topcat`
is connected only to the `10.16.0.0/16` network and `eeyore` to the `10.32.0.0/`
`16` network. So, there are other routers running RIPv2 that are not shown, but as
we have seen, their routes appear in the routing tables of other routers.

As with `beauregard` and `tigger`, `topcat` and `eeyore` are very similar in
terms of configuration. So, we consider `eeyore`. It is configured with a static

default router to beauregard (topcat would use tigger). It does not listen to RIP on its eth0 interface (there's no reason to do so), but it does broadcast so that other routers can find out about the 10.16.0.0/20 networks. It only listens to its eth1 interface for RIP broadcasts because it has nothing to offer those networks (only a default router). We won't go into the details of configuring all of the routers and hosts in the 10.16.0.0/20 (nor 10.32.0.0/20) networks, but their configuration would be similar to what we describe here and previously.

The /etc/gated.conf file for eeyore is shown in Example 11–41.

Example 11–41   /etc/gated.conf on eeyore

```
rip on {
     interface eth0 noripin ripout version 2 broadcast ;
     interface eth1 ripin noripout version 2 broadcast ;
} ;
static {
     default gateway 10.254.10.1 retain ;
} ;
```

The routing table for eeyore is given in Example 11–42. Due to the default route, it is much simpler than the others we've examined.

Example 11–42   Routing Table on eeyore

```
[root@eeyore /root]# route -n
Kernel IP routing table
Destination     Gateway          Genmask          Flags Metric Ref     Use Iface
127.0.0.1       0.0.0.0          255.255.255.255  UH    0      0         0 lo
10.254.10.0     10.254.10.10     255.255.255.0    UG    0      0         0 eth0
10.254.10.0     0.0.0.0          255.255.255.0    U     0      0         0 eth0
10.16.0.0       10.16.0.1        255.255.0.0      UG    0      0         0 eth1
10.16.0.0       0.0.0.0          255.255.0.0      U     0      0         0 eth1
10.17.0.0       10.16.0.10       255.255.0.0      UG    0      0         0 eth1
10.23.0.0       10.16.0.10       255.255.0.0      UG    0      0         0 eth1
127.0.0.0       -                255.0.0.0        !     0      -         0 -
0.0.0.0         10.254.10.1      0.0.0.0          UG    0      0         0 eth0
[root@eeyore /root]#
```

Aggregating the 10.16.0.0/20 Network

In "Configuring golden" on page 535, we described using generate to aggregate the routes to the 10.16.0.0/20 and 10.32.0.0/20 networks. We could aggregate them here (after all, this is the source of those networks) and then propagate them via RIPv2 (can't do it with RIPv1 since RIPv1 doesn't broadcast netmasks). One way of accomplishing this is to use a static aggregate route and then export it via RIP. Example 11–43 shows how this could be accomplished with additional entries in the /etc/gated.conf file for eeyore. The new entries are shown in bold.

Example 11–43   `/etc/gated.conf` on eeyore

```
rip on {
    interface eth0 noripin ripout version 2 broadcast ;
    interface eth1 ripin noripout version 2 broadcast ;
} ;
static {
    10.16.0.0 masklen 20 gateway 10.16.0.1 ;
    default gateway 10.254.10.1 retain ;
} ;
export proto rip {
    proto static {
        10.16.0.0 masklen 20 metric 2 ;
    } ;
} ;
```

Note that this configuration file causes `eeyore` to broadcast the aggregated route with a metric of 2. In fact, the actual route will cost at least 2 hops (`eeyore` and the next router); the actual number of hops may be more than 2. If you use this approach, make sure that you do *not* aggregate the routes with `generate` as shown on `golden`. Also, since the aggregate is implemented statically, all packets destined to `10.16.0.0/20` will get forwarded regardless of whether the destination actually exists.

Configuring the Hosts

Configuring the hosts in this environment is quite simple. All of the hosts in the `192.168.255.0/24` network simply need to run the client side router discovery daemon and RIPv2 in listen mode. They need to run RIP because only using router discovery would lead to a lot of ICMP redirects. This can be done with `gated` using the configuration file shown in Example 11–44.

Example 11–44   `/etc/gated.conf` on Hosts in the `192.168.255.0/24` Network

```
rip on ;
routerdiscovery client on ;
```

Every host in the `172.16.0.0/16` and `172.17.0.0/16` network simply needs a static default router which can be configured as described in Chapter 6.

Configuration of the remaining hosts and routers in the `10.16.0.0/20` and `10.32.0.0./20` networks would proceed similarly to that described in this section.

One More Thing...

Back on page 213, we promised that `gated` could be configured to properly address the RIP issue associated with the Internet gateway, G, given in the example shown in Figure 6–7 on page 206. Hopefully, it is clear how this would be done! Example 11–45 illustrates an `/etc/gated.conf` file that would do the trick.

Example 11–45   `/etc/gated.conf` for Internet Gateway G in Figure 6–7 on page 206

```
rip on {
    interface 192.29.75.251 noripin noripout ;
    interface 10.254.0.254 ripin noripout version 1 ;
    interface 10.253.0.254 ripin noripout version 1 ;
} ;
static {
    default gateway 192.29.75.250 retain ;
} ;
```

Troubleshooting with `gated`

There is a tremendous amount of troubleshooting support built into the `gated` utility. We touched on the ability to trace various activities to a file with the `traceoptions` statement. We mentioned the fact that the current state of `gated` can be dumped to `/var/tmp/gated_dump` with the `gdc dump` command or by sending a `SIGINT` signal to `gated`. We also noted that `gated` writes messages to the `daemon` facility via `syslog` (usually `/var/log/messages`). Finally, we introduced the `ripquery` utility in Chapter 6 and discussed it in more detail earlier in this chapter.

The `gated` daemon also provides a mechanism to query the running `gated` daemon, its variables, its RIB, interface list, and other internal `gated` parameters. This is called the GateD Interactive Interface (GII). In order to utilize this mechanism, you must create the user `gii` and give it a password. It is recommended that you set the shell to `/bin/false` or something similar for this account to disable native logins using `gii`. Once created, you can `telnet` to port 616. Example 11–46 illustrates.

Example 11–46   Connecting to the GII

```
[root@beauregard /root]# telnet localhost 616
Trying 127.0.0.1...
Connected to localhost.
Escape character is '^]'.
Password?
100 Gated Interactive Interface. Version gated-public-3_6
GateD-beauregard> help
100 HELP: The possible commands are:
```

Example 11–46   Connecting to the GII *(continued)*

```
100 help: Print help messages
100 show: Show internal values
100 quit: Close the session
GateD-beauregard>
```

This interface permits you to query an actively running `gated` daemon. The GII and all of the troubleshooting tools mentioned in this section are described in *Operating Gated* available at

```
http://www.gated.org/code/doc/manuals/operation_guide/
operation_guide.html
```

Summary

In this chapter, we introduced the types of protocols used for dynamic routing table management. We provided an in-depth introduction to the `gated` daemon and considered it for the implementation of RIP and router discovery. Additionally, we provided a more formal discussion of the concepts behind RIP and router discovery.

For Further Reading

Listed below are books and WWW resources that provide further information about the topics discussed in this chapter.

Books

Huitema, Christian, *Routing in the Internet*, 2nd ed., Upper Saddle River, New Jersey, Prentice Hall, 1999.

Kaufman, Charlie, et al., *Network Security: Private Communications in a Public World*, Englewood Cliffs, New Jersey, Prentice-Hall, 1995.

Mancill, Tony, *Linux Routers: A Primer for Network Administrators*, Upper Saddle River, New Jersey, Prentice Hall, 2000.

Mann, Scott, and Ellen L. Mitchell, *Linux System Security: The Administrator's Guide to Open Source Security Tools*, Upper Saddle River, New Jersey, Prentice Hall, 2000.

Perlman, Radia, *Interconnections Second Edition: Bridges, Routers, Switches, and Internetworking Protocols*, Reading, Massachusetts, Addison-Wesley, 2000.

WWW Resources

Cisco provides a wealth of networking information at

```
http://www.cisco.com/univercd/cc/td/doc/cisintwk/ito_doc/
```

12

OSPF

OSPF is a lot more complex than RIP—at least conceptually. Where RIP simply makes choices about choosing a best route based on a simple next hop metric, OSPF makes routing descisions based on the *state* of each *link* throughout the OSPF environment. A link is a (sub)network to which an interface is connected. Its state is described by various parameters including the IP address, the (sub)netmask, the cost of using the interface, and whether or not that link is up or down. Each OSPF router maintains a *link-state* database of link states throughout a collection of networks of which it is a part; furthermore, each router in a given environment has an identical copy of the link-state database. Thus, an OSPF router always has a good idea of how to move packets throughout an internetwork, whereas RIP routers only know about next hops (neighboring routers). Moreover, OSPF incorporates algorithms and configuration options that help keep its database small and help choose the best route based on a number of different parameters. Indeed, OSPF is more complex than RIP because it does a lot more. However, it turns out that configuring OSPF with gated really isn't all that more difficult than configuring RIP with gated—at least, once OSPF is conceptually understood. In this chapter, we begin with an overview of OSPF and then describe implementing it using gated.

OSPF Overview

The current implementation of OSPF is version 2 (OSPFv2), intially defined by RFC 1583. Enhancements to this version of the protocol have been made through RFC 2178 and RFC 2328, this latter RFC being the current standard. RFC 2740 defines OSPF for IPv6. Each of these RFCs exceed 200 pages in length, making their study a daunting and rather tedious task. Fortunately, the author of these RFCs, John T. Moy, has also written a book (cited in "For Further Reading" on page 612) which covers OSPF in good detail and clarifies much of what is described in the RFCs. Additionally, both *Interconnections* and *Routing in the Internet* cover OSPF conceptually. Look to these resources for the details of the protocol. In this section, we cover enough of the concepts of OSPF to enable us to configure it using `gated`.

OSPF Basics

OSPF offers a robust, mature, and flexible dynamic routing table management mechanism. In a typical TCP/IP environment it offers numerous advantages over RIPv1 and RIPv2, such as hierarchical routing table management groups (called *areas*), no counting to infinity problems, and incorporation of TOS (see Chapter 16 for a discussion of TOS and differentiated services) capabilities. Even with its additional functionality, OSPF is really no more difficult to implement than RIPv2 from a configuration standpoint. The difficulty with OSPF, although a modest one, is in the details. For that reason, we begin our discussion by considering OSPF in *flat* (no hierarchical structure) topology and then move on to building OSPF hierarchical areas in "OSPF Hierarchies and Other Routing Domains" on page 563.

OSPF uses five different types of packets to communicate with other routers and synchronize the link-state database throughout an OSPF routing environment (often called an OSPF *domain*). At a very high level, it's very simple and works as described in the following textual description; it is followed with a diagram (Figure 12–1) to help clarify these details.

Suppose an OSPF router, `foghorn`, boots. When it starts its dynamic routing table management daemon, like `gated`, it generates a multicast communication to all of its interfaces called a *hello* message. It identifies itself with a value called a *router identification* (router ID). The router ID is either a configured 32-bit number or one of the router's IP addresses. This hello message is sent to the all OSPF routers address (224.0.0.5 for IPv4). At least one other router (if such exists) that is directly connected to foghorn acknowledges the hello message with a hello message of its own. These directly connected routers are called *neighbors*. foghorn then sends a *database description request* message to each of its neighbors. These routers then respond by sending their current database description. Each description contains a summary of *link-state advertisements* (LSAs) from all of the OSPF routers in the domain. An LSA is the collection of information about a router's interface(s) and other routing information for which it is responsible—we discuss LSAs in "LSAs" on page 552. Once foghorn has a summary of the LSAs available, it requests the LSAs themselves from each of the routers using a *link-state request* message. The link-state request message is also sometimes called a *database download*. Each OSPF router that received the link-state request responds to foghorn with a *link-state update* message. Each of these messages contains the collection of all LSAs which comprise the entire link-state database. foghorn acknowledges the link-state updates with a *link-state acknowledgment*. It then responds with its own LSA (consisting of only those interfaces and routes [perhaps from other protocols] for which it is responsible) in the form of a link-state update message that it multicasts to its neighbors. The neighbors then update their link-state database to include foghorn and recompute the best routes. At this point, foghorn is considered to be *fully adjacent*[1] to its neighbors. Only when a neighbor has reached the point of considering foghorn adjacent will it install a route utilizing foghorn. After completing these tasks, these neighbors issue link-state update messages to each of their interfaces except the one from which foghorn's link-state update was received. Each link-state update message is always responded to with a link-state acknowledgment. This process, called *flooding*, repeats throughout the OSPF domain and enables each router in the domain to build an identical link-state database. Ordinarily, this process takes a few seconds at most. At the end of this process, the routers are said to be *synchronized*.

The five message types of OSPF are hello (OSPF type=1), database description (OSPF type=2), link-state requests (OSPF type=3), link-state updates (OSPF type=4), and link-state acknowledgments (OSPF type=5). All of these

---

1. Actually, full adjacency is only achieved with designated routers. See "Designated Routers and Backup Designated Routers" on page 557.

messages are carried in an IP datagram for which the IP protocol field is set to 0x59. The transport layer of the TCP/IP stack is bypassed in all OSPF communications. Most OSPF messages are sent to the destination address of 224.0.0.5 (IPv4 all OSPF routers). Special database synchronization messages are sent to the all designated OSPF routers multicast (224.0.0.6 for IPv4), which is discussed in "Designated Routers and Backup Designated Routers" on page 557. When gated starts, the system on which it is running joins the 224.0.0.5 multicast group and, if elected a *designated router* (DR) or *backup designated router* (BDR), it will join 224.0.0.6. All OSPF messages set the IP datagram TTL field (see "IPv4 Datagram" on page 93) to 1 so that the packets do not traverse routers. All packets destined to these types of multicast addresses should not be routed anyway (see "Multicast Addresses" on page 111); but the setting of the TTL ensures this behavior just the same.

Figure 12–1 illustrates the start-up synchronization process across one link between the Linux routers foghorn (router ID = 10.254.11.10) and beauregard (router ID = 10.254.1.10). While this description is somewhat repetitive given the preceding discussion, understanding this mechanism is critical to the overall understanding of implementing OSPF properly. Each of the communications is numbered to the left in the diagram.

1. foghorn initiates the communication with a hello (type=1) message announcing its availability.

2. beauregard responds with a hello acknowledgment (type=1) indicating that it recognizes foghorn as a neighbor.

3. foghorn sends a database description request message (type=2) to beauregard. This message also includes a sequence number to enable state management of these type=2 messages.

4. beauregard responds with the database description message (type=2) and incorporates the sequence number from foghorn's first type=2 message in this response.

5. foghorn next sends a database description (type=2) with itself as part of the description. The sequence number is incremented and included in this message.

6. beauregard acknowledges foghorn's description with another type=2 message carrying the incremented sequence number.

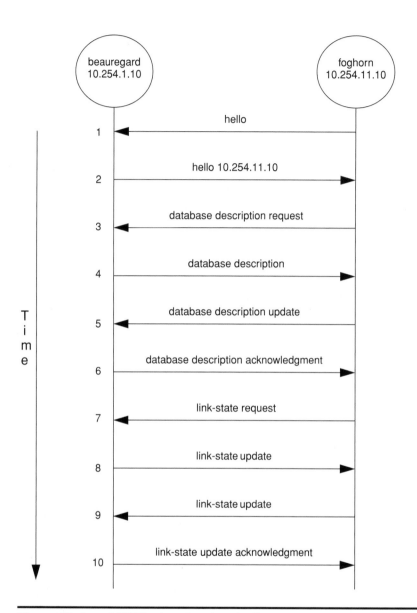

Figure 12–1   OSPF Start-up Synchronization

7. foghorn sends a type=3 link-state request message asking for the LSAs of each entry from the database description.

8. beauregard responds with a type=4 link-state update that includes all of the LSAs requested.

9. foghorn next sends a type=4 link-state update including its own LSA together with all the other LSAs.

10. beauregard acknowledges the link-state update from foghorn.

Besides the use of each message at start-up, each of the messages can be used at other times. For example, hello messages are issued by each OSPF router to all of its neighbors every 10 seconds (by default—this, and all of the parameters described as having a default value, is configurable as we see later in this chapter). If a router, R, doesn't get a hello message from its neighbor, S, within 40 seconds (by default), then S is considered down. R will generate a link-state update message to all of its other neighbors in the form of a new LSA reflecting the downed router S—this update will have the effect of initiating a flood whereby all routers in the OSPF domain can update their link-state database. When S comes back up, the process repeats.

Additionally, LSAs have a limited lifespan of 30 minutes, by default. When an LSA reaches its timeout, the originating router will issue a new LSA using a link-state update message, once again causing a flood throughout the domain. Each time a new LSA (which occurs whenever the LSA times out or the LSA changes) is sent out, each router must rebuild its link-state database and recompute all best routes. Best routes are selected based on a *cost* value associated with each route in an LSA. We describe the cost values in "Route Selection" on page 558. First, let's look at LSAs and some overhead reducing techniques of OSPF.

LSAs

LSAs contribute to the complete link-state database of an OSPF domain. The way in which LSAs are managed and the data they contain is, therefore, critical to the integrity of the database and maintaining a single, synchronized database throughout the OSPF domain. In order to understand the way in which LSAs are managed, we need to examine the LSA header. This header is depicted in Figure 12–2. Each LSA which is incorporated in the various link-state update messages is preceded by this header.

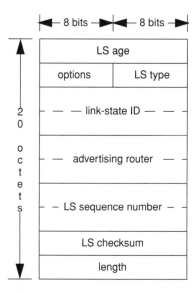

Figure 12–2   LSA Header

Table 12–1 summarizes the fields in the LSA Header.

Table 12–1   LSA Header Fields

FIELD	DESCRIPTION
LS age	Contains the age of the LSA in seconds. See "LS Age" on page 554 for further details.
options	Contains the options for the LSA. There are two options defined by RFC 1583. The E option (second lowest order bit set) specifies that the advertising router has routes outside of the OSPF domain (called *external*), and the T option (lowest order bit set) indicates that there are TOS (or differentiated service) options set in the IP header. Other options have since been defined and are discussed later.
LS type	Specifies the type of LSA. The meaning of the values in this field are described in "LS Type" on page 555.

Table 12–1   LSA Header Fields *(Continued)*

FIELD	DESCRIPTION
link-state ID	Used to uniquely identify the LSA. The identifier depends on the LS type field above and is described in "LS Type" on page 555.
advertising router	The router ID of the originating router (creator) of the LSA.
LS sequence number	The sequence number associated with this LSA. Each time a router updates an LSA this value is incremented by 1.
LS checksum	A checksum of the LSA header and contents. This value is computed by the originating router and then carried with the LSA throughout its lifespan. During flooding each router will verify the checksum. If the checksum here is different than the computed checksum, then the LSA is discarded. OSPF participants periodically verify the checksums within their link-state database to guard against hardware or software errors. If during the periodic check a checksum is found to be incorrect, then the system will reinitialize.
length	Contains the length in octets of the LSA contents and header. Minimum is 8 octets and the maximum (imposed by IP) is 65,535.

LS AGE   The LS age field indicates the age of an LSA. Routers base their updating of their own LSAs based on this field. By default, a router will advertise its LSA every 30 minutes and, thus, LSA ages are normally between 0 seconds and 1800 seconds old. Once an LSA reaches 30 minutes old, the originating router increments the sequence number, sets the LS age field to 0, and advertises the LSA to each of its interfaces.

If an OSPF router has an LSA for which the age field has reached 60 minutes (known as MaxAge), then the LSA can be removed. This is the *only* circumstance under which a router can remove an LSA that it did not create. In order to retain sychronicity, whenever a router removes an LSA under such circumstances, it floods the OSPF domain with an LSA update message incorporating the LSA with the LS age field set to 60 minutes. This causes all routers to remove this entry from their link-state database. Normally, an LSA reaches an age of 60 minutes only when the originating router has failed.

There is one circumstance under which natural aging can be circumvented. If the originating router of an LSA wants to remove the LSA from the link-state database, it can do so by setting the LS age field to 3600 seconds and sending a link-state update message to each of its interfaces. This is known as *premature aging*. Such an action might be taken, for example, if a router has an LSA for a RIP environment to which it is attached that, for some reason, is no longer reachable. The other interfaces and networks to which the router is attached remain unaffected as far as the link-state database is concerned. Only the router that originates the LSA can utilize premature aging for the LSA.

LS TYPE   There are five LS type field values defined in RFC 1583. Two types were added by other RFCs and one is proposed. Table 12–2 describes the LS type field values and in which RFC they are defined.

Table 12–2   LS Type Field Values

VALUE	MEANING	DEFINING RFC
1	Specifies that the LSA is a *router-LSA* or one which defines the state of the router's interfaces.	1583
2	Specifies that the LSA is a *network-LSA* or one which defines the type (broadcast, point-to-point, or non-broadcast—see "Supported Network Types" on page 561) of each network to which the router is attached as well as the identity of each router on each of the networks.	1583
3	Specifies that the LSA is a *network-summary-LSA*. This type of advertisement is originated by area border routers (ABRs) and contains routes to other OSPF areas. It is also used for *stub* networks (networks that have only one router to other networks).	1583

Table 12–2   LS Type Field Values *(continued)*

VALUE	MEANING	DEFINING RFC
4	Specifies that the LSA is an *ASBR-summary-LSA*. This type of advertisement is orginated by autonomous system boundary routers (ASBRs) and contains routes to the ASBR(s).	1583
5	Specifies that the LSA is an *AS-external-LSA*. This type of LSA is originated by ASBRs and contains routes to networks that are external to the AS.	1583
6	Specifies that the LSA is a *group-membership-LSA*. It contains information about multicast groups and their members. This type is used by multicast OSPF (MOSPF).	1584
7	Specifies that the LSA is an *NSSA-LSA*. These types of LSAs are used to import certain types of routes into not so stubby areas (NSSAs).	1587
8	Specifies that the LSA is an *external-attributes-LSA*. This type of LSA contains BGP routing information and is used to propagate these routes without having one or more routers participate in BGP.	proposed[*]

[*].   D. Ferguson, *The OSPF External Attributes LSA*, unpublished. This paper is referenced in RFCs 1793, 2178, and 2740.

A simple OSPF implementation, such as the one described earlier in this section, typically uses LS types 1 and 2 for the propagation of routes within the OSPF domain. If the OSPF domain incorporates connections to networks outside the domain, these are propagated as LS type 5 LSAs. We consider the use of the different LS types in "OSPF Hierarchies and Other Routing Domains" on page 563.

IMPORTANT NOTE ABOUT LSAs   A router can maintain a number of different LSAs. Some of the LSAs are those originated by the router and others are those collected from other routers. A router can update any of the LSAs in its link-state database under the following circumstances.

- As frequently as once every 5 seconds.
- Whenever a state change in an LSA occurs, such as an interface going down or a link-local router does not respond after 40 seconds.
- An LSA's LS age field has reached 60 minutes.

It is important to note that a router can only update its own LSAs except when an LSA LS age field reaches 60 minutes.

Designated Routers and Backup Designated Routers

One of the resource-saving capabilities of OSPF is that for each network, certain routers are selected to maintain communication of LSA updates and therefore the synchronization of the link-state database. These routers are the designated router (DR) and backup designated router (BDR). The purpose of the DR is to propagate link-state updates to the network for which it is the DR. In this way, each network will only receive one update each time an update is propagated. Of course, for a network with one or two routers, this feature is of little consequence, but for networks with three or more routers, it saves a lot of unnecessary OSPF traffic.

The purpose of the BDR is to take over if the DR goes down. The role of the BDR is critical since, if it didn't exist and the DR went down, none of the routers on the given network would get the updates. If a BDR assumes the role of DR, then a new BDR is immediately selected. Networks with only one router obviously cannot have a BDR. Networks with only two routers cannot select a new BDR when the DR goes down.

Effectively, once the DR and BDR have been selected for a given network, they are the only systems that will respond to hello messages on that network. This means, in particular, that routers on a network only become fully adjacent to the DR and BDR. Each of the other routers on the network are simply adjacent to each other. This merely means that they are aware of each others existence and state, but that they do not routinely exchange hellos. As we see in "Interlude: Using the `ospf_monitor` Utility" on page 595, full adjacencies are reported as full connections while adjacencies show up as two-way connections.

The DR and BDR are selected based on a priority value assigned to each router interface. If two routers have identical priorities, then the one with the higher router ID is chosen. The router with the second highest priority or router ID is designated the BDR. When configuring your routers for this selection process, you will likely want to set the priority appropriately to ensure that the best performing routers (especially, in route-intensive environments) are chosen for the DR role. We look at implementing priorities a little later in this chapter; the mechanism for this purpose is described in Table 12–4 on page 560.

Route Selection

We have already described the fact that OSPF exchanges routing information through LSAs and utilizes various messages to ensure that the collection of LSAs comprises a synchronized link-state database throughout the OSPF domain. But the link-state database is not used directly for routing. Rather, each router (indeed, each system) that has the link-state database uses it to determine what the routes to each destination should be and then populates the routing table accordingly. But how does it do this? It uses an administrator definable route *cost* that can be associated with each router interface. The only requirement for the cost value is that it be an integer between 1 and 65,535. The smaller the value, the lower the cost. The cost associated with each router interface is propagated with the LSAs enabling OSPF to choose the lowest cost path for any given destination.

Costs can be based on a variety of things. They can be simple hop counts or weighted hop counts and thereby emulate RIP. They can be assigned based on the performance of a given link. For example, a DSL connection at 256 Kbps would be assigned a higher cost than a 10 Mbps Ethernet connection. Also, since OSPF costs are associated with interfaces (and not networks), different costs can be associated with different directions across the same network. In order to determine the cost of a route from one point to another, the cost of each link (or interface) through which the packet must travel is summed. If there are multiple paths to the same destination, OSPF chooses the one with lowest cost—also known as the shortest path.

Consider the collection of interconnected routers given in Figure 12–3. Suppose that they are all running OSPF. Each of the routers in this diagram is identified by a letter to make our discussion simpler. In reality, each router with interconnecting interfaces would have an appropriate IP address. Also, each of the interfaces has a cost (shown in parentheses) associated with it. Using the diagram, you can calculate the cost of the route between two points by adding up the costs of each interface through which the packet must traverse. Costs are accumulated in an outbound direction as indicated by the arrows.

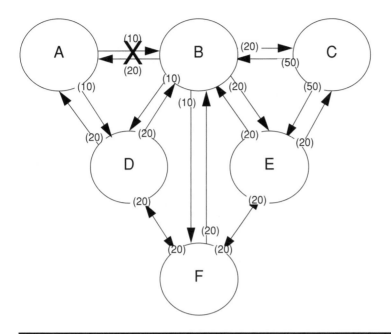

Figure 12–3   OSPF Route Selection

Note that the diagram in Figure 12–3 shows a gray X through the link between A and B. Let's consider the routing selection first as if that link were up and then as if the link were down (as shown).

ROUTE SELECTION FOR A (LINK BETWEEN A AND B UP)   If the link between A and B is up, then the lowest cost paths from A to each of the other routers is given in Table 12–3.

Table 12–3   Lowest Cost Paths for A with B Directly Accessible

DESTINATION FROM A	LOWEST COST PATH	COST
B	direct	10
C	A→B→C	10+20=30
D	direct	10
E	A→B→E	10+20=30
F	A→B→F	10+10=20

Since IP forwards packets on a hop-by-hop basis, only the next hop is put into the routing table. Thus, the routing table for A would appear as given in Table 12–4.

Table 12–4   Routing Table for A with A→B Link

DESTINATION	GATEWAY
B	A
C	B
D	A
E	B
F	B

ROUTE SELECTION FOR A (LINK BETWEEN A AND B DOWN) If the link between A and B is down then, based on Figure 12–3, the lowest cost paths from A to each of the other routers is given in Table 12–5.

Table 12–5   Lowest Cost Paths for A with B Indirectly Accessible

DESTINATION FROM A	LOWEST COST PATH	COST
B	A→D→B	10+20=30
C	A→D→B→C	10+20+20=50
D	direct	10
E	A→D→B→E A→D→F→E	10+20+20=50 10+20+20=50
F	A→D→F	10+20=30

Notice that there are two equal cost paths now from A to E. This is called an *equal-cost multipath*. Since OSPF maintains a synchronized link-state database, the router D could choose to use either B or F to reach the destination of E. This means that D could implement load balancing based on the information available from OSPF. OSPF, in and of itself, cannot provide load balancing services. To a certain extent, load balancing can be achieved through other Linux routing configuration capabilities discussed in Chapter 16.

These routes would appear in A's routing table as shown in Table 12–6.

Table 12–6   Routing Table for A without A→B Link

DESTINATION	GATEWAY
B	D
C	D
D	A
E	D
F	D

Note that the routing table change that occurred here from that shown in Table 12–4 takes place within seconds after the downed link has been identified. OSPF very rapidly synchronizes new databases around failures.

Be sure to bear in mind that while OSPF maintains complete maps of the network topology and thereby each router has complete path information about any given destination within the OSPF domain, IP does not maintain such information. Thus, it is entirely possible that a packet ends up taking a different path than originally computed by OSPF. Such an event could occur if the packet is being transmitted while OSPF flooding is taking place, so that when the packet arrived at an intermediate router, the link-state database was different. The good news is that it doesn't matter. The packet will ultimately get forwarded to its destination, even if the path it takes isn't as originally intended.

It should also be noted that OSPF can take TOS parameters into account in the calculation of paths. We discuss this capability in Chapter 16.

Supported Network Types

Everything that we have discussed to this point assumes the use of a typical TCP/IP broadcast network such as Ethernet. However, OSPF can also operate over nonbroadcast networks such as Frame Relay, X.25, or ATM. For all intents and purposes, implementing OSPF over such environments is entirely similar to broadcast networks. The major difference is that layer 2 technologies such as these that have no broadcast capabilities establish virtual circuits (connections[2]) at layer 2 through a *switching fabric*. A switching fabric is a collection of switches that forward packets based only on physical addressing. Thus, in such a case, OSPF routers need to form adjacencies by building circuits between themselves and the DR and BDR. In larger environments, this can incur a lot of overhead.

OSPF can also operate over point-to-multipoint or point-to-point environments. Sometimes it is more efficient to implement nonbroadcast networks using the point-to-(multi)point capabilities to avoid the use of a lot of circuits. In this type of environment there are no designated routers. Instead, all routers that can communicate directly with each other (that is, are on the same local network) exchange hellos and become adjacent to each other. In large environments this method can also incur a lot of overhead.

There are numerous methods for applying, and alternatives to the use of, OSPF in these types of environments. See, for example, RFC 1586 (OSPF over Frame Relay), 1793 (Extending OSPF to Support Demand Circuits), and 2332 (next hop resolution protocol [NHRP]).

Unfortunately, the public version of `gated` does not support point-to-(multi)point OSPF capabilities. If you require that functionality, you will either need to obtain a licensed version of `gated` (see Chapter 11) or use `zebra` (discussed in "GNU Zebra" on page 611).

What about NonRouters?

Systems that are not routers within an OSPF domain act very much like such systems in a RIP environment. In short, they join the multicast groups `224.0.0.5` and `224.0.0.6`, listen for all of the link-state updates, and build a link-state database that is then used to determine the best routes and modify the routing table appropriately. We consider configuring nonrouters in an OSPF environment in "Configuring the Hosts" on page 592.

---

2. Conceptually, layer 2 virtual circuit connections are the same as TCP virtual circuit connections discussed in Chapter 7.

OSPF Hierarchies and Other Routing Domains

Up to this point we have described a simple OSPF domain in which each router has a complete link-state database comprising the entire domain. As internetworks scale up in size, this approach becomes untenable. Even though the OSPF synchronization process and best route computations are fast, large environments can experience delays when the link-state database gets large. OSPF has a solution to this problem—build multiple OSPF areas within the OSPF domain.

OSPF implements a "hub and spoke" hierarchy. Effectively this means that there are two layers to the hierarchy—the networks comprising the hub (called the *backbone*) are at the top or center and the networks attached at the end of the spokes are at the bottom or on the edges. The key to this topology is that each OSPF area within the domain must directly connect to the backbone. An area's connection to the backbone may be virtual.

The point of creating OSPF areas is to reduce routing table size and route computation time. Within an area, route computation and link-state synchronization proceeds as described previously using LSAs of LS type 1, 2, and sometimes 3—this is called *intraarea* routing. Between areas, however, the LSAs advertised are LS type 3, 4, and 5 (see Table 12–2 on page 555)—this is called *interarea* routing. These are summary LSAs which, wherever possible, include route aggregation. These LSAs are smaller and reduce the overall complexity and compute resources required in synchronizing the link-state database within an area.

Areas are defined by area border routers (ABRs). Such a router is configured to participate in at least two areas by setting up the interfaces appropriately. All ABRs must have one interface that is configured to participate in the backbone even though it may be a virtual connection. All areas are uniquely identified by a 32-bit address represented in decimal dotted notation. The backbone is always identified as area 0.0.0.0. Optimally, areas ought to be configured to maximize route aggregation.

Consider the example given in Figure 12–4.

In Figure 12–4, there are five areas, three of which are directly attached to the backbone and area 0.0.1.3, which is attached to the backbone via a virtual link through the router I. Within each area, a complete link-state database exists, providing route information for all of the networks within the area. The ABRs, A, B, C, and H generate summary information about their areas and flood those routes to the backbone. Each ABR receives the flooded summary information

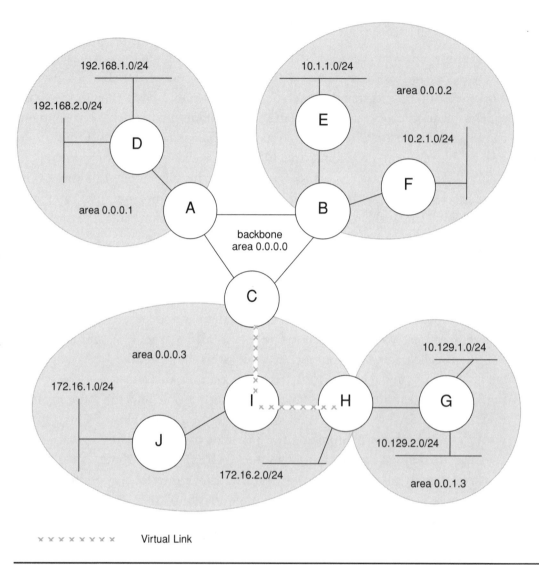

x x x x x x x x   Virtual Link

Figure 12–4   OSPF Areas

and computes interarea routes to the other ABRs for service to their areas and then floods that information into the area for which it is responsible.

Let's take a closer look at the way in which the link-state information is propagated througout this environment. Consider area 0.0.0.3. Each of the routers, C, I, J, and H, participate in link-state database synchronization by using router-LSAs (LS type=1) and network-LSAs (LS type=2). Router-LSAs are used to report the networks to which each router is attached and the DR for that network. Network-LSAs are used to identify networks and how they can be reached. They will also use summary-network-LSAs (LS type=3) to report stub networks; for instance, J will use a summary-network-LSA for the network `172.16.1.0/24` and H will do the same for `172.16.2.0/24`. The ABRs, C, J, and H, will use their knowledge of area `0.0.0.3` to create summary-network-LSAs containing only the fact that they can access the networks within area `0.0.0.3` and propagate these to routers outside the area. The routers outside the area will do exactly the same thing so that C, J, and H can advertise that they have access to the other areas. For example, C will obtain information from A that indicates that A can reach `192.168.1.0/24` and `192.168.2.0/24`. Therefore, C will generate network-summary-LSAs to area `0.0.0.3`, indicating that it can reach these two networks. As far as all the systems and routers in area `0.0.0.3` are concerned, reaching `192.168.1.0/24` or `192.168.2.0/24` requires sending the packets to C.

In fact, from Figure 12–4, it is clear that the only way to get to `192.168.0.0` is through A, so A could actually advertise that aggregate route and thereby reduce the amount of information necessary in the network-summary-LSA. This, of course, would also have the effect of reducing all the routing tables that will use this information. In larger environments, say, for example, where area `0.0.0.1` contained 40 networks, all of which began with `192.168`, the aggregation represents a substantial savings in information processing and in routing table size. Of course, A would have to be configured to do this as we see in the examples beginning in "A Flat OSPF Domain Example" on page 584. The routers B, C, and H could likewise be configured to advertise aggregate routes.

Notice that area `0.0.1.3` does not have a physical link to the backbone. In spite of the lack of direct connectivity to the backbone, H must still submit summary LSAs to the backbone. This is accomplished by tunneling through I and C so that H becomes a *virtual* member of the backbone. H's area summary LSAs thus reach the backbone routers A, B, and C and can be incorporated into their link-state databases. Similarly, H receives the summary LSAs of the routers A, B, and C so that H can propagate that information to its area. We see how to configure this capability in "The `virtuallink` Stanza" on page 583.

It is important to bear in mind, once again, that what we have described is the methodology employed by OSPF to build its link-state database. This link-state database is used to compute the best routes and then modify the routing table accordingly. The routing table *always* and *only* contains next hop information to the destination. This is particularly the case with H. Even though it has a virtual connection into the backbone, all of the packets that it sends to and through the backbone will first go to I and then to C.

Now, consider Figure 12–5, which adds an external connection to the Internet and a RIP domain to the prior example in Figure 12–4.

This example adds the router K which connects area 0.0.0.3 of the OSPF domain to an external RIP domain. The router K is called an *AS boundary router* (ASBR). It will utilize AS-external LSAs (LS type=5) to propagate routing information from the RIP domain into the OSPF domain.

Figure 12–5 also adds a connection from C to the Internet. C, therefore, also becomes an ASBR and is responsible for distributing routing information about the Internet connection. It will do so by participating in an appropriate routing table management scheme (such as BGP or a simple static default router entry) for its Internet connection and then propagating ASBR-summary-LSAs (LS type=4) to the backbone and area 0.0.0.3. These LSAs are then flooded throughout the rest of the OSPF domain by the other routers as previously described. Thus, in Figure 12–5, we have effectively defined the AS to be the OSPF domain. The RIP domain is a separate autonomous system. However, from the Internet perspective, C represents the router that leads to a single autonomous system—systems out on the Internet do not know, nor do they need to know, that multiple ASes exist in a given environment such as this. Note that C may or may not actually participate in an official AS.

Now that we have given an overview of the different LS types, let's tie things together by describing them and associating each type with the LS identification (see Table 12–2 on page 555) in Table 12–7. This table comes in handy when we consider implementation later in this chapter.

There are two special OSPF areas that we need to define.

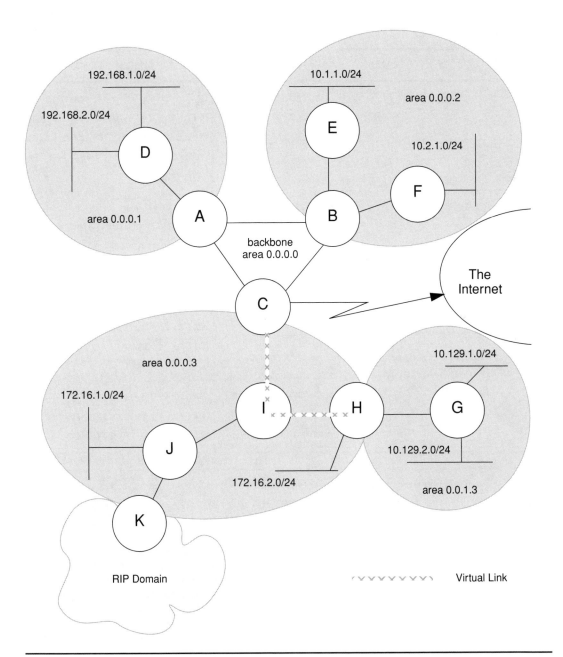

Figure 12–5 OSPF Areas and External Domains

Table 12–7   LSA Types and Identification Association

LS TYPE	LS TYPE NAME	LS ID	DESCRIPTION
1	router-LSA	The originating router ID	This LSA describes the originating router's link states. It is only issued by the router that owns the interfaces.
2	network-LSA	The IP address of the DR for that link (not necessarily the router ID)	This LSA describes the network and identifies each router attached to the network. It is only issued by the DR for the network and the DR is considered the originating router or owner of this LSA.
3	network-summary-LSA	The destination network number	This type of LSA consists of route(s) to the destination network. It is originated by an ABR or by a router connected to a stub network.
4	ASBR-summary-LSA	The router ID of the ASBR	This type of LSA consists of route(s) to the ASBR. It is originated by the ASBR.
5	AS-external-LSA	The destination network number	This type of LSA consists of route(s) to destinations external to the OSPF domain. It may simply be a default route. It is originated byt the ASBR.

Stubby and Not So Stubby Areas

RFC 1583 (and its successors) define a special type of area called a *stub* area. The purpose of a stub area is to define an area in which the routers maintain a link-state database that is as small as possible. AS-external-LSAs are not flooded into a stub area. Instead, a default route is computed by the stub ABR and propagated. Also, all summary LSAs (LS type 3 and 4) are optional in stub areas permitting the use of a default route to the appropriate router to reach networks and AS boundaries. As a consequence of the limitations imposed by stub areas, they cannot support virtual connections and must therefore always be on the outmost edge of the spoke. Considering this definition and Figure 12–5 on page 567, only areas `0.0.0.1`, `0.0.0.2`, and `0.0.1.3` could be configured as stubs. Area `0.0.0.3` cannot be a stub because it has a virtual link passing through it and it has an external domain (the RIP domain) which requires it to utilize AS-external-LSAs. Backbones can never be configured as stub areas. Configuration of stub areas is never automatic and should be reserved for those environments in which router resources are at a premium.

Due to the fairly severe limitations of stub areas, *not so stubby areas* (NSSAs) were defined in RFC 1587. The point of an NSSA was to make areas like `0.0.0.3` in Figure 12–5 on page 567 available for some of the reduced link-state database sizes by propagating a limited set of information about external routes attached to the area (in this case, the RIP domain). In this way, area `0.0.0.3` could use default routes to all points outside the area but still be able to propagate enough information about the RIP domain to properly allow access from other areas. NSSAs use the special NSSA-LSA (LS type=7) for this purpose. Unfortunately, the public version of `gated` does not support NSSAs. Thus, if you need to use them, you either must obtain a licensed version of `gated` or use `zebra`.

A Note about OSPF External Routes

OSPF views external routes in two basic categories. *Type 1* external routes are those which are imported from routing table management protocols that use compatible metrics to that of OSPF. For example, RIP metrics can be imported into the OSPF infrastructure and used by OSPF for path costing calculations. Imported static routes also fall into the type 1 category.

Type 2 external routes are those which are imported from routing table management protocols that use incompatible and more significant metrics than

OSPF. For example, routes imported from BGP contain metrics associated with reaching destinations through multiple ASes. ASBRs in OSPF will always advertise these routes with their BGP costs exclusive of the internal cost to reach the ASBR. After all, the OSPF domain represents a single AS and so the cost of reaching other ASes is more significant than the cost of reaching the ASBR within an AS.

When Should Areas Be Used?

It is very difficult to generally state when areas should be implemented as opposed to the use of a single OSPF flat domain (just the backbone). This is because so much of the decision rests upon factors that are unique to a particular environment, including administrative responsibility, organization infrastructure, geographical and topological issues, and political issues. From a strictly performance perspective, however, many router vendors recommend a maximum of 50 routers per OSPF area. Some, however, have recently advertised building OSPF areas with 350 to 500 routers! Of course, if you are using Linux systems as routers, this will have an impact on such numbers, as Linux systems ordinarily will not perform as well as dedicated routers.

In any event, deciding whether to implement multiple areas within an OSPF domain is usually dictated by both organizational needs and performance considerations. Their implementations does not substantially increase administrative overhead or configuration difficulty. In some ways, it makes troubleshooting easier because areas provide a logical breakdown of your environment and offer a way to isolate problems within or without a particular area. The primary benefit of using areas is routing table size reduction. Principally, this is accomplished by configuring routing aggregation on an ABR that is then propagated to other areas through summary LSAs instead of the more specific router- and network-LSAs.

Summary of OSPF Terms

For convenience, Table 12–8 lists many of the terms we've discussed in the preceeding sections and provides brief descriptions of each.

Table 12–8   OSPF Terms

Term	Description
link-state database	The collection of LSAs that comprise an OSPF area or domain. This database is synchronized throughout each area. If the only area is the backbone, then it is synchronized throughout the domain. This means, in particular, that every router in an OSPF area or domain contains a map of the entire area or domain in the form of the link-state database. Moreover, every router has the *exact same* map.
router ID	An identification number associated with a router. Normally, this is one of the IP addresses associated with the router. It must be unique throughout the OSPF domain.
neighbors	OSPF routers that have interfaces to the same local networks are called neighbors.
(fully) adjacent	Two OSPF routers are said to be fully adjacent, if they are: **1.** neighbors **2.** successfully synchronized as described in "OSPF Basics" on page 548 **3.** at least one of the two routers is a DR or BDR Two OSPF routers are said to be adjacent if the first two conditions above are met.
hello message	An OSPF message used to communicate with other OSPF routers at start-up and then regularly with the DR. The regular hello messages are sent out by default every 10 seconds and serve the purpose of acting as keep-alive messages.
database description request message	A request message used during the synchronization process to obtain a list of available LSAs.

Table 12–8   OSPF Terms *(Continued)*

TERM	DESCRIPTION
database description message	The response message to the database description request.
link-state request message	A request message used during synchronization seeking the collection of LSAs for the area or domain.
link-state update message	A message used in response to a link-state request or to advise neighbors of changes in one or more LSAs. These messages always cause a flood throughout the area or domain until all routers have resynchronized their link-state database.
link-state acknowledgment message	A message used to acknowledge a link-state update.
LSA	A link-state advertisement contains information about router interfaces, networks, routes to networks, and/or default route information. See Table 12–7 on page 568 for a listing of all LSA types and their meanings.
DR	A designated router is chosen for each local network (except when using point-to-multipoint OSPF). The designated router is responsible for responding to synchronization start-ups by other routers and for flooding updates to the local network.
BDR	Backup designated routers provide failover capabilities for the DR. The BDR maintains full adjacency with all routers on the local network and acts as a "hot spare" to the DR.

Table 12–8   OSPF Terms *(Continued)*

TERM	DESCRIPTION
LS age	This field in the LSA header (see Figure 12–2 on page 553) of all LSAs indicates how old the LSA is. LSAs are typically between 0 and 1,800 seconds old. Any LSA that reaches an age of 3,600 seconds (60 minutes) can be removed by *any* router in the area or domain via a link-state update. This is the only case in which an LSA can be removed by a router other than the originating router.
LS type	This field in the LSA header specifies the type of LSA that is incorporated into the message. See Table 12–7 on page 568 for a listing of all LSA types and their meanings.
link-state ID	The link-state ID is used to uniquely identify an LSA.
intraarea	Routes between routers and networks within and OSPF area are called intraarea routes.
interarea	Routes between routers and networks that cross OSPF area boundaries are called interarea routes.
type 1 metrics	Type 1 metrics are used with external routes that originate from routing table management protocols and use metrics and are compatible with OSPF cost metrics. For example, RIP and static routes utilize compatible metrics.
type 2 metrics	Type 2 metrics are used with external routes that originate from routing table management protocols and use metrics that are incompatible with and more significant than OSPF cost metrics. Routes from BGP fall into this category since they incorporate metrics that cross AS boundaries (and are therefore more significant), while OSPF metrics are always constrained to internal AS use.

Implementing OSPF with `gated`

The public version 3.6 of `gated` implements RFC 1583 for OSPFv2. While not the most recent RFC for OSPF, it captures the vast majority of functionality necessary for many OSPF implementations. Also, as we have previously noted, `gated` version 3.6 does not provide support for point-to-multipoint OSPF nor for NSSAs. If you need support for these extensions or for any of the improvements and/or enhancements in RFC 2178 and/or RFC 2328, you will need to obtain the commercial version of `gated` (see Chapter 11) or use `zebra` (see "GNU Zebra" on page 611). In this section, we consider implementing OSPF with version 3.6. Much of what is discussed here directly applies to the commercial versions of `gated` and indirectly applies to `zebra`.

We covered all of the general `gated` configuration options in Chapter 11. At this point, therefore, we only need to describe the `gated` configuration options for OSPF. Note that like Chapter 11, this section is very detailed and may be too tedious for an initial take on this topic. In such a case, feel free to skip to "A Flat OSPF Domain Example" on page 584 and read through the examples, returning to this section as necessary for the details of the various entries in `/etc/gated.conf`.

The `ospf` Stanza

The `ospf` stanza used in `gated` is fairly lengthy because it incorporates a large variety of options. Under most circumstances few of the options are necessary. Example 12–1 depicts the `ospf` syntax. The line numbers to the left are for discussion purposes and are not part of the syntax.

Example 12–1   ospf Stanza

```
1 ospf on | off [ {
2     defaults {
3             preference pref ;
4             cost defcost ;
5             tag [as] tag ;
6             type 1 | 2 ;
7             inherit-metric ;
8     } ;
9     exportlimit mzx ;
10    exportinterval time ;
11    traceoptions options ;
12    syslog [first count] [every count] ;
13    monitorauthkey pw ;
```

Example 12–1   ospf Stanza *(Continued)*

```
14    area areanumber | backbone {
15            stub [cost defcost] ;
16            networks {
17                    route-filter [restrict] ;
18            } ;
19            stubhosts {
20                    host cost cost ;
21            } ;
22            interface iface_list [cost ifcost] [ {
23                    enable | disable ;
24                    retransmitinterval time ;
25                    transitdelay time ;
26                    priority drpriority ;
27                    hellointerval time ;
28                    routerdeadinterval time ;
29                    passive ;
30                    auth [none | simple auth_key | md5 ospf_md5_key] ;
31                    secondary [none | simple auth_key | md5 md5_stanza] ;
32            } ] ;
33            interface iface_list nonbroadcast [cost ifcost] [ {
34                    pollinterval time ;
35                    routers {
36                            gateway [eligible] ;
37                    } ;
38                    retransmitinterval time ;
39                    transitdelay time ;
40                    priority drpriority ;
41                    hellointerval time ;
42                    routerdeadinterval time ;
43                    passive ;
44                    auth [none | simple auth_key | md5 md5_stanza] ;
45                    secondary [none | simple | md5 ] pw ;
46            } ] ;
47            virtuallink neighborid routerID transitarea area {
48                    interface iface_list ;
49                    retransmitinterval time ;
50                    transitdelay time ;
51                    priority priority ;
52                    hellointerval time ;
53                    routerdeadinterval time ;
54                    passive ;
55                    auth [none | simple auth_key | md5 md5_stanza] ;
56                    secondary [none | simple | md5 ] pw ;
57            } ;
58    } ;
59 } ] ;
```

In order to simplify the discussion of this stanza, we'll break it up into three parts: the `defaults` stanza, the OSPF global options, and the `area` stanza.

The `defaults` Stanza

The purpose of this stanza (see lines 2 through 8 in Example 12–1) is to set parameters for autonomous system external (ASE) routes. In other words, routes obtained from outside the OSPF AS are affected by these parameters. They apply both for importing ASE routes by an ASBR and exporting them into AS-external-LSAs by the ASBR. Importing of these routes is controlled by the `import` statement and exporting is controlled by the `export` statement. See "Import and Export Policies" on page 497 for a discussion of these statements, generally, and "Importing and Exporting OSPF Routes" on page 584 for OSPF specific details.

Any options set within this stanza apply to all ASE routes. Table 12–9 describes the options within the `defaults` stanza.

Table 12–9 Options Within the `defaults` Stanza

OPTION	DESCRIPTION
`preference` *pref*	This is the `gated` preference and specifies the priority for ASE routes. The default is 150 (see "`gated` Preferences" on page 478).
`cost` *defcost*	This sets the OSPF cost to ASE routes. The default is 1. This value may be overwritten on a per route basis in the `export` statement.
`tag [as]` *tag*	OSPF permits the use of a 32-bit `tag` field for ASE routes. OSPF does nothing with this value, but `gated` can use it to filter routes in an `export` statement. If the ASE contains AS path information, then the `as` keyword should be specified and then *tag* cannot exceed 12 bits. By default, *tag* is 0. The use of `tag` is further discussed in "Importing and Exporting OSPF Routes" on page 584.

Table 12–9   Options Within the `defaults` Stanza *(Continued)*

OPTION	DESCRIPTION
`type 1	2`	Specifies whether ASE routes use type 1 or type 2 metrics (see "A Note about OSPF External Routes" on page 569). Type 1 is the default.
`inherit-metric`	This option specifies that the ASE route metric is to be incorporated as the OSPF cost. If not specified, the `defcost` value is used and can be overwritten in an `export` statement.

It is common on ASBRs to set these defaults for imported ASE routes and then to override the exceptions in `export` statements. ASE routes *must* be exported in order for them to be propagated to the rest of the OSPF domain.

The `ospf` Stanza Global Options

This portion of the `ospf` stanza (line 9 through 13 in Example 12–1 on page 574) includes the `exportlimit`, `exportinterval`, `traceoptions`, `syslog`, and `monitorauthkey` options. The `exportlimit` and `exportinterval` options apply to ASE routes and are used to control ASE flooding by ASBRs. The reason that this is necessary is due to the fact that AS path updates can occur in large volume and more rapidly than the OSPF domain should be flooded, thus, these options provide a way to control the OSPF flooding rate and size of AS-external-LSAs (see "Configuration for `golden`" on page 607 for an example of AS path use). These options are described in Table 12–10.

Table 12–10   The `ospf` Stanza Global Options

OPTION	DESCRIPTION
`exportlimit max`	Specifies that *max* ASE routes will be flooded at any given time. This has the effect of batching ASE route floods. By default, *max* is 100.
`exportinterval time`	Specifies the maximum frequency, *time*, in seconds, with which AS-external-LSAs will be generated. The default is 1 per second.

Table 12–10 The `ospf` Stanza Global Options *(Continued)*

OPTION	DESCRIPTION
`traceoptions` *options*	The list of OSPF specific trace options. See "The `gated` interfaces Statement" on page 479 for general trace options and syntax. Table 12–11 details the trace options that are specific to OSPF.
`syslog [first count]` `[every count]`	This option can be used to limit the number of OSPF messages written to `syslog`. The `first` keyword indicates that the first *count* packets for every type of OSPF message will be logged. After that, the `every` keyword specifies that only one message per *count* packets will be logged.
`monitorauthkey pw`	This is similar to the `query authentication` statement for RIP (see "RIP Authentication with `gated`" on page 518). This authentication is used exclusively with the `ospf_monitor` utility (see "Interlude: Using the `ospf_monitor` Utility" on page 593). The authentication type is simple (passes in cleartext over the network) and *pw* can be an 8 octet value in decimal dotted notation, in hexadecimal preceeded by 0x, or in a quoted string. If not specified, no authentication is performed for `ospf_monitor` requests.

The OSPF specific trace options are provided in Table 12–11. See "The `traceoptions` Statement" on page 484 for further details on tracing.

Table 12–11 OSPF Specific Trace Options

OPTION	DESCRIPTION
`lsabuild`	Traces the creation of LSAs.
`lsatransmit` `or lsatx`	Traces transmitted LSAs.

Table 12–11   OSPF Specific Trace Options *(Continued)*

OPTION	DESCRIPTION
`lsareceive` or `lsarx`	Traces received LSAs.
`spf`	Traces the shortest path first calculations.
`debug`	Traces all OSPF activity at the debug level. This generates a lot of detail.
`packets`	Traces all OSPF packets sent and received. Can be modified with the `detail`, `send`, and `recv` parameters as described in Table 11–9 on page 486.
`hello`	Traces all hello messages. Can be modified with the `detail`, `send`, and `recv` parameters as described in Table 11–9 on page 486.
`dd`	Traces all database description messages. Can be modified with the `detail`, `send`, and `recv` parameters as described in Table 11–9 on page 486.
`request`	Traces all link-state request messages. Can be modified with the `detail`, `send`, and `recv` parameters as described in Table 11–9 on page 486.
`lsu`	Traces all link-state update messages. Can be modified with the `detail`, `send`, and `recv` parameters as described in Table 11–9 on page 486. *Warning:* As of this writing, the `lsu` option generates a syntax error and does not function correctly in `gated` version 3.6! It is documented here in the hopes that this bug will be corrected with some future release.
`ack`	Traces all link-state acknowledgment messages. Can be modified with the `detail`, `send`, and `recv` parameters as described in Table 11–9 on page 486.

The area or backbone Stanza

The area or backbone stanza (lines 14 through 58 in Example 12–1 on page 574) specifies the OSPF area(s) to which the system belongs. There is always at least one area defined (backbone, if none other is specified). Area 0.0.0.0 cannot be specified with the area keyword; the backbone keyword must be used instead. ABRs will always have at least two area stanzas or one area and one backbone stanza.

These stanzas always open with area *areanumber* or backbone statements. The *areanumber* is a 32-bit value specified in decimal dotted notation.

Within the area or backbone stanza, there are six distinct statements, five of which can have their own stanza. Each of these statements is documented in its own section below. The only statement that does not utilize a stanza is the stub statement.

SPECIFYING AN OSPF STUB AREA   The stub statement (see line 15 in Example 12–1) specifies that the area is a stub area (see "Stubby and Not So Stubby Areas" on page 569). All routers in a stub area must specify this statement or adjacencies will not form. If the cost keyword is used, then the specified *defcost* is used to associate a cost to this router as a default route. Thus, the use of the cost keyword should be restricted to ABRs. Multiple ABRs supporting a stub area can each use the cost keyword to advertise a default route. The use of *defcost* on the different ABRs can be used to set up preferred default routes within the stub area.

USING THE network STANZA   The network stanza (lines 16 through 18 in Example 12–1) is used to identify the intraarea networks for the area. The stanza can contain many *route_filter* (see "Route Filtering" on page 491) specifications for (sub)networks and their associated masks. Any network specified in the list will only be advertised outside the area in the form of network-summary-LSAs. If the keyword restrict is used for any entry, then that network is *not* advertised in a network-summary-LSA to external areas. If networks are not explicitly matched in the list within this stanza, then they are advertised in summary LSAs as well. Carefully configuring this option on ABRs can significantly reduce the amount of information included in interarea LSAs.

THE stubhosts STANZA   The stubhosts stanza (lines 19 through 21 in Example 12–1) specifies point-to-point hosts that should be advertised as reachable from this router. The host's IP address or resolvable hostname (`host`) is followed by the keyword `cost` and then the OSPF `cost` to reach this node.

BOTH FORMS OF THE `interface` STANZA The interface stanzas (lines 22 through 46 in Example 12–1) provide the method for specifying options to each interface. The `iface_list` argument accepted by the interface keyword is as described in Table 11–7 on page 480. There are two forms for this statement: one with `nonbroadcast` and one without. Using `nonbroadcast` indicates that the interface(s) listed in `iface_list` are attached to nonbroadcast networks like ATM. Most of the options for either type of statement are the same and are described in Table 12–12. Those that are peculiar to one type or the other are so noted.

Table 12–12 Options to the `interface` Stanza

OPTION	DESCRIPTION
`enable` | `disable`	Enables or disables the interface with respect to OSPF. Only used *without* `nonbroadcast`. The default is `enable`.
`pollinterval` *time*	Specifies the *time* in seconds between packets sent by a router before adjacency is established. Only used with `nonbroadcast`.
`routers`	Used to specify the list of neighbors in a `nonbroadcast` environment. Each neighbor is identified by its IP address in replace of *gateway*. If eligible is also specified, then the router can become the DR, otherwise it cannot.
`retransmitinterval` *time*	Specifies the *time* in seconds between LSA retransmissions to adjacent systems on this interface.
`transitdelay` *time*	Specifies the *time* in seconds to transmit a link-state update over this interface.

Table 12–12   Options to the `interface` Stanza *(Continued)*

OPTION	DESCRIPTION
`priority` *`priority`*	Specifies the *`priority`*, a value between 0 and 255, for this router to become the DR. Greater values indicate lower priority for becoming the DR. A value of 0 means that this router is ineligible to become the DR.
`hellointerval` *`time`*	Specifies the *`time`* in seconds between hello messages. The default is 10 seconds.
`routerdeadinterval` *`time`*	Specifies that if a router is not heard from in *`time`* seconds, it is considered to be down and a link-state update flood around this failure will occur. The default is 40 seconds.
`passive`	Specifies that OSPF packets are neither to be sent nor received on this interface.
`auth`	Sets up authentication for communication between OSPF routers. The syntax used here is identical to that described for RIPv2 in Chapter 11.
`secondary [none|simple|md5]` *`pw`*	Used for a `secondary` authentication scheme. If none is specified, then no secondary authentication is performed. The syntax of *`pw`* is like that for `monitorauthkey` as described in Table 12–10 on page 577 except that the keyword `simple` or `md5` preceding *`pw`* indicates whether or not it is a simple authentication (*`pw`* is passed in the clear) or `md5` (same as the `md5` method described in "RIP Authentication with `gated`" on page 518) authentication method.

THE `virtuallink` STANZA

The `virtuallink` stanza (lines 47 through 57 in Example 12–1) is used to establish a tunnel to areas that do not have physical connections to the backbone. This stanza can *only* be specified in a `backbone` stanza. The opening statement is of the form

```
virtuallink neighborid routerID transitarea area
```

where `routerID` is the router ID of the other end of the connection and `area` is the area number for the area for which the virtual connection is being established. A list of interfaces can be specified in the `backbone` stanza using the `interface` statement whenever configuring virtual links.

The remainder of options within the `virtuallink` stanza are the same as given in Table 12–12.

Manually Specifying `routerid`

We mentioned the `routerid` statement in "Definition Type Statements" on page 490. This statement is used to optionally set the router ID for an OSPF router. For example

```
routerid 192.168.1.1
```

would set the router ID for this router to `192.168.1.1`. If this statement is not used, then the highest IP address associated with this router would be used for its router ID.

One method for specifying router IDs is to use addresses beginning with `127` in the first octet (but `127.0.0.1` cannot be used). Using this method aids in identifying which routers are which without having to recall which IP address is being used as the router ID. This is particularly true in OSPF domains that are large and/or implement many areas. For example, `127.0.0.254` might be used as the router ID for the Internet gateway router that also connects into the OSPF backbone. (Other routers in the backbone would have router IDs of `127.0.0.`x, where $2 \le x \le 253$.) Routers in area `0.0.0.1` could use `127.0.1.`x, $1 \le x \le 255$, and so on.

Importing and Exporting OSPF Routes

Because of the way in which OSPF works, only ASEs can be imported or exported into OSPF. Thus, all OSPF import and export statements utilize the special protocol `ospfase` which indicates importation or exportation of ASE routes to OSPF. However, OSPF routes can be specified as a source of information in an `export` statement.

The general form of the `import` and `export` statements are given in Chapter 11. We consider some examples later in this chapter.

A Few Other Configuration Notes

On point-to-point connections that do not support multicasting, `gated` automatically uses unicasts for all OSPF communications to those nodes.

If you have `ipchains` configured on a router that is also going to participate in OSPF internally (or any multicasting application, for that matter), then you must add specific rules permitting communications to the appropriate mutlicast addresses (`224.0.0.5` and `224.0.0.6`). We look at `ipchains` in Chapter 14. See also the `ipchains` documentation or, for example, *Linux System Security* as cited in "For Further Reading" on page 612 for more details about `ipchains`.

A Flat OSPF Domain Example

Let's begin our implementation discussion by using the example from Chapter 11 wherein we considered a RIP implementation. The example is reproduced here for convenience. It also affords a direct implementation contrast between RIP and OSPF.

Figure 12–6 replicates the example given in Figure 11–7 on page 532.

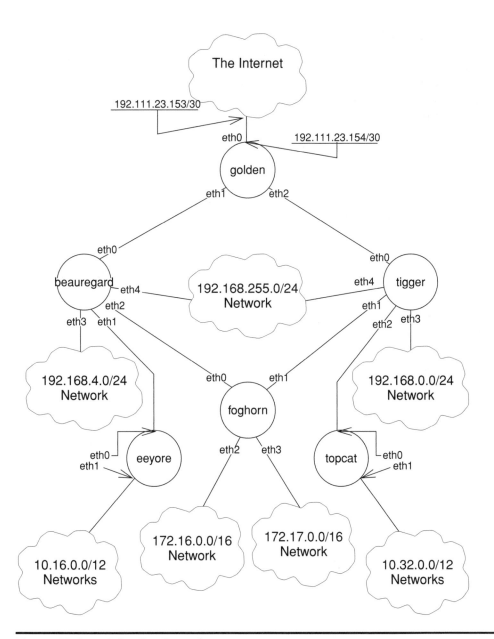

Figure 12–6   A Routing Example

To make this diagram clearer, the interfaces are labeled with device names instead of addresses. In this diagram, circles represent routers and clouds represent networks. Each router has been assigned a canonical name (shown in each circle). Table 12–13 serves to identify each router/interface/address triplet. It also shows the canonical name together with the name for each address.

Table 12–13   Figure 12–1 Canonical Name to Address Associations

CANONICAL NAME	INTERFACE NAME	HOST NAME	IP ADDRESS
golden	eth0 eth1 eth2	golden golden-1 golden-2	192.111.23.154/30 10.254.1.1/24 10.254.2.1/24
beauregard	eth0 eth1 eth2 eth3 eth4	beauregard beauregard-1 beauregard-2 beauregard-3 beauregard-4	10.254.1.10/24 10.254.10.1/24 10.254.11.1/24 192.168.4.100/24 192.168.255.100/24
tigger	eth0 eth1 eth2 eth3 eth4	tigger tigger-1 tigger-2 tigger-3 tigger-4	10.254.2.10/24 10.254.12.1/24 10.254.13.1/24 192.168.0.200/24 192.168.255.200/24
eeyore	eth0 eth1	eeyore eeyore-1	10.254.10.10/24 10.16.0.1/16
foghorn	eth0 eth1 eth2 eth3	foghorn foghorn-1 foghorn-2 foghorn-3	10.254.11.10/24 10.254.12.10/24 172.16.0.1/16 172,17,0,1/16
topcat	eth0 eth1	topcat topcat-1	10.254.13.10/24 10.32.0.1/16

Each network is assigned a network number, or range of network numbers, using prefix notation. Table 12–14 provides a listing of the networks shown in Figure 12–6.

Table 12–14   Figure 12–1 Network Descriptions

Network Description	Meaning, Use, and/or Purpose
Other Networks and the Internet	Indicates the connection to the Internet and other networks within the organization. We revisit this part of the example in Chapter 13.
`10.254.1.0/24`	This network connects the two routers `golden` and `beauregard`.
`10.254.2.0/24`	This network connects the two routers `golden` and `tigger`.
`10.254.10.0/24`	This network connects the two routers `beauregard` and `eeyore`.
`10.254.11.0/24`	This network connects the two routers `beauregard` and `foghorn`.
`10.254.12.0/24`	This network connects the two routers `tigger` and `foghorn`.
`10.254.13.0/24`	This network connects the two routers `tigger` and `topcat`.
`192.168.0.0/24`	This is the Class C network `192.168.0.0/24`.
`192.168.4.0/24`	This is the Class C network `192.168.4.0/24`.
`192.168.255.0/24`	This is the Class C network `192.168.255.0/24`.
`10.16.0.0/12`	This represents the collection of networks `10.16.0.0/16` through and including `10.31.0.0/16`.
`10.32.0.0/12`	This represents the collection of networks `10.32.0.0/16` through and including `10.47.0.0/16`.
`172.16.0.0/16`	This is the Class B network `172.16.0.0/16`.
`172.17.0.0/16`	This is the Class B network `172.16.0.0/16`.

Example Goals

For the purpose of this example, we duplicate the environment provided in "A Routing Example" on page 531. Here are our objectives.

- Make sure that each routing table is populated with routes that allow each system to connect to every other system, as shown in Figure 12–6.
- Wherever there are redundant routers, ensure that automatic failover capabilities are in place.
- The router `tigger` is slower than the router `beauregard`, so we want an automated mechanism to prefer `beauregard`.
- Keep things as simple as possible.

Effectively, these goals indicate that we want to replicate the RIP environment as closely as possible using OSPF. We should note here that aggregating routes within OSPF is not simple (it's easier to implement areas) in a flat, backbone only, OSPF environment, because OSPF handles route aggregation on area boundaries. Thus, we cannot replicate the aggregation examples used with RIP, but we will consider aggregated routes in "Examples Using OSPF Areas" on page 602.

Each of the following sections details the configuration requirements for that purpose on the various routers and hosts.

Configuring `golden`

From Figure 12–6 we see that `golden` has a single connection to the Internet. This fact needs to be propagated throughout the OSPF domain as a default route. We'll configure `golden` with a static route to the Internet and then export that route to OSPF for propagation to the domain. As before, `golden` also needs to know about all of the routes throughout the domain. Unfortunately, unlike RIP, we cannot use preferences to specify a preference for `beauregard` over `tigger` because preferences cannot be set on OSPF routes (only on OSPF ASE routes). Thus, we will have to use the OSPF `cost` value to make `tigger`'s use more costly, which we'll describe in the next section. To this end, the `/etc/gated.conf` file for `golden` is shown in Example 12–2. The line numbers shown to the left are for clarity and not actually part of the file.

Example 12–2   /etc/gated.conf File for golden

```
1   options mark ;
2   rip off ;
3   ospf on {
4       backbone {
5               interface eth0 { disable ; } ;
6               interface eth1 eth2 { priority 1 ; } ;
7       } ;
8   } ;
9   static {
10      default gateway 192.111.23.153 interface eth0 retain ;
11  } ;
12  export proto ospfase type 1 metric 2 {
13      proto static interface eth0 {
14              default ;
15      } ;
16  } ;
17  traceoptions "/var/log/gated.log" replace size 100k files 4 route ;
```

Note that at line 2, rip off is specified. This is done because the default compilation of gated (see Chapter 11) causes RIP to be automatically configured unless it is explicitly turned off. Since we're not using RIP in this example, we turn it off.

The ospf stanza, beginning at line 3, contains a backbone stanza (beginning at line 4) with two interface statements. The first interface statement disables eth0 since that interface leads to the Internet and no OSPF advertisements should be sent or received from that network. The second interface statement sets the priority of the eth1 and eth2 interfaces to 1, making them eligible with the highest possible priority to become a DR. Strictly speaking, specifying the priority of 1 is unnecessary since that is the default. However, explicitly setting such information often makes it easier to see what's going on when you are dealing with many routers in an environment.

NOTE

When you start gated configured to use OSPF, you may get a warning message about OSPF and protocol 89 from gated which appears as

```
gated[883]: task_get_proto: getprotobyname("ospf") failed, using
proto 89
```

This error message indicates that there is no entry for OSPF in the /etc/protocol file. You can remedy this issue by placing an entry such as

```
ospf  89   OSPFIGP      # Open Shortest Path First IGP
```

in the /etc/protocol file on each affected system.

The routing table on golden appears as shown in Example 12–3. Contrasting it with the one generated in the RIP environment (see Example 11–36 on page 538) shows that there are no aggregates here. Also, there are now entries for the multicast addresses 224.0.0.5 and 224.0.0.6 which were joined when gated started with OSPF configured. Otherwise, the two tables are entirely similar.

Example 12–3   Routing Table on golden

```
Kernel IP routing table
Destination    Gateway      Genmask        Flags Metric Ref   Use Iface
224.0.0.6      127.0.0.1    255.255.255.255 UGH  0     0     0 lo
224.0.0.5      127.0.0.1    255.255.255.255 UGH  0     0     0 lo
127.0.0.1      0.0.0.0      255.255.255.255 UH   0     0     0 lo
192.111.23.152 0.0.0.0      255.255.255.252 U    0     0     0 eth0
10.254.10.0    10.254.1.10  255.255.255.0   UG   0     0     0 eth1
10.254.11.0    10.254.1.10  255.255.255.0   UG   0     0     0 eth1
192.168.4.0    10.254.1.10  255.255.255.0   UG   0     0     0 eth1
10.254.12.0    10.254.2.10  255.255.255.0   UG   0     0     0 eth2
10.254.13.0    10.254.2.10  255.255.255.0   UG   0     0     0 eth2
10.254.2.0     0.0.0.0      255.255.255.0   U    0     0     0 eth2
10.254.1.0     0.0.0.0      255.255.255.0   U    0     0     0 eth1
192.168.255.0  10.254.1.10  255.255.255.0   UG   0     0     0 eth1
172.16.0.0     10.254.1.10  255.255.0.0     UG   0     0     0 eth1
172.17.0.0     10.254.1.10  255.255.0.0     UG   0     0     0 eth1
127.0.0.0      -            255.0.0.0       !    0     -     0 -
0.0.0.0        192.111.23.153 0.0.0.0       UG   0     0     0 eth0
```

Configuring beauregard and tigger

The configuration file for beauregard is very simple: just turn OSPF on and RIP off. Since golden is exporting a default route through OSPF, we do not need to configure a default as we did with the RIP example in "Configuring beauregard and tigger" on page 538. Note that the priority for beauregard is slightly lower (higher value) than that of golden to ensure that golden becomes the DR. Its configuration file is shown in Example 12–4.

Example 12–4   /etc/gated.conf on beauregard

```
rip off ;
ospf yes {
    backbone {
          interface all { priority 5 ; } ;
       } ;
} ;
```

The configuration file for tigger is slightly more complex than beauregard only because we want to make it less desirable than beauregard. This is accomplished by setting the cost to 2 (instead of the default value of 1) on those interfaces on `tigger` (`eth1` and `eth4`, see Figure 12–6 on page 585) which offer redundant routes. This has the effect of making the routes through those interfaces on `tigger` more costly than using `beauregard`, but if `beauregard` fails, they can still be used. Note that we also set the priority on all of `tigger`'s interfaces to a low priority, making it an undesirable DR. Since the DR is responsible for all the updates on its local network, a slow router is not a good choice. The configuration file for `tigger` is given in Example 12–5.

Example 12–5   `/etc/gated.conf` on `tigger`

```
rip off ;
ospf yes {
    backbone {
            interface eth1 eth4 cost 2 { priority 100 ; } ;
            interface eth0 eth2 cost 1 { priority 100 ; } ;
    } ;
} ;
```

The routing table for `beauregard` is shown in Example 12–6. The table for `tigger` would be much the same. Note that the default route exported by `golden` appears in the table. Recall that `golden` actually exports its own default (to the `192.111.23.152/30` network, see Example 12–4), but OSPF calculates the correct default to reach the exported default.

Example 12–6   Routing Table on `beauregard`

```
Kernel IP routing table
Destination     Gateway         Genmask          Flags  Metric  Ref   Use Iface
224.0.0.6       127.0.0.1       255.255.255.255  UGH    0       0       0 lo
224.0.0.5       127.0.0.1       255.255.255.255  UGH    0       0       0 lo
127.0.0.1       0.0.0.0         255.255.255.255  UH     0       0       0 lo
10.254.10.0     10.254.10.1     255.255.255.0    UG     0       0       0 eth1
10.254.10.0     0.0.0.0         255.255.255.0    U      0       0       0 eth1
10.254.11.0     10.254.11.1     255.255.255.0    UG     0       0       0 eth2
10.254.11.0     0.0.0.0         255.255.255.0    U      0       0       0 eth2
192.168.4.0     0.0.0.0         255.255.255.0    U      0       0       0 eth1
10.254.12.0     10.254.11.10    255.255.255.0    UG     0       0       0 eth2
10.254.13.0     10.254.1.1      255.255.255.0    UG     0       0       0 eth0
10.254.2.0      10.254.1.1      255.255.255.0    UG     0       0       0 eth0
10.254.1.0      10.254.1.10     255.255.255.0    UG     0       0       0 eth0
10.254.1.0      0.0.0.0         255.255.255.0    U      0       0       0 eth0
192.168.255.0   0.0.0.0         255.255.255.0    U      0       0       0 eth2
172.16.0.0      10.254.11.10    255.255.0.0      UG     0       0       0 eth2
172.17.0.0      10.254.11.10    255.255.0.0      UG     0       0       0 eth2
127.0.0.0       -               255.0.0.0        !      0       -       0 -
0.0.0.0         10.254.1.1      0.0.0.0          UG     0       0       0 eth0
```

Configuring `foghorn`, `eeyore`, and `topcat`

As with `beauregard` and `tigger`, `foghorn`'s configuration file is quite simple. It is given in Example 12–7.

Example 12–7   `/etc/gated.conf` on `foghorn`

```
rip off ;
ospf on {
    backbone {
            interface all { priority 5 ; } ;
        } ;
} ;
```

The configuration file on `foghorn`, together with the rest of our environment, results in its routing table shown in Example 12–8. Note that, once again, the default is properly computed.

Example 12–8   Routing Table on `foghorn`

```
Kernel IP routing table
Destination     Gateway          Genmask          Flags  Metric  Ref  Use Iface
224.0.0.6       127.0.0.1        255.255.255.255  UGH    0       0      0 lo
224.0.0.5       127.0.0.1        255.255.255.255  UGH    0       0      0 lo
127.0.0.1       0.0.0.0          255.255.255.255  UH     0       0      0 lo
10.254.10.0     10.254.11.1      255.255.255.0    UG     0       0      0 eth0
10.254.11.0     10.254.11.10     255.255.255.0    UG     0       0      0 eth0
10.254.11.0     0.0.0.0          255.255.255.0    U      0       0      0 eth0
192.168.4.0     10.254.11.1      255.255.255.0    UG     0       0      0 eth0
10.254.12.0     10.254.12.10     255.255.255.0    UG     0       0      0 eth1
10.254.12.0     0.0.0.0          255.255.255.0    U      0       0      0 eth1
10.254.13.0     10.254.12.1      255.255.255.0    UG     0       0      0 eth1
10.254.2.0      10.254.12.1      255.255.255.0    UG     0       0      0 eth1
10.254.1.0      10.254.11.1      255.255.255.0    UG     0       0      0 eth0
192.168.255.0   10.254.11.1      255.255.255.0    UG     0       0      0 eth0
172.16.0.0      172.16.0.1       255.255.0.0      UG     0       0      0 eth2
172.16.0.0      0.0.0.0          255.255.0.0      U      0       0      0 eth2
172.17.0.0      172.17.0.1       255.255.0.0      UG     0       0      0 eth3
172.17.0.0      0.0.0.0          255.255.0.0      U      0       0      0 eth3
172.16.0.0      -                255.240.0.0      !      0       -      0 -
127.0.0.0       -                255.0.0.0        !      0       -      0 -
0.0.0.0         10.254.11.1      0.0.0.0          UG     0       0      0 eth0
```

The configuration files and routing tables for `eeyore` and `topcat` are much the same.

Configuring the Hosts

Configuring the hosts in this environment is similar to the earlier RIP example. The major difference is that all of the hosts in the `192.168.255.0/24` network can run OSPF instead of the router discovery daemon and RIPv2 in listen mode. This can be done with `gated` using the configuration file shown in Example 12–9. This configuration will cause the host to pick up all of the necessary routes to the domain and the default router.

Example 12–9   `/etc/gated.conf` on Hosts in the `192.168.255.0/24` Network

```
rip off ;
ospf on {
    backbone {
            interface all ;
    } ;
} ;
```

Every host in the `172.16.0.0/16` and `172.17.0.0/16` network simply needs a static default router which can be configured, as described in Chapter 6.

Configuration of the remaining hosts and routers in the `10.16.0.0/20` and `10.32.0.0./20` networks would proceed similarly to that described in this section.

Interlude: Using the `ospf_monitor` Utility

The `gated` version 3.6 software includes a very useful utility that can provide a lot of information about your OSPF environment. That utility is the `ospf_monitor`. It is used to query the `gated` daemon on both the local system on which it is running and remote systems that are running OSPF. It requires a configuration file that minimally contains an IP address and hostname for each system, including the local one, that is going to be queried. This configuration file can also contain the password set by `monitorauthkey` (see Table 12–10 on page 577 for a description of `monitorauthkey`)—in fact, it must contain that password if the system in question has implemented `monitorauthkey`, otherwise that system will refuse all queries. Example 12–10 illustrates the `ospf_monitor` configuration file, which we have called `/root/ospfmon` (the configuration file can be called anything). In this case, it is configured to supply the password `foobie01` when querying `beauregard`, but there are no passwords for any of the other systems in the list. The systems can be either routers or non-routers, but it is most common to query routers.

Example 12–10   An `ospf_monitor` Configuration File

```
[root@foghorn /root]# cat ospfmon
10.254.11.1        beauregard     foobie01
10.254.1.1         golden
10.254.11.10       foghorn
10.254.12.10       tigger
[root@foghorn /root]#
```

Using this configuration file, `ospf_monitor` can now be invoked to query any of the listed systems. Example 12–11 illustrates the invocation and using the `d` command to list the systems found in the `/root/ospfmon` file.

Example 12–11   Invoking `ospf_monitor` and Displaying the Destinations

```
[root@foghorn /root]# ospf_monitor ./ospfmon
listening on 0.0.0.0.1250
[ 1 ] dest command params > d
1: 10.254.11.1    beauregard
2: 10.254.1.1    golden
3: 10.254.11.10  foghorn
4: 10.254.12.10  tigger
[ 2 ] dest command params >
```

Notice that once `ospf_monitor` has been run, it utilizes the `dest command params >` prompt. This prompt can take a number of different commands, each of which is described in Table 12–15.

Table 12–15   `ospf_monitor` Commands

COMMAND	DESCRIPTION
?	Displays the list of local commands. These are commands that are processed locally by `ospf_monitor` and do not generate queries.
?R	Displays the list of remote commands. These are the commands that query systems.
d	Lists the available destinations as read from the configuration file.
h	Prints a list of the last 30 commands executed.
x	Exits the `ospf_monitor`.

Table 12–15   `ospf_monitor` Commands *(Continued)*

COMMAND	DESCRIPTION
`@[dest] cmd`	Sends `cmd` to the specified `dest`. The valid values for `cmd` are a, c, e, h, l, A, o, I, N, and v. The value of `dest` must be the number of the destination system from the output of d. If `dest` is not specified, then the previously specified `dest` is assumed.
`.`	Repeats the last command.
`F file`	Sends all `ospf_monitor` output to `file`.
`S`	Sends all `ospf_monitor` output to standard output. This command is useful if F was used previously and you'd now like to see the output.
`a area type ls_id adv_rtr`	Requests the LSAs of the `type` specified. `area` is the OSPF area. `adv_rtr` is the routerID of the originating router. `ls_id` depends on the `type`. `type` is one of the five LSA types. Refer to Table 12–7 on page 568. **1.** router-LSA. `ls_id` must be the originating router ID. **2.** network-LSA. `ls_id` must be the originating router ID. **3.** network-summary-LSA. `ls_id` must be the destination network number. **4.** ASBR-summary-LSA. `ls_id` must be the router ID of the ASBR. **5.** AS-external-LSA. `ls_id` must be the destination network number.
`c`	Displays the cumulative log. This log is maintained internally by `gated` and contains statistics about OSPF communications and the link-state database.

Table 12–15   `ospf_monitor` Commands *(Continued)*

COMMAND	DESCRIPTION
e	Displays the cumulative error log. This log is maintained internally by `gated` and contains statistics about packets received, send, and errors.
h	Displays the list of valid next hops.
l [*retrans*]	Displays the link-state database except for ASEs. If *retrans* is nonzero, then a list of neighbors is included.
A [*retrans*]	Displays the list of ASEs.
o [*which*]	Displays the list of routes in the routing table that are managed by OSPF. The value of *which* specifies which routes are to be listed. It is one of the values from the following list. If more than one from the list is desired, then add the values together to form the *which* argument. If *which* is not specified, then all of the items listed are displayed. The term "this area" means the area to which the queried system belongs. 1 - routes to AS border routers in this area 2 - routes to area border routers for this area 4 - summary routes to AS border routers in other areas 8 - routes to networks in this area 16 - summary routes to networks in other areas 32 - ASE routes
I	Displays all interfaces configured for OSPF.
N	Displays the neighbors.
V	Displays the `gated` version.

Let's examine a few examples. We can get the entire link-state database with the 1 command, exclusive of ASE routes, which in the case of our previous example means that the default entry which comes from a static route on golden won't show up. Example 12–12 illustrates this query on beauregard. Note that for each entry, the information listed is consistent with our discussion earlier in this chapter. The Type column contains the type of LSA (Stub is type 3, Rtr is type 1, and Net is type 2). The LinkState ID column contains the link-state ID of the LSA, the AdvRouter column lists the originating router ID, Age contains the LS age of the LSA, Len is the length in octets of the LSA, Sequence is the sequence number of the LSA, Metric lists the metric (not cost!) of the entry, and Where lists where the entry came from: SpfTree means that it was calculated by the shortest path first algorithm, while Clist means that it was taken directly from the LSA. Regardless of which system is queried, this list should be the same on all OSPF routers within an area.

Example 12–12   Output of the ospf_monitor 1 Command

```
[ 4 ] dest command params > @1 1
   remote-command <l> sent to 10.254.11.1

        Source <<10.254.11.1   beauregard>>
LS Data Base:
Area: 0.0.0.0
Type LinkState ID    AdvRouter         Age  Len  Sequence   Metric Where
------------------------------------------------------------------------
Stub 172.16          10.254.11.10     2469 24   0               0 SpfTree
Stub 172.17          10.254.11.10     2469 24   0               0 SpfTree
Stub 192.168.4       10.254.1.10      2437 24   0               0 SpfTree
Stub 192.168.255     10.254.1.10      2437 24   0               0 SpfTree
Stub 10.254.13       10.254.2.10      2477 24   0               0 SpfTree
Stub 10.16           10.16.0.1        2436 24   0               0 SpfTree
Rtr 10.254.11.10     10.254.11.10     1082 72   80000160        0 Clist
Rtr 10.254.1.10      10.254.1.10       645 84   80000158        0 SpfTree
Rtr 10.254.2.10      10.254.2.10       471 60   8000014f        0 Clist
Rtr 10.16.0.1        10.16.0.1         784 48   80000014        0 Clist
Rtr 192.111.23.154   192.111.23.154   1471 48   80000157        0 SpfTree
Net 10.254.11.10     10.254.11.10     1082 32   8000000b        0 SpfTree
Net 10.254.12.10     10.254.11.10     1082 32   8000000a        0 SpfTree
Net 10.254.10.1      10.254.1.10       645 32   80000003        0 SpfTree
Net 10.254.1.1       192.111.23.154   1471 32   8000000b        0 SpfTree
Net 10.254.2.1       192.111.23.154   1471 32   8000000a        0 SpfTree
done

[ 5 ] dest command params >
```

The 1 command doesn't list any ASEs; to get those we need to use the A command. The columns are a little different here, but should be fairly straightforward. The entry is a default, as evidenced by the `0.0.0.0` destination. The `T` column here replaces the `Type` column from the previous example. Example 12–13 shows the output of the `A` command for `beauregard`.

Example 12–13   Output of `ospf_monitor` A Command

```
[ 6 ] dest command params > @1 A
  remote-command <A> sent to 10.254.11.1

    Source <<10.254.11.1    beauregard>>
AS External Data Base:
Destination     AdvRouter          Forward Addr     Age Len Sequence T Metric
------------------------------------------------------------------------------
0.0.0.0         192.111.23.154     0.0.0.0          271 36  8000010a 1       2

    Count 1, checksum sum 4462
done

[ 7 ] dest command params >
```

The `o` command provides the routing table as managed by OSPF. Different types of routes are separated into different parts of the output. Notice here that costs to destinations are listed for each entry in the `Cost` column for each type of route. This value represents the cost used by OSPF. In particular, note that the cost to the default is 3. This reflects the fact that the default was exported to OSPF on `golden` (see "Configuring `golden`" on page 588) as a Type 1 ASE route with a metric of 2, which causes that metric to be treated as an OSPF cost of 2 (Type 1 metrics, by definition, are compatible with OSPF costs—see "A Note about OSPF External Routes" on page 569). Example 12–14 displays the output.

Example 12–14   Output of the `ospf_monitor` o Command

```
[ 5 ] dest command params > @1 o
  remote-command <o> sent to 10.254.11.1

    Source <<10.254.11.1    beauregard>>
AS Border Routes:
Router          Cost  AdvRouter         NextHop(s)
--------------------------------------------------------
Area 0.0.0.0:
192.111.23.154     1  192.111.23.154    10.254.1.1

Total AS Border routes: 1

Area Border Routes:
Router          Cost  AdvRouter         NextHop(s)
--------------------------------------------------------
Area 0.0.0.0:
```

Example 12–14   Output of the `ospf_monitor o` Command *(Continued)*

```
Summary AS Border Routes:
Router       Cost AdvRouter    NextHop(s)
-------------------------------------------------

Networks:
Destination    Area        Cost Type  NextHop          AdvRouter
----------------------------------------------------------------------
-
10.254.10      0.0.0.0       1 Net    10.254.10.1      10.254.1.10
192.168.4       0.0.0.0      1 Stub   192.168.4.100    10.254.1.10
192.168.255    0.0.0.0      1 Stub   192.168.255.100  10.254.1.10
10.254.12      0.0.0.0      2 Net    10.254.11.10     10.254.11.10
10.254.2       0.0.0.0      2 Net    10.254.1.1       192.111.23.154
172.16         0.0.0.0      2 Stub   10.254.11.10     10.254.11.10
172.17         0.0.0.0      2 Stub   10.254.11.10     10.254.11.10
10.254.13      0.0.0.0      3 Stub   10.254.1.1       10.254.2.10
10.254.1       0.0.0.0      1 Net    10.254.1.1       192.111.23.154
10.254.11      0.0.0.0      1 Net    10.254.11.1      10.254.11.10
10.16          0.0.0.0      2 Stub   10.254.10.10     10.16.0.1
ASEs:
Destination    Cost E   Tag NextHop       AdvRouter
----------------------------------------------------------------------
--
0.0.0.0        3   3 c0000000 10.254.1.1   192.111.23.154
Total nets: 11
Intra Area: 5Inter Area: 6ASE: 1
done

[ 6 ] dest command params >
```

Using the `I` command yields a list of interfaces for the system. Example 12–15 illustrates. Note that the DR and BDR are listed for each local network and the system's role in that scheme is specified as well.

Example 12–15   Output of the `ospf_monitor I` Command

```
[ 8 ] dest command params > @1 I
   remote-command <I> sent to 10.254.11.1

      Source <<10.254.11.1    beauregard>>

Area: 0.0.0.0
IP Address       Type   State    Cost Pri DR                BDR
----------------------------------------------------------------------
10.254.1.10      Bcast BackupDR 1    10  10.254.1.1         10.254.1.10
10.254.10.1      Bcast DR       1    10  10.254.10.1        None
192.168.4.100    Bcast DR       1    10  192.168.4.100      None
10.254.11.1      Bcast BackupDR 1    10  10.254.11.10       10.254.11.1
192.168.255.100 Bcast DR       1     1  192.168.255.100    None
done

[ 9 ] dest command params >
```

You can use the N command to identify the neighbors of the queried system on each of its local networks. In Example 12–16, Mode indicates the DR role: if Master is specified, then the queried system is the DR, otherwise, it is not.

Example 12–16   Output of the ospf_monitor N Command

```
[ 9 ] dest command params > @1 N
  remote-command <N> sent to 10.254.11.1

    Source <<10.254.11.1   beauregard>>

Interface: 10.254.1.10   Area: 0.0.0.0
Router Id       Nbr IP Addr   State   Mode   Prio
-------------------------------------------------------
192.111.23.154 10.254.1.1   Full     Slave 100

Interface: 10.254.10.1   Area: 0.0.0.0
Router Id       Nbr IP Addr   State   Mode   Prio
-------------------------------------------------------
10.16.0.1    10.254.10.10  Full     Master 0

Interface: 192.168.4.100  Area: 0.0.0.0
Router Id       Nbr IP Addr   State   Mode   Prio
-------------------------------------------------------

Interface: 10.254.11.1   Area: 0.0.0.0
Router Id       Nbr IP Addr   State   Mode   Prio
-------------------------------------------------------
10.254.11.10  10.254.11.10  Full     Slave 5

Interface: 192.168.255.100 Area: 0.0.0.0
Router Id       Nbr IP Addr   State   Mode   Prio
-------------------------------------------------------
done

[ 10 ] dest command params >
```

The ospf_monitor has two commands that provide statistical information about OSPF activity: c and e. The c command provides information about OSPF communications and summary statistics about ASEs, LSAs, areas, and the OSPF routing table. In the list of communications in Example 12–17 note the five OSPF communication types (Hello, DB Description, Link-State Req, Link-State Update, and Link-State Ack), but also note the Monitor request Type, which collects statistics about ospf_monitor requests.

Example 12-17   Output of the ospf_monitor c Command

```
[ 10 ] dest command params > @1 c
  remote-command <c> sent to 10.254.11.1

    Source <<10.254.11.1   beauregard>>
IO stats
      Input  Output  Type
          6       0  Monitor request
        879    1471  Hello
         22      17  DB Description
          2       4  Link-State Req
         24      49  Link-State Update
         35      15  Link-State Ack
      ASE: 1 checksum sum 4462

    LSAs originated: 8received: 27
         Router: 6 Net: 2

    Area 0.0.0.0:
         Neighbors: 3Interfaces: 5
         Spf: 4 Checksum sum 4F277
         DB: rtr: 5 net: 5 sumasb: 0 sumnet: 0

Routing Table:
      Intra Area: 5Inter Area: 6ASE: 1
done

[ 11 ] dest command params >
```

The e command provides a lot of similar information about OSPF communication, and then also provides a listing of error types and the associated number of packets that fall into that category. Example 12–18 shows the output of the e command.

Example 12-18   Output of the ospf_monitor e Command

```
[ 11 ] dest command params > @1 e
  remote-command <e> sent to 10.254.11.1

    Source <<10.254.11.1   beauregard>>
Packets Received:
  7: Monitor request        888: Hello
 22: DB Description           2: Link-State Req
 24: Link-State Update       35: Link-State Ack

Packets Sent:
  0: Monitor response      1484: Hello
 17: DB Description           4: Link-State Req
 49: Link-State Update       15: Link-State Ack

Errors:
  1: IP: bad destination      0: IP: bad protocol
  0: IP: received my own packet  0: OSPF: bad packet type
  0: OSPF: bad version        0: OSPF: bad checksum
```

Example 12–18   Output of the `ospf_monitor` e Command *(Continued)*

```
0: OSPF: bad area id              0: OSPF: area mismatch
0: OSPF: bad virtual link         0: OSPF: bad authentication type
0: OSPF: bad authentication key   0: OSPF: packet too small
0: OSPF: packet size > ip length  0: OSPF: transmit error
0: OSPF: interface down           0: OSPF: unknown neighbor
0: HELLO: netmask mismatch        0: HELLO: hello timer mismatch
0: HELLO: dead timer mismatch     0: HELLO: extern option mismatch
0: HELLO: router id confusion     0: HELLO: virtual neighbor unknown
0: HELLO: NBMA neighbor unknown   0: DD: neighbor state low
0: DD: router id confusion        0: DD: extern option mismatch
0: DD: unknown LSA type           0: LS ACK: neighbor state low
0: LS ACK: bad ack                3: LS ACK: duplicate ack
0: LS ACK: Unknown LSA type       0: LS REQ: neighbor state low
0: LS REQ: empty request          0: LS REQ: bad request
4: LS UPD: neighbor state low     0: LS UPD: newer self-gen LSA
0: LS UPD: LSA checksum bad       0: LS UPD: received less recent LSA
0: LS UPD: unknown LSA type
done

[ 12 ] dest command params >
```

The `ospf_monitor` utility is a very useful tool for analyzing the network routing configuration and for troubleshooting.

Examples Using OSPF Areas

In this section, we explore the use of areas. First, we look at a simple route aggregation use of areas and then we consider a more comprehensive example.

Building an Area for Route Aggregation

Suppose that we want to aggregate the `172.16.0.0/16` and `172.17.0.0/16` routes on `foghorn` in the way we did using RIP in "Configuring `foghorn`" on page 541. One way to accomplish that (perhaps the simplest way) is to configure these networks into a separate OSPF area and then aggregate the routes for exportation into OSPF. This can be accomplished by implementing the `/etc/gated.conf` file shown in Example 12–19 on `foghorn` (see Figure 12–6 on page 585).

Example 12–19   Implementing Route Aggregation Using a Separate Area on `foghorn`

```
rip off ;
ospf on {
    traceoptions "/var/log/gated.ospf" size 100k files 4 packets ;
    area 0.0.0.3 {
        networks {
            172.16.0.0 masklen 12 restrict ;
        } ;
        interface eth2 { priority 1 ; } ;
        interface eth3 { priority 1 ; } ;
    } ;
    backbone {
        interface eth0 eth1 { priority 10 ; } ;
    } ;
} ;
aggregate 172.16.0.0 masklen 12 preference 10 {
    proto ospf {
        172.16.0.0 masklen 12 refines ;
    } ;
    proto direct {
        172.16.0.0 masklen 16 exact ;
        172.17.0.0 masklen 16 exact ;
    } ;
} ;
} ;
export proto ospfase type 1 {
    proto aggregate {
        172.16.0.0 masklen 12 ;
    } ;
} ;
traceoptions "/var/log/gated.log" size 100k files 4 all ;
```

This configuration file creates the area `0.0.0.3` and specifies that the `eth2` (`172.16.0.0/16`) and `eth3` (`172.17.0.0/16`) interfaces are within that area. In the `area 0.0.0.3` stanza, note that we use the `networks` stanza to specify that the collection of networks `172.16.0.0/12` is not to be advertised in summary LSAs by specifying the `restrict` keyword. We do that so that `foghorn` only advertises the aggregate, which is defined by the `aggregate` stanza and then exported with the `export` stanza.

The `aggregate` stanza is quite similar to the one used for RIP. It contains a `proto direct` stanza to capture the `172.16.0.0/16` and `172.17.0.0/16` networks that are local to `foghorn`. It also has a `proto ospf` stanza which is used to capture other networks in the `172.16.0.0/12` range that are advertised by other OSPF routers in area `0.0.0.3` (these don't exist in Figure 12–6 on page 585). All of these routes are grouped into a single `172.16.0.0/12` aggregate.

The aggregate is then exported by the `export` stanza. Note that the export is via the protocol `ospfase`. All routes exported into OSPF are exported as an

ASE, hence, ospfase. Type 1 metrics are used to ensure that the OSPF cost to this aggregate is computed as the cost to foghorn.

The routing table on foghorn doesn't change (recall that routes created with the aggregate statement are never used by the creator). However, other routers on the OSPF backbone will reflect the change. Example 12–20 shows the routing table on golden as illustrative of the change. The aggregate is in **bold**.

Example 12–20   Routing Table on golden with Aggregate

```
[root@golden /root]# route -n
Kernel IP routing table
Destination     Gateway         Genmask          Flags Metric Ref    Use Iface
224.0.0.6       127.0.0.1       255.255.255.255 UGH   0      0        0 lo
224.0.0.5       127.0.0.1       255.255.255.255 UGH   0      0        0 lo
127.0.0.1       0.0.0.0         255.255.255.255 UH    0      0        0 lo
192.111.23.152  0.0.0.0         255.255.255.252 U     0      0        0 eth0
10.254.10.0     10.254.1.10     255.255.255.0   UG    0      0        0 eth1
10.254.11.0     10.254.1.10     255.255.255.0   UG    0      0        0 eth1
192.168.4.0     10.254.1.10     255.255.255.0   UG    0      0        0 eth1
10.254.12.0     10.254.1.10     255.255.255.0   UG    0      0        0 eth1
10.254.13.0     10.254.1.10     255.255.255.0   UG    0      0        0 eth1
10.254.2.0      0.0.0.0         255.255.255.0   U     0      0        0 eth2
10.254.1.0      0.0.0.0         255.255.255.0   U     0      0        0 eth1
192.168.255.0   10.254.1.10     255.255.255.0   UG    0      0        0 eth1
10.16.0.0       10.254.1.10     255.255.0.0     UG    0      0        0 eth1
172.16.0.0      10.254.1.10     255.240.0.0     UG    0      0        0 eth1
127.0.0.0       -               255.0.0.0       !     0      -        0 -
0.0.0.0         192.111.23.153  0.0.0.0         UG    0      0        0 eth0
[root@golden /root]#
```

Using ospf_monitor, we can see that the aggregate is reported as an ASE route. Example 12–21 shows beauregard being queried with the A command.

Example 12–21   ospf_monitor Query Showing Aggregate as External

```
[ 4 ] dest command params > @1 A
  remote-command <A> sent to 10.254.11.1

       Source <<10.254.11.1    beauregard>>
AS External Data Base:
Destination     AdvRouter        Forward Addr   Age   Len   Sequence   T   Metric
------------------------------------------------------------------------------
0.0.0.0         192.111.23.154   0.0.0.0        1220  36    80000132   1      2
172.16/12       10.254.11.10     0.0.0.0          16  36    80000002   1      1

Count 3, checksum sum 19B05
done
```

Issuing an I query to foghorn with ospf_monitor shows the distinct interfaces in each area, as depicted in Example 12–22.

Example 12–22   `ospf_monitor` Query Showing the Two Areas on `foghorn`

```
[ 10 ] dest command params > @3 I
   remote-command <I> sent to 10.254.11.10

     Source <<10.254.11.10    foghorn>>

Area: 0.0.0.0
IP Address    Type   State      Cost Pri DR           BDR
------------------------------------------------------------------
10.254.11.10  Bcast  BackupDR 1    10  10.254.11.1    10.254.11.10
10.254.12.10  Bcast  BackupDR 1    10  10.254.12.1    10.254.12.10

Area: 0.0.0.3
IP Address    Type   State      Cost Pri DR           BDR
------------------------------------------------------------------
172.16.0.1    Bcast  DR        1    1   172.16.0.1    None
172.17.0.1    Bcast  DR        1    1   172.17.0.1    None
done

[ 11 ] dest command params >
```

Implementing Multiple Areas

Let's expand on the example given in Figure 12–6 on page 585 and consider a larger environment in which we create some OSPF areas in the OSPF domain. The example we'll consider for this section is given in Figure 12–7. This example expands on the previous one by adding additional networks and areas. In this case, however, we assign router IDs to each of the routers as given in Table 12–16.

The interfaces displayed in Figure 12–7 remain as specified in Table 12–13 on page 586, except that a new router `daffy` has been added. Its `eth0` interface has the IP address `10.16.0.254/16` and its `eth1` interface has the IP address `10.0.0.254/16`. We'll consider the `gated` configuration files on pertinent routers for each of the areas in the following sections.

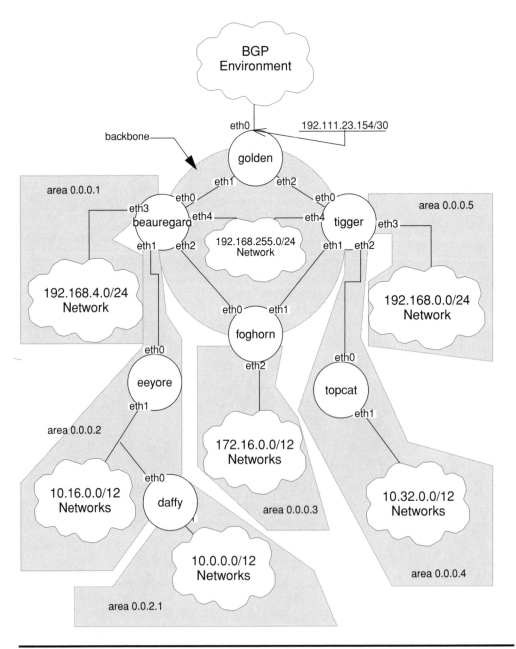

Figure 12–7   Routing and OSPF Areas

Table 12–16   Router ID Assignments for Figure 12–2

ROUTER	ROUTER ID
golden	127.0.0.254
beauregard	127.0.1.254
tigger	127.0.5.254
foghorn	127.0.3.254
eeyore	127.0.2.254
topcat	127.0.4.254
daffy	127.2.1.254

The backbone Area

In this section we'll look at the configuration files for golden, beauregard, foghorn, and tigger.

Configuration for golden

The role of golden has expanded to include a BGP routing domain. While we discuss BGP in Chapter 13, we show an example here of incorporating BGP AS path information into the OSPF domain. This is done with the bgp stanza and then placed into the OSPF domain with the export stanza. Note that the BGP routes are exported as type 2 routes, meaning that their metrics are incompatible with OSPF; furthermore, note that a metric of 2 is specified for those routes. This means that throughout the OSPF domain, these routes will always have a cost of 2. That cost will be recomputed by golden using appropriate BGP metrics. We describe the bgp stanza in more detail in Chapter 13. Except for that, the role of golden remains unchanged. Its /etc/gated.conf configuration file is shown in Example 12–23.

Example 12–23   /etc/gated.conf on golden

```
options mark ;
routerid 127.0.0.254 ;
autonomoussystem 384 ;
rip off ;
bgp on {
    group type external peeras 212 {
        peer 192.111.23.153 ;
```

Example 12–23   `/etc/gated.conf` on `golden` *(Continued)*

```
        } ;
} ;
ospf on {
    backbone {
            interface eth1 eth2 { priority 1 ; } ;
        } ;
} ;
export proto ospfase type 2 {
    proto bgp as 384 metric 2 {
            all ;
        } ;
} ;
export proto bgp as 212 {
    proto direct interface eth0 ;
    proto direct interface eth1 eth2 restrict;
    proto ospf restrict ;
} ;
traceoptions "/var/log/gated.log" replace size 100k files 4 route ;
```

The routers `beauregard` and `tigger` are very similar in their configurations. We'll look at the `/etc/gated.conf` file for `beauregard` and note the differences for `tigger`. Example 12–24 shows the configuration file for `beauregard`. It should be quite straightforward given our previous discussions and Figure 12–7 on page 606.

Example 12–24   `/etc/gated.conf` on `beauregard`

```
routerid 127.0.1.254 ;
rip off ;
ospf yes {
    traceoptions "/var/log/gated.ospf" size 100k files 4
            packets ;
    area 0.0.0.1 {
            interface eth3 { priority 1 ; } ;
        } ;
    area 0.0.0.2 {
            interface eth1 { priority 1 ; } ;
        } ;
    backbone {
            interface eth0 { priority 10 ; } ;
            interface eth2 eth4 { priority 1 ; } ;
            } ;
        } ;
} ;
```

The configuration file for `tigger` would be much the same except that, due to its slowness, a cost of 2 would be associated with the redundant interfaces `eth4` and `eth1` (both in the backbone). Also, `tigger` would have configuration entries for areas `0.0.0.4` and `0.0.0.5` instead of `0.0.0.1` and `0.0.0.2`.

The configuration file for foghorn is nearly identical to that given in Example 12–19 on page 603. The only difference is the absence of the eth3 interface. Its /etc/gated.conf file is given in Example 12–25.

Example 12–25   Implementing Route Aggregation Using a Separate Area on foghorn

```
routerid 127.0.3.254 ;
rip off ;
ospf on {
    traceoptions "/var/log/gated.ospf" size 100k files 4 packets ;
    area 0.0.0.3 {
        networks {
            172.16.0.0 masklen 12 restrict ;
        } ;
        interface eth2 { priority 1 ; } ;
    } ;
    backbone {
        interface eth0 eth1 { priority 10 ; } ;
    } ;
} ;
aggregate 172.16.0.0 masklen 12 preference 10 {
    proto ospf {
        172.16.0.0 masklen 12 refines ;
    } ;
    proto direct {
        172.16.0.0 masklen 16 exact ;
    } ;
} ;
export proto ospfase type 1 {
    proto aggregate {
        172.16.0.0 masklen 12 ;
    } ;
} ;
traceoptions "/var/log/gated.log" size 100k files 4 all ;
```

Areas 0.0.0.1, 0.0.0.2, 0.0.0.3, 0.0.0.4, and 0.0.0.5

All routers that are wholly within an area have a very simple OSPF configuration. Example 12–26 shows the /etc/gated.conf file for topcat. Each router in these areas will have an entirely similar configuration.

Example 12–26   /etc/gated.conf on topcat

```
routerid 127.0.4.254 ;
rip off ;
ospf on {
    area 0.0.0.4 {
            interface all ;
    } ;
} ;
```

Area 0.0.2.1

This area is the only one that is not directly attached to the backbone. Therefore, in addition to configuring daffy for area 0.0.0.2 and 0.0.2.1, we must also configure it with a virtual link to the backbone. That capability is configured in the backbone stanza as shown in daffy's /etc/gated.conf file in Example 12–27. Note that the routerid is beauregard's, 127.0.1.254.

Example 12–27   /etc/gated.conf on daffy

```
routerid 127.2.1.254 ;
rip off ;
ospf on {
    traceoptions "/var/log/gated.ospf" size 100k files 4 packets ;
    area 0.0.0.2 {
            interface eth0 { priority 5 ; } ;
    } ;
    area 0.0.2.1 {
            interface eth1 { priority 1 ; } ;
    } ;
    backbone {
            virtuallink neighborid 127.0.1.254 transitarea 0.0.0.2 {
                    priority 0 ;
            } ;
    } ;
} ;
```

Hosts

As with our previous OSPF example, hosts have a very simple configuration file if they are not using simple static default routes. For those hosts in the backbone, the configuration file is given in Example 12–9 on page 593. For those hosts in an area, their configuration file would appear similarly to the one shown in Example 12–28, which illustrates one from area 0.0.0.3.

Example 12–28   /etc/gated.conf on Hosts in Area 0.0.0.3

```
rip off ;
ospf on {
    area 0.0.0.3 {
            interface all ;
    } ;
} ;
```

RIP or OSPF?

The decision as to whether you ought to use RIP or OSPF is one that depends upon weighing the tradeoff of administrative overhead with greater capabilities.

If you have read, and perhaps experimented with, the topics discussed in Chapters 6, 11, and this chapter, it should be clear that implementing `routed` is much simpler than `gated`.

But, the administrative burden is only a part of the decision. In all likelihood, the bigger part of the decision is based upon the level of redundancy in and the size of your environment. Routing environments which have more than just a few redundant routes are far more robustly implemented with OSPF. Larger environments that incorporate tens of routers or more also benefit from OSPF. On the other hand, hierarchical environments with few redundancies are often more easily managed by RIP, especially since RIPv2 offers authentication and can be configured to use multicasting instead of broadcasting. Aggregating routes is arguably easier with RIP. Generating default routes, on the other hand, is probably easier with OSPF.

From the performance perspective, the tradeoff between RIP and OSPF is that where RIP generates a lot of network traffic by advertising routing tables every 30 seconds; OSPF incurs a much higher overhead on routers in that it requires synchronization of the link-state database and recalculation of all routes at each resynchronization. To some degree, the overhead incurred by OSPF can be mitigated by carefully configuring areas and stub areas. Furthermore, an argument can be made that blackbox routers and Linux systems are getting faster all the time—network bottleneck issues are of greater concern.

In short, networks with many routers and/or lots of redundant paths are obvious candidates for OSPF. Smaller environments can be more simply managed with RIPv1 using `routed`. Environments in between the two categories are good candidates for either RIPv2 or OSPF. Of course, there is also always the option of building your environment using both options appropriately in different routing domains.

GNU Zebra

An alternative to `gated` is `zebra`. Whereas `gated` is a single daemon which can be configured to implement numerous routing table protocols, `zebra` implements a daemon for each different type of protocol. Additionally, `zebra` is distributed under the GPL and is therefore unencumbered by any commercial licenses. `zebra` implements the latest RFCs for RIPv2, RIPng, OSPFv2, and

BGPv4 (all of which are available in the commercial version of `gated`). You can learn more about `zebra` by visiting their home page.

```
http://www.zebra.org/
```

Of course, the syntax for `zebra` is different than `gated`. However, the discussions in this and the preceeding chapter provide a good basis for using `zebra`.

Summary

This chapter began with an overview of the concepts of the OSPF protocol. We examined the process used by OSPF to build its link-state database and to keep it synchronized. We also described the various LSAs that comprise the link-state database and the conditions under which each type is used. We considered the requirements for implementing both a flat OSPF domain and a hierarchical OSPF collection of areas. We then looked at the implementation of OSPF with `gated` through a series of examples.

For Further Reading

Listed here are books and WWW resources that provide further information about the topics discussed in this chapter.

Books

Huitema, Christian, *Routing in the Internet*, 2nd ed., Upper Saddle River, New Jersey, Prentice Hall, 1999.

Mann, Scott, and Ellen L. Mitchell, *Linux System Security: The Administrator's Guide to Open Source Security Tools*, Upper Saddle River, New Jersey, Prentice Hall, 2000.

Moy, John T., *OSPF: An Anatomy of an Internet Routing Protocol*, Reading, Massachusetts, Addison-Wesley, 1998.

Perlman, Radia, *Interconnections Second Edition: Bridges, Routers, Switches, and Internetworking Protocols*, Reading, Massachusetts, Addison-Wesley, 2000.

WWW Resources

Cisco provides a wealth of networking information at

```
http://www.cisco.com/univercd/cc/td/doc/cisintwk/ito_doc/
```

13

BGP

Whereas OSPF and RIP are IGPs, BGP is predominantly used as an EGP. We say "predominantly" because BGP can, and sometimes is, used as an IGP. Throughout the Internet, BGP is *the* protocol for routing between ASes (interdomain routing)—when so used, it is often referred to as external BGP (E-BGP). Within ASes of ISPs, BGP is sometimes used in a manner similar to OSPF—when so used, it is often referred to as internal BGP (I-BGP).

BGP is currently at version 4 (BGPv4) and standardized by RFC 1771. The specification in that RFC is such that enhancements to BGPv4 are anticipated. Consequently, numerous enhancements have been made including, for example, confederation (RFC 1965), route reflection (RFC 2796), communities (RFC 1997), and route flap damping (RFC 2439)—we discuss each of these in this chapter. Often, a BGPv4 implementation that uses one or more of these enhancements is referred to as BGPv4+.

In this chapter, we briefly look at the concepts behind BGP and then consider implementing both E-BGP and I-BGP.

BGP Overview

As with OSPF, we will not go into a great amount of detail about the concepts behind BGP and the details of its message types and formats. That is left to other documents like RFC 1771 and the books cited in "For Further Reading" on page 657.[1] Instead, we'll hit the high points of the protocol and emphasize those things that we'll later see when we consider configuring BGP with `gated`.

We noted previously that BGP is a path vector protocol. This means that it computes routes based on AS path information and simple hop metrics. However, BGP has the capability of making more sophisticated decisions when multiple paths exist than a distance vector protocol like RIP. BGP also uses a connection-oriented mechanism for its communication, sending all of its messages over TCP. This means that BGP must have a connection with its neighbors, otherwise it will not use any routes advertised by them. Contrasted with RIP, which uses UDP and timers potentially leading to periods of time in which bad routes persist, BGP has much better knowledge of the current state of an environment. Furthermore, BGP uses AS path information to avoid looping.

Two BGP neighbors, that is, any two routers configured to use BGP, are called *peers*. The first thing two BGP peers do is establish a BGP session. This is accomplished by first establishing a TCP connection and then exchanging BGP *Open* messages. Open messages are used to exchange identification information such as each other's router ID and ASN, and to agree upon timeout periods, such as the *hold time*, which is entirely similar to the OSPF `routerdeadinterval`. Once Open messages have been successfully exchanged, the two routers are said to be in the *established* state. This session remains established until one of the two systems goes down or an error occurs. Each router expects to hear from the other within every hold time seconds.

In addition to the Open message, BGP utilizes three other message types. They are *Update, Notification*, and *Keepalive*. Update messages are used to withdraw (known as marking a route *unfeasible*) and/or advertise routes to peers. Update messages also contain *attributes*, which incorporate the power of BGP. Attributes are discussed in the next section.

Notification messages are error messages. The sending of a Notification message to a peer *must* be followed by the termination of the BGP session. There are a number of different types of error conditions that can occur. For instance, if a router configured to run BGPv3 receives a BGPv4 Open message, it will respond with a Notification message indicating that it does not recognize version 4 but does recognize version 3. The TCP connection is then dropped and must be reestablished for the negotiation of a version 3 session. Other common

---

1. See, especially, *BGP4:Inter-Domain Routing in the Internet.*

error conditions that cause Notification messages to be sent include misconfigured ASNs, problems with attributes, and AS paths that include loops. Notification messages are not sent if the pertinent router interface goes down and the session does not terminate until the hold time expires. Regardless of the cause, once a BGP router drops the BGP session with a neighbor, it will generate an Update message to all of its peers indicating that the routes through the lost neighbor are no longer available (withdrawn or unfeasible).

Keepalive messages are simple messages exchanged between peers that keep the BGP session established. During normal operation these messages are exchanged before the negotiated hold time between peers expires. The hold time will be reset upon receipt of either a Keepalive or an Update message from a peer.

Update Messages and Attributes

Update messages are the mechanism used to exchange routing information between BGP peers. Each update message contains a listing of withdrawn routes, if any, and new or updated routes. Each new or updated route is sent in the form of a network number in prefix notation. Thus, each such route could be a network, subnetwork, or supernetwork (aggregate). These routes are often referred to as *IP prefixes*. Additionally, each new or updated route has attributes associated with it.

The attributes indicate such things as the AS path for the route, the origin of the route, and the preference for the route. Attributes are either *well-known* or *optional*. If an attribute is well-known, then it has an assigned type code from IANA and must be recognized by all BGP participants. There are two types of well-known attributes: mandatory and discretionary. Mandatory attributes must be processed, while discretionary attributes can be ignored. If an attribute is optional, then it may or may not be recognized by all other BGP participants. The following subsections list and define attributes specified in RFC 1771.

Attributes are also either *transitive* or *non-transitive*. If an attribute is transitive, then the new or updated route to which it is associated can be passed to BGP peers. All well-known attributes are transitive. If an attribute is non-transitive, then the new or updated route is not passed on to BGP peers. We'll see a little later on why some routes ought to be passed on and others not.

Origin

This attribute specifies the origin of the route in the Update message. All routes must originate from some interface since this attribute indicates the source of that route. The possible origins are IGP, EGP, or Incomplete. If set to IGP, then the route was learned from an IGP, such as RIP or OSPF. If set to EGP, then the route was learned from E-BGP or possibly EGP.[2] If set to Incomplete, then the route, if not withdrawn, was most likely learned from a static entry. Origin is a well-known, mandatory, and transitive attribute.

AS-Path

This attribute contains the ASes through which the advertisement for this route has passed. Each AS that forwards this advertisement will add its ASN to the list. In this way, a BGP router can detect routing loops by examining the list of ASes in the AS-Path and determining whether its own AS is already in the list. If so, the route can be rejected. To help visualize this conceptually, consider Figure 13–1. Each circle in this diagram represents an AS, each of which is identified by its ASN. AS134 has the network `158.7.1.0/24` inside; suppose it advertises the route to AS72. In the advertisement it includes AS134 in the AS-Path. AS72 gets the advertisement and then prefixes AS72 in the AS-Path for readvertisement to AS302. AS302 could then readvertise the route to AS134 with AS302 prefixed to the AS-Path. Upon receipt, AS134 would note that it was the initial AS to advertise the route (the origin AS) and discard the advertisement.

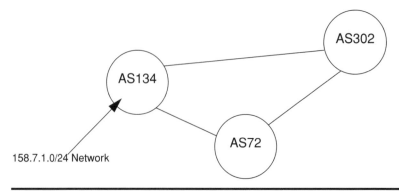

Figure 13–1   Advertising and AS-Path

---

2. The exterior gateways protocol is still used in the Internet, albeit infrequently.

It is possible for a router to accept an advertisement with its AS in the AS-Path. For example, if the `158.7.1.0/24` network were isolated from `158.7.2.0/24`, both within AS134, they could reach each other through AS72 and AS302, then the boundary routers within AS134 could be configured to accept the advertisements. This is ill-advised and discouraged as it could cause routing loops.

BGP supports route aggregation. Suppose that a BGP router for which the ASN is 418 has the AS path of 114, 87, 22 to the network `199.43.0.0/20` and the AS path of 29, 87, 22 to the network `199.43.16.0/20`. It can then aggregate these routes by advertising an AS path of 418, {114, 29}, 87, 22 to reach the network `199.43.0.0/19`. The routing tables on the recipients of this advertisement would have `199.43.0.0/19` as the destination and the BGP router in AS418 as the gateway. The sequence of AS numbers within the { } is called an *AS-Set*; the entire collection of ASNs is called an *AS-Sequence*.

The AS-Path attribute is well-known, mandatory, and transitive.

Next-Hop

Whenever a BGP router advertises a route, it includes the IP address of the next hop to reach the route. Very often, the next hop is the advertising BGP router. But suppose that the BGP router is advertising a route to a destination that goes through a different router which does not speak BGP? Figure 13–2 depicts a situation in which a BGP router, A, exports a route obtained from an OSPF router, B. In this scenario, A advertises to C that the network `144.16.9.0/24` can be reached by forwarding the packets to B. In this case, A's advertisement will indicate that the next hop is B and will set the Next-Hop attribute accordingly. It is worth emphasizing that C's routing table will cause the packets to go to B and not to A even though C got the information from A.

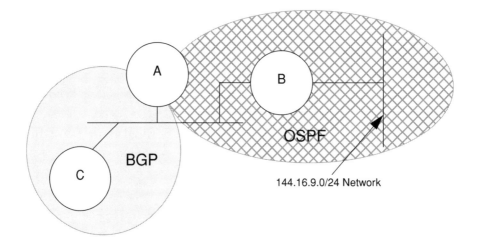

Figure 13–2   Purpose of the Next-Hop Attribute

The Next-Hop attribute is well-known, mandatory, and transitive.

Multi-Exit Discriminator

If an AS connects to another AS through two distinct routes, the Multi-Exit Discriminator (MED), an optional and nontransitive attribute, can be used to determine which route is best. For example, suppose that AS511 and AS46 interconnect through two different routers as shown in Figure 13–3. This diagram also depicts AS46 as having connections to AS2 and AS1015. Assuming that link 1 is a better route to AS1015, and link 2 is a better route to AS2, then AS46 can use a MED to advertise those facts to AS511. MEDs are metrics that are associated with routes. For example, AS46 will advertise to AS511 two routes to AS2: one through link 1 and one through link 2. In order to cause link 2 to be preferred, AS46 will assign a higher metric, by using the MED, to link 1.

Note that because MEDs are nontransitive, AS511 will not send them to the other ASes to which it is attached (depicted as circles with the ambiguous "AS" label). However, it might use MEDs to provide AS46 with best route information to the other ASes to which it is attached.

Note that MEDs can only be used when an AS has at least two distinct and direct connections to another AS.

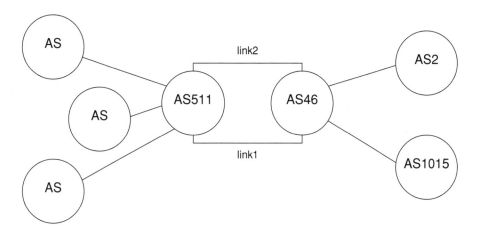

Figure 13–3   Using MEDs

One important characteristic of MEDs is that one AS is setting a preference for another AS to use. Since ASes are predominantly used in the Internet, the setting of MEDs could be used for competitive purposes. Consequently, many ISPs operating ASes will ignore MEDs from sources they do not trust—competitors, in particular.

Local-Pref

The Local-Pref attribute is similar to the MED attribute in the sense that it also carries a metric for use in specifying the preference of a given route. Its purpose, however, is to express preferences to remote destinations whenever an AS has multiple exit points. Figure 13–4 illustrates an example.

For purposes of this example, we'll focus on AS511. Notice that AS511 has multiple paths to AS2 and AS1015. Suppose that the better path to AS2 is through AS46, and that the better path to AS1015 is through AS17. In order to cause the systems and routers within AS511 to take advantage of these better paths, the Local-Pref attribute can be configured on each boundary router to specify metrics which cause the preferred routes to be used.

Notice also that AS511 has multiple paths to some ASes to which it is directly attached, such as AS80. Suppose that the direct link to AS80 is more costly (a slower link or one which costs more money) than the link to AS46. The use of Local-Pref could cause this indirect route to be preferred. However, in the

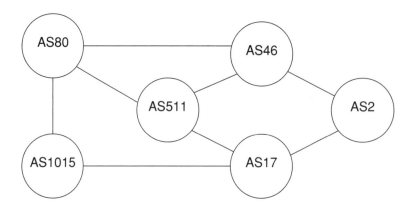

Figure 13–4   Using Local-Pref

Internet community, this could well be viewed as abusive so caution should be exercised in the use of Local-Pref for such purposes.

The Local-Pref attribute is well-known, discretionary, and transitive. This attribute is used only within an AS and is ignored when learned from another AS.

Atomic-Aggregate

The Atomic-Aggregate attribute is used to indicate that the associated route is an aggregate which should not be deaggregated. Normally, an AS will set this attribute when some portion of the aggregate cannot be reached or is not reachable by ASes listed in the AS-Path.

The Atomic-Aggregate attribute is well-known, discretionary, and transitive.

Aggregator

This is an optional, transitive attribute that can be attached to a route which has been aggregated. Only the BGP router that performed the aggregation should utilize this attribute. It contains the ASN and router ID of the router that performed the aggregation.

E-BGP and I-BGP

Thus far, we have described BGP interactions that apply to E-BGP. The primary role of I-BGP is to propagate routes learned via E-BGP within the AS. I-BGP also has the capability of propagating internal routes, just as with OSPF and RIP.

There are two rules relating to I-BGP that make E-BGP and I-BGP different. These rules are:

- I-BGP routers never insert their ASN in the AS-Path attribute.
- Any routes learned from an I-BGP router cannot be readvertised to other I-BGP routers.

The rationale behind the first bullet item is fairly straightforward. I-BGP operates *within* an AS as an IGP. Thus, it makes no sense for each I-BGP router to add its AS to the AS-Path since every I-BGP router has the same ASN.

The second bullet item warrants some discussion. Another way of expressing that statement is that the only way for an I-BGP router to learn the routes from another I-BGP router is to be a peer of that I-BGP router. The primary reason for implementing this rule is to avoid looping. The only way that BGP can avoid loops is by making sure that its own AS is not in the AS-Path. This is impossible in an I-BGP environment due to the first bullet item. In short, this means that each I-BGP router within an AS must have an established BGP session. This is called a *full mesh*.

As you can imagine, a full mesh requires a large number of BGP sessions. Since each I-BGP router must be a peer of every other I-BGP router, then each I-BGP router would need a connection to every other I-BGP router. For example, if an I-BGP environment included four routers, then each router would need three connections, one to each of the other routers. Since these connections are two-way BGP sessions, the total number of required connections in such an environment would be six. We can compute this number by observing that there are four routers, each of which has three connections, but all connections are two way, so

```
(4 x 3)/2 = 6
```

Generally, a full mesh requires the following number of connections.

```
[n x (n-1)]/2
```

where n is the number of participating routers. Thus, if the I-BGP environment contains 50 routers, there would need to be a total of 1225 BGP sessions! Clearly, this is unwieldy.

As a consequence of the high overhead associated with the I-BGP full mesh requirement in the original specification (RFC 1771), two approaches were taken to mitigate this problem. The first is route reflection, currently standardized by RFC 2796, and the second is AS confederations, standardized by RFC 1965.

Route Reflection

The idea behind route reflection is quite similar to the concept of the OSPF DR. Within an I-BGP environment some routers are designated route reflectors (RRs) and the remaining are designated route reflector clients (RRCs). Consider Figure 13–5.

The purpose of the RR is to propagate routes advertised by I-BGP RRCs. In essence, the rule about readvertising I-BGP routes is relaxed for RRs. In the diagram, the RR1 for AS511 advertises all of the routes from RRC, which acts as both an I-BGP RRC and an E-BGP router for AS511. RR1 also advertises all of the routes from RRC1 and RR2, to each other, and to RRC. Similarly, RR2 readvertises the routes it gets from RR1, RRC2, and RRC3. Note that, in this case, the number of required I-BGP sessions is reduced from 15 (for a full mesh) to five using route reflection.

In order to prevent looping, two new attributes are introduced for the use of route reflection. These are the *Originator-ID* and the *Cluster-List* attributes. Both of these attributes are optional and nontransitive. The Originator-ID attribute is used to hold the router ID of the originator of the route into the route reflection environment. An RR will never advertise a route to another router if the Originator-ID contains the router ID of the router to which it is

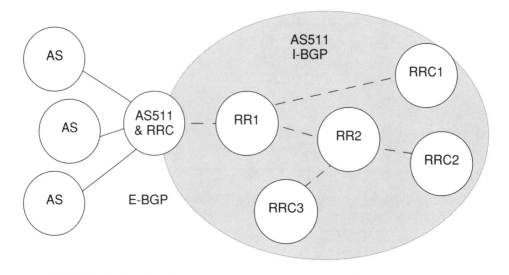

Figure 13–5   Using Route Reflection

going to make the advertisement. In other words, no sense in sending a route to the originator of the route.

The Cluster-List attribute is used to record the path the route has taken through the I-BGP. A *cluster* is the collection of an RR and its RRCs. So, in the example given in Figure 13–5, the routers RR1, RRC, and RRC1 form one cluster, and the routers RR2, RRC2, and RRC3 form another cluster. Each cluster is assigned a unique 32-bit value known as the *cluster ID*. When a cluster advertises a route, it adds its cluster ID to the Cluster-List attribute. If an RR receives a route with its cluster ID in the Cluster-List, it discards the route.

AS Confederations

Simply put, the approach that AS confederation implements is breaking up an AS into many sub-ASes (SASes). Consider Figure 13–6.

In this diagram, we see that AS511 has been split up into many SASes. Within a SAS, I-BGP runs as normal, requiring a full mesh implementation. Between SASes, a modified form of E-BGP is run, called *EIBGP*.

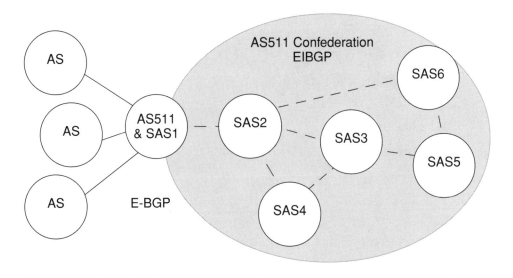

Figure 13–6   AS Confederation

The difference between E-BGP and EIBGP is as follows:

- Unlike E-BGP, the Local-Pref attribute is not ignored between SASes.
- EIBGP uses the AS-Confed-Set and AS-Confed-Sequence attributes (confederation attributes) instead of AS-Set and AS-Sequence attributes. These confederation attributes are always stripped by an AS boundary router participating in E-BGP before readvertising.
- The Next-Hop attribute does not get changed as it traverses SASes.

The first bullet item effectively takes advantage of the fact that the SASes are internal to an AS. The second bullet item implements loop avoidance within the confederation and does not leak that (unneccessary) information outside the AS.

The third bullet item essentially implements the designer's assumption that a single IGP runs throughout the confederation. This means that each SAS must have a boundary router that participates in EIBGP—there can be no SAS boundary routers that are not running EIBGP as described in "Next-Hop" on page 617. Within a SAS, just as within an AS, other protocols can be run.

BGP Route Selection

BGP route selection is fairly simple. The order of preference is:

1. the largest Local-Pref value
2. the shortest AS-Path
3. the lowest MED
4. the minimum cost Next-Hop
5. the lowest router ID

BGP always selects the route with the largest Local-Pref value first. This attribute is set by the E-BGP router for its AS or is learned from an I-BGP router. If there is more than one route with the same Local-Pref value, then the route with the shortest AS-Path is chosen. If there are multiple routes with equivalent AS-Paths, then the one with the lowest MED metric is chosen. If this still results in a tie of two or more routes, then the Next-Hop attribute is examined for the one with the lowest cost. If multiple routes still remain, then the route with the lowest router ID BGP peer is chosen.

Once a route is chosen, BGP updates the kernel routing table.

In order to accommodate these computations and advertisements, BGP maintains three separate RIBs. These are called the *Adjacent Input RIB* (AIRIB), the *Adjacent Output RIB* (AORIB), and the *Local RIB* (LRIB). The AIRIB contains the advertisements received from BGP peers. There is one such RIB for each BGP peer. The AORIB contains the routes advertised to peers. There is one AORIB for each peer. The LRIB contains the routes that have been selected and placed into the kernel routing table.

Practical Enhancements to BGP

Two major enhancements to BGP have been implemented to deal with two issues that have arisen out of its use. These are *route flap damping* (RFC 2439) and *communities* (RFC 1997).

Route Flap Damping

Suppose that, due to some problem, a link between ASes goes up and down frequently (for example, a router has a software bug and reboots frequently). Each time the link goes down, the ASes withdraw the route. When it comes back up, the route is readvertised. If this process is propagated throughout a large environment such as the Internet, it becomes problematic in that it incurs a lot of overhead in terms of rebuilding routing tables. It is called *route flapping*.

In order to mitigate the repeated propagation of this type of problem, penalties can be applied to routes that are unstable in this way—that is, routes that appear and then disappear. The penalty is increased with each flap. Once the penalty reaches a certain (configurable) level, then the route is disregarded (called *suppressed*). This is the basic procedure for *route flap damping*. Over time, the penalty is reduced if flapping desists and the route is reintroduced when the configurable threshold is reached.

Properly configuring route flap damping is critical. Waiting too long after routes have stabilized causes extended periods for access to be restored. Not waiting long enough incurs time, processor, and memory consuming activity with no useful results. See RFC 2439 for further details.

Communities

The concept of Communities, and the *Community* attribute, arose from the application of BGP to the Internet. Consider the three ISPs, with registered ASes, interconnected as shown in Figure 13–7.

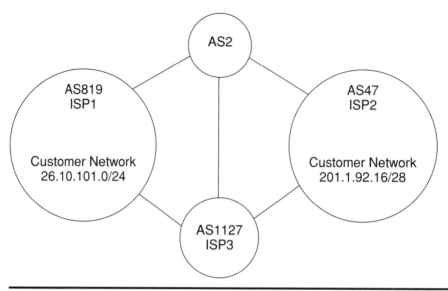

Figure 13–7   Communities

ISP1, ISP2, and ISP3 are providing connection services to the Internet for paying customers. AS2 is run by a service provider that sells Internet connectivity services to ISPs. Suppose that a host in the `26.10.101.0/24` network needs to connect to a host in the `201.1.92.16/28` network. From the diagram, ISP1 can reach ISP2 either through AS2 or through AS1127. However, AS1127 is run by ISP3, which provides the same sorts of services that ISP1 and ISP2 do. In particular, ISP3 does not want to advertise the fact that it can reach ISP2 to ISP1, unless ISP1 wants to pay for the priviledge. In short, ISP3 wants to suppress some of the routes it advertises because it only wants to allow traffic directly destined to or originated from one of its internal networks and does not want to forward packets on behalf of other ASes. Similarly, ISP1 and ISP2 do not want to advertise the reachability to other ASes.

Conceptually, what we're describing is an administrative policy. The use of the Community attribute can implement this type of policy in a BGP environment. Simply, Communities are implemented by associating one or more Community identifiers (CID) with a route. A Community identifier is expressed as *ASN:CID*, so that there is never any confusion with respect to the choice of the CID between ASes—within an AS, each CID must be unique.

For example, AS1127 could use CID 450 to identify nontransit routes. Any routes learned from AS819 would be placed into this category by associating

1127:450 as the Community attribute with the route and thus not be readvertised to other ASes. In this way, other ASes would not try to route packets through AS1127 to a destination outside of AS1127.

Unfortunately, the Community attribute is not supported by gated version 3.6. It is supported by both the commercial version of gated and the GPL'd zebra.

Implementing BGP with gated

Now that we have a basic understanding of BGP, we'll look at implementing it using gated. First, we describe the gated BGP syntax and then we look at implementing E-BGP and I-BGP.

gated BGP Syntax

In order for BGP to work, both the routerid and autonomoussystem statements must be correctly set. As with the other protocols we've discussed, BGP has its own stanza. The stanza is given in Example 13–1.

Example 13–1   BGP Stanza

```
bgp on | off
    [ {
        preference pref ;
        defaultmetric metric ;
        traceoptions options ;
        group type  external peeras ASN
              | internal peeras ASN
              | igp peeras ASN proto protocol
               routing peeras ASN proto protocol interface iface_list
              | test peeras ASN
        [nexhopself] | [ gateway gateway ]
        [ holdtime time ]
        [ indelay time ]
        [ keep  all | none  ]
        [ keepalivesalways ]
        [ lcladdr local_address ]
        [ localas ASN ]
        [ logupdown ]
        [ metricout metric ]
        [ noaggregatorid ]
        [ nogendefault ]
        [ nov4asloop ]
        [ outdelay time ]
        [ passive ]
        [ preference grouppreference ]
        [ preference2 grouppreference2 ]
        [ recvbuffer buffersize ]
```

Example 13–1   BGP Stanza *(Continued)*

```
[ sendbuffer buffersize ]
[ setpref metric ]
[ showwarnings ]
[ traceoptions options ]
[ ttl ttl ]
[ v3asloopokay ]
[ version number ]
{
  allow {
    route_filter ;
    } ;
  } ;
  {
    peer host
      [nexthopself] | [ gateway gateway ]
      [ holdtime time ]
      [ keep  all | none  ]
      [ keepalivesalways ]
      [ lcladdr addr ]
      [ localas ASN ]
      [ logupdown ]
      [ metricout metric ]
      [ noaggregatorid ]
      [ nogendefault ]
      [ nov4asloop ]
      [ outdelay ]
      [ passive ]
      [ preference pref ]
      [ preference2 pref ]
      [ recvbuffer size ]
      [ sendbuffer size ]
      [ showwarnings ]
      [ traceoptions options ]
      [ ttl ttl ]
      [ v3asloopokay ]
      [ version number ]
      ;
    } ;
} ] ;
```

The key to understanding the bgp stanza is understanding the group type statement. This statement specifies how the router behaves with respect to BGP—that is, acting as an E-BGP participant, an I-BGP participant, or both. In particular, the group type statement specifies the BGP options and attributes that are expressed to the peers within a group. In this way, multiple groups can be defined and a given router can be configured to behave differently depending upon the group. Distinctions can also be made for specific peers using the peer statement within a group type statement.

Table 13–1 describes each of the group type statements and their purpose. Only one of these specification parameters can appear in a single group type statement. However, there can be many `group type` statements within a BGP stanza. In fact, there will be one `group type` statement for each BGP peer.

Table 13–1   BGP Stanza `group type` Statements

`group type` SPECIFICATION	DESCRIPTION
`external peeras ASN`	This is used to identify E-BGP peers. The external peers specified with this statement are assumed to be reachable via a local network attached to one of the router's interfaces. If this is not the case, you will need to specify the gateway parameter to set the Next-Hop attribute correctly. `ASN` is the ASN of the peer.
`internal peeras ASN`	This is used to identify I-BGP peers. Peers must be directly connected. `ASN` is the ASN of the peer.
`igp peeras ASN proto protocol`	This is used to identify internal peers. It examines the IGP routes and advertises them via BGP only if the AS-Path attribute is not entirely represented in the IGP tags. `ASN` is the ASN of the peer. `protocol` is the protocol being used.
`routing peeras ASN proto protocol interface iface_list`	This is used to propagate external routes between I-BGP routers that are not on the same local network. `ASN` is the ASN of the peer. `protocol` is the protocol being used to resolve routes for I-BGP peer reachability. `iface_list` is the list of interfaces to which this statement applies.
`test peeras ASN`	Used for testing only. Peers and ASNs do not really need to exist.

The options to the `group type` statement and `peer` statement are given in Table 13–2. Differences in use between `group type` and `peer` are noted there as well.

Table 13–2   Options to the `group type` Statement

OPTIONS TO THE `group type` STATEMENT	DESCRIPTION
`gateway` *gateway*	Specifies the IP address to use for the Next-Hop attribute (see "Next-Hop" on page 617) instead of this router. Used whenever a peer is not on the same local network.
`holdtime` *time*	Specifies the holdtime *time* in seconds. This sets the hold time as described in "BGP Overview" on page 613. The minimum value is 3, the default is 180.
`indelay` *time*	Specifies the time in seconds that a route must be known to this BGP router before it is put in the `gated` RIB. This is a rudimentary form of route flap damping. The default is 0, disabling this feature. Normally, if this option is set, then so is `outdelay`. See "Setting up Route Flap Damping" on page 650 for a more sophisticated method of suppressing routes.
`keep all	none`	Specifies whether to keep routes with this router's ASN in the AS-Path attribute. The default is `none`, which means that all such routes are discarded.
`keepalivesalways`	Specifies that Keepalive messages are to be sent even when an Update message has been sent within the hold time. This option exists to support routers which incorrectly always require Keepalives.

Table 13–2   Options to the `group type` Statement *(Continued)*

OPTIONS TO THE `group type` STATEMENT	DESCRIPTION
`lcladdr` *addr*	Specifies the IP address on the local BGP router that is to be used by peer(s) in this group. For external peers, this address must match an interface that is on the same local network as the peer or the specified `gateway`, if used. For internal peers, this address can match any interface. In either case, incoming connections will only be accepted if this address is used. This option must be specified as part of the `group type` statement and not the `peer` statement, if the `group type` is either `internal` or `routing`.
`localas` *ASN*	Specifies the ASN that this BGP router is representing to the peers in this group.
`logupdown`	Causes a message to be written to syslog whenever this peer or a peer in this group enters or leaves the established state (see "BGP Overview" on page 613).
`metricout` *metric*	Specifies the metric for all routes sent to the peer or peers in the group. Metrics within BGP are preferred in the following order (the first being the most preferred), if they exist: **1.** The metric specified in the `export` statement **2.** `metricout` in a `peer` statement **3.** `metricout` in a `group` statement **4.** The `defaultmetric` specified in the BGP stanza For group types internal and routing, this value must be set in the `group type` statement and not the `peer` statement.

Table 13–2   Options to the `group type` Statement *(Continued)*

OPTIONS TO THE `group type` STATEMENT	DESCRIPTION
`noaggregatorid`	Forces the router ID to be set to 0 in the Aggregator attribute (see "Aggregator" on page 620) instead of the router ID of the router. This has the effect of preventing different routers within an AS from creating aggregate routes with varying AS paths.
`nogendefault`	Default routes must be explicitly generated with the `gendefault` option or using a `generate` stanza. This option prohibits a default from being generated from the updates received from this peer or peers within this group.
`nov4asloop`	Used to prevent routes with looped AS paths from being advertised to external peers. Used to prevent BGPv3 peers from getting looped routes.
`outdelay time`	Specifies the amount of time in seconds for which a route must be present before `gated` will advertise this route via BGP. This is a rudimentary form of route flap damping. The default is 0, disabling this feature. Normally, if this option is set, then so is `indelay`. See "Setting up Route Flap Damping" on page 650 for a more sophisticated method of suppressing routes. This option must be specified as part of the `group type` statement and not the `peer` statement, if the `group type` is either `internal` or `routing`.
`passive`	Prevents `gated` from trying to open a BGP session with this peer or any peer in this group. This option was incorporated to deal with bugs in BGPv3 and should not be used for BGPv4.

Table 13–2   Options to the group type Statement *(Continued)*

OPTIONS TO THE group type STATEMENT	DESCRIPTION
preference *pref*	Specifies the gated preference for this peer or peers in this group. This setting overrides that in the BGP stanza and can therefore be used to make routes learned from this group or peer more or less desirable. The default for BGP routes is 170.
preference2 *pref*	Sets a tiebreaker gated preference. Default is 0.
recvbuffer *size*	Specifies the *size* in bytes of the receive buffer. The default and maximum is 65,535 bytes. This should rarely, if ever, be needed.
sendbuffer *size*	Specifies the *size* in bytes of the receive buffer. The default and maximum is 65,535 bytes. This should rarely, if ever, be needed.
setpref *metric*	This option is used to set the Local-Pref attribute. This is not an absolute metric; instead, the *metric* specified here is used in the calculation described in "Using setpref" on page 635.
showwarnings	Causes gated to issue warning messages to syslog when receiving BGP updates incorporating duplicate routes or deletions of nonexistent routes. Normally, these updates are ignored.
traceoptions *options*	Traces the specified *options* for this peer or peers within this group. Available options are packets (all BGP packets), open (all Open messages), update (all Update messages), keepalive (all Keepalive messages), and all (packets and all modifications to gated RIB). The modifiers, detail, send, and recv (see "The traceoptions Statement" on page 484) can be used with any of these options.

Table 13–2　Options to the `group type` Statement *(Continued)*

OPTIONS TO THE `group type` STATEMENT	DESCRIPTION
`ttl ttl`	By default, `gated` sets the IP time-to-live field to 1 for all local peers and to 254 for all nonlocal peers. This option can be used to override these defaults and is especially useful for communicating with peers that drop packets for which the IP time-to-live field is 1.
`v3asloopokay`	Permits the advertisement of routes with duplicate ASNs in the AS-Path to version 3 BGP routers.
`version number`	By default, `gated` negotiates connections with peers by first trying version 4, then 3, then 2. If this option is set, then BGP will only attempt to establish a session with this peer or peers within this group to the version `number` specified, which must be 2, 3 or 4.
`allow`	Allows peer connections from any IP address that matches the `route_filter`. Numerous `route_filter`'s may be specified. The `route_filter` must be as defined in "Route Filtering" on page 491 except for `default`.
`peer host`	Used to configure a specific peer for which the IP address matches `host`. The peer statement appears within the `group type` statement and inherits the options specified within the group. All options in this table, except where noted, can be overridden in the `peer` statement.

There are three statements outside of the `group type` statement. They are global to the BGP stanza and all can be overridden by specific options in the `group type` statement. These are described in Table 13–3.

Table 13–3 BGP Stanza General Statements

STATEMENT	DESCRIPTION
`preference pref`	Specifies the `gated` preference for BGP routes. This setting can be overridden by one set in a `group type` or `peer` statement. The default for BGP routes is 170.
`defaultmetric metric`	Specifies the metric for all routes advertised by this BGP router. Metrics within BGP are preferred in the following order (the first being the most preferred), if they exist: **1.** The metric specified in the `export` statement **2.** `metricout` in a `peer` statement **3.** `metricout` in a `group` statement **4.** The `defaultmetric` specified in the BGP stanza
`traceoptions options`	Specifies the tracing options for BGP. By default, global tracing options are inherited. If specified in the `group type` or `peer` statements, these are overridden.

Using `setpref`

The Local-Pref attribute is set in `gated` for BGP routes by the following formula.

```
Local-Pref = 254 - (BGP gated preference value) + (value of setpref)
```

Here, the BGP gated preference value is the preference for BGP routes. By default, this is set to 170, but may be changed by either the `preference` statement in the BGP stanza or the `preference` statement within a `group type` statement. The `value of setpref` is set with the `setpref` statement within the `group type` statement. The value of Local-Pref will never exceed 254.

For example, suppose that you want to set the Local-Pref attribute to a value of 150 for all routes within a particular group. If the default preference for BGP routes has not been changed, this would require a `setpref` value of 66, because

```
150 = 254 - 170 + 66
```

This value is set in the BGP stanza shown in Example 13–2. It applies to all routes coming from AS712.

Example 13–2   Using `setpref`

```
routerid 127.0.0.254 ;
autonomoussystem 384 ;
bgp on {
    group type external peeras 712 setpref 66 {
        allow {
            all ;
        } ;
} ;
```

Think carefully about the choice of value used with `setpref` and how it relates to the BGP preference and, thus, the ultimate Local-Pref value. The larger the Local-Pref attribute value, the higher the preference is for the routes learned from that peer or group of peers. A larger Local-Pref value is achieved by setting a *larger* `setpref` value and/or a *smaller* BGP `gated` preference value.

Implementing BGP

In the previous chapter, we considered a simple BGP example using `group type external`. Example 13–3 repeats that example.

Example 13–3   `/etc/gated.conf` on `golden`

```
options mark ;
routerid 127.0.0.254 ;
autonomoussystem 384 ;
rip off ;
bgp on {
    group type external peeras 212 {
        peer 192.111.23.153 ;
    } ;
} ;
ospf on {
    backbone {
        interface eth1 eth2 { priority 1 ; } ;
    } ;
} ;
export proto ospfase type 2 {
    proto bgp as 384 metric 2 {
        all ;
```

Example 13–3 /etc/gated.conf on golden *(Continued)*

```
    } ;
} ;
export proto bgp as 212 {
    proto direct interface eth0 ;
    proto direct interface eth1 eth2 restrict;
    proto ospf restrict ;
} ;
traceoptions "/var/log/gated.log" replace size 100k files 4 route ;
```

The bgp stanza is quite simple here. It simply establishes a peer relationship with one external system (192.111.23.153) which is directly connected to the local 192.111.23.152/30 network. We know that the connection is local because group type external is being used. This stanza causes golden to establish a BGP session with the peer and exchange BGP routes. The peer represents AS212 while golden represents AS384.

Everything that golden learns via BGP is exported into OSPF as indicated by the export proto ospf statement. All of those routes, since they are type 2, get an absolute metric of 2.

Notice that golden offers very little to its BGP peer. This is configured by the export proto bgp statement. Within that statement, everything is restricted except for information about the eth0 interface. This is done because all of the addresses used in the OSPF domain are RFC 1918 private addresses and should not be leaked to the Internet.

This example illustrates the simplest form of BGP configuration. Basically, golden participates in BGP so that it can learn about routes external to its AS and propagate them throughout the AS. It also supplies its eth0 IP address so that external nodes can route to it. In order for the systems within AS384 to reach other ASes and for nodes in other ASes to reach inside of AS384, golden must also provide network address translation (NAT) services (see the next two chapters for a discussion of NAT).

Before we go on to more involved examples, we need to cover some specifics regarding importing and exporting routes into and out of BGP.

Importing and Exporting BGP Routes

Which routes are imported into the gated RIB and exported via BGP sessions is determined by the import and export statements, respectively. We previously considered this topic in "Importing and Exporting OSPF Routes" on page 584, however, this section serves to clarify the use of these statements for BGP.

THE import STATEMENT   The import statement begins by specifying from which protocol to import the routes. For BGP, this can be controlled by ASN or by AS-Path information. By default, all routes learned through BGP are imported into the RIB so, normally, the import statement is only used to prevent routes from being placed in the RIB or modifying their gated preference.

Example 13–4 illustrates the basic syntax.

Example 13–4   BGP import Statement Syntax

```
import proto bgp as ASN restrict ;
import proto bgp as ASN [preference pref] {
    route_filter [restrict | preference pref] ;
} ;
import proto bgp aspath aspath_regexpr origin any | egp |
    igp | incomplete restrict ;
import proto bgp aspath aspath_regexpr origin any | egp |
    [igp | incomplete [preference pref] {
            route_filter [restrict | preference pref] ;
} ;
```

There are two forms of the statement described. The first uses

```
import proto bgp as ASN
```

as the beginning portion of the statement. This form filters routes based on the ASN (given as ASN) from which the route advertisement was received. All of the routes from a particular ASN may be restricted with the restrict keyword, thereby preventing them from being placed in the RIB. All of the routes from a particular ASN can also be matched based on a route_filter (described in "Route Filtering" on page 491) and then added to the RIB, perhaps with a different preference than the default of 170 or restricted.

The second form of the import statement uses

```
import proto bgp aspath aspath_regexpr origin
```

at the beginning of the statement. Here, the aspath keyword is followed by a regular expression (given as aspath_regexpr) that can be used to match ASes contained in the AS-Path attribute. The aspath regular expression values are similar to that used for utilities like grep and are described in Table 13–4. The origin keyword is followed by one of any, egp, igp, or incomplete. The value specified is used to match the value contained in the Origin attribute with any matching all values.

Table 13–4   Regular Expression Values to the `aspath` Keyword

REGULAR EXPRESSION	MEANING
.	Matches any single character.
*	Matches zero or more of the previously matched character. For example, `.*` matches zero or more characters—in other words, it matches everything.
+	Matches one or more of the previously matched character. For example, `2+`, matches all ASes beginning with 2.
?	Matches zero or one of the previously matched character. For example, `2?`, matches 2, 20, 21, 22, ..., 29.
" "	A single space *without* the quotes. This represents AND. All of the ASes in the space-separated list must be in the AS-Path attribute for a match. For example, `201 400 54` means that all of the ASes, 201, 400, and 54 must be in the AS-Path.
|	This represents OR. At least one of the ASes in the list must be in the AS-Path attribute for a match. For example, `201 | 400 | 54` means that one of the ASes, 201, 400, and 54 must be in the AS-Path.

Suppose that we would like to import all routes except those heard from AS514 and any routes that have AS44 and AS46 in its AS-Path. Example 13–5 illustrates.

Example 13–5   Illustrative BGP `import` Statements

```
import proto bgp as 514 restrict ;
import proto aspath 44 46 origin any restrict ;
import proto bgp aspath .* origin any {
    all ;
} ;
```

Notice that in Example 13–5 all AS-Path attributes will match the last `import` statement. `gated` uses the first match. Thus, always make sure that your `import` (and `export`) statements are ordered from the most specific match to the least specific match.

WARNING

The gated documentation suggests that parentheses be used around these regular expressions. For example, (.*) instead of .*. Using parentheses in gated version 3.6 for this purpose will generate a syntax error!

THE export STATEMENT   The export statement specifies to which protocol routes are to be advertised. The inner portion of the statement specifies the source of the routes to be exported. Unlike imported routes, only routes associated with a local interface are, by default, exported via BGP. Thus, all routes must be explicitly specified in an export statement in order for BGP to advertise them. Example 13–6 provides the basic syntax for the BGP export statement.

Example 13–6   BGP export Statement Syntax

```
export proto bgp as ASN restrict ;
export proto bgp as ASN [metric MED] {
        export_list ;
} ;
```

These statements specify to which BGP ASN (given as ASN) the export statement applies. If the first form of the statement is used, that is,

```
export proto bgp as ASN restrict ;
```

then no routes will be advertised to that AS.

In the second form of the statement, the metric keyword actually specifies the MED (see "Multi-Exit Discriminator" on page 618). gated implements a 16-bit unsigned value for MED instead of the BGPv4 specified 32-bit unsigned value.

This second form of the export statement also accepts a variety of forms in the export_list. The export_list represents the source of routes for exportation via BGP and is generally described in "Import and Export Policies" on page 497. Let's consider a BGP specific example.

Suppose that you'd like to export to AS 501 routes via BGP which were obtained from BGP, OSPF, some static entries, and some specific directly connected interfaces. However, you do not want to export any routes which include AS410 and that has either an Origin attribute of incomplete or IGP. Also, there are some OSPF tagged routes (with a tag value of 2) that you want to suppress. Example 13–7 provides such a case. Line numbers provide clarity.

Example 13–7   Sample BGP export Statement

```
1   export proto bgp as 501 {
2        proto all aspath 410 origin igp incomplete restrict ;
3        proto ospf tag 2 restrict ;
4        proto bgp aspath .* origin any {
5             all ;
6        } ;
7        proto ospf {
8             all ;
9         } ;
10       proto direct interface eth0 eth1 {
11            all ;
12       } ;
13       proto static interface all {
14            all;
15       } ;
16  } ;
```

Line 1 specifies that the routes within the stanza are to be exported to AS501. Line 2 prevents any routes with AS410 in the AS-Path attribute and for which the Origin attribute is either IGP or incomplete from being included in this export. Line 3 prohibits all OSPF routes with the tag value of 2 from being included in this export.

Lines 4 through 6 cause all other BGP routes to be included in the export. Similarly, lines 7 through 9 include all other OSPF routes.

Lines 10 through 12 cause all routes associated with the specific interfaces eth0 and eth1 to be included. Ordinarily, this would happen by default, but because we are using an export statement, we must explicitly include all direct routes.

Lines 13 through 15 cause all previously defined static routes, regardless of interface association, to be included in this export.

Note that the list of export restrictions and exports are ordered most specific first to least specific. This is required, as for example, if the statement at lines 4 through 6 appeared before the restriction at line 2, then the restriction would be ignored. In other words, the first match always applies.

In the following sections, we will explore some other examples of using both the import and the export statements.

A BGP Example

If Figure 12–7 on page 606 comprised the entire network of an organization, it would not be given its own AS as depicted. Instead, a static default route for the external connection to 192.111.23.154 interface on golden would be configured and exported as described in "A Flat OSPF Domain Example" on page 584. Effectively, golden would have no knowledge, nor would it require any knowledge, of the fact that it was a part of AS212.

So, let's suppose that the example provided in Figure 12–7 is just a piece of the picture and that it is part of a larger environment. Figure 13–8 depicts a scenario in which there are two connections from the local AS (AS384) to two distinct ASes, AS212 (connected to by foghorn) and AS94 (connected to by steamboat). You can think of these ASes as ISPs which are used by AS384 for Internet connectivity. These two services could be used for redundancy and/or for access from two geographically disparate locations. Our example won't explore those issues, just the BGP configuration.

Routers are represented as rectangles and ASes as circles. Internally, routes are propagated via an IGP such as OSPF or RIP. The dashed lines between steamboat and golden indicate that the connections between these systems are not direct (that is, not on the same local network). The internal gray areas represent RIP and OSPF domains.

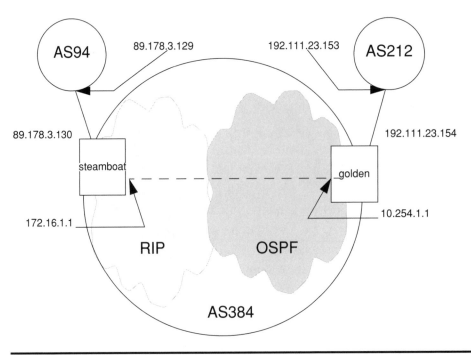

Figure 13–8   A Simple Example AS: AS384

Let's establish some goals with respect to the routers shown and involved in the BGP environment, and with respect to the routes that we would like to have propagated throughout the IGPs. The goals are as follows:

- The routers `steamboat` and `golden` must *not* advertise the fact that AS94 and AS212 can be reached through AS384.
- All internal addressing is RFC 1918 private and must not be leaked to through the ASBRs.
- The routers `steamboat` and `golden` participate in I-BGP between each other and E-BGP with the outside ASes to which they are connected.
- The routers `steamboat` and `golden` will advertise a default route internally for Internet access.

For both the routers `steamboat` and `golden`, the external interface is `eth0` (`89.178.3.130` and `192.111.23.154`, respectively) and the internal interface is `eth1`.

Now we consider `gated` configuration files that meet these goals in the next three sections. In each of these sections, we concentrate on the BGP configuration, although we also provide example configurations for IGPs as examples.

CONFIGURING `steamboat`   Given the goals described above, Example 13–8 provides a configuration file. The line numbers are added for clarity.

Example 13–8   `/etc/gated.conf` on `steamboat`

```
1   routerid 127.0.1.254 ;
2   autonomoussystem 384 ;
3   bgp on {
4           group type external peeras 94 {
5                   peer 89.178.3.129 ;
6           } ;
7           group type routing peeras 384 proto rip setpref 50 {
8                   peer 10.254.1.1 ;
9           } ;
10  } ;
11  rip on {
12          interface eth0 noripin noripout ;
13          interface eth1 ripin ripout version 2 broadcast ;
14  } ;
15  generate default {
16          proto bgp aspath .* origin any { all ; } ;
17  };
18  import proto bgp as 94 {
19          all ;
20  } ;
21  import proto bgp as 384 {
```

Example 13–8   /etc/gated.conf on steamboat *(Continued)*

```
22          all ;
23  } ;
24  export proto bgp as 94 {
25          proto bgp as 384 restrict ;
26          proto bgp as 212 restrict ;
27          proto rip restrict ;
28          proto direct interface eth0 {
29                  host 89.178.3.130 ;
30          } ;
31  } ;
32  export proto bgp as 384 {
33          proto bgp as 94 { all ; } ;
34          proto rip { all ; } ;
35  } ;
36  export proto rip metric 2 {
37          proto aggregate {
38                  default ;
39          } ;
40  } ;
```

Let's analyze this file. Lines 1 and 2 specify the router ID and ASN, respectively. These are required for BGP to work. Lines 3 through 10 reflect the fact that steamboat is participating in BGP, both externally with AS94, and internally for AS384. The E-BGP session is defined for the one peer 89.178.2.129. The I-BGP session is defined for the one peer golden (10.254.1.1). The I-BGP session is implemented with group type routing since golden and steamboat are not directly connected. This statement only defines the sessions; it is the import and export statements which define what is included in the BGP advertisements. This satisfies the third bullet item in the goals list.

Lines 18 through 23 show two import stanzas. These stanzas have the effect of importing everything learned from AS94 and from AS384 into the gated RIB. This is the default behavior so these entries are, strictly speaking, unnecessary, but they are illustrative and in larger environments make the overall BGP configuration clearer. In the next example, they will be removed.

Lines 24 through 35 illustrate the use of a BGP export statement. These statements dictate which routes get advertised to the specified BGP AS. In the first export stanza, which routes get exported to AS94 is controlled (lines 24 through 31). In that stanza, all advertisement of routes learned via BGP and RIP are suppressed. The only advertisement allowed to go out to AS94 is the one for steamboat's external interface. This satisfies the first and second bullet items in our goals list.

On the other hand, the second `export` stanza (lines 32 through 35) causes all routes learned from both BGP and RIP to be exported in advertisements to AS384. In other words, advertising everything internally is quite alright.

The fourth bullet item in the list of goals requires that default routes be propagated by `steamboat` and `golden`. The default route is generated using the `generate` stanza (lines 15 through 17). This stanza causes all routes learned via BGP to be included in the generation of a default route. Note that the `aspath` regular expression syntax described in "Importing and Exporting BGP Routes" on page 637 is used here. Use of this syntax could have been used to replace lines 25 and 26 (which is done in the next example).

Lines 36 through 40 export the default route created by the `generate` statement. Note that the protocol specified is `aggregate` and not `generate`. Whenever you need to export route(s) that have been created with `aggregate` or `generate` statements, they are always imported and/or exported as `proto aggregate`.

CONFIGURING `golden`   Fundamentally, the configuration file for `golden` is the same as that for `steamboat`. The major difference is that `golden`, unlike `steamboat`, participates in OSPF as an IGP instead of RIP. Note that, in this case, RIP is turned off. Also, the `setpref` keyword is used to set the Local-Pref attribute on these routes to be higher than those of `steamboat`. Its configuration file is given in Example 13–9. This file implements the simplifications described in the preceding section.

Example 13–9   `/etc/gated.conf` on `golden`

```
routerid 127.0.1.254 ;
autonomoussystem 384 ;
rip off ;
bgp on {
        group type external peeras 212 {
                peer 192.111.23.153 ;
        } ;
        group type routing peeras 384 proto ospf setpref 60 {
                peer 172.16.1.1 ;
        } ;
} ;
ospf on {
        interface eth0 disable ;
        interface eth1 enable ;
} ;
generate default {
        proto bgp aspath .* origin any { all ; } ;
};
export proto bgp as 212 {
        proto bgp aspath .* origin any restrict ;
```

Example 13–9   `/etc/gated.conf` on `golden` *(Continued)*

```
        proto direct interface eth0 {
                host 192.111.23.154 ;
        } ;
} ;
export proto bgp as 384 {
        proto bgp as 212 { all ; } ;
} ;
export proto ospfase type 2 metric 2 {
        proto aggregate {
                default ;
        } ;
} ;
```

FINAL NOTES ABOUT THIS EXAMPLE   As with the prior example (continued from Figure 12–7 on page 606 at the beginning of this section), both `steamboat` and `golden` must provide NAT services. Also, notice that no RIP or OSPF routes were incorporated into BGP. This is due to the fact that we want the default route to be generated solely upon BGP routes. This means, in particular, that within AS384 there must be router(s) configured to properly propagate RIP routes into OSPF and OSPF routes into RIP.

A More Complex BGP Example

Now, consider Figure 13–9 representing AS384 which interconnects with five distinct ASes. In this diagram, routers are represented by rectangles and ASes by circles. The large circle represents AS384. It connects to AS212 through the router `golden`, AS1101 through the router `collins`, AS14 through the router `springs`, AS597 through the router `omaha`, and AS94 through the router `steamboat`. These five routers are ASBRs. Additionally, there is an internal router called `central`, which we will use for route reflection. Also, `central` is responsible for incorporating all of the IGP routes into BGP for advertisement throughout AS384. For the sake of this example, all of these routers are Linux systems running `gated`.

One external router, `pyramid`, exists for the purpose of exploring an indirect connection to an external AS; in this case, the connection from `steamboat` to AS94.

The gray cloud within AS384 represents its internal networks, one collection of which is described by the example given in Figure 12–7. Since some of the internal addresses are RFC 1918 private, we'll need to be sure that they are not leaked to the Internet. The systems in this area have their routing tables updated by various IGPs and/or are configured with static entries. Notice that some of

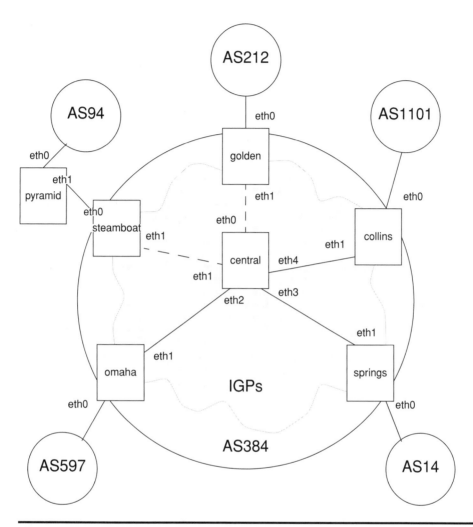

Figure 13–9   A More Complex Example AS: AS384

the lines connecting the routers internally are dashed. This indicates that they are not directly connected. The internal lines, dashed or solid, indicate the internal I-BGP sessions that are established.

For purposes of the example, assume that AS384 will route packets for AS94, AS212, and AS1101 to any destination either in or through AS384. However, AS384 will not provide the same service for AS597 and AS14. For those ASes, AS384 will only route packets which are destined within AS384 and only advertise valid internal destinations. Also, each ASBR needs to have route flap damping implemented.

As a final note, while not shown in the diagram, each of the external ASes are connected to other ASes throughout the Internet.

Table 13–5 provides IP addresses for each of the identified interfaces as well as IP addresses or networks for the ASes to which AS384 is attached. We'll use this information throughout our configuration examples.

Table 13–5   Addresses Associated with Figure 13–9

ROUTER OR AS	ADDRESSES	NOTES
golden	eth0 192.111.23.154 eth1 10.254.1.1	There is an internal router (not shown) with the IP address of 10.254.1.10 that knows how to reach central.
collins	eth0 168.5.4.2 eth1 199.77.81.18/28	
springs	eth0 48.15.38.2 eth1 199.77.81.66/28	
central	eth0 199.77.81.33/28 eth1 199.77.81.49/28 eth2 199.77.81.1/28 eth3 199.77.81.65/28 eth4 199.77.81.17/28	
omaha	eth0 176.18.92.2 eth1 199.77.81.2/28	
steamboat	eth0 89.178.3.130 eth1 172.16.1.1	There is an internal router (not shown) with the IP address of 172.16.1.10 that knows how to reach central.
pyramid	eth0 130.9.8.2/28 eth1 89.178.3.129	
AS212	192.111.23.153/30	
AS1101	168.5.4.0/24	This AS has numerous BGP routers on this network. We want to allow sessions with any or all of them.

Table 13–5   Addresses Associated with Figure 13–9 *(Continued)*

ROUTER OR AS	ADDRESSES	NOTES
AS14	48.15.38.1/28	
AS597	176.18.92.1/28	
AS94	130.9.8.1/28	

The purpose of this example is to allow us to explore the various gated configuration options for BGP and which permit the proper configuration of this environment for the correct propagation of the necessary routes. To that end, we provide the following goals which more succinctly capture the discussion in the previous paragraphs.

- All ASBRs need to be configured with route flap damping.
- All ASBRs need to be configured to prevent the leakage of RFC 1918 addresses.
- The router central needs to be configured as an I-BGP route reflector and it needs to advertise all internal routes to the ASBRs.
- The routers steamboat, golden, and collins must advertise all available routes externally.
- The routers springs and omaha must only advertise routes terminating at or within AS384 externally.

Before we look at the specific configuration for each of the routers in this example, we'll first look at setting up route reflectors and route flap damping in the next two sections. Specific configurations for each of the six routers follow these two sections.

SETTING UP ROUTE REFLECTION   Setting up route reflectors with gated is actually quite simple. It just requires that the internal AS routes be exported to the same internal AS. Example 13–10 illustrates such an entry.

Example 13–10   Route Reflector export Statement

```
export proto bgp as 384 {
    proto bgp as 384 {
    all ;
    } ;
    # other exports go here
} ;
```

Here, the routes learned via AS384 are reexported to AS384 in all BGP advertisements. We'll see route reflection in use in "Configuring `central`" on page 656.

SETTING UP ROUTE FLAP DAMPING   Earlier (see Table 13–2 on page 630), we noted that the `indelay` and `outdelay` options within the `bgp` stanza could be used to implement a rudimentary route flap damping capability. Using those options, a period of time could be set before routes became eligible for inclusion in the RIB and for advertising. While you can utilize this approach when such simplicity is acceptable, a method incorporating greater flexibility and implementing the capability described in "Route Flap Damping" on page 625 can be used. It is implemented via the `dampen-flap` stanza, which is completely separate from the `bgp` stanza. Although separate, only BGP routes are affected by the `dampen-flap` stanza. If *dampen-flap* is used, it applies to all BGP routes. Example 13–11 illustrates the syntax.

Example 13–11   The dampen-flap Stanza

```
dampen-flap {
    [suppress-above metric ;
    reuse-below metric ;
    max-flap metric ;
    unreach-decay time ;
    reach-decay time ;
    keep-history time ; ]
} ;
```

Each of the optional keywords within the `dampen-flap` stanza are described in Table 13–6. Note that the *metric* is a floating point number in units of *flaps* known as the *instability metric*. One flap accrues each time a route becomes unreachable.

Notice that the `unreach-decay` and `reach-decay` times are measures of stability of a given route (whether unreachable or reachable) as opposed to the simpler `indelay` and `outdelay` options which simply impose a time delay.

This stanza can be implemented by simply placing

```
dampen-flap { } ;
```

in the `/etc/gated.conf` file. Using this simple syntax causes the default values, as described in Table 13–6, to be utilized.

Table 13–6   Keywords within the `dampen-flap` Stanza

KEYWORD/VALUE	DESCRIPTION
`suppress-above` *metric*	The value of the instability metric at which point route suppression takes place. As long as the instability metric is at or above *metric*, then the route will not be placed into the routing table by BGP and will not be advertised even if the route is available. Default value is 3.0.
`reuse-below` *metric*	When the value of the instability metric reaches *metric* or below, then the route becomes available for use again. The default value is 2.0. This value must always be less than `suppress-above`.
`max-flap` *metric*	The value specified by *metric* is the upper limit on the instability metric. Effectively, this value is infinity for the metric and additional flaps will not be added once this limit is reached. The default is 16.0.
`unreach-decay` *time*	Specifies the *time* in seconds after which period the instability metric will be cut in half as long as the route is continuously unreachable during this time. The default is 900 and should always be greater than or equal to `reach-decay`.
`reach-decay` *time*	Specifies the *time* in seconds after which period the instability metric will be cut in half as long as the route is continuously reachable during this time. Smaller values here make the route reusable sooner. This value should always be less than or equal to `unreach-decay`. The default is 300.
`keep-history` *time*	Specifies the *time* in seconds after which route flapping records about a given route are dropped. The default is 1,800. Caution: Setting this value too high can cause unwanted consumption of memory and CPU resources.

CONFIGURING collins   Configuring collins is quite straightforward. It needs to advertise everything internally and externally. Example 13–12 illustrates, with line numbers added for clarity.

Example 13–12   /etc/gated.conf on collins

```
1    routerid 127.0.5.254 ;
2    autonomoussystem 384 ;
3    rip off ;
4    bgp on {
5        group type external peeras 1101 {
6                allow {
7                        all ;
8                } ;
9        } ;
10       group type internal peeras 384 {
11                peer 199.77.81.17 ;
12       } ;
13   } ;
14   export proto bgp as 1101 {
15       proto direct interface eth {
16                all ;
17       } ;
18       proto all aspath .* origin any {
19                10.0.0.0 masklen 8 restrict ;
20                172.16.0.0 masklen 12 restrict ;
21                192.168.0.0 masklen 16 restrict ;
22                all ;
23       } ;
24   } ;
25   export proto bgp as 384 {
26       proto direct interface eth {
27                all ;
28       } ;
29       proto bgp as 1101 {
30                all ;
31       } ;
32   } ;
```

Lines 5 through 9 cause collins to permit BGP sessions with any BGP router in AS1101 on the 168.5.4.0/28 network. This type of configuration allows for general redundancy with routers in AS1101. Lines 10 through 12 sets up a BGP session with the router central for the internal AS384.

Lines 14 through 24 specify that all routes, except RFC 1918 private addresses, are to be advertised to AS1101. Notice that all direct routes are explicitly advertised as required at lines 15 through 17. Because central (see "Configuring central" on page 656) advertises all routes discovered from other

ASes to which AS384 is attached, this satisfies the goal of allowing AS1101 to route through AS384. Also, since RFC private addresses are in use within AS384, they must be restricted from advertisement. We cannot use martians here because these routes are necessary for connectivity within AS384.

Lines 25 through 31 cause all routes to be advertised to the internal AS384.

Note that all of the statements within the export stanzas are listed with the most specific criteria first since the first match is always the match used by gated.

CONFIGURING golden   The router golden differs from collins (over and above address and router ID differences) in that it has an internal interface that uses an RFC 1918 private address (10.254.1.1/24). This means that golden must restrict the advertisement of that interface and its associated routes to AS212; it also means that its connection to central is not direct. To that end, the group type internal stanza within the bgp stanza provides a gateway for reachability to the peer central. Additionally, the export of the eth1 interface on golden is restricted from AS212.

Note that the restriction of RFC 1918 private addresses appears within the proto bgp as 384 stanza instead of the proto all aspath stanza as in Example 13–12. For this example, the results are the same and the different implementation is shown in Example 13–13 for illustrative purposes.

Example 13–13   /etc/gated.conf on golden

```
routerid 127.0.1.254 ;
autonomoussystem 384 ;
rip off ;
bgp on {
    group type external peeras 212 {
        peer 192.111.23.153 ;
    } ;
    group type internal peeras 384 {
        peer 199.77.81.33 gateway 10.254.1.10 ;
    } ;
} ;
export proto bgp as 212 {
    proto direct interface eth1 restrict ;
    proto direct interface eth0 {
        all ;
    } ;
    proto bgp as 384 {
        10.0.0.0 masklen 8 restrict ;
        172.16.0.0 masklen 12 restrict ;
        192.168.0.0 masklen 16 restrict ;
    } ;
    proto all aspath .* origin any {
        all ;
```

Example 13-13   /etc/gated.conf on golden *(Continued)*

```
        } ;
} ;
export proto bgp as 384 {
    proto direct interface eth {
            all ;
    } ;
    proto bgp as 212 {
            all ;
    } ;
} ;
```

CONFIGURING springs AND omaha   The configuration file for the routers springs and omaha is identical except for addresses and router IDs. These two routers must restrict what is advertised because we do not want to permit AS14 and AS597 to route through AS384; however, we do want them to advertise routes to AS384 including valid destinations within AS384. This is a perfect example of a situation in which the Community attribute (see "Communities" on page 625) could be used, but because gated version 3.6 does not support it, we need to explicitly set up the export statement to dictate which routes can be advertised and which cannot. Example 13-14 illustrates, with line numbers added, such a file for springs.

Example 13-14   /etc/gated.conf on springs

```
 1  routerid 127.0.4.254 ;
 2  autonomoussystem 384 ;
 3  rip off ;
 4  bgp on {
 5      group type external peeras 14 {
 6              peer 45.15.38.1 ;
 7      } ;
 8      group type internal peeras 384 {
 9              peer 199.77.81.65 ;
10      } ;
11  } ;
12  export proto bgp as 14 {
13      proto direct interface eth {
14              all ;
15      } ;
16      proto all aspath 94|212|1101|14|597 origin any restrict ;
17      proto all aspath 384 origin igp {
18              10.0.0.0 masklen 8 restrict ;
19              172.16.0.0 masklen 12 restrict ;
20              192.168.0.0 masklen 16 restrict ;
21              all ;
22      } ;
23      proto all aspath 384 origin incomplete {
24              10.0.0.0 masklen 8 restrict ;
```

Example 13–14   `/etc/gated.conf` on springs *(Continued)*

```
25              172.16.0.0 masklen 12 restrict ;
26              192.168.0.0 masklen 16 restrict ;
27              all ;
28         } ;
29  } ;
30  export proto bgp as 384 {
31      proto direct interface eth {
32              all ;
33         } ;
34      proto bgp as 14 {
35              all ;
36         } ;
37  } ;
```

The primary difference in this file compared to those considered previously for this example occur at lines 12 through 29. This is the export statment that controls the routes which are advertised to AS14. Our goal is to advertise only those routes which are legally reachable within AS384. This means that RFC private addresses must be restricted and that all routes learned from other ASes are restricted. Line 16 accomplishes the latter goal by restricting any BGP route that has one of the external ASes in its AS-Path.

Lines 17 through 28 restrict the export of RFC 1918 private addresses but allow the export of any Internet legal internal addresses satisfying the former goal. Note that this is done with two `proto all aspath` stanzas. The first, at line 17, exports all routes that have AS384 in the AS-Path and that originated from an IGP. The second, at line 23, specifies that AS384 must be in the AS-Path and that the origin of the route is incomplete. By specifying all routes with AS384 in the AS-Path attribute that originated either by an IGP or incomplete (usually a static route) exclusive of RFC 1918 private addresses, the only routes that will be exported are those that reach legal internal destinations within AS384.

The remainder of the file is as in earlier examples.

CONFIGURING `steamboat`   The configuration file for `steamboat` is nearly identical to that for `golden`. The only difference is that because `steamboat` is not on the same local network as its peer in AS94, it must specify the necessary gateway address to reach AS94. This is done within the `group type external` stanza, as shown in Example 13–15. The remainder of that file is as described for `golden`.

Example 13–15   `/etc/gated.conf` on `steamboat`

```
routerid 127.0.2.254 ;
autonomoussystem 384 ;
rip off ;
bgp on {
    group type external peeras 94 {
            peer 130.9.8.1 gateway 89.178.3.129 ;
    } ;
    group type internal peeras 384 {
            peer 199.77.81.49 gateway 172.16.1.10 ;
    } ;
} ;
export proto bgp as 94 {
    proto direct interface eth1 restrict ;
    proto direct interface eth0 {
            all ;
    } ;
    proto bgp as 384 {
            10.0.0.0 masklen 8 restrict ;
            172.16.0.0 masklen 12 restrict ;
            192.168.0.0 masklen 16 restrict ;
    } ;
    proto all aspath .* origin any {
            all ;
    } ;
} ;
export proto bgp as 384 {
    proto direct interface eth {
            all ;
    } ;
    proto bgp as 94 {
            all ;
    } ;
} ;
```

CONFIGURING `central`   The router `central` participates both in I-BGP and OSPF. Its role is to receive all BGP and OSPF advertisements from various sources and then reexport them via BGP and OSPF. Example 13–16 shows the configuration file for `central`. Its entries are quite straightforward and follow from our discussions in this and the previous chapter.

Example 13–16   `/etc/gated.conf` on `central`

```
routerid 127.1.1.254 ;
autonomoussystem 384 ;
rip off ;
ospf on {
    backbone {
            interface all ;
    } ;
} ;
bgp on {
    group type internal peeras 384 {
            allow {
                    all ;
```

Example 13–16   `/etc/gated.conf` on `central` *(Continued)*

```
                } ;
        } ;
} ;
export proto bgp as 384 {
    proto direct interface eth {
            all ;
    } ;
    proto ospf {
            all ;
    } ;
    proto bgp as 384 {
            all ;
    } ;
} ;
export proto ospfase type 2 {
    proto bgp as 384 {
            all ;
    } ;
} ;
```

Summary

We briefly discussed BGP conceptually and then looked at implementing BGP with `gated` version 3.6 in three different examples. In these examples, we also explored BGP and IGP interaction.

For Further Reading

Huitema, Christian, *Routing in the Internet*, 2nd ed., Upper Saddle River, New Jersey, Prentice Hall, 1999.

Perlman, Radia, *Interconnections Second Edition: Bridges, Routers, Switches, and Internetworking Protocols*, Reading, Massachusetts, Addison-Wesley, 2000.

Stewart, John W. III, *BGP-4: Inter-domain Routing in the Internet*, Reading, Massachusetts, Addison-Wesley, 1999.

14

ipchains: Address Translation, IP Accounting, and Firewalls

Perhaps the most compelling reason to use a Linux system as a gateway, that is, a router that interconnects two or more networks, is its out-of-the box capability to operate as a router, a packet-filtering firewall, and an address translator. Implementing these capabilities on other platforms requires additional software, often at additional cost. These Linux capabilities do not solve every problem, but they solve a great many of them. And the good news is, it gets even better with netfilter as we see in the next chapter.

In this chapter,[1] we take a look at the ipchains utility and the associated IP masquerading capability of Linux. We consider how to configure a firewall, set up a special form of address translation called masquerading, and along the way note that accounting of IP datagrams is built into the ipchains utility. The topics discussed here apply only to the 2.2.x series Linux kernels. Everything changes with the 2.4.x series kernel because ipchains is replaced with netfilter; we explore that topic in Chapter 15.

What is a Firewall?

In the context of computing, a *firewall* is a system that prevents unauthorized network communications to it, from it, and through it. The Linux ipchains is capable of establishing rules that provide a reasonably secure firewall under

---

1. This chapter is largely derived from Chapters 3, 11, and 16 of *Linux System Security* as cited in "General Security References" on page 725. Courtesy Prentice Hall, Inc.

many circumstances. It can also provide a remarkable level of flexibility in terms of selectively restricting traffic flow to, from, and through the system. Additionally, ipchains can work in conjunction with other software to provide other options not available in ipchains itself. Unfortunately, despite all of its advantages, ipchains can't solve every problem and should be viewed as a part of an overall security plan. For more information about security, generally, see the various references in "For Further Reading" on page 723.

Linux ipchains implements a packet-filtering firewall. This means that each network packet may be filtered against a set of rules. This procedure is performed in the kernel. It specifically causes the kernel to analyze each packet for source and destination IP addresses and port numbers or ICMP types and codes. A more intelligent but similar type of firewall is a stateful packet-filtering firewall. The difference between stateful filtering and ipchains is that the stateful filter can keep track of its connections and thereby distinguish packets associated with an established connection and packets that are not. While Linux ipchains is incapable of this, there is a wrapper program that can add this functionality on top of ipchains. If you need stateful capabilities, check out

```
ftp://ftp.interlinx.bc.ca/pub/spf/
```

where you will find Brian Murrell's stateful packet-filtering project.

Another type of firewall is a proxy-based firewall. This type of firewall operates as a go-between for services. All network connections destined through the proxy-based firewall terminate at the firewall. Then (if the rules allow) the proxy-based firewall will make a connection to the destination system on behalf of the originating host. The proxy-based firewall thereby manages two separate connections. We will later touch on proxy firewalls, such as Trusted Information System's Firewall Toolkit (FWTK) and NEC's SOCKSv5. It is common to implement FWTK or SOCKS in conjunction with ipchains.

Let's begin our detailed look at ipchains.

Packet Filtering

The concept of packet filtering is a fairly simple one. The contents of the headers of each network packet are checked against a series of rules. Each rule includes an action, so that, when a packet matches a rule, the action component of the rule tells the kernel what to do with the packet. In essence, we can censor network packets. In order to implement the inspection of network packets or to filter the packets, there must be software that provides the capability. The modern Linux kernel includes this capability.

The precise mechanism for packet filtering in Linux depends upon the version of the Linux kernel. The packet-filtering implementation for Linux kernels version 2.1.102 and above is `ipchains`. By default, kernel versions prior to 2.1.102 implement `ipfwadm`. Kernel versions 2.3.x and greater utilize the `iptables` utility (discussed in the next chapter) which is targeted for release with mature 2.4.x kernels. The `ipchains` mechanism is the topic of this chapter.

If you are using an earlier kernel implementation that does not include `ipchains` and you need to use `ipfwadm`, visit the site

```
http://www.xos.nl/linux/ipfwadm/
```

for documentation. The syntax and implementation of `ipfwadm` is quite similar to `ipchains` except that `ipchains` includes functionality which is not supported in `ipfwadm`. For kernel version 2.0.34 and later, you may upgrade to `ipchains` with a patch. There are three sites at which this patch may be obtained and they are referenced in "ipchains Documentation" on page 723.

Configuring the Kernel for `ipchains`

Normally, when you install a major distribution such as Caldera, Red Hat, SuSE, or Debian, the initial kernel configuration will include support for `ipchains` and IP masquerading (see "IP Masquerading" on page 689).

However, if you install with "expert" mode or you rebuild your kernel (see the *Kernel HOWTO* for a discussion of kernel rebuilding), then you will need to make sure that you select the appropriate kernel configuration parameters to support `ipchains` and IP masquerading. The configuration parameters, the proper choice (either to enable or disable), and descriptions are given in the *Linux IP Masquerade HOWTO*. Make sure that you read through that document *before* proceeding!

NOTE

As of this writing, `ipchains` is at version 1.3.9. You should be using this version to get all of the functionality described here. Visit the `ipchains` home page regularly and consider subscribing to the `ipchains` mailing list to keep up to date regarding upgrades and vulnerability reports. The `ipchains` home page and other resources are cited in "`ipchains` Documentation" on page 723.

ipchains Overview

Linux `ipchains` provides for the capability to insert rules into the kernel that will cause all network packets to be filtered against those rules. The rules are maintained in a *chain*. There are three permanent chains—they are *input, forward*, and *output*. The input chain consists of a list of rules that are applied to all incoming (entering the system) packets. The forward chain consists of a list of rules that apply to all packets that are to be forwarded (see Chapter 6 for a discussion of IP forwarding). The output chain is a list of rules that apply to all packets that are outbound (leaving the system). These three chains always exist and cannot be deleted. Each chain may be configured to invoke custom chains. By default, there are no custom chains and each permanent chain contains an allow-all-packets rule.

Let's explore the general behavior of the chains for inbound, forward, and outbound types of packets as diagrammed in Figure 14–1.

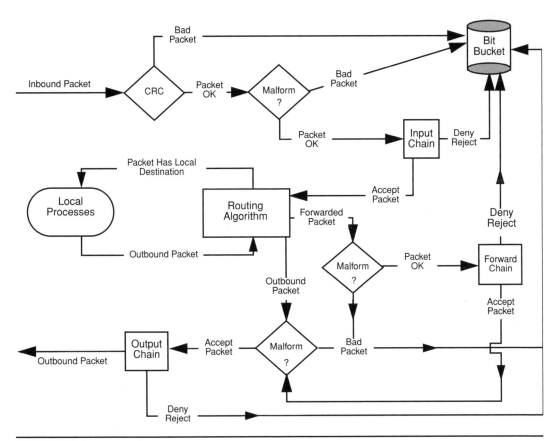

Figure 14–1   ipchains Flow of Events

Behavior of a Chain

When a packet is processed against a chain, this means that all of the Internet layer and Transport layer information, as well as the network interface involved, is compared with each rule in the chain. For the input and output chains, the rules apply to each and every interface (eth0, eth1, ppp0, lo0, etc.) on the system unless the rule specifically identifies a particular interface. If a rule matches, then the action specified by that rule will be taken. Unless the rule's action is DENY or REJECT (meaning destroy the packet—we define all of the actions in Table 14–3 on page 672), the packet passes the chain and moves on to the next step. If no rule matches, then the default rule or last rule, called a *policy*, will apply. Policies are discussed in "Setting Policies (Default Rules)" on page 682.

Malformed Packets

Before a packet is checked against a chain, it is checked for sanity; that is, all of the header information must be valid. If any information contained in any of the headers is invalid—not known to the kernel—then the packet is considered malformed and is destroyed by the kernel with no further processing. This sanity check is indicated in Figure 14–1 by the diamonds containing "Malform?".

Analysis of an Inbound Packet

When a packet arrives, the first thing that is done is a cyclic redundancy check (CRC—see Chapter 2). If the CRC does not match the one carried in the frame, the packet is destroyed (sent to the "Bit Bucket" in Figure 14–1). Otherwise, the kernel sanity check ("Malform?") is performed; if the packet is malformed, it is destroyed. If the packet is not malformed, it is processed against the input chain. The input chain will destroy the packet if it matches a DENY or REJECT rule. If the rule does not DENY or REJECT the packet, then the packet is passed on to the kernel for destination processing. This is accomplished by invoking the routing algorithm ("Routing Algorithm" in Figure 14–1—see Chapter 6 for a discussion of the routing algorithm) which determines the next step in processing by determining the destination address.

The routing algorithm determines the destination of the packet. If the destination is the local system, then it is appropriately handled, either internally by the kernel or by passing the packet on to the local process. On the other hand, if the packet is destined to another system, it must be forwarded. All forwarded packets are checked for sanity ("Malform?") and then processed by the forward chain, which either destroys the packet due to a REJECT or DENY, or passes the packet on to the output chain (after the "Malform?" check). Processing by the output chain proceeds as with the other chains—either the packet is destroyed or it is allowed to go on. If the latter, then the packet is sent to the network through the appropriate network interface.

Analysis of an Outbound Packet

If a process on the local system generates a packet that is destined for a remote host, the packet is first processed for the remote destination, then sanity checked, and then processed by the output chain. The output chain will either destroy the packet if the packet matches a DENY or REJECT rule or send it to the network through the appropriate interface.

The Loopback Interface

Packets that arrive at the loopback interface (lo0) or are destined to the loopback are treated as inbound and outbound packets, respectively. The chains may have rules that distinguish particular interfaces as we will see throughout this chapter.

Custom Chains

You can create custom chains, which are simply a list of rules, and invoke them through one of the three permanent chains. Custom chains are discussed in "Adding Custom Chains" on page 692.

Introduction to Using `ipchains`

Implementing `ipchains` can be a very complex process. It is best to start simple and then test and verify your configuration before you go on to more complex rules, such as masquerading rules. We will follow this advice by beginning with an initial description of the `ipchains` command, the permanent chains, and some simple examples. We'll move from there to examine some of the more complex features, such as custom chains and IP masquerading. Then, we'll look at some real-world examples.

The `ipchains` Command

There's really no way to simplify the introduction of the flags, options, and actions associated with `ipchains`. So, Table 14–1 lists the flags or commands, Table 14–2 describes the options or parameters, and Table 14–3 notes the actions. We will use examples throughout the remainder of this chapter to clarify the use of many of them.

Table 14–1   Flags of ipchains

Flag	Description
-A or --append	Appends one or more rules to the specified chain.
-C or --check	Checks a given packet against the selected chain. The -s, -d, -p, and -i flags are required (see Table 14–2 on page 667).
-D or --delete	Deletes one or more rules from the specified chain.
-F or --flush	Flushes all the rules in the specified chain.
-I or --insert	Inserts one or more rules in the specified chain at the specified rule number.
-L or --list	Lists all the rules in the selected chain. If no chain is specified, then all rules in all chains are listed.
-M or --masquerading	If used with -L, this flag will display all masquerading rules. If used with -S, this flag will set one or more masquerading parameters. Masquerading rules are discussed in "IP Masquerading" on page 689.
-N or --new-chain	Creates a new custom chain. The name of the new chain cannot exceed eight characters. Custom chains are defined in "Custom Chains" on page 665.
-P or --policy	Specifies the policy, or default rule, for a permanent chain. Policies cannot be specified for custom chains. This is the last rule in the chain, even though it appears first when listed with -L.
-R or --replace	Replaces a rule in the specified chain.

Table 14–1   Flags of `ipchains` *(Continued)*

FLAG	DESCRIPTION
`-S` or `--set tcp tcpfin udp`	Changes the timeout values used for masquerading. This flag requires three timeout values in seconds—*tcp* for TCP sessions, *tcpfin* for timeouts after receiving a TCP FIN packet, and *udp* for UDP timeouts.
`-X` or `--delete-chain`	Deletes the specified custom chain. There must be no rules that reference the chain you wish to delete. If you do not specify a chain, all custom chains will be deleted. Permanent chains cannot be deleted.
`-Z` or `--zero`	Zeroes out the packet and byte counters. You may use this flag in conjunction with `-L`, which will have the effect of displaying the current accounting information and then resetting the counters to 0.

Each of the flags in Table 14–1 can utilize one or more options described in Table 14–2. These options are the parameters that comprise a rule.

Table 14–2   Options to `ipchains`

OPTION	DESCRIPTION
`-b` `--bidirectional` may be used instead of `-b`	Bidirectional. Use of this flag will create a rule that applies to both source and destination IP addresses. It is the same as creating two rules with the source IP address and destination IP address reversed.

Table 14–2 Options to ipchains *(Continued)*

OPTION	DESCRIPTION

`-d [!] address[/mask]`
`[!] [port[:port]`
`--destination` may be used instead of `-d`
	This option specifies the destination IP address, `address`, for this rule. It may be an IP address, an IP network number, a resolvable hostname, or a resolvable network name (in `/etc/networks` or `/etc/hosts`). Specify the `mask` argument for network addresses. It may be either the actual netmask or the number of leftmost bits set to 1 in the mask. So, setting `mask` to `20` would be the same as setting it to `255.255.240.0`. The optional `!` is the logical NOT operator and reverses the meaning.
	The address `0.0.0.0/0` means any IP address. You may also use `0/0`.
	You may also include port number(s) or ICMP codes (described in the section, "ICMP Types and Codes" on page 683) in the optional `port` field(s). If `:` is used, then a range of ports is implied. When using `:`, the leftmost port number defaults to 0 and the rightmost to 65535, thus, `:1023` means the range of ports 0 through 1023 inclusive.

`--dport [!] [port:port]` `--destination-port` may be used instead of `-dport`	Allows for the separate specification of ports or ICMP codes.
`[!] -f` or `--fragment`	Specifies that the rule refers to fragments of a packet (see "Packet Fragments" on page 688 for a discussion of IP fragmentation). Such packets will not contain port numbers or ICMP types. The `!` reverses the meaning.

Table 14–2   Options to `ipchains` *(Continued)*

OPTION	DESCRIPTION
`-h [icmp]`	Help. If used without the optional `icmp` argument, an `ipchains` usage message will be displayed. If used with the `icmp` argument, the ICMP-named types and codes will be displayed. See "ICMP Types and Codes" on page 683 for a cross-reference of names and numbers.
`-i [!]` *name* `--interface` may be used instead of `-i`	Specifies the interface to which this rule applies. If this option is omitted, then the rule applies to *all* interfaces. The argument *name* must be the name of the interface, such as `eth0`, `eth1`, `ppp0`, etc. You may use the wildcard + to match all interfaces beginning with the specified name; for example, `eth+` will match all interfaces beginning with `eth`, like `eth0`, `eth1`, etc. If ! precedes *name*, then the rule does not apply to that interface but does apply to all other interfaces. For the input chain, specifying this option causes the rule to inspect packets incoming to that interface. For the output and forward chains, it inspects packets destined to go out the specified interface. Note that the loopback interface must be specified as `lo`.
`--icmp-type [!]` *type*	Allows for the specification of an ICMP type. Must be one of the types given by `ipchains -h icmp`. This option is identical to specifying the ICMP type with `-s`.

Table 14–2   Options to `ipchains` *(Continued)*

OPTION	DESCRIPTION
`-j target` `--jump` may be used instead of `-j`	Specifies the `target` of the rule, which may be one of the actions described in Table 14–3 on page 672 or the name of a custom chain. If a custom chain, then it cannot be the same as the current custom chain. If this option is not specified, then no action is taken when this rule is matched, but the packet and byte counters will be incremented.
`-l` or `--log`	Causes packets matching the rule to be logged via `klogd` to selector `kern.info`. Very useful option for initial setup and debugging. Be careful with this option, however, as it logs *every* packet that matches.
`-n` or `--numeric`	When listing rules, suppresses name translation. Ordinarily, `ipchains` will attempt to convert IP addresses to hostnames, port numbers to services, etc.
`-p [!] protocol` `--protocol` may be used instead of `-p`	Specifies the protocol for the rule, which may be any name or number listed in `/etc/protocols`, such as `tcp`, `udp`, or `ip`. The keyword `all`, meaning all protocols, may also be used. It is the default. The `all` protocol may not be used with `-c`. A preceding `!` reverses the meaning.

`-s [!] address[/mask]`
`[!] [port[:port]`
`--source` may be used instead of `-s`
	Identical to `-d` except that this is the source address. Also, unlike `-d`, ICMP type numbers may be specified in lieu of ports.

Table 14–2   Options to `ipchains` *(Continued)*

OPTION	DESCRIPTION
`--sport [!]` `[port:[port]]` `--source-port` may be used instead of `--sport`	Allows for the separate specification of a source port or port range.
`-v` or `--verbose`	When listing rules, this option adds additional information including, but not limited to, the interface address, rule options, and packet and byte counters.
`-x` or `--exact`	Displays the exact packet and byte counts. Ordinarily, `ipchains` rounds to the nearest 1,000 (K), 1,000,000 (M), or multiples of 1,000 M (G).
`[!] -y` or `--syn`	Only match TCP packets that have the SYN bit set and the ACK and FIN bits cleared. Such a TCP packet represents a connection attempt. The ! negates the meaning; that is, it will match return packets for an existing connection.
`--line-numbers`	Available with `ipchains` Version 1.3.9 and later. Lists the number of each rule. Must be used with `-L`.

In addition to the options described in Table 14–2, there are three other options: The `-o` option is used for passing matching packets to a device for processing by a user process (as opposed to the kernel), such as a firewall or content inspection[2] application. The `-m` option marks packets for special handling internally by the kernel. And the `-t` option is used to modify the type-of-service (TOS) field in the IP header. We consider TOS in more detail in Chapter 16.

---

2. Content inspection applications are used to examine the data portion of a network packet or packets.

Most rules will have actions. Those that don't merely act as accounting rules, collecting packet and byte counts. Table 14–3 notes the actions that may be specified for a rule. The actions are case sensitive.

Table 14–3   Actions for `ipchains`

Action	Description
`ACCEPT`	Allows the packet through.
`DENY`	Drops the packet without generating an ICMP message back to the originator of the packet.
`REJECT`	Same as `DENY` except that an ICMP message is sent to the originator. If the rule matches an ICMP packet, then `REJECT` behaves like `DENY` and no ICMP message will be sent.
`MASQ`	Only valid in the forward chain or a custom chain invoked by the forward chain. The matching packet's IP address will be set to the IP address of this host. Masquerading is discussed in "IP Masquerading" on page 689.
`REDIRECT`	Only valid in the input chain or a custom chain. The matching packet will be redirected to a local port, even if the destination IP address is for a remote host. If the default redirection port of 0 is used, then the packet will be sent to the destination port.
`RETURN`	If this action is in a custom chain, then the packet is sent to the next rule in the calling chain. If this action is in a permanent chain, then the action in the permanent chain's policy is applied.
`custom_chain`	The named custom chain is invoked.

For complete details on the flags, options, and actions, see the `ipchains(8)` man page.

`ipchains` **Syntax**

The syntax of the `ipchains` command is best understood through examples, which we provide throughout the remainder of this chapter. Generally, `ipchains` takes the form

```
ipchains -[flags] {input|output|forward|custom_chain} [options]
[action]
ipchains -M [-L|-S] [options]
```

We will examine many of the ways in which this command can be used.

Some Simple Examples

The first thing that we can do with `ipchains` is take a look at what rules are established by default. This can be accomplished with the `ipchains  -L`, as shown in Example 14–1.

Example 14–1   Listing the Default Rules

```
# /sbin/ipchains -L
Chain input (policy ACCEPT):
Chain forward (policy ACCEPT):
Chain output (policy ACCEPT):
#
```

The output of this command shows us that there are three chains (the permanent ones)—input, forward, and output. Each of these chains has the same policy, or default action, which is ACCEPT. Thus, at this point, no packets will be rejected by the kernel.

In the following sections, we'll take a look at adding and removing rules from the permanent chains.

Adding a Rule

Let's suppose that we want to completely disable FTP traffic to the host `top-cat`. We could accomplish this by commenting out or removing the `ftpd` entry in `/etc/inetd.conf` (or `/etc/xinetd.conf`, if we're using `xinetd`—see Chapter 8 for a discussion of `xinetd`). We could also accomplish this using `ipchains`, as in

```
topcat# ipchains -I input 1 -p tcp --dport ftp -j REJECT
```

This command specifies that rule number 1 be inserted (`-I`) in the input chain. That rule applies to the protocol (`-p`) TCP and all packets with the destination port (`--dport`) of `ftp`. Any packet matching this rule will be rejected. Now we have a rule that prohibits inbound `ftp` connection requests. To see that this rule has been added, let's look at a listing in Example 14–2.

Example 14–2   Listing the New Rule

```
[root@topcat]# ipchains -L
Chain input (policy ACCEPT):
target      prot opt   source        destination          ports
REJECT      tcp  ------ anywhere      anywhere             any ->    ftp
Chain forward (policy ACCEPT):
Chain output (policy ACCEPT):
[root@topcat]#
```

Notice that, even though we added the rule as rule number 1, there is no rule number associated with the rule. This becomes tedious as your rule sets get large. If you get `ipchains` Version 1.3.9 or later, you may use the command

```
# ipchains -L --line-numbers
```

to view rule numbers, but the rule numbers will not appear as you add rules.

You could also have added this rule with the command

```
# ipchains -A input -p tcp --dport ftp -j REJECT
```

Here we are using append (`-A`), which means add the rule to the end of the chain, but before the policy (which represents the last rule). In this case, the two rules are identical because the only rule in the input chain is the policy. Ordinarily, the behavior of the append and insert are quite different.

There are some additional utilities that make the generation of rules easier. See *The fwconfig GUI* and "Mason" on page 719 for further information.

Let's see what happens when a user on `pluto` attempts to `ftp` to `topcat` after adding the rule shown in Example 14–2. The result is shown in Example 14–3.

Example 14–3   Failed `ftp` Attempt Due to `ipchains`

```
pluto$ ftp topcat
ftp: connect: Connection refused
ftp>
```

Here we see that the error message `Connection refused` is sent to `pluto`. If we had used DENY instead of REJECT in the rule displayed in Example 14–2, `pluto` would never have received any message from `topcat` and the `ftp` would have eventually timed out.

SHOULD I USE DENY **OR** REJECT?   When you use REJECT in a rule and someone from the outside generates a network packet that triggers the rule, then they will immediately receive an error message such as `Connection refused`. This makes it appear as if your system is not providing that service. Perhaps this will have the effect of discouraging some crackers.

On the other hand, using DENY will cause the client system to wait for a response from the server that will never arrive. Perhaps this will have the effect of frustrating some crackers. Both DENY and REJECT may also have the effect of fooling some port scanners.

Which of the two actions you use is your call. For most of our examples, we'll use REJECT, because it is my preference.

WARNING

If you mistakenly use lowercase for the action, you will get a nonintuitive error message. For example, if we execute

```
topcat# ipchains -I input 1 -p tcp --dport ftp -j reject
```

we would get the error message

```
ipchains: No chain by that name
```

which does not indicate the problem! So beware.

Removing a Rule

We may either remove or replace a given rule. To delete or remove the rule that we have been working with, we could execute

```
# ipchains -D input 1
```

This syntax has the advantage of being simple to type. Unfortunately, when your chain contains many rules, you first have to list the rules in the chain and then manually count the rules to find out the rule number of the rule you wish to delete. As noted before, this is tedious and prone to mistakes. Fortunately, another way to delete a rule exists. Simply specify all of the options for the rule exactly as was done to add the rule, but use the -D flag as in

```
# ipchains -D input -p tcp --dport ftp -j REJECT
```

and this will delete the specific rule.

Next, let's suppose that we don't want to delete a rule, but we'd like to modify the rule. Suppose that our rule currently appears as in Example 14–2 on page 674. Suppose further that our system topcat has two interfaces. The eth0 interface is connected to the Internet and the eth1 interface is connected to the internal network. In real life, our Internet connection would be identified by a DNS hostname. However, we don't want to use fully qualified DNS names in our rules because, if the DNS resolution is broken, our rules will not work. Therefore, we'll use the hostname topcat for the Internet interface. This hostname resolves to 202.7.1.19 or our eth0 interface. So, we'd like to disallow ftp requests from the Internet to topcat, but we want to allow ftp access to topcat internally through the eth1 interface. We can use the -R flag to replace or modify the existing rule. Note that our policy action remains as ACCEPT (which is not recommended, but we'll get to that in "Setting Policies (Default Rules)" on page 682). We can modify our rule to meet the needs outlined in this paragraph, adding -i eth0, with the command

```
# ipchains -R input 1 -p tcp --dport ftp -i eth0 -j REJECT
```

Notice that we have to specify the rule number with the replace (-R) flag. There is no other way to replace a rule. Now that we have replaced the rule, let's see what -L reports in Example 14–4. We will also use -v (verbose) so that we get the ifname (interface name) column displayed.

Example 14–4   Displaying the Replaced Rule Using -L and -v

```
[root@topcat]# ipchains -L -v
Chain input (policy ACCEPT: 20083 packets, 1141062 bytes):
 pkts bytes target     prot opt   tosa tosx ifname      mark        outsize
source                 destination         ports
    1    60 REJECT       tcp  ------ 0xFF 0x00  eth0
anywhere               anywhere            any ->    ftp
Chain forward (policy ACCEPT: 0 packets, 0 bytes):
Chain output (policy ACCEPT: 2731 packets, 356485 bytes):
[root@topcat]#
```

Due to formatting constraints, Example 14–4 contains line wraps for the header and the rule. So let's go through each of the header fields and associate the value in the rule. For the purposes of this discussion, we will refer to the rule as "example rule."

The header for the example rule appears as (line wrapped due to length)

```
 pkts bytes target     prot opt   tosa tosx  ifname       mark        outsize
 source                 destination          ports
```

Table 14–4 describes each of the fields.

Table 14–4 Header Fields from Example 14–4

HEADER	DESCRIPTION
pkts	The number of network packets that have matched this rule since the rule was entered, or since the last boot, or since the last time `ipchains -Z` was executed.
bytes	The total number of bytes of all the packets that have matched this rule since the rule was entered, or since the last boot, or since the last time `ipchains -Z` was executed.
target	The action or named custom chain for the rule.
prot	The protocol for the rule.
opt	The options for the rule.
tosa	The TOS bitwise logical AND mask. Set with -t. See Chapter 16 and the resources cited in "`ipchains` Documentation" on page 723 for further details regarding this option.
tosx	The TOS bitwise logical XOR (exclusive OR) mask. Set with -t. See Chapter 16 and the resources cited in "`ipchains` Documentation" on page 723 for further details regarding this option.
ifname	The interface name to which this rule applies.
mark	The value used to mark this packet. Set with -m. See the resources cited in "`ipchains` Documentation" on page 723 for further details regarding this option.
outsize	The number of bytes that were copied to a device for handling by a user process. Applies only to rules using the -o option. See the resources cited in "`ipchains` Documentation" on page 723 for further details regarding this option.
source	The source IP address.

Table 14–4   Header Fields from Example 14–4 *(Continued)*

HEADER	DESCRIPTION
`destination`	The destination IP address.
`ports`	The source and destination ports or ICMP code and ICMP type. This field will be displayed as `sourceport -> destport` or `ICMP_code -> ICMP_type`.

Now that we know what the headers are, let's look at the fields in our example rule (in Example 14–4 on page 676) as,

```
    1    60 REJECT        tcp  ------ 0xFF 0x00  eth0
anywhere                anywhere              any ->    ftp
```

Table 14–5 lists the association between each entry and the header from Table 14–4 as well as a brief description for this example rule.

Table 14–5   Association between the Rule Header and the Example Rule

MATCHING HEADER	VALUE IN EXAMPLE RULE	DESCRIPTION
`pkts`	1	One packet has been handled by this rule.
`bytes`	60	A total of 60 octets have been processed by this rule.
`target`	REJECT	The action of this rule is REJECT.
`prot`	`tcp`	The protocol for this rule is TCP.
`opt`	------	There are no options for this rule.
`tosa`	0xFF	The TOS logical AND mask.
`tosx`	0x00	The TOS logical XOR mask.
`ifname`	eth0	The interface to which this rule applies.
`mark`	N/A	There is no mark value associated with this rule.
`outsize`	N/A	This rule does not use -o.

Table 14–5 Association between the Rule Header and the Example Rule *(Continued)*

MATCHING HEADER	VALUE IN EXAMPLE RULE	DESCRIPTION
source	anywhere	The source IP address for this rule to match is any address.
destination	anywhere	The destination IP address for this rule to match is any address.
ports	any -> ftp	The source port for this rule to match is any port. The destination port for this rule to match is `ftp` (port number 21).

Now that we know how to add, delete, and replace rules, let's go on and look at how to log packets that match a rule.

Logging

For the purpose of capturing log messages generated by `ipchains`, we will set up an entry in `syslogd`. All `ipchains` rules that specify logging will be logged with the selector `kern.info`. So we add the entry

```
kern.info          /var/log/kern.log
```

and then execute

```
killall -HUP syslogd
```

Once again, we will specify REJECT as the action so that the client gets a `Connection refused` message, and this time we also specify the -l option for logging:

```
# ipchains -R input 1 -p tcp --dport ftp -i eth0 -j REJECT -l
```

Now that we have our new rule, let's suppose that a user from 101.143.3.9 (say, `evil.org`) in the Internet attempts to `ftp` to our site.

```
[evil.org]$ ftp topcat.whatever.the.domain.is.
```

Since our rule utilizes the action REJECT, then `evil.org` will get an immediate `Connection refused`. Since our rule specifies logging, let's take a look at the log file (`/var/log/kern.log`, in our case) in Example 14–5.

Example 14–5   Log Entries Generated by Input Chain Rule 1

```
[root@topcat]# tail -f /var/log/kern.log
Aug  6 09:09:53 topcat kernel: Packet log: input REJECT eth0 PROTO=6
101.143.3.9:1025 202.7.1.19:21 L=60 S=0x00 I=181 F=0x4000 T=254
Aug  6 09:09:56 topcat kernel: Packet log: input REJECT eth0 PROTO=6
101.143.3.9:1025 202.7.1.19:21 L=60 S=0x00 I=182 F=0x4000 T=254
Aug  6 09:10:02 topcat kernel: Packet log: input REJECT eth0 PROTO=6
101.143.3.9:1025 202.7.1.19:21 L=60 S=0x00 I=183 F=0x4000 T=254
```

A log entry will be generated for every packet that matches our rule. As you might imagine, your logs will grow very quickly if you are logging many rules and/or your server is very active.

Now, let's describe the entries in the log record. Each record begins with a timestamp followed by the hostname and facility (Aug 6 09:09:53 topcat kernel: in the first log entry in Example 14–5). After that, we see Packet log:, which tells us that this log entry was generated by ipchains. The remaining fields are described in Table 14–6.

Table 14–6   ipchains Log Entry Fields

FIELD	DESCRIPTION
input	In this case, the input chain. The name of the chain in which the matching rule occurred will be listed here.
REJECT	The action (or target) of the matching rule. REJECT in this case.
eth0	The interface at which the packet arrived. In the case of an output or forward chain, this would be the outbound interface.
PROTO=6	The protocol number associated with this packet. In this case, 6 means TCP. A list of protocol numbers and names is found in /etc/protocols.
101.143.3.9:1025	The source IP address and source port number. In this case, the source IP address is 101.143.3.9 and the source port number is 1025. If the protocol is ICMP instead of a source port number, you will see an ICMP type.

Table 14–6   `ipchains` Log Entry Fields *(Continued)*

FIELD	DESCRIPTION
`202.7.1.19:21`	The destination IP address and destination port number. In this case, the destination IP address is `202.7.1.19` and the destination port number is `21`. If the protocol is ICMP instead of a destination port number, you will see an ICMP code.
`L=60`	The length, in octets, of the packet—60 octets in this case.
`S=0x00`	The TOS. If this value is `0x04` or `0x05`, then the packet must not be fragmented. If the value is `0x02` or `0x03`, then the packet is a fragment. This value of `0x00` indicates that the packet is fragmentable but is not a fragment. See Chapter 16 and the references cited in "`ipchains` Documentation" on page 723 for further details regarding TOS.
`I=181`	The IP identifier. A unique value whose primary purpose is to associate fragmented packets. In this case, the identifier is `181`. Note that the other entries in Example 14–5 have different identifiers, meaning they are not fragments of the same packet.
`F=0x4000`	This is the fragment offset. It is used to reassemble fragmented packets. See "Fragmentation and Path MTU Discovery" on page 96 for a general discussion of IP fragmentition.
`T=254`	The time to live for this packet in seconds, `254` in this case.
`[rule number]`	Linux kernel versions 2.2.10 and later will add the rule number, in brackets, of the rule that generated the log message.

All of our log entries will be similar to those defined in Table 14–6. We will look at other examples throughout this chapter.

WARNING

As noted earlier in this section, log entries are generated for each packet that matches a rule with the -l option. This will cause your log files to grow very quickly, and such log files will require special attention. See "Rule Writing and Logging Tips" on page 698 for a further discussion of log file management and tips on which rules to log.

Since we modified our rule to log all matching packets, let's see what the differences are when we list our rule. This is displayed in Example 14–6. Compare this to Example 14–4 on page 676.

Example 14–6   Verbose Listing of Our Modified Rule Specifying Logging

```
[root@topcat /root]# ipchains -L -v
Chain input (policy ACCEPT: 27472 packets, 1576415 bytes):
 pkts bytes target     prot opt    tosa tosx  ifname      mark        outsize
source                 destination              ports
    4   240 REJECT       tcp  ----l- 0xFF 0x00  eth0
anywhere               anywhere                 any ->    ftp
Chain forward (policy ACCEPT: 0 packets, 0 bytes):
Chain output (policy ACCEPT: 3012 packets, 373044 bytes):
[root@topcat /root]#
```

Note that the only difference between Example 14–4 on page 676 and Example 14–6 (besides the packet and byte counts) is that the opt column includes the l option (----l- in Example 14–6).

Setting Policies (Default Rules)

A very important rule in the permanent chains is the default rule. This rule is also called the *policy*. As noted earlier in this chapter, the default policy is ACCEPT. This policy means that if no rules explicitly match a particular packet, then the packet will be allowed through. While this type of policy may be desirable, and even required (such as at some universities and colleges) under certain circumstances, you should implement such a default rule only when absolutely necessary.

The preferred policy for all permanent chains is to disallow any packets that survive the rule base. You may accomplish this with the commands shown in Example 14–7.

Example 14–7   Establishing the REJECT Policy for Permanent Chains

```
# ipchains -P input REJECT
# ipchains -P forward REJECT
# ipchains -P output REJECT
```

You may specify any of the actions listed in Table 14–3 on page 672 (adhering to their restrictions)—with the exception of a custom chain—instead of REJECT.

You cannot use the -1 (logging) flag with -P. Because of that restriction, it is quite common to add a final catchall REJECT rule in each chain that logs any packets which reach it. We utilize such a rule in "Small Internal Network" on page 700.

The policy in Example 14–7 implements the philosophy that says: that which is not expressly permitted is forbidden. Once you have established the policy, you may go about the task of determining what you will allow and building the necessary rules. We look at an example of this process in "Small Internal Network" on page 700.

WARNING

If you are managing `ipchains` on a system over the network, make sure that you have an allow rule for the type of connection you are using *before* executing the commands in Example 14–7. Otherwise, once you execute those commands, your network connection will drop! Generally, you should always implement new rules at the console so that you do not inadvertently lock yourself out.

In any event, we strongly recommend that the only network connection you use to manage `ipchains` remotely is SSH or something similar (see the references cited in "For Further Reading" on page 723 for a discussion of SSH and its alternatives).

ICMP Types and Codes

ICMPv4 is discussed in Chapter 4. The `ipchains` utility provides a way of filtering packets based on ICMPv4 (which we reference simply as ICMP throughout this chapter). In this section, we provide two reference tables that might come in handy for your ICMP rule writing. We also provide some guidelines for choosing which ICMP types and codes to allow and deny in "ICMP Rules in a Custom Chain" on page 693.

You will likely want to disable a large number of ICMP communications relative to your external interface since many of them are used infrequently and have limited applicability to an Internet (or Intranet) connection. Some of them, such as ICMP redirects (type 5), have been used for various types of attacks. Others, such as type destination-unreachable and code fragmentation-needed, are important for overall network functionality.

Table 14–7 lists the association between ICMP type numbers used in the 2.2.x kernel and ICMP type names as output by ipchains -h icmp

Table 14–7   ICMP IPv4 Types Supported by ipchains

ICMP TYPE NUMBERS	ICMP TYPE NAME
0	echo-reply (pong)
3	destination-unreachable
4	source-quench
5	redirect
8	echo-request (ping)
9	router-advertisement
10	router-solicitation
11	time-exceeded (ttl-exceeded)
12	parameter-problem
13	timestamp-request
14	timestamp-reply
17	address-mask-request
18	address-mask-reply

Table 14–8 lists the association between ICMP code numbers used in the 2.2.x kernel and ICMP code names as output by `ipchains -h icmp`

Table 14–8 ICMP Codes Supported by `ipchains`

ICMP CODE NUMBER	ICMP CODE NAME	ASSOCIATED ICMP TYPE NAME
0	network-unreachable	destination-unreachable
1	host-unreachable	destination-unreachable
2	protocol-unreachable	destination-unreachable
3	port-unreachable	destination-unreachable
4	fragmentation-needed	destination-unreachable
5	source-route-failed	destination-unreachable
6	network-unknown	destination-unreachable
7	host-unknown	destination-unreachable
9	network-prohibited	destination-unreachable
10	host-prohibited	destination-unreachable
11	TOS-network-unreachable	destination-unreachable
12	TOS-host-unreachable	destination-unreachable
13	communication-prohibited	destination-unreachable
14	host-precedence-violation	destination-unreachable
15	precedence-cutoff	destination-unreachable
0	network-redirect	redirect
1	host-redirect	redirect
2	TOS-network-redirect	redirect
3	TOS-host-redirect	redirect
0	ttl-zero-during-transit	time-exceeded (ttl-exceeded)
1	ttl-zero-during-reassembly	time-exceeded (ttl-exceeded)
0	ip-header-bad	parameter-problem
1	required-option-missing	parameter-problem

Recall from Table 14–2 on page 667 that you cannot specify ICMP codes with the `-d` and `--dport` options, and that you cannot specify ICMP types with the `-s` and `--sport` options.

Sample ICMP Rules

We'll assume the scenario given in "Removing a Rule" on page 675, where our system `topcat` has the external IP address `202.7.1.19` associated with `eth0`. We will also assume the default `REJECT` policies set in "Setting Policies (Default Rules)" on page 682. Let's suppose that we wish to implement the following rules:

1. Allow `ping` from `topcat` to any external addresses
2. Disallow external `ping` to `topcat` and log any such attempts

Perhaps the first question to ask is, does our default `REJECT` rule really work? The answer is in Example 14–8.

Example 14–8   Failed `ping` Attempt Due to Default `REJECT` Rules

```
[root@topcat]# ping podunk.edu
PING podunk.edu (1.1.1.1): 56 data bytes
ping: sendto: Operation not permitted
ping: wrote podunk.edu 64 chars, ret=-1
^C
[root@topcat]#
```

Here, we are unable to `ping` to the Internet due to our default `REJECT` rules. If a system on the Internet attempted to `ping topcat`, it would get no response for the same reason. This latter behavior satisfies the first part of item 2 above. So we need to address item 1 and the logging part of item 2. Let's do it.

First, we'll handle item 1. We need to allow outbound `ping`, which means ICMP `echo-request`. We also need to allow inbound ICMP `echo-reply` in response to the `ping`. We can accomplish this with the commands shown in Example 14–9.

Example 14–9   Allowing Outbound `ping`

```
[root@topcat]# ipchains -A output -p icmp --icmp-type echo-request -i eth0 -j ACCEPT
[root@topcat]# ipchains -A input  -p icmp --icmp-type echo-reply   -i eth0 -j ACCEPT
```

The first command in the example appends the rule to the output chain, which allows the ICMP `echo-request` to go out `eth0` (the external interface). The second command appends the rule, which allows the inbound ICMP `echo-reply` through `eth0`.

Example 14–10 shows us a listing to verify the rules (lines wrapped due to length).

Example 14–10   Listing the Newly Added ICMP Rules

```
[root@topcat]# ipchains -L
Chain input (policy REJECT):
target     prot opt      source           destination          ports
REJECT     tcp  ----l-   anywhere         anywhere             any -> ftp
ACCEPT     icmp ------   anywhere         anywhere             echo-reply
Chain forward (policy REJECT):
Chain output (policy REJECT):
target     prot opt      source           destination          ports
ACCEPT     icmp ------   anywhere         anywhere             echo-request
[root@topcat]#
```

Let's try to `ping` `podunk.edu` again. Example 14–11 shows us that the rules work.

Example 14–11   Rules Now Allow Outbound `ping`

```
[root@topcat]# ping podunk.edu
PING podunk.edu (1.1.1.1): 56 data bytes
64 bytes from 1.1.1.1: icmp_seq=0 ttl=255 time=0.5 ms
64 bytes from 1.1.1.1: icmp_seq=1 ttl=255 time=0.5 ms
64 bytes from 1.1.1.1: icmp_seq=2 ttl=255 time=0.5 ms
^C
[root@topcat]#
```

So we have satisfied item 1. Now we need to address the logging part of item 2. The command in Example 14–12 will take care of this.

Example 14–12   A Rule that Logs All `ping` Attempts through `eth0` to `topcat`

```
[root@topcat]# ipchains -A input -p icmp --icmp-type echo-request -d topcat
-j REJECT -l
```

Let's verify. Suppose that a user at `evil.org` (`101.143.3.9`) tries to `ping` `top-cat`. Example 14–13 shows the logs generated by such activity.

Example 14–13   Log Entries Generated by Packets Matching the Rule in Example 14–12

```
[root@topcat]# tail -f /var/log/kern.log
Aug  6 18:26:17 topcat kernel: Packet log: input REJECT eth0 PROTO=1
101.143.3.9:8 202.7.1.19:0 L=84 S=0x00 I=41410 F=0x4000 T=255
Aug  6 18:26:18 topcat kernel: Packet log: input REJECT eth0 PROTO=1
101.143.3.9:8 202.7.1.19:0 L=84 S=0x00 I=41412 F=0x4000 T=255
Aug  6 18:26:19 topcat kernel: Packet log: input REJECT eth0 PROTO=1
101.143.3.9:8 202.7.1.19:0 L=84 S=0x00 I=41414 F=0x4000 T=255
```

Refer to Table 14–6 on page 680 for a description of the fields in each log entry.

An ICMP Type/Code You Should Not Block

Most modern implementations of IPv4 (Linux included) utilize MTU discovery to avoid fragmentation (fragmentation is discussed in "Packet Fragments" on page 688). MTU discovery works simply by sending packets out with the don't fragment bit set (see Chapter 4). When such a packet arrives at a system that needs a smaller-sized packet, it responds by sending an ICMP message of type `destination-unreachable` and code `fragmentation-needed` (see Table 14–7 on page 684 and Table 14–8 on page 685, respectively). If you block this communication, you will be unable to communicate with the system or network that requires the smaller packets.

In "ICMP Rules in a Custom Chain" on page 693, we will look at the most commonly allowed ICMP types.

Packet Fragments

Sometimes the data comprising a packet makes the packet too large for transmission over the network. In such a case, the packet will be fragmented into smaller packets. We discussed this phenomenon in "Fragmentation and Path MTU Discovery" on page 96. When this occurs, only the first packet will contain the full header information associated with the collection of the packets. Since `ipchains` makes its decisions based on header information, this is a potential problem.

By default, the kernel configuration parameter `CONFIG_IP_ALWAYS_DEFRAGMENT` is set to Y. This parameter causes the Linux kernel to reassemble all fragmented packets before processing. As long as this parameter is set, `ipchains` will not have to deal with fragments. Also, configuring the kernel for defragmentation with this parameter is *required* for IP masquerading support.

If you must configure your system so that it does not defragment (that is, fragments must pass through the firewall), then you must patch your kernel or upgrade to at least kernel version 2.2.11 to avoid a vulnerability. See the sites referenced in "`ipchains` Documentation" on page 723 for the patch and the details. Once you have patched or upgraded your kernel, then you can handle fragmented packets with the `-f` flag. For example, if we have the rule

```
# ipchains -A input -p tcp -s 0/0 ftp-data -d topcat -i eth0 -j
ACCEPT
```

and we need to allow second and further fragments associated with this rule through our firewall, we could utilize the rule

```
# ipchains -A input -f -s 0/0 -d topcat -i eth0 -j ACCEPT
```

We cannot be any more specific with the fragment rule because the header will not contain the source and destination ports nor any ICMP types or codes. This rule does leave us vulnerable to exploits that take advantage of the fact that fragments are passed through the firewall. If at all possible, set your firewall up to defragment.

Accounting

We've noted a number of times that the absence of `-j target` in a rule means that the rule is for accounting purposes only. Rules with a `-j target` option will also accumulate accounting data. In short, packets matching each rule will be counted and the results are viewable with the `ipchains -L -v` command. The output of that command is described in Table 14–4 on page 677. An example is given in Example 14–4 on page 676. Using this command rounds off byte and packet counts to the nearest 1,000 or 1,000,000 (as appropriate). If you add the `-x` flag and use `ipchains -L -v -x`, you will get a full reporting in bytes and packets with no rounding. You can clear all accounting data with the `ipchains -z` command.

Any rule that can be used as a filter can also be used as an accounting rule. For example, suppose that you would like to account for all incoming `telnet` connections on `topcat`. The following rule

```
# ipchains -A input -s 0/0 -d topcat 23 -i eth0 -p tcp -y
```

would do the trick. This rule neither allows nor prohibits anything. If a packet matches, that is, if a packet is destined to `topcat` at port 23 (the `telnet` port) and it is an initial connection request (due to `-y`), then the kernel will add that packet and its size in bytes to the counter for this rule. Note that if this rule did have a `-j target` option, it would still get counted.

IP Masquerading

Linux IP masquerading gives us a way to hide internal IP addresses from the external network, behind the external interface of the firewall. This is a simple form of network address translation[3] (NAT) in which many internal addresses are mapped to one external address. A more general form of NAT is available with the iptables utility discussed in the next chapter. IP masquerading does this by translating all internal addresses to the address of the external interface associated with the firewall illustrated in Figure 14–2.

Figure 14–2 depicts the Linux system topcat acting as a firewall using ipchains. It is also masquerading all internal systems as the external address 202.7.1.19. Thus, whenever an internal system, such as the MacOS box (10.1.1.5), sends a packet to the Internet, it translates the outbound packet's source IP address 10.1.1.5 to 202.7.1.19 (*masquerading*). When a packet from the Internet is destined to an internal system, such as the Windows box (10.1.1.2), topcat will translate the destination IP address 202.7.1.19 to 10.1.1.2 (*demasquerading*). Masquerading and demasquerading are implemented through ipchains. Consequently, the procedure described in Figure 14–1 on page

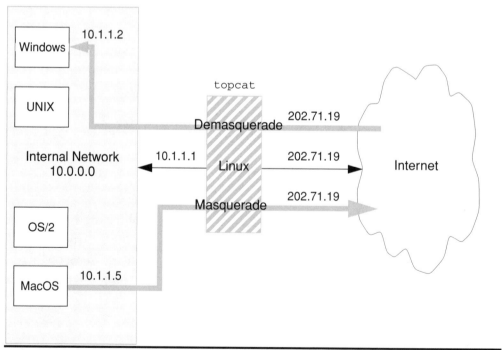

Figure 14–2   Linux IP Masquerading

---

3. Cisco refers to this as *port address translation*.

663 still applies with the following exceptions: Masquerading of addresses occurs in the forward chain prior to processing by the output chain. Masquerading rules must be specified in the forward chain. Demasquerading is performed automatically *after* processing by the input chain. Demasqueraded packets are then sent to the output chain directly, skipping the forward chain.

Figure 14–2 purposely shows a variety of operating systems in the internal network. This is to emphasize that the operating system does not matter so long as the networking protocol between `topcat` and the internal network is TCP/IP.

The rules that implement masquerading are quite straightforward. There are a few issues we must address first, however. In order to properly configure our system for masquerading, we must turn on IP forwarding (turn our system into a router—see Chapter 6). We will also want to load kernel modules to provide support for certain applications with respect to masquerading.

Kernel Modules that Support Masquerading

There are a number of kernel modules that exist for the purpose of properly handling certain applications in a masquerading environment. Some of the modules are listed in Table 14–9.

Table 14–9   Masquerading Kernel Modules

MODULE	DESCRIPTION
`ip_masq_ftp`	Properly supports `ftp` masquerading. This module takes care of both active and passive outbound `ftp` connections.
`ip_masq_raudio`	Allows for the masquerading of Real Audio over UDP.
`ip_masq_irc`	Supports the masquerading of Internet relay chat (IRC).
`ip_masq_quake`	Supports the masquerading of Quake I, II, and III and QuakeWorld.
`ip_masq_cuseeme`	Supports the masquerading of CuSeeme video conferencing.
`ip_masq_vdolive`	Supports the masquerading of VDO-live video conferencing.
`ip_masq_user`	Supports user space access to captured packets (see the `-o` option in Table 14–2 on page 667).

If you are going to implement one or more of the applications described in Table 14–9, you will need to add the module(s) with `/sbin/modprobe` (see the `depmod(1)` man page). For example, to add the `ip_masq_ftp` module, execute

```
# /sbin/modprobe ip_masq_ftp
```

This should be done prior to generating the rules.

In "Simple Internal Network Using DHCP" on page 713, we will look at placing the necessary `modprobe` command(s) into a start-up script. Load only the modules that are absolutely necessary.

Masquerading Rules

Once you have turned on IP forwarding and loaded the appropriate modules, you may add the rules necessary for masquerading. Let's suppose that our network is as depicted in Figure 14–2 on page 690 and that we wish to masquerade all of the internal addresses (network 10.0.0.0). Example 14–14 shows us the necessary masquerading rule.

Example 14–14   Masquerading All Internal Addresses

```
# ipchains -P forward REJECT
# ipchains -A forward -s 10.0.0.0/8 -j MASQ
```

The first line of this example sets the default rule in the forward chain to REJECT (we actually did this earlier). It is critical that your default forward chain policy is REJECT; otherwise, someone could potentially use your system to masquerade their activity! The second line is the masquerading rule. It will cause all connections initiated from the internal network destined to the Internet to be masqueraded by `topcat`.

Masquerading rules in conjunction with other rules will be examined in "Small Internal Network" on page 700.

Adding Custom Chains

Now that we understand the basics of `ipchains`, we'll take a look at ways in which we can organize our rules so that management is a little more organized. To this end, we may use custom chains, also known as user-defined chains. A custom chain, much like the permanent chains we've been discussing, is a collection of rules. As with the permanent chains, the rules are checked in order.

Unlike permanent chains, however, custom chains cannot have a default rule or policy. In the next section, we'll take a look at example usage of custom chains.

ICMP Rules in a Custom Chain

Let's continue with our example as depicted in Figure 14–2 on page 690. Previously, we set up rules that allowed for outbound `ping` from `topcat`; disallowed incoming `ping` requests to `topcat` and logged all such requests; and disallowed incoming `ftp` requests. The latter rule is redundant because of our default rule in all chains that denies anything which is not explicitly permitted. This rule base is listed in Example 14–10 on page 687.

Now let's create a custom chain that will accommodate the necessary ICMP rules and allow the most commonly accepted ICMP error messages. We need to worry only about the things we'll allow because of our default REJECT rule.

Recall from Table 14–1 on page 666 that custom chain names must not exceed eight characters. To create the chain, we execute

```
# ipchains -N icmperr
```

We'll add rules that allow standard ICMP error messages as shown in Example 14–15. These rules will also help if we need to troubleshoot our connection.

Example 14–15   Adding Rules to a Custom Chain

```
# ipchains -A icmperr -p icmp --icmp-type destination-unreachable -j ACCEPT
# ipchains -A icmperr -p icmp --icmp-type parameter-problem -j ACCEPT
# ipchains -A icmperr -p icmp --icmp-type source-quench -j ACCEPT
# ipchains -A icmperr -p icmp --icmp-type time-exceeded -j ACCEPT
```

Notice that we have not included our earlier ICMP rules (see Example 14–10 on page 687). This is because those rules were specific to the input and output chains. They had to be in order to meet our requirements (see "Sample ICMP Rules" on page 686). The rules in `icmperr` will be invoked by both the input and output chains.

Now that we have created the custom chain, we need to invoke the chain through one or more of the permanent chains. Here, we will add rules to the input and output chains that will invoke our custom chain. These two commands are shown in Example 14–16.

Example 14–16   Adding Rules to Invoke the Custom Chain

```
[root@topcat]# ipchains -A input -p icmp -j icmperr
[root@topcat]# ipchains -A output -p icmp -j icmperr
```

Notice that we invoke only the icmperr chain if the protocol is ICMP. While this may be obvious, if we had left off -p icmp in the two commands shown in Example 14–16, the rules would still be valid and would inspect every packet against all the rules in icmperr. Such a mistake could cause significant performance problems.

Example 14–17 shows us what our rule base looks like now.

Example 14–17   Listing of Rule Base with Custom Chain

```
[root@topcat]# ipchains -L
Chain input (policy REJECT):
target      prot opt     source            destination         ports
ACCEPT      icmp ------  anywhere          anywhere            echo-reply
REJECT      icmp ----1-  anywhere          topcat              echo-request
icmperr     icmp ------  anywhere          anywhere            any ->    any
Chain forward (policy REJECT):
Chain output (policy REJECT):
target      prot opt     source            destination         ports
ACCEPT      icmp ------  anywhere          anywhere            echo-request
icmperr     icmp ------  anywhere          anywhere            any ->    any
Chain icmperr (2 references):
target      prot opt     source            destination         ports
ACCEPT      icmp ------  anywhere          anywhere            destination-unreachable
ACCEPT      icmp ------  anywhere          anywhere            parameter-problem
ACCEPT      icmp ------  anywhere          anywhere            source-quench
ACCEPT      icmp ------  anywhere          anywhere            time-exceeded
[root@topcat]#
```

If you wish to delete a custom chain, you may do so with the -X flag. The chain must be empty in order to delete it, so you will have to flush it with -F first. Example 14–18 shows how we could delete the custom chain icmperr.

Example 14–18   Removing a Custom Chain

```
# ipchains -F icmperr
# ipchains -X icmperr
```

Antispoofing Rules

When a host sends packets with the source IP address set to other than its own for the purpose of deception,[4] it's known as IP spoofing. One way to attempt to exploit systems from outside the network is to send packets that have the source IP address of an internal system. It is a good idea to prevent this.

---

4. Except for the deception part, this is very much like what IP masquerading does.

There are two ways to prevent IP spoofing. The first and preferred method is to let the kernel routing code do it for you through source address verification. If the file

```
/proc/sys/net/ipv4/conf/all/rp_filter
```

exists on your system (and it will, by default), then you can turn on source address verification by putting a 1 into each `rp_filter` file on your system. You will have one of these files in a number of directories. A system with two ethernet interfaces would have the files shown in Example 14–19.

Example 14–19   Listing of All `rp_filter` Files

```
/proc/sys/net/ipv4/conf/all/rp_filter
/proc/sys/net/ipv4/conf/default/rp_filter
/proc/sys/net/ipv4/conf/eth0/rp_filter
/proc/sys/net/ipv4/conf/eth1/rp_filter
/proc/sys/net/ipv4/conf/lo/rp_filter
```

If you were to add another interface to the system, a new directory named after the interface would appear with the `rp_filter` and other files in it. Consequently, to automate this process, you can write a script.

The second way to prohibit IP spoofing is to write specific rules. To see how this might be done, let's consider our continuing example, as illustrated in Figure 14–2 on page 690. The `10.0.0.0` internal network is connected to top-cat via `eth1`, while `eth0` is the external interface on `topcat`. The rules in Example 14–20 will do the trick.

Example 14–20   Antispoofing Rules

```
[root@topcat]# ipchains -A input -i ! eth1 -s 10.0.0.0/8 -j REJECT -l
[root@topcat]# ipchains -A input -i eth1 -s ! 10.0.0.0/8 -j REJECT -l
```

The first rule in this example denies any packet with a source IP address beginning with 10 that arrives on an interface other than `eth1` (the internal interface). The second rule denies any packet arriving on `eth1` (the internal interface) that has a source IP address beginning with anything other than 10. This second rule keeps our internal folks honest!

WARNING

The Linux kernel versions 2.1.x and 2.2.x automatically detect and deny any packets that arrive on a physical interface but claim a source IP address beginning with 127. Unfortunately, the kernel versions prior to 2.1.x and 2.2.x do not do this. So, if you are running an older distribution with a kernel version in the 2.0.x series or earlier, make sure that you add a rule to prevent spoofing addresses beginning with 127. Such a rule could be implemented with the command

```
# ipchains -A input -i ! lo -s 127.0.0.0/8 -j REJECT -l
```

This rule will cause any incoming packet arriving at any interface other than the `lo0` interface, with a source IP address beginning with 127, to be denied and logged. Note: The specification of `lo` in the command instead of `lo0` is *not* a typographical error. The loopback interface must be specified as `lo`.

Rule Ordering Is Important!

The order of your rules is critical. Let's suppose that you want to allow the system at IP address `145.3.1.2` SSH (see "Virtual Private Networks and Encrypted Tunnels" on page 720 for information about SSH) access to `topcat`, but you do not want to allow any other TCP connections. To disallow the TCP connection attempts, you could enter the rule given in Example 14–21.

Example 14–21   Rule Rejecting TCP Connection Packets

```
# ipchains -A input -p tcp -d topcat -i eth0 -y -j REJECT
```

This rule rejects all TCP connection initiation packets (`-y`—see Table 14–2 on page 667) destined to `topcat` arriving on the external interface (`eth0`). Later on, you can decide to add the necessary rules to allow SSH. These rules are given in Example 14–22.

Example 14–22   Rules Allowing SSH

```
[root@topcat]# ipchains -A input -p tcp -s 145.3.1.2 1023:65535 -d topcat 22
-j ACCEPT
[root@topcat]# ipchains -A output -p tcp -d 145.3.1.2 1023:65535 -s topcat
22 -j ACCEPT
```

We need two rules. The input rule allows the incoming SSH connection and the output rule allows the responses.

NOTE

Notice that we restrict the port numbers that may be used by `145.3.1.2` to 1023 through and including 65535. In particular, port number 1023 is a privileged port, meaning that it requires root privilege to use it. We are allowing this because, by default, the SSH client (`ssh`) will try to use source port 1023. This behavior is generally considered undesirable because the privileged nature of the port is unique to UNIX-like systems (including Linux—for example, an unprivileged user on a Windows box could run an application using a privileged source port). You can prevent `ssh` from using privileged ports by invoking `ssh -P` on the client and then modifing these rules to accept only unprivileged ports. However, the use of `-P` will disable both RHosts and RSA and Rhosts Authentication (but still permit RSA Authentication) because SSH "trusts" the privileged source port but not an unprivileged source port. See, for example, *Linux System Security* as cited in "For Further Reading" on page 723 for the details of SSH.

So, now you try SSH from `145.3.1.2` to `topcat` and it fails. This is due to the fact that, when `ssh` is invoked from `145.3.1.2`, the first thing it does is attempt to establish a connection with `topcat`. It does this by sending a packet with the SYN bit set and the ACK and FIN bits cleared (see Chapter 7). To fix the problem, you would simply move the input rule in Example 14–22 up one, by using first the `-D` flag and then the `-I` flag with the correct rule number.

While this may seem quite straightforward, as they become more complex, it often becomes difficult to debug your chains. Often the problem has to do with the ordering of rules within a chain or rules being in the wrong chain.

Debugging rules can be quite time consuming. Your best bet, when you are stumped by a problem with your rules, is to turn logging on for the rules you suspect are causing the problem and to also use a network monitoring program like Ethereal. This may give you enough information to figure things out. As noted in Table 14–6 on page 680, rule numbers will be logged at kernel version 2.2.10 and later.

The other debugging utility at your disposal is the `-C` flag, but it is of very limited use. You must specify the parameters of the packet in order for it to check the packet against the rule base. Example 14–23 gives us two invocations where the only difference is the `-y` flag.

Example 14–23   Using ipchains -C

```
[root@topcat]# ipchains -C input -p tcp -s 110.13.1.9 1025 -d topcat 22 -i eth1
accepted
[root@topcat]# ipchains -C input -p tcp -s 110.13.1.9 1025 -d topcat 22 -i eth1 -y
denied
[root@topcat]#
```

In short, if you were trying to debug the problem presented in this section, you would probably execute the first ipchains -C command in Example 14–23. In all likelihood, this would add to your confusion, because that packet is accepted. Of course it is! It doesn't have the SYN bit set, the way the packet in the second ipchains -C command does.

Saving and Restoring Rules

You may be wondering how you can capture all these rules you've been playing with into a file for future use so you don't have to type them all in again. There's good news. You can dump your current rule set (all these commands we've been executing puts them in kernel memory) with the /sbin/ipchains-save command. For example,

    /sbin/ipchains-save > /tmp/testrules

will put all the rules in a format usable by ipchains into the file /tmp/testrules in ASCII format. You may use -v with this command to view each rule as it is saved.

To put the rules back into memory, execute

    /sbin/ipchains-restore < /tmp/testrules

You can specify the -v option here as well to get a listing of each rule as it is added. This command also permits the -f option which flushes each chain before the rules are added.

Rule Writing and Logging Tips

Your rules should, first and foremost, be based on your organization's Security Policy (see, for example, *Linux System Security* as cited in "For Further Reading" on page 723 for a further discussion of security policies). This will tell you what is and is not permitted. From there you will be able to establish a rule set.

Generally speaking, if your Security Policy permits, use DENY or REJECT as your default rule for each permanent chain. Write your ACCEPT rules by specifying as many options as possible. The following list provides some hints.

- Specify both source and destination IP addresses and ports.
- Do not use DNS names in your rules because they will not resolve if DNS is down and your rule sets will not load.
- Whenever possible, specify unprivileged ports (port numbers 1024 through and including 65535).
- Set up logging for any new rule or any rule that is still being tested. Also, log anything that should not occur.

This will limit the number of packets that might slip through; it will also make your rules easier to read and understand. We will do this in our examples later in this chapter.

Anything that should not occur, or anything you think should not occur, should be logged. It is a good idea to implement a catchall rule that is the last rule in the chain and denies everything. Such a rule should have the logging option set.

Setting up a lot of logging does have the undesirable side effect of filling up your disks and generally adding to your work load. The utilities, logrotate, logcheck, and swatch, presented in, for example, *Linux System Security* as cited in "For Further Reading" on page 723, should help considerably.

Most important, test your rule base as you build it. This will make debugging much simpler and allow for catching problems that are hidden inside a complex rule set.

Changing Rules

If you need to change your rules in any way and for any reason, it is a good idea to use blocking rules while you work on the rule set. You can do this by adding the rules

```
# ipchains -A input 1 -j REJECT
# ipchains -A output 1 -j REJECT
# ipchains -A forward 1 -j REJECT
```

and then add, modify, or delete the necessary rules. When you are done, delete the above three rules.

Alternatively, you could disable your external interface by executing

```
# ifconfig eth0 down
```

where you would replace `eth0` with the correct external interface on your system.

Make sure that you test your new rule base as much as possible before going back online.

Building Your Firewall

In this section, we will explore a simple firewall scenario and go through a detailed look at building the rules for that scenario. This example is not intended to meet the needs of any particular environment, so use it at your own risk. The primary purpose of this section is to deepen your understanding of the way in which `ipchains` and IP masquerading work.

Small Internal Network

For our first example, we'll use the scenario described in Figure 14–2 on page 690. We provide a simplified diagram in Figure 14–3 to set the stage.

For simplicity, this example will use a static external IP address. This approach provides a nice example for an internal network that must be firewalled from the rest of an organization's intranet (just change Internet to intranet in Figure 14–3). We will look at dynamically assigned IP addresses, such as

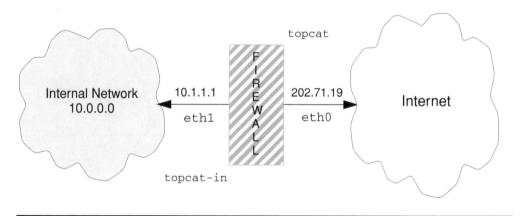

Figure 14–3   Small Internal Network Example

Point-to-Point Protocol (PPP), cable modem, and digital subscriber line (DSL) Internet connections in "Simple Internal Network Using DHCP" on page 713.

As before, `topcat` will be our Linux firewall with the external interface `eth0`, configured for the Internet IP address `202.7.1.19`, with a netmask of `255.255.255.240` (this means that our network address is `202.7.1.8`; see Chapter 4 for details about subnet masks). The external address resolves to the hostname `topcat`. The internal interface `eth1` is configured for the internal IP address `10.1.1.1`. This internal address resolves to the hostname `topcat-in`.

We'll make the following directives about what to allow and deny. This is based on our Security Policy, of course! We will assume that DNS and email services are provided by our Internet service provider (ISP). All email is retrieved via a Post Office Protocol Version 3 (POP3) server. Email must be sent via SMTP. We'll use the hostname/IP address assignments shown in Table 14–10 for our primary DNS server, secondary DNS server, and mail server.

Table 14–10   Small Internal Network Example Server Addresses

Hostname	IP Address	Purpose of Host
dnssvr1	202.7.1.225	The primary DNS server.
dnssvr2	202.7.1.226	The secondary DNS server.
mail	202.7.1.227	The POP3 server. POP3 for retrieving mail, SMTP for sending mail.
rtr-isp	202.7.1.17	The router to the ISP. Our default gateway.

DEFAULT POLICY.   Our default policy is REJECT.

INTERNAL NETWORK.   We want to allow our internal users to `ping`, `ftp`, and web-browse any Internet destination. We must masquerade because we have only the one legal Internet IP address. We also want to allow internal access to `topcat-in` via SSH only.

EXTERNAL NETWORK.   We do not want to allow any inbound connections from the Internet, so we need to configure our firewall to allow return connections only for our internal users.

Let's implement the rules to meet these requirements. We take the approach of manually executing each command for the purposes of clarifying the example. The steps are outlined beginning with "Initial Steps and the Default Policy," continuing through "Finally!" on page 713. Example 14–39 on page 714 captures the manual commands into a script.

Initial Steps and the Default Policy

In accordance with our discussion in "Changing Rules" on page 699, we take down the interfaces and then flush the chains and start with a REJECT rule. We will remove the first REJECT rule when we are finished (see "Finally!" on page 713). We also set the default policy to REJECT. These steps are shown in Example 14–24.

Example 14–24   Initial REJECT Rules

```
[root@topcat]# ifconfig eth1 down
[root@topcat]# ifconfig eth0 down
[root@topcat]# ipchains -F
[root@topcat]# ipchains -I input 1 -j REJECT
[root@topcat]# ipchains -I output 1 -j REJECT
[root@topcat]# ipchains -I forward 1 -j REJECT
[root@topcat]# ipchains -A input -i lo -s 0/0 -d 0/0 -j ACCEPT
[root@topcat]# ipchains -A output -i lo -s 0/0 -d 0/0 -j ACCEPT
[root@topcat]# ipchains -P input REJECT
[root@topcat]# ipchains -P output REJECT
[root@topcat]# ipchains -P forward REJECT
[root@topcat]# ifconfig eth1 up
[root@topcat]# ifconfig eth0 up
```

Note that we also added the two rules

```
[root@topcat]# ipchains -A input -i lo -s 0/0 -d 0/0 -j ACCEPT
[root@topcat]# ipchains -A output -i lo -s 0/0 -d 0/0 -j ACCEPT
```

to allow all communications through the loopback interface.

Now let's set up antispoofing (see "Antispoofing Rules" on page 694). We need to put a 1 in every `rp_filter` file, so we'll just use a short script as shown in Example 14–25.

Example 14–25   Antispoofing Script

```
[root@topcat]# for file in /proc/sys/net/ipv4/conf/*/rp_filter
> do
> echo "1" > $file
> done
[root@topcat]# ipchains -A input -i ! lo -s 127.0.0.0/8 -j REJECT -l
[root@topcat]#
```

For those of you using kernel versions 2.0.x and earlier, be sure to add the last command shown in Example 14–25 to prevent loopback spoofing. This rule won't hurt if you are using kernel versions 2.1.x or 2.2.x.

We must next establish IP forwarding (to allow masquerading) and load the `ftp` masquerading module. Thus, we execute the commands shown in Example 14–26. The first command, `/sbin/depmod -a`, performs a dependency check on all kernel modules.

Example 14–26   Initial Steps for Masquerading Support

```
[root@topcat]# depmod -a
[root@topcat]# modprobe ip_masq_ftp
[root@topcat]# echo "1" > /proc/sys/net/ipv4/ip_forward
```

Setting IP Masquerading Timeouts

By default, the kernel sets timeouts to 15 minutes for masqueraded sessions of all types. There are three timeout parameters that apply to masquerading: TCP timeouts, TCP FIN packet (TCP packets with the finish bit set) timeouts, and UDP timeouts (see Table 14–1 on page 666). TCP FIN timeouts should be short, so we'll use 10 seconds. UDP timeouts are related to the time between the arrival or dispatch of individual UDP packets that belong to the same communication. A good timeout range for this is somewhere between 40 and 60 seconds, so we will use 50 seconds. General TCP timeouts are based on inactivity of a session. So, if you have an established `telnet` connection, for example, and you don't use it for 15 minutes, by default, the connection will be broken. You may find it useful to increase this timeout period; we use 1 hour (3,600 seconds). The command is provided in Example 14–27.

Example 14–27   Setting the Masquerading Time-Outs

```
[root@topcat]# ipchains -M -S 3600 10 50
```

Generally Restricting Inbound Requests

We don't allow any inbound connections from the Internet, so we REJECT and log all requests to our internal network (10.0.0.0) and we REJECT all TCP SYN packets (described in "Rule Ordering Is Important!" on page 696) as our first two rules in the input chain as shown in Example 14–28.

Example 14–28   Reject All Inbound Attempts

```
[root@topcat]# ipchains -A input -i eth0 -p tcp -d 10.0.0.0/8 -j REJECT -l
[root@topcat]# ipchains -A input -i eth0 -y -p tcp -d topcat -j REJECT
```

ICMP Rules

At this point, we can deal with our ICMP requirements. We need to allow outbound ping and disallow incoming ping. We already established these rules in "Sample ICMP Rules" on page 686. But we'll be a little more careful, in accordance with "Rule Writing and Logging Tips" on page 698.

We need four rules to allow ping to go from our internal network to the Internet. Here's why. A user on a client in the 10.0.0.0 network executes a ping to a system in the Internet. The ping generates an ICMP echo-request, which goes to topcat-in (eth1) and is initially processed by the input chain. So we need a rule for that. The ICMP echo-request is then passed on to the forward chain for routing. We'll use the masquerading rule for that. Next, the packet is passed on to the output chain to head off to the Internet via eth0. We'll need another rule there.

Then the packet leaves topcat and reaches the server. The server responds with an ICMP echo-reply, which arrives at topcat (eth0) to be processed by the input chain. We'll put a rule in there. Because the address is masqueraded, it skips the forward chain and goes straight to the output chain for processing before it heads out eth1 and back to the internal client.

We also do not want to respond to ping requests from the Internet, so we'll add a rule for that—Example 14–29 provides the rules. (The numbering to the left is for illustrative purposes and will not actually appear.)

Example 14–29   Rules to Manage ping

```
1  root@topcat]# ipchains -A input -p icmp --icmp-type echo-request -i eth0
   -s 0/0 -d topcat -j REJECT
2  [root@topcat]# ipchains -A input -p icmp --icmp-type echo-request -i eth1
   -s 10.0.0.0/8 -d 0/0 -j ACCEPT
3  [root@topcat]# ipchains -A forward -i eth0 -s 10.0.0.0/8 -d 0/0 -j MASQ
4  [root@topcat]# ipchains -A output -p icmp --icmp-type echo-request -i
   eth0 -s topcat -d 0/0 -j ACCEPT
5  [root@topcat]# ipchains -A input -p icmp --icmp-type echo-reply -i eth0 -
   s 0/0 -d topcat -j ACCEPT
6  [root@topcat]# ipchains -A output -p icmp --icmp-type echo-reply -i eth1
   -s 0/0 -d 10.0.0.0/8 -j ACCEPT
```

- Rule 1 disallows any `ping` requests from the Internet. Note that we use REJECT. Recall from Table 14–3 on page 672 that DENY and REJECT are identical when the rule matches ICMP.

- Rule 2 allows client `ping`s from the internal network to pass through the input chain when they arrive at `eth1`.

- Rule 3 is the general masquerading rule. It masquerades all internal `10.0.0.0` addresses as `202.7.1.19`. This rule will masquerade all traffic and is required by all subsequent rules that permit external access.

- Rule 4 permits the `echo-request` to traverse the output chain with respect to `eth0` and head off to the destination system.

- Rule 5 allows the return `echo-reply` to traverse the input chain after it enters `eth0`.

- Rule 6 permits the `echo-reply` to pass through the output chain with respect to `eth1` and go off to the internal client.

To better understand the flow of the packet as well as the chains it passes through, it may be useful to take a look at Figure 14–4 on page 707. That diagram is specific to `ftp` and is discussed in "Rules for Allowing `ftp` from the Internal Network to the Internet," but the flow of packets through the chains is conceptually the same for all traffic through the firewall.

Now that we have taken care of `ping`, we need to set up the rules for ICMP error messages. We'll use the custom chain in Example 14–15 on page 693. Be sure to create the chain before you execute the commands given in Example 14–15. Once accomplished, we can add rules to jump to the `icmperr` chain, as shown in Example 14–30.

Example 14–30   Rules that Invoke the ICMP Custom Chain

```
[root@topcat]# ipchains -A input -p icmp -s 0/0 -d topcat -j icmperr
[root@topcat]# ipchains -A output -p icmp -s ! 10.0.0.0/8 -d 0/0 -j icmperr
```

Note that we are specifying both source and destination in these rules. In particular, we will not allow our internal network to generate ICMP messages out to the Internet.

Except for the rules in "Finally!" on page 713, the rules we add after this point are not order dependent as long as they are added *after* the ones we've added up through this section.

Rules for Allowing ftp from the Internal Network to the Internet

Based on the requirements provided in the section, "Small Internal Network" on page 700, we must allow ftp. The setup for ftp is fairly complex because it utilizes two distinct ports for communication. In active ftp mode (executing ftp from the command line), the initial packet generated by the client sets the destination port to ftp (port number 21). For responses from the server, 21 becomes the source port number. When the client requests data from the server—for example, by executing ls at the ftp prompt—the client sends the request using the ftp-data port (port number 20) as the destination port. The data request by the client causes the server to respond by requesting a connection to the client at the ftp-data port. Passive ftp (usually implemented through web browsers) allows the ftp server to choose the data port. Fortunately, we don't need to worry about passive ftp because ip_masq_ftp (see the references cited in the section, "Masquerading Documentation" on page 723) automatically takes care of it for us. But we do need to write the rules. It will help our understanding to refer to the diagram in Figure 14–4.

In order to configure this capability, we will need eight rules for ftp and one masquerading rule. The masquerading rule will be general and will apply to all connections originating from the internal network. As we step through this process, the numbers in Figure 14–4 correspond to the FTP rules noted in the following sections. The reference to masquerade in Figure 14–4 corresponds to "Masquerade Rule" on page 707.

FTP RULE 1.   A client in the internal network wants to connect to the Internet via ftp. The client will execute a command like ftp ftp.reallycool.com. This generates a packet with the source IP address from the 10.0.0.0 network and the destination port number set to ftp. It will arrive at topcat-in (eth1). So, write the rule

```
[root@topcat]# ipchains -A input -i eth1 -p tcp -s 10.0.0.0/8
1024:65535 -d 0/0 ftp -j ACCEPT
```

This rule lets the packet through the input chain. Now we need to pass it through the forward chain. Note that we limit the source ports to unprivileged ones. This is a good idea, just to be on the safe side, and we'll do it wherever possible.

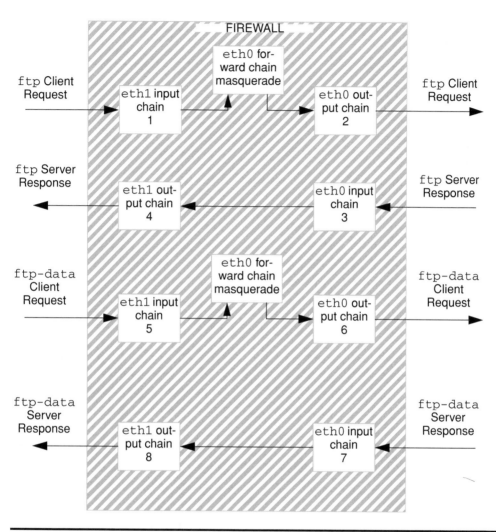

Figure 14–4   Dual Connection Requirement for `ftp`

MASQUERADE RULE.   We previously added the masquerading rule in step 2 of Example 14–29 on page 704. This is a nonspecific rule that will masquerade everything from `10.0.0.0` to `202.7.1.19` through `eth0`. The next chain to deal with is the outbound chain.

FTP RULE 2.   We need to allow the packet which was accepted by **FTP Rule 1** through `eth1` through the output chain for `eth0`. Do this with

```
[root@topcat]# ipchains -A output -i eth0 -p tcp -s topcat
1024:65535 -d 0/0 ftp -j ACCEPT
```

Note that we specify the source as topcat instead of the 10.0.0.0 network. That is because the packet has been masqueraded. At this point, the ftp request from the internal client will be able to pass through the firewall to the server in the Internet.

FTP RULE 3.   Now we need to reverse the process and allow the server to reply to the client. The server will generate a packet with the source port number set to ftp (port 21) and the destination IP address to topcat. This packet will arrive on eth0. Thus, the rule

```
[root@topcat]# ipchains -A input -i eth0 -p tcp -s 0/0 ftp -d topcat
1024:65535 -j ACCEPT ! -y
```

Since this incoming response is to a masqueraded packet, the address will be demasqueraded, the forward chain will be skipped, and the packet will be sent on to the output chain for processing.

NOTE

Since FTP Rule 3 occurs after the TCP SYN REJECT rule (due to -A) entered as the first command in Example 14–28 on page 704, ftp connection requests from the Internet will never reach this rule. But we're paranoid, so we've added ! -y to this rule. We will do this for FTP Rule 7 as well.

FTP RULE 4.   We need to allow the packet to pass back to the internal host that requested the ftp service to begin with. Accomplish this with

```
[root@topcat]# ipchains -A output -i eth1 -p tcp -s 0/0 ftp -d
10.0.0.0/8 1024:65535 -j ACCEPT
```

Notice that we may once again specify the real internal network address (as the destination this time). At this point, ftp connections will work. You will be able to login via ftp. Try it! Then, try to execute ls and watch it fail! Let's fix that next.

FTP RULE 5.   The next thing the client will want to do is establish a data connection. When the client executes an ls, get, put, etc., command, it will generate an ftp-data (port number 20) packet. This rule is identical to that in **FTP Rule 1**, except for the port.

```
[root@topcat]# ipchains -A input -i eth1 -p tcp -s 10.0.0.0/8
1024:65535 -d 0/0 ftp-data -j ACCEPT
```

Once the packet passes this rule, it will go on to the forward chain. We already set up that rule in **Masquerade Rule** on page 707, so there is nothing further to do. The packet will pass through the forward chain, the source IP address being masqueraded, and then will go to the output chain. So we'll add that rule next.

FTP RULE 6.   This step is identical to **FTP Rule 2**, except for the port. The rule is

```
[root@topcat]# ipchains -A output -i eth0 -p tcp -s topcat
1024:65535 -d 0/0 ftp-data -j ACCEPT
```

At this point the Internet ftp server can receive ftp-data requests from our internal client. Next, we need to allow the server to respond to the request.

FTP RULE 7.   This step is similar to **FTP Rule 3**. In this case, the port is ftp-data and we cannot restrict connection requests (with ! -y) because the server will request a data connection with the client. This must be allowed in order for ftp to work.

```
[root@topcat]# ipchains -A input -i eth0 -p tcp -s 0/0 ftp-data -d
topcat 1024:65535 -j ACCEPT
```

Once again, demasquerading occurs after this chain, the forward chain is skipped, and processing is passed to the output chain.

FTP RULE 8.   This rule is identical to **FTP Rule 4**, except for the port.

```
[root@topcat]# ipchains -A output -i eth1 -p tcp -s 0/0 ftp-data -d
10.0.0.0/8 1024:65535 -j ACCEPT
```

We're done! Now users on the internal network can access the Internet via ftp (that was a lot of work—ask for a raise).

Allowing DNS, POP3, and Web Access

Conceptually, every rule required for these services is like that for ftp. The basic difference is that we won't have two distinct ports to deal with. DNS and POP3 do utilize both TCP and UDP, so we will need to deal with that. We'll cover each of the services in separate subsections.

DNS RULES.   We need to allow DNS queries from internal hosts and from topcat to reach the DNS servers in the Internet. The port number for DNS is 53 and its equivalent name from /etc/services is domain. Example 14–31 provides the necessary rules. Once again, we write the rules following the flow of events shown in Figure 14–4 on page 707. (The numbers to the left are for descriptive purposes.)

Example 14–31   Rules to Permit DNS Queries

```
1   [root@topcat]# ipchains -A input -i eth1 -p tcp -s 10.0.0.0/8 -d dnssvr1
    domain -j ACCEPT
2   [root@topcat]# ipchains -A input -i eth1 -p tcp -s 10.0.0.0/8 -d dnssvr2
    domain -j ACCEPT
3   [root@topcat]# ipchains -A input -i eth1 -p udp -s 10.0.0.0/8 -d dnssvr1
    domain -j ACCEPT
4   [root@topcat]# ipchains -A input -i eth1 -p udp -s 10.0.0.0/8 -d dnssvr2
    domain -j ACCEPT
5   [root@topcat]# ipchains -A output -i eth0 -p tcp -s topcat -d dnssvr1
    domain -j ACCEPT
6   [root@topcat]# ipchains -A output -i eth0 -p tcp -s topcat -d dnssvr2
    domain -j ACCEPT
7   [root@topcat]# ipchains -A output -i eth0 -p udp -s topcat -d dnssvr1
    domain -j ACCEPT
8   [root@topcat]# ipchains -A output -i eth0 -p udp -s topcat -d dnssvr2
    domain -j ACCEPT
9   [root@topcat]# ipchains -A input -i eth0 -p tcp -d topcat -s dnssvr1
    domain -j ACCEPT ! -y
10  [root@topcat]# ipchains -A input -i eth0 -p tcp -d topcat -s dnssvr2
    domain -j ACCEPT
11  [root@topcat]# ipchains -A input -i eth0 -p udp -d topcat -s dnssvr2
    domain -j ACCEPT
12  root@topcat]# ipchains -A output -i eth1 -p tcp -d 10.0.0.0/8 -s dnssvr1
    domain -j ACCEPT
13  [root@topcat]# ipchains -A output -i eth1 -p tcp -d 10.0.0.0/8 -s
    dnssvr2 domain -j ACCEPT
14  [root@topcat]# ipchains -A output -i eth1 -p udp -d 10.0.0.0/8 -s
    dnssvr1 domain -j ACCEPT
15  [root@topcat]# ipchains -A output -i eth1 -p udp -d 10.0.0.0/8 -s
    dnssvr2 domain -j ACCEPT
```

Rules 1 through 4 accept DNS queries from the internal network through `eth1` in the input chain. Rules 5 through 8 allow those queries out to the Internet through `eth0`. Rules 9 through 11 allow the DNS responses to return through `eth0`. Note that once again we disallow TCP SYN packets. We cannot do this for UDP. Rules 12 through 15 permit the DNS responses to flow back to the internal clients.

POP3 RULES.   Next, we'll add the rules for email access. Since POP3 uses SMTP (port 25, also known as `smtp`) to send mail, we need to include those as well. We list the rules for POP3 in Example 14–32.

As with DNS, POP3 uses both UDP and TCP, so our rules allow for that.

Example 14–32   Rules to Permit POP3 Retrieval of Email

```
[root@topcat]# ipchains -A input -i eth1 -p tcp -s 10.0.0.0/8 -d mail pop-3 -j ACCEPT
[root@topcat]# ipchains -A input -i eth1 -p udp -s 10.0.0.0/8 -d mail pop-3 -j ACCEPT
[root@topcat]# ipchains -A output -i eth0 -p tcp -s topcat -d mail pop-3 -j ACCEPT
[root@topcat]# ipchains -A output -i eth0 -p udp -s topcat -d mail pop-3 -j ACCEPT
[root@topcat]# ipchains -A input -i eth0 -p tcp -d topcat -s mail pop-3 -j ACCEPT ! -y
[root@topcat]# ipchains -A input -i eth0 -p udp -d topcat -s mail pop-3 -j ACCEPT
[root@topcat]# ipchains -A output -i eth1 -p tcp -d 10.0.0.0/8 -s mail pop-3 -j ACCEPT
[root@topcat]# ipchains -A output -i eth1 -p udp -d 10.0.0.0/8 -s mail pop-3 -j ACCEPT
```

Now let's enter the rules for SMTP to allow email to be sent. These are shown in Example 14–33. Note that SMTP uses TCP only.

Example 14–33   Rules to Permit SMTP Sending of Email

```
[root@topcat]# ipchains -A input -i eth1 -p tcp -s 10.0.0.0/8 -d mail smtp -j ACCEPT
[root@topcat]# ipchains -A output -i eth0 -p tcp -s topcat -d mail smtp -j ACCEPT
[root@topcat]# ipchains -A input -i eth0 -p tcp -d topcat -s mail smtp -j ACCEPT ! -y
[root@topcat]# ipchains -A output -i eth1 -p tcp -d 10.0.0.0/8 -s mail smtp -j ACCEPT
```

WEB ACCESS RULES.   Similarly, we allow access to the World Wide Web (WWW). The port number for web access is 80 and its name is www. The rules are similar to previous rules and are shown in Example 14–34.

Example 14–34   Rules to Permit Web Access

```
[root@topcat]# ipchains -A input -i eth1 -p tcp -s 10.0.0.0/8 -d 0/0 www -j ACCEPT
[root@topcat]# ipchains -A output -i eth0 -p tcp -s topcat -d 0/0 www -j ACCEPT
[root@topcat]# ipchains -A input -i eth0 -p tcp -d topcat -s 0/0 www -j ACCEPT ! -y
[root@topcat]# ipchains -A output -i eth1 -p tcp -d 10.0.0.0/8 -s 0/0 www -j ACCEPT
```

Note that in this example we allow web access only to port 80. Many web servers will use other port numbers. If you wish to allow certain port numbers, such as 8080 and 8008, you would need to add rules similar to those shown in Example 14–34 for that purpose. If you wish to allow any port number for web access, you duplicate the rules shown in Example 14–34 with rules that specify 1024:65535 instead of www. Such an approach allows all TCP traffic initiated internally to go through the firewall. Make sure that your Security Policy permits this. For completion, we show such permissive rules in Example 14–35, but note that these are not supportive of the requirements specified in the description of our example (see "Small Internal Network" on page 700 and following subsections).

Example 14–35   Rules to Permit All Internally Initiated Traffic Using Unprivileged Ports

```
[root@topcat]# ipchains -A input -i eth1 -p tcp -s 10.0.0.0/8 -d 0/0
1024:65535 -j ACCEPT
[root@topcat]# ipchains -A output -i eth0 -p tcp -s topcat -d 0/0
1024:65535 -j ACCEPT
[root@topcat]# ipchains -A input -i eth0 -p tcp -d topcat -s 0/0 1024:65535
-j ACCEPT ! -y
[root@topcat]# ipchains -A output -i eth1 -p tcp -d 10.0.0.0/8 -s 0/0
1024:65535 -j ACCEPT
```

The use of the rules outlined in Example 14–35 does make the rule sets simpler but also represents a less restrictive implementation. These rules are not used in the subsequent Example 14–39 on page 714.

This completes the rules necessary for the required services specified at the beginning of "Small Internal Network" on page 700. It should be noted that these rules allow access to the services specified by any of our internal hosts and from `topcat` itself.

Allowing Internal SSH

The last thing we need to do to meet the requirements set forth for this example (see beginning of "Small Internal Network" on page 700) is permit SSH connections from the internal network to `topcat-in`. The port number for SSH is 22 and its name is `ssh`. This is much easier than the other rule sets since we do not need to allow the SSH connections to pass through our firewall. The necessary rules are given in Example 14–36.

Example 14–36   Rules Allowing SSH from the Internal Network to `topcat-in`

```
[root@topcat]# ipchains -A input -i eth1 -p tcp -s 10.0.0.0/8 1023:65535 -d
topcat-in ssh -j ACCEPT
[root@topcat]# ipchains -A output -i eth1 -p tcp -d 10.0.0.0/8 1023:65535 -s
topcat-in ssh -j ACCEPT
```

NOTE

If we also want to allow `topcat-in` to connect to the internal network via SSH, we could accomplish this by adding -b (bidirectional) to each of the rules in Example 14–36.

Finally!

We're nearly done! We just have a couple more steps. First, let's reject every-thing we haven't explicitly allowed and log such activity. This will make our log files grow rapidly, so we'll need to manage them as described in "Rule Writing and Logging Tips" on page 698. These are the catchall rules. We append them to the end of each chain as shown in Example 14–37.

Example 14–37   Catchall `REJECT` Rules

```
[root@topcat]# ipchains -A input -l -j REJECT
[root@topcat]# ipchains -A output -l -j REJECT
[root@topcat]# ipchains -A forward -l -j REJECT
```

Now let's remove the initial blocking rules that we input prior to modifying our chains (see "Initial Steps and the Default Policy" on page 702). Execute the commands given in Example 14–38 to accomplish this.

Example 14–38   Removing the Blocking Rules

```
[root@topcat]# ipchains -D input 1
[root@topcat]# ipchains -D output 1
[root@topcat]# ipchains -D forward 1
```

We've now implemented the firewall to meet the requirements set forth at the beginning of "Small Internal Network" on page 700. At this point, you will want to save your configuration, using `ipchains-save`, and/or write a script to rein-state this rule base at each reboot. In the next section we will look at an example set of start-up scripts that incorporates everything discussed in this example.

Simple Internal Network Using DHCP

"But," you say, "I use PPP! How do I do this with PPP?" Or maybe you use DSL, a cable modem, or some other mechanism that requires the Dynamic Host Configuration Protocol (DHCP). No problem.

Let's assume that our example is identical to that given in "Small Internal Network" on page 700. The main difference between that example and using DHCP or PPP with dynamic addressing is in the way we obtain the IP address for the external interface.

The script in Example 14–39 incorporates all of the rules we implemented in "Small Internal Network" on page 700. It uses shell environment variables to make the script more adaptable to many situations. It also adds the required rules to allow DHCP to work, and it fetches the dynamically assigned IP addresses. The script is commented, but, to make it easier, the additional entries for DHCP (PPP, DSL, cable modems, etc.) are in **bold**. If you are using DHCP, you will not necessarily use all of the entries in **bold** because some of them apply to PPP specifically. So use the entries appropriately.

Use this script, or something similar, as a start-up script to start your firewall at boot-time.

Example 14–39   Firewall Start-up Script

```
#!/bin/bash

# Begin with setting some environment variables - first PATH
PATH=/sbin:/usr/sbin:/bin:/usr/bin;export PATH

# External Interface - uncomment the one you use or set appropriately
EXIF="eth0"
# EXIF="ppp0"

# Internal Interface - set appropriately
INIF="eth1"

# DMZ Interface - set appropriately
# DMZIF="eth2"

# If you are using static IP addresses, set it below
EXIP="202.7.1.19" # topcat
# If you use DHCP, you'll need to fetch the address
# Uncomment the next line if you use DHCP, such as DSL, PPP, etc.
# EXIP="`ifconfig|grep -A 2 $EXTIF|awk '/inet/ { print $2 }'\
#       |sed -e s/addr://`"
#
# DHCP addresses are "leased" for a period of time after which
# the address may change, so make sure that this script is
# re-run each time the IP address changes. See DHCP documentation


# Now set the external broadcast address.
# This script only uses the broadcast for DHCP.
#EXBCAST="202.7.1.31"
#
# To get the broadcast address for DHCP uncomment the next line
# EXBCAST="`ifconfig|grep -A 2 $EXTIF|awk '/inet/ { print $4 }'\
#       |sed -e s/Bcast://`"

# Next set your internal IP address
INIP="10.1.1.1"    # topcat-in
#
# Now set the network variables
INNET="10.0.0.0/8"
# DMZNET="202.7.1.24/30"# Uncomment this if used
#End of variable section

# Let's be paranoid and enter blocking rules to start
```

Example 14–39   Firewall Start-up Script *(Continued)*

```
# We'll disable them at the end. Also we'll allow lo here and
# set up the REJECT policy.
ipchains -F
ipchains -I input 1 -j REJECT
ipchains -I output 1 -j REJECT
ipchains -I forward 1 -j REJECT
ipchains -A input -i lo -s 0/0 -d 0/0 -j ACCEPT
ipchains -A output -i lo -s 0/0 -d 0/0 -j ACCEPT
ipchains -P input REJECT
ipchains -P output REJECT
ipchains -P forward REJECT
#

#
# initial masquerading requirements
depmod -a
modprobe ip_masq_ftp
echo "1" > /proc/sys/net/ipv4/ip_forward
ipchains -M -S 3600 10 50
# end initial masquerading requirements

# DHCP support requires this...uncomment if necessary
echo "1" > /proc/sys/net/ipv4/ip_dynaddr
#
# anti-spoofing
for file in /proc/sys/net/ipv4/conf/*/rp_filter
do
echo "1" > $file
done
ipchains -A input -i ! lo -s 127.0.0.0/8 -j REJECT -l
# end anti-spoof

# Internet input rejects
ipchains -A input -i $EXIF -p tcp -d $INNET -j REJECT -l
ipchains -A input -i $EXIF -y -p tcp -d $EXIP -j REJECT
# end input rejects

# ICMP Custom Chain - catch important ICMP messages
#             our catch-all reject rule will drop the rest.
# First create the chain...no problem if it already exists.
# Real problems if it doesn't.
ipchains -N outputN 2>/dev/null
# Now add the rules
ipchains -A icmperr -p icmp --icmp-type destination-unreachable -j ACCEPT
ipchains -A icmperr -p icmp --icmp-type parameter-problem -j ACCEPT
ipchains -A icmperr -p icmp --icmp-type source-quench -j ACCEPT
ipchains -A icmperr -p icmp --icmp-type time-exceeded -j ACCEPT
# end ICMP Custom Chain


# ICMP rules - Allow ping out but not in.
ipchains -A input -p icmp --icmp-type echo-request -i $EXIF -s 0/0 -d $EXIP
-j REJECT
ipchains -A input -p icmp --icmp-type echo-request -i $INIF -s $INNET -d 0/0
-j ACCEPT
```

Example 14–39   Firewall Start-up Script *(Continued)*

```
ipchains -A output -p icmp --icmp-type echo-request -i $EXIF -s $EXIP -d 0/0
-j ACCEPT
ipchains -A input -p icmp --icmp-type echo-reply -i $EXIF -s 0/0 -d $EXIP -j
ACCEPT
ipchains -A output -p icmp --icmp-type echo-reply -i $INIF -s 0/0 -d $INNET
-j ACCEPT
ipchains -A input -p icmp -s 0/0 -d $EXIP -j icmperr
ipchains -A output -p icmp -s ! $INNET -d 0/0 -j icmperr
# end ICMP rules

# Masquerading Rule
ipchains -A forward -i $EXIF -s $INNET -d 0/0 -j MASQ
# end masq

# Support for DHCP client
ipchains -A input -i $EXIF -p udp -s 0/0 bootps -d 255.255.255.255 bootpc
ipchains -A input -i $EXIF -p tcp -s 0/0 bootps -d 255.255.255.255 bootpc
ipchains -A output -i $EXIF -p udp -s 0/0 bootpc -d 255.255.255.255 bootps
ipchains -A output -i $EXIF -p tcp -s 0/0 bootpc -d 255.255.255.255 bootps
# end DHCP client rules

# ftp rules
ipchains -A input -i $INIF -p tcp -s $INNET 1024:65535 -d 0/0 ftp -j ACCEPT
ipchains -A output -i $EXIF -p tcp -s $EXIP 1024:65535 -d 0/0 ftp -j ACCEPT
ipchains -A input -i $EXIF -p tcp -s 0/0 ftp -d $EXIP 1024:65535 -j ACCEPT !
-y
ipchains -A output -i $INIF -p tcp -s 0/0 ftp -d $INNET 1024:65535 -j ACCEPT
ipchains -A input -i $INIF -p tcp -s $INNET 1024:65535 -d 0/0 ftp-data -j
ACCEPT
ipchains -A output -i $EXIF -p tcp -s $EXIP -d 0/0 ftp-data -j ACCEPT
ipchains -A input -i $EXIF -p tcp -s 0/0 ftp-data -d $EXIP 1024:65535 -j
ACCEPT
ipchains -A output -i $INIF -p tcp -s 0/0 ftp-data -d $INNET 1024:65535 -j
ACCEPT
# end ftp rules

# DNS rules
ipchains -A input -i $INIF -p tcp -s $INNET -d dnssvr1 domain -j ACCEPT
ipchains -A input -i $INIF -p tcp -s $INNET -d dnssvr2 domain -j ACCEPT
ipchains -A input -i $INIF -p udp -s $INNET -d dnssvr1 domain -j ACCEPT
ipchains -A input -i $INIF -p udp -s $INNET -d dnssvr2 domain -j ACCEPT
ipchains -A output -i $EXIF -p tcp -s $EXIP -d dnssvr1 domain -j ACCEPT
ipchains -A output -i $EXIF -p tcp -s $EXIP -d dnssvr2 domain -j ACCEPT
ipchains -A output -i $EXIF -p udp -s $EXIP -d dnssvr1 domain -j ACCEPT
ipchains -A output -i $EXIF -p udp -s $EXIP -d dnssvr2 domain -j ACCEPT
ipchains -A input -i $EXIF -p tcp -d $EXIP -s dnssvr1 domain -j ACCEPT ! -y
ipchains -A input -i $EXIF -p tcp -d $EXIP -s dnssvr2 domain -j ACCEPT
ipchains -A input -i $EXIF -p udp -d $EXIP -s dnssvr2 domain -j ACCEPT
ipchains -A output -i $INIF -p tcp -d $INNET -s dnssvr1 domain -j ACCEPT
ipchains -A output -i $INIF -p tcp -d $INNET -s dnssvr2 domain -j ACCEPT
ipchains -A output -i $INIF -p udp -d $INNET -s dnssvr1 domain -j ACCEPT
ipchains -A output -i $INIF -p udp -d $INNET -s dnssvr2 domain -j ACCEPT
# end DNS rules

# POP-3/SMTP Rules
```

Example 14–39   Firewall Start-up Script *(Continued)*

```
ipchains -A input -i $INIF -p tcp -s $INNET -d mail pop-3 -j ACCEPT
ipchains -A input -i $INIF -p udp -s $INNET -d mail pop-3 -j ACCEPT
ipchains -A output -i $EXIF -p tcp -s $EXIP -d mail pop-3 -j ACCEPT
ipchains -A output -i $EXIF -p udp -s $EXIP -d mail pop-3 -j ACCEPT
ipchains -A input -i $EXIF -p tcp -d $EXIP -s mail pop-3 -j ACCEPT ! -y
ipchains -A input -i $EXIF -p udp -d $EXIP -s mail pop-3 -j ACCEPT
ipchains -A output -i $INIF -p tcp -d $INNET -s mail pop-3 -j ACCEPT
ipchains -A output -i $INIF -p udp -d $INNET -s mail pop-3 -j ACCEPT
ipchains -A input -i $INIF -p tcp -s $INNET -d mail smtp -j ACCEPT
ipchains -A output -i $EXIF -p tcp -s $EXIP -d mail smtp -j ACCEPT
ipchains -A input -i $EXIF -p tcp -d $EXIP -s mail smtp -j ACCEPT ! -y
ipchains -A output -i $INIF -p tcp -d $INNET -s mail smtp -j ACCEPT
# end POP-3/SMTP Rules

# Web Access Rules
ipchains -A input -i $INIF -p tcp -s $INNET -d 0/0 www -j ACCEPT
ipchains -A output -i $EXIF -p tcp -s $EXIP -d 0/0 www -j ACCEPT
ipchains -A input -i $EXIF -p tcp -d $EXIP -s 0/0 www -j ACCEPT ! -y
ipchains -A output -i $INIF -p tcp -d $INNET -s 0/0 www -j ACCEPT
# end Web

# SSH Rules
ipchains -A input -i $INIF -p tcp -s $INNET -d $INIP ssh -j ACCEPT
ipchains -A output -i $INIF -p tcp -d $INNET -s $INIP ssh -j ACCEPT
# end SSH

# Catch-All rules
ipchains -A input -l -j REJECT
ipchains -A output -l -j REJECT
ipchains -A forward -l -j REJECT
# end Catch-All

# Remove blocking rules
ipchains -D input 1
ipchains -D output 1
ipchains -D forward 1
# end remove
```

`ipchains` **Isn't Just for Firewalls!**

This very powerful utility can be implemented on a system with a single interface. Much of what we have described in this chapter applies to such a case, and the rules will be simpler when only a single interface is involved. For more complete security, `ipchains` should implement along with other restrictive utilities such as `xinetd` (see Chapter 8 for a discussion of `xinetd`) and SSH (see "Virtual Private Networks and Encrypted Tunnels" on page 720) on all your critical servers. Furthermore, `ipchains` can be used for simple packet accounting purposes as described in "Accounting" on page 689.

A Few More Things...

Once you incorporate ipchains rules on a system, troubleshooting becomes a bit more difficult. Very often, things stop working because you've (perhaps inadvertantly) written a rule that blocks whatever it is that you're trying to do. One of the quickest ways to determine whether or not this is the case is to shut down ipchains and then test again. This will tell you whether or not ipchains is causing the problem. In addition to the troubleshooting tips outlined in Chapter 9, when additionally using ipchains it helps substantially to turn on logging. If you log each rule and isolate the activity to the one thing or set of things you are testing, you will normally be able to quickly figure out where the problem is. Once you have completed troubleshooting the problem, you can remove the logging option on the rules. Be sure to perform your troubleshooting in a way that does not compromise your environment (that is, don't leave the Internet connection wide open) whenever possible.

Using ipchains often incurs other issues. Just because you allow a service for a given destination system with an ipchains rule doesn't mean it will work. Remember, the service must be running on the server, too. See Chapter 8 for a further discussion of network services.

Also, as you add other functionality, don't forget ipchains. For example, if you want to run BGP on your firewall, you will need to allow the BGP sessions through by writing a rule to allow it.

Supplementary Utilities

Other Examples

There are excellent examples of ipchains in the *IPCHAINS HOWTO*, TrinityOS documents, and the *Linux IP Masquerading Mini HOWTO*. These documents are cited in "ipchains Documentation" on page 723 and "Masquerading Documentation" on page 723.

Port Forwarding

There are a variety of tools that provide for the forwarding of connections from the firewall to an internal, privately addressed system. These tools support the forwarding of SMTP, www, ftp, and other services. The two major tools that support this functionality are IPPORTFW for kernel versions 2.0.x and IPMASQADM for kernel versions 2.2.x. These tools are discussed in *Linux IP Masquerading Mini HOWTO* as cited in "Masquerading Documentation" on page 723.

To learn more about IPPORTFW visit

```
http://www.ox.compsoc.org.uk/~steve/portforwarding.html
```

It turns out that IPMASQADM for kernel versions 2.2.x contains a superset of the functionality in IPPORTFW. To learn more about it, visit

```
http://juanjox.kernelnotes.org/
```

The fwconfig GUI

The fwconfig utility provides a graphical user interface (GUI) frontend to writing ipchains rules. Find out more about it at

```
http://www.mindstorm.com/~sparlin/fwconfig.shtml
```

Mason

Mason is available from

```
http://users.dhp.com/~whisper/mason/
```

This is a utility that generates rules dynamically. You set up and run Mason on the system that will be your firewall. Then you execute the allowable network-based commands to, from, and through the firewall to be. Mason dynamically collects the activity and generates rules. In this way, it is both an incredible learning tool and a rapid rule set developer. Think of the typing time you'll save!

It is not a panacea, however. The rule base Mason generates is only as secure as the quite extensively flexible configuration file it uses (/etc/masonrc). It is a tool that can save a lot of time and help you learn about ipchains, but the resulting chains require close inspection, editing, and testing before you go live with them.

Mason is well worth obtaining and using, if for nothing other than the learning experience it will provide.

The Network Mapper (`nmap`)

The Nework Mapper (`nmap`) is a very sophistocated port scanner. It can generate a variety of different types of packets. It can generate all types of normal packets like TCP, UDP, ICMP, `ftp`, and many others. It can also generate fragments and oversized packets. It is a very good utility to use to test your firewall. The bad guys will use it against you, so you should use it first. You can obtain it from

```
http://www.insecure.org/
```

Additional Firewall Software

There are two publicly available proxy-based firewall packages that operate well in conjunction with `ipchains`. They are the Firewall Toolkit (FWTK) and SOCKSv5. Both of these packages offer full-featured proxy services (although they do so in different ways) and user authentication. You can find out more about FWTK at

```
http://www.tis.com/research/software/
```

Also, *Internet Security: A Professional Reference*, cited in "General Firewall References" on page 724, contains configuration details about FWTK. SOCKS can be obtained from

```
http://www.socks5.nec.com/
```

Virtual Private Networks and Encrypted Tunnels

Related to the topic of firewalls is that of encrypted tunnels and/or virtual private networks (VPN). In order to discuss this topic, we briefly introduce some related definitions.

Cryptography is the art, or science, of secret writing. It has been widely used as a way to provide private conversations very early in human history. In the context of modern computing, it is associated with private electronic communications. It may be used to protect files, email, and various types of network connections like `ftp`, `telnet`, and `http`.

An electronic communication or, more generically, a *message* that is not disguised is called *plaintext* or *cleartext*. The process of disguising a message (in other words, making it secret) is known as *encryption* or *encipherment*; this process transforms the cleartext into *ciphertext*. Reversal of the process is called *decryption* or *decipherment.* A cleartext message, therefore, may be encrypted or enciphered into ciphertext; a ciphertext message may then be decrypted or deciphered back into its original cleartext form.[5] An algorithm that implements encryption and decryption is also known as a *cryptographic* algorithm. Such an algorithm is also often called a *cipher.* A *key* is normally a large numeric value (sometimes supplied in the form of a password or passphrase) used in conjunction with a cryptographic algorithm to either encrypt cleartext and/or decrypt ciphertext.

VPNs and encrypted tunnels are conceptually the same. They are mechanisms which encrypt all data between two nodes in an internetwork so that anyone utilizing a network sniffer such as Ethereal will be unable to easily[6] read the data. Generally speaking, the term VPN is applied whenever two firewalls build a session using cryptography. Otherwise, the more general term "encrypted tunnel" tends to be used.

There are a variety of ways to build encrypted tunnels between two nodes. One way is to use the Secure Shell (SSH). SSH is an Application layer replacement for `rsh`, `rlogin`, and `rcp`. This utility is documented in *Linux System Security* as cited in "General Security References" on page 725. A commercial version of SSH is available at

```
http://www.ssh.com/
```

A GPL version of SSH, known as OpenSSH, is available at

```
http://www.openssh.com/
```

The secure socket layer (SSL) is a very common utility used throughout the Internet today. Almost all secure web sessions are implemented using SSL which is built into every modern web browser. Originally developed by Netscape, this Transport layer utility has been modified and standardized by RFC 2246. A publicly available version of SSL, OpenSSL, is available from

```
http://www.openssl.org/
```

Another alternative is Internet Protocol Security (IPsec), standardized by a number of Internet RFCs. It implements encryption at the Internet layer of the TCP/IP stack, which enhances performance and makes it transparent to the

---

5. The International Standards Organization (ISO) 7498-2 specification prefers the terms encipher and decipher over encrypt and decrypt.

6. All encrypted data can be deencrypted given enough time. Ideally, a good cryptographic algorithm in the computing world forces decryption without knowledge of the key to take many, many computer years.

users. The major Linux IPsec implementation project is Linux free secure wide area network (FreeSwan).[7] You can find more information about Linux FreeSwan at

```
http://www.xs4all.nl/~freeswan/index.html
```

As its name implies, the software is free (distributed under the GPL) and may be downloaded from that site. As with many cryptography projects, it is being developed outside of the United States so that it can be available worldwide.

Another ongoing project is Crypto IP Encapsulation (CIPE). This purpose of CIPE is to provide a simple alternative to IPsec. It provides for encrypting connections between IP routers, including Linux. To find out more about CIPE visit

```
http://sites.inka.de/sites/bigred/devel/cipe.html
```

The Next Generation...

The good news is that ipchains is much more flexible and capable than its predecessor, ipfwadm. The other bit of good news is that the follow-on replacement to ipchains provides significant functionality enhancements. The next-generation replacement for ipchains is called netfilter and is implemented via the iptables utility. We discuss this utility in the next chapter.

Summary

In this chapter we took an introductory look at the ipchains utility. We discussed how to configure this packet-filtering software to limit connections through a Linux system connected to two different networks, to set up IP masquerading, and to perform packet accounting. We also noted a variety of other resources which further detail the use of ipchains.

---

7. RSA Data Security, Inc., has a similar commercial project called S/WAN. FreeSwan is also referred to as FreeS/WAN.

For Further Reading

`ipchains` Documentation

The *IPCHAINS-HOWTO*, written by Paul Russell, can be obtained from the LDP. It, together with patches, latest updates, and other details relating to `ipchains`, can be found at one of the three following sites:

```
http://netfilter.filewatcher.org/ipchains/
http://www.samba.org/netfilter/ipchains/
http://netfilter.kernelnotes.org/ipchains/
```

You will also find the TrinityOS resource, written by David A. Ranch, extremely valuable for this and general security-related topics. It can be found at

```
http://www.ecst.csuchico.edu/~dranch/LINUX/index-linux.html
```

Make sure that you read this, too!

Masquerading Documentation

The *Linux IP Masquerade HOWTO*, written by David A. Ranch and Ambrose Au, is available at

```
http://ipmasq.cjb.net/
```

as well as the LDP home site. This document is an absolute *must* read if you are going to use IP masquerading.

ISP Connectivity-Related Resources

You will find HOWTO documents related to ISP connections, cable modems, PPP, DHCP, and DSL at the LDP home site:

```
http://www.linuxdoc.org/
```

We provide a list of many of the pertinent documents below.

```
ADSL (mini HOWTO)
Cable-Modem (mini HOWTO)
DHCP (mini HOWTO)
DHCPcd (mini HOWTO)
ISP-Hookup-HOWTO
ISP-Connectivity (mini HOWTO)
```

General Firewall References

Atkins, Derek, et al., *Internet Security: A Professional Reference*, Indianapolis, Indiana, New Riders Publishing, 1996.

Chapman, D. Brent, and Elizabeth D. Zwicky, *Building Internet Firewalls*, Sebastopol, California, O'Reilly & Associates, Inc., 1995.

Cheswick, William R., and Steven M. Bellovin, *Firewalls and Internet Security Repelling the Wily Hacker*, Reading, Massachusetts, Addison-Wesley Publishing Company, 1994.

Kyas, Othmar, *Internet Security Risk Analysis, Strategies and Firewalls*, London, England, International Thomson Computer Press, 1997.

Siyan, Karanjit, Ph.D., and Chris Hare, *Internet Firewalls and Network Security*, Indianapolis, Indiana, New Riders Publishing, 1995.

DMZ Resources

These two books provide good background and security information related to securing Internet servers:

Garfinkel, Simson, and Gene Spafford, *Web Security & Commerce*, Sebastopol, California, O'Reilly & Associates, Inc., 1997.

Liu, Cricket, et. al., *Managing Internet Information Services*, Sebastopol, California, O'Reilly & Associates, Inc., 1994.

The following Web site contains an instructive how-to document on securely configuring DMZ systems.

```
http://ciac.llnl.gov/ciac/documents/ciac2308.html
```

Cryptography References

Electronic Frontier Foundation, *Cracking DES*, Sebastopol, California, O'Reilly & Associates, Inc., 1998.

Garfinkel, Simson, *PGP: Pretty Good Privacy*, Sebastopol, California, O'Reilly & Associates, Inc., 1995.

Kaufman, Charlie, Radia Perlman, and Mike Speciner, *Network Security: Private Communication in a Public World*, Englewood Cliffs, New Jersey, Prentice Hall, 1995.

Schneier, Bruce, *Applied Cryptography*, 2nd., New York, New York, John Wiley and Sons, 1996.

General Security References

Garfinkel, Simson, and Gene Spafford, *Practical UNIX and Internet Security*, 2nd ed., Sebastopol, California, O'Reilly & Associates, Inc., 1996.
Mann, Scott, and Ellen L. Mitchell, *Linux System Security: The Administrator's Guide to Open Source Security Tools*, Upper Saddle River, New Jersey, Prentice Hall, 2000.

15

Netfilter: Address Translation, IP Accounting, and Firewalls

In the last chapter, we described the kernel filtering utility, ipchains, for kernel versions 2.0.34 through 2.2.x. In this chapter, we look at netfilter, as implemented by the iptables utility, which replaces ipchains in kernel versions 2.3.x and later. Collectively, the kernel modules and commands that implement kernel filtering in these latest kernel versions is called netfilter. The command line utility is iptables.

As of this writing, the latest version of iptables is 1.1.1. While this version of iptables is relatively stable, the kernel versions it requires (namely, 2.3.x or later) are still in the development/testing stages and, consequently, changes are likely to occur that will affect the behavior of iptables. Bear this in mind as you read through this chapter and be sure to review the latest available documentation as cited in "For Further Reading" on page 754 before implementing iptables.

Netfilter Overview

In short, where ipchains implements three predefined chains, input, output, and forward, netfilter adds a layer of abstraction by introducing *tables* that incorporate chains. There are three tables within netfilter: filter (the default), nat, and mangle. Each of these tables contains a set of predefined chains. With the iptables utility, all chains are referred to in uppercase, unlike ipchains which uses lowercase. Each table is discussed in its own section.

In addition to the use of tables, netfilter introduces a number of other capabilities. Included are simple stateful packet filtering, port forwarding, packet filtering based on TCP flags, filtering based on incoming MAC addresses, filtering outbound packets based on user ID, much greater logging flexibility over `ipchains`, and some modest anti-denial of service (-DoS) features. Also, the netfilter package provides a number of hooks of expansion of its capabilites (see *Netfilter Hacking HOWTO*). On the downside, netfilter uses a different mechanism for NAT and, as of this writing, only the module for FTP (`ip_masq_ftp.o` for `ipchains` is now `ip_conntrack_ftp.o` for netfilter) has been rewritten for `iptables`. We examine these capabilities at various points in this chapter.

It turns out that if you have got an existing set of `ipchains` rules or the older `ipfwadm` rules, you can use those with netfilter. We discuss this capability in "Using Existing `ipchains` Rules" on page 754.

The `filter` Table

The `filter` table consists of the three built-in chains, INPUT, FORWARD, and OUTPUT. You can think of the `filter` table as being quite similar to `ipchains` altogether—however, there are some significant processing differences, as depicted in Figure 15–1. Netfilter uses the `filter` table's INPUT chain for pro-

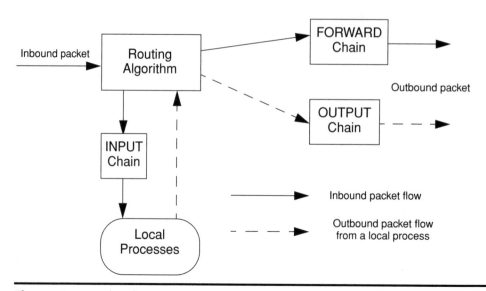

Figure 15–1   Flowchart of Chains within the `filter` Table

cessing locally destined packets only; it uses the OUTPUT chain for processing locally generated packets only; and it uses the FORWARD chain to process all packets that pass through the system.

In Figure 15–1, we see that the processing of packets by the chains in the filter table is simplified over that of ipchains. All inbound packets (solid lines in the diagram) are processed by the routing algorithm. If a packet is destined to a local process on the system, then it is filtered by the INPUT chain before being passed to that process. If, on the other hand, an inbound packet is destined to another system, then the packet will be processed by the FORWARD chain prior to departure. Finally, if a packet is generated locally and is destined to another system (dashed lines in the diagram) then, after the routing decision is made, it is filtered by the OUTPUT chain. As with ipchains (see Figure 14–1 on page 663), CRC and sanity checks are performed at each stage of processing (although not depicted in Figure 15–1).

The nat Table

The nat table also consists of three built-in chains. These chains are: PREROUTING, OUTPUT, and POSTROUTING. The nat table replaces the MASQ target in ipchains and provides substantial enhancements over the simple many-to-one IP address translation supported by ipchains. With the nat table, not only is masquerading supported, but also the more general form of network address translation (NAT), that is, translating both outbound and inbound IP addresses, is supported. This means, in particular, that internal systems can have an external presence using a registered IP address. The PREROUTING chain is used to translate addresses as soon as a packet arrives. The OUTPUT chain is used to translate addresses on packets generated locally before routing occurs. The POSTROUTING chain is used to translate addresses before they leave the system.

Figure 15–2 depicts the flow of events with respect to the nat table. We look at the interaction between the different tables in "Netfilter Flowchart" on page 731.

As with the filter table, the OUTPUT chain is only invoked when packets are generated by a local process. Inbound packets (solid lines in the diagram) are processed by the PREROUTING chain before the routing algorithm is invoked. In this way, address translation can take place before routing decisions are made. If the packet is destined to a local process, it is passed to that process (the packet will be

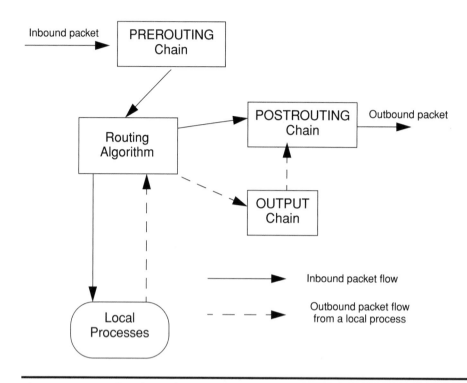

Figure 15–2   Flowchart of Chains within the `nat` Table

processed by the INPUT chain of the `filter` table first, however). If the packet is to be forwarded or it is outbound from a local process, it is filtered by the POSTROUTING chain which will apply any necessary address translation. Notice that all address translation occurs separately from filtration by other chains.

The `mangle` Table

The `mangle` table consists of two built-in chains. These are: PREROUTING and OUTPUT. The PREROUTING chain affects incoming packets before routing and the OUTPUT chain applies to locally generated packets before routing. The purpose of this table is for specialized packet alteration such as TOS bit manipulation. We consider a flowchart of the `mangle` table chains in conjunction with the others in the next section.

Netfilter Flowchart

Each of the chains described previously constitute all of the permanent chains. Each table can utilize the chains identified in the foregoing sections and, as we see in "The `iptables` Utility" on page 732, the `-t` option to the `iptables` utility specifies to which table a particular rule belongs. If no `-t` flag is used, then the default `filter` table is assumed. Rule ordering within a given chain still behaves as described in the previous chapter. The chains described for each table are distinct. Even though some of the chain names are the same across tables, each table has its own set of chains. Thus, a complete list of chains is

```
filter/INPUT, filter/FORWARD, filter/OUTPUT
nat/PREROUTING, nat/OUTPUT, nat/POSTROUTING
mangle/PREROUTING, mangle/OUTPUT
```

Figure 15–3 depicts the interaction of all eight chains. In two cases (OUTPUT and PREROUTING), more than one table uses the same chain name. In the dia-

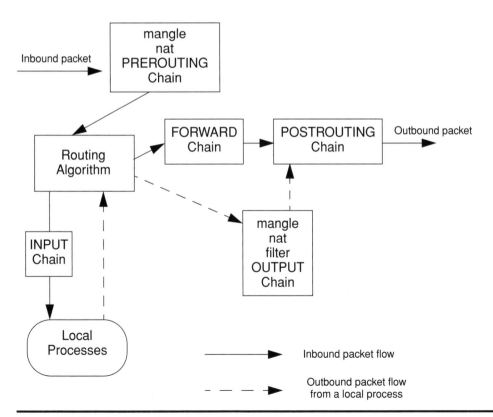

Figure 15–3   Netfilter Flowchart: Chains within All Tables

gram these tables are listed in the order that they are executed. For example, the order of processing for the OUTPUT chains is mangle/OUTPUT, nat/OUTPUT, and then filter/OUTPUT. Once again, although not shown, CRC and sanity checking is performed prior to the processing of each chain and by the routing algorithm. Perhaps the most significant difference between ipchains and netfilter, with respect to the flow of processing, is that packets that are routed through the firewall, and therefore processed by the FORWARD chains, do not have the source IP address translated until the very end. This means in particular that the rules written for the filter/FORWARD chain will use the actual IP addresses and/or port numbers involved as opposed to utilizing the masqueraded addresses (as described in Chapter 14). This certainly makes rule writing, reading, and understanding much more straightforward. Furthermore, by separating out the address translation function into the distinct chains, PREROUTING and POSTROUTING, NAT rule management becomes much easier.

Also, it should be apparent in comparing this diagram to that given in Figure 14–1 on page 663 that the processing is simplified in terms of which chain does what. Whereas with ipchains, the input and output chains are each invoked for every packet passing through a given interface, the INPUT and OUTPUT chains of netfilter are only invoked when destined to or generated by, respectively, a local process. This implementation simplifies rule writing substantially. It also reduces processing overhead.

We should point out here that as with ipchains, the predefined chains, INPUT, OUTPUT, and FORWARD, can invoke custom chains. The PREROUTING and POSTROUTING chains do not support custom chains.

The iptables Utility

The iptables command is quite similar in form to the ipchains command. It uses flags, options, and actions. Unlike ipchains, however, iptables also can use extentions to certain options. All rules introduced by the iptables command applies to a specific table (the filter table, if not specified). The general syntax of iptables is

```
iptables [-flags] [chain] [options [extentions] ] [ACTION]
```

Which flags are used determines which of chain, options, and ACTION can be or must be used. Certain options also have extentions. We describe the flags, options, extentions, and actions in the tables below. Then we consider some examples.

Flags or Commands of iptables

The available flags to iptables are given in Table 15–1. While many are the same as those for ipchains, there are some new flags like -t, which is used to indicate the table. There are also some flags that are no longer available, such as -l for logging, which has been replaced by the LOG action (described in Table 15–5 on page 744).

Table 15–1   Flags of iptables

FLAG	DESCRIPTION
-t *table*	Specifies the *table* to which the rule applies. *table* can be one of filter, nat, or mangle. filter is the default.
-A or --append	Appends one or more rules to the specified chain.
-D or --delete	Deletes one or more rules from the specified chain.
-F or --flush	Flushes all the rules in the specified chain.
-I or --insert	Inserts one or more rules in the specified chain at the specified rule number.
-L or --list	Lists all the rules in the selected chain. If no chain is specified, then all rules in all chains are listed.
-N or --new-chain	Creates a new custom chain. The name of the new chain cannot exceed 31 characters. Custom chains work identically to ipchains.
-P or --policy	Specifies the policy, or default rule, for a permanent chain. Policies cannot be specified for custom chains. This is the last rule in the chain, even though it appears first when listed with -L. This option only allows for either the ACCEPT or DROP action to be specified.
-R or --replace	Replaces a rule in the specified chain.

Table 15–1   Flags of `iptables` *(Continued)*

FLAG	DESCRIPTION
`-X` or `--delete-chain`	Deletes the specified custom chain. There must be no rules that reference the chain you wish to delete. If you do not specify a chain, all custom chains will be deleted. Permanent chains cannot be deleted.
`-Z` or `--zero`	Zeroes out the packet and byte counters. You may use this flag in conjunction with `-L`, which will have the effect of displaying the current accounting information and then resetting the counters to 0.
`-E` or `--rename-chain`	Used to rename a custom chain. Cannot be applied to one of the built-in chains. Has no effect on the contents of the chain being renamed.

Options to `iptables`

While most of the options to `iptables` are much the same as they were for `ipchains`, key functionality, such as port number specification and the SYN flag (formerly `-y`), is now specified through extentions as described in "`iptables` Extensions" on page 738. Also, the important `-l` option for logging is now a separate action described in "`iptables` Actions" on page 744. Table 15–2 describes the available options to `iptables`.

Table 15–2   Options to `iptables`

OPTION	DESCRIPTION
`-d [!] address[/mask]` `[!]` `--destination` may be used instead of `-d`	Specifies the destination IP address, `address`, for this rule. It may be an IP address, an IP network number, a resolvable hostname, or a resolvable network name (in `/etc/networks` or `/etc/hosts`). Specifies the `mask` argument for network addresses. It may be either the actual netmask or the prefix (number of leftmost bits set to 1 in the mask). So, setting `mask` to `20` would be the same as setting it to `255.255.240.0`. The optional `!` is the logical NOT operator and reverses the meaning. The address, `0.0.0.0/0` means any IP address. You may also use `0/0`. Unlike `ipchains`, port numbers cannot be specified here. See Table 15–4 on page 740 for port number specifications.
`[!]  -f` or `--fragment`	Specifies that the rule refers to fragments of a packet (see "Fragmentation and Path MTU Discovery" on page 96 for a discussion of IP fragmentation). Such packets will not contain port numbers or ICMP types. The `!` reverses the meaning.
`-h` `-j ACTION -h` `-m extended_match -h` `-p protocol -h`	Help. Using `iptables -h` outputs a general help message and listing of flags and options. Using one of the other two forms with the `-p`, `-j`, or `-m` flag provides help specific to the indicated ACTION, extended_match, or protocol, all of which are described below.

Table 15–2   Options to `iptables` *(Continued)*

Option	Description
`-i [!]` *name* `--in-interface` may be used instead of `-i`	Specifies the inbound interface to which this rule applies—that is, the interface on which packets arrive. This option is only meaningful for the INPUT, PREROUTING, and FORWARD chains. If this option is omitted, then the rule applies to *all* interfaces. The argument *name* must be the name of the interface, such as `eth0`, `eth1`, `ppp0`, etc. You may use the wildcard + to match all interfaces or those beginning with the specified name; for example, `eth+` will match all interfaces beginning with `eth`, like `eth0`, `eth1`, etc. If ! precedes *name*, then the rule does not apply to that interface but does apply to all other interfaces. Note that the loopback interface must be specified as `lo`.
`-o [!]` *name* `--out-interface` may be used instead of `-o`	Specifies the outbound interface to which this rule applies—that is, the interface through which packets leave. This option is only meaningful for the OUTPUT, POSTROUTING, and FORWARD chains. The values for *name* are as described for `-i` above.
`-j` *target* `--jump` may be used instead of `-j`	Specifies the *target* or action of the rule, which may be one of the actions described in Table 15–5 on page 744 or the name of a custom chain. If a custom chain, then it cannot be the same as the current custom chain. If this option is not specified, then no action is taken when this rule is matched, but the packet and byte counters will be incremented.

Table 15–2   Options to `iptables` *(Continued)*

OPTION	DESCRIPTION
`-n` or `--numeric`	When listing rules, this option suppresses name translation. Ordinarily, `iptables` will attempt to convert IP addresses to hostnames, port numbers to service names, etc.
`-p [!] protocol` `--protocol` may be used instead of `-p`	Specifies the protocol for the rule, which may be any name or number listed in `/etc/protocols`, such as `tcp`, `udp`, or `icmp`. The keyword `all`, meaning all protocols, may also be used. It is the default. A preceding `!` reverses the meaning. This option has extensions depending on the protocol specified as described in "`iptables` Extensions" on page 738.
`-s [!] address[/mask]` `--source` may be used instead of `-s`	Identical to `-d` except that this is the source address. Unlike `ipchains`, port numbers cannot be specified here. See Table 15–4 on page 740 for port number specifications.
`-v` or `--verbose`	When listing rules, this option adds additional information including, but not limited to, the interface address, rule options, and packet and byte counters.
`-x` or `--exact`	Displays the exact packet and byte counts. Ordinarily, `ipchains` rounds to the nearest 1,000 (K), 1,000,000 (M), or multiples of 1,000 M (G).
`--line-numbers`	Lists the the number of each rule. Must be used with `-L`.
`-m match_extension`	Specifies the `match_extension`, which may be one of `mac`, `limit`, `mark`, `owner`, `state`, `unclean`, or `tos`. These extentions are described in "`iptables` Extensions" on page 738.

`iptables` Extensions

There are two basic types of extensions that have been implemented in `iptables`. Both types are known generally as *match extensions*. Match extensions are used to further refine the matching of a packet to a rule. The primary reason for separating these extensions from options is that each extension described here is invoked through a kernel module. This gives rise to the ability to extend netfilter even further with new kernel modules. See the *Netfilter Hacking HOWTO* for further details.

The first type of extension is based on protocol (called *protocol match extensions*), and the second type uses the `-m` option (called match extensions). Each match extension (protocol or otherwise) actually invokes a module for processing. The protocol-related extension matching parameters are similar to some of the options previously described for `ipchains`. With `iptables`, these pattern-matching extensions have been expanded and are specifically associated with certain protocols. The affected protocols are TCP, UDP, and ICMP. Table 15–3 lists and describes the protocol extensions. The `-p protocol` shown in the left-most column must be specified in order for the indicated match extension to be used. In essence, `-p protocol` loads the extension module. The other extensions require the `-m` invocation.

Table 15–3   `iptables` Protocol Match Extensions

PROTOCOL SPECIFICATION	MATCH EXTENSION	DESCRIPTION
`-p tcp`	`--sport [!] [port[:port]]` `--source-port` may be used instead of `--sport`	Specifies the source port or port range. Either the service name (defined in `/etc/services`) or port number can be used. Ranges of ports are specified by `port:port`. If the leading value is absent, it defaults to 0—for example, `:1023` is equivalent to `0:1023`. If the trailing value is absent, it defaults to 65535. Whenever two values are used the range is always determined as lower value through and including higher value, regardless of order presented. Using `! port` or `! port:port` means all ports except those listed.

Table 15–3   `iptables` Protocol Match Extensions *(Continued)*

PROTOCOL SPECIFICATION	MATCH EXTENSION	DESCRIPTION

	`--dport [!]`
	`[port[:port]]`
	`--destination-`
	`port` may be used
	instead of `--dport`
		As above, except that this option specifies the destination port.

	`--tcp-flags [!]` `mask comp`	This option specifies the TCP flags to be examined. The `mask` argument is a comma-separated list of which TCP flags to check. The `comp` argument is a comma-separated list of TCP flags that are set. Possible flags are: SYN, ACK, FIN, RST, URG, PSH, ALL, and NONE. For example, `--tcp-flags ACK,FIN,RST RST` will only match TCP packets that have the RST bit set and the ACK and FIN bits unset. Using `!` matches any packet that does not have the bits set as indicated.
	`[!] --syn`	This option replaces the `-y` option to `ipchains`. It is equivilent to `--tcp-flags SYN,RST,ACK SYN` Using `!` inverts this meaning.
	`--tcp-option [!]` `number`	This matches if the indicated TCP option is set. TCP options are described in Chapter 7. Again, `!` inverts the meaning.

`-p udp`	`--sport [!]`
	`[port[:port]]`
	`--source-port`
	may be used instead
	of `--sport`
		Identical to `--sport` as specified with `-p tcp` and described above.

Table 15–3   `iptables` Protocol Match Extensions *(Continued)*

Protocol Specification	Match Extension	Description
	`--dport [!]` `[port[:port]]` `--destination-port` may be used instead of `--dport`	Identical to `--dport` as specified with `-p` `tcp` and described above.
`-p icmp`	`--icmp-type [!]` `type[/code]`	Specifies the ICMP type and code to match (see Chapter 4 for a discussion of ICMP types and codes). `type` can be a name as listed by `iptables -p icmp -h` or it can be a numeric type and code (`type/code`) for example 3/1.

The available match extensions to the `-m` flag are listed in Table 15–4. The `-m` `match_extension` shown in the leftmost column must be specified in order to use the options indicated in the middle column.

Table 15–4   `iptables` Match Extensions

Match Extension	Options	Description
`-m mac`	`--mac-source [!] addr`	This match extension module is used to match incoming MAC addresses and therefore can only be used in either PREROUTING or INPUT chains. The value of `addr` is a 48-bit MAC address in colon-separated hex notation. For example, `-m mac` `--mac-source 00:A0:CC:63:DE:EE`.

Table 15–4   `iptables` Match Extensions *(Continued)*

MATCH EXTENSION	OPTIONS	DESCRIPTION
`-m limit`		This module can be used to limit the number of matches for a specific rule. It is designed to assist in preventing denial of service (DoS) attacks and minimizing log entries. With no options, it limits matches to 3 per hour with a burst rate of 5. For example, `iptables -A FORWARD -p tcp --syn -m limit -j LOG`, permits 1 match every 20 minutes (3 per hour) with a burst of 5 matches maximum.
	`--limit rate`	Sets the rate of matches. `rate` is in the form `number/s, number/m, number/h,` or `number/d`, where number is a positive integer greater than 0, and `s, m, h,` and `d` stand for `seconds, minutes, hours,` and `days,` respectively, and each of which may be spelled out. For example, `iptables -A FORWARD -p tcp --syn -m limit --limit-rate 1/s -j ACCEPT` limits the rate of TCP connection requests forwarded to 1 match per second. Default is `3/h.`
	`--limit-burst number`	Sets the burst rate after which the limit is applied. Default is 5.

Table 15–4 `iptables` Match Extensions *(Continued)*

MATCH EXTENSION	OPTIONS	DESCRIPTION
`-m multiport`	`--source-port` `port[,port[,...]]`	This extension module matches the listed ports. The `--source-port` option indicates source ports. Ports may be specified as numbers or service names. Up to 15 can be listed.
	`--destination-port` `port[,port[,...]]`	As above except for destination ports.
`-m mark`	`--mark value[/mask]`	Used to match a mark value as set by the MARK action described in Table 15–5.
`-m state`	`--state state`	Used to match the state of a connection when the `ip_conntrack.o` module is in use. The module tracks TCP and UDP connections. The value of `state` is a comma-separated list of any INVALID (packet not associated with any known connections), ESTABLISHED (packet is associated with a known connection), NEW (packet is starting a new connection), and/or RELATED (packet is starting a new connection in association with an existing one such as an FTP data transfer or an ICMP message).
`-m unclean`		This is an experimental module that takes no options. It attempts to match unusual packets such as a packet with the TCP flags FIN, URG, and PSH set.

Table 15–4   `iptables` Match Extensions *(Continued)*

MATCH EXTENSION	OPTIONS	DESCRIPTION
`-m tos`	`--tos` *tos*	This matches the 8-bit TOS field (which can be set with the TOS action as described in Table 15–5). The value of *tos* can be one of the strings displayed by `iptables -m tos -h` or its numeric equivalent.
`-m owner`	`--uid-owner` *userid*	This module is used to match packets created by the identified owner option. It is only valid for the OUTPUT chain and there are packets (like ICMP) that have no owner. The `--uid-owner` option specifies that the packet must be created by a process owned by the indicated *userid* in order to match.
	`--gid-owner` *gid*	Specifies that the packet matches if the *gid* owns the process which created the packet.
	`--pid-owner` *pid*	Specifies that the packet matches if the *pid* matches the process which created the packet.
	`--sid-owner` *sessionid*	Specifies that the packet matches if the session group *sessionid* matches a process belonging to that group and which created the packet.

`iptables` Actions

Table 15–5 lists and describes the actions or targets to `iptables`. These are the keywords that follow the `-j` flag to `iptables`.

Table 15–5   Actions for `iptables`

Action	Description
`ACCEPT`	Allows the packet through.
`DROP`	Drops the packet without generating an ICMP message back to the originator of the packet.
`REJECT [--reject-with` *option*`]`	Same as `DROP`, except that an ICMP message is sent to the originator. This action is only valid in the `INPUT`, `OUTPUT`, and `FORWARD` chains. By default, an `icmp-port-unreachable` ICMP error message is sent. If `--reject-with` is used, then *option* can be one of `icmp-net-unreachable`, `icmp-host-unreachable`, `icmp-port-unreachable`, `icmp-proto-unreachable`, `icmp-net-prohibited`, `tcp-reset`, or `icmp-host-prohibited`. The use of tcp-reset is limited to TCP packets and causes a TCP packet to be sent with the RST bit set. If the rule matches an ICMP packet, then `REJECT` behaves like `DROP` and no ICMP message will be sent.

Table 15–5   Actions for `iptables` *(Continued)*

ACTION	DESCRIPTION
`MASQUERADE [--to-ports port[-port]]`	Only valid in the `nat/POSTROUTING` chain. This action should only be used if the masquerade address is assigned dynamically by DHCP or similar. If static address(es) are used, then `SNAT` should be used instead. This action translates the source address to the one associated with the interface out of which the packet is sent. Use of this action causes all connections to be forgotten whenever the interface goes down. This is proper since the use of dynamically assigned addresses implies no guarantees that the address will be the same when the interface comes back up. By default, `iptables` attempts to maintain source ports, but if necessary, it will translate source ports below 512 to other ports below 512; between 512 and 1023 to other ports in that range; and ports above 1023 to other ports above 1023. This behavior can be overridden by the use of `--to-ports`. The `port` or `port-port` range specified become the ports used when translating. These port translations only occur when the rule incorporates either `-p tcp` or `-p udp`.
`REDIRECT [--to-ports port[-port]]`	Only valid in the `nat/PREROUTING` and `nat/OUTPUT` chains. This action automatically redirects the packet to the local machine (`127.0.0.1`). If the `--to-ports` option is used, then the destination port number is translated to the `port` or one of the ports in the `port-port` range.
`RETURN`	If this action is in a custom chain, then the packet is sent to the next rule in the calling chain. If this action is in a permanent chain, then the action in the permanent chain's policy is applied.

Table 15–5   Actions for `iptables` *(Continued)*

ACTION	DESCRIPTION
`QUEUE`	This action is used to send matching packets up to an application. It requires the `ip_queue` module. If there is no application waiting to process the packet, then it is dropped. See *Netfilter Hacking HOWTO* for tips on writing applications for this purpose.
`LOG [--log-level level]` `[--log-prefix string]` `--log-tcp-sequence` `--log-tcp-options` `--log-ip-options`	This action captures the matching packet and logs it to facility `kern` via `syslogd` (or `klogd`, if that is running). The `--log-level` option is used to specify the `level` (see `syslog.conf(5)`). The `--log-prefix` option causes the `string` (up to 30 characters) to be prefixed to what is written to the log. The `--log-tcp-sequence` option additionally captures TCP sequence numbers (this is a big security risk if someone has access to the log file); `--log-tcp-option` additionally logs TCP options; and `--log-ip-options` additionally logs IP options.
`TOS [--set-tos tos]`	Only valid in the `mangle` table. This action sets the TOS field in the IP header to the `tos` value specified by `--set-tos`. The `tos` value can be either a numeric or character value given by `iptables -j TOS -h`.
`DNAT --to-destination ipaddr[-ipaddr][:port-port]`	Only valid in `nat`/`PREROUTING` and `nat`/`OUTPUT`. It specifies that the matching packet's (and all future packets in this connection) destination IP address is to be translated to `ipaddr`. Optionally, a range of addresses can be specified with `ipaddr-ipaddr`. If `:port-port` is used, then the destination port number will be translated accordingly for `-p tcp` and `-p udp` matches; otherwise, the destination port number is never changed.

Table 15–5   Actions for `iptables` *(Continued)*

ACTION	DESCRIPTION

`SNAT --to-source`
`ipaddr[-ipaddr][:port-`
`port]`
	Only valid in `nat/POSTROUTING`. This action specifies that the source IP address is to be changed to `ipaddr`. A range can be specified with `ipaddr-ipaddr`. The default behavior of the source port used is as described for the `MASQUERADE` action. The use of `:port-port` overrides the default behavior.

`MIRROR`	This experimental testing option inverts the source and destination IP addresses of the matching packet and retransmits the packet. It is only valid in the `INPUT`, `FORWARD`, and `OUTPUT` chains.
`MARK [--set-mark mark]`	Only valid in the `mangle` table. This action sets the `mark` value of the packet to `mark`. We examine the usefulness of this option in Chapter 16.
`custom_chain`	The named custom chain is invoked.

As with `ipchains`, if no action is specified, then the rule only acts to provide accounting information.

`iptables` Examples

Rule writing with `iptables` is quite similar to that of `ipchains`. The major difference is with respect to the fact that `iptables` implements eight distinct chains instead of three and that, as described previously, the processing of the chains is done at different points throughout the overall flow of events. In this section, we take a look at a variety of examples that highlight the differences and additional capabilities of `iptables`.

Chain Policies

Default rules or policies are handled the same way for `iptables` as for `ipchains`. The major difference is that there are eight distinct tables in netfilter for which a policy can be set. As with `ipchains`, the default policy is ACCEPT. The alternative is DROP—no other action can be set as a policy.

The policy that you set for a given table/chain depends entirely on its use. Whereas with `ipchains`, it was a good idea to set the policy for all three chains to DROP, that is not necessarily true for `iptables`. With `iptables`, the most important chain to set a default rule of DROP is the `filter/FORWARD` chain, since it behaves much like the `forward` chain for `ipchains`. The `filter/FORWARD` chain is the one that is used to filter all packets passing through the system (that is, being routed). The `filter/INPUT` chain is also a likely candidate for a default policy of DROP since this chain is used to filter packets arriving at the firewall system itself. The remaining chains' default rule is based upon use. For example, if your security policy limits outbound use, then the `filter/OUTPUT` chain would require a default policy of DROP.

Example 15–1 shows the setting of the default policy for the `filter/FOR-WARD` and `filter/INPUT` chains to DROP.

Example 15–1   Setting the Default Rule to DROP

```
iptables -P FORWARD -j DROP
iptables -P INPUT -j DROP
```

Some Basic Rules

Let's consider a simple scenario in which we want to allow `ftp` from an internal network to an external network through a system with `iptables` configured. Figure 15–4 depicts the environment. We also want to allow `ftp` access from `topcat` to the outside network. We allow nothing else out and nothing at all from the external network to the internal network. Except for outbound `ftp`,

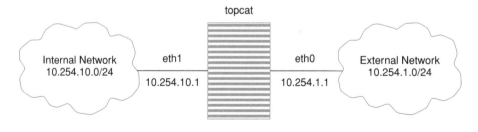

Figure 15–4   Simple `iptables` Example

nothing is allowed to or from `topcat` and the internal network. For purposes of this example, we do not consider NAT. Arguably, this is an unrealistic example, but we'll fix that a little later on.

Given our goals, consider the way that `iptables` works. In order to allow `ftp` out from the internal network, we must set the appropriate rules in the `filter/` `FORWARD` chain. We must also allow the return packets to pass through that chain. To allow `ftp` to/from `topcat`, we need to configure the `filter/INPUT` and `filter/OUTPUT` chains appropriately. Example 15–2 lists the necessary rules. The line numbers are for clarity.

Example 15–2   Sample `ftp` Rules

```
1 iptables -P FORWARD -j DROP
2 iptables -P INPUT -j DROP
3 iptables -P OUTPUT -j DROP
4 iptables -A FORWARD -s 10.254.10.0/24 -d 0/0 -m multiport -p tcp --dport
  ftp,ftp-data -j ACCEPT
5 iptables -A FORWARD -s 0/0 -d 10.254.10.0/24 -p tcp --sport ftp-data -j
  ACCEPT
6 iptables -A FORWARD -s 0/0 -d 10.254.10.0/24 -p tcp --sport ftp ! --syn -
  j ACCEPT
7 iptables -A FORWARD -j LOG --log-prefix "iptables FORWARD: "
8 iptables -A OUTPUT -o eth0 -s 10.254.1.1 -d 0/0 -m multiport -p tcp --
  dport ftp,ftp-data -j ACCEPT
9 iptables -A OUTPUT -j LOG --log-prefix "iptables OUTPUT: "
10 iptables -A INPUT -i eth0 -s 0/0 -d 10.254.1.1 -p tcp --sport ftp-data -j
  ACCEPT
11 iptables -A INPUT -i eth0 -s 0/0 -d 10.254.1.1 -p tcp --sport ftp ! --syn
  -j ACCEPT
12 iptables -A INPUT -j LOG --log-prefix "iptables INPUT: "
```

Each of the rules listed here can be executed individually from the command line or put into a script. Lines 1 through 3 set the policy to DROP on the three `filter` table chains. Lines 4 through 7 are the `filter/FORWARD` rules which deal with packets that are forwarded by `topcat`. Line 4 allows any packet from the internal network to anywhere else as long as the destination port is either `ftp` or `ftp-data`. Line 5 permits `ftp-data` connections through to the internal network. Line 6 allows `ftp` communications back through to the internal network as long as they are not attempts to initiate a connection. Line 7 logs everything else that passes through the `filter/FORWARD` chain. This latter logging rule is likely to capture an excessive amount of information, so we'll use limits in the next section.

Lines 8 through 12 list the `filter/OUTPUT` and `filter/INPUT` rules. These rules are effectively the same as those in the `filter/FORWARD` chain except that they apply to packets generated by a local process on `topcat` that are headed outbound (`filter/OUTPUT`) and packets destined to `topcat` (`filter/INPUT`). Note that the rules specify `eth0` as the interface, which has the effect of only allowing `ftp` to the external network. Nothing is allowed in to `topcat`, except `ftp` return packets, and nothing is allowed out from `topcat` to the internal network.

Example 15–2 approaches rule writing in the same way that `ipchains` would have worked. In the next section, we'll take a look at connection tracking to minimize rules and improve overall security.

Connection Tracking

We can actually simplify the `filter/FORWARD` rules given in Example 15–2 by using connection tracking. Example 15–3 illustrates. Once again, line numbers are for clarity.

Example 15–3   Sample `ftp` Rules with Connection Tracking

```
1 modprobe ip_conntrack
2 modprobe ip_conntrack_ftp
3 iptables -P FORWARD -j DROP
4 iptables -P INPUT -j DROP
5 iptables -P OUTPUT -j DROP
6 iptables -A FORWARD -m state --state ESTABLISHED,RELATED -j ACCEPT
7 iptables -A FORWARD -m state --state NEW -s 10.254.10.0/24 -d 0/0 -p tcp -
  -dport ftp -j ACCEPT
8 iptables -A FORWARD -m limit -j LOG --log-prefix "iptables FORWARD: "
9 iptables -A OUTPUT -o eth0 -s 10.254.1.1 -d 0/0 -m state --state ESTAB-
  LISHED,RELATED -j ACCEPT
10 iptables -A OUTPUT -m state --state NEW -o eth0 -s 10.254.1.1 -d 0/0 -p
   tcp --dport ftp -j ACCEPT
11 iptables -A OUTPUT -m limit -j LOG --log-prefix "iptables OUTPUT: "
12 iptables -A INPUT -i eth0 -s 0/0 -d 10.254.1.1 -m state --state ESTAB-
   LISHED,RELATED -j ACCEPT
13 iptables -A INPUT -m limit -j LOG --log-prefix "iptables INPUT: "
```

The big difference here compared to Example 15–2 is that the `state` match extension is used. Because the RELATED keyword in the rules using `-m state` handles the return `ftp-data` connections, there is no need for specific rules allowing return packets with a source port of `ftp-data`. Notice that lines 1 and 2 cause the `ip_conntrack` and `ip_conntrack_ftp` modules to be loaded into the kernel. These modules are necessary for the use of the `state` match extension. Lines 3 through 5 set the policy for the `filter` table chains to DROP, as before.

The `filter/FORWARD` chain has been reduced from four rules to three. Line 6 is the rule that allows all existing packets associated with an existing connection through due to the ESTABLISHED keyword. The RELATED keyword permits all related communications, including ICMP and `ftp-data` packets. Line 7 specifies that the only allowed outbound connection is `ftp`. Line 6 appears before line 7 because fewer packets will match the latter rule. While the reduction in the number of rules from four to three is not terribly significant here, there would be a substantial amount of saving in a case where many types of connections were allowed. For instance if you wanted to allow `ftp`, WWW, and `telnet` access, the rule at line 7 could be simply changed to

```
iptables -A FORWARD -m state --state NEW -m multiport -s
10.254.10.0/24 -d 0/0 -p tcp --dport ftp,www,telnet -j ACCEPT
```

in order to accommodate the other ports.

The `filter/OUTPUT` and `filter/INPUT` chains in Example 15–3 are similiar to what we've already described. Note that all of the logging rules utilize the `-m limit` match extension. This causes the logging of packets to be reduced as described in "iptables Actions" on page 744. It has the effect of reducing the log size and mitigating denial of service attacks designed to overfill the log files.

As with the previous example, all of the rules and commands in this example can be executed manually at the command line or put into a script.

NAT Rules

Now, let's look at a more realistic example. Consider Figure 15–5. Suppose that `topcat` has the Internet address `199.2.8.17/28` associated with `eth1` and, further, that the entire range of addresses `199.2.8.18` through and including `199.2.8.29` are available. We'll assume that these addresses were assigned by an ISP and that the router within the ISP to which `topcat` connects is `199.2.8.30`.

In this example, there is a public WWW server and an FTP server. These servers are accessible via the addresses `199.2.8.18` and `199.2.8.19`, respectively, from the Internet for the sole purpose of WWW and FTP. So our `iptables` rules

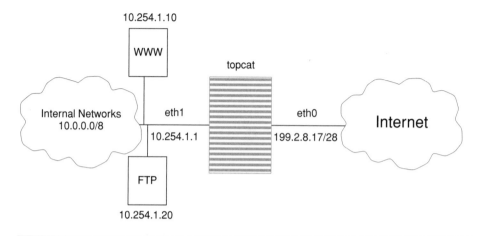

Figure 15–5 More Realistic `iptables` Example

will need to incorporate NAT for that purpose. Additionally, suppose that the security policy permits all nodes in the internal network to access the Internet. No access to internal systems from the Internet is permitted except for return connections and access to the WWW and FTP servers. Allowing the internal systems to connect to the Internet requires NAT rules as well. For this example, we'll leave out the logging rules.

Example 15–4 shows the rules that could be used to set up topcat for this example. Again, the line numbers are for clarity.

Example 15–4 Using NAT

```
 1 modprobe iptable_nat
 2 modprobe ip_nat_ftp
 3 modprobe ip_conntrack
 4 modprobe ip_conntrack ftp
 5 iptables -P INPUT -j DROP
 6 iptables -P FORWARD -j DROP
 7 iptables -P OUTPUT -j DROP
 8 iptables -t nat -A PREROUTING -d 199.2.8.18 -j DNAT --to-destination
   10.254.1.10
 9 iptables -t nat -A PREROUTING -d 199.2.8.19 -j DNAT --to-destination
   10.254.1.20
10 iptables -t nat -A POSTROUTING -s 10.254.1.10 -j SNAT --to-source
   199.2.8.18
11 iptables -t nat -A POSTROUTING -s 10.254.1.20 -j SNAT --to-source
   199.2.8.19
12 iptables -t nat -A POSTROUTING -s 10.0.0.0/8 -j SNAT
13 iptables -A FORWARD -m state --state ESTABLISHED,RELATED -j ACCEPT
14 iptables -A FORWARD -s 10.0.0.0/8 -d 0/0 -m state --state NEW -j ACCEPT
```

Example 15–4 Using NAT *(Continued)*

```
15 iptables -A FORWARD -s 0/0 -d 10.254.1.10 -m state --state NEW,ESTAB-
   LISHED,RELATED -p tcp --dport www -j ACCEPT
16 iptables -A FORWARD -s 0/0 -d 10.254.1.20 -m state --state NEW,ESTAB-
   LISHED,RELATED -p tcp --dport ftp -j ACCEPT
17 iptables -A OUTPUT -m state --state NEW,ESTABLISHED,RELATED -j ACCEPT
18 iptables -A INPUT -m state --state ESTABLISHED,RELATED -j ACCEPT
19 iptables -A INPUT -i eth1 -s 10.0.0.0/8 -d 10.254.1.1 -m state --state
   NEW -j ACCEPT
```

Lines 1 and 2 cause the necessary kernel modules for NAT to be installed. Lines 3 through 7 are as described previously. Lines 8 through 11 provide the necessary NAT rules for the WWW and FTP servers. The PREROUTING rules translate the Internet addresses back to the internal addresses for arriving packets while the POSTROUTING rules provide the translation for the source addresses for outbound packets. Note that because of the order of execution of the various PREROUTING and POSTROUTING chains, all rules regarding internal hosts are written using the actual IP addresses (not the translated ones as with ipchains) in the FORWARD chain.

Line 12 is the rule that translates the source IP address for all internal nodes (except the WWW and FTP servers). SNAT is used here because the external address of 199.2.8.17 is fixed (that is, DHCP or similar is not used). All packets to the Internet from such internal systems will appear as if they came from 199.2.8.17. As with ipchains, the reverse translation is done automatically.

The remaining rules are quite similar to those we've described in earlier examples.

NOTE

Just setting up the NAT rules for translating 10.254.1.10 to 199.2.8.18 and 10.254.1.20 to 199.2.8.19 is *not* sufficient. This is due to the fact that, by default, topcat is not configured to pay attention to 199.2.8.18 or 199.2.8.19. The simplest way to resolve this is to configure IP aliases (as described in Chapter 4) for those two addresses and associate them with eth0 on topcat.

Using Existing `ipchains` Rules

Once the distributions start shipping kernel version 2.4.x (currently, it is anticipated that this will occur in 2001), you can expect to be able to use `iptables`
reliably. Also, at that time, you can use your existing `ipchains` rules if you so
desire. This can be accomplished with

```
modprobe ipchains
```

which causes the `ipchains.o` module to be loaded into the 2.4.x kernel. Of
course, many of the extra benefits of `iptables`, like connection tracking, will be
unavailable. However, it makes for a nice transition if you need to put off converting your rules to `iptables` for a time.

Summary

In this chapter, we took a brief, introductory look at `iptables`, the replacement
for `ipchains` in the Linux 2.4.x kernel series. We highlighted the major differences between `iptables` and `ipchains`, pointing out the advantages of `ipta-
bles`. We also considered a number of examples. As this document goes to
publication, both `iptables` and 2.4.x kernels are becoming much more stable.

For Further Reading

Documentation supporting `iptables`, at this time, is limited to HOWTOs.
The three HOWTOs are:
   Linux 2.4 NAT HOWTO
   Linux 2.4 Packet Filtering HOWTO
   Linux 2.4 Netfilter Hacking HOWTO
All of these documents, together with the latest `iptables` source code and
patches, can be found at any one of the following three sites.

```
http://antarctica.penguincomputing.com/~netfilter/
http://www.samba.org/netfilter/
http://netfilter.kernelnotes.org/
```

16

iproute2 and Other Routing Topics

If you have been impressed with what Linux can do based on the previous chapters, then hang on to your hat because there is much, much more. The power and flexibility of the IP implementation within the Linux kernel has no match in any other widely available computer operating system. The features described in this section are normally only available on dedicated systems such as dedicated routers and switches—at substantially higher cost. There are, of course, limitations to the Linux implementation. Dedicated routers or switches can be tuned, both in hardware and software, for their specific purpose, whereas Linux carries a lot of additional baggage to support a full-featured user operating system that generally runs on generic low cost hardware.

In this chapter, we briefly introduce the advanced routing capabilities built into the Linux kernel including traffic control (controlling which packets are processed first), tunneling (sending packets through network(s) that do not or cannot process certain types of communications), and routing policies (causing routing decisions to be made based on data other than just the destination IP address). We also look at configuring the kernel for these capabilities and specifically tuning the kernel for routing. Additionally, we touch on turning a Linux system into a switch and mention using Linux as a WAN router.

Routing and iproute2

As of the 2.2.x version of the Linux kernel, considerable enhancements to the kernel networking components have been made. This includes enhancements to the internal TCP/IP stack and a number of additional features. Although largely not well documented, the feature set includes three major categories: routing policies, traffic control (including quality of service [QoS]), and tunneling.

Routing policies permit the configuration of rules that cause routing decisions to be made in ways other than the default longest or best match method (as described in Chapter 6). This is accomplished by virtue of the fact that the Linux kernel actually maintains multiple routing tables. New routing tables can be created and specific rules can be used to direct the kernel to process matching packets by a specific rule. Viewing and configuring these routing tables and rules can only be accomplished with the `ip` command (discussed beginning with "The `ip` and `rtmon` Commands" on page 765) which is part of the iproute2 suite of tools. The iproute2 package is available from

```
ftp://ftp.inr.ac.ru/ip-routing/
```

but is already a part of all major distributions.

QoS capabilities within the Linux kernel provide the capability of determining how and when to process packets after the routing decision has been made. This functionality provides support for priority processing, bandwidth allocation, and scheduling and queueing of packets utilizing a variety of different algorithms. These features must be configured using the `tc` command (discussed in "Traffic Control" on page 818), which is also a part of the iproute2 package.

Tunneling, from the perspective of IP, is the process of putting an IP header (the *outer* header) on a packet that already has an IP header or something similar (the *inner* header) in another protocol. The purpose is to provide the outer IP header for intermediate routers that do not understand what is in the inner header. Linux supports simple IP in IP encapsulation and generic router encapsulation (GRE), both of which are described in "Tunneling" on page 814.

In summary, the major features and benefits of the Linux 2.2.x and later kernel with respect to networking are:

- Routing policy rules
    - rules based on destination IP address
    - rules based on source IP address

- rules based on TOS
- rules based on `mark` value set by `ipchains` or `iptables` (called *FWMARK*)
- rules based on incoming NIC
- Traffic Control
  - filter packets based on TOS, FWMARK, IP header fields, and/or protocol
  - queue and schedule filtered and unfiltered packets for transmission based on a variety of algorithms
- Tunneling
  - IP in IP
  - IPv4 and/or IPv6 through IPv4 GRE
  - Multicasting through IPv4 GRE

In order to take advantage of the capabilities, the kernel must first be configured to provide the appropriate services. To that end, we consider some of the necessary kernel parameters, followed by a discussion of the syntax of the various iproute2 commands, and then look at implementation examples.

Reconfiguring the Kernel

Whether you simply want to tune your system for routing or you want to take advantage of some of the many advanced routing features (as described above) available in the Linux kernel, you will need to reconfigure the kernel. Kernel reconfiguration simply involves setting up a configuration file that tells the kernel which options to turn on and which additional kernel modules to make available. This process is initiated by using `make config`, `make menuconfig`, or `make xconfig` in the `/usr/src/linux` directory. Each of these commands is equivalent in that it produces a `.config` file in `/usr/src/linux` that is subsequently used to rebuild the kernel. The `make config` command provides an ASCII interface that tends to be tedious to use. Using `make menuconfig` provides a curses[1] interface while `make xconfig` provides a similar interface through the X window

---

1. The `curses` library provides a suite of calls that permits controlling of a terminal screen. Originally designed for cathode ray tube (CRT) terminals. See the `curses(3)` man page for further details.

system. These latter two are preferred because they make identifying and selecting particular features much easier. We will use `make menuconfig` in our examples.

The overall process of reconfiguring and rebuilding the kernel is as follows:

```
make menuconfig
make dep
make clean
make bzImage
cp /boot/vmlinuz-2.2.14 /boot/oldvmlinuz
cp /boot/System.map-2.2.14 /boot/oldSystem.map
cp /usr/src/linux/arch/i386/boot/bzImage /boot/vmlinuz-2.2.14
cp /usr/src/linux/System.map /boot/System.map-2.2.14
make modules
make modules_install
reboot
```

Here, we are assuming that the kernel version is 2.2.14 and that the newly built kernel is also 2.2.14—substitute the appropriate kernel version for your system. Also, note that if you are building a different kernel version, you will need to create the appropriate links in `/boot`. In order to make easy use of `oldvmlinuz` (which is retained in case the new kernel is broken), make sure that you configure `/etc/lilo.conf` appropriately and run `/sbin/lilo`. See the `Kernel-HOWTO`, the `lilo.conf(5)` man page, and the `lilo(8)` man page for further details.

In order to proceed with the reconfiguration, we need to know which kernel features and/or modules to enable so that the appropriate options can be chosen when `make menuconfig` is run. A fairly complete list with descriptions is available in the file `Configure.help` in `/usr/src/linux/Documentation/` directory. Table 16–1 summarizes the features and modules with which we are concerned and represents a subset of `Configure.help`. The option column in the table lists the option as it appears in `menuconfig`.

Table 16–1   Some Kernel Configuration Options Pertinent to Routing

OPTION	DESCRIPTION
IP: advanced router	Sets the `CONFIG_IP_ADVANCED_ROUTER` parameter in the `.config` file. This option actually doesn't effect the kernel at all, but does cause other options like IP: policy routing to be offered. Use this option if you want many of the options below.

Table 16–1   Some Kernel Configuration Options Pertinent to Routing *(Continued)*

OPTION	DESCRIPTION
IP: policy routing	Sets the CONFIG_IP_MULTIPLE_TABLES parameter in the .config file. This option allows for the use of additional routing tables and, in particular, allows for routing decisions to be made based on the source IP address as well as the destination IP address.
IP: equal cost multipath	Sets the CONFIG_IP_ROUTE_MULTIPATH parameter in the .config file. This option permits the setting of multiple paths for a given destination. The decision about which path to use is set by other, non-deterministic parameters.
IP: use TOS value as routing key	Sets the CONFIG_IP_ROUTE_TOS parameter in the .config file. This options allows for the use of the TOS bit settings in the IP header in routing decisions.
IP: use FWMARK value as routing key	Sets the CONFIG_IP_ROUTE_FWMARK parameter in the .config file. This option allows for the use of mark values set by ipchains or iptables in routing decisions.
IP: verbose route monitoring	Sets the CONFIG_IP_ROUTE_VERBOSE parameter in the .config file. This recommended option causes additional messages to be written to klogd.
IP: large routing tables	Sets the CONFIG_IP_ROUTE_LARGE_TABLES parameter in the .config file. Specify this option if you expect a given routing table to contain more than about 64 entries.
IP: fast network address translation	Sets the CONFIG_IP_ROUTE_NAT parameter in the .config file. This options permits NAT through the internal routing function. It is a stateless implementation designed for address transitioning and support of routing policy rules.

Table 16–1   Some Kernel Configuration Options Pertinent to Routing *(Continued)*

OPTION	DESCRIPTION
IP: optimize as router not host	Sets the CONFIG_IP_ROUTER parameter in the .config file. This option disables host optimizing capabilities of certain NIC device drivers.
IP: tunneling	Sets the CONFIG_NET_IPIP parameter in the .config file. This option permits the tunneling of IP through IP. The purpose of this kernel feature is to allow a system to tunnel through other network(s) and participate in a LAN that is physically remote. This option makes a loadable kernel module available.
IP: GRE tunnels over IP	Sets the CONFIG_NET_IPGRE parameter in the .config file. This option is the configuration of generic routing encapsulation (GRE). Currently, the Linux kernel supports IPv4 and IPv6 through IPv4 tunnels set up with this kernel feature. It also permits multicasting through the tunnel. GRE was originally developed by Cisco. This option makes a loadable kernel module available.
IP: broadcast GRE over IP	Sets the CONFIG_NET_IPGRE_BROADCAST parameter in the .config file. This option permits sending broadcast messages through a GRE tunnel. This is useful if you want to create a LAN through a WAN. That implementation requires that the IP: multicast routing option also be set. This option makes a loadable kernel module available.

Table 16–1   Some Kernel Configuration Options Pertinent to Routing *(Continued)*

OPTION	DESCRIPTION
Bridging (EXPERIMENTAL)	Sets the `CONFIG_BRIDGE` parameter in the `.config` file. This option allows Linux to act as a bridge or switch. Each NIC in the Linux system can be configured to be a switch port. The code supports the IEEE 802.1 spanning tree algorithm. In order to use this capability, the configuration tools at `ftp://shadow.cabi.net/pub/Linux` are also required. This software is still experimental and thus not guaranteed to work.
Routing messages	Sets the `CONFIG_RTNETLINK` parameter in the `.config` file. This option causes the kernel to write routing messages to the character device file `/dev/route` which can be read programatically. If you use this option, you must create the file manually with `# mknod /dev/route c 36 0`
WAN router	Sets the `CONFIG_WAN_ROUTER` parameter in the `.config` file. This option permits the use of WAN devices so that a Linux system can act as a WAN router between, for example, Ethernet and X.25, frame relay, or high speed serial interfaces. You must additionally select the appropriate device driver for the WAN interface being used—these kernel options can be found under Network device support→WAN interfaces when using `menuconfig`. This option makes a loadable kernel module available.

Table 16–1   Some Kernel Configuration Options Pertinent to Routing *(Continued)*

OPTION	DESCRIPTION
Fast switching	Sets the `CONFIG_NET_FASTROUTE` parameter in the `.config` file. Enables NIC to NIC transfers (currently only supported by the `tulip` driver). This can really speed up the passing of packets and is quite useful with the Bridging option above. Use of this option, however, completely bypasses all firewall filtering.
Forwarding between high speed interfaces	Sets the `CONFIG_NET_HW_FLOWCONTROL` parameter in the `.config` file. This option permits hardware flow control when high speed NICs are used in systems with slower CPUs (for example, a 10 Mbps Ethernet NIC can overwhelm a 120 Mhz Pentium). Currently, only the tulip driver is supported. This option should be useful for Gbps NICs when driver support becomes available.
QoS and/or fair queueing	Sets the `CONFIG_NET_SCHED` parameter in the `.config` file. This option permits the ability to utilize different algorithms for determining which packets get routed first. These different algorithms are embodied in the scheduler and queue options set below. This option requires the iproute2 `tc` command in order to set up classes of packets that can then be assigned different routing priorities.
CBQ packet scheduler	Sets the `CONFIG_NET_SCH_CBQ` parameter in the `.config` file. This option sets up the class-based queueing (CBQ) algorithm. CBQ can be implemented to utilize other scheduling algorithms (called *disciplines*). This option makes a loadable kernel module available.

Table 16–1   Some Kernel Configuration Options Pertinent to Routing *(Continued)*

Option	Description
CSZ packet scheduler	Sets the CONFIG_NET_SCH_CSZ parameter in the .config file. This option configures the Clark-Shenker-Zhang (CSZ) packet scheduling algorithm. It currently does not work. This option makes a loadable kernel module available.
The simplest PRIO pseudo scheduler	Sets the CONFIG_NET_SCH_PRIO parameter in the .config file. This option enables a simple bandwidth priority scheduler. This option makes a loadable kernel module available.
RED queue	Sets the CONFIG_NET_SCH_RED parameter in the .config file. This option sets up the random early detection (RED) packet scheduling algorithm. This option makes a loadable kernel module available.
SFQ queue	Sets the CONFIG_NET_SCH_SFQ parameter in the .config file. This option enables the stochastic fairness queueing (SFQ) packet scheduling algorithm. This option makes a loadable kernel module available.
TEQL queue	Sets the CONFIG_NET_SCH_TEQL parameter in the .config file. This option configures the true link equalizer (TLE) packet scheduling algorithm. This option makes a loadable kernel module available.
TBF queue	Sets the CONFIG_NET_SCH_TBF parameter in the .config file. This option sets up the token bucket filter (TBF) packet scheduling algorithm. This option makes a loadable kernel module available.

Table 16–1   Some Kernel Configuration Options Pertinent to Routing *(Continued)*

OPTION	DESCRIPTION
QoS support	Sets the `CONFIG_NET_QOS` parameter in the `.config` file. This option has no effect on the kernel but provides the remaining options listed in this table except Traffic shaper for quality of service (QoS) support.
Rate estimator	Sets the `CONFIG_NET_ESTIMATOR` parameter in the `.config` file. This option causes the kernel to keep statistical information regarding the rate of traffic flow through each NIC. This information can then be used by QoS scheduling.

Packet classifier API	Sets the `CONFIG_NET_CLS` parameter in the `.config` file. This option provides class support for the CBQ algorithm. The following options should also be set, if CBQ support is desired:
	`CONFIG_NET_CLS_ROUTE`
	`CONFIG_NET_CLS_FW`
	`CONFIG_NET_CLS_U32`
	`CONFIG_NET_CLS_RSVP`
	`CONFIG_NET_CLS_RSVP6` (only required for IPv6)
	`CONFIG_NET_CLS_POLICE`

Traffic shaper (EXPERIMENTAL)	Sets the `CONFIG_SHAPER` parameter in the `.config` file. This experimental code permits the control of outbound packets. It requires the `shapecfg` command and works similarly to iproute2 and CBQ. This option makes a loadable kernel module available.

In the next section, we consider which of these options are required for particular functionality and briefly describe the commands used to implement these capabilities.

iproute2 Commands: `ip`, `rtmon`, `rtacct`, and `tc`

The iproute2 distribution includes the four utilities `ip`, `rtmon`, `rtacct`, and `tc`. The `ip` command is a more finely grained replacement for `ifconfig` and `route` as well as the utility for creating routing policy rules and tunnels. The `rtmon` command can be used to capture routing information for future analysis. The `ip` and `rtmon` commands are introduced in the next section and further explored in "Routing Policies" on page 804.

The `rtacct` command is used to provide summary information about ingress packets. It is described in "Realms and the `rtacct` Command" on page 804.

The `tc` command is used to configure QoS capabilities. It is introduced in "Example Using the `tc` Command" on page 825 and further described in "Traffic Control" on page 818.

The `ip` and `rtmon` Commands

The basic syntax of the `ip` command is

```
ip [ -options] object [ command [ arguments ] ]
```

where `options` are modifiers affecting general `ip` behavior, and output, always preceded with a `-`. `object`, determines to what the `ip` command will apply and is one of `link`, `address`, `neighbor`, `route`, `rule`, `maddress`, `mroute`, or `tunnel`. `command` is an action and available actions depend upon the object specified. `arguments` are action modifiers.

The `ip` command is rather complex, so we break it up into components. In Table 16–2, we list the major objects of `ip`, a brief description, and which kernel options are required to support it. Next, we'll look at the `options` of the `ip` command. The specific use and syntax of each `object` and its associated `commands` and `arguments` are described when it is discussed.

Table 16–2   Major Subcommands of `ip`

IP OBJECT	KERNEL OPTIONS	DESCRIPTION
`ip link`	default settings provide functionality	Functionally similar to `ifconfig`. Used to modify NIC parameters and/or get information about a NIC except for the IP addresses.

Table 16–2   Major Subcommands of `ip` *(Continued)*

IP OBJECT	KERNEL OPTIONS	DESCRIPTION
`ip address`	default settings provide functionality	Functionally similar to `ifconfig`. This command and the command above, taken together, can replace the `ifconfig` functionality. Used to modify, delete, or add IP addresses to a NIC. Supports aliasing and IPv6. Expands upon `ifconfig` capability by adding scope of address parameter.
`ip neighbor`	default settings provide functionality	Functionally similar to the `arp` command. Supports both IPv4 ARP and IPv6 ND.
`ip route`	*required*: IP: advanced router, IP: policy routing, IP: equal cost multipath *optional*: IP: fast network address translation, IP: large routing tables	Functionally similar to the `route` command except substantially more capable and flexible. Used to list, modify, delete, or add entries to any of the routing tables on the system. Note that the `route` command is only capable of operating on a single routing table which is actually a combination of two distinct routing tables.
`ip rule`	*required*: IP: advanced router, IP: policy routing *optional*: IP: use TOS as routing key, IP: use FWMARK as routing key, IP: fast network address translation	Used to show and maintain the routing policy database.
`ip maddress`	default settings provide functionality	Used to list, modify, add, or delete multicast addresses.

Table 16–2   Major Subcommands of `ip` *(Continued)*

IP OBJECT	KERNEL OPTIONS	DESCRIPTION
`ip mroute`	*required*: IP: multicast routing, IP: advanced router, IP: policy routing *optional*: IP: large routing tables	Used for managing the multicast routing cache.
`ip tunnel`	*required*: IP: tunneling, IP: GRE tunnels over IP, IP: broadcast GRE over IP	Used to build IP tunnels. IP in IP tunnels are supported by the IP: tunneling kernel option and are essentially Linux specific. GRE tunnels are more widely implemented (on Cisco, other routers, and other OSes) and therefore are generally preferred.
`ip monitor`	*required*: IP: verbose route monitoring	Used to continuously monitor the state of devices, addresses, and routes. Often used in conjunction with `rtmon`.

All of the objects can be abbreviated by using a sufficient number of leading characters to uniquely identify it. For example, `address` can be abbreviated to `a`; `rule` to `ru`; and `route` to `ro`. Note that the commands, `ip link`, `ip address`, `ip neighbor`, and `ip maddress` can be used with no kernel modifications in a 2.2.14 or later kernel.

The options to the `ip` command are shown in Table 16–3.

Table 16–3   Options to the `ip` Command

OPTION	DESCRIPTION
`-V` or `-Version`	Prints the version number of the `ip` command.
`-s`, `-stats`, or `-statistics`	Adds additional output to the command. Additional output can be obtained with multiple instances of this option—multiple instances must include the `-`, for example, `# ip -s -s link list eth0`

`-f inet|inet6|link`
`-family can be used instead`
`of -f`
	If this option is not specified, then `ip` determines the protocol family identifier based on other arguments or defaults to `inet`. `inet` is for IPv4, `inet6` is for IPv6, and `link` is for no networking protocol.

`-4`	Short for `-f inet`.
`-6`	Short for `-f inet6`.
`-0`	Short for `-f link`.
`-o` or `-oneline`	Causes each record to be printed per line. Useful for scripting or processing with `wc`, `grep`, `awk`, or `sed`, but not very readable.
`-r` or `-resolve`	Use DNS names instead of IP addresses. By default, `ip` does not use names.

NOTE

You can always get syntax help for the `ip` command by using `help`. For example, `ip help` gives general syntax for the `ip` command; `ip link help` provides syntax for the `link` object; and `ip link set help` yields specific syntax details for the `set` command of the `link` object. The `help` option can be used in this way for all of the objects and their commands.

The `ip link` Command

The `ip link` command is used to configure NICs and view current configurations of NICs. It does not deal with IP addresses. It takes two commands, `set` or `show`, each of which accepts arguments peculiar to the command. The `set` command can be abbreviated as `s` and the `show` command is equivalent to `list`, `lst`, `sh`, `ls`, and `l`.

Let's consider the show command first. Its syntax is

```
ip link show [dev name] [up]
```

where the optional keyword `dev` is followed by a specific device name such as `eth0`, `pp0`, or `tr0`; and `up` specifies that only interfaces marked with the UP flag should be listed. If no arguments are specified, then all interfaces are shown (somewhat similarly to `ifconfig -a`). Example 16–1 illustrates.

Example 16–1   Output of `ip link show`

```
# ip link show
1: lo: <LOOPBACK,UP> mtu 3924 qdisc noqueue
   link/loopback 00:00:00:00:00:00 brd 00:00:00:00:00:00
2: eth0: <BROADCAST,MULTICAST,UP> mtu 1500 qdisc pfifo_fast qlen 100
   link/ether 00:60:94:b9:83:0a brd ff:ff:ff:ff:ff:ff
3: eth1: <BROADCAST,MULTICAST,UP> mtu 1500 qdisc pfifo_fast qlen 100
   link/ether 00:50:ba:d7:f8:14 brd ff:ff:ff:ff:ff:ff
4: eth2: <BROADCAST,MULTICAST,UP> mtu 1500 qdisc pfifo_fast qlen 100
   link/ether 00:a0:cc:61:84:a5 brd ff:ff:ff:ff:ff:ff
5: eth3: <BROADCAST,MULTICAST,UP> mtu 1500 qdisc pfifo_fast qlen 100
   link/ether 00:a0:cc:63:de:ee brd ff:ff:ff:ff:ff:ff
6: tunl0@NONE: <NOARP> mtu 1480 qdisc noop
   link/ipip 0.0.0.0 brd 0.0.0.0
7: gre0@NONE: <NOARP> mtu 1476 qdisc noop
   link/gre 0.0.0.0 brd 0.0.0.0
#
```

The output in Example 16–1 is quite similar to that of `ifconfig`, although in a slightly different format and with some additional information. Note that each output entry is numbered with each number representing a distinct device—this number is called the *interface index* and uniquely identifies the interface. The device name (i.e., `lo`, `eth0`, etc.) is the first entry after the number, followed by the flags in angle brackets. The flags are as described in Chapter 4. Next is the MTU.

After the MTU is `qdisc`, which stands for queueing discipline. The string following `qdisc` identifies the queueing algorithm used for the given interface. Available queueing algorithms are described in "Queueing Disciplines" on page 822. There are two special strings for `qdisc`: `noqueue`, which means that no queueing is performed for the interface, and `noop`, which means that the interface discards all packets sent to it (this is known as *blackhole* mode). If a valid queueing algorithm is specified, then `qlen` appears and indicates the transmit queue length of the interface in packets.

After `qlen`, the link type is specified. Entries such as `link/localhost` and `link/ether` indicate the localhost and ethernet interface(s), respectively. Note that in Example 16–1, `link/ipip` and `link/gre` exist (supported by the kernel) but are not currently configured. These entries are for tunnels and are discussed in "Tunneling" on page 814. After the link type entry is the physical address of the interface (if one exists) for most interfaces. Following the physical address is the keyword `brd`, for broadcast, followed by the layer 2 broadcast address.

Additional statistical information can be obtained with `-s`, as shown in Example 16–2. Note that the statistics given are identical to that from `ifconfig`.

Example 16–2   Output of `ip -s link show`

```
# ip -s link sh
1: lo: <LOOPBACK,UP> mtu 3924 qdisc noqueue
    link/loopback 00:00:00:00:00:00 brd 00:00:00:00:00:00
    RX: bytes  packets  errors  dropped overrun mcast
    589644     11766    0       0       0       0
    TX: bytes  packets  errors  dropped carrier collsns
    589644     11766    0       0       0       0
2: eth0: <BROADCAST,MULTICAST,UP> mtu 1500 qdisc pfifo_fast qlen 100
    link/ether 00:60:94:b9:83:0a brd ff:ff:ff:ff:ff:ff
    RX: bytes  packets  errors  dropped overrun mcast
    26169597   68853    0       0       0       0
    TX: bytes  packets  errors  dropped carrier collsns
    6292765    65747    0       0       0       2
3: eth1: <BROADCAST,MULTICAST,UP> mtu 1500 qdisc pfifo_fast qlen 100
    link/ether 00:50:ba:d7:f8:14 brd ff:ff:ff:ff:ff:ff
    RX: bytes  packets  errors  dropped overrun mcast
    460638     1467     0       0       0       0
    TX: bytes  packets  errors  dropped carrier collsns
    2748642    35248    0       0       0       0
4: eth2: <BROADCAST,MULTICAST,UP> mtu 1500 qdisc pfifo_fast qlen 100
    link/ether 00:a0:cc:61:84:a5 brd ff:ff:ff:ff:ff:ff
    RX: bytes  packets  errors  dropped overrun mcast
    103440394  751512   0       0       0       0
    TX: bytes  packets  errors  dropped carrier collsns
    88299629   778665   0       0       0       2151
5: eth3: <BROADCAST,MULTICAST,UP> mtu 1500 qdisc pfifo_fast qlen 100
    link/ether 00:a0:cc:63:de:ee brd ff:ff:ff:ff:ff:ff
    RX: bytes  packets  errors  dropped overrun mcast
    774096     5895     0       0       0       0
    TX: bytes  packets  errors  dropped carrier collsns
    3105372    38488    0       0       0       0
6: tunl0@NONE: <NOARP> mtu 1480 qdisc noop
    link/ipip 0.0.0.0 brd 0.0.0.0
    RX: bytes  packets  errors  dropped overrun mcast
    0          0        0       0       0       0
    TX: bytes  packets  errors  dropped carrier collsns
```

Example 16–2   Output of `ip -s link show` *(Continued)*

```
             0           0          0         0          0         0
7: gre0@NONE: <NOARP> mtu 1476 qdisc noop
    link/gre 0.0.0.0 brd 0.0.0.0
    RX: bytes   packets   errors    dropped overrun mcast
    0           0         0         0       0       0
    TX: bytes   packets   errors    dropped carrier collsns
    0           0         0         0       0       0
#
```

Adding another `-s` option to the command cases the receive and transmit errors to be categorized by type, as shown in Example 16–3. The error type headings are really Ethernet types, but remain unchanged for other network interfaces and other interface types will use them for different meanings undocumented outside of the source code. Note that we use `list` instead of `show` to illustrate its equivalence.

Example 16–3   Using an Extra -s Option with `ip link list`

```
# ip -s -s link list
1: lo: <LOOPBACK,UP> mtu 3924 qdisc noqueue
    link/loopback 00:00:00:00:00:00 brd 00:00:00:00:00:00
    RX: bytes   packets   errors    dropped overrun mcast
    590344      11780     0         0       0       0
    RX errors: length  crc       frame     fifo    missed
               0       0         0         0       0
    TX: bytes   packets   errors    dropped carrier collsns
    590344      11780     0         0       0       0
    TX errors: aborted fifo      window    heartbeat
               0       0         0         0
2: eth0: <BROADCAST,MULTICAST,UP> mtu 1500 qdisc pfifo_fast qlen 100
    link/ether 00:60:94:b9:83:0a brd ff:ff:ff:ff:ff:ff
    RX: bytes   packets   errors    dropped overrun mcast
    26176105    68923     0         0       0       0
    RX errors: length  crc       frame     fifo    missed
               0       0         0         0       0
    TX: bytes   packets   errors    dropped carrier collsns
    6298031     65818     0         0       0       2
    TX errors: aborted fifo      window    heartbeat
               0       0         0         0
3: eth1: <BROADCAST,MULTICAST,UP> mtu 1500 qdisc pfifo_fast qlen 100
    link/ether 00:50:ba:d7:f8:14 brd ff:ff:ff:ff:ff:ff
    RX: bytes   packets   errors    dropped overrun mcast
    461266      1469      0         0       0       0
    RX errors: length  crc       frame     fifo    missed
               0       0         0         0       0
    TX: bytes   packets   errors    dropped carrier collsns
    2751528     35285     0         0       0       0
    TX errors: aborted fifo      window    heartbeat
               0       0         0         0
4: eth2: <BROADCAST,MULTICAST,UP> mtu 1500 qdisc pfifo_fast qlen 100
    link/ether 00:a0:cc:61:84:a5 brd ff:ff:ff:ff:ff:ff
    RX: bytes   packets   errors    dropped overrun mcast
    105144701   764429    0         0       0       0
```

Example 16–3   Using an Extra -s Option with `ip link list` *(Continued)*

```
      RX errors: length   crc       frame    fifo     missed
                 0         0         0        0        0
      TX: bytes  packets   errors    dropped carrier collsns
      89422722   791359    0         0        0        2208
      TX errors: aborted fifo       window   heartbeat
                 0         0         0        0
5: eth3: <BROADCAST,MULTICAST,UP> mtu 1500 qdisc pfifo_fast qlen 100
      link/ether 00:a0:cc:63:de:ee brd ff:ff:ff:ff:ff:ff
      RX: bytes  packets   errors    dropped overrun mcast
      776153     5924      0         0        0        0
      RX errors: length   crc       frame    fifo     missed
                 0         0         0        0        0
      TX: bytes  packets   errors    dropped carrier collsns
      3111311    38554     0         0        0        0
      TX errors: aborted fifo       window   heartbeat
                 0         0         0        0
6: tun10@NONE: <NOARP> mtu 1480 qdisc noop
      link/ipip 0.0.0.0 brd 0.0.0.0
      RX: bytes  packets   errors    dropped overrun mcast
      0          0         0         0        0        0
      RX errors: length   crc       frame    fifo     missed
                 0         0         0        0        0
      TX: bytes  packets   errors    dropped carrier collsns
      0          0         0         0        0        0
      TX errors: aborted fifo       window   heartbeat
                 0         0         0        0
7: gre0@NONE: <NOARP> mtu 1476 qdisc noop
      link/gre 0.0.0.0 brd 0.0.0.0
      RX: bytes  packets   errors    dropped overrun mcast
      0          0         0         0        0        0
      RX errors: length   crc       frame    fifo     missed
                 0         0         0        0        0
      TX: bytes  packets   errors    dropped carrier collsns
      0          0         0         0        0        0
      TX errors: aborted fifo       window   heartbeat
                 0         0         0        0
[root@foghorn linux]#
```

The `ip link set` command is used to set interface parameters, except for the IP address, in a manner quite similar to `ifconfig`. The syntax for the command is given in Example 16–4.

Example 16–4   Syntax of `ip link set`

```
ip link set [dev] iface_name up | down | arp { on | off } |
      dynamic { on | off } |
      multicast { on | off } | txqueuelen packets |
      name newname |
      address lladdr | {broadcast|peer} llbaddr |
      mtu mtu
```

Table 16–4 lists the arguments to the `ip link set` command as shown in Example 16–4.

Table 16–4   Arguments to `ip link set`

ARGUMENT	DESCRIPTION
`[dev]` *iface_name*	Specifies the *iface_name*, such as `eth0`, `ppp0`, or `tr0`. Use of the `dev` keyword is optional. Specifying the interface name is *required*.
`up`	Enables the interface to send and receive packets.
`down`	Disables the interface from sending and receiving packets. It is good practice to down an interface before making other changes and, in some cases, is required.
`arp {on|off}`	`arp on` enables the interface to send and receive ARP packets; `arp off` disables this capability. The interface must be down in order to use this argument.
`dynamic {on|off}`	Turns the DYNAMIC flag `on` or `off` (for IPv6 autoconfiguration).
`multicast {on|off}`	Enables sending and receiving multicast packets with on; disables with `off`.
`txqueuelen` *packets*	Sets the transmit queue length in *packets*. `txqueuelen`, may be abbreviated as `txqlen`.
`name` *newname*	Sets the name of the device to *newname*. Normally, this is only done with virtual interfaces like tunnels. Only use this operation when the interface is `down` and before any addresses have been assigned (if addresses have already been assigned, reassign them after the name change).
`address` *lladdr*	Sets the link layer (layer 2) address, *lladdr*, for the interface.

Table 16–4   Arguments to `ip link set` *(Continued)*

ARGUMENT	DESCRIPTION
`broadcast|peer llbaddr`	Sets the link layer broadcast address, *llbaddr*, for the interface. If `peer` is used, then this is the peer address for a point-to-point link.
`mtu mtu`	Sets the MTU.

Use of the `ip link set` command is, except for the syntax, entirely similar to `ifconfig` as described in Chapter 4.

The `ip address` Object

The `ip address` command is used to set, modify, delete, or show the IPv4 and IPv6 addresses, and aliases, associated with an interface. The commands available are `add`, `delete`, `flush`, and `show`. We consider each one below.

IP ADDRESS SHOW   This command lists the same information about interfaces as does `ip link show` and adds information about IP addresses. Listing information about all interfaces is illustrated in Example 16–5.

Example 16–5   Output of `ip address show`

```
# ip address show
1: lo: <LOOPBACK,UP> mtu 3924 qdisc noqueue
    link/loopback 00:00:00:00:00:00 brd 00:00:00:00:00:00
    inet 127.0.0.1/8 brd 127.255.255.255 scope host lo
2: eth0: <BROADCAST,MULTICAST,UP> mtu 1500 qdisc pfifo_fast qlen 100
    link/ether 00:60:94:b9:83:0a brd ff:ff:ff:ff:ff:ff
    inet 10.254.1.11/24 brd 10.254.1.255 scope global eth0
3: eth1: <BROADCAST,MULTICAST,UP> mtu 1500 qdisc pfifo_fast qlen 100
    link/ether 00:50:ba:d7:f8:14 brd ff:ff:ff:ff:ff:ff
    inet 10.254.12.10/24 brd 10.254.12.255 scope global eth1
4: eth2: <BROADCAST,MULTICAST,UP> mtu 1500 qdisc pfifo_fast qlen 100
    link/ether 00:a0:cc:61:84:a5 brd ff:ff:ff:ff:ff:ff
    inet 172.16.0.1/16 brd 172.16.255.255 scope global eth2
5: eth3: <BROADCAST,MULTICAST,UP> mtu 1500 qdisc pfifo_fast qlen 100
    link/ether 00:a0:cc:63:de:ee brd ff:ff:ff:ff:ff:ff
    inet 172.17.0.1/16 brd 172.17.255.255 scope global eth3
6: tun10@NONE: <NOARP> mtu 1480 qdisc noop
    link/ipip 0.0.0.0 brd 0.0.0.0
7: gre0@NONE: <NOARP> mtu 1476 qdisc noop
    link/gre 0.0.0.0 brd 0.0.0.0
#
```

Note that the only difference between using `ip address show` and `ip link show` is the addition of one line, beginning with `inet` in this case, for each of the configured interfaces. The keyword `inet` indicates that these values are for IPv4. Following the `inet` keyword is the IP address together with its prefix, followed by `brd` and the IP broadcast address. After that is the `scope` of the address.

The address scope can be one of `global` (default), `site` (IPv6 only), `link`, or `local`. These terms have the same meaning as described in Chapter 5.

There are a number of arguments associated with `ip address show` which may be used to filter the output. The general syntax is given in Example 16–6.

Example 16–6   General Syntax of `ip address show`

```
ip address show [[dev] iface_name] [scope scope_value] [to prefix]
       [label pattern] [dynamic | permanent] [tentative] [deprecated]
       [primary | secondary]
```

Each of the arguments in Example 16–6 is described in Table 16–5.

Table 16–5   Arguments to `ip address show`

ARGUMENT	DESCRIPTION
`[dev]` *iface_name*	Specifies the *iface_name*, such as `eth0`, `ppp0`, or `tr0`. Use of the `dev` keyword is optional.
`scope` *scope_value*	Lists all entries with the specified *scope_value*.
`to` *prefix*	Lists all entries matching *prefix*, which is a network address in prefix notation. See Example 16–7.
`label` *pattern*	Lists all entries matching the string *pattern*. The string uses shell semantics. See Example 16–8.
`dynamic	permanent`	IPv6 only. Entries with the DYNAMIC flag were configured through IPv6 autoconfiguration. Specifying `dynamic` shows only those entries with the DYNAMIC flag set; `permanent` shows all entries without the DYNAMIC flag set.
`tentative`	IPv6 only. A tentative address is one which has not yet passed or did not pass the duplicate address detection check. This option lists only those.

Table 16–5   Arguments to `ip address show` *(Continued)*

ARGUMENT	DESCRIPTION
`deprecated`	IPv6 only. A deprecated address is one which is still valid for existing connections, but cannot be used for new connections. This option lists only those types of addresses.
`primary	secondary`	List only primary or secondary addresses.

To illustrate the `to` *prefix* argument, Example 16–7 matches all entries that have an IP address beginning with 172. Note that the use of the prefix notation with this argument does not have to match a real network.

Example 16–7   Using the `to` *prefix* Argument with `ip address show`

```
# ip addr show to 172/8
4: eth2: <BROADCAST,MULTICAST,UP> mtu 1500 qdisc pfifo_fast qlen 100
    inet 172.16.0.1/16 brd 172.16.255.255 scope global eth2
5: eth3: <BROADCAST,MULTICAST,UP> mtu 1500 qdisc pfifo_fast qlen 100
    inet 172.17.0.1/16 brd 172.17.255.255 scope global eth3
#
```

Example 16–8 shows the usage of the label argument in conjunction with the quoted string `"eth*"`, which matches all entries beginning with `eth` in the label.

Example 16–8   Using the `label` *pattern* Argument with `ip address show`

```
# ip addr show label "eth*"
2: eth0: <BROADCAST,MULTICAST,UP> mtu 1500 qdisc pfifo_fast qlen 100
    link/ether 00:60:94:b9:83:0a brd ff:ff:ff:ff:ff:ff
    inet 10.254.1.11/24 brd 10.254.1.255 scope global eth0
3: eth1: <BROADCAST,MULTICAST,UP> mtu 1500 qdisc pfifo_fast qlen 100
    link/ether 00:50:ba:d7:f8:14 brd ff:ff:ff:ff:ff:ff
    inet 10.254.12.10/24 brd 10.254.12.255 scope global eth1
4: eth2: <BROADCAST,MULTICAST,UP> mtu 1500 qdisc pfifo_fast qlen 100
    link/ether 00:a0:cc:61:84:a5 brd ff:ff:ff:ff:ff:ff
    inet 172.16.0.1/16 brd 172.16.255.255 scope global eth2
5: eth3: <BROADCAST,MULTICAST,UP> mtu 1500 qdisc pfifo_fast qlen 100
    link/ether 00:a0:cc:63:de:ee brd ff:ff:ff:ff:ff:ff
    inet 172.17.0.1/16 brd 172.17.255.255 scope global eth3
#
```

IP ADDRESS ADD   This command is used to set IP addresses or create aliases. Its syntax is

```
ip address add dev iface_name [local address] [peer address]
[broadcast address] [label name] [scope scope_value]
```

Table 16–6 describes the arguments.

Table 16–6   Arguments to `ip address add`

ARGUMENT	DESCRIPTION
`dev` *iface_name*	Specifies the *iface_name*, such as `eth0`, `ppp0`, or `tr0`. In this case, the `dev` keyword is required.
`local` *address*	Specifies the *address* to set. IPv4 addresses are specified in decimal dotted notation followed by the prefix. IPv6 addresses are specified as colon-separated 16-bit hex values followed by the prefix. If you do not specify the prefix, then `/32` is assumed for IPv4 and `/128` for IPv6!
`peer` *address*	Sets the address of the remote endpoint for point-to-point interfaces. *address* is as defined for `local` above.
`broadcast` *address*	Sets the broadcast address. Unlike `ifconfig`, the broadcast address is *not* automatically set when the IP address is set. In this case, *address* can be either +, used to initially set the broadcast based on IP address and netmask, or -, used to recompute the broadcast.
`label` *name*	Used for IP aliases. *name* must be a valid alias name of the form *iface_name*:*alias*, for example `eth0:2` or `eth1:2net`.
`scope` *scope_value*	Sets the scope of the address. *scope_value* must be a numeric value unless the file `/etc/iproute2/rt_scopes` exists and contains the previously defined scope names. This file is part of the distribution and can be found therein and copied if not already located in the above referenced directory. The default *scope_value* is `global`.

Using `ip address add` is quite straightforward. Consider Example 16–9. Here, the interface `eth0` is brought down, a new address and broadcast address is set, and the interface is brought up again.

Example 16–9   Changing or Setting an IP Address with `ip address add`

```
# ip link set eth0 down
# ip -4 addr add dev eth0 local 172.17.1.1/16 broadcast +
# ip link set eth0 up
```

Note that the use of `-4` in the `ip addr add` command is not strictly necessary since the addresses used would cause the kernel to determine that IPv4 was being used.

Adding an IP alias is quite simple. Example 16–10 illustrates creating an alias on `eth0`.

Example 16–10   Creating an IP Alias with `ip address add`

```
# ip -4 addr add dev eth0 local 192.168.254.1/24 brd + label eth0:1
# ip addr show eth0
2: eth0: <BROADCAST,MULTICAST,UP> mtu 1500 qdisc pfifo_fast qlen 100
    link/ether 00:60:94:b9:83:0a brd ff:ff:ff:ff:ff:ff
    inet 10.254.1.11/24 brd 10.254.1.255 scope global eth0
    inet 192.168.254.1/24 brd 192.168.254.255 scope global eth0:1
#
```

IP ADDRESS DELETE   Deleting addresses proceeds as expected with this command. Its syntax and argument definitions are identical to that of `ip address add`, except that the command is `ip address delete`. Example 16–11 illustrates removing the alias created in Example 16–10.

Example 16–11   Removing an IP Address with `ip address delete`

```
# ip addr del 192.168.254.1/32 label eth0:1 dev eth0
[# ip addr show eth0
2: eth0: <BROADCAST,MULTICAST,UP> mtu 1500 qdisc pfifo_fast qlen 100
    link/ether 00:60:94:b9:83:0a brd ff:ff:ff:ff:ff:ff
    inet 10.254.1.11/24 brd 10.254.1.255 scope global eth0
#
```

IP ADDRESS FLUSH   This command utilizes the same arguments as `ip address show`. Unlike that command, however, `ip address flush` requires at least one argument. Its purpose is to remove all IP addresses based on the criteria indicated by the specified argument(s). Example 16–12 illustrates the removal of all IPv4 addresses with 10 in the first octet. The use of `-s -s` provides more verbose output.

Example 16–12   Flushing IP Addresses

```
# ip -s -s addr flush to 10/8
2: eth0    inet 10.254.1.11/24 brd 10.254.1.255 scope global eth0
3: eth1    inet 10.254.12.10/24 brd 10.254.12.255 scope global eth1

*** Round 1, deleting 2 addresses ***
*** Flush is complete after 1 round ***
#
```

WARNING

The use of `ip address flush`, and indeed, other `ip object flush` commands, can be very dangerous. Be very certain that you know what will be flushed before you execute the command.

The `ip neighbor` Object

The `ip neighbor` command is used to view and manipulate the ARP cache which can contain either IPv4 ARP entries and/or IPv6 ND entries. It accepts the commands `add`, `change`, `replace`, `delete`, `flush`, and `show`. We consider the syntax of each.

`ip neighbor show`   This command is similar to `arp -a`. It shows the entries contained in the ARP cache. The syntax for this command is

```
ip neighbor show [[to] addr] [dev iface_name] [unused] [nud state]
```

It takes the arguments listed in Table 16–7.

Table 16–7   Arguments to `ip neighbor show`

ARGUMENT	DESCRIPTION
`[to]` *addr*	Specifies the IPv4 or IPv6 address of the neighbor. Use of the keyword `to` is optional.
`dev` *iface_name*	Specifies the interface name.

Table 16–7   Arguments to `ip neighbor show` *(Continued)*

ARGUMENT	DESCRIPTION
`unused`	Lists entries that are not currently in use.
`nud` *state*	This argument specifies the neighbor unreachability detection (nud) state of the entry. The state variable can be one of these values: `none`—state of the neighbor cannot be determined and is unreachable. `incomplete`—the entry is in the process of being resolved. `reachable`—the neighbor is reachable and the entry is subject to standard ARP cache timeouts. `stale`—the entry is valid but may be unreachable at this point and the kernel will check at the next use. `delay`—a packet has been sent to a stale entry and the kernel is awaiting confirmation. `probe`—the timer associated with a delay entry expired and the kernel has initiated ARP or ND communications. `failed`—the resolution attempt related to the probe state has failed. `noarp`—valid entry for which no confirmation will be attempted. `permanent`—administratively controlled valid entry not subject to ARP cache timeouts.

Example 16–13 illustrates the use of `ip neighbor show`.

Example 16–13   Output of `ip neighbor show`

```
# ip neigh sh
10.254.1.10 dev eth0 lladdr 00:a0:cc:5f:75:82 nud stale
10.254.1.1 dev eth0 lladdr 00:20:af:dc:28:1f nud stale
172.16.13.10 dev eth2 lladdr 00:a0:cc:58:69:05 nud stale
172.16.1.3 dev eth2 lladdr 08:00:20:16:07:a8 nud reachable
#
```

Adding `-s` to this command yields reference and timing information regarding each entry. Example 16–14 illustrates. The value after `ref` is the number of processes that are using this entry. The triplet after `used` is a collection of three timers, each separated by /. The values are *used*/*confirmed*/*updated*. Thus, 5/1/1 means that the entry was used 5 seconds ago, confirmed 1 second ago, and updated 1 second ago.

Example 16–14   Output of `ip -s neighbor show`

```
# ip -s n sh
10.254.1.1 dev eth0 lladdr 00:20:af:dc:28:1f ref 2 used 456/456/456 nud stale
172.16.13.10 dev eth2 lladdr 00:a0:cc:58:69:05 ref 2 used 5/1/1 nud reachable
172.16.1.3 dev eth2 lladdr 08:00:20:16:07:a8 ref 1 used 19/19/1069 nud reachable
#
```

`ip neighbor {add,change,replace}`   These commands create, modify, or replace ARP and/or ND records. The syntax takes one form for standard entries and a slightly more simplified form for proxies, as shown in Example 16–15.

Example 16–15   Syntax of `ip neighbor {add, change, replace}`

```
ip neighbor add | change | replace [to] addr [lladdr lladdr]
       [nud permanent | noarp | stale | reachable ] [dev iface_name]
ip neighbor add | change | replace proxy addr [dev iface_name]
```

Each of the arguments are described in Table 16–8.

Table 16–8   Arguments of `ip neighbor {add, change, replace}`

ARGUMENT	DESCRIPTION
`[to] addr`	Specifies the IPv4 or IPv6 address of the neighbor. Use of the keyword `to` is optional.
`lladdr lladdr`	Specifies the layer 2 address of the neighbor.

Table 16–8   Arguments of `ip neighbor {add, change, replace}` *(Continued)*

ARGUMENT	DESCRIPTION
`nud permanent | noarp` `| stale | reachable`	Specifies the state of the ARP or ND entry. `permanent` means that the entry is not subject to timeouts, this is the default; `noarp` means that the entry is valid, administratively added, but will not be verified via ARP or ND; `reachable` means that the entry is valid and is subject to the timeout periods associated with the ARP cache (see Chapter 3 for a discussion of ARP cache timeouts)—such entries have usually been discovered by ARP or ND; and `stale` means that the entry is valid, but may have exceeded the timeout and was not reverified by ARP or ND. Local interfaces are reported as `stale`. Dynamically discovered entries which are `stale` will shortly be removed. These are the only states that can be set administratively. All other states described in Table 16–7 can only be set internally by the kernel.
`dev iface_name`	Specifies the interface name.
`proxy addr`	Specifies the IPv4 or IPv6 of the neighbor for which to proxy.

Adding entries using the `ip neighbor add` command proceeds similarly to the `arp` command (discussed in Chapter 3). Example 16–16 illustrates adding a permanent entry. Since `permanent` is the default state when manually adding entries, the use of `nud permanent` is not required.

Example 16–16   Adding an ARP Entry with `ip neighbor add`

```
# ip neigh add 10.254.1.21 lladdr 08:00:69:08:0a:1c dev eth0
# ip neigh show
172.16.88.22 dev eth2 lladdr 08:00:69:0c:c7:ad nud stale
10.254.1.1 dev eth0 lladdr 00:20:af:dc:28:1f nud stale
172.16.13.10 dev eth2 lladdr 00:a0:cc:58:69:05 nud stale
172.16.1.3 dev eth2 lladdr 08:00:20:16:07:a8 nud reachable
10.254.1.21 dev eth0 lladdr 08:00:69:08:0a:1c nud permanent
#
```

Example 16–17 shows changing the state of an entry from `permanent` to `reachable`, and therefore subjecting the entry to timeouts. Note that the entry for `172.16.88.22`, which was `stale` in Example 16–16, has now been removed by the kernel.

Example 16–17   Changing the State of an ARP Entry

```
# ip neigh chg 10.254.1.21 lladdr 08:00:69:08:0a:1c nud reachable dev eth0
# ip neigh sh
10.254.1.1 dev eth0 lladdr 00:20:af:dc:28:1f nud stale
172.16.13.10 dev eth2 lladdr 00:a0:cc:58:69:05 nud stale
172.16.1.3 dev eth2 lladdr 08:00:20:16:07:a8 nud reachable
10.254.1.21 dev eth0 lladdr 08:00:69:08:0a:1c nud reachable
#
```

`ip neighbor delete`   This command is used to remove entries from the ARP cache. Its syntax and arguments are the same as `ip neighbor add` except that the `nud` and `lladdr` arguments are ignored. Deleted entries are not removed immediately, but are marked for removal at the next time the kernel flushes the cache of old entries. Entries deleted in this way that are in use will not be removed until the using process terminates the connection. An example of removing the entry associated with `10.254.1.21` is

```
# ip neigh del 10.254.1.21 dev eth0
```

WARNING

Attempts to delete or change entries with `nud` state `noarp` may cause the kernel to try to start resolving the entry using ARP or ND even when the interface is set to `NOARP`.

`ip neighbor flush`   This command is used to flush entries from the ARP cache. It uses the same arguments as `ip neighbor show`. Without arguments, however, `ip neighbor flush` does nothing. It operates as described for `ip neighbor delete` with respect to the way in which entries are removed. `ip neighbor flush` will not remove entries that are either `noarp` or `permanent`. As an example, the following will remove the entry with the IP address `10.254.1.21`.

```
# ip neigh flush 10.254.1.21
```

The `ip maddress` **Object**

The commands associated with this object are used to `add`, `delete`, or `show` multicast addresses. Note that IP multicast addresses can only be added programmatically and that `ip maddress add` and `ip maddress delete` can only be used to effect layer 2 multicast addresses. However, `ip maddress show` lists both layer 2 and layer 3 multicast addresses.

The `ip maddr show` command lists the multicast addresses of all interfaces. This command accepts one argument, the interface name which can be optionally preceded with the `dev` keyword. Example 16–18 illustrates. Note that this interface is participating in OSPF (see Chapter 12).

Example 16–18   Output of `ip maddress show`

```
# ip maddr sh eth0
2:eth0

link   01:00:5e:00:00:06

link   01:00:5e:00:00:05

link   01:00:5e:00:00:01

inet   224.0.0.6

inet   224.0.0.5

inet   224.0.0.1
#
```

IP multicast addresses can be suppressed by using the `-0` option as shown in Example 16–19.

Example 16–19   Output of `ip -0 maddress show`

```
# ip -0 maddr sh eth0
2:eth0

link   01:00:5e:00:00:06

link   01:00:5e:00:00:05

link   01:00:5e:00:00:01
#
```

The `ip maddress add` and `ip maddress delete` have the following syntax:

```
ip maddress add | delete [address] lladdr [dev iface_name]
```

where *lladdr* is the layer 2 multicast address optionally preceded by the `address` keyword, and *iface_name* is the interface name which must be preceded by the keyword `dev`. For example,

```
# ip maddr add 01:00:5e:00:00:11 dev eth0
```

adds a multicast address layer to eth0 and

```
# ip maddr del 01:00:5e:00:00:11 dev eth0
```

removes it.

The `ip mroute` Object

This object consists only of the show argument. At the time of this writing, multicast routing tables cannot be added manually and can only be added through a multicast routing table daemon. The syntax for the `ip mroute show` command is

```
ip mroute show [[to] prefix] [iif iface_name] [from prefix]
```

where *prefix* specifies the multicast address(es), in prefix notation, to list, optionally preceded by the `to` keyword; `iif` *iface_name* specifies the interface on which multicast packets are received; and `from` *prefix* specifies the source IP address(es), in prefix notation, of the multicast route.

The `ip route` Object

This object is used to manage the kernel routing tables. Whereas the `route` command only operates on, what appears to be, a single routing table, `ip route` can be used to manipulate multiple tables. In reality, the kernel can maintain up to 255 routing tables; two, known as `local` and `main`, exist by default and appear as one table to the `route` command. The tables are numbered (within the range 1 through 255), but can be given names in the file `/etc/iproute2/rt_tables`—the `local` table is 255 and `main` is 254; these two associations are hard coded. The `route` command sees these two tables as one.

Each entry in the routing table has a *key* by which it is uniquely identified. The key consists of the destination network number and prefix, an optional TOS value (described in "TOS, Differentiated Services, and Integrated Services" on page 819), and a preference (described in this and subsequent sections). Each route key refers to a record in a routing table. Each routing table entry consists of the necessary information to forward packets (as described in Chapter 6) and required and/or optional attributes (described in the following sections) which refine the route entry's use. The required and optional attributes depend upon the route *type*. Route types supported by the Linux 2.2.x series kernels are listed and described in Table 16–9. Their use is detailed in the sections throughout the remainder of this chapter.

Table 16–9   Route Types

TYPE	DESCRIPTION
unicast	The route entry specifies reachable actual paths to the destinations associated with the network number.
unreachable	The route entry specifies an unreachable destination. Any packets matching this route are discarded and an ICMP host unreachable message is generated.
blackhole	The route entry specifies an unreachable destination. Any packets matching this route are discarded and no ICMP message is generated.
prohibit	The route entry specifies an unreachable destination. Any packets matching this route are discarded and an ICMP communication administratively prohibited message is generated.
local	The route entry specifies a reachable destination assigned to this host. Packets are looped back and locally delivered.
broadcast	The route entry specifies a reachable broadcast destination. Matching packets are sent through the appropriate local interface.
throw	The route entry specifies a special control route that is used with policy rules. Any packets matching this type of entry are processed in accordance with the policy rules. If no policy rules exist, or if policy routing is disabled, then all matching packets to this type of entry are discarded and an ICMP net unreachable error message is generated.
nat	The route entry of this type specifies that network address translation must be performed prior to the forwarding of a matching packet.

Table 16–9   Route Types *(Continued)*

TYPE	DESCRIPTION
`anycast`	The route entry specifies that the destination is an IPv6 anycast address. This type is *not* implemented in Linux 2.2.x kernels.
`multicast`	The route entry specifies that the destination is a multicast address. This type of entry only appears in multicast routing tables.

Beginning with "Routing Policies" on page 804, we consider the capabilities of multiple routing tables and the use of `ip route` in more detail. In this section, we provide the syntax of the commands associated with `ip route`.

The `ip route` object accepts `add`, `change`, `replace`, `delete`, `show`, `flush`, and `get`. We describe the syntax and arguments of each in the following sections.

`ip route {add,change,replace}` The syntax of the `ip route {add,change,replace}` command is provided in Example 16–20.

Example 16–20   Syntax of the `ip route {add,change,replace}`

```
ip route add | change | replace [to] [type] nprefix | nat addr [tos tos]
    [metric | preference pref] [table tableid] [dev iface_name] via addr
    [src addr] [realm realmid] [mtu [lock] mtu] [window wsize]
    [rtt nbr] [nexthop nexthop] [scope scope_val] [protocol rtproto]
    [onlink] [equalize] [append] [prepend]
```

Table 16–10 describes the arguments shown in Example 16–20.

Table 16–10   Arguments to `ip route {add,change,replace}`

ARGUMENT	DESCRIPTION
`[to] [type] nprefix`	The value of *nprefix* is the network number or host address in prefix notation and represents the destination address of the route. It may be preceded with the optional keyword `to`. The special keyword `default` can be used as nprefix instead of `0/0` (IPv4) or `::/0` (IPv6). If *type* is not specified, then the default type is `unicast`. See Table 16–9 for a description of route types.

Table 16–10   Arguments to `ip route {add,change,replace}` *(Continued)*

ARGUMENT	DESCRIPTION
`tos` *tos*	Specifies the TOS value associated with this route. Either an 8-bit hexadecimal value or an identifier from `/etc/iproute2/rt_dsfield`. TOS is discussed in "TOS, Differentiated Services, and Integrated Services" on page 819. Note that the default TOS is 0 (or not set). Route entries with a 0 TOS value can match a packet with a nonzero TOS value if no better match is found.
`metric` | `preference` *pref*	Specifies the preference value of the route. *pref* is an arbitrary 32-bit value with smaller values having higher preference.
`table` *tableid*	Specifies the *tableid*, which can be a number between 1 and 255 inclusive, or a string defined in `/etc/iproute2/rt_tables`, to which this route is added or belongs. If not specified, then for route types `local`, `broadcast`, and `nat`, the *tableid* defaults to `local`; for all other route types, it defaults to `main`.
`dev` *iface_name*	Specifies the output interface name.
`via` *addr*	For route types other than `nat`, this option specifies the *addr* of the nexthop router (referred to as gateway with respect to the `route` command). For route type `nat`, *addr* is the (first, if a block of addresses is translated) translated IP address.
`src` *addr*	Specifies the source IP address to prefer when sending packets matching the route.
`realm` *realmid*	Specifies the realm to which this route belongs. *realmid* can be a number or a string from `/etc/iproute2/rt_realms`. Realms are discussed in "Realms and the `rtacct` Command" on page 804.

Table 16–10   Arguments to `ip route {add,change,replace}` *(Continued)*

ARGUMENT	DESCRIPTION
`mtu [lock] mtu`	Specifies the `mtu` of the route. This value can be overridden by kernel PMTU unless the keyword `lock` is used, in which case PMTU is disabled for this route.
`window wsize`	Specifies the maximum burst TCP window size (described in Chapter 7) in bytes.
`rtt nbr`	Specifies the RTT estimate. In actuality, this is the initial TCP retransmission timeout.
`nexthop nexthop`	Specifies the nexthop of a multipath route. The `nexthop` value is of the form `[via addr] [dev iface_name] [weight nbr]` where `addr` is the actual nexthop router, `iface_name` is the output interface, and `nbr` is an arbitrary number reflecting the relative bandwidth or quality of this route.
`scope scope_val`	Specifies the scope of the destination(s) of this route. `scope_val` can be a number or string from `/etc/iproute2/rt_scopes`. If this argument is not specified, then the scope of the destination(s) is/are `global` for all `unicast` route types; `link` for `broadcast` route types or unicasts that are on the same local network (link local); `host` for all `local` route types.
`protocol rtproto`	Specifies the routing protocol associated with this route. `rtproto` can be a number or string from the file `/etc/iproute2/rt_protos`.
`onlink`	Specifies that the route should be treated as if it is directly attached to a local link even if it is not. This argument is often used with tunnels.
`equalize`	Specifies that this route participate in packet-by-packet randomization with multipath routes. Without this option, packets will always use the same route.

Table 16–10   Arguments to `ip route {add,change,replace}` *(Continued)*

ARGUMENT	DESCRIPTION
`append`	Adds the route to the end of the routing table.
`prepend`	Adds the route to the top of the routing table. IPv6 cannot use this option.

ip route delete   This command is used to delete routes. It uses the same arguments as `ip route add`. There must be enough information, in the form of arguments, for the command to identify a unique route, otherwise, it fails. Examples are given later in this chapter.

ip route show   This command is used to list the entries in the routing table(s). Its syntax is given in Example 16–21.

Example 16–21   Syntax of `ip route show`

```
ip route show [[to] [root | match | exact] nprefix] [tos tos]
       [table tableid] [cloned | cached]
       [from [root | match | exact] prefix] [protocol rtproto]
       [scope scope_val] [type type] [dev iface_name] [via prefix]
       [realm realmid | realms fromrealm/torealm]
```

Each of the arguments in Example 16–21 is described in Table 16–11.

Table 16–11   Arguments to `ip route show`

ARGUMENT	DESCRIPTION
`[to] [root | match | exact]` `nprefix`	Lists matching routes. The value of `nprefix` is the network number or host address in prefix notation and represents the destination address of the route. The `to` keyword is optional. The `root` keyword specifies that `nprefix` is to match all routes not shorter than `nprefix`. The keyword `match` specifies that `nprefix` is to match all routes not longer than `nprefix`. The keyword `exact` matches routes exactly with `nprefix` and is the default. Examples are given below.

Table 16–11   Arguments to `ip route show` *(Continued)*

ARGUMENT	DESCRIPTION
`tos` *tos*	Lists only routes matching the given *tos*, which is a number or string from `/etc/iproute2/rt_dsfield`.
`table` *tableid*	Lists routes in the matching *tableid*, which is a string or number in `/etc/iproute2/rt_tables` or the special values: `all`, meaning list all tables, or `cache`, meaning list the routing cache (see Chapter 6 for a description of the routing cache).
`cloned` | `cached`	These two keywords are synonymous and are equivalent to `table cache`.
`from [root` | `match` | `exact]` *prefix*	Lists routes for which the source address matches *prefix*. The keywords `root`, `match`, and `exact` are as described for the first entry in this table.
`protocol` *rtproto*	Lists routes matching *rtproto* which is a number or string from `/etc/iproute2/rt_protos`.
`scope` *scope_val*	Lists routes matching *scope_val* which is a number or string from `/etc/iproute2/rt_scopes`.
`type` *type*	Lists routes matching the route *type* as described in Table 16–9 on page 786.
`dev` *iface_name*	Lists routes that transmit via this interface.
`via` *prefix*	Lists only routes that match *prefix* for the nexthop (gateway) routers.
`realm` *realmid* | `realms` *from-realm/torealm*	Lists only routes matching this or these realms.

Let's consider some examples that help clarify the use of some of the arguments described in Table 16–11. Example 16–22 illustrates the use of the `table all` argument. Some lines wrap due to formatting constraints.

Example 16–22   Output of `ip route show table all`

```
# ip ro sh table all
224.0.0.6 via 127.0.0.1 dev lo  proto gated  scope link
224.0.0.5 via 127.0.0.1 dev lo  proto gated  scope link
127.0.0.1 dev lo  scope link
10.254.12.0/24 dev eth1  proto gated  scope link
10.254.2.0/24 via 10.254.1.1 dev eth0  proto gated
10.254.1.0/24 dev eth0  proto gated  scope link
172.16.0.0/16 dev eth2  proto kernel  scope link  src 172.16.0.1
172.17.0.0/16 dev eth3  proto kernel  scope link  src 172.17.0.1
unreachable 172.16.0.0/12  proto gated
unreachable 127.0.0.0/8  proto gated  scope link
default via 10.254.1.1 dev eth0  proto gated
broadcast 127.255.255.255 dev lo  table local  proto kernel  scope link  src 127.0.0.1
local 172.16.0.1 dev eth2  table local  proto kernel  scope host  src 172.16.0.1
broadcast 172.16.0.0 dev eth2  table local  proto kernel  scope link  src 172.16.0.1
broadcast 10.254.12.0 dev eth1  table local  proto kernel  scope link  src
10.254.12.10
local 10.254.1.11 dev eth0  table local  proto kernel  scope host  src 10.254.1.11
local 172.17.0.1 dev eth3  table local  proto kernel  scope host  src 172.17.0.1
broadcast 10.254.1.255 dev eth0  table local  proto kernel  scope link  src
10.254.1.11
broadcast 172.17.0.0 dev eth3  table local  proto kernel  scope link  src 172.17.0.1
broadcast 172.17.255.255 dev eth3  table local  proto kernel  scope link  src
172.17.0.1
broadcast 172.16.255.255 dev eth2  table local  proto kernel  scope link  src
172.16.0.1
broadcast 10.254.12.255 dev eth1  table local  proto kernel  scope link  src
10.254.12.10
broadcast 127.0.0.0 dev lo  table local  proto kernel  scope link  src 127.0.0.1
broadcast 10.254.1.0 dev eth0  table local  proto kernel  scope link  src 10.254.1.11
local 127.0.0.1 dev lo  table local  proto kernel  scope host  src 127.0.0.1
local 10.254.12.10 dev eth1  table local  proto kernel  scope host  src 10.254.12.10
local 127.0.0.0/8 dev lo  table local  proto kernel  scope host  src 127.0.0.1
#
```

The output shown in Example 16–22 lists the contents of all routing tables (but not the routing cache) on the given system. Each record begins with the route type (see Table 16–9 on page 786) except for those records that are of type `unicast`. Following the route type is the destination. After the destination follows a series of attribute names and values, all of which have been described here or previously in Chapter 6. The final value is the nexthop router or gateway. Note that a number of entries are of `proto gated`, meaning that they have been added to the table dynamically by the `gated` daemon. Also, note the `unreachable` aggregate entry for `172.16.0.0/12`. This entry is created on this system and propagated via OSPF (see Chapter 12) to other routers, but is not used by this system since it has direct links (route type `local`) to the `172.16/12` networks.

To illustrate the distinction between `root` *nprefix* and `match` *nprefix*, first consider Example 16–23 which shows the use of the `match` keyword. In this example, we are matching all routes with a destination of `10/8` or shorter (less specific). Compare the results here with those of Example 16–22. All routes beginning with 10 in the first octet have more than 8 significant bits in the network portion of the address in Example 16–22 and, thus, Example 16–23 returns the default entry.

Example 16–23   Using `ip route show match`

```
# ip ro sh match 10/8
default via 10.254.1.1 dev eth0  proto gated
#
```

On the other hand, by using the keyword root with the same `10/8` match prefix, all routes to `10.254.x/24` will match as illustrated in Example 16–24.

Example 16–24   Using `ip route show root`

```
# ip ro sh root 10/8
10.254.12.0/24 dev eth1  proto gated  scope link
10.254.2.0/24 via 10.254.1.1 dev eth0  proto gated
10.254.1.0/24 dev eth0  proto gated  scope link
#
```

Now, let's take a look at a routing cache. Example 16–25 shows the routing cache from the same system as viewed in Example 16–22.

Example 16–25   Viewing the Routing Cache with `ip route show table cache`

```
# ip ro sh table cache
172.16.13.10 from 172.16.0.1 dev eth2
    cache  mtu 1500 rtt 300
local 10.254.1.11 from 10.254.1.11 dev lo
    cache <local>  mtu 3924 rtt 300
169.238.64.2 from 172.16.88.22 via 10.254.1.1 dev eth0  src 172.16.0.1
    cache <src-direct>  mtu 1500 rtt 300 iif eth2
broadcast 172.17.255.255 from 172.17.55.22 tos 0x10 dev lo  src 172.17.0.1
    cache <local,brd>  iif eth1
198.29.75.75 from 10.254.1.11 via 10.254.1.1 dev eth0
    cache  mtu 1500 rtt 300
172.16.88.22 from 192.26.51.194 dev eth2  src 10.254.1.11
    cache  mtu 1500 rtt 300 iif eth0
172.16.88.22 from 192.26.51.193 dev eth2  src 10.254.1.11
    cache  mtu 1500 rtt 300 iif eth0
172.16.1.3 from 172.16.0.1 dev eth2
    cache  mtu 1500 rtt 300
local 10.254.1.11 from 10.254.1.1 dev lo  src 10.254.1.11
    cache <local,src-direct>  iif eth0
172.16.88.22 from 169.238.64.2 dev eth2  src 10.254.1.11
    cache  mtu 1500 rtt 300 iif eth0
```

Example 16–25   Viewing the Routing Cache with `ip route show table cache` *(Continued)*

```
local 10.254.1.11 from 198.29.75.75 dev lo   src 10.254.1.11
    cache <local>   iif eth0
198.29.75.112 from 172.16.88.22 via 10.254.1.1 dev eth0   src 172.16.0.1
    cache <src-direct>   mtu 1500 rtt 300 iif eth2
172.16.88.22 from 198.29.75.112 dev eth2   src 10.254.1.11
    cache   mtu 1500 rtt 300 iif eth0
local 127.0.0.1 from 127.0.0.1 dev lo
    cache <local>   mtu 3924 rtt 300
multicast 224.0.0.5 from 10.254.1.11 dev eth0
    cache <local,mc>   mtu 1500 rtt 300
multicast 224.0.0.5 from 10.254.12.10 dev eth1
    cache <local,mc>   mtu 1500 rtt 300
broadcast 172.16.255.255 from 172.16.88.22 dev lo   src 172.16.0.1
    cache <local,brd,src-direct>   iif eth2
192.26.51.194 from 172.16.88.22 via 10.254.1.1 dev eth0   src 172.16.0.1
    cache <src-direct>   mtu 1500 rtt 300 iif eth2
broadcast 172.17.255.255 from 172.17.1.3 dev lo   src 172.17.0.1
    cache <local,brd,src-direct>   iif eth3
local 172.16.0.1 from 172.16.13.10 dev lo   src 172.16.0.1
    cache <local,src-direct>   iif eth2
multicast 224.0.0.5 from 172.17.0.1 dev eth3
    cache <local,mc>   mtu 1500 rtt 300
multicast 224.0.0.5 from 172.16.0.1 dev eth2
    cache <local,mc>   mtu 1500 rtt 300
local 172.16.0.1 from 172.16.1.3 dev lo   src 172.16.0.1
    cache <local,src-direct>   iif eth2
local 127.0.0.1 dev lo   src 127.0.0.1
    cache <local>   mtu 3924 rtt 300
multicast 224.0.0.5 from 10.254.1.1 dev lo   src 10.254.1.11
    cache <local,mc>   iif eth0
broadcast 172.16.255.255 from 172.16.1.3 dev lo   src 172.16.0.1
    cache <local,brd,src-direct>   iif eth2
#
```

The routing cache (described in Chapter 6) contains a listing of all currently used routes. Similar to the output of `ip route show table all`, each record begins with the route type (except for type unicast) and the pertinent destination address. Wherever there is a `from` keyword, the address following it specifies the host involved in the communication. The address following the `src` keyword specifies the address of the source of the route. The address following the `via` keyword is the address of the nexthop router. The `rtt`, `dev`, and `mtu` keywords and the values following them are the RTT, interface, and MTU, respectively. The interface name following the `iif` keyword indicates the interface on which packets related to this route are expected to arrive. Although not appearing in this example, there are two other keywords that can show up: `expires` followed by a timeout value indicates that the entry will expire after the indicated number of seconds, and `error`, which appears on `reject` routes indicating the error code that is to be translated into an appropriate ICMP message.

Note that there are some special values within < and > after the keyword cache. These values are called *cache flags* and are described in Table 16–12.

Table 16–12   Cache Flags

FLAG	DESCRIPTION
local	Route causes packets to be delivered locally. This is the case for loopback, broadcast, and multicast (for which the host is a member) routes.
reject	This route is bad and cannot be used. The keyword error and appropriate error code will appear in the entry for this record.
mc	The destination is a multicast address.
brd	The destination is a broadcast address.
src-direct	The source address is on a local interface.
redirected	The entry was created by an ICMP redirect.
redirect	Use of this route will generate an ICMP redirect.
fastroute	The route can be configured to use the fastroute capability. See Fast switching in Table 16–1 on page 758.
equalize	Use of multiple routes is in use on this (and at least one other) entry.
dst-nat	Destination address requires NAT.
src-nat	Source address requires NAT.
masq	Source address requires masquerading.
notify	A change or deletion to this route will generate notification. This flag is not functional in 2.2.x series kernels.

If the -s option is added to the command shown in Example 16–25, then the following fields will additionally appear.

- users—the number of processes using the entry
- age—the number of seconds ago that this route was used
- used—the number of times this route was looked up since its creation

ip route flush   This command is used to flush the routes or routing table specified by arguments. The arguments used are identical to that of `ip route show`. If no arguments are given to `ip route flush`, it prints a usage message. For example,

```
ip -4 route flush scope global type unicast table cache
```

will remove all global, unicast, IPv4 routes from the routing cache. Use of the `-s` flag provides more verbose output.

ip route get   This is a special command that effectively simulates sending (doesn't actually send) a packet to a specified destination. This command will often cause a new entry to be placed into the routing cache. Its syntax is provided in Example 16–26.

Example 16–26   Syntax of `ip route get`

```
ip route get [to] addr [from addr] [tos tos] [iif iface_name]
    [oif iface_name] [connected]
```

Each of the arguments shown in Example 16–26 are described in Table 16–13.

Table 16–13   Arguments to `ip route get`

ARGUMENT	DESCRIPTION
`[to]` *addr*	Specifies the destination address.
`from` *addr*	Specifies the source address.
`tos` *tos*	Specifies a TOS value to match in the route.
`iif` *iface_name*	Specifies the interface on which packets arrive. If this option is specified, the kernel pretends that it received a packet from *iface_name* and is forwarding it.
`oif` *iface_name*	Forces the packet to use the specified interface as the outbound device.
`connected`	If `from` is not specified, then this argument causes the kernel to set the source address for this test to the most preferred one based on existing tables and policy rules.

Let's examine the behavior of the `ip route get` command. Example 16–27 shows getting a route to the address `24.1.8.33`. The first command in this example proves that the entry is not currently in the routing cache; the `ip route get` command is then executed. Note that its output of that command is the same as `ip route show`. The last command in Example 16–27 repeats the first, showing that a new entry has indeed been entered into the routing cache due to the `ip route get` command.

Example 16–27   Using `ip route get`

```
# ip ro sh 24.1.8.33 table cache
# ip ro get 24.1.8.33
24.1.8.33 via 172.16.0.1 dev eth0   src 172.16.13.10
    cache  mtu 1500 rtt 375ms
# ip ro sh 24.1.8.33 table cache
24.1.8.33 via 172.16.0.1 dev eth0   src 172.16.13.10
    cache  mtu 1500 rtt 375ms
#
```

The `ip rule` Object

The purpose of this object is to control the *routing policy database* (RPDB), which in turn controls the route selection algorithm. The RPDB consists of rules that can make decisions about routing packets depending upon the source IP address, destination IP address, TOS, `mark` value set by `ipchains` or `iptables`, and the incoming interface. These four components comprise the match key of the rules within RPDB. It should be noted that because the mark value can be used in the RPDB, routing decisions can also indirectly be made based on any values that `ipchains` or `iptables` can check. Thus, the RPDB provides a powerful and flexible mechanism for controlling whether or not and how packets get routed.

It is very important not to confuse the RPDB with routing tables. The RPDB consists of a set of rules that dictate which routing tables are used, whereas the routing tables are used by the kernel to select a route for each packet. Effectively, the Linux 2.2.x series kernel selects routes based on the longest (most specific) match. The RPDB controls which routing table(s) the kernel searches and thereby indirectly controls the selection. We consider examples of this functionality beginning with "Routing Policies" on page 804. In this section, we define the command syntax for this object.

Each rule in the RPDB is of a particular rule type. These types are described in Table 16–14 and represent a subset of route types (see Table 16–9 on page 786).

Table 16–14   Rule Types

TYPE	DESCRIPTION
unicast	This rule type causes the routing table to return a matching unicast route.
blackhole	This rule type causes the packet to be discarded and no ICMP messages to be generated.
unreachable	This rule type causes the packet to be discarded and an ICMP network unreachable message to be generated.
prohibit	This rule type causes the packet to be discarded and an ICMP communication administratively prohibited message to be generated.
nat	This rule type causes the source address of the packet to be translated.

The `ip rule` object accepts the three commands, `add`, `delete`, and `show`, each of which is discussed in the following two sections.

ip rule {add,delete}   The `ip rule add` and `ip rule delete` commands are used to add and delete rules from the RPDB, respectively. The general syntax of this object is

```
ip rule add | del selector action
```

where `selector` represents one or more arguments used to match packets and `action` represents one or more arguments that dictate what to do with a matching packet. Table 16–15 lists the possible arguments for `selector` and `action`, and distinguishes between them by specifying in the column *Operation* as to whether the argument is for use in either the `selector` or `action` role.

Table 16–15   Selector and Action Arguments to `ip rule {add,delete}`

ARGUMENT	OPERATION	DESCRIPTION
`from prefix`	selector	Sets the source IP address `prefix` in prefix notation to match.
`to prefix`	selector	Sets the destination IP address `prefix` in prefix notation to match.
`iif iface_name`	selector	Sets the incoming interface `iface_name` to match. Using this argument, packets originating from the localhost can be distinguished from packets to be forwarded.
`tos tos`	selector	Sets the `tos` value to match.
`fwmark mark`	selector	Specifies the `mark` value, from `iptables` or `ipchains`, to match.
`priority prio`	selector	Sets the priority of the rule. Each rule must have a unique priority.
`table tableid`	action	Specifies the routing table to use for route selection if the rule is matched.
`realms [srcrealm/]dstrealm`	action	Specifies the realm(s) to select if the rule is matched.

Table 16–15   Selector and Action Arguments to `ip rule {add,delete}` *(Continued)*

ARGUMENT	OPERATION	DESCRIPTION
`[type]` *type*	action	Specifies one of the types in Table 16–14. Note that `reject` is synonymous with `blackhole`. Type `nat` requires an address argument and is described next. *type* can be optionally preceded with the keyword `type`.
`nat` *addr*	action	Translates source address to *addr* which may be the start of a block of addresses.

NOTE

Once rules are added they are not automatically read internally by the kernel. In order to force a read of rules after the RPDB has been modified, execute `ip route flush cache`.

`ip rule show`   This command is used to list the RPDB. It takes no arguments. Example 16–28 shows the default RPDB.

Example 16–28   Using `ip rule show`

```
# ip ru sh
0:      from all lookup local
32766: from all lookup main
32767: from all lookup 253
#
```

The output of the command has the following form.

```
priority:from source [to dest] lookup tableid [map-to addr]
```

Here, `priority` is the priority of the rule (lower values have higher priority), followed by a colon. The `from` keyword precedes the source IP address, `source`, to match. Here, the special keyword `all` is used, meaning that all packets match. If the rule was written with a destination IP address (`dest`) match, that address would appear after the `to` keyword. The `lookup` keyword precedes the *tableid*—if this rule matches, then *tableid* is used for route selection. Finally, if the rule is for NAT, then the translated address (*addr*) will appear after the map-to keyword.

Note that there are three tables shown in Example 16–28, each configured by default at system start-up. The table local is always the first table to be searched (priority 0). It consists of routes for local and broadcast addresses and its rule can neither be deleted nor modified. The table main is the normal routing table consisting of non-policy routes. Its rule can be overridden by higher priority rules and can also be deleted. The rule associated with table 253 (also known as default—if /etc/iproute2/rt_tables is copied from the distribution, then this table will be identified as default in the RPDB) is empty, by default. It is used for special post-processing of packets if default rules do not match. It can be deleted.

The `ip tunnel` **Object**

The ip tunnel object is used to add, change, delete, and show tunnels which are infrastructures that encapsulate packets in IPv4 packets. In this section, we describe the syntax of the ip tunnel commands and subsequently consider examples in "Tunneling" on page 814. In particular, examples of the ip tunnel show command, which displays all tunnels, is shown in that latter section.

ip tunnel {add,change,delete} These commands are used to add, change, and delete tunnels, respectively. The syntax of the command is given in Example 16–29.

Example 16–29 Syntax of ip tunnel {add, change, delete}

```
ip tunnel { add | change | del } [[name] tname]
    [mode ipip | gre | sit ] [ remote addr ] [ local addr ]
    [iseq | oseq | seq] [ikey | okey | key key] [icsum | ocsum | csum]
    [ttl n] [tos tos] [nopmtudisc] [dev iface_name ]
```

Each of the arguments associated with the commands given in Example 16–29 are described in Table 16–16.

Table 16–16   Arguments of `ip tunnel {add,change,delete}`

ARGUMENT	DESCRIPTION
`name` *tname*	Specifies the tunnel name, *tname*.
`mode ipip| gre | sit`	Specifies the type of tunnel. `ipip` is the Linux specific IP in IP tunnel; `gre` is for a GRE; and `sit` is IPv6 in IPv4 tunnel.
`remote` *addr*	Specifies the remote IP address of the tunnel, known as the *remote endpoint*.
`local` *addr*	Specifies the local address of the tunnel. This is the *local endpoint*.
`iseq | oseq | seq`	Serializes the packets flowing through the tunnel. `iseq` requires that all ingress packets are serialized; `oseq` causes serialization of all egress packets; `seq` is both. As of this writing, these options are *not* functional.
`ikey | okey | key` *key*	Used only with GRE tunnels. Specifies the *key*, a 32-bit value often expressed in decimal dotted notation, to use at the endpoints of the tunnel. Only holders of the *key* can successfully use the tunnel. The keyword, `key`, specifies that the *key* is to be used for both inbound and outbound packets. `ikey` specifies inbound only; `okey` specifies outbound only.
`icsum | ocsum | csum`	Specifies that checksums are to be included with packets. `icsum` indicates that checksums are to be checked on all inbound packets; `ocsum` sends checksums with all outbound packets; `csum` does both.
`ttl` *n*	Specifies a fixed time-to-live (TTL) value, $1 \leq n \leq 255$. The default value is 0, a special value meaning that the TTL is inherited.

Table 16–16   Arguments of `ip tunnel {add,change,delete}` *(Continued)*

ARGUMENT	DESCRIPTION
`tos tos`	Specifies the `tos` value (see "TOS, Differentiated Services, and Integrated Services" on page 819). The default behavior is to inherit the TOS.
`nopmtudisc`	Specifies that PMTU is not to be performed on this tunnel. By default, PMTU is enabled. Note that this option cannot be specified if the `ttl` option is used.
`dev iface_name`	Specifies the interface to which the tunnel is bound. If this option is used, then all tunneled packets will be routed through *iface_name*, even if there is a better route or when the route to the endpoint fails.

`ip monitor` and `rtmon`

The `ip monitor` command is different than other `ip object` objects in that it is a command. It can be used to monitor state changes in the various routing tables. It can perform this task continuously or on demand in conjunction with the `rtmon` command. The syntax of the `ip monitor` command is

```
ip monitor [file file] [all | object_list]
```

where *file* is the name of a file containing binary formatted messages generated by `rtmon` and *object_list* is a space-separated list of object types to monitor. The monitorable object types are `link`, `address`, and `route`. The special keyword `all` is equivalent to `link address route`. If `ip monitor` is invoked without any commands, then it monitors all objects continuously until a `Ctrl-C` is executed.

The `rtmon` command is used to write routing table state changes to a file. Its syntax is

```
rtmon file file [all | object_list]
```

The arguments are identical to those for `ip monitor` except that the file argument is required. This command can be used in a start-up script executed prior to interface configuration to maintain a complete log of routing table state changes. For example,

```
rtmon file /var/log/rt_state.log
```

The file `/var/log/rt_state.log` can then be viewed anytime with `ip monitor`.

Realms and the `rtacct` Command

In larger environments, such as those using OSPF and/or BGP, routing tables can get quite large. Packet accounting and route use becomes a fairly complex task quite quickly when the tables get large and even more complex when multiple tables are used due to the implementation of routing policies. In order to simplify some of these accounting tasks and, perhaps, also to collect routes into an aggregate for policy implementation, realms can be used.

A realm is nothing more than an identifying number (and name, if `/etc/iproute2/rt_realms` is used). Specific packets can be identified by almost any field in the IP header (as described in the next section) and then associated with a realm based on a matching rule. Realms can then be added to the appropriate routing table(s) as source and destination routes. Furthermore, a patched version of `gated` can accommodate propagating realm oriented routes. This patched version is available at

```
ftp://ftp.inr.ac.ru/ip-routing/
```

The `rtacct` command is used to obtain accounting information about realms. Only ingress traffic is counted and it is maintained in `/proc/net/rt_acct`. With no arguments, `rtacct` displays the statistics for all realms. One or more realm identifiers or names (in a space-separated list) can be used as arguments to `rtacct` causing the output to consist of statistics for only those realms listed. Example 16–30 illustrates.

Example 16–30   Output of `rtacct`

```
# rtacct internal
Realm          BytesTo          PktsTo          BytesFrom        PktsFrom
internal       1589326          1089            1908247          1016
#
```

Routing Policies

Throughout the Internet and within most internal networks, routing decisions are made primarily based on the destination IP address and sometimes additionally based on the TOS field of the IP header. With the use of routing policies, this approach can be expanded significantly to cause routing decisions to be made based on a wide variety of parameters including, specifically, destination IP address, source IP address, TOS value, and anything that can be marked by `ipchains` or `iptables`. Implementation of routing policies is largely accomplished through the use of the `ip route` and `ip rule` objects, the syntax of which are described earlier in this chapter. In this section, we consider the creation of routing policies that can be used to modify the routing decision process under a variety of circumstances. The examples provided here simply scratch the surface of these Linux capabilities.

Source IP Address Decisions

Consider a Linux router, `topcat`, with two external interfaces, `eth0` via a 256 Kbps connection and `eth1` via a 1 Mbps connection (these could be DSL connections, for example). These external interfaces could lead to the Internet or to an internal internetwork; for this example it doesn't matter; just suppose that each external interface can reach all destinations. Suppose also that `topcat` has an internal Ethernet interface, `eth2`, that connects to the internal Ethernet network. This internal network is nicely divided into two subnetworks, Engineering (`172.16.1/24`), the users of which infrequently connect to the external networks, and Sales (`172.16.10/24`), the users of which frequently connect to the external network. Figure 16–1 depicts this scenario.

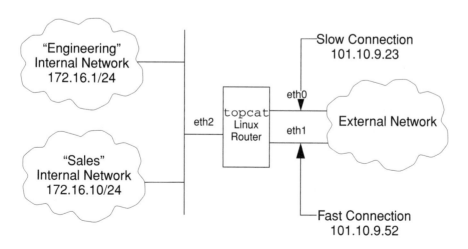

Figure 16–1   A Simple Routing Policy Example

Given this description, it is desirable for `topcat` to forward all packets originating from Engineering through `eth0` and all packets from Sales through `eth1`. This can be accomplished by creating rules that cause the kernel to use distinct routing tables based on the source IP address. To that end, we first create two table names and put them in `/etc/iproute2/rt_tables`, as shown in Example 16–31. The example also shows the contents of the `/etc/iproute2/rt_tables` file—note the reserved values. The only purpose for adding the entries here is so that table names (`Eng` and `Sales`, in this case) can be used instead of numbers (`100` and `101`).

Example 16–31   Adding Entries to `/etc/iproute2/rt_tables`

```
# echo "100 Eng" >> /etc/iproute2/rt_tables
# echo "101 Sales" >> /etc/iproute2/rt_tables
# cat /etc/iproute2/rt_tables
#
# reserved values
#
255     local
254     main
253     default
0       unspec
#
# local tables
#
100 Eng
101 Sales
#
```

Next, we create the rules as illustrated in Example 16–32. The example first adds the two rules and then lists all of the rules. The choice of priority values in this case is arbitrary, except that the values must be less than `main` and `default` so that they are processed first, since `main` likely has a default router entry. Rule priorities become more significant as more rules are added. The two rules added tell the kernel that whenever a packet has a source IP address that matches `172.16.10.0/24`, then use the routing table `Sales`; for source IP addresses matching `172.16.1.0/24`, use the routing table `Eng`.

Example 16–32   Adding Rules to the RPDB

```
# ip ru add from 172.16.10/24 table Sales priority 250
# ip ru add from 172.16.1/24 table Eng priority 300
# ip ru list
0:      from all lookup local
250:    from 172.16.10.0/24 lookup Sales
300:    from 172.16.1.0/24 lookup Eng
32766: from all lookup main
32767: from all lookup default
#
```

Now, we need to create the routing tables and put entries in them to allow the rules in Example 16–32 to function. Example 16–33 provides the commands. The `ip route flush cache` command has the effect of activating the rules immediately.

Example 16–33   Adding the Routes

```
# ip route add default via 101.10.9.23 dev eth0 table Eng
# ip route add default via 101.10.9.52 dev eth1 table Sales
# ip route flush cache
```

That's it! All packets originating from `172.16.1/24` will exit through `eth0` and all packets from `172.16.10/24` will exit through `eth1`. Unfortunately, there is no way on `topcat` to control the return packets—accomplishing that requires a cooperative effort with the administrators of the routers in the external network. If you have that cooperation (such as, it is all part of the same company), then techniques such as those described in this chapter can be used. If you do not have that cooperation, then using DNS is likely the only sure way to get return packets through the correct interface.

NOTE

All of the commands shown in this and subsequent sections are only effective until the next reboot. In order to cause them to survive reboots, they must be put into an appropriate start-up script.

The example given in Figure 16–1 on page 805 is fairly simplistic and certainly presents the unlikely scenario that the network topology matches desired routing path usage. In the next two sections, we consider ways to accomplish goals similar to those presented here by using `mark` and TOS values instead of just the source IP address.

Mark Values

In the previous two chapters, we described the capability of setting the mark value on packets using `ipchains` and `iptables`, respectively. Any packets marked by these tools can subsequently be used by rules in the RPDB. Let's see how this works.

Consider Figure 16–2. The scenario here is the same as in Figure 16–1 except that the internal network is not nicely separated by use (thus, it is depicted as a single cloud).

To illustrate the flexibility of this feature, we begin by considering marking packets simply based on specific service types. To that end, suppose that we want all HTTP traffic to go through the fast connection and all FTP and telnet traffic to go through the slow connection. This is accomplished through the following steps.

1. Write `ipchains` or `iptables` rules to mark the specified packets.
2. Place rules in the RPDB that cause the kernel to use a routing table that forces traffic through the appropriate interface based on mark values.
3. Place the appropriate routes into the routing tables defined in step 2.
4. Flush the routing cache to effect the changes.
5. Once tested and verified, put the commands affecting the above four steps into a start-up script.

Effectively, these steps are entirely similar to those outlined in the previous section except that we additionally need to set up the appropriate rules in `ipchains` or netfilter. The `ipchains` rules in Example 16–34 show sample rules that meet the requirements—this is not a complete list of rules, just those that set the `mark` values. Here, we are using a `mark` value of 1 for the high speed connection, and 2 for the slower connection.

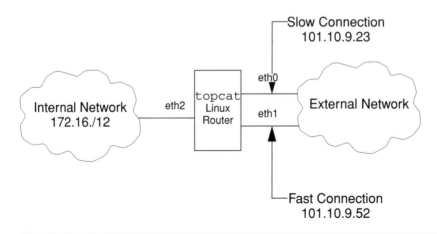

Figure 16–2   Routing Policy Using `mark` and/or TOS values

Example 16–34   Using `ipchains` to Set mark Values

```
# ipchains -A input -i eth2 -p tcp -s 172.16.0.0/12 -d 0/0 www -j ACCEPT -m 1
# ipchains -A input -i eth2 -p tcp -s 172.16.0.0/12 -d 0/0 telnet -j ACCEPT -m 2
# ipchains -A input -i eth2 -p tcp -s 172.16.0.0/12 -d 0/0 ftp -j ACCEPT -m 2
# ipchains -A input -i eth2 -p tcp -s 172.16.0.0/12 -d 0/0 ftp-data -j ACCEPT -m 2
```

The same thing can be accomplished with netfilter using `iptables` as shown in Example 16–35. Again, only the rules associated with marking the packets are shown.

Example 16–35   Using `iptables` to Set mark Values

```
# iptables -A PREROUTING -t mangle -p tcp --dport www -i eth2 -s 172.16/12 -d 0/0 -j MARK --set-mark 1
# iptables -A PREROUTING -t mangle -m multiport -p tcp --dport ftp,ftp-data,telnet -i eth2 -s 172.16/12 -d 0/0 -j MARK --set-mark 2
```

Now that the `mark` values are set, we can write rules for the RPDB to cause the kernel to use appropriate tables. These are shown in Example 16–36. First, the new table names are added to `/etc/iproute2/rt_tables` and then the rules are added and listed. The table numbers are arbitrary. The priority values used are arbitrary except that they must be less than 32766.

Example 16–36   RPDB Fast and Slow Rules

```
# echo "100 Slow" >> /etc/iproute2/rt_tables
# echo "101 Fast" >> /etc/iproute2/rt_tables
# cat /etc/iproute2/rt_tables
#
# reserved values
#
255     local
254     main
253     default
0       unspec
#
# local tables
#
100 Slow
101 Fast
#
# ip ru add fwmark 1 table Fast priority 250
# ip ru add fwmark 2 table Slow priority 300
# ip ru list
0:      from all lookup local
250:    fwmark 1      lookup Fast
300:    fwmark 2      lookup Slow
32766: from all lookup main
32767: from all lookup default
#
```

Finally, let's put the routes in the tables defined above and flush the cache to effect these changes. Example 16–37 illustrates.

Example 16–37   Adding the Routes for `Slow` and `Fast` Tables

```
# ip route add default via 101.10.9.23 dev eth0 table Slow
# ip route add default via 101.10.9.52 dev eth1 table Fast
# ip route flush cache
```

We can take this process even further with `iptables`. Suppose that we want to base the routing decisions on specific users. Since `iptables` allows for the matching of packets based on userID (when available), this can be done. For example, the command below illustrates marking packets with the value 3 for the user with a UID of 553.

```
# iptables -A PREROUTING -i eth2 -m owner --uid-owner 553 -s 172.16/
12 -d 0/0 -j MARK --set-mark 3
```

Now, rules can be placed in the RPDB to match packets with the mark value of 3 and the routing decision for those types of packets can be set up distinct from other packets as previously described.

Using mark values can also allow for post processing decisions regarding transmission of matching packets.

Masquerading Multiple Addresses

In Chapter 14, we described how to use masquerading with `ipchains`. That mechanism is limited to a single address. Suppose that you've been assigned the range of Internet registered addresses `192.129.75.32/28` by an ISP and that you'd like to configure a network environment as depicted in Figure 16–3. Here, `192.129.75.34` is the IP address associated with `eth0` on the Linux router `top-cat`, which is running a 2.2.x series kernel. The goal is to have all nodes in the internal network masqueraded to that address and to additionally have the WWW server masqueraded to `192.129.75.35` and the FTP server to `192.129.75.36`.

There are two ways to configure `topcat` to support the masquerading scheme shown in Figure 16–3. The first method involves upgrading the kernel on `top-cat` to 2.4.x and implementing `iptables` as described in the previous chapter. As of this writing, such an approach would require a significant amount of work. Once the major distributions start shipping version 2.4.x kernels, the effort will be lessened considerably.

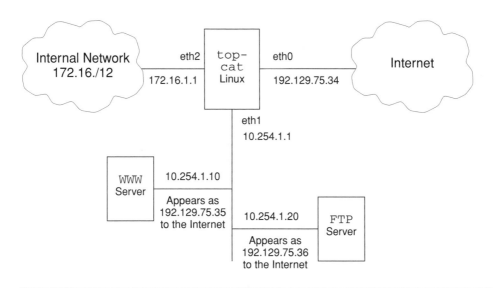

Figure 16–3   Masquerading to Multiple Addresses

The second approach is to configure the RPDB in conjunction with `ipchains` so that addresses are masqueraded correctly. This approach requires the following steps.

1. Configure `ipchains` to perform masquerading as described in Chapter 14.
2. Configure `topcat` to listen to the two new masqueraded addresses. The simplest way to accomplish this is with IP aliases as described in Chapter 4. Once this is accomplished, unique DNS entries can be used for access by nodes in the Internet.
3. Configure rules in the RPDB to cause the kernel to route packets from the WWW server and FTP server via the appropriate addresses.
4. Create the appropriate routing entries to support step 3.
5. Create route entries that allow communication between the internal network and the WWW and FTP servers.
6. Flush the routing cache to effect the changes.
7. Once tested, put the commands in an appropriate start-up script.

The steps outlined here are conceptually similar to those for the previous two examples, except for step 5, which requires two additional rules that we will describe shortly. Presuming that the `ipchains` configuration is already complete, Example 16–38 illustrates the commands necessary to complete steps 3 through 6. Line numbers are added for clarity.

Example 16–38   RPDB Rules to Support Multiple Masqueraded Addresses

```
 1 # echo "102 WWW" >> /etc/iproute2/rt_tables
 2 # echo "103 FTP" >> /etc/iproute2/rt_tables
 3 # cat /etc/iproute2/rt_tables
 4 #
 5 # reserved values
 6 #
 7 255    local
 8 254    main
 9 253    default
10 0      unspec
11 #
12 # local tables
13 #
14 102 WWW
15 103 FTP
16 #
17 # ip ru add from 10.254.1.10 to 172.16/12 table main priority 98
18 # ip ru add from 10.254.1.20 to 172.16/12 table main priority 99
19 # ip ru add from 10.254.1.10/32 table WWW priority 100
20 # ip ru add from 10.254.1.20/32 table FTP priority 101
21 # ip ru list
22 0:     from all lookup local
23 98:    from 10.254.1.10 to 172.16.0.0/12 lookup main
24 99:    from 10.254.1.20 to 172.16.0.0/12 lookup main
25 100:   from 10.254.1.10 lookup WWW
26 101:   from 10.254.1.20 lookup FTP
27 32766: from all lookup main
28 32767: from all lookup default
29 #
30 # ip route add default via 192.129.75.35 dev eth0 table WWW
31 # ip route add default via 192.129.75.36 dev eth0 table FTP
32 # ip route flush cache
```

The essential difference in this example is that the rule priorities are significant. There are four rules added to the RPDB at lines 17 through 20. The first two, at lines 17 and 18, specify that if packets arrive from either the WWW server (10.254.1.10) or the FTP server (10.254.1.20) and are destined to the internal network, then they are to be routed using the main routing table. The latter two rules, at lines 19 and 20, specify that any packets from the WWW or FTP server are to be routed through the external addresses 192.129.75.35 or 192.129.75.36 using the special routing tables WWW and FTP, respectively. The rules at lines 17 and 18 must have a higher priority (lower priority value), otherwise packets to the internal network will get routed by way of the external interface.

Note that the `main` routing table must have appropriate routing entries in it in order for routing between the WWW and FTP servers and the internal network to proceed normally. This could be accomplished through static entries or through the use of a dynamic routing table management daemon.

Once these settings have been tested, they can be put into a start-up script to be executed prior to the interfaces being brought up.

Route NAT

We previously noted that NAT can be accomplished with the `ip route` object. This capability, known as *route NAT,* is stateless and designed specifically to facilitate routing policies and ease transitions to new addresses. It cannot be used for managing active sessions like FTP. Each address that is translated through this mechanism must be uniquely mapped in a one-to-one (one real address to one translated address) fashion or all addresses must be masqueraded to one address.

Setting up a translated address with route NAT is straightforward. For example, a route can be added to the `main` routing table with

```
# ip route add nat 192.129.75.35 via 10.254.1.10 dev eth0
```

This command causes `192.129.75.35` to be treated as if it were an aliased address to the `eth0` device. The system will answer ARP queries related to it, and any packets received on `eth0` destined for `192.129.75.35` will be translated to `10.254.1.10` prior to forwarding.

In order to cause packets from `10.254.1.10` to be translated before they exit `eth0`, a policy rule such as

```
# ip ru add from 10.254.1.10 nat 192.129.75.35 table main prio 102
```

would need to be added to the RPDB. It is important to note that the priority specified for this rule should be lower (larger value) than rules for internal routing as described in the previous section.

This methodology could also be used to employ NAT only under certain circumstances. For example, `mark` values could be employed to identify packets that are to be translated and then rules configured to NAT only those packets. See the preceding sections for details.

Tunneling

The purpose of a network *tunnel* is to encapsulate unroutable packets into a routable packet. Generally, there are three major situations in which this might be the case.

- Packets that utilize a protocol other than that being used in the local network
- Broadcast packets that need to be sent through an NBMA network
- Packets of the same protocol but participating in a remote LAN

In each of these cases, packets are being encapsulated twice, which increases overhead. Additionally, for tunnels to work properly, the tunnel must be configured at two points—that is, a tunnel device must be configured both locally and remotely, known as the *local endpoint* and *remote endpoint*, respectively. The tunnel represents a virtual link between the endpoints. The packets are routed as normal between the endpoints due to the extra encapsulation. Special processing occurs at the endpoints themselves. Figure 16–4 conceptually depicts a network tunnel.

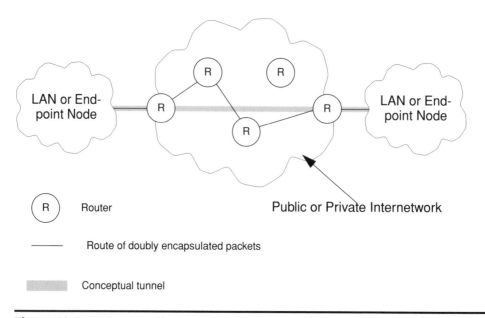

Figure 16–4   Conceptual Tunnel and Actual Route of Packets

Linux supports the configuration of each type of tunnel in the bulleted list above by way of three different virtual device types. These virtual device types are known as *modes*. The three modes are `ipip`, `gre`, and `sit` (initially described in Table 16–16 on page 802). Mode `ipip` is a Linux specific virtual device that can be used to build IPv4 in IPv4 tunnels. It is primarily used for configuring systems to participate in remote LANs. This method of tunneling has been available in Linux since the series 1.3.x kernels. Using `ipip` requires that both endpoints run Linux.

Modes `gre` and `sit` are both used to configure GRE tunnels. Originally developed by Cisco, GRE tunnels have been widely adopted as somewhat of a defacto standard. In Linux, mode `sit` is used to build a special IPv6 in IPv4 tunnels (a special case of different protocols). Mode `gre` is used to build all other GRE tunnels, including other protocols through IP and broadcasts over NBMA networks. Regardless of tunnel type, the module `ip_gre.o`[2] is required. Now, let's consider some examples.

IPv4 within IPv4 Tunnels

Consider the scenario depicted in Figure 16–5. The system `nomad` is a host that needs to participate in the `10.254.12.0/24` network. It connects through an intermediate network via `89.16.2.18` to reach `192.129.75.14`, which is the address of the router `R1` that connects directly to the `10.254.12.0/24` network. Using the `ip_gre` module and the `ip` utility, `nomad` can be configured to participate in `10.254.12.0/12` as if it were a local node by using a GRE tunnel.

In order to build the tunnel between nomad and `R1`, we need to configure a mode `gre` device on both systems and add appropriate routes to permit packets to flow through the tunnel. We step through the process on `nomad` first. We begin by making sure that the `ip_gre` module is loaded.

```
# modprobe ip_gre
#
```

Next, we configure the tunnel device called `greA`

```
# ip tunnel add greA mode gre remote 192.129.75.14 local 89.16.2.18
#
```

---

2. The modules `ipip.o` and `new_tunnel.o` are still available in the 2.2.x series kernels. These modules can be used in conjunction with the `ifconfig` utility to build `ipip` tunnels; however, it is likely that these modules will be dropped from future releases.

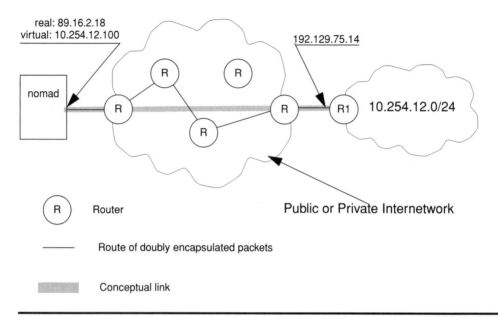

Figure 16–5   IPv4 in IPv4 Tunnel

Now, we add the address that will allow `nomad` to participate in the `10.254.12.0/24` network.

```
# ip addr add 10.254.12.100/24 dev greA
#
```

The link needs to be brought up with `ip link`

```
# ip link set greA up
#
```

Finally, we add the route for the tunnel. In the case of `nomad`, we'll assume that it has a default router entry as its only entry in the routing table. By simply adding this one, it becomes preferred over the default for all traffic destined to `10.254.12.0/24` because this entry represents a longer match.

```
# ip route add 10.254.12.0/24 dev greA
#
```

That completes the configuration for `nomad`. We can view the routing table entries created with `ip route ls` as shown in Example 16–39.

Example 16–39   Routing Table `main` on `nomad`

```
# ip route ls
10.254.12.0/24 dev greA  proto kernel  scope link  src 10.254.12.100
89.16.2.0/16 dev eth0  proto kernel  scope link  src 89.16.2.18
127.0.0.0/8 dev lo  scope link
default via 89.16.2.1 dev eth0
#
```

The configuration for `R1` proceeds similarly except that the routing entry needs to be a host entry. Example 16–40 illustrates the commands with the host route for `nomad` as the last command. Unless there are rules in the RPDB specifying otherwise, the routing entry for `nomad` on `R1` will always prevail as the longest match (in fact, in this case, it is the most specific match possible). Note that on `R1` the tunnel is called `greB`. There is nothing sacred about the naming, and in all likelihood the choices are made to clarify the tunnel's purpose.

Example 16–40   Commands to Set up Tunnel `greB` on `R1`

```
# modprobe ip_gre
# ip tunnel add greBA mode gre remote 89.16.2.18 local 192.129.75.14
# ip link set greB up
# ip route add 10.254.12.100/32 dev greB
```

Once configuration on both `nomad` and `R1` are complete, `nomad` is effectively a member of the `10.254.12.0/24` LAN. After the configuration is tested and known to be correct, the commands can be put into an appropriate start-up script. Note that this example could be replaced with one using mode `ipip` as long as both endpoints are Linux systems. Using GRE is recommended, however, since it is more widely implemented on other operating systems, such as Cisco IOS.

Configuring other types of IPv4 in IPv4 tunnels can be accomplished in a similar fashion. If the two endpoints of the tunnel represent different networks (for instance, if `nomad` had the IPv4 address `10.254.15.100/24`), then the routes added with `ip route add` would need to be adjusted accordingly; otherwise, the procedure is the same.

IPv6 within IPv4 Tunnels

In order to utilize mode `sit` tunnels (IPv6 within IPv4), both endpoints of the tunnel must support IPv6 through the necessary kernel configuration in addition to tunnel support.

Suppose that you want to join the 6bone using the system R1 in Figure 16–5 on page 816. Further suppose that 192.129.75.14 is a registered Internet address and that 212.177.81.1 is the address of a router that is connected to the 6bone and the address that represents the remote endpoint of the tunnel. Finally, suppose that the 6bone administrator has assigned the IPv6 address 3ffe:848:5:5:5:b6:14:23/96 for R1 to participate in the 6bone. On R1, the tunnel, and appropriate route, can be configured as illustrated in Example 16–41 (line wraps are due to formatting constraints).

Example 16–41   Commands to Configure IPv6 in IPv4 Tunnel on R1

```
# ip tunnel add 6bone mode sit remote 212.177.81.1 local 192.129.75.14 ttl 255
# ip link set 6bone up
# ip addr add 3ffe:848:5:5:5:b6:14:23/96 dev 6bone
# ip route add 3ffe::/16 dev 6bone
```

The final command in this example adds a routing entry that will cause all IPv6 packets having 3ffe in the first 16 bits to be forwarded through the tunnel. This IPv6 address represents the current 6bone test address space. Of course, the administrator for the router with the 212.177.81.1 address must configure an appropriate endpoint for this to work (but if you register for 6bone participation, as described in Chapter 5, it will be done).

Traffic Control

In the simplest sense, network traffic control means the purposeful restriction of the movement of packets throughout a network either or both in terms of the rate of flow and the paths used. Ordinarily, there is some purpose behind the controlling of traffic. For instance, you might want to have enough bandwidth so that an audio stream could flow uninterrupted. This type of service would require a dedicated portion of bandwidth along a given path and is known as a quality of service (QoS). On the other hand, while electronic mail doesn't require a specific amount of bandwidth nor is it normally time critical data, it does require a high level of reliability. Thus, the resources a given packet needs is often dictated by the type of application. Packets need to be categorized based on the resource needs of the packet in order for any traffic control system to appropriately manage it. This can be managed in many ways and, as noted in "TOS, Differentiated Services, and Integrated Services" on page 819, standardization efforts are underway. Additionally, although perhaps obvious, traffic control throughout a network requires the cooperation of many, if not all, of the routers involved.

Traffic control, as implemented in the Linux 2.2.x and 2.4.x kernels, is comprised of filters, flow control, and queues. Filters are used to select network traffic while queues are used to determine the order in which network packets are sent. The combination of these two components permits the establishment of control over network data flow. In the previous examples, we examined imposing rudimentary traffic control by way of filtering packets on `mark` value and then sending packets through specific interfaces depending on those values. Using the `mark` value and `ipchains` or `iptables` is one example of a filter. Special filters can be created and used to determine how packets are placed in specified queues using the traffic control capabilities of Linux.

Each network interface has at least one packet queue associated with it—by default, it is a first-in, first-out (FIFO) queue. The FIFO nature of the queue is its rule or algorithm or filter, also called the *queueing discipline*, imposed on the packets within the queue. Queueing disciplines can be quite complex and provide great flexibility. Filtering and routing policies can provide a very finely grained approach to traffic control. In "Queueing Disciplines" on page 822 and "Example Using the `tc` Command" on page 825, we take an introductory look at these filtering and queueing capabilities.

TOS, Differentiated Services, and Integrated Services

The TOS value was initially specified in RFC 791 (see Chapter 4). While subsequent RFCs dealt with TOS and the general issue of prioritizing network packets, the entire approach lay dormant for some 20 years. As the Internet has grown and demand for high bandwidth and/or real time applications has increased, the concept of providing a way of categorizing network traffic and treating it based on some scheme of prioritization has begun to flourish. While TOS provided an initial glimpse into the classification of network traffic, it proved to be too limited. The first push toward a more useful method came in the form of integrated services as embodied in RFC 1633. This concept attempted to provide guaranteed bandwidth services for applications like Real-Audio, but did not really address other types of services. A more general concept of differentiated services is defined in RFC 2474 as a proposed standard and, furthermore, implementing integrated services into differentiated services is given in RFC 2998.

The service type field was originally defined in RFC 791 and further refined by RFC 1349 (TOS) and RFC 1812 (Precedence field). The RFC 1349 version of the service type field is shown in Figure 16–6. This field is depicted as svc typ in the IPv4 header as shown in Figure 4–1 on page 93. Note that RFC 1349 refers to this entire octet as the TOS octet—even though only the 4 bits shown are used for TOS values. You can read RFC 1349 for a definition of these fields—these definitions are relevant now only for historical purposes[3] as RFC 2474 currently defines the use of this field and the IPv6 traffic class field. It is interesting to note that the use of the Precedence field was defined in RFC 1812 and was used widely. Consequently, provisions are made in RFC 2474 to accommodate RFC 1812 Precedence field definitions. Note that MBZ means "must be zero."

The IPv6 traffic class field was simply defined as an 8-bit field in RFC 2460 and left to a future RFC(s) for definition. RFC 2474 defines a differentiated services field which gives meaning to the IPv6 traffic class field. This definition obsoletes the RFC 1349 definition and applies to both IPv4 and IPv6. Figure 16–7 depicts the 8-bit differentiated services field which replaces the 8-bit type of service field (RFC 1349) in IPv4 and the 8-bit traffic class field (RFC 2460) in IPv6.

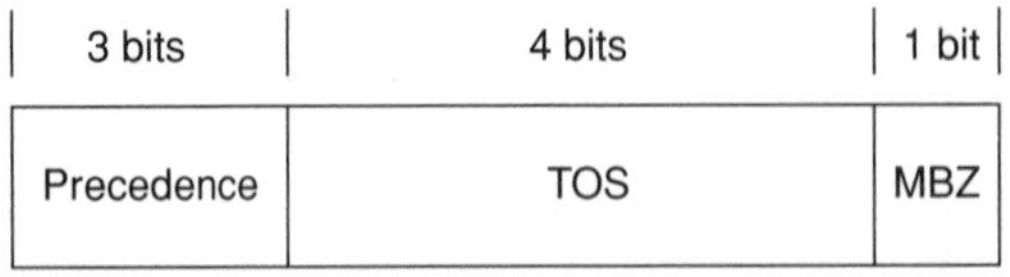

3 bits	4 bits	1 bit
Precedence	TOS	MBZ

Figure 16–6   RFC 1349 Type of Service Field

---

3. Linux, and most routers, allow for the setting of at least a part of this octet in whatever way a user chooses. Thus, if you aren't depending on the interpretation of this field by systems outside of your administrative control, you can use RFC 1349 or any other definitions you choose.

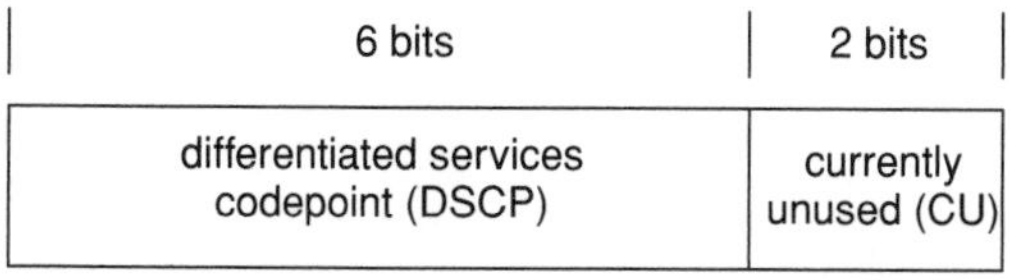

Figure 16–7   RFC 2474 Differentiated Service Field

RFC 2474 defines the use of the 6-bit DSCP field as indicated in Table 16–17. The Standard values (any DSCP with the last bit set to 0) utilize the RFC 1812 precedence value definitions in the leftmost 3 bits—this is required by RFC 2474. The remaining bits in Standard values have recommended, but not required, treatment specified in RFC 2474.

Table 16–17   DSCP Value Definitions

VALUE X = 0 OR 1	DEFINITION
xxxxx0	Any DSCP value with the last bit set to 0 is a standard value and is defined in RFC 2474. We refer to any value of this form as *Standard*. The meanings and actions associated with these values must be adhered to throughout the Internet.
xxxx11	Any DSCP value with the last two bits set to 1 is for local use (LU). The definitions for these values are entirely up to local administrators.
xxxx01	Any DSCP value with the last two bits set to 01 can also be used for local use, however, these values may be allocated for other purposes in the future and, therefore, it is suggested that they are not used.

Table 16–18 lists the definitions of the leftmost 3 bits of the DSCP also known as the Precedence values. Generally, these bits are used to determine the priority of a given packet. The remaining bits are used to provide a finer level of prioritization.

Table 16–18   Precedence Values

LEFTMOST 3 BITS OF DSCP	DESCRIPTION
111	Precedence 7. Routing protocol keep alive.
110	Precedence 6. Used by IP routing protocols.
101	Precedence 5. Express forwarding (EF). This precedence causes a packet to make use of the guaranteed bandwidth that is reserved specifically for such high priority packets.
100	Precedence 4. Assured forwarding (AF) Class 4. This precedence is relative to the next three. Packets marked with this precedence are not guaranteed any bandwidth, but will be treated preferentially over any lower precedence. And so it is for each of the next three in turn.
011	Precedence 3. AF Class 3.
010	Precedence 2. AF Class 2.
001	Precedence 1. AF Class 1.
000	Precedence 0. No special handling. Best effort delivery.

The purpose of the DSCP is that it causes routers to treat a given DSCP in the same way each time. If all routers do the same thing throughout a given network, then higher priority packets will indeed get preferential treatment. The details of DSCP use and the implementation of DSCP is a book unto itself. In the next two sections, we consider the most major of these details.

Queueing Disciplines

One way in which DSCP values can be accommodated is to use routing policies as described in "Routing Policies" on page 804. Another, more efficient, method is to implement queueing disciplines (QDs). QDs are much more powerful and can do much more than simply prioritize traffic based on DSCPs. A queueing discipline incorporates one or more of queues, filters, and classes. Figure 16–8 depicts the default FIFO queueing discipline. This QD has no filters or classes, only a queue that operates by processing packets on a FIFO basis.

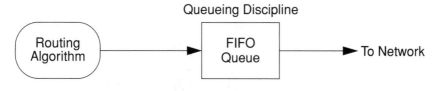

Figure 16–8   The FIFO Queueing Discipline

QDs can be much more complex; if controlling traffic is the goal, then the QDs will include filters and classes and, often, other QDs. Filters are used to determine into which class a packet should go. An example of a modestly complex QD is one that separates packets into high and low priority. This type of queueing discipline would have a filter that distinguishes packets as either low or high priority, probably based on a DSCP value, and then places the packet into an appropriate class. Each class then submits the packet to another queueing discipline for final processing and submission to the NIC. Figure 16–9 illustrates. Queueing disciplines are commonly stacked in this way to filter out packets in a very finely grained way.

Note that the "High Rate QD" in Figure 16–9 must have an upper bound that is less than the throughput of the device. Otherwise, it would be possible to starve the FIFO QD. An example of such a high priority, maximum rate enforcing QD is the token bucket filter (TBF) QD which imposes a maximum limit of 1 Mbps. This is a QD that is implemented and available with Linux 2.2.x and later series kernels.

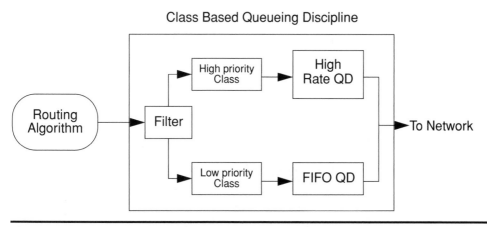

Figure 16–9   The Class Based Queueing Discipline

There are many other QDs available in Linux. Table 16–19 lists a number of them with their descriptions. Note that these QDs must be enabled in the kernel and that the algorithms supporting the QDs are mostly kernel modules. See Table 16–1 on page 758 for a listing to the kernel options.

Table 16–19   Queueing Disciplines

QD	DESCRIPTION
CBQ	Used for splitting traffic into multiple classes. Always used with at least one filter and one class.
Prio	Similar to CBQ in that it is used for splitting traffic into separate categories. Commonly used with TBF and FIFO.
FIFO	The default QD. Use whenever a simple queue is needed.
TBF	Frequently used as a QD for a class. Used when limiting the output rate is necessary.
TEQL	Used to concatenate multiple network connections into one virtual connection.
RED/GRED	Used for early detection of congestion and (hopefully) avoidance.
SFQ	Uses stochastic and round-robin to "fairly" treat packets.
DSMARK	Used for controlling traffic based on the DSCP.

Quite often, QDs use filters. Table 16–20 lists a number of filters available to these QDs in the standard Linux 2.2.x and later kernel.

Table 16–20   Common QD Filters

FILTER	DESCRIPTION
rsvp	Specifies the use of the Resource Reservation Protocol (RSVP). See RFC 2205 for a description of this protocol and RFC 2998 for a discussion of implementing RSVP in a differentiated services environment.

Table 16–20   Common QD Filters *(Continued)*

FILTER	DESCRIPTION
u32	Specifies that anything in the IP header can be used for filtering.
fw	Filters based on FWMARK values.
route	Filters based on tag values in routing table.
tcindex	Filters based on internal tag.
police/estimator	Special filters most commonly used to restrict rates of flow. Often applied to ingress packets whereas other filters are used on egress packets.

For further details about the topics discussed in this and the previous section, please see the references cited in "For Further Reading" on page 829.

Example Using the `tc` Command

In this section, we look at a very simple example. Suppose that using `ipchains` or `iptables`, all packets have a `mark` value of 1 or 2. Example 16–42 illustrates the use of CBQ to route higher priority traffic through a higher rate connection. In this case, the high rate outbound connection is 30 Mbps via `eth0` while the slower connection operates at 1.5 Mbps via `eth1`. Line numbers are added for clarity. Note that lines 1 through 4 wrap.

Example 16–42   Simple CBQ Illustration

```
1 tc qdisc add dev eth0 root handle 1: cbq bandwidth 100Mbit avpkt 1000
  cell 8
2 tc qdisc add dev eth1 root handle 1: cbq bandwidth 100Mbit avpkt 1000
  cell 8
3 tc class add dev eth0 parent 1:0 classid 1:1 est 1sec 2sec cbq bandwidth
  100Mbit rate 30Mbit allot 1514 cell 8 weight 1 prio 5 maxburst 20 avpkt
  1000 bounded
4 tc class add dev eth1 parent 1:0 classid 1:2 est 1sec 2sec cbq bandwidth
  100Mbit rate 1500Kbit allot 1514 cell 8 weight 1 prio 5 maxburst 20 avpkt
  1000 bounded
5 tc filter add dev eth0 protocol ip handle 1 fw classid 1:1
6 tc filter add dev eth1 protocol ip handle 2 fw classid 1:2
```

Lines 1 and 2 set up the CBQ QDs for each interface. Lines 3 and 4 add a class each for the CBQs. Lines 5 and 6 are the filters. Line 5 matches all packets for which the `mark` value is 1 due to the `handle 1 fw` matching string. Similarly, line 6 matches all packets for which the `mark` value is 2.

It should be clear from this simple example that the implementation details of traffic control are quite complex. Adding to that fact, documentation is fairly limited. See "For Further Reading" on page 829 for more details regarding the `tc` command as well as traffic control in general.

The Real Routing Algorithm

It should be clear from the discussion in this chapter and the routing algorithm presented in Figure 6–2 on page 194 that there are some details not provided in that previous description. In particular, from our discussion of routing policies, we now know that, if configured, there are multiple routing tables and an RPDB. Also, although not directly a part of the routing algorithm, we now know that outbound interface choices and traffic flow can be controlled by `tc` commands and inbound packets can be filtered (policed). Furthermore, in the previous two chapters, we considered the use of `ipchains` and `iptables`, respectively, which can alter which packets get routed and how they get routed.

Clearly, the way in which packets are processed through a Linux router can be very complex. The complexity offers a great deal of flexibility and, consequently, describing the interrelationships of these various capabilities is quite difficult. However, it is very useful to get a perspective on these interrelationships and it is in that spirit that Figure 16–10 is given. This figure depicts the flow of events for packets passing into, through, and out of a Linux router.

In Figure 16–10, all ovals indicate a decision point and address a topic previously discussed. These decision points are what makes routing in the Linux kernel both complex and flexible. Note that all of the decision points can cause a packet to be destroyed. The shaded area indicates the decision processes within the kernel that historically represent the routing algorithm.

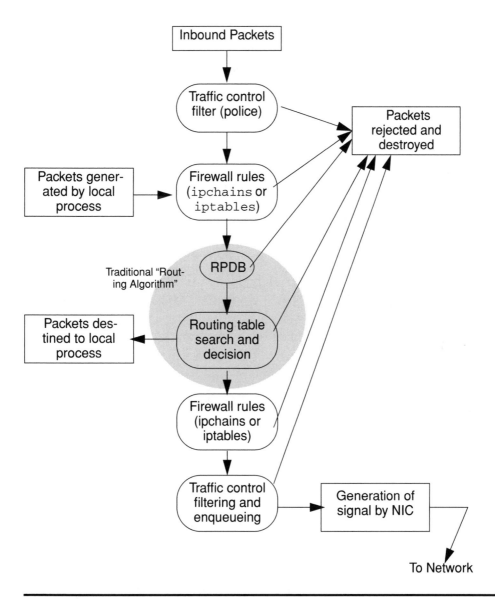

Figure 16–10   Flow of Packets for a Linux Router

Although Figure 16–10 appears to be anticlimatic, it represents a tremendous amount of detail—the majority of material in this book, in fact. And some of the topics (such as traffic control and `iptables`) only receive light treatment in this book. Figure 16–10 actually represents an extraordinary capability. And the Linux kernel embodies this capability.

Switching

Now that we have covered the concept of routing, we can make some general comments about switching (also referred to as layer 2 routing). The concept of switching, at the highest level, is to apply routing functionality at layer 2 of the TCP/IP stack. The advantage of doing such a thing is performance. Being able to move packets from point A to point B without having to interpret the IP header would be a big advantage. The problem is that at layer 2, only the physical or MAC address is available.

As a consequence of the layer 2 limitation, numerous schemes have been implemented to permit routing functionality to be implemented among switches at layer 2. The most common scheme has been *tagging*. Tagging is simply a way of adding additional information to the Ethernet frame that indicates which switch to use as the next hop. This extra information is removed by a switch when it prepares the packet for delivery to a destination that does not understand the tags—in particular, this is commonly true when the packet is delivered to the end node. Conceptually, this notion is the same as routing, in that local routing decisions are always about to which router (or end system) to send the packet next.

As you might imagine, the topic of switching represents yet another book (or collection of books). There are a number of resources in "For Further Reading" on page 829; for a good introduction on the topic, see *High-Speed Networking with LAN Switches* as cited there.

Tuning Linux for Routing

We really have not addressed the issue of tuning Linux for routing at all. Nor have we discussed setting up Linux as a WAN router. The reason for this omission is quite simple. The book, *Linux Routers*, as cited in "For Further Reading" on page 829, covers these topics, including the Linux router project, in great detail.

Summary

This chapter covers the iproute2 suite of tools. These tools can be used to set up routing policies, IP tunnels, and control traffic. We took a fairly detailed look at routing policies, introduced tunneling, and briefly presented traffic control with references. Additionally, we pointed to references for such topics as switching and tuning Linux for routing.

For Further Reading

Listed below are books and WWW resources that provide further information about the topics discussed in this chapter.

Books

Held, Gilbert, *High-Speed Networking with LAN Switches*, New York, New York, John Wiley & Sons, Inc., 1997.
Mancill, Tony, *Linux Routers: A Primer for System Administrators*, Upper Saddle River, New Jersey, Prentice Hall, Inc., 2000.

WWW Resources

You will find information about iproute2 and many useful links at

`http://snafu.freedom.org/linux2.2/iproute-notes.html`

The Advanced Routing HOWTO offers some additional information and can be found at

`http://www.ds9a.nl/2.4Routing/HOWTO/`

The following site focuses on differentiated services and the iproute2 `tc` utility. There is also a mailing list to which you can subscribe.

`http://lrcwww.epfl.ch/linux-diffserv/`

Currently, the mailing list is the best source of information about the `tc` tool.

Index

Symbols

Numerics

A

B

J

K

L

O

R

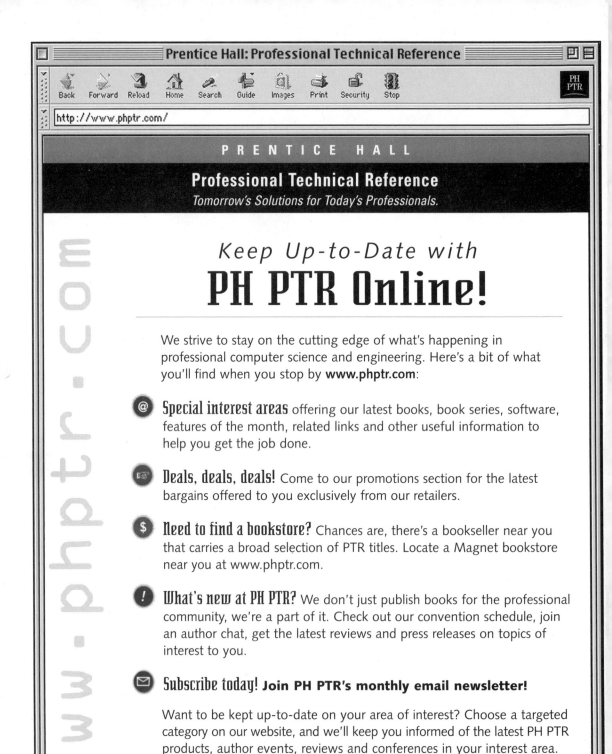